W9-BOL-250

ALSO BY JOHN M. BARRY

The Ambition and the Power:
  A True Story of Washington

The Transformed Cell:
  Unlocking the Mysteries of Cancer
  (with Dr. Steven Rosenberg)

RISING

The Great Mississippi Flood

and How

TIDE

of 1927

It Changed America

JOHN M. BARRY

Simon & Schuster

PUBLIC LIBRARY
EAST ORANGE, NEW JERSEY

DISCARD

977
B279
cop.1

 SIMON & SCHUSTER
Rockefeller Center
1230 Avenue of the Americas
New York, NY 10020

Copyright © 1997 by John Barry
All rights reserved,
including the right of reproduction
in whole or in part in any form.
SIMON & SCHUSTER and colophon are
registered trademarks of Simon & Schuster Inc.
Designed by Edith Fowler
Manufactured in the United States of America

10 9 8 7 6 5 4 3 2 1

Library of Congress Cataloging-in-Publication Data

Barry, John M.
   Rising tide : the great Mississippi flood of 1927
and how it changed America / John M. Barry.
      p. cm.
   Includes bibliographical references (p. 481) and
index.
   1. Floods—Mississippi River Valley—History—
20th century.   2. Flood control—Mississippi River
—History.   3. Mississippi River Valley—History
—1865-   4. Humphreys, A. A. (Andrew
Atkinson), 1810–1883.   5. Eads, James Buchanan,
1820–1887.   I. Title.
F354.B47   1997
977'.03—dc21   96-40077   CIP
ISBN 0-684-81046-8

27.50
4/17/97
RJt

For Anne and Rose and Jane

Contents

And the rain descended, and the flood came, and the wind blew,
and beat upon that house;
and it fell, and great was the fall of it.

—MATTHEW 7:27

Calgary

Regina
C

Winnip

A

Milk

Missouri

Missouri

NORTH DAKOTA

Helena

MONTANA

Bismarck

Yellowstone

Little

Big

Horn

SOUTH DAKOTA

Missouri

Cheyenne

Pierre

White

IDAHO

Wind

Missouri

WYOMING

Niobrara

NEBRASKA

North Platte

Cheyenne

Platte

Platte

Lincoln

NV

South

Republican

Salt Lake City

Denver

Kansas

UTAH

COLORADO

KANSAS

Arkansas

Las Vegas

Wichita

CA

ARIZONA

Canadian

OKLAHOMA

Albuquerque

Oklahoma City

NEW MEXICO

Red

Dallas

TEXAS

Mississippi River Drainage Basin

0   500

Scale of Miles

MEXICO

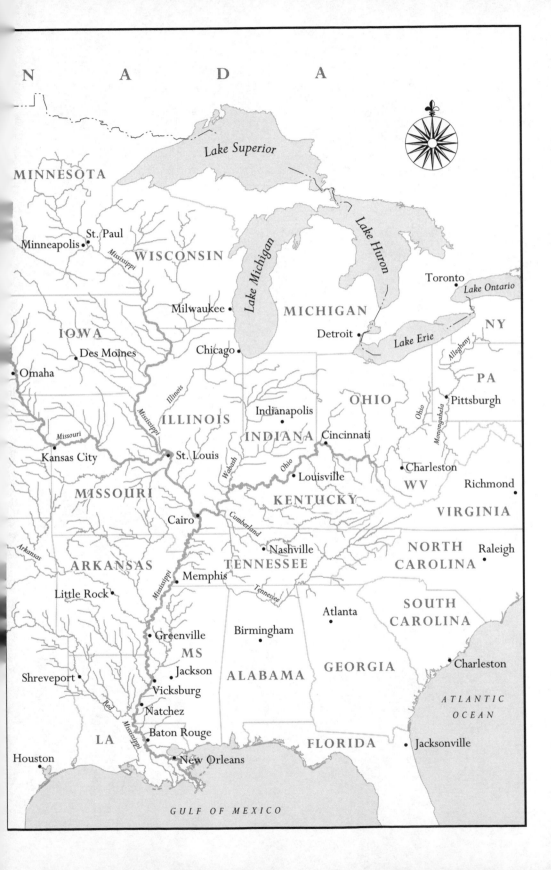

N A D A

MINNESOTA

Lake Superior

St. Paul
Minneapolis
Mississippi
WISCONSIN

Lake Michigan

Lake Huron

Toronto
Lake Ontario

MICHIGAN

NY

Milwaukee

Detroit

Lake Erie

IOWA

Chicago

Des Moines

Omaha

Illinois

PA

Ohio

Pittsburgh

Mississippi

ILLINOIS

Indianapolis

OHIO

Allegheny

Monongahela

Missouri

Kansas City

St. Louis

INDIANA

Wabash

Cincinnati

Ohio

Louisville

Charleston

WV

Richmond

MISSOURI

KENTUCKY

VIRGINIA

Cairo

Cumberland

Nashville

NORTH
CAROLINA

Raleigh

Arkansas

ARKANSAS

TENNESSEE

Tennessee

Mississippi

Little Rock

Memphis

SOUTH
CAROLINA

Atlanta

Birmingham

Greenville

MS

Mississippi

Shreveport

Jackson

GEORGIA

Charleston

Vicksburg

ALABAMA

Red

Natchez

*ATLANTIC
OCEAN*

Mississippi

Baton Rouge

LA

FLORIDA

Jacksonville

Houston

New Orleans

GULF OF MEXICO

Prologue

O<small>N THE MORNING</small> of Good Friday, April 15, 1927, Seguine Allen, the chief engineer of the Mississippi Levee Board in Greenville, Mississippi, woke up to the sound of running water. Rain was lashing the tall windows of his home near the great river with such intensity that the gutters were overflowing and a small waterfall poured past his bedroom. It worried him. He was hosting a party that day, but his concern was not that the weather might keep guests away. Indeed, he knew that the heavy rain, far from decreasing attendance, would bring out all the community's men of consequence, all as anxious as he for the latest word on the river.

Tributaries to the Mississippi had already overflowed from Oklahoma and Kansas in the west to Illinois and Kentucky in the east, causing dozens of deaths and threatening millions of acres of land. The Mississippi itself had been rising for weeks. It had exceeded the highest marks ever known, and was still rising. That morning's *Memphis Commercial-Appeal* warned: "The roaring Mississippi river, bank and levee full from St. Louis to New Orleans, is believed to be on its mightiest rampage. . . . All along the Mississippi considerable fear is felt over the prospects for the greatest flood in history."

Now it was raining again. Hours later, with the rain heavier yet, the men of consequence appeared at Allen's door. Even LeRoy Percy appeared.

No man mattered more in the Mississippi Delta, or perhaps anywhere the length of the river, than he. Sixty-seven years old, still imperious, thick-chested and vital, with measuring eyes, a fin-de-siècle mustache, silver hair, and frock coat, he seemed a figure from an earlier age. If so, he had been a ruler of that age, and in the Mississippi Delta he ruled even now. Not only a planter and lawyer but a former U.S. senator, an intimate of Teddy Roosevelt and William Howard Taft, and a director of railroads, the Carnegie and Rockefeller Foundations, and a Federal Reserve bank, Percy's political and financial connections extended beyond Washington and New York to London and Paris. Only his closest friends addressed him by his first name.

At Seguine Allen's party that afternoon it was "Senator Percy, how are you?" and "Senator Percy, good to see you," and "Senator Percy, do you think the levees will hold?" Percy began to answer, but, as if to mock anything he might say, thunder shook the house, wind rattled the windows, and the rain suddenly intensified. The party fell silent. Men and women listened, holding food and cocktails—the Greenville elite separated themselves from hill-country Baptists by ignoring Prohibition with great show—uneaten and unsipped in their hands. The rain pelted the roof, the windows. The sounds of the black musicians echoed hollowly, then the musicians too fell silent before the great booming cracks of thunder and pelting rain.

It had rained heavily for months. Henry Waring Ball, whose social rank fell somewhere between friend and retainer of the Percys, had recorded it in his diary. On March 7 it had been "rainy"; March 8, "pouring rain almost constantly for 24 hours"; March 9, "rain almost all night"; March 12, "after a very stormy day yesterday it began to pour in torrents about sunset, and rained very hearty until 10. . . . [At] daylight, a steady unrelenting flood came down for four hrs. I don't believe I ever saw so much rain"; March 18, "a tremendous storm of rain, thunder and lightning last night, followed by a tearing wind all night. . . . Today is dark, rainy and cold, with a gale blowing"; March 19, "rain all day"; March 20, "still raining hard tonight"; March 21, "Quite cold. Torrent of rain last night"; March 26, "Bad. Cold rain"; March 27, "still cold and showery"; March 29, "very dark and rainy"; March 30, "too dark and rainy to do anything." April 1, "Violent storm almost all night. Torrential rains, thunder, lightning, high winds"; April 5, "much rain tonight"; April 6, "rain last night of course."

Finally, April 8, Ball wrote that "at 12 it commenced to rain hard. I have seldom seen a more incessant and heavy downpour until the present moment. I have observed that the river is high and it is always raining . . . we have heavy showers and torrential downpours almost every day and night. . . . The water is now at the top of the levee."

Since then, the Mississippi River at Greenville had risen higher than it ever had before. Now came this new rain, the heaviest yet.

Indeed, no one present at Allen's party knew it, but the storm of Good Friday, 1927, was extraordinary for its combination of intensity and breadth. That day the great storm would pour from 6 to 15 inches of rain over several hundred thousand square miles, north into Missouri and Illinois, west into Texas, east almost to Alabama, south to the Gulf of Mexico. Greenville would receive 8.12 inches of rain. Little Rock, Arkansas, and Cairo, Illinois, would receive 10 inches. New Orleans would receive the greatest rainfall ever known there; in eighteen hours officially 14.96 inches fell, more in some parts. That amount, in less than a day, exceeded one-quarter the average precipitation New Orleans received in an entire year.

Senator Percy, do you think the levees will hold?

Allen addressed the question, reminding everyone that the levees were far stronger than they had ever been. They had held a record flood in 1922. They would hold this one. They would have the fight of their lives, but the levees, Allen assured everyone, would hold.

Percy suggested that they inspect the levees right now. Perhaps the storm would uncover a weakness they could address. Others nodded. Two dozen men, including Allen, put on their gun boots and raincoats, piled into their cars, and drove the few blocks to the center of downtown, where the levee rose up abruptly. A few decades earlier the levee had been blocks farther west, but one day the river had simply devoured it, taking much of the old downtown as well. Since then the city had covered the levee adjacent to downtown with concrete to prevent a further loss to the river and to serve as a wharf, and the men drove up the slope of the levee itself, parking on its crest, even with third-story windows in the office buildings, high above the city streets, high above millions of acres of flat, lush Delta land. A hundred yards upriver, where the concrete ended, a work gang of a hundred black men under one white foreman struggled in the driving rain to fill sandbags. For hundreds of miles on both sides of the river, other black work gangs were doing the same thing. Then Percy, Allen, and the others climbed out of their cars; leaning against the wet wind, their boots seeking a purchase on the soaked concrete, they faced the river.

It was like facing an angry dark ocean. The wind was fierce enough that that day it tore away roofs, smashed windows, and blew down the smokestack—130 feet high and 54 inches in diameter—at the giant A. G. Wineman & Sons lumber mill, destroyed half of the 110-foot-high smokestack of the Chicago Mill and Lumber Company, and drove great chocolate waves against the levee, where the surf broke, splashing waist-high against the men, knocking them off-balance before rolling down to the street. Out on the river, detritus swept past—whole trees, a roof, fence posts, upturned boats, the body of a mule. One man working on the levee recalled decades later, "I saw a whole tree just disappear, sucked under by the current, then saw it shoot up, it must have been a hundred yards away. Looked like a missile fired by a submarine."

The river seemed the most powerful thing in the world. Down from the Rocky Mountains of Colorado this water had come, down from Alberta and Saskatchewan in Canada, down from the Allegheny Mountains in New York and Pennsylvania, down from the Great Smokies in Tennessee, down from the forests of Montana and the iron ranges of Minnesota and the plains of Illinois. From the breadth of the continent down had come all the water that fell upon the earth and was not evaporated into the air or absorbed by the soil, down as if poured through a funnel, down into this immense writhing snake of a river, this Mississippi.

Even before this storm, levees along every significant tributary to the Mississippi had been shouldered aside by the water. In the East, Pittsburgh had seen 8 feet of water in city streets; in the West, outside Oklahoma City, 14 Mexican workers had drowned. And the Mississippi was still swelling, stretching, threatening to burst open entirely the system designed to contain it.

At the peak of the great Mississippi River flood of 1993, the river in Iowa carried 435,000 cubic feet of water a second; at St. Louis, after the Missouri River added its waters, it carried 1 million cubic feet a second. It was enough water to devastate the Midwest and make headlines across the world.

In 1927, a week after and a few miles north of where Percy and the others stood upon the levee, the Mississippi River would be carrying in excess of *three* million cubic feet of water each second.

LeRoy Percy did not know the immensity of the flood bearing down upon him, but he knew that it was great. His family had fought the river for nearly a century, as they had fought everything that blocked their transforming the domain of the river into an empire, an empire that had allowed its rulers to go in a single generation from hunting panther in the cane jungle at the edge of their plantations to traveling to Europe for opera festivals. The Percys had fought Reconstruction, fought yellow fever, fought to build the levees, all to create that society. Only five years earlier, to preserve it, LeRoy had fought the Ku Klux Klan as well. He had triumphed over all these enemies.

Now the river threatened those triumphs, threatened the society his family had created. Percy was determined that, even if the river burst the levees, that society would survive. He had power, and he would do whatever was required to preserve it.

Four hundred miles downriver from Greenville, the Mississippi flowed past New Orleans. There, a handful of men were Percy's peers, hunting and investing and playing poker with him, and belonging to the same clubs. Some were men of the Old South, controlling hundreds of thousands of acres of timber or sugar cane or cotton. Some were men of the New South, financiers and entrepreneurs. Some, like Percy, bridged those worlds. For decades they had controlled New Orleans and the entire state of Louisiana.

The river threatened their society too. And like Percy, they would do whatever was required to preserve it.

Their struggle, like Percy's, began as one of man against nature. It became one of man against man. For the flood brought with it also a human storm. Honor and money collided. White and black collided. Regional and national power structures collided. The collisions shook America.

On the levee in downtown Greenville, the men watched the river rage for a few more minutes. The rain stung. The river was, literally, awful. Yet they took a certain pride in its awfulness, in the greatness of the river. Confronting it made them larger. For a few more minutes, frozen by it, they stood there.

When they left, neither Senator Percy nor anyone else, not even Seguine Allen, the host, returned to the party. They would not go home for hours; some would not go home for days. They had work to do.

Part One

THE ENGINEERS

CHAPTER ONE

THE VALLEY of the Mississippi River stretches north into Canada and south to the Gulf of Mexico, east from New York and North Carolina and west to Idaho and New Mexico. It is a valley 20 percent larger than that of China's Yellow River, double that of Africa's Nile and India's Ganges, fifteen times that of Europe's Rhine. Within it lies 41 percent of the continental United States, including all or part of thirty-one states. No river in Europe, no river in the Orient, no river in the ancient civilized world compares with it. Only the Amazon and, barely, the Congo have a larger drainage basin. Measured from the head of its tributary the Missouri River, as logical a starting point as any, the Mississippi is the longest river in the world, and it pulses like the artery of the American heartland.

To control the Mississippi River—not simply to find a modus vivendi with it, but to control it, to dictate to it, to make it conform—is a mighty task. It requires more than confidence; it requires hubris. It was the perfect task for the nineteenth century. This was the century of iron and steel, certainty and progress, and the belief that physical laws as solid and rigid as iron and steel governed nature, possibly even man's nature, and that man had only to discover these laws to truly rule the world. It was the century of Euclidean geometry, linear logic, magnificent accomplishments, and brilliant mechanics. It was the century of the engineer.

Two engineers in particular spent most of their lives and much of the nineteenth century attempting to control the Mississippi River.

Andrew Atkinson Humphreys labored for eleven years over a massive and revolutionary report about the river that, combined with bloody triumphs in the Civil War, earned him the position of chief of the U.S. Army Corps of Engineers and an international reputation. In

Vienna, Paris, and Rome, royal scientific societies made him an honorary or corresponding member. In the United States he became an incorporator of the National Academy of Sciences, Harvard gave him an honorary doctorate, and the *American Journal of Science and the Arts* called his report "one of the most profoundly scientific publications ever published . . . a monument [to] unwearied industry and accuracy."

James Buchanan Eads had a reputation even greater. In 1876, *Scientific American* spoke of his "commanding talents and remarkable sagacity," termed him a "man of genius, of industry, and of incorruptible honor," and called upon him to seek the presidency of the United States. In 1884, Britain's Royal Society of the Arts awarded him the Albert Medal; others so honored had included Napoleon III, Louis Pasteur, Lord Kelvin, and Sir Henry Bessemer. In 1932 deans of American colleges of engineering named him one of the five greatest engineers of all time, ranking him with the likes of Leonardo da Vinci and Thomas Edison.

Humphreys and Eads were the two most powerful and influential engineers ever to work on the Mississippi River. Both intended to leave a mark on the river and on the land and people beside it. But each wanted to leave *his* mark, and only his. And they disagreed over nearly everything involving the Mississippi.

One had genius; the other had power. Eads' pleasure was to make the river obey his will. Humphreys' pleasure was to stop him, and implement his own plans for the river. Their fight turned bitter with hatred, and their disagreement split the Mississippi valley and put technical engineering arguments on front pages across the nation. The consequences of their fight are still felt on the Mississippi today.

LIFE DID NOT TREAT James Eads kindly starting out, but he was not one who accepted reverses. In the winter of 1833, thirteen years old, Eads arrived in St. Louis with his mother and two sisters. His father, a dreamer and a drifter, would appear later. As their steamboat approached the wharf, the boiler exploded, and the steamer sank. Terrified and freezing, coughing up water so muddy that one could taste its grit, the family was pulled from the river. It was Eads' first intimate experience with the Mississippi River, and he would not forget it; years later, it was said, he chose the point where he reached shore that night to begin his great conquest of the river.

That first winter the family was destitute. To help support his family, James sold apples on the street and never again attended school. But he learned, with St. Louis itself his teacher.

The city represented a bizarre, uniquely American mix of raucous frontier and European sophistication, and it taught boldness, confidence, and breadth of vision. With the Mississippi River before it, with a thousand miles of empty green prairie and the Missouri River stretching west behind it, the city sat at the nexus of North and South, East and West. Its location had already attracted and helped make such legends as Mike Fink, king of the river in keelboat days; Kit Carson, the frontier scout; and John Jacob Astor, the Manhattan organizational mastermind whose vast western enterprises made him the richest man in America. On the street men spoke French, Polish, Italian, German; by 1860, 40,000 Germans would live there. Creoles recently returned from Paris wore French fashions, while white men and Indians recently returned from the Rockies wore buckskin. For always in St. Louis there was the West. While Washington Irving was impressed with the city's gardens overflowing with trees and flowers, the sound of harpsichords muted by closed windows, its old French neighborhood, its coffeehouses and billiard halls, he and other eastern visitors were astounded by the casualness with which people traveled to the Rocky Mountains.

Eads, apprenticing in the streets, near the docks where goods were traded, amid the bustle of peddlers and wagons and spontaneous auctions, learned business first: salesmanship; the difference between honest dealing and sharp practice; and the fact that a piece of information could make a man a fortune, if a man had the sophistication to understand it and the guts to risk all for it. He watched fortunes made and lost, and saw that a man's character could turn losing positions into winning ones, and the reverse.

He also learned from books. The owner of a mercantile house hired him to run errands, was impressed by his mind, and allowed him to use his library after work. Here Eads spent night after night. Mathematics and geometry interested him the most—the angles of things, the relationships of things. He experimented with equations, read every mathematical treatise he could find, exhausted the library, experimented in a workshop of his own. He made a six-foot-long working model of a steamboat complete with engines and boilers, a working model of a sawmill, a working model of a fire engine, a working electrotype machine.

He had the passion of the lonely, an intense focus on the few things he cared about. He taught himself chess, became one of the city's best players, and engaged in simultaneous games allowing his opponents a board but playing himself without one. There was something lonely about chess as well, and brutal, and he gave no quarter.

But with chess and machinery, it was as if when he beheld a thing he saw deep inside it, as if in his mind he took it apart and put it back together. He understood weaknesses, flaws, tensions, strengths. His understanding went beyond the merely mechanical to the internal logic of a thing, and even beyond that to fundamental principles that dictated a result.

By now Eads' father, Thomas, had appeared in St. Louis. Thomas had spent his adult life moving, first down the Ohio River, now up the Mississippi, staying in one place long enough to try a trade—farmer, boardinghouse keeper, merchant—and fail. Then he had moved on, always westward, always closer to the frontier. Such was the pattern of his life. After three years in St. Louis he wanted to move on again. With his family he boarded one more steamboat, taking his wife and daughters along, and steamed farther into the wilderness, to try again.

James chose to remain in St. Louis, alone. Unlike his father, he dug in, rooted, persisted; he would center the rest of his life on St. Louis and the Mississippi River. He was determined, whatever the price, to succeed. The man who gave him his first adult job as "mud clerk," the lowest officer on a steamboat, would remember Eads' "towering ambition."

He was sixteen years old.

HIS FIRST SUCCESS would have satisfied most men. In achieving it, he acquired an understanding of the Mississippi no man shared.

He began a salvage business. At the time, boiler explosions, snags, fire, giant whirlpools that could swallow a small steamboat, and even pirates made travel on the river so dangerous that a French visitor called a trip on the Mississippi "more dangerous than a passage across the ocean, not merely from the United States to Europe, but from Europe to China." A shipper said, "The history of the world presents no example of an amount of destruction of loss of property and loss of life equal to that which yearly occurs on the western rivers."

Salvage operations existed on some rivers and on the Great Lakes. None existed on the Mississippi because of unique difficulties: light does not penetrate the muddy Mississippi more than a few inches, so men had to operate blind, and the river made locating wrecks nearly impossible, both because currents could quickly move them far downstream and because the enormous sediment load the river carried could quickly bury a boat under tons of sand.

Eads believed he could solve the problems. He designed a new salvage vessel modeled after snag boats built by Captain Henry Shreve. Shreve, a giant on the river, had created the steamboat age by designing a boat with engine and boilers above deck, thus creating shallow-draft vessels—small steamboats might draw as little as one foot of water—that could navigate both the Mississippi and its far shallower tributaries. In another engineering feat Shreve even altered the channel of the Mississippi itself—and opened a controversy that lasted a century—by creating a "cutoff," carving a straight channel through an S curve in the river, shortening and straightening it and accelerating the movement of water. The snag boats he built had derricks capable of lifting great trees out of the water, and he used them to clear the river and tear up a great 40-mile-long raft of timber that clogged the Red River.

Like Shreve's snag boats, Eads' salvage craft would use twin hulls connected by a flat platform, and a derrick. But the derrick was farther back from the bow and the hulls farther apart to allow Eads' boat to straddle a sunken cargo and, with improved leverage, to lift it. To allow men to spend long periods on the river bottom searching for hulls, Eads also designed a diving bell and, although men already worked underwater using various kinds of snorkel-like apparatuses, he is generally credited as its inventor.

Barely twenty-two years old, without introduction of any kind but with drawings in hand, Eads walked into the St. Louis offices of boatbuilders Calvin Case and William Nelson and showed them his designs. Short, thin, intense, Eads impressed with his precision, which extended to meticulous dress. "From young manhood," wrote an admirer, "he had felt that it was due to one's self and one's friends to look one's best; and he had also realized the practical value of good appearance."

Then he asked them to build a ship and several diving bells for him—for free. In payment he offered to make them partners in the salvage business he intended to start. His enthusiasm, energy, and compelling logic made success seem inevitable. Andrew Carnegie himself would later marvel at "the personal magnetism of the man. . . . It is impossible for most men not to be won over to his views, for a time at least." Case and Nelson agreed to his proposal.

Before the vessel was finished, Eads was offered a contract to salvage several hundred tons of lead. He took it, and soon demonstrated his willingness to commit his entire soul to, even risk his life for, his own idea.

With his boat not ready, he jury-rigged a crane on another and hired a professional diver with experience on the Great Lakes who brought his own equipment. But when the diver went down, the current brushed him aside. Repeated attempts proved useless. Eads went to a nearby town, bought a 40-gallon whiskey barrel, and converted it to his diving-bell design. The diver refused to enter the water in it. Eads put on the bell and descended to the bottom. The experience changed him, and through him man's policy toward the Mississippi River, forever.

Without light, Eads could not see the river. He felt it. The bottom sucked at him while the current embraced him in darkness and silence. The current also buffeted, whipped, bullied, pulled. A diver had to lean against it, push against it. Unlike the wind, it never let up. He later wrote: "I had occasion to descend to the bottom in a current so swift as to require extraordinary means to sink the bell. . . . The sand was drifting like a dense snowstorm at the bottom. . . . At sixty-five feet below the surface I found the bed of the river, for at least three feet in depth, a moving mass and so unstable that, in endeavoring to find a footing on it beneath my bell, my feet penetrated through it until I could feel, although standing erect, the sand rushing past my hands, driven by a current apparently as rapid as that on the surface. I could discover the sand in motion at least two feet below the surface of the bottom, and moving with a velocity diminishing in proportion to its depth."

Once on the bottom, he located the lead, tied a cable around one 70-pound pig at a time, and raised it. His business quickly boomed. Master of a vessel, he became known as "Captain Eads," and soon operated a fleet of salvage boats. Always he was improving them. Several could empty a sunken steamboat of water with centrifugal pumps of his design, then raise the entire ship from the bottom. From the great sandbars that formed at the river's mouth in the Gulf of Mexico north to Iowa, Eads personally salvaged wrecked ships and walked the bottom of the Mississippi River. He came to know the river and its currents in ways more intimate than any captain or any pilot or any engineer. The river had unveiled secrets to him alone. Already his vision had gone beyond mechanical devices. He was beginning to formulate theories about the river, and about the great forces within it.

In 1845, at the age of twenty-six, Eads married and left the river briefly. He sold his business to his partners and started the first glass factory west of the Mississippi. It failed quickly, the only real failure of his life. At the age of twenty-seven, owing $25,000, he borrowed $1,500 more, bought back a share of the salvage business, and returned to the water. He quickly recovered financially, telling his wife, Martha, that they need not join the gold rush to California since they had found gold on the river bottom.

He seemed to hate the separation from his wife. When away, he worked incessantly, even Christmas Day and in all weather. "It requires little short of a hurricane to keep me from working," he wrote her. His wife sent poems back, calling to him. In "To an Absent Husband" she pleaded, "[C]ome to our cottage—my husband come home / . . . come to thy children, . . . thy wife."

Yet he could not leave the water. His company owned twelve boats, and usually they worked different locations. He captained one boat and hired men to run the others. He could have hired another captain and spent far more time with his wife. Instead, he continued to work the river and dive himself. His passion seemed divided now, between his family and the Mississippi.

He remained away for weeks, even months, at a time. His only son died; still he stayed out on the river. His wife fell ill, and he wrote her: "I do hope and pray my beloved wife that I will never again so long as life lasts, leave you even for a day when you are as ill as when I left you. It is almost totally inexcusable." But he did stay away. Finally, they went on vacation to Vermont. Returning home aboard a steamboat in 1852, Martha died of cholera. Eads was thirty-two years old. He left his two baby daughters with his sister-in-law and went back on the river.

More than ever he poured himself into his work. Despite the dozen ships and several hundred men under him, he continued to dive himself. He did so with a new fury, going, an assistant worried, into "dangerous and exposed places where the men refused to go." While his fortune grew on land, he walked the river bottom, alone in the silent and turbulent darkness. And then in 1853, a year after his wife died, saying he was ill, he gave up diving forever and entered the surface world.

IN ST. LOUIS, Eads made his presence felt. His salvage operation had already made him known throughout the Mississippi valley, but now he reached even wider. In 1856, when the federal government stopped removing snags from the Mississippi, he bought the government snag boats for $185,000 and proposed to do the same job. Lobbying efforts in Washington the following year failed to get a government contract—Mississippi Senator Jefferson Davis opposed giving one to a man "whose previous pursuits gave no assurance of ability to solve a problem in civil engineering." So Eads formed a syndicate of fifty insurance companies stretching from New York to New Orleans to finance his operation privately. Also in 1856 his mother's first cousin James Buchanan, for whom Eads was named, was elected president of the United States.

One year later, at the age of thirty-seven, Eads retired with a fortune exceeding $500,000 in cash, again blaming ill health. But he remained active. He was now a man of substance, owner of a mansion with parklike grounds on Compton Hill. His friends included congressmen, senators, publishers, big businessmen. Demonstrating what seemed more a sense of responsibility than love, he married his widowed cousin, who had four children; they had no children together, and he spent little time with her. He became a founding director of the St. Louis Philharmonic Society. He was active in the St. Louis Merchants Exchange (the city's chamber of commerce). He became involved in railroads, director of a major bank. He had come very far indeed from the boy who sold apples on the street.

In 1860, James Buchanan Eads was forty years old, his face framed by whiskers that met under his chin, and bald. He was sensitive about his baldness and rarely appeared in public without a skullcap. Though he looked frail, his years working the river had given him, one observer noted in surprise, "iron muscles." Everything about him, from his clothes to his desk, was disciplined, clean, and orderly to the point of obsessiveness. "Really he seems to have been a point too precise," his grandson said. "He was just the opposite to those geniuses whose great brain shows itself by a sloppy exterior. Eads was never sloppy, even at home." In a photograph from the period he appears wise, possessing a kind of inner peace, yet he also seems intense, ascetic, with a disciplined and driven air.

He was also hard, his hardness creating turbulence around him. Others would call him unreasonable and rigid. He conceded nothing and pursued everything with ferocity. Even when playing chess with his grandson, he yielded nothing, and advised, "Never let even a pawn be taken." In later photographs he usually appeared tight-lipped; one man described his mouth as "shut[ting] so emphatically that it made plain his intention to do, in spite of all, what he believed could and should be done. [His mouth] admitted no trifling. When it spoke seriously it spoke finally."

And he was still willing to risk everything on himself. With a cheerfulness that understated the price he was willing to pay, he wrote, "Fortune favors the brave. 'Drive on' is my motto."

He had created, in his own person, a great and powerful machine capable of extraordinary accomplishment. Emerson Gould, a steamboatman and investor who knew Eads for sixty years, later wrote: "Whatever credit is due him as an engineer, or for his mechanical and inventive genius, all sink into insignificance when compared to his ability as a *financier*. Upon that all his success depended. . . . His ability to avail himself of the skill, of the experience and the brains of all with whom he came in contact, was phenomenal and enabled him to succeed in any mechanical proposition suggested. . . . To plan and execute, no man was his equal."

The machinery of Eads' person was lying dormant, unused, restless. The Civil War was about to change that.

As SOME IN MISSOURI talked of secession, Eads and a handful of powerful men including Edward Bates, Francis Preston Blair, Benjamin Gratz Brown, and James Rollins met regularly in each other's homes to plot stratagems to keep Missouri in the Union, and strategy in case of war. Bates would become Lincoln's attorney general; Blair, whose father edited the *Washington Globe* (his home, Blair House, lies across the street from the White House and is now used to house visiting heads of state), Brown, and Rollins would become U.S. senators. Eads argued for building ironclad steamboats, seizing the Mississippi River, and dividing the South. The others listened.

In April 1861, immediately after the firing on Fort Sumter, Bates, already in Lincoln's cabinet, sent Eads a note marked "confidential. . . . Be not surprised if you are called here suddenly by telegram. If called, come instantly." A few days later Eads was in Washington, presenting detailed plans for ironclads to Lincoln and the cabinet. Both the War Department and the Navy listened attentively. When the Army requested bids to build seven ironclad gunboats, Eads made the low bid and promised to deliver the boats in sixty-five days. He won the contract.

Eads had never built a gunboat or worked with metal and needed thirty-five boilers, twenty-one steam engines, hundreds of tons of metal, and thousands of board-feet of lumber. He had no shipyard, no machine shop, no foundry, no factory, and lacked the capital to begin, but within two weeks he had 4,000 men in St. Louis working seven days a week, with more thousands working in machine shops as far away as Cincinnati. When the government failed to pay him as required by the contract, Eads used personal funds and money raised from friends to pay subcontractors.

Although he could not deliver the seven gunboats in sixty-five days, he did deliver eight in one hundred days. The eighth one was the queen of his salvage fleet converted into a monster ship of war, 200 feet long with a 75-foot beam—wider than any oceangoing vessel. When it and the other ships arrived late in 1861 in Cairo, Illinois, for final outfitting, Commodore Andrew Foote reported to the quartermaster general that it "is greatly superior to any gunboat I have ever seen. Every officer here pronounces her the best gunboat in the Union."

Eads arrived in Cairo himself with his warships and gave Ulysses S. Grant, a brigadier general waiting to push south, and his officers a tour of the ironclads. Grant had no intellectual curiosity and seemed sometimes dull and torpid, but he got along well with Eads and shared one trait with him. When he moved toward his purpose, his energy rumbled with volcanic and frightening force, powerful enough to move not only men but events. The ships seemed like Grant somehow: lumbering, squat, ugly, angry-looking, and sinister, and if slow and difficult to maneuver upstream, they also moved with inexorable power. Troops called them "turtles." And Grant was grateful that Eads, who still owned the boats—the Army had not paid for them—allowed them into combat. They performed magnificently. In February 1862, with minimal involvement of Grant's infantry, the gunboats bombarded Fort Henry on the Tennessee River and Fort Donelson on the Cumberland River. The forts surrendered, marking the first major Union victories of the war and significantly enhancing Grant's reputation.

Eads' reputation grew as well. During the war he built twenty-five ships, and Admiral David Farragut, before the battle of Mobile Bay, pleaded with Navy Secretary Gideon Welles, "Only give me the ironclads built by Mr. Eads, and we will see how far Providence is with us." Eads also designed a rotating, steam-driven gun turret that became an engineering classic and precursor to modern battleship guns. The Navy quickly chose it over the turret designed by John Ericsson for his better-known but inferior ironclad, the *Monitor,* and also asked Eads to go to Europe to study navy yards there. He was received everywhere, including by Bismarck in Prussia, and possibly had access to the secretive Krupp works, where experiments with steel weapons and new steel-making processes were being conducted. American ordnance experts with whom he worked definitely had that access.

As the war ended, James Eads was among the most prominent and powerful men in the entire Mississippi valley. Eight hundred guests attended the wedding in 1867 of his daughter to the son of a former mayor; police were needed to hold back throngs of the uninvited curious. He put together a syndicate to buy the National Bank of Missouri, the largest bank in the West, served as president of the

Mound City Life Insurance Company, controlled a railroad that was reaching west to Kansas City and north into Iowa's grainfields, and cofounded a company to bridge the Missouri River. In 1871 the book *Great Fortunes and How They Were Made* devoted an entire chapter to Eads in a section titled "Capitalists"; other chapters in the section considered the likes of Cornelius Vanderbilt, John Jacob Astor, and Daniel Drew.

The war proved Eads brilliant and formidable. But the war had also created opportunity for another man, a man with whom Eads would fight a personal war for control of the Mississippi River.

CHAPTER TWO

ANDREW ATKINSON Humphreys was born in 1810, the only child of a Philadelphia family of means and position. From boyhood he assumed that attention and prominence were his right. Often a disciplinary problem, he refused to return to one schoolmaster "who used the rod unmercifully," so his parents changed his school, then changed it again, and again. When his father was away in Europe, his mother was unable to handle him and he "ran wild." At sixteen years of age, the age at which Eads went his own way in St. Louis, Humphreys entered West Point. If taming him seemed an odd usage of the U.S. Military Academy, made possible only by his family's connections, nonetheless he thrived.

The Army Corps of Engineers then ran West Point, and Humphreys enjoyed the intellectual challenges of engineering. In fact, he loved challenges and combat of all kinds, embraced contests, competed with vigor. Unlike Eads, whose inner convictions allowed him to stand alone against the world, Humphreys saw himself largely in the mirror of others' eyes. He wanted to achieve singularity, to stand out, and, even more, to be recognized for these things; he was driven by his desire for glory, and glory is a reflection of the world's view. His only problem at West Point was discipline, and demerits for infractions lowered his class rank, but he graduated thirteenth in a class of thirty-three.

Life after West Point was a disappointment. Not yet twenty-one years old upon graduation, he craved action. He found none in Army routine. Assigned to desolate Provincetown, Massachusetts, surrounded by giant sand dunes and facing the gray and wintry Atlantic, he found neither his intellect nor his courage engaged. He sought refuge by exploring scientific questions on his own, dismissing his routine duties as "a source of great discontent to me. I am constantly yearning to return to those contemplations which I hope will lead to some substantial good. . . . I had reached that point where everything was unsettled. I felt like one who from the ground has caught a glimpse of a beautiful sky and had felt a soft kissing wind. . . . My duty is constantly calling me away to pursuits which I feel are not of that importance. . . . It makes me look upon my labor as a dull, uninteresting task and I go about it with disgust."

His frustrations would only increase. Sent to fight Seminole Indians in Florida in 1836, he became so ill that he had to resign from the Army. It was not a disgrace, but it rankled. He worked as an engineer, a field exploding with opportunity, but in 1839 he sought and received appointment as a first lieutenant in the Corps of Topographical Engineers, a then-separate military unit. It brought him new frustration. In his mid-thirties, an age at which most men who will achieve significant things have begun to emerge—by then Eads was both wealthy and known the length of the Mississippi River—Humphreys had done nothing.

The less he accomplished, the more the measures of rank and title mattered. Assigned to Washington, he devoted himself to personal advancement by cultivating politicians and maneuvering within the Army. First he blocked a rival from receiving a plum appointment by having him accused of conduct unbecoming an officer. Then Humphreys usurped the functions of his own superior, the prominent explorer J. W. Abert, who protested bitterly to the secretary of war that Humphreys' action constituted a "serious irregularity . . . seriously injurious to the discipline and subordination of the Corps." But Humphreys' high-placed friends protected him from retribution. Senator John Crittenden of Kentucky may well have had Humphreys in mind when he castigated Washington-based Army engineers as "capitoline guards, half officer, half civilian, 'sprinkled with the dandy,' who were dancing attendance at the skirts of Congressmen, . . . never seen in the hour of danger, and found only where favors were to be had."

Yet Humphreys truly had abilities and wanted to demonstrate them. In 1845 he maneuvered for detached duty as an aide to Professor A. D. Bache, an internationally renowned scientist who headed the U.S. Coastal Survey. Later he recalled: "I went to science because the ordinary military routine nearly killed me; I was so restless and impatient under it, that any pursuit that required thinking would have been an acceptable change."

The Coastal Survey did far more than simply map the coastline. It and similar offices drew blueprints for the country's development, especially for the construction of infrastructure—harbors, roads, canals, railroads, bridges. Finally, Humphreys had a position he could embrace with enthusiasm. For six years he did more than well, making in Bache a great and important friend.

But despite all his good work on the Coastal Survey, the world was threatening to pass him by. Even within the Army, Humphreys was being passed by. He had twice had the opportunity to fight a war, against the Seminoles and in Mexico, and while his fellow officers had tested their courage and tasted blood, he had, on the first occasion, returned home ill and, on the second, remained in Washington with Bache.

At forty he had brown hair that could appear golden in a certain light, and steadfast steely blue eyes. In photographs, his shoulders are broad, his mustache bristling, his hands large and thick-fingered. Nothing about him appears relaxed. He always seemed on the edge, always ready to explode. Charles A. Dana, later assistant secretary of war, described him as "very pleasant to deal with, unless you were fighting against him, and then he was not so pleasant." Dana also called him "intolerant" and capable "of the most distinguished and brilliant profanity" in the Army.

Then, in 1850, Humphreys saw his main chance.

FOR DECADES the increasingly populated states of the Mississippi valley had been demanding that the national government address navigation and flood problems on the Mississippi River. Conventions in Cincinnati in 1842, in Memphis in 1844, in Chicago in 1847 (where 16,000 delegates overwhelmed a city of 10,000) had pressured Washington to act. At last, to keep the West, the upper Mississippi valley, from forging a political alliance with the South and spurred on by a flood in 1849 that inundated much of the lower Mississippi valley—including New Orleans itself—eastern politicians acceded to the demands, and Congress ceded millions of acres of federally owned "swamp and overflowed lands" to the states.* The states were to sell this land and spend the proceeds on flood control. And floods were not the only river problem. At the mouth of the Mississippi enormous sandbars often blocked access to the Gulf of Mexico. Sometimes fifty ships waited there for the sandbars to dissipate enough to allow passage into or out of the river; the largest ships sometimes waited as

---

* Louisiana received 9.5 million acres, Arkansas 7.7 million, Missouri 3.4 million, and Mississippi 3.3 million.

long as three months. The sandbars were choking the trade of the entire valley. Solutions were not obvious. Controversy existed over every aspect of river engineering, including both how best to control floods and open the river's mouth.

So on September 30, 1850, Congress authorized a survey of the lower Mississippi, from Cairo, Illinois, to the Gulf of Mexico. The aim was to discover the laws governing the Mississippi River and to determine how to tame it.

The survey would be a monumental work, by far the most important of its kind ever conducted anywhere in the world, and it would break new ground in science. If successful, it would also frame the development of virtually the entire Mississippi valley, from Bismarck, North Dakota, to Pittsburgh, Pennsylvania, as well as the lush alluvial lands, the most fertile lands in the world, from Cairo to the Gulf.

Humphreys desperately wanted to perform the Mississippi survey. With considerable understatement he wrote when officially requesting the assignment, "It is a work which I should desire, as it is one of much difficulty and of great importance." Unofficially, he beseeched the congressmen he had earlier cultivated, used old family political connections, employed every professional allegiance. Bache personally lobbied the cabinet for him and wrote Secretary of War Charles Conrad: "To sound knowledge [Humphreys] joins a practical turn. . . . He is cautious in obtaining data, energetic in using them when obtained, is not likely on the one hand to run into unnecessary refinement or on the other to mistake rough guesses for accurate conclusions." Conrad recalled Humphreys from detached duty and appointed him to the job.

Ecstatic, home now in the Army, Humphreys had found "the work of my life."

BUT HUMPHREYS was about to become a pawn in a war between military and civilian engineers that would continue for a century. This conflict threatened both Humphreys personally and the Army Corps of Engineers itself, and it reflected the growing importance of a profession—the first of the technocratic disciplines—that would largely define the nineteenth and early twentieth centuries.

Until the 1830s, West Point dominated American engineering. West Point offered the only academic training in the field in America, and Army engineers were a true elite. Only the top two cadets of each West Point class were allowed to enter the Corps of Engineers, while only the top eight cadets in each class could enter the separate Corps of Topographical Engineers. (Humphreys had fallen short of this mark but, after establishing himself as a civilian engineer, the corps commander personally selected him.)

But these few could hardly supply the nation's needs. Engineers who left the Army were besieged by job offers, and a civilian profession was developing through apprentice programs, especially on the Erie Canal. In 1835, Rensselaer Polytechnic Institute first granted a degree in engineering. By 1850 so did Michigan, Harvard, Yale, Union, and Dartmouth. Meanwhile, technical knowledge was advancing at an exponential rate, and civilian engineers began denigrating their military counterparts for their rigid and dated training.

Of all the civilian engineers in America, the most renowned was Charles Ellet, Jr. Ellet was exactly Humphreys' age but entirely unlike him. Charming, athletic, brilliant, handsome, and arrogant, he would risk his own life simply to steal a scene. Ellet had, as a future time would say, charisma.

At seventeen, already an assistant canal engineer, Ellet had complained there were "not above 3 Engineers who can be called men of science in the United States." So he taught himself French, saved his money, solicited the help of Lafayette and the American ambassador to France, and, while Humphreys attended West Point, was admitted to the best engineering school in the world, the École des Ponts et Chaussées in France. He returned in 1829 the only engineer in the United States with a European education, and promptly proposed bridges across the Potomac and across the Mississippi at St. Louis. Neither project went beyond talk, but he did bridge the Schuylkill River at Philadelphia, and followed that with a 1,010-foot-long suspension bridge, then the longest in the world, across the Ohio at Wheeling, West Virginia. (It would later collapse.) While this bridge was under construction, Ellet became the first to cross the gorge at Niagara Falls. Initially, he strung a wire cable, hung a basket from it, got in, and pulled himself across, remarking, "The wind was high and the weather cold, but yet the trip was a very interesting one to me—perched up as I was two hundred and forty feet above the Rapids." Then he built a catwalk of planks without guardrails, and was the first to cross it too, driving a horse and carriage, standing up like a charioteer, speeding and swaying, and transforming himself into a legend.

In 1850 he had just finished both the Wheeling bridge and a survey of the Ohio River. He had developed theories about the Ohio he believed applicable to the Mississippi as well, and now sought the assignment already given to Humphreys.

The entire civilian engineering profession and its supporters in Congress demanded that the government give Ellet the job. The War Department and its allies lobbied bitterly and intensely to allow Humphreys to proceed. In the end, President Millard Fillmore directed that the $50,000 appropriation for the survey be divided between the two men. Each was to operate independently and produce a separate report.

Humphreys, representing not only himself but the entire Army, was in a competition. He was determined to win it.

"AT THE MOUTH of the Missouri, the Mississippi river first assumes its characteristic appearance of a turbid and boiling torrent, immense in volume and force . . . [which] impart to it something of sublimity," wrote Humphreys, describing the survey's goals, "yet the Mississippi is really governed by laws, the development of which was the first object of these investigations."

The force did seem sublime in its immensity. Mass and velocity determine the force of any moving object. Volume determines a river's mass. Slope, chiefly, determines its velocity. The steeper the slope to the sea, the steeper the fall and, hence, the greater the speed, or the velocity, of the current. The Corps of Engineers defines the starting point of the lower Mississippi River as the confluence of the Mississippi and the Ohio at Cairo, Illinois, 290 feet above sea level. The river in its natural state flowed 1,100 miles from there to the Gulf (its many curves lengthen the straight-line distance of 600 miles), giving it an average slope equal to 290 feet, the height, divided by 1,100 miles, the distance, or slightly over 3 inches to the mile. In long stretches the slope drops below 2 inches a mile. The Mississippi, and even more so the lower Mississippi, runs through some of the flattest land in the world. This gentle slope that moves the tremendous volume of water in the Mississippi to the sea suggests that the river moves sleepily through the belly of America. The suggestion is false.

The river's characteristics represent an extraordinarily dynamic combination of turbulent effects, and river hydraulics quickly go beyond the merely complex. Indeed, studies of flowing water in the 1970s helped launch the new science of chaos, and James Gleick in his book on the subject quotes physicist Werner Heisenberg, who stated that on his deathbed he would like to ask God two questions: why relativity? and, why turbulence? Heisenberg suggested, "I really think God may have an answer to the first question."

Anything from a temperature change to the wind to the roughness of the bottom radically alters a river's internal dynamics.

Surface velocities, bottom velocities, midstream and mid-depth velocities—all are affected by friction or the lack of friction with the air,
the riverbank, the riverbed.

But the complexity of the Mississippi exceeds that of nearly all
other rivers. Not only is it acted upon; it acts. It generates its own
internal forces through its size, its sediment load, its depth, variations
in its bottom, its ability to cave in the riverbank and slide sideways
for miles, and even tidal influences, which affect it as far north as
Baton Rouge. Engineering theories and techniques that apply to other
rivers, even such major rivers as the Po, the Rhine, the Missouri,
and even the upper Mississippi, simply do not work on the lower
Mississippi, which normally runs far deeper and carries far more
water. (In 1993, for example, the floodwaters that overflowed, with
devastating result, the Missouri and upper Mississippi put no strain
on the levees along the lower Mississippi.)

The Mississippi never lies at rest. It roils. It follows no set
course. Its waters and currents are not uniform. Rather, it moves
south in layers and whorls, like an uncoiling rope made up of a
multitude of discrete fibers, each one following an independent and
unpredictable path, each one separately and together capable of snapping like a whip. It never has one current, one velocity. Even when
the river is not in flood, one can sometimes see the surface in one spot
one to two feet higher than the surface close by, while the water swirls
about, as if trying to devour itself. Eddies of gigantic dimensions can
develop, sometimes accompanied by great spiraling holes in the water.
Humphreys observed an eddy "running *upstream* at seven miles an
hour and extending half across the river, whirling and foaming like a
whirlpool."

The river's sinuosity itself generates enormous force. The Mississippi snakes seaward in a continual series of S curves that sometimes approach 180 degrees. The collision of river and earth at these
bends creates tremendous turbulence: currents can drive straight
down to the bottom of the river, sucking at whatever lies on the
surface, scouring out holes often several hundred feet deep. Thus the
Mississippi is a series of deep pools and shallow "crossings," and
the movement of water from depth to shallows adds still further force
and complexity.

High water—a flood—makes river dynamics more volatile and
enigmatic. In some parts of the river high water raises the surface seventy feet above low water. By raising the surface in relation to sea level,
high water can thus increase the slope of the river by 25 percent or
more. And velocity depends upon the square of the slope. The river's

main current can reach nine miles an hour, while some currents can move much faster. During floods, measurable effects of an approaching flood crest can roar downriver at almost eighteen miles an hour.

And, for the last 450 miles of the Mississippi's flow, the riverbed lies *below* sea level—15 feet below sea level at Vicksburg, well over 170 feet below sea level at New Orleans. For this 450 miles the water on the bottom has no reason to flow at all. But the water above it does. This creates a tumbling effect as water spills over itself, like an enormous ever-breaking internal wave. This tumbling effect can attack a riverbank—or a levee—like a buzz saw.

But the final complexity of the lower Mississippi is its sediment load, and understanding it was the key to understanding how to control the river.

Every day the river deposits between several hundred thousand and several million *tons* of earth in the Gulf of Mexico. At least some geologists put this figure even higher historically, at an average of more than 2 million tons a day.

By geological standards the lower Mississippi is a young, even infant stream, and runs through what is known as the Mississippi Embayment, a declivity covering approximately 35,000 square miles that begins 30 miles north of Cairo to Cape Girardeau, Missouri— geologically the true head of the Mississippi Delta—and extends to the Gulf of Mexico. At one time the Gulf itself reached to Cape Girardeau, then sea level fell.

Over thousands of years the river and its tributaries have poured 1,280 cubic miles of sediment—the equivalent of 1,280 separate mountains of earth, each one a mile high, a mile wide, and a mile long—into this declivity. Aided by the falling sea level, this sediment filled in the embayment and made land. Throughout the Mississippi's alluvial valley, this sedimentary deposit has an average thickness of 132 feet; in some areas the deposits reach down 350 feet. Its weight is great enough that some geologists believe its downward pressure pushed up surrounding land, creating hills.

There were two basic, and to some extent contradictory, approaches that engineers historically embraced to protect this valley from floods: levees or outlets. Levees confined the Mississippi; outlets released it. Levees represented man's power over nature; outlets represented man's accommodation to nature. Which approach was the right one depended largely upon the answer to the question of what caused the river to carry more sediment, and what caused it to deposit sediment it already carried.

A LEVEE IS NOTHING MORE than earth mounded into a hill to contain water. Babylonians leveed the Euphrates. Rome leveed the Tiber and Po. By 1700 the Danube, the Rhône, the Rhine, the Volga, and other European rivers had levees, while Holland made the most extensive use of them (a levee and a dike are the same thing).

The Mississippi creates natural levees. When the river overflows, it deposits the heaviest sediment first, thus building up the land closest to the river. Generally, these natural levees extend for half a mile to a mile from the riverbank. "Bottomlands" farther away are lower and often marsh and swamp. New Orleans was founded on a natural levee, and its French Quarter is the highest ground in the region. By 1726, artificial levees with a height ranging from four to six feet also protected the city.

But levee building never stopped; levees were extended above and below New Orleans, then to the opposite bank. Those levees increased the pressure on old ones. The reason is simple: when the river was leveed on only one bank, in flood it simply overflowed the opposite bank. But with both banks leveed, the river could not spread out. Therefore, it rose up. Thus the levees, by holding the water in, forced the river higher. In turn, men tried to contain the flood height by building levees still higher. By 1812, levees in Louisiana began just below New Orleans and extended 155 miles north on the east bank of the river and 180 miles on the west bank. By 1858, levees on the two sides of the river totaled well over 1,000 miles.

In some stretches the levee rose to a height of 38 feet. These heights changed the equations of force along the river. Without levees, even a great flood—a great "high water"—meant only a gradual and gentle rising and spreading of water. But if a levee towering as high as a four-story building gave way, the river could explode upon the land with the power and suddenness of a dam bursting.

From the first, some critics argued that building the levees higher simply increased the dangers should a crevasse, or levee break, occur, and insisted that a means to lower flood heights be used in conjunction with levees. There were three main ways to lower the flood level. One was to build reservoirs on tributaries to withhold water from the Mississippi during floods. A second was to cut a line through the sharp S curves of the river; these cutoffs would move the water in a shorter and straighter line, increase its slope, and hence its speed (a book arguing for cutoffs would later be titled *Speeding Floods to the Sea*). A third way was to let water escape from the river through outlets. All three proposals had detractors, but outlets had the most—because it also had the most advocates.

As early as 1816, proposals were made to create artificial outlets, also called spillways or waste weirs, on the east bank of the Mississippi near New Orleans. One proposal called for a spillway above the city to drain Mississippi floodwater into Lake Pontchartrain, while another called for one below the city to drain into Lake Borgne. Both "lakes" are really more akin to saltwater bays and empty into the sea, and at the proposed sites the river flowed within five miles of them.

Simple logic drove the argument for outlets. Removing water from the river would lower flood levels, proponents of the scheme insisted, just as removing the plug in a bathtub lowered the water level there.

Critics of outlets who instead insisted upon levees, and levees only—it soon became known as the "levees-only" position—generally subscribed to an engineering theory developed from observations of the Po made by the seventeenth-century Italian engineer Guglielmini. Guglielmini argued that alluvial rivers, like the Mississippi, always carried the maximum amount of sediment possible, and that the faster the current, the more sediment the river *had* to carry. His hypothesis further argued that increasing the volume of water in the river also increased the velocity of the current, thus compelling the river to *pick up* more sediment. The main source for this sediment had to be the riverbed, so confining the river and increasing the current forced a scouring and deepening of the bottom. In effect, adherents of this theory argued, levees would transform the river into a machine that dredges its own bottom, thus allowing it to carry more water without overflowing.

Levees-only advocates argued that outlets, by allowing water to escape from the river, were counterproductive since they removed volume from the river, lowered the slope, and caused the current velocity to slow. This not only prevented the current from scouring out the bottom, but actually caused the deposit of sediment—thus raising the bottom and in turn the flood height. According to the levees-only theory, using outlets was like taking water out of a bathtub, then dumping so much gravel into it that the tub ended up holding less water. The levees-only hypothesis argued that outlets, rather than lowering the flood height, would actually raise it.

In an 1850 report to the Louisiana legislature, a professor of engineering endorsed the hypothesis: "Concentration of force increases the abrasive power. . . . Levees confine and concentrate the waters, concentrate and increase the force, therefore increase the abrasion, therefore the capacity of the channel. . . . Outlets diffuse the waters, reduce the abrasive force, and therefore reduce the capacity of the channel."

Strict adherents of Guglielmini's theory even called for closing natural outlets to force even more water into the main channel of the Mississippi, claiming the increase in volume would also increase its scouring effect.

In fact there was no doubt that levees did increase current velocity, which in turn did increase the scouring out of the channel. But the question was, how much? Floods might carry twenty times the low-water volume of the river. Could levees increase scour enough to accommodate that much water?

As Humphreys observed soon after arriving in New Orleans: "The public mind here is bewildered by the contradictory opinions given by the Engineers in the state as to what ought and ought not to be done. One says cut-offs is the only means of protecting the country. Another says cut-offs will ruin the country, make levees only. . . . A third says make outlets. Each one quotes opinions of foreign engineers and partial facts and pretended facts respecting the Mississippi to support his views. No wonder the legislature does nothing." Ellet and Humphreys—rather, Ellet *or* Humphreys, whoever won their contest—would decide the issue.

AT THE TIME, few would have bet against Charles Ellet in any competition. But the survey was not the work of *his* life, nor did he intend to spend long at it. He had already developed his ideas studying the Ohio, and, even with his wife and children beside him, he disliked New Orleans. In March 1851, not long before he returned north to write his report, he told his mother: "We have been to see Jenny Lind [who was managed by P. T. Barnum] and I must admit we paid a full price for that music. . . . I have pretty near come to the conclusion that instead of controlling these floods I would do service to the work to sweep away . . . New Orleans with all its boardinghouses, grog shops, and music to boot."

Humphreys had arrived in Louisiana at the same time as Ellet. He came alone, without his family. He never saw Jenny Lind. He worked. While Ellet was preparing to leave, Humphreys was writing a colleague: "I cannot understand how any man can be willing to assume charge of a work without making it his business to know everything about it from A to Izzard. . . . Having got to work I am ready to go into it up to the armpits."

The next few months would be the truest of Humphreys' life. He proceeded deliberately, exploring every issue in exquisite detail, compiling mountains of data, rejecting anything that threatened the integrity of his findings. He protected the survey's integrity at all times, for example resisting pressure to hire one assistant who was "a most active partisan of levees only, to the exclusion of outlets, and his mind is biased. He could not perceive the force of any factor or argument on the other side."

For the moment, Humphreys believed truth would make his reputation. He asked himself such questions as "What is the reason that the Po—and the Mississippi—do not carry gravel to their mouths when their velocities in floods are more than sufficient, according to the books? Answer? Make a profile of the bottom and see." He literally chewed on the problem, tasting mud dredged from the bottom, 150 feet deep, as if it had some mystery to impart, noting, "The clay itself has a somewhat gritty feel between the teeth and a peculiar taste."

He also chose two outstanding deputies: Caleb Forshey and Lieutenant G. K. Warren. Forshey was a professor of mathematics and engineering and a leading expert on the river; Warren, later a prominent explorer, had just graduated from West Point and had declined an offer of a mathematics professorship there to work on the survey. Humphreys gave each of them detailed instructions; the three each took charge of a work party and proceeded independently, hundreds of miles apart, recording rigorous measurements and observations.

It was hard work, physical work, being constantly out on the river. Humphreys was precise, dressed always in full uniform. On the water there was no relief from the sun. Spring was hot. Summer was hotter. The heat drove him nearly mad. But the work exhilarated! How it must have felt to stand on the bank of the Mississippi in the middle of the nineteenth century, to push one's way through a wild and thick jungle of cane, vines, and willow, to hear the animal sounds mixed with the rush of water, to see water a mile wide, boiling, dark, and angry, two hundred and more feet deep, to watch it thunder and roll south at a speed so great a boat with six men at oars could not move upstream. How godlike it must have felt to a man who intended to find a way to command it.

Humphreys carefully tested generally accepted theories and found them all wanting. The levees-only theory seemed particularly flawed, and these flaws suggested that outlets would best control floods. He discovered that, for example, contrary to the predictions of Guglielmini and the levees-only theory, the Mississippi did not always carry its maximum sediment load, and water moving at a higher velocity did not necessarily carry more sediment, per unit of volume, than water moving at a slower velocity. He reported, "The opinions of Frisi, Gennete, Guglielmini, and various others adverse to outlets with the facts respecting the Rhine and the Italian rivers, the Po, the Rhône, etc. cited by them . . . do not apply to the condition of things here."

Increasingly confident that his investigations might leave a great mark on science, he wrote in March 1851, "Facts of great interest are developing constantly—*new facts* too that bear upon hydraulic questions of the first importance." In April he added, "Never was there a finer field for a man!" In May he remained excited: "You see how I shall have to upset pretended facts."

But he was also becoming erratic. He worked intensively, then more than intensively. The work obsessed him, unbalanced him, pushed him to the margin. He stopped writing his wife because it distracted him. He tried to buy a steamboat for the sole purpose of conducting a few soundings. He tongue-lashed his assistants for speaking with outsiders, even though they had simply been trying to glean information about Ellet. He himself talked to reporters. He basked in their attention, basked in their portrayal of him as a major figure so much that his superiors reprimanded him for talking so much to the press.

The reprimand was a sudden and disconcerting blow. Then came a far heavier one. Deep into summer, rumors filtered into Louisiana that Ellet had nearly finished his report. Soon after, Humphreys collapsed and returned to Philadelphia for an extended recuperation.

It seems to have been a nervous breakdown. The attending physician diagnosed "a lesion of Enervation of the whole system, produced by excessive mental exertion and intense application to business."

In October 1851, Humphreys still lay in bed. And Ellet officially submitted his report.

Time would prove it an extraordinary document, lacking in hard data but brilliant and intuitive. Ellet began by noting that if floods were controlled, then "the lands which are now annually over-flowed . . . would possess a value that it might seem extravagant to state; while the annual loss and distress of the present population caused by the inundations of the river can scarcely find a parallel, excepting in the effects of national hostilities." He also warned that "future floods throughout the length and breadth of the delta, and along the great streams tributary to the Mississippi, are destined to rise higher and higher, as society spreads over the upper states, as population adjacent to the river increases, and the inundated low lands appreciate in value."

Then he discussed river engineering, seizing the scientific glory Humphreys had foreseen for himself by showing that the theories of the famous Europeans "fail to give results in close agreement with recognized facts. It has therefore been deemed advisable, indeed necessary, to derive new and better formulae from a wider range of experiments."

He dismissed the levees-only theory as "a delusive hope, and most dangerous to indulge, because it encourages a false security." Indeed, he blamed levees for exacerbating the problem: "The water is supplied by nature, but its *height* is increased by man. *This cause is the extension of the levees* [his italics]."

Finally, he proposed a comprehensive approach to control floods, including improving levees, enlarging natural outlets, and adding artificial outlets and reservoirs.

Humphreys had expected his own report to set policy toward the Mississippi River forever. Instead, he lay in bed impotent. He had no response to Ellet. Indeed, Humphrey's superior, Lieutenant Colonel Stephen Long, could only write, "The continued illness of [Captain Humphreys] renders him unfit for the laborious task of collating and reporting on the proceedings."

The Army's office of the Mississippi survey closed. Logs, instruments, and data were shipped to Louisville to be stored and gather dust.

Yet Humphreys swore he would complete his work. He had become not merely Ellet's rival now, but his enemy.

CHAPTER THREE

ELLET PUBLISHED his report as a book and distributed it nationally to politicians and engineers. His stature and triumph grew, driving Humphreys past the point of toleration, making him more determined to produce a masterpiece himself.

In 1853, to escape Ellet's success, Humphreys, though still recuperating, used his political connections to obtain orders to study European deltaic rivers. He spent eighteen months there, making observations, meeting with Europe's leading hydraulic engineers. But they asked him about Ellet's report too. When he returned home, he published—at his own expense—a pamphlet attacking Ellet methodology, calculations, and conclusions.

Upon his return in 1854, Humphreys' close friend Secretary of War Jefferson Davis gave him a prime assignment: overseeing surveys for transcontinental railroads. This he did well; his office laid out four routes through the mountains, each one of which would later be used. But the Mississippi obsessed him. He continued to follow every development and assemble information, always planning to write his report. In 1857, after several years of intense politicking, Humphreys succeeded in reopening the Mississippi survey office in Washington.

He still had to give most of his time to other assignments, but he obtained all his old data from storage, reviewed it, and handpicked a young lieutenant named Henry Abbot, whom he sent to the Mississippi to perform new measurements from Kentucky to Louisiana. In 1860, Humphreys was finally ready to begin writing his report. As the nation prepared to go to war, he isolated himself in his office in the new five-story Winder Building, at Seventeenth and F Streets, just behind the War Department. Through the winter of 1860, Humphreys was there, working through the night, night after night, rarely emerging from his office. As the cold weeks turned into spring, as state after state seceded from the Union, as war talk filled Washington, Humphreys worked, his only respite his view of the Mall, an enchanted carpet of green interspersed with great forest oaks and pines and twisting private paths past boscage and flower beds. West Point classmates and friends clasped hands and separated, knowing that they would be called upon to kill each other. Humphreys had no time for such partings. While he made clear to superiors that he was "desirous of taking part at the earliest day practicable in military operations," he focused only upon his report. He was desperate not to leave "the work of my life in an unfinished condition. I was deeply anxious to complete [it]. A few hours . . . under such circumstances became important."

In this, Jefferson Davis ironically helped him again. Hostility lingered in the Union Army over Humphreys' friendship with Davis. On April 12, 1861, Confederate forces fired on Fort Sumter and war broke out, but Humphreys was not given immediate combat responsibility.

While the nation went to war, Humphreys engaged in hostilities too, only his were personal. His report was his weapon. He had never been generous to rivals. He now became ruthless. If earlier, while gathering information, Humphreys had pursued pure truth, now he saw himself as having been wronged by Ellet. His own son conceded that his father "schooled" himself "not to feel love, friendship, or sympathy, but wrong, injustice, and misrepresentation." Ellet had cheated him out of glory. What if Humphreys could show that Ellet was mistaken?

On July 21, 1861, Union forces were routed at the first battle of Bull Run. Soon afterward Humphreys submitted his report to the secretary of war. To prevent its loss in the confusion of war and his own possible death, he also had one thousand copies printed immediately by a Philadelphia publisher.

The report quickly won attention and praise in Europe. In the United States, both the Union Army and the southern states along the river had other priorities. But the war would eventually give Humphreys' report the greatest imaginable weight.

LIKE VIRTUALLY ALL West Point graduates, Humphreys advanced rapidly, in eight months rising from captain of engineers to brigadier general and commander of a combat infantry division. And in combat Humphreys showed the iciness of a man who saw others as a means to his end. He displayed his temperament chiefly in letters to his wife, where a portrait emerges of a man enormously prideful and enormously sensitive to position, while his desire for glory showed itself in war.

When Theodore Lyman, a young Union officer, encountered him for the first time, he found "an extremely neat man . . . continually washing himself and putting on paper dickeys . . . an extremely gentlemanly man. . . . There was never a nicer old gentleman"— Humphreys was fifty-two—"and so boyish and peppery that I continually wanted to laugh in his face." Then on December 14, 1862, at Fredericksburg, Virginia, Lyman saw a different Humphreys, a chilling Humphreys, and said of him, "I do like to see a brave man, but when a man goes out for the express purpose of getting shot at he seems to me in the way of a maniac."

Fredericksburg was Humphreys' first real battle. The Confederate Army under Lee sat behind a stone wall atop a steep high bluff, overlooking open ground. The Union General Ambrose Burnside (whose trademark whiskers later became known as "sideburns") ordered his troops to charge.

It was one of the great bloody blunders of the war. Yet in it a strange detachment surrounded Humphreys, a penumbra of raw ego.

Division after division charged and fell back. Then came Humphreys' turn. His soldiers fixed bayonets. One of his officers told the rawest, youngest recruits to remain in the rear. Humphreys called them stragglers and ordered them forward with the rest of his troops. He then bowed to his staff, said, "Gentlemen, I shall lead this charge. I presume, of course, you will wish to ride with me?" With him at their head, they started up the hill.

After the battle he wrote his wife: "I led my division into a desperate fight and tried to take at the point of a bayonet a stone wall behind which a heavy line of the enemy lay. The heights just above were lined with artillery that poured upon us round shot, shell, and shrapnel; the musketry from the stone wall made a continuous sheet of flame. We charged within 50 yards of it each time but the men could not stand it."

Still, he told her, "The charge of my division is described by . . . some general officers [as] the grandest sight they ever saw, and that as I led the charge and bared my head, raising my right arm to heaven, the setting sun shining full on my face gave me the aspect of an inspired being. . . . I felt gloriously, and as the storm of bullets whistled around me, and as the shells and shrapnel burst close to me in every direction with hissing sound, the excitement grew more glorious still. Oh, it was sublime!"

To an old friend he added, "I felt like a young girl of sixteen at her first ball. . . . I felt more like a god than a man. I now understand what Charles XII meant when he said, 'Let the whistling of bullets hereafter be my music.' "

As an afterthought, he noted, "In ten or fifteen minutes I lost more than 1,000 officers and men." The casualties exceeded 20 percent of his command. Five of his seven staff officers were shot off their horses. Yet only the glory mattered to him. "The division has made such reputation as will make the fortunes of many of its officers," he wrote.

Only one thing seemed to have perturbed him. After the battle a fellow officer noted, "General Humphreys with his usual bland smile appeared on a small gray horse, which was of a contrary and rearing disposition; but the General remarked that he had had three valuable horses killed under him, and now he would get only cheap ones."

More heavy fighting followed. His division shrank from 7,000 men to 3,684. In a series of letters to his wife there is no mention of the horrors they, and he, had gone through, only reports of praise of himself. "It is acknowledged throughout this army," he wrote, "that no officer ever did as much with troops of short term of service as I did with these, and . . . that no one else would or could have done as much."

He was given a new division. At Gettysburg there was more bloodshed. A Union officer watching from a distance reported: "The space occupied by the division of Humphreys was the vortex of a cauldron of fire, the crater of a volcano of destruction . . . every horse killed and every man in the battery having fallen at his post. Against the weakened, struggling lines of Humphreys . . . Confederates were pressing with eager yells, trampling the wounded Union men under their feet."

Humphreys, himself unscathed, only noted with pride, "The newspaper correspondents have congratulated me too and said the handsomest things." A few weeks later he was promoted to major general and transferred. In his farewell speech to his troops he said nothing of them, their blood, nor even what they had achieved together. He spoke only of himself: "Why, anyone who knows me intimately knows I had more of the soldier than a man of science in me. I did not go to pure science or book science for that would soon have been unendurable, but to science that partook of practicable application, and looked besides to greater application eventually . . . in the development of the resources of the country."

Humphreys' new post was chief of staff to General George Meade, commander of the Army of the Potomac. But staff officers received no glory. Quickly discontented, he complained, "I prefer infinitely command of troops to this position of Chief of Staff. It suits me in nothing, my habits, my wishes, my tastes. I hate to be second to anyone."

Again: "My mortification at seeing the men over me and commanding me who should have been far below me has destroyed all my enthusiasm and I am indifferent. . . . How much I could say! I have hardly begun yet."

And again: "I know that as a Division Commander I have done what no other Division Commander ever has done, and I know that my example has taught others what to do."

And again: "I have good reason to believe that if it was left to each of the Corps of this Army to say who should command them, I should be chosen in preference to any other."

Later, ignoring the illnesses that had forced him to leave active service for long periods, he even bragged of physical superiority, claiming, "I do not believe there was a stronger man physically in the whole Army than myself, and but few equally strong."

In 1864, General Grant was placed over Meade. Humphreys became even more disenchanted: "The reputation justly due to those labors, responsibility and deeds will go to General Grant, and not to General Meade, much less to myself. General Grant will reap all the glory, all the reputation of success, and share none of the obloquy of disaster if such should befall us."

If Humphreys' hopes in the war were not realized, neither were his fears. He ended the war not on Grant's staff but as one of Grant's corps commanders, chasing Lee down, with considerable power within the Army. His report on the river gave him more.

During the war his report had been hailed throughout Europe. Now, after the war, his own country gave him honors enough to satisfy even him. Every major scientific society in the nation elected him to membership, joining the many in Europe that had already done so. Both the scientific and lay press heaped praise upon him. Dozens of newspapers wrote encomiums like that of the *New Orleans Daily Crescent:* "Its publication constitutes an epoch in hydrographical science. . . . General Humphreys, in spite of so many previous failures on the part of so many eminent scientific men, succeeded."

Humphreys' report would in fact become the single most influential document ever written about the Mississippi River. Indeed, it would become one of the most influential single engineering reports ever written on any subject. It would have such influence both because of the position Humphreys would soon attain and because of its quality. It included hundreds of pages of drawings, graphs, and raw data on sandbars, on riverbanks, on levees, on every imaginable river phenomenon, along with critical analyses of several centuries of scientific literature.

The title alone was a monument to thoroughness: it began *Report upon the Physics and Hydraulics of the Mississippi River* and went on for ninety words. For brevity, it became known as "Humphreys & Abbot" (he graciously credited his assistant Lieutenant Henry Abbot as coauthor), *Physics and Hydraulics*, or simply the *Delta Survey*.

More important, the report appeared in the first great age of science, a time when science was redefining the world, when man believed nature was governable and scientists were daily promulgating new laws to subdue it. The telegraph had made communication virtually instantaneous. Already there were plans to lay a cable across the Atlantic, binding Europe and America unimaginably close. In 1859, Charles Darwin's *Origin of Species* appeared. In Europe, Louis Pasteur was probing the world of microbiology, and Pasteur had written, "I am on the verge of mysteries, and the veil is getting thinner and thinner."

Humphreys saw his own work ripping away the veils that had shrouded the great river, and promulgated his own laws to govern it. He declared that he had found "the crowning proof of the exactness of the new formulae as applied to water moving in natural channels. . . . It establishes beyond reasonable doubt, first that the same laws govern the flow of water in the largest rivers and in the smallest streams; second, that the new formulae truly express these laws; and, third, that the formulae heretofore proposed do not express them even approximately."

Humphreys considered his methodology, observations, and conclusions irrefutable, and on his title page indirectly rebuked other engineers—especially Ellet—for theorizing without data, when he quoted Benjamin Franklin: " 'I approve much more your method of philosophizing, which proceeds from actual observation, makes a collection of facts, and concludes no further than those facts warrant.' "

Science, however, is a process. Humphreys considered his own work final, proclaiming, "Every river phenomenon has been experimentally investigated and elucidated. Thus every important fact connected with the various physical conditions of the river and the laws uniting them being ascertained, the great problem of protection against inundation is solved. At the mouths of the river, a similar course has resulted in the development of . . . the principles upon which the plans for deepening the channels over them should be based."

To CONTROL FLOODS, levees-only advocates called for confining the river to increase the volume of water, hence increasing the current velocity and scour, thereby deepening the channel.

Ellet had called for the reverse approach, building outlets and reservoirs to decrease the floodwater the river carried.

Humphreys' own observations seemed to favor outlets as well. His report repeatedly dismissed the levees-only approach, stating, "The investigations of the Delta Survey have rendered untenable that position [that] the exclusive use of levees . . . lowered the flood by deepening the bed." Again, "The legitimate consequences which result from Guglielmini's theory are all contrary to observation." Again, "Measurements demonstrate with a degree of certainty rarely to be attained in such investigations, that the opinions advanced by these writers are totally erroneous."

Significantly, he warned that calls by levees-only advocates for closing natural outlets of the Mississippi, especially the Atchafalaya River, "would, if executed, entail disastrous consequences." Regarding artificial outlets, he wrote: "The investigations of the Delta Survey prove that outlets, in the few localities where they are practicable, may be made to reduce the floods to any desired extent in certain divisions of the river. . . . [S]o far as the river itself is concerned, they are of great utility. Few practical problems admit of so positive a solution."

Since this analysis suggested that Ellet was correct, Humphreys demolished Ellet personally. "The task of criticism is always ungrateful," Humphreys wrote unctuously, "and had [Ellet's report] been proposed by an obscure writer, it would have remained unnoticed. Coming, however, from a civil engineer so well known as Mr. Ellet, and furnishing, as it does, the basis [of] practical conclusions believed to be most erroneous and most mischievous, it cannot be passed by in silence."

Then he attacked. He damned Ellet with a mocking faint praise, calling Ellet's work on the Ohio River "admirably executed, as far as the field work was concerned, but . . . the computation . . . seems to be a repetition of Destrem's misapplication of Prony's rule."

He also lashed out: "Mr. Ellet shows he does not understand the essential requirements"; "the exactness of measurement deemed essential in the operations of this Survey was not attempted by Mr. Ellet"; "Mr. Ellet's opinion is based on erroneous measurements"; "the discharge of the Mississippi calculated by Mr. Ellet, cannot be relied upon as very accurate."

Finally, after reviewing recommendations made over the course of three centuries by engineers from Italy, France, Switzerland, Austria, Britain, and the United States, Humphreys concluded, "Mr. Ellet's is the worst ever suggested."

Ellet had called for outlets. If Ellet's recommendations were the worst ever suggested, how could Humphreys recommend outlets?

He could not.

Humphreys had begun his survey with intellectual curiosity and honesty. But he had also always intended to write a masterpiece. No masterpiece can merely confirm another's findings. *I hate to be second to anyone,* he had said. He would not be second. Instead, he would become corrupt. The corruption did not infect his data—even today his data are considered reliable and instructive—but it did infect his reasoning and his recommendations.

The reasoning was key. He convinced himself of the validity of two new arguments against outlets that not even levees-only advocates had raised. Like a deus ex machina, they allowed him to alter the direction in which his own scientific observations pointed.

First, he claimed that outlets risked creating a new main channel for the river. Humphreys' own deputy Forshey, the man who provided the raw data that went into the analysis, had earlier called this fear "groundless," but Forshey was now, after the war, relying on Humphreys for patronage and did not protest.

Second, Humphreys insisted that creating outlets would cost too much for the benefits gained. There may have been considerable validity to this argument in 1861, but the cost-benefit equation would change as more land was developed. Humphreys made no mention of that.

So Humphreys rejected outlets, and Ellet with them. "It has been *demonstrated,*" he concluded, his italics implying that no reasoning man could dispute him, "that no advantage can be derived either from diverting tributaries or constructing reservoirs, and that the plans of cut-offs, and of new and enlarged outlets to the Gulf, are too costly and too dangerous to be attempted. The plan of levees, on the contrary, which has always recommended itself by its simplicity and its direct repayment of investments, may be relied upon for protecting all the alluvial bottom lands liable to inundation below Cape Girardeau."

Humphreys continued to reject the engineering hypothesis that underlay the levees-only idea. He continued to warn that the closing of natural outlets would be disastrous. Yet he was recommending that levees, and levees only, be used to contain the Mississippi River and its floods. He had found a facile way to reconcile his conclusion with seemingly contradictory analysis and data.

And who could challenge him? Certainly no one in the South. People along the river were destitute, exhausted physically, emotionally, and financially. The war had ripped enormous gaps in the levees, either through erosion or sabotage by Union forces. Humphreys' first assignment after the war was to inspect the Mississippi levees, and he recommended the federal government spend several million dollars to rebuild them. Though Congress did not appropriate the money, no southerner would antagonize this new friend. And behind him he had the weight of the U.S. Army.

Ellet could not protest. He had been killed during the war, commanding a Union ram on the Mississippi. Humphreys seemed to stand alone, where he had always wanted to be. And he would soon have the power to enforce his will upon the nation.

CHAPTER FOUR

In 1866, HAVING CHAMPIONED the Army against civilian critics and having been honored by scientific societies throughout the world, Andrew Atkinson Humphreys became chief of engineers of the U.S. Army. Ironically, by then there was no scientist left within him. Only the soldier remained.

He cared now only about obedience, power, and rank. Rank in particular obsessed him. The Army shrank after the war, and officers returned to their permanent rank. Some brevet major generals became captains again. Humphreys, a brevet major general, fell only to brigadier general, a rank that automatically went with his command. Yet he resented even this. He began lobbying congressmen to make the chief of engineers a major general, arguing that his duties were "far more onerous, extensive, and responsible than of any department commander." Unsuccessful in that, he then asked the secretary of war that he "be relieved from duty as Chief of Engineers and assigned to command under my brevet rank," although he soon wrote to "beg leave to withdraw" that request.

Inside the Corps his rule was absolute. He sought to have all engineering officers formally "detached" from the Army, thus making them answerable only to him. This effort earned him a reprimand, but he still sent a chilling message to underlings when one of the Corps' civilian engineers, a man named Daniel Henry, invented a new instrument to measure water outflow; it gave far more precise results than a method Humphreys himself had developed for the Delta Survey. A scientist would have welcomed the advance, and the innovation was important enough to be displayed later at the 1876 Philadelphia Centennial Exhibition. But when Henry used the new method in Army work, Humphreys relieved Henry's military commander—a general—of his command for allowing its use, and forced Henry out of his job.

Humphreys tolerated no criticism. Even less would he tolerate a rival. But a rival far more formidable than anyone he had ever encountered was emerging.

Humphreys and this rival would soon meet in a great collision over control of the Mississippi River. The rival was James Buchanan Eads. Their collision began over a bridge.

THE CONSTRUCTION of what came to be known as the Eads Bridge at St. Louis was an epic in itself. The story began with money, and commerce. Prior to the Civil War, steamboats from St. Louis could navigate 15,510 miles of rivers, and an enormous and growing river trade seemed to quarantee the city's future, helping the city grow from a population of 77,860 in 1850 to 160,773 in 1860 and 310,864 in 1870. Of railroads, the *Missouri Republican* said in 1854, "It may be properly assumed that trade, shipping, or business cannot be diverted by mere artificial means, from channels which nature . . . [has] given it . . . nor can any amount of capital supply the place of the rivers which constitute her great highways."

But capital built railroads and railroads made Chicago explode. Its population skyrocketed from 4,479 in 1840, to 29,963 in 1850, 109,260 in 1860, and, officially, 298,977 in 1870. (Chicagoans charged, probably correctly, that St. Louis boosters manipulated the 1870 numbers to keep Chicago from surpassing St. Louis in population.)

The competition between the two cities, and between steamboats and railroads, was vicious. It came to a head when railroads bridged rivers. The first bridge across the Mississippi came in 1856 at Davenport, Iowa. Poorly designed, it was promptly hit by a steamboat, which sank (Eads salvaged it). St. Louis interests financed a famous lawsuit, seeking to tear down the bridge as a hazard to navigation. Abraham Lincoln argued for the railroad. His success—actually, a hung jury—was a major blow to river transport, and to St. Louis.

But as a result, the Corps of Engineers demanded, and Congress gave it, authority to review future bridges over the Mississippi to ensure their safety to shipping.

The Civil War meanwhile cut off St. Louis from much Mississippi River trade. Chicago took up the slack, and more. In 1860, not a single Chicago mercantile house did $600,000 worth of business a year; in 1866, with several bridges across the upper Mississippi open or under construction, twenty-two Chicago firms did over $1 million worth of business. The St. Louis Merchants Exchange finally recognized that without a railroad bridge across the river at their city, its business would evaporate; the exchange asked Eads to chair a subcommittee to reconcile bridge and steamboat interests.

Though long identified with steamboats, Eads was intrigued with bridging the Mississippi. He knew more about the river than any man who had ever lived. His experience with ironclads and naval artillery had taught him much about iron, and even about the then experimental metal steel.

After studying the problem, Eads proposed an arched bridge made of steel with either one span of at least 600 feet, or two of at least 450 feet. At the time he made this recommendation, not a single steel bridge existed anywhere in the world; in addition, the proposed arches would be the longest in the world. But on April 18, 1866, in the Merchants Exchange Building, his subcommittee adopted his proposal unanimously. Such was the faith St. Louis businessmen had in Eads.

An existing company already owned a state charter to build a bridge, but after a year in which it made no move toward actual construction, Eads and his associates bought it. He became the company's chief engineer. Suddenly, things began to move swiftly.

First, Eads met with his old friend Missouri Senator Benjamin Gratz Brown, who won congressional authorization for the bridge over opposition from ferries, steamboats, railroads with established connections, and Chicago politicians. The authorization passed, Brown said, only because it stipulated at least one span of at least 500 feet or two of at least 350 feet, which was considered "impossible. . . . In fact, the utterance was then and there boldly made that the genius did not exist in the country capable of erecting such a structure."

Eads had never built any bridge, and this would have the longest arches ever built, with a material never before used for such a purpose—indeed, the British then forbade the use of steel in bridges. It would span the Mississippi *below* the mouth of the Missouri, after that river's tremendous volume joined the upper Mississippi. No bridge on the upper Mississippi itself nor anywhere else crossed a comparable flow of water.

Yet in an expression of almost suicidal self-confidence, Eads decided to design this bridge himself. He did hire outstanding assistants, including Henry Flad and W. Milnor Roberts, who both later became presidents of the American Society of Civil Engineers. But the basic design was his, many of the calculations his, many of the technical innovations his.

His plans called for a center arch 520 feet wide resting on piers sunk to bedrock, and two side arches 502 feet wide. The key to success would be steel. Steel was as revolutionary as his plans. Though Eads probably knew more about steel than any engineer in the world, and most metallurgists, it was still a new medium; not until 1867—the year Eads committed himself to the metal—was the open-hearth process even developed.

This did not reassure. Bridges built by experienced engineers, including Ellet, across lesser rivers had already collapsed, costing lives and money. In fact, roughly one out of every four bridges built in this period collapsed. The cost estimate for the St. Louis Bridge approached $6 million. Almost certainly it would rise. Eads would need to find capital not only in New York and Boston, but in London and Paris. To build investor confidence Eads hired as consulting engineer Jacob Linville, former bridge engineer for the Pennsylvania Railroad and president of the Keystone Bridge Company, which Linville and Andrew Carnegie had formed. But after examining the plans in July 1867, Linville said: "I cannot consent to imperil my reputation by appearing to encourage or approve its adoption. I deem it entirely unsafe and impracticable."

Linville's criticism was only one blow. A few weeks later a rival bridge builder tried to undermine further Eads' ability to raise capital by convening a meeting in St. Louis of twenty-seven engineers. Their report announced "unqualified disapproval of spans of five hundred feet . . . for which there is no engineering precedent"; it was printed as a pamphlet and distributed nationally.

Yet Eads never took a backward step. Elmer Corthell, a third Eads assistant who later became president of the American Society of Civil Engineers, wrote of him: "It is absolutely certain that no obstacle of an engineering, financial or any other kind ever for a moment disturbed or discouraged him. His complete knowledge of the conditions and the forces he was dealing with gave him unfaltering faith in the plans of the work, and yet there was something more than knowledge. . . . There was genius of the highest order that gave to him unalterable determination . . . and a sublime faith in what he always believed were the clearly written laws of the Creator."

Eads answered his critics three ways.

First, he fired Linville and eliminated the position of consulting engineer.

Second, he gathered in the financial resources at his immediate command—mostly investors who had faith in him personally—and, on August 21, 1867, began construction of a cofferdam even as the twenty-seven engineers met. Supposedly, he chose as the site the same spot on which he had first landed in the city, dragged wet and destitute from the river three decades before.

Third, he prepared his first report to the bridge company directors. The report, actually an open letter to investors, typified Eads. Much of the force of his personality lay in his ability to explain the most esoteric science in terms an intelligent layman could grasp. The report began, "Anyone who can be made to understand the principles of all mechanical powers, the lever, can readily comprehend the explanation I propose making." Step by step, each one laid with mathematical certainty atop the preceding, he presented his plans. Reaction around the world in engineering journals was, finally, universal praise. Newspapers published the plans. They were talked about everywhere.

And he applied his charm. He charmed the roughest of men working on the bridge; although he always carried a knife and pistol around them, they addressed him as "J.B." and he competed with them in weight-lifting contests on the blacksmith boat—he finished second. He was professional and focused on the task in the extreme, explaining, for example, that an employer must "have constant control of his temper, and be able to speak pleasantly to one man the next moment after having spoken in the harshest manner to another, and even to give the same man a pleasant reply a few minutes after having corrected him. Self must be left out of the matter entirely, and a man or boy spoken to only as concerns his conduct; and the authority which the controller has over the controlled, used only when absolutely necessary, and then with the utmost promptness."

More important, he charmed investors in New York, London, and Paris. His logic made the boldest goal seem attainable. His enthusiasm made it seem inevitable. Even Andrew Carnegie was charmed and first became involved in international finance selling the bridge's bonds in London.

The bridge rose. In the late 1860s and early 1870s, nearly 2,000 men were swarming about on twenty-four large derrick-equipped barges and boats and scaffolding as the steel and masonry took shape. (Thirteen men who worked as deep as 125 feet below the surface would die of caisson disease, later known as the bends, caused by nitrogen bubbles forming in the blood under pressure; problems continued until Eads' personal physician cut the shifts to forty-five minutes.) Thousands more worked in quarries in New England and machine shops and foundries in Pittsburgh, Wheeling, and Philadelphia.

But the money pressure did not abate. The estimated cost was soon up to $9 million. In one crisis the arches had to be closed by a certain date or the bridge would collapse financially. Temperatures of 100 degrees had caused the steel to expand, making it too long by fractions of an inch. Eads was in London negotiating a new loan from Junius Morgan, J. Pierpont's father, when his assistants wired that even applying hundreds of tons of ice had failed to cool and contract the metal. Eads had anticipated the problem and wired back the solution (telescoping the metal and screwing it into place, in the same way one might adjust a shower rod). Eads astounded Morgan when he, supremely confident of success, left for Paris without waiting to hear the result.

Eads made only one compromise. The same Jacob Linville whom he had fired as a consultant was president of the Keystone Bridge Company, an iron and steel contractor. His partner was Carnegie. Both Linville and Carnegie had close ties to the Pennsylvania Railroad, which was represented on the bridge company's board. Eads also needed Carnegie's financial connections. So Eads made the Keystone company chief contractor. Carnegie knew the pressures on Eads and repeatedly squeezed him, demanding new financial concessions and secretly maneuvering to control—and milk—every subcontract. Typically, Carnegie wired one steel maker not to inform Eads "about our confidential efforts to throw the steel contract your way . . . no one knows about this in St. Louis and no one should know."

But Eads pushed Carnegie as well. Eads was demanding, demanding of everyone, demanding of seemingly impossible standards. Each individual piece of key materials—not random samples from a production run—was tested. Eads' assistant Flad invented a testing machine capable of detecting deformations of 1/200,000 of an inch, a heretofore unimaginable tolerance. In one instance, the Keystone factory worked for six months to produce a single steel plate good enough to test. It failed.

To William Taussig, chairman of the bridge company—Eads was nominally only chief engineer—Carnegie complained, "The very machinery to make the raw material has in large part to be created. . . . Your man of decided real genius is the most difficult to deal with practically. . . . Nothing that would please and that does please other engineers is good enough. Capt. Eads must only require the custom of the trade. . . . You must keep Eads up to requiring only what is reasonable and in accordance with custom."

Eads cared nothing for custom. He drove on, turning to another company that pioneered chrome-alloy steel, a product he helped develop. The bridge rose up and reached across the river.

Then, abruptly, six years after Congress had specifically authorized the bridge and years after the Corps of Engineers had approved the plans for it and construction had begun, the Corps threatened to tear the bridge down.

IN REALITY, the Army's objection had little to do with the bridge. It had to do with who would control the Mississippi River.

The fight for control began on May 13, 1873, when Eads read a resolution he had written, endorsed by the city's businessmen, to a huge river convention in St. Louis attended by a dozen governors, more than one hundred members of Congress, and several thousand delegates representing every commercial interest in the Mississippi valley.

The bridge made Eads the biggest man at the convention. The sight of it was more eloquent than any acclaim, and it was the talk of the delegates. Its piers had long since been sunk to bedrock, and now its steel arches, like dancers whose outstretched arms did not quite touch each other, extended across the great river, while hundreds of men teemed about on giant derricks and great workboats.

But Eads said nothing about the bridge. Instead, he addressed the problems at the mouth of the Mississippi River, where sandbars were choking commerce.

The bars were not a new problem. In 1718 the French had noted, "It is necessary, by all sorts of methods, to open the entry of the river." In 1859, General Winfield Scott, commander of the Army, had examined the sandbars and found thirty-eight ships in the river trying to get into the Gulf, twenty-one in the Gulf waiting to get into the river, and three ships aground on the bar itself; another fifty ships were waiting to depart New Orleans. One of the ships at the bar had been waiting eighty-three days. Bad as that situation was, the problem —like the floods—was growing worse. Larger and larger ships were being blocked more and more often.

The Corps of Engineers had been trying different approaches for forty years to solve the problem. None had succeeded. Only recently the Corps had pronounced the sandbar a permanent, immovable barrier. So it planned to outflank it by building a canal to connect the river to the Gulf. The canal idea had gained nearly universal support throughout the Mississippi valley, from Louisville to Davenport and especially in New Orleans, where the issue of the sandbars was of vital concern.

So his words were controversial, even inflammatory. When Eads rejected the canal idea, he declared, "The solution of this problem, it is believed, will be achieved . . . by a system of jetties."

Eads called for constructing two parallel piers far out into the Gulf. This would narrow the river and increase its current, and Eads believed that the concentrated current would cut its own channel through the bar. In 1837, Eads had watched this happen in St. Louis. Sandbars had grown into tree-covered islands so large that they threatened to cut the city off from the river. Robert E. Lee, then a captain in the Army engineers, had built a jetty into the river that directed the force of the main channel against the islands. They had quickly melted away. Now Eads wanted to do the same thing at the Mississippi's mouth.

Eads made few converts at the convention. But after the convention many delegates, including Eads, members of Congress, and reporters from major Mississippi valley and eastern papers, traveled to New Orleans to examine the sandbar.

There Captain Charles Howell of the Corps of Engineers, author of the report calling for the canal, took them on a two-hundred-mile roundtrip to the mouth of the Mississippi. Eads spent the entire trip explaining to an interested audience why jetties were superior to the canal. Howell, increasingly irritated by this civilian who questioned the judgment and authority of the Army engineers, immediately reported the interference to Humphreys.

Humphreys was already warding off plans pushed by critics to create a U.S. Geological Survey and transfer to it the Army's authority to survey the West, and—an even more serious attack—to transfer control of the Mississippi River from the Corps to a new commission of both Army and civilian engineers. In resisting these proposals, Humphreys had advised a subordinate: "We must get ready for a combat at the next session [of Congress]—not only defensive but offensive if necessary. . . . The contest must be sharp and merciless."

He had won those contests. In triumph he turned to Eads.

Eads considered his comments about the canal and jetties impersonal, a question of science, efficiency, and truth. Humphreys considered them a personal insult directed at the single greatest failure, and embarrassment, of the Corps.

But Humphreys had never engaged a man like Eads. In his own way Eads was colder than Humphreys, far larger of vision and thus impersonal. Eads was, said a friend, "a bitter and unrelenting foe. . . . To him the unfolding of great and correct principles was more than personal friendships. His beliefs were his friends."

HUMPHREYS INTENDED to teach Eads a lesson, and his weapon was the Army's authority over obstacles to navigation on the Mississippi. He wielded that weapon when a formal complaint about the bridge was filed with Secretary of War William Belknap by the Keokuk Steamboat Company and several ferries, each of which would be hurt by competition from the bridge. Belknap, who later resigned after the House voted to impeach him over an unrelated matter, was from Keokuk and a partner of the steamboat line's owners. The charge was that some of their steamboats had smokestacks too high to fit under the bridge. Ten years earlier a solution to this problem had been found: smokestacks could simply be hinged, and lowered when passing under bridges.

Although the bridge complied precisely with the earlier congressional legislation and plans for the bridge had been widely discussed for years and approved by both Belknap's predecessor and Humphreys himself, now, a few weeks after Eads first criticized the canal idea, Humphreys ordered a board of Army engineers to investigate the complaint.

Major G. K. Warren was the board member closest to Humphreys. His own career, once filled with such promise, had been derailed a few days before Appomattox when he had been unfairly relieved of his command. He had not only worked under Humphreys on the Delta Survey but fought beside him during the war, and Humphreys was helping him convince a board of inquiry that he should not have been relieved. Warren may also have felt personal animosity toward Eads. Eads was suing Warren's brother-in-law Washington Roebling, the great engineer building the Brooklyn Bridge; Eads had given Roebling a tour of his own work, and Roebling had then used caissons similar to Eads' design. Finally, Warren himself was building a railroad bridge at Rock Island, Illinois, which would compete with the St. Louis bridge.

The Army board convened at St. Louis on September 2, 1873, without officially informing the bridge company of its inquiry and while Eads was in England raising capital. In a small room with Warren suggesting appropriate answers, bridge opponents presented two full days of choreographed testimony. Then Warren drafted a statement for bridge opponents to sign saying that "the river interests" considered the bridge "a serious obstruction to navigation."

Only then, late on a Friday afternoon and minutes before the scheduled end of the hearing, was Taussig, chairman of the bridge company, invited to speak. He asked for an additional day of hearings to allow experts and steamboatmen who did not object to the bridge to testify, requesting "as many *hours* as the complainants had had *weeks* with which to prepare their testimony."

Warren snapped, "If a thousand steamboat men should come and say that this bridge was no obstruction, it could not change my opinion." The request for another day of testimony was denied.

A week later the board issued its report. Humphreys quickly approved it. It was merciless indeed. Eads had criticized a canal near the river's mouth. The Corps would now ram a canal down his throat. The report not only concluded that the bridge would obstruct navigation but stated: "The Board have very carefully considered the various plans proposed for changing the present structure but find none of them satisfactory. They would therefore recommend that a canal be formed behind the east Abutment of the Bridge."

Humphreys was ordering Eads to build a canal with a drawbridge so ships could go around his bridge. It was an absurdity, but Humphreys had the authority to require it. Only an order from the secretary of war or the president, or an act of Congress, could prevent it.

From Europe, Eads began his counterattack, generating a flurry of condemnations of the Corps by steamboat owners and captains. Then he returned and, with Taussig, went to Washington.

On an unseasonably hot morning in the fall of 1873, they walked into the White House and with some trepidation asked to see President Grant. Just before the war Taussig had blocked the hiring of the then-struggling Grant as superintendent of county roads in St. Louis County, ironically because his father-in-law was a prominent southern sympathizer. The preceding year Eads had publicly supported Horace Greeley for president, against Grant. But Eads and Grant had always liked each other. And Eads had smoothed the way with Grant's private secretary General Horace Porter. Porter, who had captured Jefferson Davis at the end of the war, was leaving the government; he and Eads would soon reach a secret agreement giving Porter a share of Eads' profits on a venture he was about to propose.

Grant received Eads warmly, clasping his hands in both of his own. But he addressed Taussig as "Judge," his title when he rejected Grant's job application—an indication that Grant remembered. Taussig froze. Then Grant laughed, saying he bore no grudges, "since I prefer my present position to that one."

They sat in Grant's office while a steward served coffee. Eads recounted everything that had happened, along with the technical issues. Grant sat back, listening. He knew Humphreys well enough from the war. After half an hour he summoned his secretary of war.

Within moments Belknap appeared. He saw Eads and blanched. Grant asked curtly: Did the bridge not conform to the congressional legislation? Had it not already received approval from the War Department? Belknap conceded both points, but pleaded for Grant to review the papers relating to the case. Coldly, Grant said: "I do not care to look at the papers. You certainly cannot remove this structure on your own judgment. . . . If your Keokuk friends feel aggrieved let them sue the Bridge. I think, General, you had better drop the case."

Belknap reddened, bowed briefly, and left.

A few weeks later Grant was in St. Louis. He visited Eads at the bridge. The great arches were complete but only narrow planks connected them, where the roadway would be. It was a cold damp November day. They took a walk single file along the planks with the wind blowing, each of them holding their hats, walking past whistling wire ropes, the white-capped river far below them. Grant was in good cheer. They retired to the work shed. Eads opened brandy and they drank, smoked cigars, and played cards, and spoke of the past.

DESPITE GRANT'S ORDER, Humphreys did not quit. In January 1874 the Corps issued a new report, rejecting as insufficient its own earlier recommendation of a canal, calling the bridge a "badly designed . . . monster . . . Justice demands that the bridge must come down."

The bridge would not come down. Eads simply ignored the order. The bridge opened July 4, 1874, on schedule, with a great celebration attended by 300,000 men and women. It spanned the river with clean and powerful symmetry, the design as simple and elemental as the river itself, and it would carry trains for a century. An extraordinary architectural and engineering achievement, Richard Kirby and Philip Laurson in their book *The Early Years of Modern Civil Engineering* call it "[O]ne of those remarkable advances which speed the progress of an art or science . . . an achievement out of all proportion to its size." The tremendous attention focused on the bridge created instant confidence in steel and helped fuel an explosion in demand for it. In 1867, when Eads started construction, America produced 22,000 tons of steel; in 1874, when he finished, America produced 242,000 tons. But no tribute could say more than Louis Sullivan, the first great modern architect, father of the phrase "form follows function." (To him, function included not only utility but man's aspirations and ideals.) As a child in Chicago, he said, his "soul became immersed" in the bridge. "I followed every detail of design, every measurement . . . with the intensity of personal identification

... here was Romance, here again was Man, the great adventurer, daring to think, daring to have faith, daring to do."

EVEN BEFORE THE BRIDGE OPENED, Eads embarked upon another great adventure. He had begun his career riding on the surface of the Mississippi. Then he had penetrated its depths, walked its bottom. His bridge had gone deeper than the bottom, into the bedrock below it, while enveloping it above. Now he intended more: to make the river obey his will and to transform it into a tool for his own use. If in the course of pursuing this new adventure Humphreys happened to be destroyed, that would be, as they said in New Orleans, lagniappe.

CHAPTER FIVE

T HE STRUGGLE between Eads and Humphreys had become personal, rich with hatred and contempt. At stake was far more than their respective reputations, or how engineers dealt with sandbars at the mouth of the Mississippi River. At stake was the future of the millions of people who were settling in its natural floodplain. And at stake was money. The river meant money, both the money that came from trade throughout the Mississippi valley and the possible development of its floodplain. For the river itself had created enormous potential wealth in the land beside it, depositing sediment—some of the deepest and lushest soil in the world—across its floodplain. In 1857 a geologist predicted: "Whatever the Delta of the Nile may once have been will only be a shadow of what this alluvial plain of the Mississippi will be. It will be the central point—the garden spot of the North American continent—where wealth and prosperity culminate."

But the trade was limited as long as the river choked its mouth with sandbars, and the land was worthless as long as the river overflowed it at will. In the 1870s the river did just that. The war was one reason. Grant, in his campaign against Vicksburg, had cut levees, including the single strongest in the country. "On the second of February, [1863,] this dam, or levee, was cut," he later wrote. "The river being high the rush of water through the cut was so great that in a very short time the entire obstruction was washed away.... As a consequence the country was covered with water."

His act had exposed several thousand square miles to inundation, and it remained naked to the river. The poverty of southern states prevented either repairing destroyed levees or maintaining good ones. At Bonnet Carré, a few miles above New Orleans, the river broke through the levee in 1871; the crevasse would remain open, pouring water into nearby Lake Pontchartrain every flood season, until 1882.

Since the war the lower valley had gone backward, and land that had once produced wealth had gone back to jungle. Development had become a national issue as northern investors became interested. Even Massachusetts Congressman Nathaniel Banks, a Union general, called for action: "If we make the river what it ought to be we will make 40,000,000 acres of the best cotton and sugar lands on the face of the earth in consequence of the necessary improvement of the river —40,000,000 where now 1,000,000 exists. It is inseparable from and incidental to the improvement of the Mississippi river."

DESPITE EADS, Humphreys seemed in a position to dictate engineering policies toward the river. He had always nurtured his relations with Congress, and had the infrastructure of the War Department behind him. In January 1874 a board of Army engineers formally considered Captain Howell's report calling for a canal from the Mississippi to the Gulf. This board, which included Warren and, despite an obvious conflict of interest, Howell himself, first rejected Eads' call for jetties because they had been "exhaustively treated" by Humphreys in his *Physics and Hydraulics* "and there is nothing more to add." The board then endorsed Howell's plan.

The board's vote was 6 to 1, the lone dissenter the board's chairman, Colonel John Barnard, who urged further study of jetties. Barnard had actually once declined appointment as chief of engineers, urging that his mentor Fred Delafield be appointed instead. Delafield had been named, but when he retired, Barnard was not offered the post again. Humphreys was. And Humphreys immediately began making Barnard's life difficult. Barnard later called Humphreys' appointment "my death blow. . . . Every door to promotion or recognition closed."

Barnard's dissent would later give Eads leverage, but for the moment Humphreys ignored it. On January 15, 1874, just as the Corps was demanding the St. Louis bridge be torn down, Humphreys advised Congress: "The canal is the only project that will meet the commercial, naval, and military demands of the United States. Its feasibility has never been doubted by anyone, and only on account of its cost have other methods been heretofore recommended. These other methods have always been regarded as experiments, and the reliance has been that, if they failed, the canal, as a final resort, was certain. I believe the time has come when that which appears certain should be tried first."

●

ENGINEERS HAD in fact tried everything and failed. The problem was unique. The Mississippi was not alone in having sandbars block its mouth. Bars also blocked other deltaic rivers, including the Danube, the Rhône, the Vistula, and the Maas. But the Mississippi was the only river in the world that had "mud lumps." Likely caused by the extreme weight of new sediment settling on the bottom, they could rise suddenly enough to lift a ship as it passed, and they usually had a volcano-like cone spewing gasses and liquid mud. Humphreys' *Physics and Hydraulics* described them as "masses of tough clay, varying in size from mere protuberances looking like logs sticking out of the water to islands several acres in extent. They attain height from three to ten feet above the Gulf. Salt springs are found upon them, which emit inflammable gas."

The Corps of Engineers had begun its efforts to open a shipping channel through the bars in 1837. Like the French, the Spanish, and the State of Louisiana before the Corps, it tried dragging harrows across the bar to stir it up, then dredging. After eighteen years of watching the Corps fail, the New Orleans magazine *De Bow's Review* in 1855 called for jetties, noting: "If a fleet of 1,728 boats, each freighted with 500 tons of mud, were to sail down the river daily and discharge it into the Gulf of Mexico, it would be no more than the equivalent to the average daily operation of the river. A well-constructed dredge of 16 horse-power, under favorable circumstances, will raise 140 tons of mud an hour."

Finally, in 1856, with a unanimous vote from the West and South, Congress overrode a presidential veto and appropriated $330,000 to open the river. The Corps hired a contractor to try jetties, but after two years of work an Army inspector found "only a scattering of piles . . . [that] remain to mark the position of the dam which was to control the 'mighty river.' "

In disgust, the *New Orleans Picayune* condemned jetties as "a foolish attempt . . . so useless that its continuance should awaken remonstrance from all whose interests are identified with the commercial prosperity of the city of New Orleans."

The Army voided the contract with the jetty builders and hired a famous dredge, the *Enoch Train,* to clear the way. Its hull added water like a modern submarine to lower itself and two huge propellers into the bar; the propellers were to churn up the bottom and make removal of the mud easy. But the ship's engines lacked enough power to turn the propellers in the heavy mud. Next a scraper dredge designed by an Army engineer was used. It broke. In 1860 the Army tried harrows, and failed.

As soon as the war ended, demands from southerners and westerners to open the river's mouth began anew. In 1867, at a huge river convention at St. Louis, Eads demanded the "improvement of the Mississippi River and its great tributaries. . . . Not a dollar should be voted by the representatives of this great Valley for any public works while these great rivers remain neglected." Two years later, at another convention in Louisville, former Union General William Vandever warned, "The West is waking up! The child has become a man, and a mighty man at that! . . . The Mississippi is our institution. . . . We say to the politician, if you are not loyal to it, we will abolish you. . . . The North and the South will shake hands on that."

Under intense political pressure, Humphreys put his faith in two new monster dredges built expressly to attack the sandbar. The first was the *Essayons,* completed in 1868. Her name meant "Let us try" and was the motto on the emblem of the Corps of Engineers. She tried, which is all one can say for her.

On her maiden voyage to the bar, as she pulled away from the New Orleans dock, the *Essayons'* engines broke down. She drifted into a wharf and shattered a yawl. Two weeks later, after two more false starts, the ship finally left New Orleans. It took her two weeks to travel the hundred miles downstream to the river's mouth. A log floating with the current would travel the distance in no more than a day and a half. Once there, the dredge worked for two days, then returned to New Orleans for repairs. Nonetheless, an Army engineer reported, "I am well satisfied, and her final success needs no further demonstration to my mind."

But in three out of the next ten months, the *Essayons* worked at the bar not a single day; in the other seven months she worked from one and a half to fifteen and a half days. In March 1869 the *New Orleans Picayune* snorted: "It is idle for us to rely upon the government dredge machine. . . . [T]he most she can do is break her propeller, and steam up to the city for another."

Two years later the Army dredges were still breaking down regularly. In 1871 a New Orleans businessman wrote Humphreys, "[T]he *Essayons* has done nothing. . . . From last October 28th to date April 19th, she has worked in November, 47 hours 30 minutes, December 18 hours 55 minutes, January 27 hours, February 13 hours 55 minutes, March 20 hours 15 minutes, and been up in the city 70 days. . . . Is not the West and the Mississippi River of enough consequence to be heard at the War Department?"

Humphreys scribbled on the letter, "This is a tissue of falsehood." But the information in it came from the log of the *Essayons.*

Whenever the channel was open, the Corps claimed success. One prominent New Orleans businessman was less sure, telling a Corps officer that a ship captain "told me yesterday there was eighteen feet of water over Southwest Pass. I asked what had caused that —he said 'God.' How do you account for it?"

Captain Charles Howell, who was in charge, blamed failure on sabotage by tugboats, which dragged ships across the bar for outrageous fees; an open channel would put them out of business. Once Howell complained to Humphreys that a tugboat tried "to run the *Essayons* down." In fleeing, she broke more blades. He became a laughingstock. It infuriated him.

The New Orleans Chamber of Commerce, with the weight of commercial bodies throughout the Mississippi valley behind it, demanded a new approach. Since jetties had already failed, it insisted that the Corps try an idea first proposed in 1832: a canal connecting the river to the Gulf. A board of Army engineers had given it serious consideration in 1838. The Chamber declared, "Its construction is a necessity for the commerce of the Mississippi Valley."

Finally, tired of failure, Howell and the Corps adopted the canal idea as their own. Virtually the entire Mississippi valley backed the plan.

BUT ON FEBRUARY 12, 1874, Eads arrived in Washington from St. Louis and made an extraordinary promise. The canal proposed a shipping channel 18 feet deep. Eads told congressmen and reporters he could build jetties that would produce a shipping channel *28 feet deep,* deep enough to accommodate the largest oceangoing ships. Almost as important, he promised a channel 350 feet wide, allowing ships room to pass freely; in contrast, the canal would force ships to queue in single file. He also offered to build his jetties for $10 million, compared to the estimated $13 million total cost for the canal.

Then Eads made the most extraordinary offer of all. He proposed to build the jetties at his own risk. The government would pay him nothing until he achieved a channel 20 feet deep, 2 feet deeper than the canal's goal. Then he would get $1 million, and $1 million more for each additional 2 feet in depth until 28 feet was reached; the remaining $5 million would be paid out in the future for maintenance.

Yet Eads' offer was condemned throughout the Mississippi valley, nowhere more so than in New Orleans, a city desperate to build up its port. Congressman J. Hale Sypher of Louisiana expressed a widely held view when he warned that the people of the Mississippi valley "are not in condition of mind to tolerate further nonsense. . . . The safe rule for Congress to follow is the precedent established and followed for twenty-five years—to act upon the [Army] engineers' reports authorized by Congress." In New Orleans, Caleb Forshey, Humphreys' former assistant on the Delta Survey, asked the *New Orleans Picayune,* "Can it be possible at this late date, after 35 years of tampering with dredges, jetties, and stirrings, the Congress can be staggered by the proposition of any man, and especially one who has never given the subject personal investigation?" Editorially, the *Picayune* added, "Never was an honest proposition more inopportune."

Even the Missouri congressional delegation rejected Eads' jetties and supported the canal.

Had the idea come from any other individual, it would likely have died. But it came from Eads. Earlier, in the face of intense opposition from so-called bridge experts, he had persevered. Now the bridge, weeks away from opening, stood as one of the engineering triumphs of the century. He would persevere again.

"In talking over any project he gave it long, careful and thorough examination, looking at it from all sides," said one of his assistants. "When once his mind was made up it never changed; once having stepped forward he never took a backward step, no matter what obstacles confronted him; his faith never wavered. . . . He never became discouraged for a moment, no matter how dark it looked."

To convince Congress to accept his proposal, Eads first had to reverse the position of his own Missouri delegation. To do so he returned briefly to St. Louis, met with editors, reporters, bankers, manufacturers, and shippers and swung them to his side. Armed with a barrage of publicity and wires of support from the state's most powerful men, he went back to Washington and began a lobbying campaign as skillful as any of the twentieth century. Results were immediate.

On February 9, 1874, Missouri Congressman William Stone had introduced a bill calling for the canal. On February 22 he introduced a bill calling for Eads' jetties. Stone's reversal marked the switch of the entire state delegation. From this solid core Eads reached outward, to other Mississippi valley congressmen and to other newspapers, while his close friends in the Blair family—one was a senator, another ran the *Washington Globe*—and Missouri Senator Carl Schurz, a former Union general who knew Humphreys well and had contempt for him, weighed in. Relentlessly, Eads buttonholed members of Congress, playing cards with them, dining with them, drinking with them, joking with them, and, when needed, testifying before them. "Socially Mr. Eads was one of the most charming men who ever came to Washington," observed the *New Orleans Times-Democrat,* while the *New York Times* reported that he was "using all those peculiar methods so well-known to those having long experience in working up legislation such as he is now attempting to secure . . . dinners, costly bouquets and baskets of flowers sent to their wives." He also bought influence, for example, in return for lobbying help, secretly agreeing to share his profits with James Wilson, an engineer close to Belknap as well as to many members of Congress and even Humphreys.

Slowly, he gathered support and, one at a time, votes.

Humphreys fought back. Both Eads and Humphreys knew that the winner of the battle over the jetties would determine policy for the entire Mississippi River. So Humphreys tried to push through canal legislation quickly, citing the fact that on March 31 forty-seven ships were waiting at the mouth of the Mississippi to enter or leave the river.

The debate over engineering details grabbed the attention of the nation. Through the spring and summer of 1874 newspapers spread hydraulic theories across front pages, not only in river cities such as St. Louis, New Orleans, Davenport, and Cincinnati but in Chicago, Boston, and New York. Congressman Stephen Cobb of Kansas called Mississippi River improvements the single most vital issue for his constituents. Massachusetts Congressman Rockwood Hoar demanded action.

And increasingly, the debate became one of civilian versus military engineers. Privately, even some Army engineers were aghast at Humphreys' position. One was Barnard, the sole dissenting vote on the board that recommended the canal. He confided to General C. B. Comstock: "I need not say this is for your eyes alone. . . . The plan submitted to the Chief Engineer by Howell and by him to the board simply ignored the engineering science of the present. . . . The incompetence from first to last with which the thing has been handled by the [Corps] has thrown it irrevocably into the hands of politicians."

Civilian engineers saw the issue as an opportunity to strip the Corps of its power. For years they had attacked it as rigid, even incompetent. West Point had been using the same engineering textbook since 1837 (and would use it for two more years), a period of enormous and rapid technological change that included such advances as the telephone. Now with a specific issue and a champion, members of the American Society of Civil Engineers exerted what pressure they could on Ead's behalf.

Meanwhile, one senator declared: "Every attempt that has ever been made to induce the Corps of Engineers . . . to listen to the recommendations made by the ablest civil engineers in the country has been resisted with an obduracy that is beyond belief. I state it here from my own knowledge that the Chief of Engineers has refused to allow any civil engineer to approach him who differed from him in opinion."

A second senator echoed him: "Thirty-seven years ago the Engineer Department of the Army took the matter in hand, and . . . today the depth of water is no greater than it was then. In other words, they have effected nothing. . . . The civil engineers . . . , men who have tunnelled mountains, run our railroad tracks thousands of feet above the level of the sea, built the foundation of our magnificent bridges, and whose triumphs are among the most resplendent of our glorious Republic—we insist that they shall have an opportunity to offer their genius and skill to the country."

But calls for more power to civilian engineers only made Humphreys dig in further. He insisted that jetties would have to fail for several reasons. The land near the mouth of the river was too soft to sustain the jetties' weight, he argued, and therefore they would sink into the ocean bottom. Even if they did not sink, his second argument was that "the real bed of the river, upon which rest the moving sandbars" was composed of a "hard, blue, or drab-colored clay . . . nearly insoluble, resisting for years the strong current of the Mississippi." If that argument proved in error, Humphreys had still a third: even if the jetties cut a deep channel through the bar itself, the river would simply deposit its sediment further out in the Gulf, beyond the jetties, creating a new bar. Thus the jetties would have to be extended ad infinitum. Humphreys informed Congress, "The annual advance will not be less than 1200 feet."

But Eads knew the river in a way that separated him from Humphreys and all other men. Humphreys may have tasted the clay dredged up from the bottom of the river. Eads had spent years walking along that bottom, had been embraced by the river, had come as close to being part of it as it was possible to do and live. He had salvaged wrecks on the sandbar itself, walked the bottom there. He *knew*. He called Humphreys' views "absurd."

Some Eads opponents charged that jetties would confine the river so much they would raise flood heights in New Orleans—the identical objection to the levees-only policy voiced by its opponents. Paul Hebert, former governor of Louisiana and a West Point graduate, pleaded to senators: "We have laid before you the results of science and experience; we come now with prayer. Would you, can you, honorable Senators, at such a moment contemplate or tolerate the half insane proposition of strangers who can know nothing of our inexorable enemy, to dam his waters at the mouth by jetties that must inevitably send back the flood waters like a tide to the very city of New Orleans or beyond . . . ? Do not, we pray, permit us to be destroyed." And Forshey confessed that the Mississippi had caused "disasters and failures" in his own projects and warned Congress that the river would similarly teach Eads "modesty and humility in the presence of the gigantic torrent."

Eads responded with scorn: "Disasters and serious accidents are always evidence of bad engineering. I have no confession of disaster or failure to make, for in my dealings with the Mississippi I have had none . . . I am sure I have not learned 'modesty and humility in the presence of the gigantic torrent.' Nor do I believe that it can be controlled by modesty and humility. . . . I believe [man] capable of curbing, controlling and directing the Mississippi, according to his pleasure."

Then, carefully, logically, in testimony before a Senate committee and in well-distributed writings, he rebutted every argument against him. And always there was his unanswerable offer: if he did not succeed, the government paid nothing.

Immediately after Eads' testimony, Louisiana's Senator Rodman West, a longtime canal advocate, announced his support of jetties. The New Orleans Chamber of Commerce condemned him as a traitor and mounted an effort to defeat him; meanwhile, his conversion marked the complete rout of Humphreys in the Senate.

Humphreys still had strength in the House. The day the House voted, Humphreys circulated a letter stating that recent measurements proved his theory that a new sandbar would develop beyond the jetties. Also, despite his earlier charge that the jetties would cost $23 million, he now claimed that Eads' offer of $10 million would give him a profit of $7 million.

The House rejected jetties and passed the canal bill. The Senate refused to consider a canal. The two houses finally compromised by creating a new board of engineers including three from the Army, three civilians, and one from the U.S. Coastal Survey. This board spent six months studying the bar as well as jetties in Europe. Eads, though not in direct contact with them, followed them through Europe. In January 1875, by a vote of 6 to 1, the board recommended jetties.

But it did not give Eads total victory. Just before the Mississippi reaches the sea, it splits into three main channels, or passes. He had offered to build jetties for $10 million at Southwest Pass, which carried most of the river's water and, hence, its potential power. The board estimated the cost for construction and twenty years' maintenance there at $16,053,124, and therefore recommended building jetties at the South Pass, where it estimated the cost would be $7,942,110.

Eads did not want to work at South Pass. It was the smallest and shallowest of all the river's main outlets. He feared that a current powerful enough to dig a channel 28 feet deep and several hundred feet wide could destabilize not only the jetties but the pass itself. And at Southwest Pass, nature provided 14 feet of water over the sandbar. At South Pass, only 8 feet of water covered the bar. Finally, a shoal in the river blocked access to South Pass; removing the shoal would be more difficult than building the jetties themselves.

He made a counterproposal, offering to build the jetties, again at the larger Southwest Pass, for $8 million, $2 million less than his earlier offer and less than half the board's estimate. And he guaranteed to deepen the channel to 30 feet instead of 28.

But now that Eads had won on the principle of the jetties, Humphreys and congressional allies spread more rumors about excessive profits and wrote a new jetties bill so restrictive that they believed Eads must reject it. In a memo to Humphreys, an aide explained: "The accompanying discussion of Mr. Eads' project has for its chief object the presentation of an argumentum ad hominem which . . . does not aid in solving scientific questions. . . . The suggestions of what the bill should be, of course, do not imply a desire that it should pass, but merely to suggest amendments that would defeat the purpose of its projector and render it unacceptable to him."

This bill required Eads to use the South Pass, produce a 30-foot-deep channel, and do it for $5 million, with an additional $1 million to be held in escrow for up to twenty years. He would receive nothing until Army engineers certified that a channel 20 feet deep existed—2 feet deeper than the goal of the canal. For this he would get only $500,000. Subsequent payments would be made in 2-foot increments until 30 feet was reached. Then Eads would receive $100,000 a year for maintenance for twenty years.

If Eads refused to accept the terms, the Corps of Engineers would build the jetties. If Eads was wrong, he would be ruined both financially and professionally. Even if his engineering theory was correct, the financial strictures could make his success impossible. But if he succeeded, his success would be total.

Eads accepted.

Meanwhile, on March 23, 1875, at a victory dinner in St. Louis attended by 400 powerful men, Eads made a speech that epitomized the nineteenth century's linear certainty, and its hubris: "If the profession of engineer were not based upon exact science, I might tremble for the result. . . . But every atom that moves onward in the river . . . is controlled by laws as fixed and certain as those which direct the majestic march of the heavenly spheres. Every phenomenon and eccentricity of the river, its scouring and depositing action, its caving banks, the formation of the bars at its mouth, the effect of the waves and tides of the sea upon its currents and deposits, are controlled by laws as immutable as the Creator, and the engineer needs only to be assured that he does not ignore the existence of any of these laws, to feel positively certain of the result he aims at."

Then Eads promised to "undertake the work with a faith based upon the ever-constant ordinances of God himself, and so certain as He will spare my life and faculties for two years more, I will give to the Mississippi river, through His grace, and by application of His laws, a deep, open, safe, and permanent outlet to the sea."

Great as that goal was, even more was at issue. And Humphreys, not a man to have for an enemy, was not finished.

CHAPTER SIX

A YEAR BEFORE Eads' victory dinner, in the spring of 1874, the Mississippi River had overflowed from Illinois south. It had devastated the lower Mississippi region and focused the nation's attention fully on the great river. In response, the government had created the U.S. Levee Commission to decide upon a river control policy to prevent future floods.

G. K. Warren, the Humphreys loyalist who had tried to destroy Eads' bridge, chaired it; other members included Henry Abbot, coauthor with Humphreys of *Physics and Hydraulics,* and Paul Hebert, the former Louisiana governor who was then lobbying against the jetties. Despite the importance of its charge, this commission conducted no fieldwork, made no measurements, visited no sites. Its sole source of information was the Humphreys and Abbot report; it did not even review any observations or measurements made by others. Unsurprisingly, its conclusions conformed to Humphreys' earlier ones.

As Humphreys had, it rejected reservoirs, cutoffs, and the engineering theory associated with the levees-only policy, saying, "The idea that the river would scour its bed deeper if confined . . . [is] erroneous." As Humphreys had, it emphasized the importance of keeping all natural outlets open, and it was "forced unwillingly to" reject artificial outlets because of the cost. As Humphreys had, it stated flatly, "The alluvial regions of the Mississippi can only be reclaimed by levees."

The report appeared in January 1875. The 1874 flood and this report had not entered directly into the debate over the jetties, and until his jetty contract was secure, Eads refrained from comment on it. But then he attacked. Dismissing the entire report and its recommendations, he urged, in effect, the use of jetties on the entire river.

His reasoning superficially resembled the theory that levees would increase current velocity and scour out the bottom. But there was an immense difference. Levees were built back from the river's natural banks, sometimes more than a mile back. The river had to overflow its banks before the levees could begin to confine it; as a result, any force generated by this confinement was dissipated over an area far greater than the river's natural channel. Also, levees only confined the river during floods. Thus, levees could increase current velocity for only a few weeks each year—and not necessarily every year.

This was a crucial point. Neither Humphreys nor Ellet had ever disputed the fact that a faster current increased scouring of the bottom. The question was, how much? The river in flood carried several orders of magnitude more volume than when it was at low water. Levees did confine floods, and did increase scour, but could levees cause enough increased current and scour to accommodate a flood?

Humphreys, Ellet, and Eads all agreed that levees could *not* do so. But Eads proposed to concentrate the river's force constantly, year-round. He planned to invade the river, to build not levees back from the banks but jetties *in the river's channel*. These would constrict the water year-round, even at low water, and apply a constant scouring of the bottom. He also called for cutoffs to create a far straighter and faster river. All this, he was certain, would significantly deepen the river.

He declared: "By such correction the flood . . . can be permanently lowered, and in this way the entire alluvial basin, from Vicksburg to Cairo, can be lifted as it were above all overflow, and levees in that part of the river rendered [superfluous]. . . . *There can be no question of this fact, and it is well for those most deeply interested to ponder it carefully before rejecting it; for the increased value given to the territory thus reclaimed can scarcely be estimated.*"

Eads was directly contradicting Humphreys, the U.S. Levee Commission, and the entire Corps of Engineers. If the jetties in South Pass succeeded, Eads would clearly try to apply his theory to the length of the river, and make the Corps irrelevant.

IN EARLY MAY 1875, Eads arrived in New Orleans. He had delayed starting work until the end of the flood season, and the city that had earlier fought him now waited anxiously. Upon his arrival he was entertained at the Canal Street mansion of Dr. William Mercer, who used the same gold service for Eads that he had used for the Grand Duke Alexis of Russia during Mardi Gras three years earlier. The city council formally applauded Eads' "grand enterprise," while the

Chamber of Commerce, the Cotton Exchange, the Merchants' Exchange, the Ship and Steamship Association, and others of prominence hosted a reception at the St. Charles Hotel, which called itself the most elegant in the country. There, under the chandeliers sat Creoles and Americans, carpetbaggers and Confederates, fanning themselves with the printed menus commemorating the occasion. One thing brought them together—money.

In a toast simultaneously blunt and gracious, General Cyrus Bussey announced: "Captain Eads has fought his way with an address and vigor and courage which deserve unqualified admiration. Against the most persistent misrepresentations that ever beset any human endeavor, against ignorance, angry and false witness, he has at last brought his efforts to a successful termination. . . . That he has the sympathy of the community in this hour of his triumph, and at the outset of the enterprise, is eminently fit and proper. That he did not have it when it was most sorely needed, Captain Eads can afford to forget. The struggle is over."

The struggle was not over.

Eads had always loved the river and knew it more intimately than he had ever known any man or woman. He knew it in private ways that would never be known by any river captain, by any fisherman, by any levee contractor, by any engineer. He had buried his hands in the rich silt of its bottom, wandered blind in its depths, and come as close to breathing it as a man could do and live. The river had taken him from his family and wrapped itself around him. Now, finally, in his great pride, he had determined that he would command it, the great, great river, the Mississippi itself.

But Humphreys had said: *Anyone who knows me intimately knows I had more of the soldier than a man of science in me. . . . We must get ready for a combat. . . . The contest must be sharp and merciless.*

THE MORNING AFTER the reception and Bussey's toast, Eads, his contractor James Andrews, a determined and bold man who had worked with him on the bridge, and two other engineers left behind the city's elegance and proceeded downriver aboard a small steamer.

Below New Orleans the river resembles a 100-mile-long arm crooked at the elbow, narrowing gradually, to Head of Passes. There the river divides into three main channels, Southwest Pass, Pass à l'Outre, and South Pass, each extending like a long thin finger—the land separating the passes from the sea is as narrow as a few hundred yards—out into the Gulf.

At Head of Passes the party crossed over a shoal and entered the finger that was South Pass. It ran in an almost perfectly straight line 700 feet wide for 12.9 miles. Along its banks were dense, impenetrable reeds, 10 to 12 feet high, interrupted by an occasional copse of willow trees in the upper reaches. This was, geologically, truly the river's delta, created as the Mississippi River deposited its immense sediment load. It was the newest land in North America, a mixture of water and earth so soft that, except for the banks immediately adjacent to the pass, it could not support a man's weight. The animal life was primitive; muskrats and minks, herons and gulls and ducks, and snakes. The closer to the Gulf, the more desolate and solitary the marsh became, the grayer the reeds and grasses.

Upon reaching the sea, they anchored, rowed to shore, and walked on the beach. The Gulf surf lapped gently, but the jetties would have to withstand the most violent hurricanes. In the already steamy heat, clouds of mosquitoes, gnats, and sand flies began to swarm around them. Then they climbed the lighthouse.

It was the only elevation for 100 miles. From it they could see the whole country. River, land, and sea were barely differentiated. Every inch of land within view could be overflowed by tides or the river. Out in the Gulf, beyond the pass, the sandbars and mud lumps were in the process of becoming land. For miles beyond the bars, out into the sea, the Mississippi continued to have an identity. Half a century earlier a European visitor had described the scene: "The first indication of our approach to land was the appearance of this mighty river pouring forth its muddy mass of waters, and mingling with the deep blue of the Mexican Gulf. I never beheld a scene so utterly desolate as this entrance of the Mississippi. Had Dante seen it, he might have drawn images of another Bolgia from its horrors."

South Pass was dying, becoming land, shoaling at its entrance and exit. Eads needed to produce a channel with a continuous depth of 30 feet. For a distance of 12,000 feet, more than 2 miles, the depth was less than that. At high tide, the deepest water over the bar itself was 9 feet, and the bar was 3,000 feet thick.

But after three days of study the Eads party left more confident than ever. Light, silty sand made up the bar; Eads was certain a strong current could easily cut through it. Equally important, deep water lay beyond the bar, and a strong coastal current ran across it, so sediment flushed out by the jetties would either sink or be swept away. Any unspoken concern in Eads' heart about the formation of a new bar beyond the jetties vanished.

Upon their return to New Orleans, Eads was so confident

that he wrote his New Orleans attorney, Henry Leovy, whose clients included Jefferson Davis, about plans for a railroad to the mouth of the river: "[T]ransfers of cargoes of grains from barges into ships can be made quite as cheaply as by elevator in the City and with an important saving in port charges. . . . I believe the stock of the [rail]road would become quite valuable. I am willing to make some arrangement, mutually beneficial, by which I received stock in exchange for land at Port Eads, as I own ten miles front on each side of the pass with the riparian right out to sea on both sides of the channel."

He also promised a channel deep enough to use by July 4, 1876, thirteen months away. An assistant told the *Picayune,* "Assurance of success is absolute."

REGARDLESS OF his engineering, however, if Eads could not raise capital, or if he had to pay too high a premium to attract it, he would fail. This was his weakness, and here Humphreys aimed his attack.

To raise money, Eads organized the South Pass Jetty Company. Investors in it would be paid only if the jetties succeeded. But then they would receive double their investment plus 10 percent interest. He capitalized the company at $750,000 but planned to raise only what was needed to keep work going until the first government payment. Raising the money was not easy. He exhausted his own contacts, then urged Elmer Corthell, a young Brown University graduate still in New England who would become resident engineer at the jetties, to make "any 'bloated bondholder' or 'money aristocrat' *wish* he had a hand in" by telling anyone who had $100,000 to invest that Eads would negotiate a private, even more lucrative deal.

Andrews & Company, of which Eads was a minority owner, agreed to supply all equipment—pile drivers, barges, steamers, housing, office space, materials, and labor—and build and place all piling, plus 450,000 cubic yards of stone and wood fillers, for $2.5 million. Eads believed this would be enough to get a 26-foot-deep channel.

Eads would pay Andrews & Company nothing until 60,000 cubic yards of material were in place, at which point Andrews would get $300,000. The company was guaranteed one-half of all subsequent government payments until it was paid.

Like Eads himself, the company's majority owner, James Andrews, moved quickly. Andrews had first seen the bar in late May 1875. On June 12 he left New Orleans with several dozen men and a steam tug pulling a pile driver and three flatboats, one for boarding workers and two loaded with material to build housing. They arrived in a steaming marsh, and were promptly tormented by small gray motile clouds of biting insects.

One of Andrews' first acts was to establish direct communication by telegraph with New Orleans, and soon equipment and supplies began arriving at what ultimately became Port Eads, a small town complete with hotel, offices, and boardinghouses for 850 men. For now the men lived on the boarding boat; no liquor was allowed. There was no relief from the insects and heat, not even in the water; water moccasins kept the men from swimming.

Only five days after Andrews arrived at the river's mouth, on June 17, he drove the first piles into the floor of the ocean. The work went quickly. In one day they could drive 176 piles. Lumber came from Mississippi and New Orleans; crushed stone, discharged from ships as ballast, came from New Orleans; limestone carried in fleets of twelve to twenty barges at a time came from 1,400 miles upriver, quarried from the blue and gray limestone bluffs of the Ohio River at Rose Clare, Indiana.

By September 9 the guide piling for the east jetty was finished, and extended in a lonely curve of wood two and one-third miles into the Gulf. The job was executed with extraordinary precision; the piles farthest from land's end were located within a few inches of their planned site. Work on the west jetty had already begun.

Next came the heart of the jetty: the fascine mattresses. These were made of willow tree trunks, which were thin, flexible, and straight. The trunks were to be linked, secured to the guide piling, and sunk. Eads expected the river to deposit sediment upon them and eventually make them impermeable. Then they would do their work.

Harvesting the willows was the worst work. The trees came from 6,000 acres of land 30 miles upriver and formed only 40 years earlier, when fishermen, seeking a quicker route to the Gulf, had cut a canal there. The river had quickly overwhelmed the lock, and forced an opening 1,400 feet wide and initially 80 feet deep. This opening became known as "the Jump," but after the first surge of water the river had begun depositing sediment and making land. The trees had grown rapidly on it.

To get to the area the men traveled on a barge where they slept stacked in bunks. Ventilation was as good as Eads could design, but in the near-tropical heat and with swarming mosquitoes, nights were awful. Days were worse. The men, half-naked, without shade, chopped down trees and dragged them, at every step sinking—sometimes shoulder-deep—into the soft mud, 200 yards to waiting barges. Moccasins and leeches made the water and marsh frightening.

Once the barges were full, tugs towed them to the sandbar. There, on an inclined, 100-yard-long platform, men constructed the mattresses of willow trees.

Upon this construction depended Eads' success. The river would rip apart an improperly built mattress. And in the construction process itself lay Eads' profit.

The board of engineers had anticipated his using willow mattresses but had estimated the cost based on techniques developed by the Dutch, who intertwined the willows, virtually weaving them together.

Eads and Andrews designed a different process, and later patented it. They first laid out strips of yellow pine 20 to 40 feet long, 6 inches wide, and 2.5 inches thick. These strips were bolted together, and the willow trees were laid within them. Other layers, each one at a right angle to the proceeding one, were added, then more strips of yellow pine were bolted on top, and the whole thing was lashed together. The resulting mattress was 100 feet long, 35 to 60 feet wide (depending upon where it would be placed), and 2 feet thick.

Workers could make and launch it in two hours. The Dutch method required two days to do the same. It was this innovation that had allowed Eads to offer to build the jetties at Southwest Pass at one-half the board's estimate.

A tug towed the barge to the guide pilings. The men then launched the mattresses, covered them with stone, and sank them in layers—as many as sixteen layers.

In less than a year Andrews drove all the guide piles and laid much of the mattressing. The jetties were incomplete walls of willows, not yet filled in with sediment and consolidated. But already they were succeeding. They were compressing the current, increasing its force, and deepening the channel.

Yet Eads had received no payments and his initial capital was running out. To attract more, he hired the luxurious steamer *Grand Republic* for her maiden voyage, May 2, 1876, to carry investors and the press to the jetties. Traveling amid the glamour of the grand steamer, dining on exquisite preparations of oysters, shrimp, and beef, he sensed only goodwill and excitement on the trip from New Orleans.

Meanwhile, Charles Howell, whom Humphreys had recently promoted to major, was 30 miles away dredging Southwest Pass, still trying to achieve 18 feet of water there. Howell certainly knew of the *Grand Republic*'s visit and its purpose. He had no role in inspecting the jetties, and an official inspection mandated by Eads' contract and to be conducted by a visiting team of surveyors was scheduled in only a few days. Yet Howell dispatched an assistant in a steam launch who, in full view of Eads' guests, took repeated soundings at the South Pass. This assistant, instead of returning to Howell, disembarked at Port Eads. A few hours later the *Grand Republic* also stopped at Port Eads. Howell's man, carrying charts, boarded her. During the long trip back to New Orleans, feigning reluctance, he stood in the saloon allowing reporters to pry his findings from him.

Eads claimed South Pass was 16 feet deep at high tide. The soundings, official measurements by Army engineers, showed 12 feet. More important, they also showed a new sandbar forming 1,000 feet beyond the jetties. If the soundings were correct, they proved Humphreys right and doomed the jetties to failure.

THE NEWS shot northward up the Mississippi valley. Stock in the jetty company collapsed. Howell pressed his attack in the New Orleans papers, accusing Eads of bilking investors. Suddenly, for the first time since his wife died, Eads was desperate.

He tried to negotiate a loan. Without it the project could collapse. But to get it, he needed the findings of the official inspection to refute Howell. The Army engineer who sounded the pass refused to give Eads the results, insisting he could only give them to General C. B. Comstock, who had come to Port Eads from Detroit expressly for the survey. Eads asked Comstock for them. Comstock too refused, saying he "had no authority to divulge my report."

Eads immediately wired Secretary of War Alphonso Taft, "Please instruct General Comstock, now at Port Eads, to sound channel between jetties with me . . . and furnish results promptly. Major Howell has published a misstatement affecting public confidence in my work, and this information is required in justice to myself, and the public."

Taft did not reply. Comstock left. Eads appealed to the superintendent of the Coastal Survey for results of separate soundings it had conducted—using Eads' own launch for them. He was refused. He appealed to the secretary of the treasury and was informed, "General Comstock will give all information required by law."

The law required Comstock's report to go to Humphreys, then to the secretary of war, then to Congress, and only then to the public. The results would not appear for months.

Eads' loan negotiations collapsed. By the time the official results were scheduled to become public, there might be no jetty company left.

Eads had one last chance at a rebuttal. On May 12, 1876, the oceangoing steamer *Hudson* was due at the mouth of the river. She was 280 feet long and 1,182 tons, and drawing 14 feet, 7 inches.

E. V. Gager was her captain, and Eads' friend. He had once said he hoped to captain the first oceangoing ship through the jetties. Never would there be a better time. When she arrived, Eads, the pilot, and a few reporters boarded her outside the bar. The pilot reported that his earlier soundings had indicated sufficient water in the jetties for her to use them, but the tide had turned since then and was falling fast. He could not recommend the attempt.

Every moment the water was growing shallower. Gager did not hesitate, waved the pilot away, and ordered, "Head her for the jetties."

The pilot obeyed.

Three hundred men understood what was happening, and its significance. Everywhere, on the barges sinking willows, on the shore at Port Eads, on the launches, on the *Hudson* herself, men ceased what they were doing and watched silently. In a calm sea, with swells barely whitening against the jetties, all was still. Only the ship moved.

"Shall we run in slow?" the pilot asked.

"No!" Gager snapped. "Let her go at full speed."

The engines churned. She seemed almost to leap forward. At full ahead, Corthell later wrote, "on she came like a thing of life."

Her speed increased still further. If Howell's soundings were correct, she could destroy herself, rip a great gouge out of her bottom. Faster she went, the great white bow wave climbing higher up her hull, her wake swamping the Gulf's swells, steaming onward, racing the falling tide down through the two-and-one-third-mile-long channel. As Corthell recalled, "As long as she carried that 'white bone in her teeth,' the great wave that her proud bows pushed ahead of her as she sped onward—we knew that she had found more than Major Howell's twelve feet."

Then she was through! On the *Hudson,* on the barges, at Port Eads, the men erupted in cheers, and kept cheering, and kept cheering, and kept cheering. She stopped at Port Eads for a brief celebration. The reporters wired their stories the length and breadth of the country. The channel was open!

"No event in the whole history of the jetties gave us such intense pleasure and satisfaction as the successful passage of this beautiful ship through the jetties," Corthell said. "It is not too much to say that Capt. Gager, who took the risk and responsibility of this trial trip, greatly assisted the enterprise in one of its darkest hours; for the stubborn facts brought out by his brave action could not be gainsaid. They restored confidence in the jetties, and the much-needed loan was soon afterward secured for the further prosecution of the work."

Meanwhile, Eads was pressing Congress for help. It passed a resolution demanding the release of the official survey. The secretary of the treasury obeyed.

The survey showed 16 feet of water in the channel, and no bar forming beyond the jetties.

YET EADS' financial squeeze and his problems with the government continued. Despite his achieving the required depths, several times the government delayed payment until the cabinet debated the question. One such debate lasted three days, ending only when the attorney general informed the cabinet that the government had to pay.

At one point, out of money, Eads wired Corthell, "Discharge the whole force except those necessary to protect property, unless they are willing to work on certificates, payable on receipt of 22 foot payment." Seventy-four of seventy-six men agreed.

Only the work went well. The South Pass had been surveyed for 150 years; no prior survey had ever found more than 9 feet of water over the bar. Eads officially achieved a 20-foot-deep channel October 4, 1876. Oceangoing ships began routinely using his still-unfinished channel.

Eads then built a new series of dikes, which increased the slope of the river from .24 foot per mile to .505 foot per mile, producing, according to the Army report, "a marked scour in the channel." On March 7, 1877, Comstock reported 23.9 feet of water there.

The law stipulated that Howell's dredging at Southwest Pass must end whenever the jetties achieved an 18-foot channel. Howell continued dredging in violation of the law. But on August 22, 1877, his appropriations ran out. There would be no more. The dredging ended.

Even then, financial pressure on Eads continued. Ultimately, he lobbied Congress to accelerate the payment schedule, and added to his usual lobbyists Grant's former secretary Porter, the Union general who had captured Jefferson Davis, and P. G. T. Beauregard, the Confederate general who fired on Fort Sumter to begin the Civil War, whom he paid $5,000. Congress finally pushed forward payment.

Now Eads turned his attention to Humphreys.

EADS WANTED a civilian commission independent of the Corps of Engineers to govern the Mississippi River. Although civil engineers and their supporters had called for one for years, it was now being spoken of as "the Eads commission."

In response, Humphreys lashed out with blind enmity, insisting in a letter to Congress, despite all data, that a new sandbar was forming beyond the jetties: *The results actually attained at the South Pass disprove the views advanced by Mr. Eads, and confirms those of the Engineer Department. Hence, any claim that he shall be intrusted with the control of the Mississippi River, in so far as it rests upon the results thus far achieved by him, has no proper basis."*

Eads had had enough. He wrote an article for *Van Nostrand's Engineering Magazine,* had it reprinted as a pamphlet, and distributed it to congressmen, reporters, and engineers across the country. It was entitled, "Review of the Humphreys and Abbot Report."

It was a crushing article. Eads derisively subtitled sections, "The Laws of Gravity Ignored"; "How the Wonderful Discovery Was Made"; "No Relation Between Cause and Effect!" He used Humphreys' own data to deliver blow after blow, describing Humphreys' calculations as "totally wrong," "mathematically . . . a blunder that would disgrace a boy in High School," and, finally, "The mistake made by Humphreys and Abbot is one unpardonable in the merest tyro in the science of dynamics."

Two years earlier a Prussian engineer had written an article in the same magazine also attacking Humphreys and Abbot's original report. The two men had written a forty-three-page rebuttal. But now Abbot warned against replying to Eads at all, arguing, "a reply might advantage him. . . . [M]ake an end of it."

At Humphreys' insistence, Abbot did finally write a rebuttal. It was ignored by all except Humphreys' most loyal supporters.

In the midst of these exchanges, Humphreys received more blows. The National Academy of Sciences urged the creation of the U.S. Geological Survey to survey the West—work formerly done by the Corps of Engineers. Humphreys, an original founder of the academy, resigned from it. As he had before, he fought the proposal in Congress. But no longer did he have the power to ward off passage of the legislation.

Then on June 28, 1879, Congress created the Mississippi River Commission, a mix of Army and civilian engineers, to control the entire river. Both private individuals and state governments would have to obey it. Upon the bill's passage, Humphreys resigned as chief of engineers and retired from the Army, effective June 30.

Exactly one week later, U.S. Army Captain Micah Brown certified that the South Pass channel had reached the final goal, a depth of 30 feet.

On July 11, the *New Orleans Daily Times* announced: "The work is done. Human patience and courage and industry, backed by an indomitable and untiring will, and informed and directed by human skill, have applied the forces of nature to the accomplishment of an end too vast for mere artificial agencies. Man has used the tremendous river which uncontrolled has been its own oppressor and imprisoner, and has now become its own liberator and saviour. There is no achievement of mechanical genius which compares with it in the splendor of its economies or in the magnitude of its results. There is no parallel instance of man's employment of the prodigious energies of nature in the realization of his aims. It stands alone in these respects as in the almost incalculable possibilities which it has brought within our reach."

IN 1875, WHEN EADS BEGAN work on the jetties, 6,857 tons of goods were shipped from St. Louis through New Orleans to Europe. In 1880, the year after he finished, 453,681 tons were shipped by that route. New Orleans rose from the ninth-largest port in the United States to the second-largest, trailing only New York. (In 1995, by volume of cargo greater New Orleans ranked as the world's largest port.)*

Yet the impact of the jetties on the Mississippi River far exceeded that of anything else that had happened at the river's mouth. That impact would be felt through the Mississippi River Commission.

It never became, formally or informally, "the Eads Commission." Though Humphreys and the War Department could not pre-

* The Corps soon took credit for the jetties, saying as early as 1886, "The present successful results might have been obtained years before Mr. Eads took hold of the work if Congress had not handicapped the Corps. . . . It is certainly unjust to blame the Engineer Corps because its recommendations were not followed." In 1924 the chief of engineers officially informed the secretary of war: "The Army Engineers did not oppose the jetties. As a matter of fact, the plan for the construction of the jetties was originated by the Corps of Engineers, and Captain Eads merely carried out plans which had been previously discussed." It also soon became clear that, as Eads had predicted, South Pass was too small to accommodate heavy shipping traffic and that the larger Southwest Pass had to be opened. In 1893, Eads' former assistant Corthell offered to do the work on the same terms as had Eads: he would receive nothing unless successful. This time the Corps outmaneuvered Corthell and was given the task, but twenty-one years later the channel was still only 27 feet deep. "The plan did not prove to be successful," conceded Major General Lansing Beach, chief of engineers.

vent the establishment of the commission, they did succeed in having Congress stipulate that Army officers outnumber civilians on it by three to two, that an Army officer serve as president, and that this officer report to his military superior, the chief of engineers. Eads was named to the commission, but he could not dominate it. In 1882 he resigned to protest its compromises.

Science, he knew, does not compromise. Instead, science forces ideas to compete in a dynamic process. This competition refines or replaces old hypotheses, gradually approaching a more perfect representation of the truth, although one can reach truth no more than one can reach infinity.

But the Mississippi River Commission never became a scientific enterprise. It was a bureaucracy. The natural process of a bureaucracy, by contrast, tends to compromise competing ideas. The bureaucracy then adopts the compromise as truth and incorporates it into its being. The military hierarchy in the river commission exacerbated these bureaucratic tendencies. Over time, as Army engineers staffed nearly all key posts, the commission lost any real independence from the Corps of Engineers. And with rare exceptions, the Army controlled even civilian appointments.

The commission took positions, and the positions became increasingly petrified and rigid. Unfortunately, these positions combined the worst, not the best, of the ideas of Eads, Ellet, and Humphreys.

Both Eads and Humphreys opposed outlets. Ellet proposed them. Ellet was right. But the commission opposed outlets.

Both Eads and Humphreys opposed building reservoirs. Ellet had proposed them. Ellet was right. But the commission opposed reservoirs.

Eads wanted to build cutoffs, believing they had enormous impact on floods. Humphreys and Ellet opposed cutoffs. Eads was right. The commission followed Humphreys and Ellet.

Yet the greatest and most dangerous mistake of the Mississippi River Commission still lay elsewhere—in its position on the levees-only policy. Almost inconceivably, the commission arrived at a position that Eads, Humphreys, and Ellet had all violently rejected. It did so by compromising and mushing together its analysis over time. It embraced Humphreys' levees-only idea and justified the decision by citing *Physics and Hydraulics*. But, as years passed, commission engineers ignored his reasoning and espoused the theory that levees would cause the river to scour out the channel enough to accommodate floods. Ellet had called this idea "a delusive hope, and most dangerous to indulge." Humphreys had proved the theory "untenable." Eads too had rejected it, distinguishing between the scouring effects of "contraction works" built into the river channel and levees far back from the banks.

On this one point, Eads, Humphreys, and Ellet all concurred. Nonetheless, the levees rose, confining the river while failing to increase velocity enough to deepen the channel. No reservoirs were built, as Ellet had wanted. No outlets were built, as Ellet had also wanted, and as even Humphreys would likely have accepted, as the cost-benefit equation changed with development. No cutoffs were built, as Eads had wanted. Only levees were built.

So the water rose higher. In turn, the levees rose higher; as more lands were reclaimed and water was cut off from it, the water also rose, and so on, and so on. At College Point, Louisiana, 40 miles above New Orleans, a levee 1.5 feet high had held the flood of 1850, a flood Humphreys investigated in detail; by the mid-1920s the levee exceeded 20 feet. At Morganza, Louisiana, a levee 7.5 feet high had held the flood of 1850; by the mid-1920s it towered 38 feet, nearly the height of a four-story building.

By the 1920s, the commission went further. To increase the volume of the Mississippi River, without building the contraction works Eads had demanded, it began closing all natural outlets. This policy, Humphreys had warned, "would, if executed, entail disastrous consequences."

THE MISSISSIPPI RIVER is wild and random. High water magnifies its wildness. It also magnifies its power. At its head, as Army engineer D. O. Elliot said, the river "is held in place . . . by the gorge in the Commerce hills. Its mouth in the Gulf of Mexico is fixed by the works of man. Between these points it writhes like an imprisoned snake constantly seeking to establish and maintain a state of equilibrium, between its length; its slope; and the volume and velocity of its discharge."

In the century of the engineers the study of this writhing river began as a scientific enterprise. The resulting policy became a corruption of science. Indeed, the policy was scientific only in that it began an immense, if unintended, experiment with the forces of the river.

For thousands of centuries the river had roamed over its alluvial valley, its vast natural floodplain. The Mississippi River Commission, certain of its theories, constrained the river within levees, believing that the levees alone, without any other means to release the tension of the river, could hold within narrow banks this force immense enough to have spread its waters over tens of thousands of square miles, where millions of people would settle.

The Mississippi River Commission promised protection to this great valley, a valley filled with the richest earth in the world. It was earth rich enough that men would risk everything for it. Given just the promise of protection, large men willed that the valley would hum with money, and culture, and industry. And they waited to discover whether the great unintended experiment of the levees-only policy would prove a success or a failure.

Part Two

SENATOR PERCY

CHAPTER SEVEN

I̲N 1841, TWENTY-YEAR-OLD Charles Percy abandoned an Alabama
plantation worth a quarter of a million dollars and headed deep
into the lush wilderness of the Yazoo-Mississippi Delta. He loaded
furniture, equipment, supplies, mules, overseers, and slaves onto
barges and flatboats, traveled down the Tennessee River to the Ohio,
stopped briefly near Paducah, Kentucky, before continuing down the
Ohio to the Mississippi, then proceeded two hundred more miles
down it. Finally, he and his entourage unloaded near what would
become the city of Greenville, Mississippi, then cut their way fifteen
miles through a jungle of vines and cane twenty feet high to Deer
Creek and some of the very finest land in all the Delta. They soon
built a house with ceilings so high that even in dead summer its center
hall was "a very cave for coolness and emptiness," and waited for
barrels of whiskey, oranges, brandy, and oysters that had already
been ordered from New Orleans to arrive.

The Percys were home, home in the Yazoo-Mississippi Delta
—known throughout America as simply "the Delta." It is a region
that conjures dark things in the mind. It has been called the South's
South, Mississippi's Mississippi, the most southern place on earth.
There, over the next century, the Percys became giants, generations
of men who led both the South and the nation. These giants in turn
spawned generations of writers, including William Alexander Percy,
whose work remains in print half a century after his death, and
Walker Percy, an award-winning novelist important enough to be the
subject of literary biographies. The family story includes men who
lived lives like Faulkner's Sartoris, only larger, and who were well
known to Faulkner. It also contains men with dark secrets, dark
enough and complex enough for a Faulkner novel. Some, haunted by
death, died young and by their own hand.

T. S. Eliot wrote that the sea is around us, but the river is in us. The Mississippi River ran through everything that the Percys did. And the Percy story was intertwined not only with the river but with race, and power, and money, and evil. These were wild forces, yet the Percys did not simply represent a time and class. They tried to put bridles on these forces and command them. Others ruled much larger personal empires like fiefdoms. Yet the Percys were the most commanding of all the planters and, in their own way, the most ambitious, more ambitious even than Eads or Humphreys.

Eads and Humphreys struggled with each other, and to contain the river. The Percys built upon what Eads and Humphreys had done by transforming the potential that the river had created into an entire society, extending far beyond their own holdings, and by making it conform to their own special vision. This immense task required them to contain both the river and great social forces sweeping through the nation. Yet, for a time at least, they succeeded.

THE DEMESNE the Percys shaped out of the river's potential was the Yazoo-Mississippi Delta. Resembling an elongated diamond, this Delta begins just below Memphis, widens to nearly 70 miles near the head of the Yazoo River (which means "river of death") at Greenwood, Mississippi, and extends south 220 miles to Vicksburg, where the Yazoo empties into the Mississippi. The Mississippi created this land, for thousands of years depositing ineluctably sweet topsoil, dense with nutrients and washed down from the rest of the continent, making a lush saucer of 7,000 square miles, almost twice the size of Connecticut. Then, as if marking its ownership, the river splayed sideways across the Delta; the Sunflower, the Tallahatchie, the Yalobusha, Deer Creek, now all tributaries of the Mississippi, all transverse it and once served as the main channel for either the Mississippi or the Ohio.

The Delta was wild and the river kept it so. In 1837 a European visitor observed the Mississippi as it roiled through this region and was chilled: "It is not like most rivers, beautiful to the sight . . . not one that the eye loves to dwell upon as it sweeps along, nor can you wander along its bank, or trust yourself without danger to its stream. It is a furious, rapid, desolating torrent, loaded with alluvial soil. . . . Pouring its impetuous waters through wild tracts, it sweeps down whole forests in its course, which disappear in tumultuous confusion, whirled away by the stream now loaded with the masses of soil which nourished their roots, often blocking up and changing the channel of the river, which, as if in anger at its being opposed, inundates and devastates the whole country round. . . . It is a river of desolation, and instead of reminding you, like other rivers, of an angel which has descended for the benefit of man, you imagine it a devil."

The land, wrote another traveler, was "a jungle equal to any in Africa," with dense forests of cane and "giant trees" from which hung "great clinging vines of wild grape and muscadine." The density of growth suffocated, choked off air, held in moisture and a pulsing heat, was so thick a horse and rider could not penetrate; even on foot one needed to cut one's way through. Only the trees, some one hundred feet high, burst above the choking vines and cane into the sunshine. Stinging flies, gnats, and mosquitoes swarmed around any visitors. One pioneer reported killing fourteen bears in eight days. Another warned of wolves and "the fetid alligator, while the panther basks at [the river's] edge in the cane-brakes, almost impervious to man . . . nearly as large as a young calf. They are the most savage looking animal I ever saw. Their strong sinewy legs with large hooked claws like a cat could tear a man to pieces in a trice if they chose to."

The wild animals, the rattlesnakes and water moccasins, the yellow fever and malaria, made it, worried one settler, "almost worth a man's life to cast his lot in the Swamp."

Yet the river had made it worth the risk. The river left gold in the Delta. It was gold the color of chocolate, gold that was not in the earth but was the earth. Elsewhere one measures the thickness of good topsoil in inches. Here good lush soil measures tens of feet thick. A 1901 report published by the American Economic Association said, "Nature knows not how to compound a richer soil." A 1906 scientific assessment concluded that the nutrients in the soil were unexcelled by those of any other soil in the world.

The Delta, however, overwhelmed individual farmers. To take the land from the river, to clear it, drain it, and protect it, required an enormous outlay of capital and labor. From the first the Delta demanded organization, capital, entrepreneurship, and gambling instincts. It was a place for empire, and the Percys intended to transform what the river had created into empire.

At first, they and a few others only clung to narrow strips of the highest ground, the natural levees, usually within half a mile of the Mississippi and its tributaries. They carved fields out of jungle, built levees—rarely more than two or three feet high—and planted cotton. The vast and impenetrable interior remained an untouched offering.

By 1858, 310 miles of levees protected the Delta from the

Mississippi. They protected adequately, largely because the Arkansas bank had weaker levees, or none at all. In floods the river simply overflowed the Arkansas side. So Delta planters began to thrive. After levee improvements, assessed values in five Delta counties leaped from $7,792,869 in 1853 to $23,473,115 in 1857.

Yet the region remained almost entirely wild. Even its settled parts resembled the frontier more than the plantation society of older parts of the South. It boasted few if any estates like those of Natchez, built on cotton wealth downriver, nor was it favored by the elegant sprawling oaks that shaded the mansions on the vast sugar plantations of Louisiana. In 1861 an area that later became three large Delta counties had not a single school, not a single church. That same year Humphreys' report referred to the entire Delta simply as "that great Swamp." The Delta was still, warned a man who perhaps saw too deeply into it, "a seething lush hell."

AT AGE THIRTY, ten years after coming to the Delta, Charles Percy died. His younger brother W. A. Percy took charge of family affairs. Like his father a Princeton graduate with a law degree from the University of Virginia, this Percy understood power and had few illusions. He had opposed secession but immediately after Mississippi seceded raised a regiment of Confederate volunteers, became its colonel, and during the war earned the nickname "the Gray Eagle." It fitted him. At twenty-eight he came home from the war deep-voiced, white-haired, aloof, and steely-eyed, but also charming. A cold efficiency lay beneath that charm.

He came home to desolation. Federal troops had flattened virtually every town in the Delta. Grant in his efforts to conquer Vicksburg had destroyed numerous levees. Others had disintegrated without maintenance. In the spring of 1865 the Mississippi flooded and miles of additional levees were breached. Much of what had survived Union troops was washed away. In all of Bolivar County not a single town remained; its most populous town, Prentiss on the river, left no trace of having ever existed. Wilderness was rapidly reclaiming cleared land. Blue cane fifteen and sometimes twenty feet high, vines, even willow trees grew where cotton had once risen taller than a man's head. Returning soldiers found "a wilderness and a waste. . . . Our lands had grown up in bushes. . . . A desolate scene presented itself."

The first priority was to rebuild the levees. In December 1865, W. A. Percy reorganized the levee system, convincing the governor and the state legislature to create a new levee board, legally unencumbered by old levee board debts or bonds. (The state simultaneously created a "Liquidating Levee Board" that built no levees, only raised money to pay off old debts at pennies on the dollar.) It was an effort to bring order out of the chaos left by the war. Percy naturally controlled the active levee board; this gave him power. The board spent more money than any other enterprise in the area on everything from attorney fees, bond commissions, and printing contracts, which guaranteed that certain newspapers would support a board while others would oppose it, and it kept its deposits in favored banks— especially the one on whose board Percy sat.

Never forgetting the levees, Percy then began to address other needs as well, helping to organize a railroad that crossed the state from east to west. Almost immediately it became the most profitable of Mississippi's sixteen railroads, largely because Percy also helped get public bond issues to pay for its expansion. Ultimately, J. P. Morgan's Southern Railroad bought it.

The levee boards and the railroads would soon link W. A. Percy and, largely through him, all the Delta's interests and complexities to the financial markets of New York and London, and the political market of Washington. Meanwhile, his influence inside Mississippi spread, particularly over the nexus of race, money, and power. In 1879, when Eads was finishing the jetties, Percy had relatively little to show for his influence. Only a fraction—less than 10 percent—of the Delta was developed. But the flow of events was moving Percy's way.

IT WAS THE GILDED AGE, the age of robber barons and great Wall Street manipulators, of vast fortunes and dominating eastern capital. The spirit of the age spread south and infected southern crusaders who now hoped to use commerce to do what the Confederate armies could not—defeat the North—creating a "New South." Led by people like James De Bow in New Orleans, editor of *De Bow's Review,* and Henry Grady of the *Atlanta Constitution,* southerners made economic development a sacred call.

The weapon was cotton still, both growing it and, now, bringing great textile factories to the South. The *Memphis Daily Appeal* called cotton "more a king today . . . than ever before." Grady declared that cotton had put the South "on the threshold of a prosperity more brilliant than any in the past," and the masthead of his newspaper proclaimed, "The foremost branch of American industry is the culture and manufacture of cotton."

In 1880, Grady estimated that if the twenty counties bordering the Mississippi River between Memphis and Baton Rouge were fully developed—the undeveloped land lay largely in the Yazoo-Mississippi Delta—they could produce more cotton than the entire American crop of that year, a record harvest that exceeded the prewar peak by over a million bales.

Eads' success allowed Grady to make that prediction, for the establishment of the Mississippi River Commission promised protection from floods. The commission would set standards, oversee construction, supply funds to nearly bankrupt states and local levee boards. As a result, northern and foreign capital, which was building textile mills in the Carolinas, steel mills in Alabama, and rail junctions in Georgia, suddenly saw profits in Delta cotton fields.

Eads' influence extended further. As he began work on the jetties, he noted, "To facilitate trade, two great agencies are absolutely requisite . . . *Transportation and Finance,* and they are so inseparable . . . that the first may be not inaptly termed the bone and sinew and the last the nerve and brain of Commerce."

Indeed, in the nineteenth century transportation and finance were virtually identical. Railroads *were* capital, the physical incarnation and representation of Wall Street. And by making New Orleans into a great port, the Eads jetties compelled this capital to bend toward it, to build a web of track paralleling the rivers that flowed south. Where track was laid, development followed.

The single railway most important to the lands along the Mississippi River was the Illinois Central, headquartered in New York, where its executives were major Wall Street figures. It was a symbiotic relationship. In the mid-1870s, the company fell into desperate financial straits; its directors, gambling everything on the success of the jetties, invested the company's scarce resources in a line to New Orleans. With Eads' triumph, the Illinois Central's traffic jumped 500 percent in three years, and profits gushed forth. The road's president, Stuyvesant Fish, called the extension to New Orleans "the salvation" of the company and committed the railroad to the region. (Years later, Chauncey Depew of the New York Central Railroad demanded to know why Fish was "stealing" business from New York for New Orleans. Fish replied, "I [am] only trying to get for New Orleans what New York and other northern ports had stolen from it during and immediately after the Civil War.")

Simultaneously, Percy was helping craft tax and land policies to tie railroads, especially the Illinois Central, directly to the rich land the river had created. During the economic chaos accompanying Reconstruction, 2,365,214 Delta acres—nearly all of it undeveloped, totaling more than half the entire Delta—had been forfeited to the state for back taxes. In 1881, with the river commission generating new confidence, with cotton prices rising, and with Percy pushing from backstage, the state made two huge land deals.

First, it sold 774,000 acres of the Delta to a railroad that had laid not a single mile of track and owned not a single locomotive. But this road did have a franchise and state tax exemptions worth millions of dollars, and it ultimately became the Yazoo & Mississippi Valley Railroad, the Y&MV, later called "the yellow dog" in blues songs after the color of its trains. The Y&MV was wholly owned by the Illinois Central and shared the same directors.

A few weeks after the first sale, the state sold 706,000 acres of Delta land for $2,500 in cash plus nearly worthless old levee board bonds that had a face value of only $45,954.22. Title to this land went through several hands before ending up with the Southern Railroad, controlled by J. P. Morgan.

Now large capitalists owned the land, men who had created vast fortunes and who intended to use the Delta to make more. And the Delta began to explode into flower.

Town after town sprang into existence around a tiny depot. The *History of Bolivar County* reads like a litany to the Y&MV railroad: "The coming of the railroad in 1884 marks the beginning of the Boyle community." "Gunnison first saw the light in a cotton field, Nov. 18, 1889, when the foundations of the . . . depot was [*sic*] laid at . . . the plantation owned by Arvin Gunnison." "The life of Benoit began in the year 1889 with the coming of the Y.&M.V. Railroad." If a town could not attract a railroad or grow up around a depot, it might simply relocate: "The entire town [of Concordia] moved south three miles to greet the welcome railroad."

DEVELOPMENT PAID. The veins of chocolate-colored gold the river had deposited meant money, not simply the kind of bare living that poor whites scratched out of the land elsewhere in the South—a living so poor that they were losing their lands and being forced to work in mills—but serious money, money for the railroads, money for the planters, money for the suppliers, money for the cotton factors, money even for blacks. Even through a depression in the 1880s, the Y&MV Railroad poured forth profits. And it grew. In 1890, 235 miles of its track traversed the delta. In 1903, 816 miles crisscrossed it, and the expansion continued. One stretch of road was known as "the Pea-vine" because its circuitous route zigzagged from plantation to plantation, each having its own station; when there were dances, a locomotive pulling one or two cars would run through the night, stopping to pick up belles or their young men at their plantations and waiting if they were not ready, delivering them to the party, delivering them home at dawn. If this seemed inefficient, profits were enormous. The Y&MV soon became more profitable, Fish confided, "than the Illinois Central taken as a whole."

Two-thirds of the world's cotton supply came from the American South. The river had made Delta soil so lush that without fertilizer it produced far more than other land did with fertilizer, even the black loam of Alabama. Often Delta yields doubled and tripled that of other soils. Delta cotton, for reasons of climate and soil, even had some resistance to the boll weevil, which had entered Texas from Mexico in 1892, spread east at 40 to 70 miles a year, and was devastating the rest of the southern crop.

In the early 1900s, world textile manufacturers began to fear a cotton famine. British and northern investors poured ever more cash into the Delta. Development required three things: protection from the river, transportation into the interior, and labor. Increasingly, labor shortages were limiting the Delta's growth. No area of the South was more short of labor than it.

In the South, of course, the issue of labor was inextricably bound up with race. It was also inextricably linked with the society the Percys intended to create. On the issue of labor, the Percy family would play more of a role than on any other.

THE DELTA had always been too wild for one man or one family to subdue, and from the first, settlers had brought slaves and organization with them. Immediately after the Civil War, Mississippi and other southern states tried to resolve labor and racial questions by passing a "Black Code" that effectively reestablished slavery. One Mississippi provision required blacks to sign annual labor contracts or be arrested for vagrancy; the local government would then sell their services to contractors. Congress reacted to such laws with anger and instituted "Radical Reconstruction," setting up new state governments that threw out those laws and putting a buffer of federal power between southern whites and blacks.

Percy recognized both the economic problems and the need to accept a new order, and advocated a solution. Planters had land but no cash. Blacks had labor but no land; they also resisted working in gangs under a foreman, which smacked of slavery and overseers. So Percy, who understood both the capital shortage and the importance of making labor content in order to maximize efficiency, advocated sharecropping. One man even credited Percy with inventing the system, and contemporaneous reports in other southern states did attribute the system's beginnings to Mississippi. Planters supplied land; blacks supplied labor and gained some independence. Profits were theoretically split fifty-fifty (the cropper got more if he had his own mules), making blacks and whites partners and by implication comparable if not equal. However abusive sharecropping later became, because of the system's implied partnership of white and black, initially whites resisted it while blacks welcomed it.

Sharecropping may have helped alleviate the Delta's desperate shortage of labor in another way. Planters and their labor agents were scouring the rest of the state and the South recruiting former slaves, promising—and delivering—better pay and treatment than elsewhere. The new system may have helped attract blacks, for in a steady stream they came. From one Mississippi county outside the Delta, a single Delta plantation recruited 500 workers. From Columbus, Mississippi, near the Alabama line, 100 black workers left for the Delta in a single week. From Uniontown, Alabama, 250 blacks boarded a single train, heading for the Delta. From Virginia, the Carolinas, and Georgia as well, thousands of blacks came.

The advocacy of sharecropping was not the only reflection of Percy's sensitivity to the inefficiencies of racial animosity. As Reconstruction dragged on, as the federal government became less and less willing to support black rights with Army bayonets, Percy, like most southern white leaders, became increasingly aggressive in his efforts to seize power back from Republicans and Negroes. But he did not want to frighten away either labor or northern investors. Elsewhere across the South, Democrats took power by murdering hundreds of blacks—including dozens in the Delta—intimidating thousands away from the polls, and perpetrating massive vote fraud. But Percy prevented the Ku Klux Klan from operating in his own Washington County and no murders were reported there; on one occasion, Percy waded into a crowd to stop the lynching of a black man accused of murdering a white. He also offered blacks minor county offices on a "fusion" ticket, and enlisted Cassius Clay, a Kentucky newspaperman and prewar abolitionist, to urge Negroes to vote for his slate. Then he formed a Taxpayer's League that spread rapidly across the state and demanded a rollback of taxes. Though not above vote fraud, he considered violence counterproductive; it disturbed unnecessarily. More smoothly than elsewhere, Democrats "redeemed" Washington County.

Percy, now a power statewide, prepared the trumped-up articles of impeachment which forced Adelbert Ames, the last Reconstruction governor, to leave the state. Yet after serving one term as speaker of the state legislature, Percy never again ran for office and even declined appointment as a U.S. senator (although only after arranging for a close ally to be named). He preferred to exercise power backstage while concentrating on transforming the river's land into a New South empire.

In the Delta in general, and particularly in Percy's Washington County, blacks continued to be relatively well treated, at least compared to most of the South. When a former Percy slave killed a white man, he was not lynched; instead, he was tried and acquitted. In 1877, when a white man boasted of murdering a black, a mob of whites lynched *him*, while the *Times* of Greenville, the county seat, announced, "Public sentiment excuses the lynching."

A more important test of sentiment came in 1879 with the first great migration of blacks out of the South, the "Exodus" to the "promised land" of Kansas. Outside the Delta, Mississippi whites cheered the departure; one paper hoped "that thousands [of Negroes] will follow . . . till the whites have a numerical superiority in every county in Mississippi." But in the Delta, planters threatened to seize boats and barges to keep labor from crossing the Mississippi River; a former governor called for creating local committees to protect black rights "with unceasing vigilance"; and a convention of planters warned blacks that they would "be subjected [to prejudice] in a greater degree at any other place on the American Continent" than in the Delta.

Kansas turned out not to be the promised land. In the end, more blacks entered the Delta from elsewhere in the South than left in the exodus. The crisis ended and growth continued.

Then in 1888, at the age of fifty-three, Colonel W. A. Percy, the Gray Eagle, died. Through his fingers had run nearly every thread of power or investment in the region. His son LeRoy stepped forward to replace him. He would do more than merely that.

EVEN BEFORE his father's death, LeRoy had emerged as a young man to watch. Like his father, he was not a sentimentalist. Like his father, he . . . *understood* things. After graduating from the University of the South at Sewanee, Tennessee, he, like his father and grandfather, attended the University of Virginia Law School—and finished a three-year program in one year, in time to be admitted to the bar on his twenty-first birthday. Fittingly, his first significant client was the state's second levee board (the first was headquartered in Greenville), which was organized in the northern Delta and hired him as its attorney although he was only twenty-four years old and did not live in the area this board controlled. By the early 1900s he was a prominent attorney whose plantations exceeded 20,000 acres, on the verge of eclipsing anything his father had done.

He had a thick chest, a handlebar mustache, and, though only in his early forties, a full head of silvery hair. Handsome in only a general sort of way and of average height, still he had a remarkable presence. His eyes pierced and chilled and, when he was in good humor, sparkled. He had grown up used to people deferring first to his father and then to himself, and his bearing assumed precedence and deference. When he spoke, he expected that others would give his words weight. If they failed to, this was their failure, not his.

In all his dealings he sought every advantage, including small ones, and gave no quarter. When his sister-in-law left her purse on a train, he demanded the $8 it had contained from the president of the Pullman Company. A monogram on goods purchased in Venice was a "disappointment" and required compensation. A resort in North Carolina must "quote a lower rate," in return for which he promised "much more patronage from this section . . . if I am pleased." When he brought the first concrete road to Washington County, he saw to it that it ran directly past his plantation. He also had expectations. His brother committed suicide, and when his brother's boy entered Stanford, LeRoy wrote him a long paternal letter that concluded, "While, if you should ever need help, if I am in a position to extend it and thought you deserved it, I will probably do so, I have never felt the obligation to take care of any able-bodied grown man."

Yet if he focused on small things, he also saw the world in wide-angle. Occasionally, he fell into a deep moodiness, sometimes exploded in inexplicable rages. He had passion; he also had the coldness both to see what some might call "the greater good" and to sacrifice whatever or whoever was necessary to achieve it. He had a sense of irony, and with it came the ability to step back and see himself and his class as if from a distance. He opposed requiring lawyers to attend law school because "it has a tendency to build up snobbishness in the profession and to keep poor men out of it." And he advised another nephew about to leave for Europe: "I think the 3rd class travelling is absolutely all right. I have been on many big ships where the 3rd class passengers, composed largely of school teachers and young students, were much more interesting people than the other classes. There is a feeling of comradeship and also an amount of intelligence which does not prevail upstairs."

LeRoy's father had represented the Illinois Central and helped found a small railroad. The Illinois Central would pay LeRoy more than it paid any outside attorney in the country, except one Wall Street lawyer who worked nearly full-time for it, and he would serve on the board of J. P. Morgan's Southern. His father had been speaker of the Mississippi legislature and declined a U.S. Senate seat. LeRoy would hunt with President Teddy Roosevelt, be a friend of three justices of the United States Supreme Court (two of them chief justices), become a U.S. senator, a director of a Federal Reserve bank, a director of the Rockefeller Foundation, a trustee of the Carnegie Foundation.

In 1885, LeRoy had his first child, a son, and named him William Alexander Percy after his own father. Young Will was never close to his father but idolized him and recalled, "He read *Ivanhoe* once a year. . . . He was kin to Hotspur and blood brother to Richard Coeur de Lion, and he looked the part. . . . [T]o the day of his death he was beautiful, a cross between Phoebus Apollo and the Archangel Michael. He could do everything well except drive a nail or a car; he was the best pistol-shot and the best bird-shot, he was the fairest thinker and the wisest, he could laugh like the Elizabethans, he could brood and pity till sweat covered his brow and you could feel him bleed inside. He loved life, and never forgot it was unbearably tragic."

His son also recalled, "No one ever made the mistake of thinking he wasn't dangerous."

Young Will had reason to know. His father lay at the center of a great web of power he had woven that stretched from its center in Greenville not only to Jackson and New Orleans but outward, to Washington, New York, even London. In the Delta, the web hung heavily from the bluffs of Memphis to the bluffs of Vicksburg, glistening with moisture from the Mississippi River. Young Will would lie in this web as well. He would lie trapped and poisoned in it.

CHAPTER EIGHT

LeRoy Percy had a clear conception of the society he intended to build. It would be a great agricultural factory that chested its way into the forefront of the New South, more humane than, but every bit as efficient as, the textile mills in North Carolina or the coal mines in Alabama. It would have rich and poor and little middle, but it would provide opportunity. It would be a place in which a superior civilization might flourish. And, although Percy was not burdened by sentimentality, he expected this society to adhere to a code of honor. If ruled by an elite, that elite would take care of its less fortunate members.

Building this society seemed possible. Its center would be Greenville, a town that even took advantage of disaster when, in the late 1800s, the river swung sideways and block after block of downtown collapsed into the river. Lawyers and cotton brokers moved their offices back, while the levee board and the Mississippi River Commission built a new levee, then poured concrete over it to protect it from the currents. This created a huge sloping wharf hundreds of yards long that helped make the port the busiest between Memphis and New Orleans. By the turn of the century, demand for cotton was steadily increasing. Between 1900 and 1904 alone the number of world cotton spindles jumped by 12 percent. In 1904 a "bull clique" of New Orleans traders drove cotton to 17.5 cents a pound, its highest price in decades and four times the price of just six years earlier. Meanwhile, young Greenville gentlemen frolicked; mimicking Sir Walter Scott, until World War I they tied ladies' scarves to their lances and galloped at full speed in jousting tournaments.

Yet before Percy's ideal society could be realized, one problem remained. Capital and transportation needs were being met, making labor the key to everything. Too much of the wealth the river had created, the most fertile land in the world, remained jungle. Levees were rising higher and capital was pouring into the Delta, but there was no labor to clear it, nor enough to farm what was cleared. This was true despite the benefits blacks were gleaning from what Percy was trying to do. Probably a higher proportion of Delta farms were owned by blacks than was the case anywhere else in the country; large numbers of these black owners had sharecroppers themselves. But even this opportunity had not lured the workers needed to the Delta. Percy declared: "The South must not be dependent for its prosperity upon the negro. There is not enough of him, and what there is is not good enough."

So he began looking for a source of white labor. In so doing he hoped not only to supply the region's needs but also to somehow escape "the Negro question." One breed of whites he would not recruit: the poor whites from small farms in Alabama or Georgia or the Mississippi hills who were being driven off the land by economics. Percy did not seek them for two reasons: he considered them inferior to blacks, and he believed their presence would exacerbate rather than ease any racial tension.

Instead, he and Charles Scott, possibly the Delta's single largest planter, asked Illinois Central president Stuyvesant Fish for help: "We are without sufficient labor to work that which is already cleared. These conditions grow more and more acute each year. . . . [We] must turn elsewhere for a new supply of farm laborers."

Fish had every reason to help. By then he and Percy had become friends. They also used each other. Bred to power and wealth, Fish was descended from the original Dutch founders of New York City; his father, Hamilton, had been governor of New York, a U.S. senator, and secretary of state (descendants would represent the same New York district in Congress from 1910 until 1994). Stuyvesant himself controlled banks and insurance companies as well as railroads, and ranked among the shrewdest and most influential players on Wall Street. His uses to Percy could be many. In turn, Percy helped the railroad legally and politically in Mississippi and Louisiana, where most of its profits lay. He also helped Fish personally when Fish and several partners created a giant plantation in the Delta; these partners included Speaker of the House "Uncle Joe" Cannon, the most dictatorial speaker in history, and Senator William Allison, chairman of the Senate Appropriations Committee.

Personal relations aside, Fish recognized that, with less than one-third of the Delta developed, clearing more land could greatly enhance Illinois Central profits. The railroad itself still had hundreds of thousands of Delta acres for sale, and it also had a land settlement department that began operating in the 1850s when the railroad received a federal land grant, the first to any railroad, of 2.5 million acres.

Fish promised Scott and Percy the Illinois Central would "leave no stone unturned" in the search for labor. In addition, Fish instructed a deputy to accept any suggestions about stimulating immigration from "the Delta's three leading planters, John M. Parker, Charles Scott, and LeRoy Percy."

PERCY, PARKER, AND SCOTT all had plantations just outside Greenville, all traveled often to Europe, and all moved in the highest circles politically and socially in New York, Washington, and New Orleans. Scott would run for governor of Mississippi. Parker would become governor of Louisiana. Percy would become a U.S. senator. Their friendship, particularly that between Parker and Percy, would become an axis around which much that happened in the Delta would revolve.

The three men had ideas, and so did the Illinois Central's land commissioner. They talked. The land commissioner changed the region's name on railroad circulars from "the Yazoo Delta" to "the Yazoo Valley" to avoid connotations of floods. He urged Dutch, English, and German stockholders to tell their countrymen of the opportunity there. He sent an exhibition train loaded with products of Delta soil to the Midwest. He had the railroad give away thousands of free passes to midwestern farmers to examine the Delta. He went to Iowa, Michigan, Ohio, Wisconsin, and elsewhere to extol Delta soil, and distributed tens of thousands of copies of a pamphlet, *The Call of the Alluvial Empire,* that cited head-high cotton and "an experimental demonstration yielding 220 bushels an acre" of corn. In the Midwest a yield of 40 bushels an acre was excellent.

But the wild had not changed. Making farms of it still required economies of scale, while the railroad was committed to selling its own land in lots the size of Midwest farms. And there was something dark about Mississippi, something dark and deep that men did not want to venture into. Despite a decade of effort, only a few hundred white farmers moved to the Delta.

Immigrants were then pouring into America by the millions, filling northern cities and factories, providing cheap, good, white labor. Percy decided to recruit Italians. In the 1870s, Delta planters had made a concerted effort to bring in Chinese from Hong Kong and from the labor gangs of the intercontinental railroads. The Chinese had left the fields, many opening tiny grocery stores, over fifty in Greenville alone. (Unable to speak English, they provided their almost exclusively black clientele with a pointer for picking out merchandise.) But Percy was not deterred by this failure. He decided to recruit large numbers of Italians to the Delta. If they succeeded as sharecroppers, tens of thousands might follow. Then the Delta would hum like the vast factory he envisaged, and the labor problem would disappear. So would the Negro problem. The Italian government agreed to cooperate, and John Parker urged President Teddy Roosevelt to listen to Percy's "eloquence on the subject."

PARKER AND ROOSEVELT had had similar childhood experiences and had become friends. Parker, an asthmatic and weak child, had learned judo, performed hard manual labor, bred fighting cocks, and avoided church. He grew tall, proud, determined, and successful, and became president of the New Orleans Cotton Exchange and the New Orleans Board of Trade and a director of the Illinois Central; he went back and forth between Mississippi and his mansion in the New Orleans Garden District.

Through Parker, Percy also became a friend of Roosevelt. Roosevelt understood the South; his mother was a Georgia aristocrat and two of his uncles had fought for the Confederacy. Both he and Percy loved to hunt, with Percy traveling as far as Alaska to shoot and Roosevelt traveling even farther. They were both direct, humorous, charming, charismatic. No one could dominate a room like Roosevelt; his energy simply filled it. But Percy's presence in a room was felt too. LeRoy's son Will, while attending Harvard Law School, met Roosevelt and judged him "scarcely a genius . . . [but] the biggest man I have ever seen outside of private life." In private life, Will considered his father bigger.

Percy met Roosevelt on a bear hunt Parker organized, a gathering of money and power in the Delta wilderness, including the president, two cabinet secretaries, Percy, Fish, and several others. (Governor Andrew Longino had been invited but, having just annoyed Percy over legislation involving the Hartford Insurance Company, was never informed of the time or place of the hunt, and so was left behind.) The guide was Holt Collier, born a slave of the Percy family.

The hunt itself was brutal and intimate. The dogs cornered the first bear in a lagoon surrounded by tall cane; there the bear stood at bay. Collier and Parker found it there and wanted Roosevelt to have the first kill. So Collier roped the bear to prevent its escape. Then Roosevelt arrived. He refused to shoot it. Parker also disdained a distant kill, instead circling behind the bear as dogs leaped at its front, then ramming his hunting knife under the bear's ribs and into its heart. It was November and crisp. Parker stood there, his chest heaving, his hands dripping blood, his boots covered with mud, as the bear died.*

After this hunt, Percy routinely dined with Roosevelt whenever he visited Washington. There Percy and Parker could count among their friends an extraordinarily powerful grouping: both the Republican Speaker of the House and the House Democratic leader John Sharp Williams, a Delta planter from Yazoo City, along with the Republican chairman of the Senate Appropriations Committee and the president. Parker confided that he never "made any direct request of President Roosevelt for that would embarrass him." Instead, he and Percy would go through back channels to "Speaker Cannon and whatever was desired would be realized."

Percy's experiment with Italian labor would soon force him to call upon his powerful friends.

THE EXPERIMENT took place at the vast, 11,000-acre Sunnyside Plantation in Chicot County, Arkansas, directly across the Mississippi River from Greenville. The plantation already had its own railroad and a telephone line to Greenville in 1898, when the O. B. Crittenden Company, Greenville cotton factors, took it over. The company's partners were Crittenden, Percy, and Morris Rosenstock (whose grandson is Civil War historian Shelby Foote). Percy was not the first to bring Italians there. Sunnyside's previous owner had started doing so in 1895, but after only a few months he had died in an accident in New York. Then malaria and yellow fever had struck the Delta. The tiny Italian colony had disintegrated.

Percy was intent on succeeding. He and Scott personally went to Italy to recruit workers and hire labor agents. In all, they brought several thousand Italians to the Delta, not all for Sunnyside. They performed well enough that in 1904 Percy boasted to the *Manufacturer's Record* that Italians were "in every way superior to the negro. . . . If the immigration of these people is encouraged, they will gradually take the place of the negro without their being any such violent change as to paralyze for a generation the prosperity of the country."

Soon 47 Delta plantations were working as many as 180 Italian families each. Alfred Stone, a Percy friend and neighbor who was both an agricultural and social scientist, had earlier written in *Publications of the American Economic Association,* "Every step taken in the development of this section has been dependent upon,

* A *Washington Post* cartoonist portrayed the president refusing to shoot a cute bear cub. It became "Teddy's bear." A German toy manufacturer sent dozens of small stuffed bears to the White House and launched a product that is still selling.

and marked by, an increased negro population." Now Stone seconded Percy's opinion: "It is always difficult to get a negro to plant and properly cultivate the outer edges of his field—the extreme ends of his rows, his ditch banks, etc. The Italian is so jealous of the use of every foot for which he pays rent that he will cultivate with a hoe places too small to be worked with a plough."

But the Italians did not consider the experiment so successful. The South did not welcome them. The most grievous incident occurred in 1891, when a corrupt New Orleans police chief involved himself in Mafia rivalries and was murdered; a jury was supposedly either bribed or frightened into acquitting the murderers. The next day many of the city's young leaders—including John Parker—issued a "call for action"; in response a crowd stormed the jail and lynched eleven Italians, including those just acquitted. The incident was hardly isolated. A year later three Italians were lynched in Hahnville, Louisiana; in 1899 five were lynched in Tallulah, Louisiana; in 1901 two were murdered outside Percy's own Greenville. In 1907, after another violent incident in Mississippi prompted the Italian government to demand an investigation, the governor informed the State Department that the victim deserved his fate because he was "a very dirty, low-caste Italian, of the 'Dago' type—very mouthy . . . causing [others] to be discontented with their work."

Though some Italians at Sunnyside were making money—in six years a single family saved $15,000 in cash—most were sinking into debt and growing bitter. Percy squeezed his tenants hard, charging "flat" annual interest of 10 percent on all advances, whether borrowed for one month or twelve, a routine practice in Mississippi but one that violated Arkansas law. Yet Percy ended the practice only after his manager warned, "I think we are taking some risk. . . . [Tenants are] making very close investigations about this point."

One Italian answered with a pamphlet titled *Don't Go to the Mississippi,* warning that there Italians would find only "slavery and fever"; he distributed it in New Orleans and Italy. In December 1906 a barn at Sunnyside exploded into flame. It was arson; the Italians were learning the revenge of the poor white.

In response, men with guns began patrolling the plantation. Some Italians were beaten. Some ran off. Tensions escalated.

When a labor agent tried to help some unhappy Sunnyside tenants relocate, Percy warned him "an unfriendly attitude on my part would be an injury to you." And when Percy learned some Sunnyside Italians were at the Greenville train depot, he told other planters not to take them on and sent a manager to intimidate them into returning.

Federal law prohibited "debt peonage," forcing people to work to pay off debts. Percy was pushing against the edge of the law. Federal law also prohibited advancing travel expenses and bringing in foreign workers under contract. Percy believed he had found a loophole in this law; more likely he had violated it.

Then Percy's partner Crittenden pushed beyond the edge of the law. Two Italian tenants walked into his office, announced they were leaving for jobs in Alabama coal mines, and promised to repay money owed. They walked out, but Crittenden followed with a Greenville policeman and forcibly pulled them off a train and returned them to Sunnyside.

In the spring of 1907, complaints from the Italians reached Italian Ambassador Baron Edmondo Des Planches. To co-opt him and regain their customary control of the situation, Percy, Charles Scott, Stuyvesant Fish, and others invited Des Planches to tour the plantation. Percy showed off the families whose acreage was highly profitable, pointed out the modern cotton gin, the railroad, the office for the doctor who was on call, the place reserved for Catholic services. Others tactfully let Des Planches know that Percy's wife, Camille, was Catholic. Afterward in Greenville, already a city with a sophistication beyond its small size, Percy hosted a dinner for the group at the Mirror Restaurant, an opulent restaurant run by two Italians that resembled Antoine's in New Orleans. Percy, an engaging and cultured host, entertained with grace and elegance and seemed to win Des Planches over. As Des Planches was leaving, he clasped Percy's hand and said, "Mr. Percy, I assure you we will send you Italians, who not only will make good farmers but will make good first class American citizens."

Des Planches had shown Percy his diplomatic face. There was another. He had a keen eye and saw deeply. He had seen the shacks in which many of the sharecroppers lived and the long rows of cotton assigned to each family, and he had stopped to try almost undrinkable water. He understood enough. Back in Washington he reported: "The Italian immigrant at Sunnyside is a human production machine. He is better off than the black man, more perfect than the black man, but like the black man still a machine." He demanded a Justice Department investigation, and specifically asked that Mary Grace Quackenbos conduct it.

MARY QUACKENBOS was strong, tough even, yet oddly naive and vulnerable. Heiress to a modest fortune, she had founded the People's Law Firm in New York to protect immigrants. As a private individual and at considerable personal risk, she had uncovered conditions of virtual slavery in turpentine and timber camps in Florida and handed over the evidence to the Justice Department, which prosecuted, then hired her as the first female U.S. attorney. Her contest with LeRoy would pit federal law against both Percy's friendship with Roosevelt and, in effect, all southern society.

From the first their relationship was one of mutual charm, mutual deceit, mutual determination, and, perhaps, even mutual respect. Upon her arrival in Greenville in July 1907, Percy seemed to extend both personal and professional courtesy to her. He hosted a dinner in her honor and gave her warm letters of introduction to X. O. Pindall, governor of Arkansas, and Charles Scott. But Percy also wrote a private letter warning Scott that her queries would be "endless and tedious" and wondering how to prevent her from "convers[ing] freely with the Italians."

She too operated with guile at dinner, playing the disarmed and disarming guest, saying she so enjoyed Mrs. Percy that she wondered if Mrs. Percy could accompany them on a tour of Sunnyside. Yet she had already dispatched an undercover agent to the plantation to seek evidence against her host. (The investigator was arrested for trespassing.) Soon she went to the plantation herself, slept in a sharecropper's shack with no screens on windows or doors, was besieged by mosquitoes, and drank the red, iron-laden water.

She returned with accusations of wrongdoing, yet still told her superiors, "Mr. Percy appears to be a man of common sense." She asked him to improve plantation conditions and rewrite tenant contracts, and he agreed to some changes. But when she pushed for more, he refused. Meanwhile, she had threatened one of Percy's labor agents with a long jail sentence for violating contract labor laws unless he confessed and helped her. She broke him, and his confession implicated Percy himself.

Percy reacted immediately. Her notes, including those of interviews with potential witnesses, disappeared from her room at the Cowan Hotel in Greenville. They were then "recovered" (Percy's mocking word) and returned to her by Thomas Catchings, a retired congressman and a close Percy associate. Percy seemed to be telling her she could not touch him, that she was powerless, not only in the Delta but in Washington.

At the time, Percy himself was with President Roosevelt in Memphis, at the largest river convention ever held. More than 10,000 attended. Boosters in every town along every river in the upper Mississippi valley, anticipating the opening of the Panama Canal, were dreaming of direct shipments to South America and the Orient. Roosevelt's high-pitched voice had pierced the hall. He approved the building of empires and called for great massive dams to generate hydroelectric power, irrigation projects to reclaim the dry West, and flood control too. Roosevelt proclaimed, "The whole future of the nation is directly at stake." The crowd cheered and cheered, although Roosevelt's own Army Corps of Engineers was trying to—and would —kill the legislation to carry out his plan.

Roosevelt then spent a week on Parker's plantation relaxing, hunting, fishing, and talking politics. Percy was with him for much of that time too.

Quackenbos knew of Percy's friendship with Roosevelt. It put enormous pressure on her. It drove her forward. She would not be intimidated. Instead, she showed her own power. Earlier she had written Attorney General Charles Bonaparte that the situation "at Sunnyside is not exactly peonage as I understand it." The settlers were making profits, often substantial profits. An assistant attorney general had also visited Sunnyside and found none of the systematic brutality and viciousness "we have seen in cases found in other states."

Now she returned to Sunnyside to spend another night with a tenant family. A foreman ordered her off the property. She refused to obey unless Percy himself told her to leave in writing. Before sunrise the next day a young black man delivered her a note from Percy doing so.

She left but sent Percy a note accusing him of "untrustworthiness and ungentlemanly behavior." They were two accusations that would have most enraged him, and also revealed the delicate balance between her feminine and professional roles. But she also declared, "I have a perfect right to go upon the Sunnyside property, at any time," and warned him not to interfere "with my duty as a government official."

Nine days later she sent an even stronger response, contained in a wire on October 25, 1907, to Attorney General Charles Bonaparte: "O. B. Crittenden arrested for peonage."

EARLIER THAT YEAR the Delta had survived a major flood of the Mississippi River. Although tens of thousands of acres had gone under, by and large the levees had held. Percy had worked hard in confronting that enemy at his front. He understood now that Quackenbos was an enemy at his rear, capable of threatening not only him personally but the relationship of the entire Delta with the financial markets and Washington.

She was proving a powerful adversary. Not satisfied with the weight of the Justice Department, she also used the press. Northern and Washington newspapers were sensationalizing what were plainly leaks from her. It was the age of muckraking and, like all ages, of scandalmongering, of exposing evil, of bringing down the mighty. It worried him.

But Mary Quackenbos was attacking only a wrong, and a relatively small one at that. To block her attack, Percy would use something far larger as a shield. The shield was the lot of the Negro in Mississippi, an evil that was to the wrong she accused him of as a supernova is to a streetlight.

Percy was no crusader on race. The preceding Christmas, when sharecroppers were signing contracts for 1907, he had warned his foreman that blacks considered him "rough with labor. . . . A difficulty at this time would be fatal to filling the place up. . . . [T]ake now what you would not be willing to do after." He had excepted "a negro named Toler [who] is doing the place a great deal of injury. I don't mind your being rough with Toler if you find him on the place." And Percy, like other planters, virtually bought and sold black sharecroppers, paying off their debts as the price of acquiring them as tenants. Typically, he wrote one fellow planter: "I would be willing to pay his account if you are willing for him to leave. I would not even write you about the matter, but he says it is your custom to let them leave whenever they are dissatisfied. If you care to turn him loose, call me over the phone."

And like many men of his class and time, he fully embraced Social Darwinism and considered blacks unable to compete with whites. He noted, "Those negroes who do receive higher education . . . in course of time, under the inexorable working out of the 'survival of the fittest' they will have to go to the wall."

This put him squarely in the mainstream of contemporary thought. Roosevelt tempered Social Darwinism with the Social Gospel—decrying "cutthroat competition" and embracing social work—but still used competition to define even friendship. Of a tennis partner Roosevelt said, "If conditions were such that only one could live he knows that I should possibly kill him as the weaker of the two and he, therefore, worships this in me." Although he dined with Booker T. Washington in the White House, arousing a fury of outrage in the South, he also said he wanted to "see the South back in full communion" with the rest of the nation, adding that in keeping with Social Darwinism, "The Negro . . . must take his chances like the rest."

Percy agreed with that sentiment. But if the idea of social equality with blacks was as abhorrent to him as it was to others of his class, and if he expected blacks to lose a competition, he also believed that each man had to join in that competition. And he viewed a black man as just that, a *man*.

This set him apart. When a dispute erupted on his Trail Lake Plantation between the white manager and black tenants, it was the black tenant Lewis Levi whom Percy addressed as a man of honor and trust: "I am counting on you to use your influence with the hands for the benefit of the place, as you said you would do. I hope that I will find things straightened out when I get back. . . . I believe I can rely upon you to do what is right." And it was the white manager whom Percy patronized and instructed: "You want to get as many of the hands satisfied as you can. . . . Treat Levi and the other negroes you think are against you exactly like you do the others, give them an equal chance to do day work, etc."

Such an insistence on fair play was rapidly losing favor. In 1903, Mississippi had elected James K. Vardaman, "the Great White Chief," governor. He was the first man in Mississippi to realize, in the sense of "making real," the politics of race hatred. Tall, with a massive head and long black hair draped like a cape over his shoulders, he always wore an immaculate white suit, mastered every stage, was charismatic and demagogic to all, and was demonic and frightening to his many rivals and enemies.

As governor, Vardaman raised expenditures on white education and regulated railroads and corporations, Percy's clients, but Percy initially supported him because they agreed on levee board appointments. But he also patronized him. Percy told a friend: "The fundamental trouble with Vardaman is that he honestly believes money is an evil to be guarded against . . . that Spartan simplicity, virtue and poverty are the virtues which should be emulated. It all comes of an untrained mind grappling with economic questions and trying to be original. . . . Between barbarism and Wall Street I believe he rather leans toward barbarism."

But then Vardaman began to exhibit a truly barbaric side. He denounced the education of blacks as "a positive unkindness because it renders him unfit for the work which the white man has prescribed and which he will be forced to perform." Besides, it made no sense to have education "dissatisfy [the Negro] and then kill him if he undertakes to enjoy the prerogatives of citizenship." He called blacks "lazy lying lustful animal[s] which no amount of training can transform into a tolerable citizen."

Appalled not only by Vardaman's comments but by the support they engendered, Percy believed that the time had come to respond. At a meeting of the Mississippi Bar Association in Vicksburg he made a remarkable speech. In it, he was very consciously preparing the ground for what would become a long war over race, a war that would last until the end of his life and beyond. He believed that his position represented civilization and decency, that Vardaman's represented evil. If his position also represented self-interest—even if the experiment with Italian sharecroppers proved successful, the Delta would still need black labor and Vardaman was threatening to drive blacks away—he considered that perfectly consistent with morality.

Ultimately, the Mississippi River would show that in race matters Percy's self-interest was not consistent with morality, and the river would force him to choose. In the meantime, his views on race were as progressive as those of any mainstream figure in the nation.

Percy began his speech with the observation "[t]hat man is a lover of his country, and a true patriot, who humbly strives to do his duty and to discharge the obligations of citizenship in that locality to which Fate may have assigned him." It therefore behooved him to act. He continued: "An erroneous statement, oft repeated by those high in place, if permitted for long to go uncontradicted, soon passes current as axiomatic truth. . . . Such an erroneous statement has come much into vogue in the South, and especially in Mississippi in regard to the negro and education. . . . The statement is daily heard that education ruins the negro. . . . I deny that any man is rendered worse by having his intelligence quickened, his mental horizon widened." It was a long speech. It affirmed the moral reasons for educating blacks and treating them fairly and honestly, including the fact that abusing blacks corrupted whites. Another reason for education was money. "The negro must be educated," he concluded. "But not as a matter of justice to him alone is his education necessary, but because the industrial development of the South demands it."

His speech would have impact. Jacob Dickinson, a former assistant U.S. attorney general and general counsel of the Illinois Central, a man Percy described as "an intense southerner," sent a copy of the speech to Roosevelt.

Roosevelt already trusted Percy and respected him. He also liked him. Only a few weeks earlier Percy had stopped at the White House to say hello. Roosevelt had greeted him cordially and urged him to return for lunch the next day, when he had talked of hunting and his fight with Edward Harriman, whom Percy knew well from Harriman's days as vice president of the Illinois Central. Finally the president had laughed: "Percy, by George, I like the Kaiser, he is a fine fellow. If you would put him down in Chicago he would carry his ward but the Czar would not. He would be president of the Mugwump Society." Now, Roosevelt, fully understanding the political forces at work in the South and understanding the storm Percy was calling down upon his own head, forwarded Percy's speech to the *Outlook,* the country's leading Progressive magazine, which published it. On August 11, 1907, he sent Percy a note saying, "I hailed that article of yours with genuine delight. I have long since become convinced that while in each section of the country there are wrongs to be remedied, . . . the only effective way to remedy them . . . [is] to back the man on the ground who is acting well and wisely. My dear sir, as an American I felt I owed you a debt of gratitude."

It was into that relationship that the arrest of Percy's partner intruded.

SOON AFTER his partner's arrest Percy left for Washington. When he needed action there, he usually relied upon either his own congressional delegation, which included the House Democratic leader, or Speaker Cannon. But Congress could not help in this matter. Only two men, the attorney general or the president, could.

So Percy met first with Attorney General Charles Bonaparte. The meeting went badly. He wrote home, "I believe he will give what trouble he can in the premises." Only Roosevelt remained.

Percy had never asked a favor of the president, refusing, as he told one man who sought his help, to make a "social acquaintance the basis of a request for political favors." But he did not hesitate to discuss policy with Roosevelt. Only days earlier Percy had urged Parker to join him in asking Roosevelt to help southern banks through the Panic of 1907. Whether because of them or not, Roosevelt did move $50 million of federal deposits into those banks.

Now Percy called at the White House. Roosevelt knew the subject of the visit and saw him at once. Percy had prepared for this meeting as thoroughly as for any court appearance. He would not confuse business with friendship and refrained from any talk of hunting or mutual friends. Instead, he presented his brief, explaining, "You are fully aware of the absolute necessity for immigration to the Delta section of Mississippi, Louisiana, and Arkansas, that the country is less than one-third developed and its development absolutely arrested for lack of labor."

Mary Quackenbos was threatening this immigration despite, he charged, her "most profound and remarkable ignorance. . . . There was not a condition, a custom, a form of contract, or a crop raised about which she had the slightest information." Percy cited specific errors she had made, including a grossly overestimated calculation of Sunnyside's profits based on her stunningly mistaken belief that the plantation produced two cotton crops a year.

He did not ask the president to quash the grand jury that would consider indicting his partner. He did not fear the law, he said, nor did Quackenbos care about the law. Indeed, he argued, "Her manner was that of a 'Lady Bountiful' dispensing alms, a philanthropic humanitarian, a doctrinaire, seeking to remove poverty wherever she finds it . . . without discrimination as to whether that poverty is due to unjust treatment or oppression, or is the result of necessary conditions and environment." It was simply the world, a hard world, which caused the immigrants' pain, he argued. Not even the South. The world. The fitter survive.

But if the legal process did not worry him, he continued, the press did. Quackenbos was leaking her report in bits and pieces to the press. Washington papers were suggesting that charges of "sensational character" would be made, and the southern press was reprinting the stories.

He then made three requests. First, believing that "the publication at this time of an unfavorable Government report would be absolutely fatal to any chance of securing immigration," he asked that "no publicity be given [her report] and no action be taken on it by the government until it be verified." Second, he asked that an investigation by *"men* of practical understanding" be conducted, and, third, that she not be sent south again.

Roosevelt listened closely. He approved of Quackenbos. When Florida congressmen had earlier erupted in outrage over her investigation of turpentine camps, Roosevelt had backed her absolutely. Just recently, he had sent a newspaper clipping about her offending southern timber interests to Bonaparte with the notation "very amusing." But Roosevelt trusted Percy. That was not something easily achieved or discounted.

After a moment he gave Percy the answers he wanted. Quackenbos would be removed from the investigation. There would be no publication of her report unless it was verified.

Then the president invited Percy to dinner. Percy declined. Few people would decline an invitation to dinner with the president, fewer still who had just won a favor from him. It was part of what Roosevelt liked about Percy.

IN A NARROW SENSE Percy had succeeded. A federal grand jury in Jackson, Mississippi, refused to indict Crittenden, despite a charge from the judge almost requiring them to do so. Quackenbos was reassigned, and all copies of her report were removed from Justice Department files.

A few weeks later Percy invited Stuyvesant Fish and Jacob Dickinson to join him at Sunnyside. "Fish are biting, Mint is growing, soft breezes blowing," he beckoned.

Meanwhile, Roosevelt asked Harvard historian Albert Bushnell Hart to investigate Sunnyside. In a letter expressing simultaneously doubts about feminism, concerns about having removed Quackenbos, and the limits of his own power, he wrote, "I am very uneasy about . . . [her] unsoundness of judgment which is both hysterical and sentimental. . . . The fact is that on these southern plantations we are faced with a condition of things that is very puzzling. Infamous outrages are perpetrated—outrages that would warrant radical action if they took place in Oyster Bay or Cambridge; but where they actually do occur, the surroundings, the habits of life, the sentiments of the people, are so absolutely different that we are in reality living in a different age, and we simply have to take this into account in endeavoring to enforce laws which cannot be enforced save by juries." Hart investigated and exonerated Percy.

Yet Percy actually had failed. The State Department forwarded Quackenbos' report to the Italian government in confidence. Throughout Italy the government put up signs in railroad depots warning emigrants away from the Delta. The Austrian government simply forbade emigration there.

Of 8 million people entering the United States from foreign countries between 1892 and 1906, only 2,697 claimed Mississippi as their destination. Most were Italians brought over for Percy's experiment. There would be few more.

There was something dark about Mississippi, darker even than the rest of the South. And it would grow darker still.

Percy concluded, "Italian immigration has not been a success . . . principally because the people of the Delta accustomed for a good many years to handling negro laborers are not fit to handle any other."

But the Delta was still starved for labor. In 1907 the boll weevil crossed the Mississippi River. The Delta suffered, but not as much as elsewhere; its climate and soil gave its cotton some resistance to the weevil. Demand for Delta cotton only increased. Percy observed wryly: "There is no labor . . . with which to develop [the state]. Mississippians have no idea of doing any work themselves and nobody else on God's green earth is thinking about coming here or can be made to contemplate such a dire possibility."

To seize land from the river, to build his society, more than ever Percy needed labor. In the South labor had always, one way or another, come down to race. Percy had tried to escape that tar pit. He had failed, both in recruiting independent white farmers from the Midwest and white sharecroppers from Europe. The future of the Delta and of whites like Percy was wedded to the black race more than ever, however much men of either race resisted.

CHAPTER NINE

IN 1903, THE YEAR Vardaman was elected governor, even W. E. B. Du Bois, the great black leader who was then considered a radical, commended "the representatives of the best white Southern public opinion," adding "[A] partially undeveloped people should be ruled by the best of their stronger and better neighbors for their own good, until such time as they can start and fight the world's battles alone."

In effect, Du Bois was calling upon men like LeRoy Percy to protect the Negro from emerging southern demagogues and the mob. In order to attract labor to build his society, Percy was doing just that, with some success. Percy's friend Alfred Stone told the American Economic Association: "If I were asked what one factor makes most for the amicable relations between the races in the delta I should say without hesitation the absence of a white laboring class, particularly of field laborers. . . . There were no small [white-owned] farms, no towns, no manufacturing enterprises, no foothold for the poor white, who is here a negligible, if not an absolutely unknown quantity."

This did not make the Delta the promised land. Lynchings did occur there—one occurred even in Percy's own Washington County —and they reverberated through the region's overwhelmingly black population, which in some areas exceeded 90 percent of the total. And, few places in the South saw more brutality than Delta levee camps. The camps were often isolated, surrounded by jungle, where one or two white men controlled a hundred "of the most reckless meanest niggers in the world," according to William Hemphill, a young engineer from the North who worked above Greenville and who also worked on the Panama Canal. He found the camps hellish. "You have seen a swarm of gnats bunched together. You can form some idea of how thick the mosquitoes are here . . . I killed a blue-striped scorpion which I found in my bedclothes." But mostly he found violence: "The way these levee niggers shoot one another is something fearful. One got shot in a crap game last night. It didn't even stop the game. If one of the white foremen shoots a couple of niggers on the works and it is by no means an unheard of or infrequent thing the work is not stopped. . . . The long arm of the law does not reach [here]." Once a levee contractor even murdered "the Mercy Man," a white man who issued fines for mistreating mules. On the levees mules were worth more than blacks. Black levee workers recited a saying, "Kill a mule, buy another. Kill a nigger, hire another."

Yet the Delta did offer blacks at least relative promise. Judge Robert R. Taylor of Indiana, a member of the Mississippi River Commission, pointed out that levees, by allowing the mining of the river's wealth, also allowed "the negro to better his condition. . . . In considerable and increasing numbers he is buying land and becoming an independent cultivator. . . . Nowhere else in the South are as favorable opportunities offered to the black man as in the reclaimed Mississippi lowlands, and nowhere else is he doing as much for his own up-lifting."

Percy and the men with whom he dominated the region, and particularly Washington County, did create something special—at least given the times. Largely because of Percy, who was on the board of one bank and influenced others, lenders did not hesitate to offer blacks mortgages. In 1900 blacks owned two-thirds of all Delta farms, probably the highest proportion of black land ownership in the country. Also largely because of Percy, Greenville had black policemen, a black justice of the peace, and every mailman in the city was black. In 1913 the Census Bureau concluded that the plantation organization was "more firmly fixed in the Yazoo-Mississippi Delta than in any other area of the South." But even sharecropping could offer opportunity. Alfred Stone founded an agricultural experiment station to develop better cotton and, as a social scientist, kept meticulous records of his settlements with sharecroppers. (He would also later make Mississippi the first state to enact a sales tax.) In 1901 the average family on his plantation cleared $1,000 after all expenses were deducted, and in 1903 they cleared roughly $700.

Mississippi outside the Delta contrasted sharply with this picture. There, whites were driving blacks off the land, burning down their barns, whipping them, forcing them to sell at a loss, murdering them. In one Mississippi county 309 men, including the sheriff, were indicted; some towns bragged that they were "nigger-free." More important was an outbreak of lynchings of almost incomprehensible viciousness. Ho Chi Minh, then a French journalist, collected clippings that included headlines such as, from the *New Orleans States,* "Today a Negro Will Be Burned by 3,000 Citizens," and from the *Jackson* (Mississippi) *Daily News,* "Negro J.H. to Be Burnt by the Crowd at Ellistown This Afternoon at 5 P.M." The *Vicksburg Evening-Post* reported the lynching of a black husband and wife accused of murdering a white man: "The blacks were forced to hold out their hands while one finger at a time was chopped off. The fingers were distributed as souvenirs. The ears of the murders [*sic*] were cut off. Holbert was beaten severely, his skull was fractured, and one of his eyes, knocked with a stick, hung by a shred from the socket. . . . [A] large corkscrew. . . . was bored into the man and woman . . . and then pulled out, the spirals tearing out big pieces of raw, quivering flesh." Then the crowd burned them at the stake, after partially filling their mouths and nostrils with mud to prevent a fast death from smoke inhalation.

Vardaman, the governor, fed on, and fed, the hatred. Although he sent troops to prevent one lynching, he also said it did not matter whether innocent blacks were lynched since "[t]he good [Negroes] are few, the bad are many, and it is impossible to tell what ones are . . . dangerous to the honor of the dominant race until the damage is done." Once he stated, "We would be justified in slaughtering every Ethiop on the earth to preserve unsullied the honor of one Caucasian home." Another time he said, "If it is necessary every Negro in the State will be lynched; it will be done to maintain white supremacy."

Percy had already attacked Vardaman's race-baiting, most publicly in the speech that Roosevelt had so liked. Since then Vardaman's rhetoric had only grown more barbaric. When Vardaman began pursuing a seat in the United States Senate, Percy moved to block him, denouncing his racial views as "infamous," condemning his willingness to use race "to inflame the passions and hatred of his audience, hoping out of it to gain a few paltry votes."

At first, Vardaman tried to conciliate Percy, writing: "My dear Percy, . . . I believe I can be elected by a handsome majority and do not want to be cut out of the opportunity. . . . I wish you would come down to see me."

Instead, Percy devoted himself to helping John Sharp Williams defeat Vardaman in 1908. Williams was Democratic leader of the U.S. House and had given the keynote speech at the Democratic National Convention. He could move crowds too. Yet he won by only 648 votes out of 118,344 cast. The Delta alone then had a black population of at least 171,209, and a white population of 24,137, but of course only a few hundred blacks—if that many—still voted.

But Vardaman, despite his loss, had changed the equation of power in Mississippi. The change was not wholly obvious. In the Delta and in Washington, D.C., Percy's might was still tangible, like a hard muscle one could touch. In the Delta even Williams, himself owner of a Delta plantation, paid homage. When his son, an engineer with a degree from MIT, needed business introductions, Williams thought his own influence insufficient and wrote Percy, "I wish you would give [my son] some letters to Delta people . . . so he may have a fair opportunity to present his proposition." In Washington, Anselm McLaurin, the other Mississippi senator, asked Percy to intervene with Roosevelt on a personal matter. Percy was happy to have the president do a kindness for the senator. Nor did Roosevelt's departure end Percy's influence. Despite opposition from the Army Corps of Engineers, he still arranged the appointment of Charles West, engineer of the Greenville Levee Board, as one of the five members of the Mississippi River Commission. And Speaker Cannon and Senator Allison continued to listen to him, especially on levees. Once, at Percy's request and to protect levees, Cannon had even, in violation of the seniority principle, removed a congressman from one committee and replaced him with another.

Yet paradoxically, in between the Delta and Washington, in the state capital of Jackson, Percy's power was becoming circumscribed. In the hill country of eastern Mississippi, in the piney woods of the southeast corner of the state, in the central and southwestern parts of the state, small white farmers who scratched a living from hill-country farms that took twice the effort to produce half the cotton as Delta soil resented his client corporations, resented the big Delta planters and the foreign and northern investors who owned tens of thousands of alluvial acres, resented the planters also for drinking—Mississippi passed prohibition in 1908—gambling, a general lack of God-fearingness, and because, the poorer whites well knew, the planters had contempt for them. Governors elected with their votes rarely allied with Percy. One governor was advised upon taking office to "whip" Percy and his friends: "You cannot conciliate them and retain your self-respect. They demand nothing short of the earth."

As a result, Percy was forced to retreat to the Delta, where he still had the votes to humble any adversary. He wanted only one thing from these governors: they appointed the levee board, and he wanted a say in those appointments. Usually, he got a say, even if he had to go through a third party to do so.

But the river was not the only rising force that threatened to inundate Percy's Delta. And Percy, not levees, would have to hold this new force back.

In 1910, Senator McLaurin died in office, leaving two years of his term unfilled. The state legislature would choose his successor. The leading candidate, by far, was Vardaman.

Percy again threw everything he had into preventing Vardaman's elevation to the Senate. Everything he had tried to build was at stake. Vardaman threatened "the welfare of the state and the peaceful relationship existing between the races," Percy protested. Defeating him would be "a life and death struggle." And this time Percy decided to run himself.

THE CONTEST was one in which backroom deals and maneuvers, not popular vote, would decide the winner. To counter Vardaman's overwhelming lead, Percy joined with his rivals and enemies to settle on a common strategy. First, they decided that, although the state legislature did not contain a single Republican, and although the legislators would be using the legislative chamber for votes, the legislators would meet formally as a party caucus to choose a Democratic nominee. This allowed secret balloting, so a legislator could vote against Vardaman without risking his constituents' wrath. Only for the formal election of the senator—ratifying a selection already made —would they legally convene as a legislature. Vardaman supporters immediately condemned this stratagem as "the Secret Caucus." Second, to dilute Vardaman's strength they encouraged favorite-son candidates to run. Third, they agreed that candidates who dropped out should urge their supporters not to switch to Vardaman but instead to rally around whatever opponent seemed strongest.

On the first vote Vardaman received 71 votes, more than double his closest rival. Percy received 13. But Vardaman's opponents totaled 99 votes. Vardaman fell short of a majority. The fight had begun.

It became a grand show for Jackson, the state capital that had only just become a city. In 1900 its population had been 7,000; in 1910 it was 21,000. Although streets were unpaved, streetcars ran throughout it. Automobiles were so common they no longer frightened horses and mules. There were wooden sidewalks that lasted for several years before they rotted. Great stone buildings were rising. Department stores sold suits for $125—the annual salary of most Mississippi teachers. The Edwards House charged $2 a night, an enormous sum; there the large Percy party took suites of rooms.

James Buchanan Eads was named by the deans of American engineering colleges as one of the five greatest engineers of all time, with the likes of Leonardo da Vinci and Thomas Edison. He fought the Army Corps of Engineers for control of policy toward the Mississippi River. Eads was, said a friend, "a bitter and unrelenting foe. . . . To him the unfolding of great and correct principles was more important than personal friendships. His beliefs were his friends."

TWO PHOTOS: U.S. ARMY CORPS OF ENGINEERS

Andrew Atkinson Humphreys wrote a study of the Mississippi River that won international scientific acclaim and earned him the post of chief of the Army Corps of Engineers. He was also one of the bloodiest Union generals in the Civil War. After losing twenty percent of his command in fifteen minutes in a fruitless charge, he wrote, "I felt like a young girl of sixteen at her first ball. . . . I felt more like a god than a man." Before confronting Eads he said, "We must get ready for combat. . . . The contest must be sharp and merciless."

COURTESY OF THE AUTHOR

EADS JETTIES
AT SOUTH PASS *of the* MISSISSIPPI.

BIRDS EYE VIEW.

The dispute between Eads and Humphreys exploded first over how to open the mouth of the Mississippi to shipping. The hearts of Eads' jetties were made of these mattresses of willow tree trunks fastened together. Similar mattresses were used later to protect riverbanks from erosion. The year Eads began work, 6,857 tons of goods were shipped from St. Louis to Europe. The year after he finished, 453,681 tons went by that route.

LESLIE'S ILLUSTRATED WEEKLY, APRIL 14, 1877

U.S. ARMY CORPS OF ENGINEERS

In essence, levees are nothing more than mounds of earth. But they need to be engineered carefully. This is a muck ditch, which melds the levee seamlessly to the ground. The war between Eads and Humphreys resulted in a compromise "levees-only" policy, meaning that only levees would be used to contain the Mississippi River.

LeRoy Percy was a U.S. senator, a hunting partner of Teddy Roosevelt, a friend of two chief justices of the Supreme Court, a governor of a Federal Reserve Bank, and a trustee of the Carnegie and Rockefeller Foundations. He helped transform the Mississippi Delta into a vast empire, then defended this empire against all enemies.

TWO PHOTOS: MISSISSIPPI DEPARTMENT OF ARCHIVES AND HISTORY

The Ku Klux Klan parading through downtown Columbus, Mississippi, in 1922 or 1923. When the Klan was electing the mayors of Portland, Oregon, and Portland, Maine, and dominating such states as Indiana and Colorado, Percy confronted and defeated the Klan in the heart of the Delta.

TWO PPHOTOS: LIBRARY OF CONGRESS

The beginning of a crevasse in Illinois that flooded thousands of acres. The narrowness of the levee was typical in this stretch of the river. Levees further south—such as the one in the photo below—were far wider and stronger.

Fighting to save the levee outside Lakeport, Arkansas. The wooden wall built along the levee crest protects from wave wash, sandbags raise the levee's height, and men are laying planks on the slope and covering them with sandbags to prevent sloughing. This levee was roughly a mile back from the river's natural banks, which the river had already overflowed. The fight here succeeded, but only because across the river a levee break flooded Percy's Delta, turning 180,000 people into refugees.

The beginning of a crevasse in Louisiana. The water left the town of Melville covered with sand drifts up to twenty feet deep.

LIBRARY OF CONGRESS

U.S. ARMY CORPS OF ENGINEERS

The Cabin Teele crevasse in Louisiana, just below Vicksburg, Mississippi, soon after the break. Already the water has uprooted the forest immediately in its path, and the break soon widened. This single break flooded the land for seventy miles to the west, to Monroe, Louisiana, creating another 120,000 refugees.

In Louisiana, as elsewhere, as the water rose inside houses, thousands of people had to chop their way through to rooftops or cling to trees, waiting for rescue. Unseasonably cold temperatures and incessant rain caused many deaths.

Most of the flooding in Arkansas came from tributaries to the Mississippi. In Clarendon, water rose to the rooftops. Several of these buildings were floating.

Holly Bluff, Mississippi, south of Greenville.

TWO PHOTOS: LIBRARY OF CONGRESS

ILLINOIS CENTRAL RAILROAD

With the river on one side, and the flood on the other, the levee itself provided the only high ground. Here refugees piled everything they could save onto the crest of a levee.

LIBRARY OF CONGRESS

J. MACK MOORE COLLECTION, OLD COURTHOUSE MUSEUM, VICKSBURG

Refugees shortly after arriving in Vicksburg. One group of black refugees, before being allowed off a barge onto dry land, was ordered to sing Negro spirituals. They refused. Finally, National Guard officers let them disembark.

COURTESY LUCILE BAYON HUME

COURTESY LAURA BAYON

Mr. and Mrs. James Pierce Butler, Jr. Butler was president of the South's largest bank and of the elite Boston Club. He manipulated the state and federal governments into dynamiting the levee outside New Orleans—flooding out thousands of people—to relieve pressure on the city. Mrs. Butler, queen of the Mystic Club in 1927, is wearing a gown reputed to cost $15,000. The governor's salary was $7,500.

COURTESY OF THE AUTHOR

The Sam Zemurray house at 2 Audubon Place, a private street, on the corner of St. Charles Avenue, one of the most elegant boulevards in America. Zemurray, an immigrant, started his career collecting rotting bananas on the wharf and ended up president of the United Fruit Company. He was never admitted to any of the city's private clubs. Also living on Audubon Place were J. Blanc Monroe and Rudolph Hecht.

In 1920s New Orleans, three men's clubs—the Louisiana Club, which has been called the most exclusive club in the country, the Boston Club, and the Pickwick Club—represented not only social and financial power, but political power as well. This is the foyer of the Pickwick Club.

TWO PHOTOS: TULANE UNIVERSITY

Each year the crowning moment of Carnival comes when Rex, the public King of Carnival, leaves his ball to attend that of Comus, whose identity is secret and who occupies the pinnacle of society. The motto of Comus is *Sic volo, sic jubeo,* "As I wish, thus I command."

LIBRARY OF CONGRESS

The April 29, 1927, dynamiting of the levee at Caernarvon, thirteen miles below New Orleans, flooded thousands of residents of two Louisiana parishes out of their homes. To get permission from the U.S. government to carry out the dynamiting, the mayor of New Orleans and fifty leading businessmen promised to pay crevasse victims for all losses. The dynamite also exploded the levees-only policy.

COURTESY DOROTHY BENGE

Manuel Molero was barely literate but highly intelligent. He became one of the South's most prominent bootleggers, led two parishes in a confrontation with the New Orleans power structure over the dynamiting, and later developed tax strategies copied by Chase Manhattan Bank. This photo was taken during one of his campaigns for sheriff against the Meraux machine.

J. Blanc Monroe, descendant of two U.S. presidents and New Orleans' most powerful attorney, argued before the Louisiana State Supreme Court that the promises made by the city to repay victims of the dynamiting "are irrelevant to this case."

COURTESY THOMAS LEWIS

Chicago Daily Tribune FINAL EDITION

0,000 FLEE FLOODS; 27 DIE

DIKES CRUMBLE, 150,000 MORE ARE IN DANGER

THE COMMERCIAL APPEAL.

EENVILLE FLOODED; PEOPLE FLEE FOR LIVES; LEVEES SNAP UNDER STRAIN LEAVING PATH OF DEATH AND DESTRUCTION IN WAKE OF WORST FLO

ST. LOUIS POST-DISPATCH

FINANCIAL EDITION

MISSISSIPPI FLOOD AREA EXTENDS AS DIKES FAIL

Banner.

Nashville

ESCENT CITY'S FATE IN BALANCE

DYNAMITE AGAIN USED TO AID WAR ON FLOOD

mes·Picayune

US BOATS,' PLEADS MURPHREE

CRAFT NEEDED IN EVACUATION OF GREENVILLE

The Courier-Journal.

The Minneapolis Morning Tribune

THOUSANDS TRAPPED BY FLOOD

D; 9,000 MILES FLOOD

Plan to Walk Out

ESTIMATES WATER'S T APPROACH

The New York Times.

172,000 MORE IMPERILED; COOLIDGE CALLS ON NATION TO DOUBLE FLOOD RELIEF

The 1927 Mississippi River flood dominated the front pages of the nation's news-papers for weeks. It stripped the society bare and left a legacy affecting local and national politics, race relations, demographics, and even geology.

Red Cross vice chairman James Fieser, Secretary of Commerce Herbert Hoover, and Secretary of War Dwight Davis. Hoover chaired a special cabinet committee that handled the emergency. Before the flood, Hoover's presidential ambitions were at a low point. Favorable news coverage trans-formed him into a front-runner. He said, "I shall be the nominee probably. It is nearly inevitable."

RED CROSS, COURTESY OF PETE DANIEL

WILLIAM ALEXANDER PERCY LIBRARY

William Alexander Percy, a poet and war hero. In Greenville, Mississippi, Will's orders nearly caused a scandal threatening Hoover's presidential ambitions.

Will Percy, Hoover, and LeRoy Percy on the boardwalk above the flood water in Greenville.
MISSISSIPPI DEPARTMENT OF ARCHIVES AND HISTORY

LIBRARY OF CONGRESS

Chaos reigned in Greenville. With local planters refusing to evacuate their labor force, 13,000 black refugees were crammed into a camp stretching seven miles up the Greenville levee. Here they are being vaccinated.

TWO PHOTOS: MISSISSIPPI DEPARTMENT OF ARCHIVES AND HISTORY

There were too few tents, not enough food, no dry clothes. This is the city viewed from the levee, several weeks after the flood.

A group of men here await work assignments on the Greenville levee. Tags attached to their collars kept track of inoculations, work assignments, and what plantation they came from. The levee became a work camp, where food and supplies for 50,000 people and thousands of heads of livestock were unloaded for distribution throughout the Delta. Black men were not allowed to leave, and they were forced to work without pay.

COURTESY TUSKEGEE UNIVERSITY

As news spread in the north of a possible scandal over treatment of refugees, Hoover asked Robert Russa Moton, head of Tuskegee Institute, to organize a commission to investigate the charges.

The Colored Advisory Commission, said one of its members, comprised "some of the most conservative men in America." Claude Barnett, head of the Associated Negro Press, is in the first row, second from left. Several believed that Hoover was planning to do "something in behalf of the negro more significant than anything which has happened since Emancipation." In return, the commission would do all in its power to help him become president.

COURTESY TUSKEGEE UNIVERSITY

In Greenville itself, blacks responded to abuse by organizing the General Colored Committee. Levye Chapple was one of its leaders.

COURTESY SYLVIA JACKSON

U.S. ARMY CORPS OF ENGINEERS

Vice President of the United States Charles Dawes slept through this train wreck after his visit to the Mississippi state convention of the American Legion in July. The engineer was killed. President Coolidge, despite repeated personal pleas from governors, senators, congressmen, and private individuals, never visited any of the flooded territory.

MISSISSIPPI DEPARTMENT OF ARCHIVES AND HISTORY

Where the current was strongest, it ripped apart buildings and towns as it tore through them. Along with muck eight inches thick, snakes, frogs, and tens of millions of crawfish, this is part of the flood's leavings in Greenville.

U.S. ARMY CORPS OF ENGINEERS

General Edgar Jadwin, who told Congress that the Mississippi River in its natural state did not flood the Yazoo-Mississippi Delta. The congressman from the Delta replied, "That is news to us." Nonetheless, the Jadwin Flood Control Plan became law.

COURTESY OF THE AUTHOR

During the Depression, Will Percy spent $25,000 to put this statue over his father's grave. It marked the end of a culture.

HOOVER LIBRARY

Hoover and his wife, Lou Henry, during the 1928 presidential campaign. In the White House he used the same policy approach to the Depression that he had employed during the flood.

Huey Long's inauguration. In an election held a few months after the flood, aided by a statewide antipathy toward the existing power structure, Huey Long (LEFT) easily defeated incumbent governor O. H. Simpson (RIGHT), who had approved the dynamiting of the levee.

LOUISIANA STATE MUSEUM

Despite a state prohibition law, whiskey flowed freely both in the Percy headquarters and in the Lemon Hotel, which Vardaman, a prohibitionist, used for his headquarters. But only Percy had real money. He and his brothers Walker and Willie, prominent attorneys in Birmingham and Memphis who came to Jackson to help, represented many of the major corporations doing business in the South.

There was business to do. The Mississippi legislature was a swamp, "timid and third-rate," thick with petty men greedy for small things. But the pettiness and greed kept the anti-Vardaman coalition together over an amazing six weeks, with votes taken, on the average, more than once each day. It was six weeks of chicanery, drinking, prostitution, deal-making, vote-peddling, and corruption. The legislature adjourned for Mardi Gras, as dozens of members took the Illinois Central to New Orleans, some no doubt on Percy-supplied but illegal railroad passes. At one point the members adjourned the caucus, convened as the legislature, passed a law creating seventy-nine new county attorneys so that the anti-Vardaman governor had more offices with which to buy votes, then adjourned as a legislature and reconvened as a caucus.

Vardaman never received less than 65 votes nor more than 79. But gradually, support began to coalesce around Percy. One after another, other contenders dropped out while still opposing Vardaman. After fifty-seven ballots the coalition agreed to support Percy, who would face Vardaman alone. Sitting on the floor of the legislature, Percy leaned over to his campaign manager and said, "Crump, let's just put it to the touch."

Percy won, 87 to 82. Vardaman ran back and forth around the rostrum, screaming that his opponents were "black as the night that covers me!"

The caucus then convened as the legislature and officially elected Percy 157 votes to 1. The one went to John C. Kyle, not Vardaman, who would set no precedent of splitting the Democratic Party.

The next day, February 25, 1910, Percy returned to Greenville at 7:05 P.M. Two brass bands met the train, men and women shook cowbells, fireworks exploded. A parade began, led by torch-carrying men, then the bands, then a procession of all the twenty-six automobiles in Greenville, then marchers. Thousands of people lined the streets; it seemed the entire Delta had gathered, many more than the population of Greenville. The parade ended at the Opera House. It was chaos. "Swinging perilously from the railing around the balcony was a perfect sea of shouting men yelling for Greenville's favorite son," reported the *Memphis Commercial-Appeal*. A dozen men spoke, but none could be heard. Strangely, the excitement did not energize Percy, who had stood in the car so exhausted that friends worried he might fall out. When he rose, a roar shook the hall. Quieting the bedlam, he held up his hands and said, "I am not going to make a political speech tonight—not because I am tired—but because I don't have to. I'm among friends at home. I have been away from you for seven weeks, and those weeks seem like so many years, and tonight I know as I have never known before, as I never realized how I could know, the full meaning of 'home sweet home.' "

IN WASHINGTON not only John Sharp Williams but Roosevelt, Jacob Dickinson, the former Illinois Central counsel who was now secretary of war, and Edward White, the chief justice of the Supreme Court— Percy and he were frequent poker players at the exclusive Boston Club in New Orleans—made Percy at home.

But he had won little respite for the Delta. In a year and a half he would have to face Vardaman again, this time in a statewide primary.

While Percy began making himself at home in Washington, Vardaman began campaigning before huge, frightening crowds. Vardaman declared: "This is a contest for supremacy between the man whose toil produces the wealth of this country, and the favored few who reap the products of that toil. I expect to win by the largest margin ever received in Mississippi."

Meanwhile, the *Jackson Democrat-Star* called "the Secret Caucus . . . the most disgraceful political farce ever enacted at our state capital." The *Columbus Dispatch* avowed, rightly, that Vardaman's defeat "was brought about by a hundred men, representing . . . the corporations of the state, . . . the money of the state." The *Laurel Ledger* denounced "the multiplicity of influences that culminated in [Vardaman's] defeat."

Then Theodore Bilbo, a state senator, emerged. A hater who would later, as a U.S. senator, publicly use words like "kikes," "dagos," and "niggers" (in 1995 at the Million Man March, Louis Farrakhan invoked Bilbo's name as a symbol of racism), Bilbo accused a Percy supporter of having attempted to bribe him to vote for Percy. The accused man won easy acquittal—the jury stayed out eighteen minutes. But the charges compounded the public revulsion over the caucus. And Bilbo announced his own candidacy for lieutenant governor. The campaign had begun.

Underneath lay the issue of race. And Percy, who had sought

a Senate seat tenaciously, seemed diffident. For months he delayed putting together a campaign organization and constantly displayed political insensitivity. A *New York Times* reporter described him as "suave and dignifiedly courteous" to his equals, "condescending but still affable" to those beneath "his estimate of himself on birth or money," but "overbearing toward the hoi-polloi beneath his altitudinous orbit." Far worse, in one speech, LeRoy equated Negroes and poor whites: "They say I'm a big Greenville aristocrat, and don't care anything about the common man. There are people on my place, white and dark, who have lived there all their lives. I've taken care of them, and I'll continue to take care of them."

Outside the Delta, angry crowds heckled him. They wanted to know about his black servants, about his hunting on the Sabbath, about his churchgoing, about his drinking, about his wife's Catholicism.

Percy reciprocated with contempt. The crowds were peasants, *Anglo-Saxons,* while the Percys considered themselves descended from nobles, the Norman conquerors of the Anglo-Saxons, from Harry Percy, Shakespeare's Hotspur. At one rally, LeRoy's son Will "looked over the ill-dressed, surly audience, unintelligent and slinking, and heard him appeal to them for fair treatment of the Negro. . . . They were the sort of people who lynched Negroes, that mistake hoodlumism for wit, and cunning for intelligence, that attend revivals and fight and fornicate in the bushes afterwards." LeRoy himself, interrupted during a speech with shouts of "Hurrah for Vardaman!" "Hurrah for Bilbo!," called the crowd "cattle" and "rednecks."

Vardaman reacted with mockery, arriving at rallies on carts drawn by oxen while his supporters began wearing red ties. "We are the low-brows! We are the rednecks! Rah for Vardaman!" the crowds shouted.

On July 4, 1911, Percy addressed the angriest crowd yet at Lauderdale Springs, where he distastefully shared a platform with Bilbo. Five thousand people were seething before him. Will described the scene: "When Father rose to speak he was greeted by a roar of boos, catcalls, hisses, and cries of 'Vardaman! Vardaman!' . . . The din was insane and intolerable. . . . I was glad to observe Billie Hardie with his pistol across his lap. Father faced that obscene pandemonium, paused for the courtesy of silence, and when he did not receive it, his eyes narrowed. Then burning cold insults poured from his lips, he jeered them as cowards afraid to listen, and dared them to keep on."

Finally, the crowd fell silent while all the vileness of the campaign welled up in LeRoy. He did not give a speech. He unleashed a torrent of vitriol, first on Vardaman. Then he pointedly turned his back on Bilbo, called him a liar, tongue-lashed him while Bilbo reddened, compared standing near him to picking up a "striped caterpillar" out of the muck and swallowing it "to see how strong my stomach was." In a final mockery, the crowd cheered and cheered.

Vardaman received 79,369 votes in the 1911 primary, and Charlton Alexander, who entered the race when Percy showed weakness, received 31,490. Percy, the incumbent senator, got 21,521. Bilbo won his race with comparable ease.

One could hardly suffer a more crushing loss. Teddy Roosevelt wrote Percy: "My dear Senator, I am sure you would be pleased if you knew how men who in the right sense of the word are gentlemen in public life, in entirely different sections of the country, men such as Cabot Lodge of Massachusetts . . . have talked about your being in the Senate, and then about your leaving it. It was a piece of national good fortune to have you in the Senate; it is a calamity from the standpoint of the nation that you have been beaten."

ELSEWHERE IN THE SOUTH, others like Vardaman—or worse—were also winning elections, men like Tom Watson in Georgia, Thomas Heflin in Alabama, Ben Tillman in South Carolina. (When Roosevelt dined with Booker T. Washington in the White House, Tillman warned it "will necessitate our killing a thousand niggers before they will learn their place again.")

The men of Percy's class had ruled in their own interest and in class interest. But they had had a code of honor and only, at worst, personal hatreds. They were better than those who were replacing them, who had a darkness in the soul.

The Percys of the world, the patricians, the "Bourbons," the "best" white men to whom even Du Bois looked for protection, still controlled the money of the South, but only in a narrow strip of the Delta and in the state of Louisiana did they still control the politics. Of seventy-nine counties in Mississippi in 1911, Percy carried only five, all in the Delta, which represented less than half of it. Only in Washington County did he win an absolute majority. Percy's empire, and that of all the old aristocracy of the South, had shrunk to one county.

Even the river brought home the change. In 1912 the Mississippi rose higher than it ever had. It spilled over in many places, crashed through in others. In Greenville, Percy helped organize a flood fight and held his front against the river. But just above Washington County, the *New York Times* reported, an engineer who ran out of sandbags "ordered . . . several hundred negroes . . . to lie down on top of the levee and as close together as possible. The black men obeyed, and although spray frequently dashed over them, they prevented the overflow that might have developed into an ugly crevasse. For an hour and a half this lasted, until the additional sandbags arrived."

The men were convicts, and the *Times* called the idea "brilliant." But Percy did not approve. To him men were economic units competing with other men, not with sandbags. He would not have other such incidents. No local paper mentioned it. With new energy Percy concentrated on maintaining in the Delta, or at least Washington County, the society he had envisioned.

After leaving the Senate for the last time, Percy wrote a friend: "If I can keep this small corner of the United States in which I reside, comparatively clean and decent in politics and fit for a man to live in, and in such a condition that he may not be ashamed to pass it on to his children, I will have accomplished all that I set out to do. A good deal has been written about 'shooting for the stars.' I have never thought much of that kind of marksmanship. . . . I rather think it is best to draw a bead on something that you have a chance to hit. To keep any part of Mississippi clean and decent in these days, is a job that no man may deem too small."

CHAPTER TEN

LeRoy Percy had in fact sculpted a remarkable world, an island of order and reason in a sea of entropy and chaos. Yet it was not without its own internal inconsistencies, and combined equal parts of frontier and sophistication.

At the outbreak of World War I the Delta was still the Wild West of the South. More than 60 percent of the land remained wilderness, with bears still invading cornfields and wolves devouring livestock. Like the West, and unlike the already settled South, it had few churches, few schools, much drinking (despite statewide prohibition), and violence. Violence and passion were everywhere, bred in its endlessly flat earth. Standing on cleared land one saw all sky, and a man had to stand straight and tall, had to feel his own pride intruding upon the sky, or he would sink into the mud. One did not turn the other cheek in the Delta. Neither black nor white turned the other cheek. The homicide rate in Mississippi dwarfed that of the rest of the nation, and the Delta's dwarfed that of the rest of Mississippi. More than 75 percent of Delta blacks in the state penitentiary had been convicted of murder or attempted murder, double the percentage for black prisoners from outside the Delta. Whites also killed. Judge Percy Bell observed that before state prohibition, "Shootings were comparatively frequent around [Greenville] saloons, and few if any white men were indicted or tried."

Incongruously, cotton had simultaneously created an elite whose sons went to Harvard, Princeton, and Cornell and traveled the world; in 1914 several Greenville planters attending the annual Wagner festival in Bayreuth, Germany, were stranded by the outbreak of war. After the war, with cotton prices soaring, the best Delta land brought $1,000 an acre, making the Percy land suddenly, if only briefly, worth several hundred million of today's dollars. Even the social elite of New Orleans considered Greenville exceptional. Leonidas Pool, a New Orleans bank president who frequently played cards with Percy at the Boston Club and occasionally hunted with him, was Rex, King of Mardi Gras, in 1925. When his daughter moved to Greenville, he told her, "You are going among the aristocrats of the earth."

By the 1920s, Greenville had become "The Queen City of the Delta," with twelve miles of paved streets. Its population reached 15,000 souls, all nestled close to the river. Downtown teemed with life. Barges piled with goods docked at the concrete wharf, warehouses burst with cotton, trucks and spavined mules pulled supplies. The city had one French and two Italian restaurants, twenty-four-hour coffee shops, bowling alleys and pool halls and movie theaters. The biggest entertainers, including Enrico Caruso and Al Jolson, regularly stopped at the Opera House or the even larger People's Theater. Enough Chinese lived in Greenville that a tong war erupted. The four-story Cowan Hotel was the state's finest. The Armour Packing Company, the largest meatpacker between Memphis and New Orleans, distributed fresh meat throughout the Delta and into the hill country. Three cotton exchanges each had a wire to Liverpool, New Orleans, New York, and Chicago. The Greenville Cotton Compress, a huge operation owned by Percy, baled cotton and sold it directly to international buyers. Fourteen trains a day arrived in Greenville at the Y&MV railroad station; six more trains arrived daily at the Columbus & Greenville station. Four oil mills, the smallest covering two city blocks, crushed cotton seed. Half a dozen sawmills worked the great masses of logs floated to them; the two largest each made 150,000 board feet of lumber a day.

The city's most exclusive gathering place was the Swan Lake Club, a shooting club outside the city. Since anyone in the Delta acceptable for membership already belonged, no guests were allowed who lived within a hundred miles. The Greenville Country Club was new; it and the Mississippi Club were for the fine families, and unlike other cities—including nearby Greenwood—both had Jewish members. (Only the Garden Club excluded Jews.) The Elysian Club, a two-storied yellow brick building with a vast porch, held dances renowned throughout the Delta; fans were placed behind a 300-pound block of ice to blow air over it and cool the room, and a hedge in front was used to hide corn whiskey. W. C. Handy, one of the fathers of the blues, frequently played there. The Elks Club, a step down the social scale, concentrated on poker, and a Rotary club met. There were few speakeasies but plenty of liquor; men carried whiskey in brown bags and snuck away to dark corners to drink it straight or with a chaser of Coke or water. And there was one club that only Percy and a few other gentlemen patronized. On the edge of the city was the home of a beautiful, light-skinned black woman whose daughters were equally beautiful and even lighter. Elegant and charming, she often played hostess to Percy. He and others would stay deep into the night, usually playing cards.

More than half of Greenville's population was black, and there were two black neighborhoods. If young men from one entered the other, trouble followed. Newtown lay north of downtown; there "blacks tried to be citified, uppity," according to one black man. Southside was more working-class. Most blacks worked on the river, or in the sawmills, or as servants for whites. By 6 A.M. the streets were alive with maids and cooks and chauffeurs heading to white folks' homes. Several black doctors and dentists had offices in two buildings on the edge of downtown. There was a black printer, a black-owned newsstand serving whites, several black funeral home operators, black shoe repairmen. A black bank was nurtured largely by money from black prostitutes who serviced white men only. Their brothels flourished just east of downtown, near Broadway and Nelson, across from the pride of the black community, Mt. Horeb Church, a small but magnificent stone structure. A block away, there were black juke joints and pool halls and gambling joints. There was liquor, and women, and the blues. And there were knives, razors, and pistols.

On Saturdays downtown was packed. From all around the county both whites and blacks poured into it to shop, or look—really just to socialize. On Saturdays a single drugstore could sell 1,400 ice-cream cones. Young men took their girls to the Kandy Kitchen for confections. Opposite it was a spot called "passion corner."

In the 1920s, Greenville was a thriving small metropolis, and, like most ports, more cosmopolitan than neighboring communities. But what set Greenville apart was the imprint that Percy and those few who allied themselves with him had imposed.

GREENVILLE'S SCHOOLS epitomized the difference. In 1920 the city spent $85 per white pupil, double the state's second-most-generous locality; five Mississippi counties in the hills spent less than $5 per white child, while one spent only $2.75. The teachers and facilities were outstanding, and for its size Greenville produced an extraordinary number of writers, including LeRoy's son William Alexander Percy and great-nephew Walker Percy,* David Cohn, Ellen Douglas, Beverly Lowry, Charles Bell, and Shelby Foote.

For blacks, Greenville schools were, relatively, even more special. The city spent $17 per black child, compared to 68 cents in another district. At the same time that many Mississippi politicians opposed teaching blacks arithmetic and reading, Greenville public schools offered blacks Latin. Lizzie Coleman, principal of the black high school, intimidated students and teachers into excelling. She made each teacher raise $150 a year for the school, and also said, "I don't believe in the melting pot." But she knew how to survive. During the week she bought groceries from two black men; on Saturdays she bought steaks from Will Reed, a white man, on Washington Avenue. The steak was more expensive, but that did not matter. Because of her good relationships with whites, when black teachers asked school superintendent E. E. Bass to stop calling them by their first names in front of their students, he agreed to address them in school as "Mr.," "Mrs.," or "Miss." Greenville was also state headquarters for several black fraternal organizations, including the Pythians and the Masons, and Percy had even sued a white fraternal organization on their behalf and won.

In addition, before settling upon whom to support for office, Percy and a few others whites routinely met with black community leaders to ask their opinions; though few Greenville blacks could vote, this process did give them some voice in the election.

If Greenville reflected Percy's values, however, reflections are the thinnest of veneers. By the 1920s the city was growing beyond him. To a friend who had moved away, he observed, "Our town has grown some in population, and improved much in comfort and attractiveness, but there were more men and women possessing individuality, personality and charm in the dear dead days when you knew it, than there are today."

One demographic change was the arrival of whites from the Mississippi hill country. The prosperity of the Delta brought them. The oil mills and sawmills and office supply stores and meatpacking plants brought them. The hill country was home to the whites who elected Vardaman and Bilbo. With them came different values. And with them came the Ku Klux Klan.

●

* Walker Percy and his two brothers were children of LeRoy's nephew; they were orphaned, and Will adopted them.

THE 1920S KLAN had roots that ran deep in America. It was racist, anti-Catholic, and anti-Semitic. Yet it represented not only bigotry, but a desire to find an anchor in a sea of change, to shrink the large world into a smaller, more understandable one. For men and women who were middle-aged in the 1920s had lived through more change than did citizens during any other period in American history.

The nation was both striding into and resisting the modern age. Robert Goddard was demonstrating the practicality of rockets; talking pictures reached movie screens; radio linked the country together for the first time; even television came into existence. So did national advertising, national brands, and national fads and chain stores—in 1923 more Mah-Jongg sets than radios were sold, while Woolworth's had 1,500 stores.

Simultaneously, in what seemed almost another country, fundamentalists were rejecting science and trying to outlaw the teaching of evolution. National Prohibition arrived, and its passage embodied a union of the strangest bedfellows: the emerging force of moralistic and muscular Christianity lay down with the dying force of Progressives who believed in the perfectibility of man and the ability of rational human engineering to control behavior.

The tensions contained within those two nations—the one surging forward, the other clenching tight—grew out of more fundamental shifts. The nineteenth century had seen tremendous change, but it was a time of certainty and rules. Nature's laws appeared fixed and certain. If science had begun to undermine faith in God, the theory of evolution still guaranteed a happy future. Herbert Spencer, the author of the phrase "survival of the fittest," proclaimed, "The ultimate development of the ideal man is logically certain."

The twentieth century would be a century without certainty. In 1905, Albert Einstein published his theory of relativity and exploded the mechanistic universe. Soon the reliability of engineering gave way to the "uncertainty principle" of physics. In 1909, Sigmund Freud came to Worcester, Massachusetts, to lecture at Clark University and show Americans that nothing was as it seemed. Meanwhile, women were winning the right to vote, entering the workforce in large numbers, and forcing a reassessment even of gender.

As the intellectual base upon which the world rested shifted, its moral pillars cracked. A new sexuality suffused the nation. In 1908 skirts touched the floor; in 1915 the word "flapper" entered the language; in 1924 skirts touched the knee. The automobile and radio altered the experience of time and distance; the automobile also created sexual opportunities. In 1919, barely 10 percent of cars were enclosed; by 1927, 82.8 percent were. Jazz music was suggestive, wild, lewd. In the nineteenth century, virtually every school in the country used McGuffey's Readers, anthologies that taught morality as much as reading, including the story of George Washington and the cherry tree. By Teddy Roosevelt's presidency McGuffey's Readers were losing favor. Instead, *The Rubáiyát of Omar Khayyám* was selling millions of copies; it sang of seduction and youth and the infinite present. Social commentator Mark Sullivan noted, "Many an American adult in the 1920s remembered as a landmark the day he read Omar's line, 'I myself am Heaven and hell.' "

The essential character of America was changing as well. In 1870, America's population was 40 million, 72 percent of whom lived in small towns or on farms. Between 1900 and 1915, 15 million immigrants flooded the United States. Mostly from eastern and southern Europe, the new immigrants were different from most Americans already here. They were truly foreign, strange in religion, darker in complexion. And 1920 marked the first time that more than half of America's population, now 110 million, lived in cities. It was frightening, deracinating.

This was not the America in which those who were adults in the 1920s had grown up. The nation's very identity seemed under assault, and an aching for community developed. The first organized outgrowth of this longing came in Chicago in 1905, when a group of men trying to re-create the sense of small-town community started the Rotary Club; it required members to address each other by their first names.

Then, during the World War, President Woodrow Wilson turned the desire for community into something foul by encouraging, manipulating, and exploiting the nation's fears. His administration warned of hidden enemies undermining the nation, enemies to be found and cast out. George Creel ran Wilson's propaganda machine and demanded "100% Americanism." At his peak 150,000 people worked under his umbrella. (John Parker once walked into the White House and told Wilson that in the entire civilized world there was "no more arbitrary ruler.") One newspaper editor complained, "Government conscripted public opinion as they conscripted men and women and materials. . . . They mobilized it. They put it in charge of drill sergeants. They goose-stepped it."

Creel's words created a hysteria. Beatings occurred across the nation. Near St. Louis a German-American defended Germany in an argument; a mob stripped him naked, wrapped him in an American flag, dragged him through the streets, and lynched him.

Congress, ignoring the Constitution, passed the Sedition Act, which made it illegal—punishment was twenty years in jail—to "utter, print, write or publish any disloyal, profane, scurrilous, or abusive language about the government of the United States . . . or any language intended to . . . encourage resistance to the United States."

Wilson's attorney general, A. Mitchell Palmer, "the Fighting Quaker," prosecuted more than 2,000 people for violating this and related acts. He also developed a nation of informers by helping create the American Protective League, whose 12,000 local units spied on neighbors and coworkers. Other groups, such as the National Security League and the Allied Loyalty League, also fed names to the government.

In Greenville, Mississippi, LeRoy Percy looked on with contempt. He wrote his friend Dickinson, a former secretary of war: "If this country lives through the scholarly idiocy of the present administration, Providence must certainly be watching us. If we could only swap the well-turned sentences of Wilson for the homely wisdom of Cleveland or Lincoln." He also believed that an opportunity existed to pass federal anti-lynching legislation, which he had long supported, "at the close of the war as an expression of the kindly feeling of the nation toward the negro race." Percy was misjudging the times.

DESPITE PEACE, 1919 opened with Judge Kenesaw Mountain Landis sentencing Wisconsin Congressman Victor Berger and several others to twenty years in prison for sedition. (The House voted 309 to 1 to expel Berger; he won the special election to fill the open seat and the House refused to swear him in.) The Supreme Court upheld several earlier sedition convictions, including the ten-year prison sentence of Socialist Eugene Debs, who the next year would receive 915,000 votes for president. Oliver Wendell Holmes wrote the opinion calling the Sedition Act constitutional, arguing that the First Amendment did not protect speech if "the words used . . . create a clear and present danger."

Then came violence. In Washington, in Chicago, in twenty-six major cities, race riots erupted. Far more blacks than whites died. In Elaine, Arkansas, north and across the Mississippi River from Greenville, black sharecroppers were being systematically cheated. They formed a union. When a deputy sheriff fired into a building where they were meeting, the blacks returned fire, killing him. A pogrom commenced, until 500 regular Army troops imposed martial law. Five whites and, officially, 11 blacks died, although the NAACP claimed 200 blacks were killed. No whites were charged, but courts sentenced 54 blacks to prison and 12 to death (the Arkansas Supreme Court blocked the executions); in none of the cases did a jury deliberate more than seven minutes.

Strikes brought violence too. Few unions had struck during the war. In 1919 strikes shook the country. Two in particular seemed dangerous, threatening America with the chaos then wracking Germany, Poland, and Italy. One was a general strike of more than 100 unions in Seattle. The other was a police strike in Boston.

Unions were castigated as un-American. The *Chicago Tribune* warned, "It is only a middling step from Petrograd to Seattle." The *Salt Lake City Tribune* asserted, "Free speech has been carried to the point where it is an absolute menace." The *Washington Post* wrote: "Silence the incendiary advocates of force. . . . Bring the law's hand down. . . . Do it NOW!"

In New York, 400 servicemen ransacked the Socialist paper *The Call* and beat up everyone there. Six days later Governor Al Smith signed a bill forbidding the display of red flags.

In Indiana a jury deliberated two minutes and acquitted a man for murdering an immigrant who yelled, "To hell with the United States."

In Weirton, West Virginia, police forced 118 immigrants, members of the International Workers of the World, the Wobblies, to kiss the American flag.

Anti-foreign feeling was so strong that it affected even supposedly international Communists: the United States had two Communist parties, one with mostly native-born members, one with a membership 90 percent immigrant.

The American Legion was formed, its constitution stated, "to maintain law and order" and "to foster and perpetuate a one hundred percent Americanism." Within months it had 1 million members, and its commander ordered the organization to "be ready for action at any time . . . against these extremists who are seeking to overturn a government."

In Centralia, Washington, the local American Legion attacked a Wobbly office. Three Legionnaires died. Others later dragged Wesley Everest, a fellow veteran but a Wobbly, from jail. They beat him, cut off his testicles, then cut off his penis. He begged: "For God's sake, men, shoot me. Don't let me suffer like this." They hung him from a bridge first, then shot him. The coroner judged it suicide: "He . . . jumped off with a rope around his neck and then shot himself full of holes."

The left fought back. Bombs exploded outside Attorney General Palmer's Washington home, and at the homes of the mayor of Cleveland and several judges. In New York City, a post office employee found sixteen more bombs, addressed to J. P. Morgan, J. D. Rockefeller, Oliver Wendell Holmes, and several senators.

At a cabinet meeting President Wilson turned to his attorney general and said, "Palmer, do not let this country see Red."

Palmer named a young J. Edgar Hoover to run a new Intelligence Division within the Justice Department. Within a few months, Hoover had a card file on 200,000 "radical" organizations. Palmer himself hoped to ride the anti-Red wave all the way to the White House, and said: "I myself am an American and I love to preach my doctrine before 100% Americans because my platform is undiluted Americanism. . . . Each and every [radical] is a potential murderer or a potential thief. . . . Out of the sly and crafty eyes of many of them leap cupidity, cruelty, insanity, and crime; from their lopsided faces, sloping brows, and misshapen features may be recognized the unmistakable criminal type."

The paroxysms ended on January 1, 1920, when the Justice Department conducted raids in 33 cities and arrested 6,000 "dangerous aliens." Three guns and no explosives were found. Yet in Hartford, Connecticut, anyone who visited the jailed aliens was also arrested.

LATER THAT YEAR Republican Warren G. Harding won the presidency saying, "America's present need is not heroics but healing; not nostrums but normalcy; not surgery but serenity."

A new Congress, seeking to prevent further dilution of 100 percent Americanism, passed "emergency" laws restricting immigration. Percy, ever concerned with the labor supply, unsuccessfully urged former Senate colleagues to defeat the bill, arguing that their fears were "fancied and certainly far distant," that the danger of Bolshevism was "not real," that "the crippling of the manpower of this nation is the one thing which will check its prosperity, check it effectually and for an indefinite duration."

But much of the nation wanted to smother change. *The Fundamentals,* a book financed by an oil millionaire and espousing a literal interpretation of the Bible, was published, and the World's Christian Fundamentals Association was organized. Christian fundamentalism began a war against the teaching of evolution.

Perhaps at no other time in American history, even including the 1960s, did so wide a gap develop between a mainstream culture that clung to its certainties and American intellectuals. Sinclair Lewis mocked Main Street, while F. Scott Fitzgerald declared "all Gods dead, all wars fought, all faiths in man shaken."

The mainstream defended itself. The magazine of the U.S. Chamber of Commerce editorialized: "Dare to be Babbitt! . . . Good Rotarians live orderly lives, and save money, and go to church, and play golf, and send their children to school. . . . Would not the world be better with more Babbitts and fewer of those who cry, 'Babbitt!'?"

An article in *American Magazine* simply attacked anything that stood out. Entitled "Why I Never Hire Brilliant Men," it explained, "[B]usiness and life are built upon successful mediocrity."

Normalcy reassured; sameness was comfortable; to be average meant to be secure.

When Dr. Hiram Wesley Evans, a dentist, became Imperial Wizard of the Ku Klux Klan, he defined himself as "the most average man in America."

D. W. GRIFFITH's *Birth of a Nation* appeared in 1915. Its epic sweep, its driving narrative, its technical magnificence, and its length revolutionized Hollywood. Before it, movies rarely lasted more than thirty minutes and cost a nickel or less to attend (hence the name "nickelodeon"). *Birth of a Nation* cost $2 and ran for three hours. Yet in city after city lines stretched for blocks. By the end of World War I, nearly 25 million tickets had been sold.

Thomas Dixon had written the novel *The Clansman* upon which the film was based. It portrayed blacks during Reconstruction as virtual jungle beasts who stole from, brutalized, and raped whites. It portrayed the Ku Klux Klan as mythic heroes fighting for decency and honor. He explained: "The real big purpose of my film was to revolutionize northern sentiment by [our] presentation of history. . . . Every man who comes out of our theaters is a Southern partisan for life."

The film had many critics and sparked many demonstrations. To counteract the criticism, Dixon showed it at the White House to his college classmate Woodrow Wilson, telling him the film marked "the launching of the mightiest engine for moulding public opinion in the history of the world." After viewing it, Wilson, a southerner who had segregated the previously integrated federal bureaucracy, said: "It is like writing history with lightning. My only regret is that it is all so terribly true."

A few days before the film's 1915 opening in Atlanta, Colonel William Joseph Simmons climbed Stone Mountain, burned a cross, and announced the rebirth of the Klan.

At the time, Simmons sold memberships in the Woodmen of the World for a living, and the Woodmen—not the military—had made him a colonel. He also belonged to eleven similar groups, and when asked his profession he replied, "I am a fraternalist."

Simmons' sale of memberships in his new Klan went slowly until, in 1920, he signed a contract with Edward Clarke and Mary Elizabeth Tyler, whose Southern Publicity Association had raised money for the Red Cross and the Anti-Saloon League of America. The three agreed that new Klan members would pay an initiation fee of $10. Of that, Clarke and Tyler would get $8, out of which they paid $4 to "kleagles," full-time commission salesmen, for each recruit, and small commissions to other Klan officers. Eventually, 1,200 kleagles were on the road. Membership exploded.

The Klan's message combined the binding forces of hyperpatriotism and moralistic Christianity with the excluding forces of disdain for elites, cities, and intellectuals. And of course the Klan preached hatred of Catholics, blacks, foreigners, and Jews. The world, the Klan said, was falling apart, but a crusading Klan would put things right. One Klansman proclaimed: "It is going to drive the bootleggers forever out of this land. It is going to bring clean moving pictures . . . clean literature . . . protect homes. It means the return of old-time Southern chivalry and deference to womanhood; it means that 'the married man with an affinity' has no place in our midst."

The message struck home. By the early 1920s at least 3 million Americans belonged to the Invisible Empire; some estimates were as high as 8 million. It had 300,000 members in Ohio, 200,000 in Pennsylvania. It seized control of state governments in Colorado and Indiana, where one scholar estimates between one-quarter and one-third of all native-born white males belonged. It elected the mayors of Portland, Oregon, and Portland, Maine. It recalled the governor of Oklahoma, dominated parts of California, and passed a state law in Oregon requiring Catholic children to attend public schools.

There were two Americas now, one accepting and advancing into the insecurity of an uncertain age and one holding back and searching for something to grasp onto. And the two nations were growing further apart. "The world broke in two in 1922 or thereabouts," observed Willa Cather.

In 1922 the Invisible Empire entered the demesne of LeRoy Percy.

CHAPTER ELEVEN

In Greenville the tone of race relations was shifting. Before World War I, when a court outside Washington County ordered Nathan Taylor, a black Greenville attorney, to stand in the gallery with black defendants, white Greenville attorneys objected and protected him from a sheriff who tried to beat him. In 1920, Taylor was elected president of the National Equal Rights League. One night four white men tied his hands behind him, rowed him out to vicious whirlpools in the middle of the Mississippi River, and told him he was leaving Greenville one way or another. Taylor moved to Chicago and became the first black there to run, though unsuccessfully, for Congress.

A year after the Taylor incident, a Klan klavern was organized in Washington County. Its leaders were ambitious men, men who intended to use the Klan to become bigger men.

Percy had run the county for as long as anyone could remember. Deep into the night the lights often stayed on in his law office in the Weinberg Building, where he sat down with a few men to decide who would serve as county supervisor, or city councilman, or mayor, or state senator. Notably absent from those meetings was LeRoy's son and law partner Will, a war hero and a poet. Usually present were Joe Weinberg, a wealthy Jewish banker, planter Alfred Stone, and Billy Wynn, younger than Will and also a war hero, a comer with his own law firm who also owned a Mississippi River ferry on which passengers could play slot machines. Their support nearly always meant victory; their opposition meant defeat. "Percy would almost draft people he wanted to run for office," recalled one man. "I'd walk by and look up and see the lighted window and think, 'They're running the city up there.' "

The men organizing the klavern believed it was time for that to change. By early 1922 the Klan had already taken over the Mississippi hill country, the central part of the state, and penetrated even the Delta counties of Bolivar and Coahoma north of Greenville, Sunflower to the east, Issaquena to the south.

The klavern met for weeks without Percy's knowledge, itself a sign of weakness and change. Years before, nothing of consequence could have been kept secret from him. Then the klavern arranged for Colonel Joseph Camp, one of the most successful of the Klan's organizers, to hold a recruiting rally at the county courthouse.

IN FEBRUARY 1922, Percy could look out his office window across the levee and see the Mississippi River rising. It had been several years since the last flood, and the river worried him. It took priority over everything—except, just for the moment, the Klan.

The Klan was personal. His wife, Camille, was Catholic; her parents had emigrated from France to New Orleans, then come upriver to Greenville after the Civil War. And the kind of men who joined the Klan, men whom his son Will described as "the inflammable, uneducated whites whom the best part of our lives is spent in controlling," had humiliated him once already, during his Senate campaign.

After that Senate campaign, LeRoy had retreated to Washington County. Now the Klan was challenging him in his home. His father had kept the Klan out of the county even during Reconstruction. Now, no matter what happened in the rest of Mississippi, even in the rest of the Delta, LeRoy Percy would tolerate no rebellion in Washington County. If the Klan spread there, it would shatter the society he had struggled to build.

Immediately upon learning of the planned Klan rally, he called to his office influential men who opposed the organization. They decided that when the recruiter spoke, Percy would answer him, and they would try to pack the rally with Klan opponents. Typically, to a planter scheduled to be out of town on business, Percy sent a special delivery note explaining the plan: "A Ku Klux orator is booked to speak at the courthouse Wednesday evening at seven o'clock. . . . We concluded to pass resolutions condemning the Ku Klux Klan. . . . It would be advisable for you to attend. . . . It is very essential that we put through the resolution by a large majority."

The Klan had reserved the courthouse for March 1, 1922. That evening the crowd, not knowing who was friend or enemy, seethed inside the massive Victorian building. The black neighborhood, the black brothels for the white men, the juke joints, the pool halls, were within a few blocks, but no blacks were in view. Percy called for the county sheriff to chair the meeting. The sheriff said simply, "Colonel Camp will now address you."

Tall and angular, with square sharp shoulders, Camp had a riveting energy. He pumped his arms, pounded fist against lectern, strode the length of the platform and back, preaching pride: Pride in America! Pride in Mississippi! Pride in the white race! Then he began to preach hate. Who killed Garfield and McKinley? *A Catholic*. Who had bought land opposite West Point as well as in Washington? *The Pope*. Jews were organized! Catholics were organized! Niggers were organized! The only people in America who weren't organized were *the Anglo-Saxons*! Debauchery, lechery, drinking, horrors that he hardly dare speak of were going on right here in Washington County. *God* wanted it to stop. *The Klan* would stop it. They were a million strong, and growing stronger every day.

Camp finished in an uproar. Many clapped and shouted for him. Others broke into a loud chant: "Percy!" "Percy!" "Percy!"

Camp had given hundreds of speeches, recruited thousands of men. Never before had any man answered him.

Percy did. He spoke for an hour, mixing logic and sarcasm. His message was simple. They were a community whose members loved one another. He smiled with sarcasm and held out his hands to "this eminent orator, this *colonel,* under what flag he won his title or what battlefield he trod we know not." He spoke of his Jewish partner and snorted that Camp was right, "There are times I think he needs straightening out." Listeners laughed. This Jew had loaned Gentiles in the county $150,000 at less than half the market interest rates. "Don't you know that Jew ought to be regulated." He was "alarmed" about "this Catholic encroachment on our Government. . . . Do you know that after ten years of domination by that grand hierarchy of the Church . . . they have managed to get hold of our city government? . . . They have got Boots, as constable. . . . Took them ten years to get this far. Where will a hundred years take them?"

Still, his concern was not "this war on Catholics and Jews. . . . They can take care of themselves. But I know the terror this organization embodies for our negro population and I am here to plead against it. . . . The shifting of the population from the South to the North—you cannot stop that trend. It is going on as the result of industrial call to better opportunity. You cannot stop it, but you can expedite it. Instead of making it a matter of 35 years or 50 years, during which the South can readjust itself, you can make it an exodus within a year. . . . You can make three parades in the county of Washington of your Ku Klux Klan and never say another word and you can start the grass growing in the streets of Greenville."

He concluded angrily, denouncing this "gang of spies and inquisitors," then pleading: "Friends, let this Klan go somewhere else where it will not do the harm that it will in this community. Let them sow dissension in some community less united than is ours. Let this order go somewhere else if there is any place it can do any good. It can do no good here."

Dr. J. D. Smythe, officer of a bank on whose board Percy served, seized the moment. He rose and offered a resolution that he and Percy had drafted: "Be it resolved by the citizens of Washington County, Mississippi, in mass meeting assembled, that we do hereby condemn that organization called by itself the Ku Klux Klan, but having no connection with the real Ku Klux Klan, which, having served its usefulness, was dissolved many years ago. . . . Its impertinent assumption of the right to judge the private life of American citizens . . . is against the spirit of free institutions and the traditions and laws of our country, and is unAmerican."

With a loud roar, by voice vote the resolution passed. Camp was shaken and asked for protection. With elaborate courtesy an Irish Catholic policeman escorted him back to the Cowan Hotel.

PERCY'S SPEECH was reprinted in newspapers from New York to Houston. Leading Greenville blacks signed a letter to him reading: "If we had Mr. Percy in every county of the state there would be no Klan and the less fortune [*sic*] people would not be terrorized. . . . The colored people will feel much safer and more willing to live here and go on in trying to develop this our state of Mississippi." The Knights of Columbus distributed thousands of copies of the speech. Ellery Sedgwick, the *Atlantic Monthly* editor who had visited Greenville as a guest of LeRoy and Will, ran it as an article. Letters of praise and requests to speak poured in from around the country. Percy always declined, telling those who invited him that it would have "much stronger effect" for a "local man to reply."

But Percy knew his fight had not ended. Preparing for an extended struggle, he contacted three newspaper clipping services for information on the Klan. And he seemed to consider the fight a last stand of his class. To a friend he confided, "The eagerness with which . . . this Ku Klux Klan folly is received in the South . . . is a reflection of the fading away of the old aristocracy of the South, which with its many faults and weaknesses is yet far and away the best thing the South has yet produced. In the olden days as gentlemen we were something of a success. In the latter days as money seekers we are sorrowful figures in the competition with the more highly trained brains of the East and the more virile and unscrupulous products of the West. . . . [H]e is an optimist indeed who today can name the day or point the way" to the disappearance of the Klan.

Indeed, the night after being humiliated by Percy, Camp had spoken in Bolivar County, just upriver from Greenville, and announced that the Knights of Columbus had paid Percy, *whose wife was a Catholic*, $1,000 to confront him. Two weeks later the *Leland Enterprise,* located in the Klan's Washington County stronghold, published a letter from the Klan: "To all Flag and Liberty Loving, Law Abiding Citizens: In the name of our venerated dead, . . . We are going to make this a place in which you will be glad to rear your children. . . . To bootleggers, gamblers, and all other law-breakers, We are making an appeal at this time to clean up. . . . There are married men in this town who are not treating their wives right, we know who you are, . . . change your way. . . . To the boys who take girls out automobile riding, and park their cars by the roadside: Had you ever thought that what you do, some other boy is entitled to do with your sister? . . . To the Negroes: We are your best friend, but we wish you to do right. . . . We have our eyes on you, and we are many; we are everywhere. . . . Dated this the Deadly Day, of the Wailing Week, of the Sorrowful Month. . . . Yours for a better country, Knights of the K.K.K."

THE TOWN OF MER ROUGE lay a little more than 60 miles south of Greenville, across the Mississippi River in northeastern Louisiana. Less than 10 miles from it was the town of Bastrop. Both towns were in Morehouse Parish (in Louisiana, counties are called parishes), but the hostility between them was palpable. Mer Rouge had the same alluvial soil as Greenville, and it was home to planters who traveled, gambled, whored with black women, mocked Prohibition, mocked the Baptists, and mocked the Klan. But political power in the parish had already shifted from the planters to populists; the parish was in the part of Louisiana that served as the base for Huey Long, then a rising politician.

Bastrop sat beyond a ridge that was just high enough—about 15 feet—to contain the river's floods and thus prevent the deposit of lush soil. The town epitomized the industrial New South, with gritty mills, poor whites who had been forced off the land, and a narrow-minded middle class. The Klan did not so much take over Bastrop as embody it, and J. K. Skipwith, the local Exalted Cyclops, was a former Bastrop mayor. Since 1889, on a per capita basis, more lynchings had occurred in Morehouse Parish than in any other county in the United States. One mob had bound a black man's hands and legs and placed him inside the body of a dead cow with only his head sticking out, so he would die slowly while insects and birds were attracted to the moisture of his eyes, mouth, and nostrils, and crawled in his ears.

The Bastrop Klan specifically warned the sons of two Mer Rouge planters, Watt Daniel and Thomas Richards, to stop drinking and whoring, especially with black women. Daniel and Richards replied by publicly mocking the Klan.

On August 24, 1922, a baseball game and barbecue in Bastrop drew 4,000 celebrants. The Klan set up a roadblock and backed cars up for one and a half miles looking for the two men. They were found in a car with three others. All five were flogged. Three were released. Daniel and Richards never returned. John Parker was governor.

Their wives begged Governor Parker to investigate. He tried, but the parish sheriff insisted the men were alive. Parker asked for federal assistance from U.S. Attorney General Harry Daugherty, a political hack. (He was Harding's campaign manager and in February 1920 had predicted that the Republican National Convention would deadlock, and that party leaders would meet in a "smoke-filled room" in the middle of the night to choose Harding; his prediction came true and his phrase entered the language.) Daugherty would resign amid scandal a year later and had no interest in involving the White House in the Klan issue. He refused aid unless Parker formally declared that he had lost control of the state.

Parker was prideful. A few months earlier the Mississippi River had flooded a million acres of Louisiana and left 40,000 people homeless. The entire Louisiana congressional delegation had pleaded with him to ask for federal aid, or at least help from the national Red Cross. He had refused to do either, stating, "Louisiana has issued no call for help and will not."

Yet now Parker humbled himself and did as Daugherty required. He also vowed "a fight to the finish [against the Klan]. . . . It is now my solemn duty to whip them. . . . When we have in Louisiana an outside organization seeking to control this state politically, seeking to be prosecutor, judge, jury and executioner in one, seeking to take the place of constituted law, then I tell you that it's incumbent on your executive, if he is a man, to stamp that organization out."

Justice Department investigators found evidence of murder, along with proof that parish law enforcement and court officers belonged to the Klan. Yet Daugherty refused to pursue the matter unless the Louisiana legislature passed a resolution requesting it to do so, an impossibility. In November 1922, Parker went to Washington to plead personally for more help. He received none.

Meanwhile, the Louisiana Klan invited the press to a mass Klan initiation, erected wooden headstones on the lawn of the governor's mansion, and tied up Parker's dog. Their message: they could do anything.

Then two bodies were found in Lake Lafourche in Morehouse Parish. Each man had broken arm and leg bones; their hands and feet had been cut off or mashed off; each had had his penis and testicles cut off.

No convictions were ever obtained. And Skipwith, Bastrop's Exalted Cyclops, began campaigning across the river in Percy's Delta.

IN FEBRUARY 1923, organizers of a massive anti-Klan rally in Chicago invited Governor Parker and Percy to speak. Percy declined, but Parker, making it plain that a refusal would personally embarrass him, wired Percy, "You have been extensively billed for a speech with me. . . . Will meet you at Blackstone Hotel. Don't fail." Percy could not refuse his old friend. But his speech fell flat and he never again spoke outside Washington County.

Inside it he fought. The Klan's presence was threatening everything he had built in the Delta and every hope he had for it. He told his old colleague Jacob Dickinson: "I am intensely uneasy about the labor, uneasy for fear the negroes may not stay with us even to make this crop. . . . I regard the menace from the weevil, great as it once seemed, slight compared to the migration of the negroes from the South."

When a friend argued that confrontation strengthened the Klan and that, if unopposed, it would collapse of its own absurdity, Percy replied: "Nothing that is founded on pure absurdity can long survive, but . . . [i]t was unopposed in Indiana. It is said that it has 360,000 members there. It named the last United States Senator and all the state offices. It was unopposed in Oregon and swept the state. It has been unopposed, to come nearer home, in Bolivar, Coahoma, and Hinds counties. It has charge of all three counties. . . . It has been openly opposed in only two places in the United States: in Greenville and by John Parker in Louisiana."

And despite opposition, it had already infested Washington County. Ray Toombs, the county prosecutor, was the local Exalted Cyclops, and Klansmen occupied such county offices as superintendent of schools, circuit court clerk, chancery court clerk, supervisor of roads, tax assessor, two of the five-member Board of Supervisors, even county health officer. None had been elected as Klan candidates, but they now intended to sweep the county openly. Here, as across the country, the Klan was using techniques like the "decade," which required every Klansman to urge ten people to vote for the Klan candidate.

In March 1923 the Klan began holding election rallies around the county. Its target was Percy himself. "No man in the county ought to have a boss," one minister who supported the Klan told his congregation, "especially one who hasn't opened the Bible in ten years."

Percy, the banker and physician J. D. Smythe, and others organized the Washington County Protestant Committee of Fifty Opposed to the Ku Klux Klan. The committee excluded Catholics and claimed independence from Percy, declaring that he was not an officer of it, and stating that "Senator Percy has never written even one word of any article published by this committee."

The claims fooled no one. The power behind the group was Percy's. The force that drove the group was Percy's. The room it met in was in the same building as his law office, a few doors away. At an early meeting of the committee, Percy had listed five points all had to affirm. The final one: "All agree to stay and fight to the finish."

The Klan rallies continued. "The Big Cheese," Toombs called Percy at one in Leland, proclaiming, "The day of Kings has passed."

To REPLY, Percy announced a public meeting on April 23, 1923. It was hot the way only the Delta gets hot, but all day men and women poured into town in anticipation, coming in cars, in wagons, on horses, on mules. They found business to do with cotton brokers and farm suppliers, or lined up at one of the soda fountains, or sinned in moderation by climbing the stairs of the Elks Hall to gamble on cards, or sinned greatly by visiting women.

Then they trooped to the People's Theater and stood impassively waiting, the crowd thickening past 2,000. The moment the doors opened, they filled the benches, crowded the aisles, pressed against the back railings. Some had come to see a show, some to listen and decide; some knew what they thought one way or the other and had brought guns. The conjoined elbows and knees and smoke and spit and sweat put the crowd in a foul mood. So did the alcohol: the sinners who drank it became more insolent; the prohibitionists who reviled it grew enraged at its proximity. By the time the meeting began, the crowd was surly, tense, explosive.

Percy took it over. He gave a speech full of love, and a warrior's speech. He stood dressed formally as always, stiff, solid, barrel-chested, implacable, the ferocity of his eyes his only sign of passion. He declared, "The day of kings may have passed, but the day when wizards will rule Washington County will never come!"

He spoke of unity, of decency, of fairness, of humanity. He reminded his listeners that a few years earlier when the blacks went to war, "We prayed to the same God that they might come back to us. . . . And then only one year ago when we fought the Mississippi River flood, we fought it united together. Now, can't you let us say to those negroes who want to stay with us that we never meant to hurt you, that we have taken this thing out of our midst and, standing here united, we pledge this as a safe place to live out your lives?"

In the heat, sweat shone on his face, making him seem brilliant and glistening as it reflected the electric lights. To those who wanted to allow the Klan to run its course, he warned: "When the mighty Mississippi River charges against these levees, if you don't fight it it will run its course, but behind that course it will leave devastated fields." From the stage, as if from a pulpit, he pointed out the Klan leaders, Toombs and others, and the crowd stared at them. But Percy did not damn the Klansmen. He pleaded with them: "People know you, have honored you, you have lived with us, we have known you as friends. Is not there one among you who can say, 'I have made a mistake in going into it?' . . . Can't you come back and take part with us in the life of this community? I say to you, come back, come back and place us back where we were, come back to your father's house."

Then suddenly he turned hard, warning, "But if you won't, if 'Ephraim is joined to his idols,' I tell you we are going to clean you up from top to bottom."

He lashed the Klan as evil and absurd, sneering at the Klan's claim that the Mer Rouge murders were committed by Irish Catholics on the pope's order. Then he switched to mockery: "[Klansmen] are guilty of one grave defect. They are lacking in a sense of humor." The audience began to laugh and he had them. "You know humor is the saving grace of human life. It enables you to get a proper perspective, size things up in their true proportion." He mocked the Klan's leadership: two men were claiming to be Imperial Wizard and fighting over hundreds of thousands of dollars. He read a letter that the Klan claimed the pope had sent to the Knights of Columbus, challenging any Klansman present to say he believed the letter was real, scoffing, "They dare not do it because they know they will write themselves down as blithering idiots." He compared the Klan's titles to "some colored society . . . Genii, Grand Dragons, Hydras of Realms, Grand Goblins, Grand Titans and Furies of Provinces, Giants, Exalted Cyclops and Terrors of Klantons. . . . And yet keeping a brother in black out of the order, the only person who can really enjoy it. Don't you know that no full grown white man ought to be allowed to indulge in that stuff?"

His audience was laughing, laughing. Then, finally, he denounced the Klan as spies, liars, cowards. And he announced, "If I've said anything untrue about the Klan, and there's a Klansman here with the courage of a red worm, he'll stand up and deny it."

Eyes flaming, Percy stared out at the crowd. It was silent. He was finished. The theater emptied.

PERCY CONTINUED to campaign relentlessly, gathering one vote at a time, leaning on people, leaning hard. He wrote Alfred Stone: "[A] letter from you to the Klan bunch might be of service. . . . No one could write such a letter with any hope of doing any good except yourself." Stone promptly published a pamphlet that began: "Senator Percy has no knowledge whatever of my purpose to make the following statement. . . . In fact, I am taking this step at the risk of offending him."

And over and over Percy condemned the Mer Rouge murder and Skipwith, who also continued to campaign in the Delta. One night in a rainstorm a man came to his door, claimed his car had broken down, and asked Percy to come help him. Despite having never seen him before, Percy was about to do so when several men, including the sheriff, arrived for a poker game. The visitor ran off.

Privately, Will Percy gave Toombs a message. Will had little in common with his father, though, even at thirty-seven years old, he still lived at home. Despite being his father's law partner, he had not yet made a mark in Greenville, and his father likely suspected he was homosexual. Yet they did share a ferocity, and now Will told Toombs: "If anything happens to my father or any of our friends, you will be killed. We won't hunt for the guilty party. So far as we will be concerned the guilty party will be you."

Meanwhile, LeRoy exploited the incident. In a letter to Toombs published in the Greenville paper and the *Memphis Commercial-Appeal,* he accused the Klan of plotting "my personal injury or death. . . . You claim the Klan has eyes everywhere and knows everything and that its object is to cooperate with officers of the law. Will you cooperate with Sheriff Nicholson in the location of this man?"

Percy was wearing down the Klan. In Toombs' final pre-election statement even he, the Exalted Cyclops, implicitly repudiated the Klan himself by appealing for votes from his "friends among the Jews [and] Catholics" in the county.

Voter turnout was the largest in the county's history. Anti-Klan candidates won control of the Board of Supervisors, county offices, and the courts. But the margins were narrow—a single vote in one race—and Toombs was reelected. For county superintendent of education, a Klansman defeated E. E. Bass, who had made Greenville's schools the best in the state. Five candidates had run for sheriff; a runoff pitted Percy's candidate against a Klansman.

For three weeks the campaign, more intense than ever, continued. As the ballots were counted, a crowd gathered outside the court-house, the same building where the confrontation had begun. People milled about, quiet and apprehensive. Percy sat in an office inside for a while, then chatted with supporters, then went home to play cards. At 9 P.M. a man rushed down the courthouse steps, bellowing, "We've won! We've won! God damn the Klan!"

As Will recalled, "A tremendous uproar came to us from the street. We rushed out on the gallery. From curb to curb the street was filled with a mad marching crowd carrying torches and singing. They swarmed down the street and into our yard. . . . Father, nonplused . . . laughed, 'They don't seem to have any idea of going home and I haven't a drop of whiskey in the house—at least I'm not going to waste my *good* liquor on them.' "

Despite Prohibition, "Adah and Charlie dashed off in their car and returned with four kegs. Father called to the crowd: 'Come on in, boys,' and into the house they poured. That was a party never to be forgotten. . . . Our Ku Klux neighbors stood on their porch watching—justified and prophesying Judgment Day."

FROM AROUND THE COUNTRY congratulations poured in upon Percy. One letter came from former President and then–Chief Justice William Howard Taft. He and Percy knew each other well, and with former Secretary of State Elihu Root were working together on a project for the American Bar Association. Taft told him, "I mourn the fact that you are not in Washington continuing to represent your state, but the work you are doing at the place where it is to be done is perhaps more important."

Percy replied: "You can scarcely understand the sense of relief experienced by the people of this community as a result of the Klan defeat. . . . The amazing spread of it seems to be an indictment of democracy, but at best the maintenance of any form of government worthwhile means a constant struggle. . . . No class of American citizenship can escape responsibility for the rise of the Klan, but no class seems to have been more recreant to its duty as the protestant [sic] ministry. The repudiation of this sulking, cowardly, unAmerican, un-Christian, organization as the champion [of] protestantism should have been instantaneous and wide spread and such a repudiation would have sounded its death knell . . . [but] the rank and file of the Baptist and Methodist ministry has either acquiesced in it or actively espoused it."

The Klan of the 1920s represented something frightening in America, frightening because it ran so close to the mainstream. Across the country, lawyers, doctors, and ministers—successful men, ambitious men, middle-class men—supported the Klan.

The Klan's target was not really blacks. No politician was proclaiming racial equality. Even Calvin Coolidge, raised in Vermont, stated, "Biological laws shows us that Nordics deteriorate when mixed with other races." The Klan's target was change. Out of fear, the Klan enforced a populist conformity. In addition, as in Greenville, Klansmen generally tried to pry power out of the hands of the strongest and wealthiest men in a community, the men who had always run things. Percy was tired of fighting this battle. He even blocked plans to locate the new Delta State College, a normal school, in Greenville because he expected it to attract poor whites who would strengthen his enemies. Instead, in 1925 the school went to Cleveland, in neighboring Bolivar County.

In the larger sense, Percy sarcastically compared "the Klan virus" to "the good old days when [William Jennings] Bryan was the demagogue" and the Klan of the 1920s does fit uncomfortably close to America's populist tradition.

American populism has always been a complex phenomenon containing an ugly element, an element of exclusivity and divisiveness. It has always had an "us" against a "them." The "them" has often included not only an enemy above but also an enemy below. The enemy above was whoever was viewed as the boss, whether a man like Percy, or Wall Street, or Jews, or Washington; in the 1920s the enemy below was Catholics, immigrants, blacks, and political radicals.

The Klan continued to run strong nationally after Percy's rare victory over it. It was in 1924 that it elected the mayors of Portland, Oregon, and Portland, Maine. That same year Percy tried to address the 1924 state Democratic convention; after complex parliamentary maneuvers finally gained him recognition, the convention erupted in tumult and he was shouted down.

He turned his attention to "mak[ing] it more difficult for the Democrats to evade the Klan proposition" at their national convention. The Democrats had hoped to avoid the issue, as the Republicans had. But William Pattangall, attorney general of Maine, proposed a platform plank condemning the Klan. His proposal lost by a vote of $542\frac{3}{20}$ to $541\frac{3}{20}$. The fight split the party and made the Democratic presidential nomination worthless. It took 103 ballots to nominate John Davis, who was crushed by Coolidge. Pattangall himself lost reelection.

A year later the Klan remained strong. In 1925, Colorado Judge Ben Lindsay wrote Percy, who was advising him on anti-Klan tactics: "I really believe there is nothing in the entire history of the South that shows such sudden and devastating sweep as [the Klan] has achieved in Colorado. This secret order has functioned as almost the entire state government from state militia to the last constable."

Yet the 1920s Klan did collapse. It did so because it was not conceived as a political movement but as a scheme to make money selling memberships and regalia. It brought terrible forces together, like a magnifying glass concentrating the sun's rays, but no leader with a political vision emerged to focus that power and make it explode into flame. Instead, its leaders wrestled scandalously over profits, embarrassing its members. Then David Stephenson, Indiana's Klan leader who had amassed $3 million, was convicted of rape and murder; expecting a pardon and not receiving it, he revenged himself by revealing the corruption of dozens of Klan-backed politicians, including the governor and the mayor of Indianapolis, several of whom were also jailed. The Klan faded away.

Percy belonged to the large world. By 1925 he was a governor of the Federal Reserve Bank at St. Louis, a trustee of the Carnegie Foundation for International Peace, on the board of directors of the Rockefeller Foundation, companion of presidents of great northern universities. Though a Democrat, he often dined with the chairman of the Republican National Committee and was routinely consulted by black Mississippi Republicans about appointments Republican presidents made in the state.

Yet what he cared about most remained the Delta. He had shown absolute focus, and a certain ruthlessness, in his fight against the Klan. It had made him a hero to many across the country. He had built a society and he would protect it against any enemy—even if it made him reviled. The great invincible enemy was of course the river.

CHAPTER TWELVE

THERE IS NO SIGHT like the rising Mississippi. One cannot look at it without awe, or watch it rise and press against the levees without fear. It grows darker, angrier, dirtier; eddies and whirlpools erupt on its surface; it thickens with trees, rooftops, the occasional body of a mule. Its currents roil more, flow swifter, pummel its banks harder. When a section of riverbank caves into the river, acres of land at a time collapse, snapping trees with the great cracking sounds of heavy artillery. On the water the sound carries for miles.

Unlike a human enemy, the river has no weakness, makes no mistakes, is perfect; unlike a human enemy, it will find and exploit any weakness. To repel it requires an intense, nearly perfect, and sustained effort. Major John Lee, in the 1920s the Army district engineer in Vicksburg who would in 1944 make the cover of *Time* as an important World War II general, observed, "In physical and mental strain, a prolonged high-water fight on threatened levees can only be compared with real war."

In 1922 the Mississippi River was rising. Soon after LeRoy Percy began his struggle with the Klan, the river reached extreme high water and threatened all the tens of thousands of square miles in the river's floodplain. Even more than the Klan, it threatened the society LeRoy Percy had built, and it turned both his focus and that of his Klan opponents to the river, temporarily unifying them again.

And there was something new and frightening about this flood. For more than forty years the Mississippi River Commission had set standards and contributed money to build levees. For most of that time the overwhelming majority of the people in the Mississippi valley had trusted the commission and its strategies. Now some were accusing it of flawed strategies that exposed the valley to danger.

To understand the threat to the Delta and to all the floodplain, one has to understand both this criticism and what man had done in the years since James Eads had triumphed over Andrew Humphreys.

ALTHOUGH for very different reasons, Eads and Humphreys had both rejected the theory that levees alone caused a significant deepening of the channel. It was the only thing they had agreed upon. Yet, beginning a few years after both had left the scene, Mississippi River Commission engineers began to meld Humphreys' arguments for levees with Eads' arguments about the effect of current. The result was a bastardization of both their arguments, and a theory that both Eads and Humphreys had not only rejected but condemned: in 1885 the commission stated flatly, and repeated thereafter, "Levees designed to limit the high water width of the river, by concentration of the flood discharge of the channel, . . . secure the energy of the flood volume in scouring and enlarging the channel."

This pure expression of the levees-only theory was now policy. Few people along the lower Mississippi disputed this policy because Congress, throughout the nineteenth century and into the twentieth, resisted spending money on "internal improvements" on fiscal and constitutional grounds. So those who wanted money for levees embraced the claim that levees deepened the channel and thus aided shipping and interstate commerce, a clear federal responsibility. For forty years, congressmen and senators, governors and state and local politicians, local levee boards, contractors, planters, and cotton brokers all became wedded to and defenders of the commission's policy.

Meanwhile, the commission itself, although created specifically to inject civilian input into Army thinking, had fallen under the influence of Army engineers. Its president was an Army officer who reported to the chief of Army engineers. The commission did include two civilians and employed civilians, but Army engineers, who had neither special background nor training in the problems of the Mississippi River, made all important decisions. They were not scientists asking questions. They were soldiers serving a regular tour of duty. By the 1920s, after decades of adherence to the levees-only policy, few officers questioned it.

So for decades the river commission followed a policy of sealing the river off from its natural reservoirs and outlets. This both opened up millions of acres to development, reinforcing the political support for levees-only, and increased the volume of water in the river along with the current. But the stronger current did not seem to dredge out the bottom enough to compensate. Floods that carried less water were rising higher than earlier ones that had carried more. In 1912, for example, a flood devastated the lower Mississippi region. Though carrying far less water than the great flood of 1882, it smashed height records on seventeen of the eighteen river gauges from Cairo to the Gulf.

This contradicted the predictions of the levees-only theory, but the Corps ignored the findings. After the 1912 flood a few civilian engineers tried to reopen the debate about levee policy, chief among them James F. Kemper, a thin, intense young man to whom the cause became an obsession. The commission ridiculed him. Later Kemper recalled, "I was not accustomed to ridicule and it hurt to the bone." But as he persisted, abuse supplanted ridicule. "That was more to my liking. I rather like to fight."

When he presented his arguments to a meeting of engineers in New Orleans, General Arsène Perrilliat patronized him: "The alluvial stream is a gigantic hydraulic dredge. . . . Just as your arm will have its muscles developed if you exercise it and train it intelligently, so if the Mississippi River is guided intelligently . . . by a levees-only policy . . . it will grow in section so that it will carry floods to the sea, where we want them to go, without damage to us."

Then came the 1913 flood. The *New York Times* estimated 2,000 dead in Ohio alone. Fifty died in Hamilton, 150 in Zanesville, 200 in Dayton, and at least that many in Columbus. When the same waters reached the lower Mississippi, deaths were few but economic damage was vast.

The deaths of northern whites sensitized the country in ways that deaths of black sharecroppers did not, and Percy took advantage of the disaster to push Congress to increase appropriations for levees and, for the first time, to do so solely for flood control—no longer using the pretense of aiding shipping. He spent weeks in Washington leading a consortium of interests, and wrote home that he "succeeded in getting a favorable report . . . [and] its passage."

A few civilian engineers also opened savage attacks on the river commission and the Corps. Yielding finally to the pressure, the commission agreed to conduct "new" studies of cutoffs, reservoirs, and outlets. But the respective reviews lacked scientific integrity.

The "study" of cutoffs, for example, reviewed old arguments and observations—originally made between 1831 and 1848—regarding two cutoffs in Louisiana. It collected no new data and performed no experiments. Its conclusion affirmed the old policy: it rejected cutoffs.

The issue of reservoirs was handled similarly. Reservoirs had been a pet proposal of Humphreys' archenemy Charles Ellet, and in 1874, Humphreys had convened a board of Army engineers to investigate them. That board had rejected reservoirs but conceded, "The question of absolute practicality could only be decided by a series of extensive and elaborate surveys, for which neither funds nor time were available."

In the ensuing forty years not a single such survey had been made, yet the "new" study again unequivocally condemned the idea. Ohioans who had just suffered a disastrous flood ignored the findings and built their own reservoir system. Army engineers opposed it and warned it would not succeed, but, since no federal money was involved, they could not block it. (Over the next three-quarters of a century, these reservoirs would prove successful.)

Then came the question of outlets, also called spillways. The deaths in 1913 had frightened New Orleans; the city had demanded a new study. Mississippi River Commission secretary Major Clarke Smith did collect fresh data and confessed, "[T]here is no doubt that a spillway would reduce extreme flood heights at New Orleans." Still, he recommended against building one because "its use would be rare . . . and the expense great."

The commission published his conclusion but, despite repeated requests from civilian engineers, refused to release his new data. And the formal commission response to the call for spillways came in 1914 from commission member J. A. Ockerson. Ockerson revealed the openness of his mind when he said that he conducted his study solely to calm people in New Orleans, adding, "Whether their fears are groundless or not, whether based on facts or not, it justifies a review." Ignoring both the commission's new data and Humphreys' old data, he declared: "Guglielmini confirmed the opinion as to the little utility of spillways for reducing flood heights. . . . It is difficult to find a reason for any change at this time."

Guglielmini had made his observations on the Po River centuries earlier. Humphreys himself had stated that the results predicted by Guglielmini's theory "are all contrary to observation."

The engineering review thus left the levees-only policy in force. The only policy impact of the 1912 and 1913 disasters was to force the Mississippi River Commission to set new standards for levees, making them higher and thicker. Then in 1920, in accord with its theory that called for increasing the volume of the Mississippi River, the commission began sealing the river off from Cypress Creek.

●

CYPRESS CREEK was located on the west bank of the Mississippi, about 35 miles by river (less than half that in a straight line) above Greenville and 15 miles below the mouth of the Arkansas, which drains a basin stretching deep into the mountains of New Mexico and Colorado.

The 1916 Mississippi River flood was not a great flood, but during it 336,000 cubic feet of water each second escaped from the Mississippi into Cypress Creek. This amount exceeds the flow of the Danube in flood, far exceeds Niagara Falls in flood, and more than doubles the flow of the flooding Colorado River.

The water that escaped into Cypress Creek inundated a huge natural reservoir, and eventually found its way into the Boeuf, Ouachita, or Red Rivers, thence to the sea either by returning to the Mississippi or going down the Atchafalaya River, the greatest outlet of the Mississippi.

Closing Cypress Creek sparked controversy. James Kemper and a few others argued that increasing the volume of the Mississippi by 300,000 second-feet or more was madness. He insisted that the closure would raise the flood height 6 feet higher than it would otherwise be.

To prove his case he and others tried to convince the Corps to build a hydraulics laboratory for studying the river. It was not a new idea, but General Lansing Beach, chief of engineers, rejected it, explaining: "The art of dam construction is so far advanced in this country that a national hydraulic laboratory is not necessary to advance that science. . . . I particularly desire to emphasize my opinion that the hydraulic laboratory proposed would have no value whatever in solving flood control."

As Kemper later observed, "It is so much easier to believe than to think; it is astounding how much more believing is done than thinking. It is more astounding that an honest study was not made of conditions resulting from [the levees-only policy]. Not only was essential data not available but it appeared as though the failure to acquire it was deliberate. The determination to carry out this impossible theory was so great that, with many, it appeared to be an obsession."

The obsession was proving dangerous. The Corps of Engineers and the Mississippi River Commission closed the Cypress Creek outlet in 1921. No longer could Mississippi River water escape into Cypress Creek.

BY MID-MARCH 1922, shortly after LeRoy Percy first spoke against the Klan, Kemper was predicting a record or near-record flood. At the time, he stood alone in that prediction.

On April 10 in Greenville, the river rose unexpectedly over the 50-foot mark on the gauge, just inches below the all-time record of 50.8 feet.* Water already "in sight"—i.e., upriver or in tributaries— would keep the Mississippi rising for at least two more weeks.

On April 11 the gauge at the foot of Canal Street in New Orleans, more than 400 miles downriver from Greenville, also neared a record. Along the entire length of the lower Mississippi, people grew tense, fearing they were in for the battle of their lives.

The next day in Louisiana a call went out for volunteers to guard the levee at night. In Mississippi identical efforts had already begun. Armed men walked every inch of the levee watching for weak points; they also watched for dynamiters. If the levee yields on one bank of the river, those on the opposite bank are suddenly safe.

On April 15 the river at Greenville rose to 51 feet—a record —and continued rising.

Each hour the river drained more resources, more energy, from the people along it. Supplies of sandbags were exhausted. The men stacking them were exhausted. Money was exhausted.

On April 19, Percy once again addressed a mass meeting con- vened in the People's Theater. The Klan fight was put on hold; the river took precedence. This address contained no rhetoric and little pleading. He stated the facts. Already the levee board had expended all of its funds. There was no money for sandbags, for barge fuel, for lumber, for any of the other things a high-water fight required. They needed to work together, he said, to pool all that they had, to make all their labor available, to devote *all* their resources to this fight. Hundreds of people listened to him, and they organized in smaller groups, each agreeing to feed levee workers, or arrange for timber, or supply shovels.

Percy stripped his own cotton compress and plantations of laborers and sent them to the levee under the command of his man- ager, Charlie Williams, an expert flood fighter. Tens of thousands of men were fighting the river, filling and stacking sandbags, building "mud boxes"—planks nailed together at the crown of the levee, backed up by sandbags—to protect against wave wash, searching for signs of sloughing or of the river undermining the levee.

Meanwhile, Percy was asking bankers across the country for money; he also, with nine other leading Delta planters, one from each affected county, created the West Mississippi Flood Committee to mount an emergency lobbying effort in Washington. As a result, up

* Zero on river gauges originally marked low water, without reference to river depth; a 50-foot reading meant the river was 50 feet above the low-water mark.

and down the river mayors, the heads of levee boards, and bank presidents rained telegrams on Congress. Read one wire: "Everything possible is being done to hold the levees from ravages of highest water in histroy [sic] but with funds exhausted by the river commission and levee board they cannot expect to hold the situation. . . ." Read another: "Without the $2 million . . . the fight will be hopeless in this district. With sufficient funds we have every prospect of winning this fight." Within days, Congress appropriated $1 million for the emergency.

The levees were holding, but the river was so high that tributaries could not empty into it; instead, the Mississippi forced its own waters back up their mouths. The flooding covered parts of six Delta counties and turned 20,000 Delta people into terrified refugees. "People from Belzoni to Vicksburg flooded by backwater," pleaded a new wire to Congress. "Conditions desperate without food or means of escape. . . . Suffering growing daily more widespread and acute. Believe only relief organized by government on large scale can equal emergency."

There was no more federal relief. At Greenville the river, far above the old record, was still rising. Virtually every male black within miles was working on the levees. Meanwhile, the flood poured south.

IN 1922, NEW ORLEANS was a city of 450,000 people. At its back lay Lake Pontchartrain, 22 miles across and 50 miles wide, and at its front lay the river. No bridge crossed the river, much less the lake. Roads were poor in the best of circumstances, worse than useless in heavy rain. The only way out of the city was rail; a flood would cut even that connection. In an emergency the city would be impossible to evacuate or escape.

The Mississippi River Commission's official New Orleans flood gauge was at Carrollton Bend near Tulane University, where St. Charles Avenue, one of the most elegant streets in America, intersects with Carrollton Avenue. The 1912 flood had set the record height of 21 feet at Carrollton. On April 14 the 1922 flood registered 21.3 feet at Carrollton, and rising. The crest was still hundreds of miles upriver.

At the foot of Canal Street in downtown New Orleans, the U.S. Weather Bureau maintained its own gauge. On April 25 it registered 22.7 feet, with the crest still far upriver. The river rose above rooftops, to the top of the levee. In places it rose above the levee. City engineer John Klorer, in a highly confidential report to the mayor, warned: "At Octavia there is low levee as well as levee deficient in cross-section. . . . At Louisiana Avenue the levee occupied by the Celeste Street shed is below the present stage of the river by 18 to 24 inches. . . . [The river] is being held out by a line of sandbags plus loose dirt. . . . There is not enough progress being made by the present forces."

Three thousand city workers and the National Guard frantically struggled to raise the levees higher. Far above New Orleans, when a levee board president discovered a dangerous section of levee and begged Governor Parker for a few men to patrol it, Parker refused: "We are in a most desperate fight here and need every man we are able to secure."

At the Esplanade wharf at the edge of the French Quarter, the Mississippi curved around a sharp bend greater than 90 degrees. There the overwhelming weight and momentum of the water coming downriver threw itself directly against the levee. The turn is so sharp that the water surface on the outside of the bend rises a foot higher than on the inside, as if banking around a racetrack, and the currents generate such force that they make this bend the deepest spot on the river, 240 feet deep. On Esplanade Street 100 yards from the levee, the cobblestones suddenly broke apart and a cone of earth shaped like a miniature volcano thrust upward and water began to shoot out of it. It was a sand boil, caused by the tremendous pressure of the water pushing its way underneath the levee; the muddy water it spewed forth meant that earth from the levee was being shot into the air. An emergency crew built a ring of sandbags to contain the water until pressure equalized.

New Orleans had four competing daily newspapers, each run by men who used their papers as tools in a competition for influence and power. The *New Orleans Times-Picayune* was the oldest, the largest, the most conservative, the most powerful. Earlier, when the river equaled the all-time record at Carrollton, it had printed the news on page 15 in a one-paragraph story. The flooding of Arkansas City, 10 miles below the now-closed Cypress Creek outlet, had been kept out of the papers entirely. Now no newspaper published news of the sand boil on Esplanade.

The silence did not calm the city. And the *Times-Picayune* had to report what the competing *Item* put on page 1: Isaac Cline, the highly respected chief of the regional office of the U.S. Weather Bureau, was predicting a record stage of 22.6 feet at Carrollton and warning, "I cannot say whether the present prediction will be final or not." Soon Cline raised his prediction to 23 feet, almost a foot and a half above the old record.

New Orleans Mayor Andrew McShane announced that the city was in no danger. Simultaneously, he notified all city workers to hold themselves in readiness for emergencies, and said that twenty-four-hour patrols of the levees were being conducted for 100 miles upriver.

The Port of New Orleans ordered all ships to proceed at slow speed to prevent wakes from washing over levees and sandbags. An anonymous telegram to Governor Parker published in the press gave a more forceful warning: "Notify the barge line that if the state cannot stop this we will. The next boat that comes down at such high speed will need two pilots, as we intend to kill the first one. Our guards are armed with Winchesters and they have orders to shoot to kill."

The crest was still at least a week away, a week of ever-rising water. Major R. T. Cotner, the New Orleans district engineer for the river commission, affirmed, "The levees are better and stronger now than at any time in history." But were they strong enough?

ON APRIL 24, the levee crevassed at Myrtle Grove, Louisiana, 50 miles downriver from New Orleans in a region with few inhabitants. On April 26, near Ferriday, Louisiana, across the river from Natchez, Mississippi, two tiny sand boils, barely an inch in diameter and shooting water only a foot high, erupted. Less than five minutes later, the levee abruptly caved into the river. Soon the breach exceeded 1,000 thousand feet in width. The river roared through it in giant billows, waves exploding as high as the tops of trees, forcing 20,000 people from their homes.

Engineers were stunned. The crevasse broke at a spot more than a mile from the river's natural banks, where the water seemed still. No current had attacked the levee. The weight of the river alone, pressing against the levee for weeks, had caused the collapse.

In New Orleans outright panic erupted. Hundreds of people, not trusting the papers, came to the levee to see the river themselves. They left terrified. The water licked at the top of the levee; indeed, for long stretches it stood higher than the levee. Only sandbags held it. And the river was still rising.

On April 27, levee breaks upriver forced the *New Orleans Times-Picayune* for the first time to put the flood on page 1. Its editorial tried to calm the frightened city: "As for the high water situation, both state and federal engineers give us reassuring reports. The levees are in better shape than they have ever been in. . . . This newspaper assumes that the expert and seasoned guardians of the levees know what they are talking about. In our judgment the official assurances justify a reasoned and sane confidence."

Twelve miles below New Orleans at a place called Poydras in St. Bernard Parish, the Mississippi River, after running in a straight line for several miles, took another sharp turn. Louisiana state engineers described the area as "the bight of a big bend in the river, where the full effect of the strong current was felt."

There, also on April 27, also without warning, less than an hour after a guard had inspected the levee and found no problem, the levee imploded. It happened almost precisely at a site, barely 5 miles from an inlet of the Gulf of Mexico, that had long been considered for an artificial spillway. St. Bernard and neighboring Plaquemines Parishes were flooded. Rumors of sabotage swept the two parishes.

By luck the Poydras crevasse killed no one, but it ultimately reached a width of 1,500 feet and dug a hole 90 feet deep where the levee had been. The levee itself added 25 feet of height. That meant that a moving mountain of water nearly 1,500 feet wide and up to 115 feet high—as high as an eleven-story building—exploded onto the land.

AFTER THE POYDRAS CREVASSE, the river at New Orleans fell rapidly, as if a plug had been pulled out of a sink. With collective and immense relief, all New Orleans watched the river fall. All along the city's waterfront, from the most fashionable homes a few blocks from the river on St. Charles Avenue and in the Garden District, through the downtown business district, down to the working-class slum of the French Quarter, down to the wharves and industrial areas below that, down past the largest sugar refinery in the world, the water level fell. It fell 6 inches in a day, when it had been rising with the crest still upriver. It fell 2 feet in three days, when it had been rising with the crest still upriver. By the time the crest arrived, so much water was pouring out through the Poydras crevasse that the river did not even approach the record set earlier.

Meanwhile, far upriver in Greenville, the crest had set a new record height of 52 feet. The people of the Delta had waged a tremendous struggle. Their levee system had held. Backwater flooding had created tens of thousands of refugees, but the levees had held.

After the flood, engineers interpreted these events differently.

THE MISSISSIPPI RIVER COMMISSION and the Corps of Engineers believed that the 1922 flood proved that their ancient fight with the Mississippi River had nearly ended, and that they would soon see themselves crowned as victors. They insisted that the crevasses in Louisiana had come in substandard levees. They bragged that for the first time in history a record-setting Mississippi River flood had passed from Illinois to the Gulf without a single break in a levee built to commission standards. The 70,000 homeless in three states had been the victims of either substandard levees or backwater.

So the Mississippi River Commission turned its attention to completing its work: seeing that all levees met its standards for grade and section, and laying plans to close the final and greatest outlet of the Mississippi—the Atchafalaya River.

But if the commission was congratulating itself and saw final victory in the near future, other engineers, especially James Kemper, looked at the 1922 flood and saw imminent danger.

The 1922 flood had broken no records for height and had threatened no levees above Cypress Creek, but it had broken records on every single gauge below Cypress Creek, from Greenville all the way to the Gulf of Mexico. Critics of the Army argued that the closure of Cypress Creek had raised flood heights dangerously high.

Walter Sillers, Sr., head of the levee board based in Greenville, warned both Percy and Charles West, whose appointment to the Mississippi River Commission Percy had engineered, "A situation has been created in the upper part of the Mississippi Levee District which, in my opinion, is a menace and endangers . . . all of the counties of the district." Kemper pointed out: "The Mississippi River Commission closed off Bayou Plaquemine, and they closed off Bayou Lafourche. They have closed off everything that can be closed. They closed Cypress Creek, all under the same policy, and every closure has raised the flood stages to a stage higher than they were before. . . . In 1850 the levee at Raccourcci was required to be 8 feet high. It is well above 30 feet now. At Morganza, a levee of 7.5 feet held the flood of 1850. It had 38 feet of water against it this year. Forty miles above New Orleans the levee that held the flood of 1850 was 1.8 feet high. Now it must be 20 feet high."

Water runs to the sea. If an obstacle—such as a dam or a levee—prevents water from flowing where gravity would send it, then the water's mass and potential energy builds. The greater the force applied in an effort to block water from its natural flow, the greater will grow the mass of water so blocked, and the greater will become the potential power of its energy. The engineer of the levee district immediately north of Greenville, stated, "[W]e are in reality facing a condition and not a theory."

The Corps clung to its theory.

IF PEOPLE UPRIVER VOICED CONCERN, in New Orleans they were desperate.

Kemper warned loudly that New Orleans had escaped disaster in 1922 only because the flood had, despite its record height, carried far from record volume. He pointed out that, measured in cubic feet per second, twelve floods in the preceding forty years had exceeded the 1922 flood.

The terrible flood of 1882 had carried 2,250,000 cubic feet per second. The 1912 and 1913 floods had each carried 2,000,000 cfs. The 1922 flood had carried not quite 1,750,000 cfs. Kemper believed that 1922 did not even suggest the forces that the Mississippi could unleash.

What would happen if a flood as great as those of 1912 and 1913, much less 1882, moved down the river with Cypress Creek closed? What would happen if the river commission proceeded with its plan to close the last outlet, the Atchafalaya—thus increasing the volume of water passing New Orleans by approximately one-third?

More than ever, Kemper was convinced New Orleans needed a spillway for emergencies. He believed the experience of the Poydras crevasse proved his case. He began to fight, hard, for his beliefs, and was now joined by far more powerful allies.

Jim Thomson threw his weight behind Kemper. Long interested in the river, Thomson owned two New Orleans newspapers, the *Morning Tribune* and the afternoon *Item*. He was also well connected in Washington; he had worked in several presidential campaigns and, using family like a medieval potentate cementing alliances, became the son-in-law of the Speaker of the House and the brother-in-law of a senator, with his niece married to a senator. He contacted the presidents of every bank in the city, the Cotton Exchange, the Board of Trade, the Association of Commerce, and union leaders, then formed them all into the Safe River Committee of 100. Together their connections stretched from Washington to Wall Street.

For the next five years Thomson pushed Presidents Harding and Coolidge, the War Department, and the Congress to require the river commission to build a spillway.

General Beach, head of the Army engineers, responded by charging that New Orleans' interests wanted a spillway only to save money. The city's port infrastructure—docks, railroads, grain elevators, cotton warehouses, wharves—had been built to the old Mississippi River Commission standard. Raising it all to the new commission standard would cost millions of dollars, and the federal government would pay none of it. Beach also warned, "Some one has apparently started a propaganda, judging by the letters which are reaching this office. . . . Indiscriminate accusations against adopted methods can only result in harm." When the criticism did not stop, he threatened the city, subtly intimating that he might advise "capitalists" to invest in competing ports like Mobile or Baton Rouge instead of New Orleans.

But his critics persisted. Finally, at a meeting on spillways in August 1922 in New Orleans, Beach told the businessmen present, "If it were my property, I would rather blow a hole in a levee, if conditions became serious, and let the water take care of itself, rather than [pay to] build it and pay $250,000 a year continually in interest charges [for bonds] and the additional cost of maintenance."

The chief of Army engineers was recommending that his audience blow up a levee and flood its neighbors. It seemed an astounding position for him to take. In taking it he was conceding that they were right, that a spillway would work.

Later that year Thomson had a New Orleans congressman introduce a bill calling for a study of a "comprehensive" approach to the river, including reservoirs, cutoffs, and spillways. Before hearings on the bill, LeRoy Percy maneuvered unsuccessfully to work out a unified position among the levee boards of the lower river.

The hearings were acrimonious. Engineers called each other liars. Percy weighed in. On all technical issues he relied on Charles West, his man on the river commission, and West, like the other commission members, opposed spillways. So Percy had the Greenville Chamber of Commerce contact chambers in Vicksburg; Helena, Arkansas; Tallulah, Louisiana; and elsewhere to lobby against spillways. After four years of bitter fighting, Congress created a "spillway board" to conduct a new study and resolve the issue. The board scheduled a visit to New Orleans in the spring of 1927. It would arrive with the greatest flood ever known.

Part Three

THE RIVER

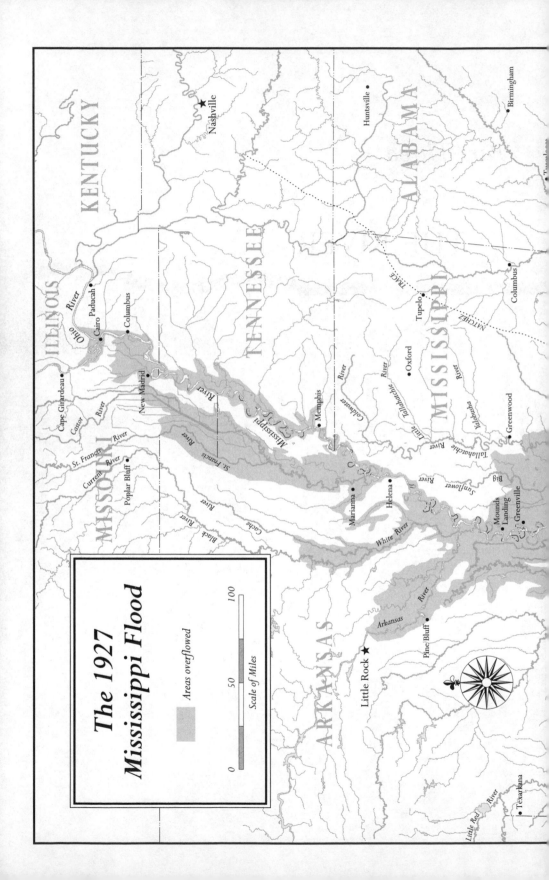

The 1927
Mississippi Flood

Areas overflowed

Scale of Miles

0   50   100

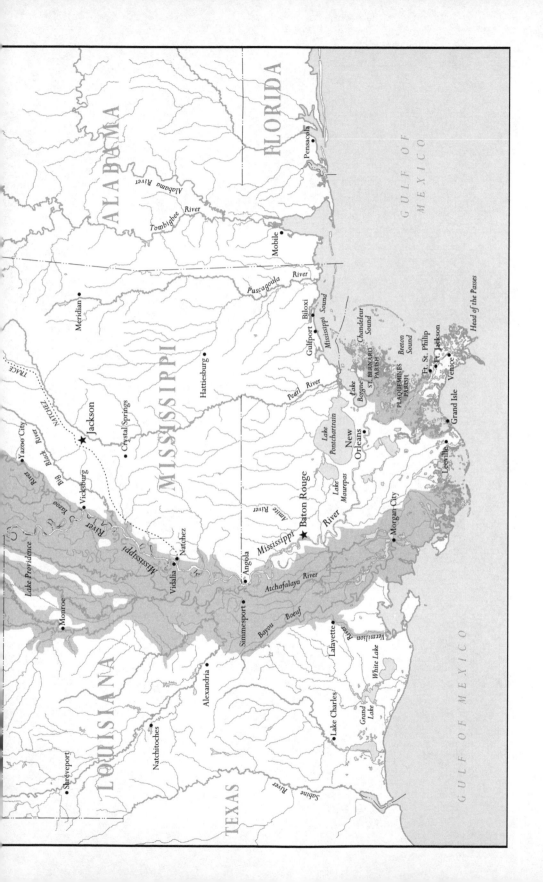

CHAPTER THIRTEEN

In 1543, GARCILASO DE LA VEGA, a member of Hernando de Soto's expedition, was one of the first white men to see the Mississippi River. He recorded its power: "Then God, our Lord, hindered the work with a mighty flood of the great river, which . . . came down with an enormous increase of water, which in the beginning overflowed the wide level ground between the river and the cliffs"—meaning the river's banks, which towered above the river at low water—"then little by little it rose to the top of the cliffs. Soon it began to flow over the fields in an immense flood, and as the land was level, without any hills, there was nothing to stop the inundation. On the 18th of March, 1543, . . . the river entered with ferocity through the gates of the town of Aminoya [an Indian village near the present site of Greenville, Mississippi]. It was a beautiful thing to look upon the sea that had been fields, for on each side of the river the water extended over twenty leagues"—nearly 60 miles—"of land, and [within] all of this area . . . nothing was seen but the tops of the tallest trees. . . . These floods occur every fourteen years, according to what an old Indian woman told us, which can be verified if the country is conquered, as I hope it will be."

IN THE LATTER PART of August 1926, the sky darkened over much of the central United States and a heavy and persistent rain began to fall. Rain pelted first Nebraska, South Dakota, Kansas, and Oklahoma, then edged eastward into Iowa and Missouri, then into Illinois, Indiana, Kentucky, and Ohio. Great cracks of lightning seemed almost to break open the sky, booming thunder made buildings quiver, and the wind rattled windows and tore away anything loose. Rain poured from the sky in sheets. Even in the intervals when the rain ceased, the darkness did not lift. The sky was impenetrable and uniform, the clouds themselves lost in gray.

The great storm lasted for days. Finally it broke and the sun shone, but within forty-eight hours a second low-pressure system heavy with moisture moved up the Mississippi valley and poured precipitation over this same region. It was followed by still another storm system. In the last fourteen days of August 1926, an area covering several hundred thousand square miles received little relief from drenching rain.

The rain drowned crops and ruined harvests. Though it fell in the dry season, it saturated the soil and filled the riverbeds. The rivers rose. On September 1, water poured over the banks of dozens of streams and flooded towns from Carroll, Iowa, to Peoria, Illinois, 350 miles apart. All the land in between lay heavy, wet, and glistening, reflections of silver drowning the green of crops and grass.

Still more rain fell. On September 4 floods deluged much of Nebraska, Kansas, Iowa, Illinois, and Indiana, killing four people. The Mississippi River rose rapidly in the upper Midwest and washed out bridges and railroads. A few days later there was another storm. Flooding stretched from Terre Haute, Indiana, to Jacksonville, Illinois. Seven more people died.

The rains continued. Storms hung over the region. On September 13, the Neosho River roared through southeastern Kansas, killing five, causing millions of dollars in damages. In Illinois a flood rammed a tree through an oil pipeline, setting it ablaze, spreading fire on the water.

In northwestern Iowa, 15 inches of rain fell in three days over the Floyd River valley, the Sioux River valley, the Dry Creek valley. With the land already saturated and the streams bursting, this water exploded over the riverbanks, drowning ten, inundating 50,000 acres that included Sioux City, adding millions of dollars more in damages. On September 18, the national headquarters of the American Red Cross sent its special disaster team to Iowa, while the waters near Omaha rose to threatening levels.

When the rains began, they had first relieved the region of the summer's heat. As they persisted, they had irritated, then depressed. Now they frightened. People could do nothing but watch their crops drown and their rivers rise and, reminded of their own impotence and of the power of God and nature, pray.

In many a church preachers spoke of the rain as a sign from God of man's wickedness. Even without a preacher's sermon, the good, decent folk of the prairie had to be thinking of the story of Noah, of the end of the world, of the coming of judgment.

All through the month of September and into early October it rained. Floods followed in Nebraska, South Dakota, Oklahoma. The Neosho River in Kansas and 600 miles to the east the Illinois River in southern Illinois rose to their highest levels in history. Flooding in those two states was the greatest and most disastrous ever—an extraordinary occurrence in October, when rivers normally run low.

The Mississippi itself grew fat and swollen, until it too over-flowed above Cairo. Tens of thousands more acres went under water.

Along the 1,100 miles of the lower Mississippi, from Cairo to the Gulf, only levees were in place to contain the energy of the river. For the length of that levee line the great earthworks seemed an impregnable fortress, towering two and three stories above the flat delta land. The Mississippi River Commission had pride and confidence in them.

Indeed, that year, even while threatening clouds formed over much of the drainage basin of the Mississippi River, General Edgar Jadwin, new chief of the Army Corps of Engineers, had for the first time officially stated in his annual report that the levees were finally in condition "to prevent the destructive effect of floods."

But the gauge readings were disturbing. The U.S. Weather Bureau noted that the average reading through the last three months of 1926 on every single river gauge on each of the three greatest rivers of North America, the Ohio, the Missouri, and the Mississippi itself —encompassing nearly 1 million square miles and stretching the width of the continent—was the highest ever known. The Weather Bureau later stated, "There was needed neither a prophetic vision nor a vivid imagination to picture a great flood in the lower Mississippi River the following spring."

But that fall no one at the Weather Bureau or the Mississippi River Commission correlated or even compiled this information. The individuals who made the readings simply noted them and forwarded the information to Washington.

The gauge at Vicksburg, which lay at the foot of the Delta and roughly halfway between Cairo and the Gulf, was even more disturbing. In October the Vicksburg gauge usually hovered not far above zero, a low-water mark. Only six times in history had the river exceeded 30 feet on the Vicksburg gauge in October. Each time, the following spring saw a record or near-record high water.

Usually, records on gauges are broken by inches, rarely by more than a foot. No October reading had ever broken 31 feet. In October 1926, the gauge at Vicksburg exceeded 40 feet.

Late in October the rain ceased. Those watching the river relaxed.

Six weeks later unusually violent storms carrying heavy precipitation began pelting the Mississippi valley again. On December 13, in South Dakota the temperature fell 66 degrees in 18 hours, followed by an intense snowstorm. Helena, Montana, received 29.42 inches of snow. In Minnesota snowdrifts of 10 feet were reported. As the storm swept south and east, 5.8 inches of rain fell on Little Rock in one day, with Memphis reporting 4.11 inches and Johnson City, Tennessee, near the Virginia line, 6.3 inches. By Christmas, 1926, heavy flooding had begun.

To the west, three children drowned in Arkansas as the continuing rains turned streams into torrents. To the east, the Big Sandy River, dividing West Virginia and Kentucky, overflowed. The Cumberland River rose to the highest level ever recorded and flooded Nashville. The Tennessee River rose to near record levels and flooded Chattanooga. At least sixteen people died in Tennessee, with thousands homeless over Christmas. The Yazoo River, running through the heart of the Mississippi Delta, overflowed and left hundreds more homeless. Goodman, Mississippi, had the highest water in thirty years. The Illinois Central, running north-south, and the Columbus & Greenville, running east-west, both suspended railroad traffic across Mississippi.

The chief, but by no means sole, determinant of how dangerous a flood will be is the height of its crest. This crest is not a wave but a gradual swelling; it is by definition simply the highest point to which a river rises. Flood height depends on several factors, with volume of water only the most obvious. Another is the speed with which a crest moves downriver. The slower it moves, the more dangerous it is: slower floods exert pressure on levees for a longer time, and slower floods carrying the same volume of water rise higher.

Common sense explains why. Floods are measured in cubic feet per second, also known as "cfs" or "second-feet," a dynamic measure of both volume and force. (When considering issues like storage and irrigation, engineers instead use the static measure of "acre-feet"; 1 acre-foot of water covers 1 acre of land with water 1 foot deep. Although 1 second-foot of water flowing for one day almost exactly equals 2 acre-feet, the two terms represent different concepts and do not equate easily.)

The number of second-feet is obtained by multiplying the average speed of the current times the river's "cross section." A large river might have a width of 1,000 feet and an average depth of 10 feet; its cross section would measure 10,000 square feet. If the current is moving at 10 feet each second—almost 7 miles per hour, a current fast enough that a person would have to break into a run to keep pace with driftwood floating downstream—then the river would be carrying 100,000 cubic feet per second. If the current slowed to 5 feet per second, the cross section of the river would have to double to pass the same 100,000 cfs. The river would have to either spread wider or rise higher, or both. Similarly, if the current accelerated to 15 feet per second, the river could accommodate the same 100,000 cfs with a cross section one-third smaller. So the slower the current, the bigger the cross section—and the higher the flood height—need be. The faster the current, the smaller the cross section—and the lower the flood height—need be.

Current velocity depends on the slope of the river toward sea level and on conditions in a particular stretch of river. In some reaches the river flows in a straight line and moves faster; in others it constantly collides with bends or rough spots on the bottom and slows down. Friction—with wind, the riverbank, the riverbed, sediment pushed along the bottom or carried in suspension—can influence current velocity. So can tides, whose influences on the Mississippi reach north of Baton Rouge, and other factors.

Even in a particular locality, the average speed of a river current is just that, an average. In midstream, water contends with less friction than near the banks and generally moves faster; water 20 feet deep faces less friction than on the surface, and so on. On the Mississippi violent differences in currents can create undertows that pull 100 feet straight down, or whirlpools as large as 800 feet long and 200 feet across, large enough to swallow trees, flotsam, or boats. As Ellet observed, "It is no unusual thing to find a swift current and corresponding fall on one shore towards the south, and on the opposite shore a visible current and an appreciable slope towards the north."

Floods increase the height of the river—in some sections of the Mississippi the average high-water mark may be 50 feet higher than low water—and therefore increase the slope and the speed of the current. If the river is low, and a sudden surge of water is poured into it, the current speeds up. But if the river is already high when more water enters, the river can act like a dam, forcing the additional water to pile up and slow down. Backwater flooding occurs when the main river is so high a tributary cannot empty into it; water from the main river can actually push water upstream into the tributary.

A classic study reveals how flood crests can move at very

different speeds. It compared two different flood crests flowing down the same 307 miles of river, from Cairo, Illinois, to Helena, Arkansas, in 1922.

In one case the flood crest poured into the river at Cairo when the Mississippi was low and swept downriver at a speed almost double the average current velocity of the river. The crest, in effect, was a separate layer of water that skidded down the top of the river, traveling the 307 miles in three days.

In the second case the crest entered the lower Mississippi when the river was already high and flooding, and the river dammed up the new flood crest. The new crest moved only one-third as fast as the average speed of the whole river, and took eight days to go the same 307 miles. This crest was, in effect, a layer of water that had to wait for the river channel to empty out before it could flow south. In the meantime, it rose higher than it otherwise would have.

There is no standard speed for a flood. Engineers have observed a maximum sustained current velocity in the Mississippi of 13 feet per second, roughly 9 miles an hour. The power of a mass several miles wide and 100 or more feet deep moving at 9 miles per hour is, literally, awful. And a Corps study concludes that, in a large lower Mississippi flood, "stage transmission" averages 419 miles a day. (The stage is the height of the river surface as measured by gauges up and down the river.) This does not mean that a flood crest covers 419 miles in a day, but some of the force of an approaching crest—some indication of it—travels downriver at almost 18 miles an hour.

The most dangerous floods are those that contain several flood crests. The first crest fills the storage capacity of the river, causing later ones to rise higher than they otherwise would. Meanwhile, the river's pressure on the levees intensifies. In 1927 the U.S. Weather Bureau station at Cairo, Illinois, noted ten distinct flood crests moving down the Mississippi.

CHAPTER FOURTEEN

O**N NEW YEAR'S DAY**, 1927, the Mississippi River reached flood stage at Cairo, the earliest for any year on record. Then the storms abated. As Congress reconvened, representatives from Mississippi, Alabama, and Tennessee wired their respective governors to find out if they should seek federal aid for the flooded districts. The governors unanimously wired back that no help was needed.

Meanwhile, several events early in the year were signaling the passing of an age. The *Kate Adams,* the last of the old Mississippi packets, burned in Memphis. Even the violently anti-southern black newspaper *Chicago Defender* wrote lovingly, "To plantation people —both races alike—the 'Kate' was a living creature, whose sonorous whistle, audible as far as 20 miles inland, was the signal for joyous cries. Straightening from their tasks at the sound, cotton pickers with grinning faces would shout across the field 'Yer comes the lovin' *Kate.*' "

In Greenville, Granville Carter, a black man, retired. He could not read but had run a newsstand and bookstore for both races downtown since 1880. The *Greenville Democrat-Times* editorialized, "Carter entered business on what was at the time Front St. That street and Mulberry Street have gone into the river. . . . He sold school books to girls learning their ABCs. He was always trusted. There are a great many people who say [the colored man] is beaten up and given no chance in Mississippi. The case of Carter is a complete refutation of their statements. The people of Greenville are always ready to acknowledge service, whether from black skin or white skin." But neither black nor white took over Carter's store. It closed.

In New York, Walter Gifford, president of the American Telephone & Telegraph Company, made the first regular long-distance telephone call from New York to London, while Commerce Secretary Herbert Hoover participated in the first public demonstration of television as picture and sound traveled from New York to Washington.

In Washington, talk about the 1928 presidential race had already begun. If Coolidge chose not to run again, ex-Governor Frank Lowden of Illinois was the favorite. Other likely GOP candidates were General Leonard Wood, who had been expected to win the 1920 nomination, Senate Majority Leader Charles Curtis, and Vice President Charles Dawes. One man not considered a serious contender was Herbert Hoover.

In California, Charlie Chaplin's divorce was a running story. America's newspapers, newly taken with celebrity, published accounts on page 1.

At the same time, in Arkansas the state senate overwhelmingly rejected a bill, passed by the House, outlawing the teaching of evolution.

In Fulton, Kentucky, a police sergeant was shot and killed by a Negro in an Illinois Central station. The sergeant had gone into the station to clear out the "hoboes, stragglers and floaters who drift in and use the place." The shooting occurred at midnight. The Negro was killed in the subsequent gun battle.

In Columbus, Mississippi, a Negro attacked a police officer with an ice pick. According to the *Jackson Clarion-Ledger,* the police officer was "questioning" him in the police station about a burglary, and the Negro was heard to shout, "You hain't got de only gun in de world. Jes' give me dat icepick an' I'll show you who comes out of here alive." Also in Columbus, the *Clarion-Ledger* reported, "The local Klan of the Ku Klux having just recently come into possession of reliable information that a notorious dive known as the 'Blue Goose' had become a nuisance to residents of the city, visited the place a few nights ago and found only a small quantity of liquor."

In Amite, Louisiana, fifty miles north of New Orleans, several farmers were indicted on charges of kidnapping a family of Negroes at gunpoint, taking them into Mississippi, and selling the whole lot for a twenty-dollar bill; the Negroes were forced to work without pay for weeks under armed guards.

The *Memphis Commercial-Appeal* ran a long story on the Delta & Pine Land Company, a cotton plantation of 60,000 acres, the largest in the world. British investors had pieced the plantation together a few years before and, said the paper, turned the rich soil into a giant, efficient factory: "Almost the first person employed on the property was a physician instructed to stamp out malaria and venereal diseases in the shortest possible time. . . . A competent civil engineer was on the job almost as soon as the doctors. . . . There are thirty-one negro churches on the company properties . . . elementary schools . . . an agricultural high school is under consideration . . . a modern fully equipped tenants hospital. . . . A newspaper is issued weekly for the benefit of the negro population . . . with a paid circulation of 1300 a year confined almost entirely to the tenants of the property."

Plantation headquarters lay in Scott, Mississippi, fifteen or so miles north of Greenville, near a sharp and dangerous bend in the Mississippi River and just below the closed Cypress Creek outlet. The river's tremendous mass collided with the bend at Scott, generating enormous and complex forces and putting intense pressure on the levees. In fact, the area was considered one of the weakest spots anywhere on the river's levee system.

In New Orleans in January the first Mardi Gras balls were being held. They were exclusive affairs for the season's finest debutantes. Unfortunately, a major Carnival parade had to be aborted. "Cornets, trombones, bass horns filled with water from the driving rain," reported the *Times-Picayune*. "Proteus, Monarch of the Sea, with his parade less than half completed decided the downpour was too heavy and turned his pageant back to the den." It was the heaviest rain in fifty-two years. The storm covered half the continent and made the paper's front page: "From the Rockies to the Ozarks a blanket of snow was being laid tonight . . . in some places the heaviest of the winter."

The storms had returned.

PITTSBURGH, where the confluence of the Allegheny and Monongahela Rivers form the Ohio, was flooded on January 23; five days later the Ohio flooded downtown Cincinnati. That crest took twenty-nine days to travel from Pittsburgh to New Orleans; a second flood at Pittsburgh on March 1 took thirty-eight days to go the same distance. The storage capacity of the Mississippi was filling.

The Illinois River at Beardstown, Illinois, had reached flood stage on September 5, 1926. It would remain in flood for 273 of the next 307 days. On every gauge from Cairo to New Orleans, the Mississippi itself reached flood stage early, often the earliest on record; it would remain in flood for as long as 153 *consecutive* days.

Water reaching the river was piling higher, rising against already saturated levees. Unseasonably high stages the preceding fall had prevented many of the levee repairs and maintenance normally carried out at low water. Now along the length of the levee system the weight of the river grew, its weight pushing outward against the levees, seeking its floodplain.

By February 4, the White and the Little Red Rivers had broken through levees in Arkansas, flooding more than 100,000 acres with water 10 to 15 feet deep and leaving 5,000 people homeless.

A week later New Orleans received 5.54 inches of rain in twenty-four hours. Similarly heavy rains deluged much of the lower Mississippi valley, generating violent local floods that killed thirty-two people.

In New Orleans, Colonel Charles L. Potter, chairman of the Mississippi River Commission, said reassuringly, "Although river stages along the Mississippi are high for this time of year, no serious trouble with flood waters is expected this spring unless more rain than usual falls in the upper valley and tributaries."

March opened with a severe blizzard striking Wyoming, Colorado, Kansas, and Nebraska, and parts of Oklahoma, Missouri, and Texas. The storm then swept east and dumped record snowfall in Virginia, North Carolina, and Tennessee, where buildings gave way under the weight. Farther south it rained.

The Tennessee River flooded for the second time in a few weeks, covering highways and sweeping one railroad bridge away, severing communication. In Mississippi on March 15 the *Jackson Clarion-Ledger* reported, "The virtual flood of rain which fell Saturday did considerable damage to highways and railroads, crippling service throughout the state." The next day, March 16, an additional four inches of rain fell, and the Mississippi National Guard was mobilized to guard the levees.

The storms turned violent. Between March 17 and March 20, three different tornadoes in the lower Mississippi valley killed forty-five people. High winds whipped the Mississippi into whitecaps and sent waves crashing into the levees; the waves did severe damage, virtually tearing off the crown of some sections.

In every levee district on the river, supplies were laid in and men met to plan the deployment of their forces. In January, Seguine Allen, the chief engineer of the Mississippi Levee Board, headquartered in Greenville and with jurisdiction over 184 miles of riverfront, had pleaded with Major John Lee, in charge of the Mississippi River Commission's Vicksburg office, for money to raise the low spots in his district. On March 23, Allen arranged delivery of dozens of generators, hundreds of feet of wire, and four railroad cars full of hundreds of thousands of empty cotton sacks, each one 20 inches wide and 36 inches long. The generators and wire were to string lights on the levee at night so work could proceed twenty-four hours a day. The sacks were for sandbagging; the levee board could return them, if not used, without charge. LeRoy Percy, a governor of the St. Louis Federal Reserve Bank, talked to bankers at the Chase Bank in New York, at the Canal Bank—the largest in the South—in New Orleans, and elsewhere in case emergency loans to several levee boards became necessary. He did not want to lose to the river for lack of resources.

Major Donald Connolly was in charge of the Mississippi River Commission's Memphis district, which included 450 miles of river, from Cape Girardeau, Missouri, to the mouth of the White River in Arkansas. He declared, "If the river does not go any higher than has been forecast by the meteorologist at Memphis, no serious trouble with the United States levee system is anticipated."

To those along the river Connolly's comment did not reassure. They knew that Weather Bureau policy limited meteorologists' forecasts of river heights to "all the water in sight," i.e., to precipitation that had already fallen. Therefore the Weather Bureau predictions routinely understated actual river stages. In addition, Connolly was claiming only that levees the federal government helped maintain on the Mississippi itself were safe. Hundreds of miles of state, local, and private levees existed. Indeed, the day after he spoke, levees along the St. Francis River broke in three places, pouring waters into Missouri and Arkansas.

IT WAS AS IF THE MISSISSIPPI was growing and swelling and rising in preparation, gathering itself for a mighty attack, sending out small floods as skirmishers to test man's strength. Those who knew the river always felt that it seemed a thing alive, with a will and a personality. In 1927 its will seemed intent on sweeping its valley clean of man.

From Cairo to the Gulf, the 1,100 miles where the river was mightiest and angriest, people readied themselves. Major Lee had taken charge of the Vicksburg district only the preceding July and had no experience with the Mississippi. Still, he was a man of order and discipline (attending Episcopal services daily and as often as three times on Sunday) and was an outstanding organizer. He had been preparing for months for what he considered the equivalent of war. Already engineers under him had walked each foot of the 800 miles of levees in the district—400 miles on each bank—and mapped weak areas so he could deploy resources.

His army numbered 1,500 full-time levee workers, including six levee contractors who each operated camps where one or two white men worked 100 to 200 black laborers. These were isolated, violent, and brutal places. (One camp operator named Charlie Silas may have been the original "Mr. Charlie," slang for a white boss in blues songs, who was reputed to routinely murder black workers and throw their bodies into the river.) But the levee contractors moved earth. Ten modern levee machines, each one looking like a giant dinosaur, also moved mountains of earth in a few days. Quarter boats served as highly mobile levee camps. Ten separate groups of men were working on revetting the riverbank, protecting it from the currents by covering it with willow mattresses much like the ones Eads had used for the jetties. The Corps had begun experiments laying asphalt and concrete over the riverbank as well. And in an emergency Lee and the local levee boards could call upon virtually all the plantation labor within miles of the river, a total labor force—an army—approaching 30,000.

On April 1, Lee mobilized nearly all of these forces and put them to work on the levees. He also summoned Navy seaplanes and Army observation planes to inspect miles of levee quickly, and communicate to men on the levee out of reach of telephones. Armed guards were also patrolling the entire levee line. They were needed.

Violence was erupting. Marked Tree, Arkansas, was a rough lumber town on the St. Francis River, surrounded by rich alluvial lands. In early February a 4-foot-deep cut in the top of the levee was discovered. Armed men began patrols there. On April 6 the guards shot four men trying to plant 105 sticks of dynamite. The town promised a reward of $500 for the "higher ups." This would not be the only shooting to erupt along the levee line; it was merely the first.

In Greenville, meanwhile, Percy once again stripped his own plantations and his cotton compress of labor and put Charlie Williams, manager of his compress, in charge of the flood fight. Williams, an expert hunter and fisherman as well as an expert on levees, had started a training camp early in the year to teach men flood-fighting techniques. It was the first such formal training ever conducted on the river, but Williams was expecting the battle of his life and wanted to be ready. He also planned "concentration camps" on the levee, complete with field kitchens and tents, for thousands of plantation laborers to live while they fought the river. These same camps would double as refugee centers, if the worst happened.

In New Orleans hundreds of men had started topping the levee January 17. A hole in the levee near a ferry landing had developed and been sealed. An emergency bulkhead had been placed across Bayou St. John and had already been washed out and repaired. Twenty-four-hour patrols began in March. John Klorer, a city councilman and experienced river engineer, reported confidentially that

7,000 linear feet of levees, considerably more than a mile, fell short of safe margins. Danger areas included such central locations as Poydras Street downtown and Bienville, Toulouse, Dumaine, and Governor Nicholls Streets in the French Quarter.

James Kemper and Jim Thomson, whose Safe River Committee of 100 represented every interest in New Orleans, went again to Washington to press anew for policy changes. Together they again protested the Mississippi River Commission's plans to close off the Atchafalaya, the final natural outlet of the Mississippi. Kemper warned: "It is apparent to any competent engineer . . . that this closure would result in the collapse of the levee system below the Arkansas [River] on the first great flood. . . . It is now *fight or drown.*"

BY LATE MARCH four separate flood crests had passed Cairo. On March 25, the gauge there reached the highest stage ever known. On March 29, the Laconia Circle levee, the oldest in Arkansas, sloughed into the Mississippi. It was not a federal levee, but it was a good one, and its collapse was ominous. Engineers sounding the bottom to gauge river depth could find none.

The same day local, regional, and national officials of the American Red Cross gathered in Natchez, Mississippi, to plan refugee camps, anticipating that local resources would not be able to handle the disaster they expected. Already the Yazoo and Sunflower Rivers were rampaging through the Delta, and the White and St. Francis Rivers were miles wide in Arkansas.

Connolly in Memphis said, "All levees are in fine condition and we expect no trouble." Lee in Vicksburg said, "It is not believed that the new rise in sight will necessitate emergency topping at any point. The organization is functioning perfectly in all sectors." Captain W. H. Holcombe, head of the Mississippi River Commission's New Orleans district, said, "No serious trouble is expected."

Privately, Lee was preparing for the worst, asking eleven postmasters for a "report on relief they would need in their vicinity in case" the levee broke. Tributary streams and backwater flooding had made thousands homeless. Mississippi Governor Dennis Murphree had sent a desperate wire to the War Department, pleading for tents and supplies.

In the West, a storm March 31 killed two in Oklahoma City, crippled railroads, and inundated highways. At St. Louis the Mississippi rose 6 feet in twenty-four hours and, to the south, poured into Cape Girardeau. In the east, the Ohio from the mouth of the Kanawha in West Virginia to Kentucky was rising 2 feet every twenty-four hours. The Y&MV Railroad sent twenty-five freight cars to

Natchez to house refugees. At Columbus, Kentucky, on the Mississippi, 3,000 men were sacking the levee.

From Cairo south, every levee board was operating on a twenty-four-hour basis. The weather was unseasonably cold, the temperature dipping into the thirties, even in the Delta. The men working on the levees huddled around fires and drank coffee during their few minutes off. Every foot of levee was patrolled by armed guards looking for signs of weakness or saboteurs. Thousands of men, mostly black plantation workers taken from the fields or impressed randomly by police from the streets of towns like Greenville, were living in camps on the levee or on barges tied up to the levee. The rain continued, drenching and chilling them. Day after day, hour after hour, they filled sandbags, carried them up the slope of the levee, stacked them; the wet earth made the sandbags heavier than normal, over 100 pounds.

In early April there were already 35,000 refugees, almost all along tributaries. But the Mississippi itself, a waking giant, was pressing outward against the levees, and it was swelling.

IN APRIL the rains continued. It rained harder and longer than anyone could recall over a vast area. Even the rains of the preceding year seemed light beside these days of darkness.

The *Memphis Commercial-Appeal* for the first time began to register doubts about the Army engineers' reassurances. Water in sight guaranteed record stages and rain was still falling. On April 8 it observed: "The outlook was gloomy now. . . . A couple of big tows which went down the river yesterday came very near to bursting the levee. They travelled at midstream and sent in waves running five to ten feet high." Even so, Major Connolly was still insisting: "The government levees are safe. We do not expect a break anywhere along the line of our levees, although some of the private levees may give way. The situation is well in hand."

But storms that very day devastated a wide area. *New York Times* headlines blared, "Eleven Killed Many Hurt in Midwest Flood; Great Area in Oklahoma and Kansas Is Inundated; [Railroad] Traffic Is Paralyzed; Three Trains Are Wrecked . . . Missouri-Kansas-Texas passenger train number 22, northbound from San Antonio, struck a washout at St. Paul, Kansas, the engine and ten cars going into a flooded ditch. . . . Many Southeast Kansas streams went to the highest stage on record after the downpour last night and early today. . . . Streets in Erie, Kansas, became a raging torrent four feet deep. . . . Late today the Neshobo [*sic*] River levee burst, flooding thousands of acres. . . . At Independence, Ks., the Verdigris River reached the highest stage on record and was still rising. The Neshobo [*sic*] River continued to rise. . . . Railroad service was paralyzed and was out on many Missouri Pacific, Frisco, Rock Island, Missouri-Kansas-Texas, and Santa Fe lines. . . . Late reports from Columbus, Kentucky, told of movements of inhabitants to higher ground when the waters of the Mississippi virtually reached the top of the embankment. . . . Handbags [sic] were being placed to prevent overflowing of the stream, which is now five miles wide here."

Outside Oklahoma City the Canadian River killed fourteen Mexicans; in El Dorado, Arkansas, the Ouachita River killed four in one family.

As of April 9, 1927, the upper Mississippi River from Iowa south was in flood; the Ohio below the mouth of the Green was in flood; the Missouri from Kansas City east was high; the St. Francis, Black, and White Rivers approached record levels; and the Arkansas was the highest since 1833. Below the Arkansas, the Ouachita, Black, and Red Rivers were rising; the Yazoo, Sunflower, and Tallahatchie in Mississippi, in flood for three months, were rising. And the Mississippi below the mouth of the Arkansas, also long since in flood, was rising.

More than 1 million acres of land were already under water. Downtown Cincinnati and Pittsburgh had been flooded. Oklahoma City was threatened. More than 50,000 flood refugees were living in tents or boxcars in Oklahoma, Missouri, Illinois, Kentucky, Tennessee, Arkansas, and Mississippi.

The record height along the Mississippi below Cypress Creek had been reached in 1922. Most levees had held—barely, perhaps, but they had held—that year. Already the unusual simultaneity of rising tributaries made it certain that the Mississippi would exceed the 1922 mark.

The rain continued. Connolly continued to insist: "We are in condition to hold all the water in sight. . . . This is a vastly different feeling than was expressed back in 1922. Then everyone was anxious but kept plugging away to prevent further breaks in the levees. Now they seem to have that easy confidence that the levees will hold, but will give every assistance should there be a break in the line."

IN NEW ORLEANS, Guy Deano, head of the Orleans Levee Board, confidentially informed Klorer, the city councilman and engineer: "From the forecast we are given to understand the water level will reach . . . extreme high water. Under the law the levee board authorities are authorized to proceed under the extreme emergency."

Publicly, every person in authority in New Orleans proclaimed absolute confidence. So did the newspapers. The *Times-Picayune* hardly mentioned the local situation and downplayed river news elsewhere. Earlier, Jim Thomson's two papers had used the high water as a weapon to increase support for spillways. Now, as the danger of the flood grew real, his papers too were quiet.

On April 13 tornadoes ripped through twelve states, accompanied by heavy rains. Under cover of the violent storm, a levee in Arkansas was dynamited, although the explosion did little damage since levee guards opened fire before the saboteurs could lay the charge properly.

On April 15, 1927, Good Friday, the *New York Times* reported: "Great Flood Peril Along Mississippi; Huge Mass of Water Is Rushing Southward Threatening to Inundate a Vast Territory . . . From Cairo to the sea, the most menacing flood in years was sweeping down the Mississippi River and its tributaries tonight. High stages from Evansville, Indiana, to Cairo, Illinois, increased volume from smaller streams above Cairo, and the unloading of heavy surplus of the Arkansas and White Rivers presaged a stage that may equal or surpass the records in 1922. . . . The guardians reported the great dykes in fine condition, but they placed men and machines at strategic points to reinforce any weakness which may develop under the immeasurable weight."

The *Memphis Commercial-Appeal* said simply, "The roaring Mississippi river, bank and levee full from St. Louis to New Orleans is believed to be on its mightiest rampage." It added, "Government engineers are confident that the government levees will withstand the floodwaters."

Already from Oklahoma and Kansas in the West to Illinois and Kentucky in the East, rivers were overflowing. The Mississippi was rising, high and fast. The Army had sent 275 barrack-size tents to Natchez for refugees. As much as 15 feet of water covered 2 million acres in Arkansas.

Arkansas Senator T. H. Caraway wired Secretary of War Dwight Davis: "Every available house and box car and tent at Helena and all of Phillips County is in use to house refugees from the overflowed section and still hundreds unprovided for. . . . Situation demands immediate action."

Tennessee Senator Kenneth McKellar wired Secretary Davis: "Floods breaking levees this district many rendered homeless. . . . How soon could you send [supplies] here. . . . Answer tonight."

That morning, as Greenville levee engineer Seguine Allen prepared to play host to LeRoy Percy and others for his Good Friday party, the great storm began.

Never had the sky been more brooding. In parts of Oklahoma and Texas temperatures dropped 30 degrees in a few hours. In Mississippi and Louisiana the damp cold hung like January in the air. For hundreds of miles angry winds whistled, whipping across flat land, whipping the Mississippi until waves pounded levees. Men and women shivered, frightened by the dark and the winds, and stayed inside. The skies grew blacker, as black as an eclipse. But an eclipse lasted only for a moment. These clouds blacked out the sun for hours; the only light came from the great cracks of lightning, the only sound from great claps of thunder.

On April 15, in eighteen hours 15 inches of rain fell on New Orleans; some parts of the city received more. The total rain, in less than a day, exceeded one-quarter the city's average annual precipitation of 55 inches. It was a terrifying reminder of the power of nature. Up to 4 feet of water stood in the streets. Photographs of it flashed around the country; photo captions, even in the *New York Times*, mistakenly stated that the river had flooded the city.

In the ten years from 1916 through 1926, not a single storm had poured as much precipitation on New Orleans as did any of five storms that struck in the first four months of 1927.

Nor was the rain localized. Between 10 and 12 inches fell as far north as Cairo, west past Little Rock, east past Jackson. Near Hickman, Kentucky, the Mississippi River rose higher than ever before—7 *feet* higher.

The river had leaned against the levees for weeks now, in many places for months, saturating them, pressing against them. Seepage was seen the entire length of the system. Dozens of tributaries, small and large, east and west—the Tennessee, the Cumberland, the Yazoo, the Ohio in the east; the Arkansas, the White, the St. Francis, the Canadian, the Missouri in the west; and a hundred others—had burst onto the land. Water was spouting out of the containment system as if through holes punched in a hose. The river was still swelling, threatening to burst open the containment system entirely. The private and state levees on tributaries had already been overwhelmed. Only the U.S. government–standard levees still held. But the Mississippi was only now receiving the great runoff from the lower valley, and the great flood from its tributaries.

The 1882 flood covered 34,000 square miles—more than the combined area of New Hampshire, Vermont, Connecticut, Massachusetts, and Rhode Island—to an average depth of 6.5 feet. The river was now carrying far more water than in 1882.

CHAPTER FIFTEEN

In the absence of a rampaging river, the "government" levees seemed immense, formidable, impregnable. They were massive earth works, thicker than any before and rising three feet higher than the highest water ever known along each stretch of the river. In 1882, one mile of levee contained an average of 31,000 cubic yards of earth. In 1912, the average mile of levee contained 240,000 cubic yards. In 1927, commission standards called for an average of 421,000 cubic yards per mile, 13.5 times the 1882 standard and almost double that of fifteen years before. Levees meeting this standard extended most of the length of the lower Mississippi.

Though made of earth, they were precisely engineered. Between the river and the levee lay the batture, the barrow pit, and the berm. The batture was the land between the river's natural bank and the levee; often a mile or more wide, it was usually forested (even if that required planting willows) to protect the levee from current scour and waves. Then came the barrow pit, from which the earth came to build the levee; the wheelbarrows used in early levee construction gave it its name, although it was also called the "borrow" pit. It served as a dry moat; the river had to fill it before reaching the levee itself. This pit, generally 300 feet wide and 14 feet deep at its deepest point, closest to the river, had a gradual slope of ten on the horizontal to one on the vertical up to the berm. The berm was flat ground, usually 40 feet wide, between the barrow pit and the toe of the levee.

The levee itself was the fortress, the great redoubt, its bulk melded carefully and seamlessly through a muck ditch into the ground upon which it was built. The crown was flat, at least 8 feet wide, and the sides had a three-to-one slope, so a levee 30 feet high would be at least 188 feet wide—the 8-foot-wide crown plus two sides, each 90 feet wide. The entire levee was planted with tough-textured and thickly rooted Bermuda grass to hold the soil. No other growth was allowed, so that inspectors could easily locate any weak spots during a high water.

On the land side of the levee, a banquette reached halfway up the crown and buttressed it, like a man leaning his weight against a door to hold it shut. The banquette slope was ten to one close to the crown and four to one near the toe: thus a 30-foot-high levee with a banquette was nearly as wide as a football field, not including the barrow pit or berm. The Mississippi River Commission paid two-thirds of levee construction costs; local levee boards paid one-third and provided rights-of-way and land, in effect a fifty-fifty cost-sharing.

At low water, when a person standing on the levee could not even see the distant river, the levee system seemed impregnable in-deed. But it was not impregnable.

A dozen things can cause a levee to collapse. A single piece of wood, a branch, left in a levee during construction could cause disas-ter if it rots and creates a cavity. Burrowing animals, even crawfish nests, also create cavities. The river will find such flaws and can enlarge them enough to cause a massive levee to collapse.

Soil could be a weakness. No levee district could afford to transport the enormous amounts of earth needed, so each used the soil at hand. If it was light and sandy, the levee needed much support and was highly vulnerable to wave wash and water pouring over its top.

The current, roaring downriver at 10 miles an hour, can scour out the levee base, eat away at it. High winds or passing barges can send waves that pound the levee with surf, ripping out chunks of earth, gouging out holes knee-deep, destroying walls of sandbags.

But the biggest danger is simply pressure, constant unrelenting pressure. Water, in seeking its own level, does not simply run over the top of a container; it presses against the side. A rising Mississippi presses against a levee with immense and increasing weight. The longer the river lies against the levee, the more saturated and weaker the levee becomes, and the more likely part of it will slough off. Such a slide increases the chance that the tremendous weight of the river can push it aside. Sand boils also result from pressure; the weight of the river pushes water underneath the levee. This water then erupts like a miniature volcano behind the levee, sometimes 200 yards be-hind it. When a sand boil shoots up clear water, it is not dangerous. But when the water is muddy, the boil is eroding the core of the levee.

Each of these dangers could be handled, at least in theory. But men had to do everything right, and they had to do so twenty-four hours a day. As long as a flood lasted, the river could only grow stronger, the levees weaker. Since the river was relentless, men had to be relentless. Since nature missed nothing, made no mistakes, and was perfect, men had to miss nothing, make no mistakes, and be perfect.

Even then, even if they matched nature's perfection, even if they matched the river's relentlessness, if the river rose high enough, it would still overwhelm all they had done.

Building levees higher also increased by orders of magnitude the potential energy of a crevasse. At Poydras in 1922, river currents had gouged out a deep enough hole to create that moving mountain of water, 115 feet high and 1,500 feet wide. It had all the power of a dam bursting. Conceivably, a crevasse could generate even more force.

WEEKS EARLIER Charlie Williams had divided the levee near Greenville into sectors half a mile long, then gave each sector a captain who organized his own guards and labor. In total, the workforce numbered close to 10,000. At known weak spots tent cities holding as many as several thousand men were set up at the base of the levee. Shock troops lived on barges that fed and slept 400 men and got them to weak spots in a hurry. Wires were strung for lights and telephones to allow twenty-four-hour operation and quick communication. Percy worked with others behind the scenes, assuring that logistics went smoothly, talking to West on the river commission to make sure it was doing everything possible.

As the river rose, even before the Good Friday rains, the levee guards changed. They had been black. Bill Jones, a black man, recalled, "They gave me a shotgun and told me, 'Don't let nobody from the Arkansas side come over.'" But Jones had allowed fishermen from Arkansas near the levee; he had not shot them. "They took the shotgun away from me. 'You ain't no damn good,' they said."

Now the guards were white, mostly World War I veterans. Tough, gritty men defending their homes, they did shoot. The *Greenville Democrat-Times* reported, "An attempt to dynamite [the levee] . . . near here was discovered by national guardsmen last night. A pitched battle followed the discovery and three men were shot."

But if black men did not guard the levees, they worked on them. The whites liked to think a flood fight represented the best of the community, all of it pulling together. Instead, it simply reflected the nature of power in the community, shorn of pretense. LeRoy Percy understood this. In 1922, just after the Klan fight began, he had invited Ellery Sedgwick, the editor of the *Atlantic,* to visit: "Nothing could be more interesting, so far as racial study goes, than to see five or six thousand free negroes working on a weak point under ten or twelve white men, without the slightest friction and of course without any legal right to call upon them for the work, and yet the work is done not out of any feeling of obligation but out of a traditional obedience to the white man."

Just inspecting the levee was hard physical work. Not only the crown but the slope had to be examined. The earth would suck a man's boots off his foot. Just walking was exhausting. White men did that generally.

Black men raised the levee. Where waves were eroding the crown, they built mud boxes, a wall of planks several feet high buttressed with sandbags, or sometimes simply stacked sandbags, laying them carefully like bricks. Each weak spot required thousands of sandbags, each one filled by hand, carried by hand, placed by hand. To fill a sandbag, two men held it, a third shoveled earth into it, then tied it. Dry, each filled sandbag weighed from 60 to 80 pounds; wet earth weighed much more. Bending over to fill one quickly became backbreaking. Carrying them up the long slope of the levee wore men down quickly. Only ten earth-moving levee machines were available for 800 miles of levees. There were few mules. There were only black men. But the white men did not treat them like men.

Bill Jones remembered, after his shotgun was taken away, carrying sandbags up the levee. A black man beside him slipped and fell; he fell the wrong way, into the river, and disappeared, his body never recovered, never even looked for. Work went on without interruption.

Duncan Cope, a white foreman, recalled: "They had a bunch of niggers over there . . . beating them with a stick and holding a pistol on them and couldn't get nothing done. . . . They asked me if I wanted a pistol and a stick. I told them no. I knew all those niggers. . . . I divided them up in groups, made one bunch fill the sacks, one bunch cull them, and one bunch lay them on. And I got them singing and working, and in about a day's time I had that levee sacked."

Get them singing and working; leave the stick and the pistol alone. The white man had learned that much.

There was no relief from the work. There could be none. The river took no rest. And while blacks did the most physical labor, everyone worked. The American Legion ran kitchens at the levee camps, cooking thousands of meals a day. Foremen, all white, levee guards, mostly white, and levee workers, all black, could get a cup of coffee in the middle of the wilderness during breaks. But the breaks were brief. The men worked hour after hour, and day after day.

The river kept rising. All the rivers kept rising, rising and swelling and overflowing and bursting levees.

Saturday, April 16, at Dorena, Missouri, 30 miles below Cairo, 1,200 feet of the government levee on the Mississippi River crumbled. The Mississippi River Commission had repeatedly insisted, "There has never been a single break nor a single acre of land flooded by a break on a levee constructed according to Government specifications for grade and [cross-]section."

It could say that no more. The river poured through the breach, tearing down trees, sweeping away buildings, and destroying faith.

THE COLLAPSE of the Dorena levee sent a chill all the way down the Mississippi River to New Orleans. The single crevasse flooded 175,000 acres. Few were reassured by Connolly's statement, "We feel confident that the other [government] levees will withstand the floodwaters." Virtually everywhere along the lower Mississippi— except in New Orleans—people had embraced the judgment of the river commission and the Army engineers. Now these people watched the river continue to rise, even with hundreds of thousands of second-feet pouring out of the river through the crevasse, and were afraid.

Arkansas Senator Caraway wired Secretary of War Davis: "At Forest City . . . 5000 people without shelter and without food. Both ought to be supplied immediately. Similar help is being extended to Tennessee although not one tenth its area as compared to Arkansas is overflowed." The Mississippi Flood Control Association wired Davis that another 6,000 refugees in Helena, Arkansas, were "absolutely without food."

That day the *New York Times* reported: "Seven more die in flood along the Mississippi. . . . Additional levees broke today on both the Missouri and Illinois shores . . . at Big Lake in northeastern Ark., and at Whitehall Landing in Ark. on the St. Francis River. . . . Additional rainfall in the Missouri and Upper Valleys threatened even higher stages. . . . Somebody's house passed through Memphis today en route to the Gulf of Mexico. . . . In St. Louis thousands of weary men tonight continued their struggle to strengthen the levees against what threatened to be the greatest and most damaging flood in the history of the lower valley. Other thousands of men, women, and children were refugees under the care of the Red Cross."

The head of disaster relief for the American Red Cross moved to the flood zone and wired headquarters in Washington that they faced "the greatest flood in history." In fact, this flood had barely begun.

SATURDAY, APRIL 16, as the river began to crash through at Dorena, LeRoy Percy sat down in the levee board office in Greenville for an emergency meeting with Charlie Williams, General Curtis Green, head of the Mississippi National Guard and spokesman for the governor, and every member of the levee board, including Walter Sillers, Percy's only real political rival in the region. Percy and Sillers had already asked Mississippi Governor Dennis Murphree to send convicts from Parchman Penitentiary to the levee.

Murphree owed both of them politically, Percy in particular. Years before, Murphree had been a strong supporter of Vardaman against Percy, and Murphree had become governor the preceding month, when his predecessor died of cancer. But Percy—because Bilbo was expected to run for governor—had willingly forgiven him and immediately offered support, advising him to announce immediately for reelection: "This is the psychological hour for you. Favorable results eventuate more frequently from acting at the psychological moment than from any other given cause. Those who do so are called lucky; they should be called wise."

Murphree had sent the convicts and promised to devote himself to helping the Delta. Now in Murphree's name Green offered every resource the state had. The next day Murphree himself pleaded with War Secretary Davis for supplies and tents to be sent to Greenville.

Vivian Broom worked in the levee board headquarters, listening to the men constantly on the phone repositioning barges, juggling manpower, seeing to supplies of sandbags. "The levee board was a madhouse," Broom said. " 'Is the levee going to break? is the levee going to break?' Mr. Elam—the assistant chief engineer—kept on saying no. . . . That place was a madhouse, payrolls, crowds of people running through, phones calling."

Florence Sillers Ogden's father, Walter Sillers, was on the levee board. She recalled, "They kept sending for labor. They sent convicts, they sent everyone they could find. Labor everywhere and trucks were just running through [filled with workers]."

In towns on both sides of the river, every morning the police ran patrols through the black neighborhoods and grabbed black men off the street to send them to the levee. If a black man refused, he was beaten or jailed or both; more than one man was shot. In Greenville, from the corner of Broadway and Nelson Streets, every morning trucks full of black men left, depositing a new load of workers fifteen miles upriver. Two or three times a day the trucks went up there. Wynn Davis, a black man, drove the trucks, and says, "The first of April I started carrying people up there. Never saw any white people on the levee working. I only saw the people I carried up."

Frank Hall, a white engineer, was then twenty-four years old: "They gave me charge of a stretch of levee. When I got there water was running over the top. I had a hard time keeping labor because we weren't organized. The feeding was almost nil in some places. Where farmers had their own camps and crews and brought in their own labor they were able to do a better job with their labor than we were with labor picked up by the police department."

The Mississippi was three miles wide between the levees, darker and thicker and more wild than any man, red, black, or white, had ever seen it. Detritus of the flood—tree branches and whole trees, part of a floor, a roof, the remains of a chicken coop, fence posts, upturned boats, bodies of mules and cows—raced past.

Levee engineers publicly continued to display confidence, but a disastrous crevasse was inevitable. The question was where. If the Mississippi broke through on the Arkansas bank, where levees averaged eighteen inches lower than Mississippi's, or far enough south of Greenville, then Washington County might survive. News of every crevasse added to their hope. Near Pine Bluff, a crevasse on the Arkansas River doomed another 150,000 acres. Good news, for that water would not threaten Greenville. On April 19, the Associated Press reported "the attempt to save the levees on the White River has been virtually abandoned." More good news, for Greenville anyway. That same day, near New Madrid, Missouri, the levees burst apart, opening a mile-wide gap. That water would flood as much as 1 million more acres in Missouri and Arkansas. Good news again for Greenville, lessening the pressure at least temporarily. But much of that water would return to the Mississippi. Timing was everything; when the water arrived was everything.

The crest would not reach New Orleans for at least three weeks, but that same day, April 19, near the site of the 1922 Poydras crevasse, levee guards in St. Bernard Parish shot three suspected dynamiters, killing one.

Charlie Williams ordered the automobile ferry from Mounds Landing, a dozen miles above Greenville, to Arkansas City to stop running. Automobile traffic weakened the levee; no more would be allowed. Thirty years earlier this had been the site of a small town called Huntington, where a railroad ferry had operated. A flood had washed the entire town and ferry operation away.

At that spot the levee was particularly and unavoidably vulnerable. Just above the landing the river ran in a straight line for several miles, gathering force and momentum. Then it curved around a 90-degree bend. The water there was in tumult; it boiled. It collided with the bank and generated terrific, literally terrifying, currents. Their swirl threw up waves that made no sense, that came from opposite directions and crashed against each other. The surface of the river rose and fell from one spot to the next, exploding into eddies and whirlpools. As Ellet had reported in 1851: "The apparent slope is everywhere affected by the bends on the river, and the centrifugal force acquired by the water in sweeping around curves, and by the eddies which form on the opposite side. The surface of the river is not therefore a *plane*, but a peculiarly complicated warped surface."

Mounds Landing lay not far below the mouth of the Arkansas, and just below where the Mississippi River Commission had closed the Cypress Creek outlet.

THE WHITE RIVER is 720 miles long and the Arkansas 1,459 miles long; together they drain 189,000 square miles and flow into the Mississippi a few miles apart. By April the area between them was entirely submerged.

At their mouths the greatest pressure on the levees began. Even before the Good Friday rains, both the White and the Arkansas had burst through their levees and reached record levels. The rains loosed unimaginable power.

In Little Rock a Missouri Pacific Railroad bridge trembled as the current of the Arkansas tore at its pillars. To steady it engineers parked an engine and twenty-one coal cars on it. The trembling continued; the vibration ignited the coal. Just as the fire started, the bridge crumbled into the river. Great clouds of steam billowed forth. In the roar of the river itself the tremendous hissing was barely audible. No trace of the spans or the cars could be found later.

In the great Mississippi River flood of 1993, the upper Mississippi River at Keokuk, Iowa, carried 435,000 cubic feet of water a second, a record; the old record, set in 1851, was 365,000 second-feet. Downriver from there in 1993, at the mouth of the Missouri, the Mississippi at St. Louis carried 1,030,000 second-feet. (The record of 1,300,000 second-feet was set in 1844.)

The channel of the lower Mississippi, below Cairo, Illinois, can generally accommodate 1,000,000 second-feet without difficulty. In 1927 the Mississippi River at Cairo was carrying at least 1,750,000 second-feet, and possibly 2,000,000. The Arkansas was carrying 813,000 second-feet, almost one-third more than it had ever carried before, while the White approached 400,000 second-feet. James Kemper personally inspected the area. So did engineers of the American Railway Engineering Association. They independently estimated that the Mississippi at the mouth of the Arkansas was carrying in excess of 3,000,000 cubic feet per second.

From the mouth of the Arkansas south, on both banks of the river, the levees trembled. In the worst sections, behind the levees dozens of sand boils spouted water, the weight of the river pushing through every weakness.

Everywhere men were racing to top the levee, racing both the rising river and their counterparts on the opposite shore. Bags averaged 6 inches in thickness. Men had raised the levee at least three bags high for much of the levee line above Greenville, and the Mississippi River lay washing at the top. That meant the river was 1.5 feet higher than the levee.

Levee engineers, for the first time on a large scale, tried a desperate measure. They pumped billions of gallons from the river onto the land, hoping the additional weight of water would stabilize and buttress the levee, preventing sand boils and sloughing.

In the areas it was tried, the new technique did help, but violent storms continued. On April 19, tornadoes tore across four states to the west, killing 31 people. On April 20 those same storms struck the lower Mississippi region. Percy's friend Henry Ball recorded in his diary: "Stormy tonight with a gale blowing and heavy rain threatened every moment. Hard on levees. Heaven spare us!"

The gale was worse than the rain. Great waves pounded the sandbags and the levee. Men tried to protect it with log booms, but the waves snapped the chains connecting the logs and tossed them into the air; individual logs repeatedly crashed down onto the levee like pile drivers.

The cold rain continued. Water poured out of the Arkansas, poured out of the White, both rivers still rising; upriver, above Memphis, the Mississippi itself was still rising.

Walter Sillers was in charge of one section of the levee. His daughter accompanied him on an inspection tour of the part near their home. It terrified her: "I'd never seen anything like that before and I've been in a good number of high waters.... There were streams ... of water running through there all up and down the side of that levee. . . . In front of our house, you can see right across there at the levee, the water was up at the top, running over the top. And the boats would go by and you could see the men's knees as they were standing in the boat, from across the levee. . . . They had sacks up there but the water was just running, trickling through them. My mother said she was standing there and saw the reeds moving on the levee, so she went up to see what it was, and it was the water coming over the levee."

The next day Sillers went down to inspect the levee at Mounds Landing. His daughter asked him, "Is it as bad as Lake Vermilion? It just couldn't be, could it?"

"It's worse," he said.

"Well I don't see how it can last."

"It will not. It's not going to last."

The *Jackson Clarion-Ledger* reported: "Forces were redoubled on levees north of Greenville late today, as the Mississippi River, lashed into fury by the strong winds, battered at the great dykes. . . . Five thousand men labored in a driving rain to place sandbags on the top in the places where the water is almost even with the top. 'No material damage has been done,' Major A. J. Paxton, commanding the national guard troops in Greenville, declared. 'We expect to hold the levee.' "

In fact, upriver from Mounds Landing, water was running over the top of the levee. The sandbags seemed to be holding. But two hours later, for a two-mile stretch the river was pouring over the tops of the sandbags.

That night Seguine Allen told the planter B. B. Payne, "You get all your labor and bring 'em to the levee and work on the sacks."

Payne snorted, "That's not going to do you a bit of good for the simple reason the river's rising an inch an hour. All the labor in Washington County won't do you any good."

Bill Jones and Moses Mason were piling sandbags near Mounds Landing. The levee, Jones recalled, "felt like jelly. The levee was just trembling." When he looked, for a moment, into the dark water of the river, "The water was just boiling."

"It was just boiling up," Mason remembers. "The levee just started shaking. You could feel it shaking. You could watch the water —everything was wet, but it was like the water was raising dust."

Earlier that day the gauge at Cairo had reached 56.4 feet, almost 2 feet higher than the record set a few weeks earlier. The reading did not reflect the record amounts of water downriver pouring into the Mississippi from the Arkansas and the White.

In Vicksburg, Major Lee noted that that night: "From dark until dawn came calls for help [from the entire levee line]. It rained heavily that night and at dawn we tried to get our big Navy seaplane started. It was waterlogged and it took us over an hour to get away."

Florence Ogden remembered, "All night long we heard the tramp of gun boots through the house. The guards would come into the house to get coffee. It just simply poured down that night. You never heard such a rain in your life. And they began calling for labor, labor, labor, send us labor, early in the morning, before day."

At Mounds Landing itself, 450 men in one camp were struggling to increase the height of the sandbag wall six more inches. The Mississippi was threatening to pour over the top. The men had no time to build a proper base. The waves pounded the levee and washed over them as they worked. They were freezing—the temperature was in the low forties. At a site a mile north the situation seemed even more dangerous; several thousand more men were working there.

At 3:30 A.M., Lieutenant E. C. Sanders, in charge of the National Guard contingent at Mounds Landing, named Camp Rex, toured two and a half miles of levee. Frequently, he stepped into holes more than knee-deep, dug out by waves. In innumerable places water was seeping through the levee. At the northern edge of his sector a guard reported a sand boil. Sanders went to inspect it and discovered a geyser of water as thick as a man's leg. He had no labor to spare and telephoned the next base up to take care of it; they did. He also noted a low spot in the levee caused by automobile traffic.

At 4:30 A.M. a new contingent of men arrived and Sanders put them to work setting up tents for even more men. At 6:30 word flashed down—a small break in the levee had appeared.

In a car he rushed to the scene. Water 12 inches deep and 24 inches wide was gushing through the low spot he had noted earlier.

He ran to awaken the labor, rushed another man to a nearby plantation "to arouse the labor" there, notified other camps on the levee. All had their own problems yet sent men. Within half an hour 1,500 men were working on the low spot. By then the flow of water had grown to the size of a roaring stream.

"The negroes ran to the break also," Sanders wrote in his official report, "but as they arrived they soon became demoralized and ran away. It then became necessary for the civilian foreman and my detachment to force the negroes to the break at the point of guns."

Hundreds of blacks, held by guns, began risking their lives for someone they had to see as a white fool. Under the guns they filled sandbags, threw them into the breach, passed them down the line to men standing in the breach. The water poured through in a growing torrent, washing the sandbags away as fast as they threw them in. Under their feet the levee quivered, shook. The breach was wider, deeper. The river was overflowing the levee along a front of several miles.

Charlie Williams arrived on the scene. He could do nothing. The river was still rising.

Mason remembers, "You could see the earth just start boiling. A man hollered, 'Watch out! It's gonna break!' Everybody was hollering to get off. It was like turning a hydrant on—water was shooting forward."

Men began running. Everyone was yelling at the top of his voice. At that moment Sanders was on the phone to his commander in Greenville, Major A. G. Paxton, saying, "We can't hold it much longer— There she goes!"

Williams remembered that the levee "just seemed to move forward as if 100 feet of it was *pushed out* by the river."

A man named John Hall was handling the phones in the levee board office, relaying information, dispatching materials. When word came to him about the break, he went in to see Seguine Allen, the chief engineer. "I took him the message and the old man just sat there and cried."

Word spread instantly amid confusion. Many papers initially reported the break as having occurred at Stops Landing, a few miles north. Cora Campbell told historian Pete Daniel, "I was ... right where it broke. My husband, he was working on that levee. . . . I run and run and run. . . . The bells was ringing and the whistles was blowing. Oh it was a terrible time. We made it to the levee."

The levee was the only land. The rest would soon be water. At plantations all through the district bells rang, dogs barked, cows bellowed, people hurried about gathering necessities—most had long since built scaffolds in their houses and moved furniture onto it. In Greenville at 8 A.M., the fire whistle and every whistle at every mill began to blow, and every church bell rang. Immediately water pressure dropped to nothing as thousands of people tried to fill their bathtubs with a supply of drinking water.

At 12:30 P.M., Thursday, April 21, Lee wired General Edgar Jadwin, head of the Corps of Engineers, "Levee broke at ferry landing Mounds Mississippi eight A.M. Crevasse will overflow entire Mississippi Delta."

Things would never be the same again.

CHAPTER SIXTEEN

THE ROAR OF THE CREVASSE drowned all sound. It carried up and down the river for miles, carried inland for miles. It roared like some great wild beast proclaiming its dominance. Men more miles away felt the levee vibrate under their feet and feared for their own lives.

There is no accurate count of the number of men swept to their deaths as the levee broke. The Red Cross listed two dead. The *Memphis Commercial-Appeal* said, "Thousands of workers were frantically piling sandbags . . . when the levee caved. It was impossible to recover the bodies swept onward by the current at an enormous rate of speed." The *Jackson Clarion-Ledger* reported, "Refugees coming into Jackson last night from Greenville . . . declare there is not the slightest doubt in their minds that several hundred negro plantation workers lost their lives in the great sweep of water which swept over the country." Judge R. C. Trimble, an eyewitness, said he did not expect the bodies to be recovered for days, if ever. The Associated Press quoted National Guard Sergeant Henry Bay, who was in charge of the rescue and "estimated that more than 100 negroes had been drowned in the flood waters." The only official account, that of the National Guard officer at the crevasse site, stated only, "No lives were lost among the Guardsmen."

The crevasse was immense. Giant billows rose to the tops of tall trees, crushing them, while the force of the current gouged out the earth. Quickly the crevasse widened, until a wall of water three-quarters of a mile across and more than 100 feet high—later its depth was estimated at as much as 130 feet—raged onto the Delta. (Weeks later, engineer Frank Hall sounded the still-open break: "We had a lead line one hundred feet long, and we could find no bottom.") The water's force gouged a 100-foot-deep channel half a mile wide for a mile inland.

It was an immense amount of water. The crevasse at Mounds Landing poured out 468,000 second-feet onto the Delta, triple the volume of a flooding Colorado, more than double a flooding Niagara Falls, more than the entire upper Mississippi ever carried, including in 1993. The crevasse was pouring out such volume that in 10 days it could cover nearly 1 million acres with water 10 feet deep. And the river would be pumping water through the crevasse for months.

ON THE RIVER ITSELF the crevasse created a maelstrom. Hundreds of workers climbed onto a barge below the break to escape, and a tugboat began to push it downstream. The engines strained and the barge and boat trembled, yet they were being sucked *upstream*, toward the crevasse. "Let's put all the niggers on the barge and cut it loose," a man said. Charlie Gibson, a retired levee contractor so feeble that he had to be carried about in a chair but whose advice was so valuable that he had been brought to the levee anyway, ordered: "We ain't goin' to cut the barge loose. I'll shoot you if you try that. If we go, we go together."

They escaped by angling across to the Arkansas shore. The *Pelican,* a Mississippi River Commission steamboat, was not so lucky later that day at a far smaller levee break in Arkansas. In full sight of thousands of workers and refugees, the current sucked the *Pelican* toward this crevasse. Desperately trying to stop, the captain rammed his bow into the levee. The levee collapsed and the *Pelican* capsized, was dragged through the crevasse rolling over and over. In one of the most heroic acts of the flood, a black man named Sam Tucker jumped into a rowboat alone—no one would join him—and headed for the break. The current lifted his boat and rocketed him through the turbulence. Somehow he survived, followed the steamer, and a mile inland picked 2 men out of the water. They were alive; 19 others drowned. The amount of water pouring through this break paled when compared to Mounds Landing. Yet the *Memphis Commercial-Appeal* wrote, "It was as if [the steamer] had been carried over Niagara Falls."

Meanwhile, the water from Mounds Landing was roaring inland. E. M. Barry recalled: "[T]he water was leaping, it looked like, in rapids thirty feet high. And right in front of the break was the old Moore plantation house, a big mule barn, and two big, enormous trees. And when we came back by there [a few hours later] everything was gone."

For three miles inland from Mounds Landing the river scoured out the land—today a large, deep lake still remains as a legacy—but even as the mountain of water flattened, spread out, and slowed, its force remained terrifying. It tore out trees, made splinters out of thousands of thin sharecropper cabins, crushed or undermined and then swept away houses and barns.

Cora Walker, a black woman, lived a few miles south of the break. Her home lay beside the toe of the levee. "An airplane kept flying over, real low, backwards and forwards, . . . told us we better get to the levee. A lady was coming to the levee, had a bundle of clothes on her head and a rope around her waist leading a cow." Suddenly, the water arrived, tearing south. "She and the cow both drowned. . . . Just as we got to the levee we turned back and saw our house turned over. We could see our own place tumbling, hear our things falling down, and the grinding sound. And here come another house floating by. The water was stacked. The waves were standing high, real high. If they hit anything, they got it. Every time the waves came, the levee would shake like you were in a rocking chair."

One planter a few more miles inland stood on his veranda and watched along the rim of the horizon "the flood water approach in the form of a tan colored wall seven feet high, and with a roar as of a mighty wind."

In Leland, twenty-five miles from the crevasse, Mrs. D. S. Flanagan watched the flood come "in waves five or six feet deep and just rolling and rolling. I never had seen it come like that, so dangerous looking, in all the floods I had been in. There was a Negro standing on the railroad track below the oil mill, and, when the water hit that track, it just washed out all the way under the track, the Negro into it, and he was never seen again."

The water rolled over and over itself, lifting trees, mules, roofs, dogs, cows, and bodies, rolling forward, the water filthy, liquid mud, churning, spitting brown foam and froth. Sam Huggins recalled: "When that levee broke, the water just come whooshing, you could just see it coming, just see big waves of it coming. It was coming so fast till you just get excited, because you didn't have time to do nothing, nothing but knock a hole in your ceiling and try to get through if you could. . . . It was rising so fast till peoples didn't get a chance to get nothing. . . . People and dogs and everything like that on top of houses. You'd see cows and hogs trying to get somewhere where people would rescue them. . . . Cows just bellowing and swimming. . . . A lot of those farmhouses didn't have no ceiling that would hold nobody."

Newman Bolls said that the water moved with such force that behind one large tree the ground was dry—the current broke around it. In that space a cow and its calf stood bellowing with a deep, plaintive sound. Later, when the current lessened, water filled the sanctuary; the animals drowned. They were joined by others. In the quiet of the new sea, animals by the hundreds were floating.

Those who understood the river's power abandoned their homes and left their doors and windows open to let the water flow through and lessen resistance; closed doors forced buildings to bear the full current. In Winterville, several families gathered together in what seemed a sturdy house. The current swirled around it, scoured out a hole 25 feet deep underneath it, and the house collapsed. The Associated Press reported, "23 white women and children, marooned, in one house . . . were drowned in the Mississippi flood, says a report made public today by [Seguine] Allen. . . . Urgent warnings to all people living between here and Vicksburg nearly 100 miles . . . were issued by Maj. Allen. 'Wall of water going south is very dangerous and unless people move to levees quickly, they will be drowned.' "

The superintendent of the Illinois Central in Greenville had scattered dozens of boxcars on Delta sidings for emergency shelter. Fred Chaney, outside Greenville, had been getting phone reports of the advance of the crevasse water and moved into a boxcar. "At 9:00, we could hear the rustle of waters in the woods a mile north of our box car haven. It sounded not unlike the first gust of wind before an on-coming storm and a shiver shot up and down my spine as the rustling noise grew louder and its true significance plumbed the depths of my mind."

It took three days for the water to reach L. T. Wade, deep within the Delta. But when it arrived, it covered the horizon. And it still came in force: "The water just came in waves, just like a big breaker in the ocean, coming over this land. It was a really frightening thing to see something like that. It didn't follow the . . . It just came right on over and rolled over."

"The situation is far worse than can possibly be imagined from the outside," stated General Green from Greenville. "It is the greatest disaster ever to come to this section and we need help from the federal government to prevent the worst kind of suffering."

For God's Sake, Send Us Boats! was the headline blared across page 1 of the *New Orleans Times-Picayune,* quoting a plea from Mississippi Governor Dennis Murphree: "For God's sake send us boats. It would be impossible to overestimate the distress of the stricken sections of the state. Back from the levees, where the land is flooded by backwaters, people are living on housetops, clinging to trees, and barely existing in circumstances of indescribable horror.

The only way we can get them out of there is by boat and we haven't the boats at present. Please try to make the people of New Orleans realize how urgent this is."

In fact, it was nearly indescribable. Mounds Landing was the greatest single crevasse ever to occur anywhere on the Mississippi River. It would flood an area 50 miles wide and 100 miles long with up to 20 feet of water. It would put water over the tops of houses 75 miles away in Yazoo City. A total of 185,459 people lived in the region that would be flooded by it. Virtually all of them would be forced out of their homes; 69,574 would live in refugee camps, some for as long as five months. The Red Cross would feed an additional 87,668 outside the refugee camps—jammed into shelters ranging from elegant hotels to boxcars. Most of the remaining 30,000 would flee the Delta.

There would be many other crevasses to come, devastating hundreds of thousands more people downriver.

GREENVILLE SEEMED SAFE. The river levee protected the city from the Mississippi, and a rear protection levee protected it from water that came from a crevasse such as this one. Even before the Mounds Landing break, the city had actually pulled hundreds of black men off the river levee and put them to work raising the protection levee. But people were afraid. Within three hours after the crevasse special trains began carrying people out of town.

All that day police rounded up hundreds more black men and carried them to the protection levee. Levee board engineers assured citizens it would hold, assured them the city itself would not be flooded.

Waiting, the city seethed with anxiety and activity. LeRoy Percy spent the day as he had spent the preceding several days, at the levee board office on the phone. He had called planters who had refused to send their sharecroppers to the levee and demanded that they do so. He had spoken with Lewis Pierson, president of both the Irving Trust Company in New York and the U.S. Chamber of Commerce about organizing a national campaign for legislation to settle the river problem once and for all. He had involved his peers in New Orleans, bankers and lawyers with whom he hunted and played cards at the Boston Club, about the same issues. He had once again assured nervous bankers in New York and St. Louis that any money advanced for sandbags, lumber, and wages—blacks on the levee were paid 75 cents a day, less than they got to pick cotton—would be repaid. He had spoken to executives of the Illinois Central, arranging for supplies and more empty boxcars to use for shelter in case of the worst. His son had helped him in all this.

Now the levee board headquarters became even more a beehive, the National Guard headquarters a great Army camp preparing for war. Large Army tents were going up on the levee and giant kitchens were being built to feed thousands of refugees and workers. Trucks rattled through the streets carrying laborers and supplies. Hammers were pounding boats together in the lumber mills. Police and guardsmen impressed every black male they saw and sent them to the protection levee.

The crevasse water first encountered the Greenville protection levee deep into the night. "The water was just rolling, like an ocean wave," said Levye Chapple, a leader of the black community who was sacking the protection levee. It struck the way the sea strikes against rocks, with violence, roaring, shooting up waves 12 and 15 feet high, jumping over the levee, sweeping away sandbags, backing up and rising higher. Within moments the water had climbed to a depth of 8 feet—the same as the levee—while oceanlike swells rolled over it. Still deeper water was coming. Most workers ran. Chapple—along with dozens of others—had guns pointed at him and stayed, working as the swells washed over him, washed the sandbags away, washed over the levee. Finally, as the levee gave way, he shouted, "Everybody run for your life!"

At 3:10 A.M. the fire whistles and church bells in Greenville sounded, and suddenly the streets were thick with people running to churches, to city hall, to the courthouse, to commercial buildings, and to the only dry land left—the river levee itself.

In the city streets the water initially retained the same ferocity as outside the city. Huge oil tanks from the Standard Oil storage facility in the northern part of the city came rolling down the street. Lamar Britton, a black woman, recalls, "You could see waves coming in big as you, five-, six-feet-high surf, rolling over, like the ocean, rolling chicken coops, mules, cows mixed up in it."

Britton's neighborhood—the bottomlands, the black section—soon had 15 feet of angry roiling water. The buildings acted like breakwaters. A few blocks away, Mrs. Henry Ransom, a white woman, saw a still-violent but calmer scene: "The water was coming in just in a whirling fashion, and there were plenty cows, and it was a bale of cotton . . . on the bales of cotton there was chickens . . . there was horses and mules coming down the street in this water . . . this current . . . the water was just spreading."

Up to 10 feet of water inundated downtown. For weeks the

current through the heart of the city, at the intersections of Broadway with Main, Nelson, and Washington Streets, would remain violent and deadly; like crisscrossing rapids, currents collided in spray, capsizing boats, drowning several people.

In the best neighborhoods, on the highest ground, the water came gently. It snaked up streets, running first in the gutters, filling them, spilling into the street, rising steadily, climbing steps and porches, but often stopping at the door. The highest ground in the city had only a foot of water.

WHEN THE FIRE WHISTLE BLEW, the Percys knew what it meant. Everyone in Greenville knew what it meant.

In the darkness of early morning, in his vast quiet house, LeRoy Percy had to face the great disaster he had always feared and fought to prevent. Now it had come. It threatened to end the life he had known, end the life he had tried to build, not only for himself, but for all of the Delta. The river was seizing the Delta back. LeRoy was sixty-seven years old, but he would concede nothing yet, not even to the river. At whatever cost, he was determined to preserve what he had built.

Meanwhile, the river rolled South.

AS GREAT AS THE DISASTER of Mounds Landing was, the flood had not even begun to exhaust itself. All the water flooding the Delta would be funneled by hills back into the Mississippi River at Vicksburg, a hundred miles south. From there, reenergized, the flood would continue downriver, shouldering levees aside.

The *Memphis Commercial-Appeal* warned: "Louisiana waits with fear and foreboding. . . . In St. Bernard Parish, below New Orleans, the section in which the crevasse of 1922 occurred, levees were being patrolled by guards armed with shotguns and all strangers were halted." The guards were fur trappers who trusted no one and would not hesitate to use their shotguns. They had already shot at least four men who had come too near the levee.

But the men who ran New Orleans—indeed, ran the entire state of Louisiana, or at least what they cared about in it—did not now contemplate anything so unsophisticated as sabotage. They had power, and, like LeRoy Percy, they intended to exercise it to protect their interests.

On the day that newspapers from Portland, Maine, to San Diego, California, put the Delta's plight on page 1, in New Orleans the headline of the *Morning Tribune* read, "Coolidge in Conference on Spillway." The story made no reference to the meeting a few years before, when the head of the Corps of Engineers had advised that New Orleans businessmen should, instead of building a spillway, simply dynamite the levee in an emergency. But the men of consequence in New Orleans recalled that advice. One site long considered for a spillway, of course, was in St. Bernard.

The struggle against the river had begun as one of man against nature. It was becoming one of man against man.

Part Four

THE CLUB

CHAPTER SEVENTEEN

In New Orleans each lamppost on Canal Street, which local boosters claimed was the widest street in the world, bore a plaque engraved FRENCH DOMINATION, 1718–1769, SPANISH DOMINATION, 1769–1803, CONFEDERATE DOMINATION, 1861–1865, AMERICAN DOMINATION, 1803–1861, 1865 —. The inscription suggested something secret about the city, that New Orleans was willing to yield on its surface, but that the real city lay deeper, that from behind a mask it had seen everything, and that it intended to survive.

No American city resembled it. The river gave it both wealth and a sinuous mystery. It was an interior city, an impenetrable city, a city of fronts. Outsiders lost themselves in its subtleties and intrigues, in a maze of shadow and light and wrong turns. Houses were built with faux stone fronts facing the street; the faux stone did not extend to the sides. Modern poker, the most secretive of games, was invented there. New Orleans had not only whites and blacks but French and Spanish and Cajuns and Americans (the white Protestants) and Creoles and Creoles of color (enough to organize their own symphony orchestra in 1838) and quadroons and octaroons.

Each group lived an apparently separate existence. In the mid-1920s, the Vieux Carré, or French Quarter, was mostly a gritty working-class slum where people spoke French as often as English. Women lowered baskets to the street to grocers who loaded them with food and added a pint of gin. Artists and writers had taken to the area, seduced by its cheap rents. Oliver Lafarge wrote his Pulitzer Prize–winning *Laughing Boy* there; Faulkner began writing there, encouraged by Sherwood Anderson, who entertained visitors like Theodore Dreiser, Alice B. Toklas, Gertrude Stein, and Bertrand Russell. One of Anderson's friends even wrote a book about Paris without ever having visited it, instead using New Orleans as his model; Parisians read it, Anderson reported, with "delight." The smells of the docks hung over the whole area: sickly sweet rotting bananas—the United Fruit Company was the single largest user of the port—and the more intimate smell of the dozens of bakeries making bread. The finest restaurants—Antoine's, Galatoire's, Arnaud's, Broussard's—were there, and so were working-class cafés. In Jackson Square at Billy Cabildo's, for 50 cents one got an enormous bowl of homemade soup, boiled beef, an entree, dessert, and coffee. The square itself was surrounded by hedges where prostitutes took clients.

Downriver from the French Quarter lived working-class whites. They made their living from the port, from sugar and timber mills, from great slaughterhouses.

The social elite, those with whom LeRoy Percy hunted and played poker, lived upriver in the great homes on St. Charles and in the Garden District. There maids waxed the grand ballrooms by sitting on towels and sliding across the floor. Chauffeurs picked up teenaged girls for lavish parties where a black jazz band—one included Sweet Emma—entertained. Fine young men took young ladies to Furst & Kramer's downtown; it had a pastry counter, a candy counter, a soda fountain, a marble fountain in the middle of the room, cages of songbirds everywhere, and every box of candy carried the slogan "Happiness in every box." On Canal Street at Katz & Besthoff drugstore, soda jerks delivered ice-cream sodas to cars parked on the street. Well-dressed doormen at Maison Blanche and Holmes department stores knew all the chauffeurs and called for them by name as their employers came out.

But underneath this perfect order lay a drumbeat. It was heavy and sensual. Most streets, even uptown, were graveled, not paved. The ice man sang and sweated delivering blocks of ice. Wagons rolled past the houses selling fruits and vegetables, sometimes three men on a cart creating a melodic, contrapuntal effect. Louis Armstrong said: "Yeah, music all around you. The pie man and the waffle man, they all had a little hustle to attract people. . . . The junk man had one of them long tin horns they celebrate with at Christmas—could play the blues and everything on it."

Only recently, jazz had been born from deep in the bowels of the city, its beat emerging from the African jungle into Congo Square, then spreading to the whorehouses of Storyville, where Jelly Roll Morton and the Spasm band, possibly the original jazz combination, and a little later Louis Armstrong, played. At its peak, Storyville had had two newspapers and its own Carnival ball, and the best houses had advertising brochures. One claimed to be "without a doubt, one of the most elegant places in this or any other country. . . . Miss Lulu stands foremost, having made a lifelong study of music and literature." There were also one-dollar "cribs" that were less than elegant, and women who threw mattresses down in doorways less elegant still. It had closed in 1919 by order of the Secretary of the Navy, still exercising wartime authority, but its legacy lingered, only spreading the women and houses and music into other neighborhoods. "Jazz is all the same—not anything new," said Armstrong. "At one time they was calling it levee camp music, then in my day it was ragtime. When I got up north, I commenced to hear about Jazz, Chicago Style, Dixieland, Swing—all refinements of what we played in New Orleans. I always think of them fine old cats way down in New Orleans—Joe and Bunk and Tio and Buddy Bolden—and when I play my music, that's what I'm listening to. . . . You want to feel the smell—the color—the great 'OH MY' feeling of the jazzmen and stomp around in the smoke and musk of the joints."

One joint in particular was called the Frenchman's, where musicians gathered after work, usually not until 3 A.M. Jelly Roll Morton recalled, "It was only a back room, but it was where all the greatest pianists frequented. . . . The millionaires would come to listen to their favorite piano players. . . . People came from all over the country and most times you couldn't get in." Across the street a drugstore sold cocaine; newsboys sold three marijuana cigarettes for a dime.

If all these societies seemed separate, they were not. Personal, social, political, and financial histories ran deep, connecting everyone. And perhaps more than any other city in America, New Orleans was run by a cabal of insiders, and everything from politics to the money the jazz musicians made depended upon them. Looking on as if from behind a two-way mirror, these insiders watched and judged and decided.

THERE WERE LAYERS of insiders, and folds within layers, with position largely defined by Mardi Gras. "Mardi Gras runs New Orleans," said one socialite. "It separates people."

The celebration itself—the balls, masking, street partying— began in the 1700s. In 1857 men of the finest families organized the first pageant of Comus. By the 1920s the city's Christian male elite belonged to at least one, usually more, of the exclusive "krewes"— Comus, Rex, Momus, the Atlanteans, and Proteus.

The commoners, those not inside, had only the parades. Even in the 1920s, several hundred thousand people lined the parade routes, and the krewes marched at night except for Zulu, the black parade, which marched Mardi Gras morning, and Rex, which followed later in the day. The night parades were led by a cadre of flambeau carriers, black men carrying torches burning oil, dripping fire on the streets. Then came horsemen all masked, then float after float, each an elaborate creation in line with that year's theme; the krewe members on the floats, all men, passed by high above the crowds, looking down at a horde of screaming people seeking attention and favor, elbowing for position, stretching out their hands in supplication, begging to be thrown a trifle. For the moment the krewe members truly felt like royalty.

Not every krewe paraded, but each gave a Carnival ball. They were the peak of the social season and doubled as debutante balls. Men planned every aspect of them, and they suffocated differences. One Carnival historian wrote, "There is perhaps no other city in America where men are social arbiters. . . . The most prominent gentlemen of the city abandon their urgent business obligations to spend their hours considering who shall be invited to their ball. Demand for these invitations surpasses all bonds of reason, and throws the commercial and professional life of the city into chaos. . . . No qualities whatever are of any force unless an invitation is requested [by a krewe member] and issued through regular channels, and there are no other channels. This strict care in the list of guests may find occasional resentment, but no injustice is done. Any request that is refused was already in doubt beforehand. If a member's request is not granted, he knows the reason and seldom has cause to be dissatisfied when he learns it. . . . Carnival is generous but in its social aspects protects its own. Wealth is no consideration, nor is ancestry unless supported by becoming character. . . . Instead of listening to the voice of scandal, Carnival hushes it, even where scandal looks to the masquerades for pabulum."

Carnival mattered. National Book Award winner Walker Percy, a Greenville Percy and Boston Club member, would later observe, "[Carnival] queens are chosen by the all-male krewes at sessions which can be as fierce as a GM proxy fight. New Orleanians may joke about politics and war, heaven and hell, but they don't joke about society." One prominent New Orleans attorney speaks of a friend who was president of the Louisiana bar, president of the Chamber of Commerce, and president of the Dock Board, which runs the port of New Orleans, "Yet he values most that his daughter was queen of Comus."

Rex, nominally "King of Carnival," was the public face of

Mardi Gras; his identity was announced. But the real king was Comus, whose identity was secret; at midnight Mardi Gras day, Rex and his court left their own ball to attend that of Comus. Secrecy added to the cachet. The queen of one important ball notes, "Often the men don't even tell their wives who is what."

The motto of Rex is *Pro bono publico*—"For the good of the public." The motto of Comus is *Sic volo, sic iubeo*—"As I wish, thus I command."

John Parker was Comus. Every Rex since 1888 has belonged to the Boston Club.

As EXCLUSIVE as the Carnival balls were, membership in the clubs of New Orleans marked the real insiders, for the krewes had a larger membership than the clubs. The city's first club was formed in 1832, four years before New York's Union Club. In 1842 the Boston Club, named after a card game, was founded, and several men, including Louisiana Senators John Slidell and Judah P. Benjamin, subsequently a Confederate cabinet officer and then adviser to Queen Victoria, belonged to both the Boston and Union Clubs. Then came the Pickwick Club and the Louisiana Club. All were exclusive, but the Louisiana Club has been called the most exclusive club in the country; only members were allowed within its walls. In 1905, President Teddy Roosevelt visited New Orleans during a yellow fever epidemic. It was an act of heroism that won the city's heart—in the preceding century, the disease had killed 175,000 people in Louisiana alone—and the Louisiana Club gave a luncheon in his honor. But before even the president, himself from one of the nation's grandest families, could enter the club, he had first to be made an honorary member. The club president at the time was Edward Douglass White, then a justice and later chief justice of the U.S. Supreme Court.

From the beginning the clubs mixed power and society. In 1874 an organized army of Confederate veterans, including White, defeated the largely black city police force in a pitched battle and overthrew the Reconstruction government. (Federal troops later restored it to power.) Of the Pickwick Club's 161 members, 116 fought in the battle, and the plans for the uprising "were largely formulated under the roof, within the walls, and by members of the Boston Club, screened from the public eye by the sanctity of the club walls," according to the *New Orleans Times-Democrat,* which added, "The Boston Club [is] composed of gentlemen who know what's what . . . and stands today, as it has always stood, at the forefront of the social system of New Orleans."

Half a century later the only thing that had changed was the role of the Jews. The first Rex, in 1872, was Jewish. Jews belonged to the Country Club and the Southern Yacht Club, the second oldest in the country. The most socially prominent law firms and banks had Jewish partners and board members, and Jews and gentiles socialized.

Yet Jews occupied a complex never-never land in New Orleans society. By the 1920s the clubs and Carnival excluded Jews, except for a few token members of Rex (but Jews were never in the royal court). The exclusion was gradual, beginning in the late 1800s and early 1900s as immigrants from eastern and southern Europe, including Hasidic Jews, seemed to threaten the nation's ethnic and racial identity. New Orleans, despite its Catholic heritage, showed a violent bias against Italian immigrants. Immigrant Jews were far more foreign; even native New Orleans Jews discriminated against them. Immigrant Sam Zemurray became president of the United Fruit Company and built one of the greatest mansions on St. Charles Avenue but was never accepted into the elite all-Jewish Harmony Club because, says the daughter of one of the city's oldest and wealthiest Jewish families, "he spoke with an accent."

Carnival snubbed even elite Jews. One prominent Jewish woman recalls, "Mother used to get invitations to all the balls but it just stopped." The exclusion was punctuated with an insult. Rex stopped along his parade route for a toast at suitably important places. These stops had always included the Harmony Club. But one year, probably 1913 or 1914, with a crowd of Harmony members waiting in the street and a waiter holding a tray of glasses, Rex went right on by. The Jews would never wait for him again, and Rex would never stop again. Later, Baron de Rothschild was in New Orleans during Carnival, and society ladies prostrated themselves before him. While he was Jewish, he had been received in all the real courts of Europe. In New Orleans he was invited neither to any club nor to any ball of Carnival royalty. Jews continued as partners and intimate friends with men who were Rex and Comus and president of the Boston Club. But a line had been drawn. Jewish members of the elite resented it bitterly, although to avoid embarrassment on both sides they routinely vacationed outside the city during Carnival.

Jews had been among the Boston Club's founders—Judah Benjamin was Jewish—and one served as club vice president as late as 1904. But by the 1920s the Boston Club had no Jewish members (nor did it in 1996). One Boston Club member bragged of his club's "spirit of noblesse oblige." But he also spoke of a harder racial edge: "Your club man must have a sense of the fitness of things. A club in its membership must follow Darwin's law of natural selection. In club life as in all other activities only the fittest survive."

In 1927 every bank president in the city but one—believed to be a Jew, although he denied it—belonged to the Boston Club. Charles Fenner, whose investment firm later merged into Merrill, Lynch, Pierce, Fenner, and Smith, was a club past president. John Parker belonged. So did LeRoy Percy; whenever he came to New Orleans, a limousine picked him up and took him to the club, where he played poker. (Gentlemen all, no one even kept careful track of money. After one game Percy sent a check of several thousand dollars to cover his losses, noting, "The aggregated amount may be three [hundred] out of line on either side, but any way, this will do to go on account." Another time the club manager wrote Percy to ask what he had won because "there is a discrepancy in the sheet"; the club had several hundred dollars too much and the manager was trying to find to whom it belonged.) The club men had power.

But these men were not like Percy. His vision extended deeper and wider than theirs. Unlike Percy, these rulers of New Orleans did not initiate or create, did not grow or make or build things. Bankers and lawyers, they judged what other men grew or made or built. Their power was over money itself, and whether to give it to those who produced or created. It had always been that way. From the city's earliest days New Orleans had close ties to the money centers of New York, Boston, Philadelphia, London, Paris. English bankers began living full-time in New Orleans in the early 1800s.

As a result, before the Civil War, on a per capita basis New Orleans was the wealthiest city in America. In the 1920s it remained —by far—the wealthiest city in the South. Its Cotton Exchange was one of the three most important in the world. Its port was second only to New York. Its banks were the largest and most important in the South. According to a Federal Reserve study, New Orleans had nearly twice the economic activity of Dallas, the South's second-wealthiest city, and between double and triple that of Houston, Atlanta, Memphis, Louisville, Richmond, or Birmingham.

The city's power over money also meant its power extended far outside the city itself. Percy recognized this himself when he, Parker, and several others organized the Staple Cotton Cooperative Association to control prices by limiting production. In 1926, Percy urged several New Orleans bank presidents and financiers, all but one of whom were members of the Boston Club, to force "a compulsory reduction in acreage" by refusing to lend money to planters who exceeded their crop allotments. "[S]uch an agreement made among the bankers would at once be accepted as effective and immediate relief would follow."

A few other organizations, such as the Board of Trustees of Tulane University, indicated even closer proximity to the inside of New Orleans than did club membership. But the most interior institution in this city of insiders wielded the power of the establishment in a way unique in the United States, and probably the world. This organization was serious, not social, and did include an occasional Jew. It controlled New Orleans in the way that really counted: it controlled the money.

THE BOARD OF LIQUIDATION of the City Debt was initially created to handle the huge debt left over from Reconstruction. Mississippi, led by LeRoy's father William Alexander Percy, had, similarly, created the Liquidating Levee Board, which built no levees but did eliminate old levee bonds by paying only pennies on the dollar, and then was abolished. But New Orleans, which produced few goods and grew no crops, had to retain the confidence of investors in New York, Boston, and London; the city had to pay off its bonds in full. So New Orleans bankers in 1880 created the Board of Liquidation and gave it extraordinary powers. (It operates today with many of those powers.)

First, every day the city deposited *all* the money it collected in taxes in the board's bank accounts. The board paid off whatever notes and interest were due, then gave any money left over to the city government. In the 1920s, payments on bonds absorbed between 39 and 45 percent of all city taxes, leaving little for the city to spend on anything else.

Second, the city could issue no bonds—not for schools, not for roads, not for lighting—without the board's consent.

But the most extraordinary aspect of the board was its composition. It had nine members: the mayor and two councilmen served ex officio, while six "syndicate" members, who made all real decisions, served for life. And the board was "self-perpetuating." When a syndicate member died or resigned, surviving syndicate members picked a successor.

Though the mayor, the governor, and the voters had no say over who became a syndicate member, the syndicate members dictated decisions about nearly all large public expenditures. Elected officials controlled only current operating budgets. The syndicate members answered to no one but themselves—and their colleagues in the clubs.

Between 1908 and 1971 only twenty-seven men served as syndicate members; virtually all were either bankers or bank directors. Twenty-four of the twenty-seven belonged to at least one of the exclusive clubs; most belonged to several. At least two of the other three, probably all three, were Jewish.

In the 1920s three men in particular had strong voices on the Board of Liquidation. One was James Pierce Butler, Jr., a towering gangly man who headed the Canal Bank, the largest bank in the South and the only southern bank listed among the world's largest; it also had intimate ties with the Chase in New York. Butler was a president of the Boston Club. A second man was Rudolph Hecht, president of the Hibernia Bank, who had a reputation for brilliance and arrogance; in 1921 he had received the *Times-Picayune* Loving Cup, given annually by the paper to the citizen who had contributed most to the city in the preceding year, for his work as president of the Dock Board. Later he became president of the American Bankers Association. The third man, J. Blanc Monroe, was an unyielding litigator who dominated the board of the Whitney Bank; he combined social connections with real abilities to become the city's most powerful lawyer. LeRoy Percy knew all three well, both through clubs and business.

In 1927, Butler sat snugly at the center of the New Orleans world of money, society, and power. His position was signified by the treatment given him by the Mystic Club, a Mardi Gras organization called "ultra-exclusive . . . [with] a reputation among fastidious people for presenting the most elaborate and most successful costumed entertainments of America." That year the club put on a Mardi Gras ball whose theme came from a movie starring Rudolph Valentino and Doris Kenyon. Booth Tarkington, who wrote the movie, also wrote the pageant for the ball; the same jewels worn in the film by Valentino and Kenyon adorned Mystic's king and queen. The queen's gown was said to cost $15,000, double the $7,500 annual salary of the governor of Louisiana. The *Times-Picayune*, the paper that was run by and served as the voice of money and society and authority, ran photographs of all but the Mystic Club's queen on its society pages; the photograph of the Mystic Club queen appeared on page 1. She was Mrs. James Pierce Butler, Jr.

CHAPTER EIGHTEEN

AFTER THE 1922 FLOOD the chief of the Army Corps of Engineers had advised the New Orleans financial community that, if the river ever seriously threatened the city, they should blow a hole in the levee. In the years since, those words had never left the consciousness of either the people in St. Bernard and Plaquemines Parishes, who would be sacrificed, or those who dealt with the river in New Orleans. Both groups had been monitoring the river closely all year. As early as New Year's Day the *St. Bernard Voice* had warned, "Flood Water Is Coming Down!" And in late January, hydraulics engineer James Kemper wrote a report on the river situation for newspaper publisher James Thomson.

No layman in New Orleans spent more time on river policy than Thomson. Five years earlier he had organized the Safe River Committee, and ever since he had been pushing hard in Washington to change the policy toward the Mississippi. It seemed, however, he had adopted the river issue at least partly to make himself a larger figure in New Orleans, to push himself into the inner sanctums.

Thomson was not a member of the club and wondered why. An ancestor had tutored John Marshall, and he had run a paper in Norfolk, Virginia, then bought the *New Orleans Item* and moved to the city in 1907. He started a second paper in New Orleans, the *Morning Tribune,* and became a director of a midsized bank, while in Washington he remained a confidant of senators as well as his father-in-law, Speaker of the House Champ Clark. But none of that was good enough for New Orleans. Perhaps he was kept in New Orleans' outer reaches because he lacked appropriate style. Tall, with a disproportionately large head, he liked to be called "Colonel" despite his lack of military experience. In hot weather he often stripped off his shirt in his office, treating those who worked for him to the sight of his pale white skin and soft body. Or perhaps he was excluded because he had criticized the Board of Liquidation for allowing banks with whom it deposited millions of dollars of the city's tax receipts to pay no interest to the city (after a lengthy campaign, banks finally did begin paying interest), and for favoring certain banks—the Canal, the Whitney, and the Hibernia—with these deposits.

Whatever the reason, his exclusion bothered him. His only child had died. His place in the city mattered. Charles "Pie" Dufour, a Boston Club member and writer who worked for him, said: "Thomson was an ambitious man, always seeking acceptance from the establishment and never quite getting it. He moved in the establishment but always tentatively. . . . He was on a tightrope, a treadmill."

His river campaign allowed him to insinuate himself into the establishment. Once he had brought Butler, Hecht, and Lonnie Pool, the president of the Marine Bank & Trust Company who ruled Carnival as Rex in 1925, to Washington to see President Harding. Harding had listened to a presentation by Kemper and had promised action, but died before he could keep his promise.

Still, when a dinner was given celebrating the twentieth anniversary of Thomson's ownership of the *Item,* the governor, the Louisiana congressional delegation, present and former mayors, even a senator from Wisconsin attended. Blanc Monroe and Jim Butler did not. Nor did a single person associated with the *Times-Picayune.* It was a snub from the social elite, a snub that only made Thomson more determined to penetrate into the city's decision-making. His knowledge of the river was his battering ram. For the report Kemper gave him in January 1927 was not good news.

The weakest levees in the state lay just thirty miles upriver, Kemper said, outside the jurisdiction of the Orleans Levee Board. A crevasse there could send water pouring into the city from the rear as had happened in 1849, the last time New Orleans had been flooded. New Orleans had a rear protection levee but "it offers protection in name only," Kemper warned. As for the city levees themselves, the river had already begun to strain them. At a ferry landing uptown a hole in the levee had developed and needed immediate attention, while four and a half miles of city docks fell below the Mississippi River Commission's grade for height. But the biggest problem was the new Industrial Canal, built to connect the river and Lake Pontchartrain. The height of its locks, Kemper said, "was based on a miscalculation in slope. The Mississippi River Commission and the Dock Board have concluded there is a four foot drop over the 10 miles between Carrollton and the canal. It is no more than one foot, eight inches. A flood equal to that of 1922 will overtop the locks by four feet."

The turbulence this would generate could rip the locks, and the levee there, apart. They required immediate attention.

Kemper also explained that, paradoxically, a great flood would not threaten the city because it was certain to overwhelm levees upriver. The river would then spread over the land, lower the flood height at New Orleans, and eliminate any danger for the city, although it would devastate the rest of the lower Mississippi valley. Kemper's chief concern, in terms of New Orleans, was actually a lesser flood, one higher than 1922 but not so high as to breach levees above the city.

Thomson had made Kemper his personal engineering expert and put his newspaper's weight behind him in many fights, but he chose to reject Kemper's insistence that a great flood would not threaten New Orleans. The rejection would have vast impact. Meanwhile, he informed members of the Safe River Committee of Kemper's opinion on the narrower question of the city's levees.

Soon after Mardi Gras a Dock Board engineering report also warned of trouble: "The levee between Canal Street and Esplanade Avenue is not up to Mississippi River Commission grade and section." Those blocks included the entire French Quarter. It added, "Serious settlements have taken place [here]. . . . Mistakes at this time would have far-reaching consequences."

By mid-March the public was paying close attention to the river. People needed no report; they simply climbed the levee and looked. The river was high and angry. Hundreds of men were working on the levees, and hundreds more were being hired. Railroads were putting their own crews to work on the levees as well. In one area railroad crews built an emergency bulkhead; within weeks waters washed part of it out. It was repaired, sacked, and additional revetment added.

In late March, John Klorer, the city councilman and former river engineer, personally inspected the levees, walking their entire length on both banks for the third time in four weeks. Though an elected official, he gave his report to Thomson, not to the mayor or the council. He cited "decided improvement" overall, but noted that 7,000 feet of the levee line still fell short of safe margins and "should be taken in hand promptly."

On April 4, in St. Bernard Parish, twenty-four-hour patrols of the levee by armed guards began. The 1922 crevasse at Poydras remained fresh in the minds of everyone in the parish. Meanwhile, the Weather Bureau forecasts of flood stages continued to rise, from 20.8 feet to 21.5 feet, 4 inches below the record.

On April 8, with the flood approaching a record upriver, the New Orleans chapter of the Red Cross began building two hundred boats and setting up forty-one relief stations to be scattered throughout New Orleans to feed and clothe thousands of people, in case of the worst.

No word of this activity appeared in any New Orleans paper. As the Mississippi grew more threatening, New Orleans papers gave it less space. This lack of news attention was no accident.

THREE MEN determined what went into newspapers in the city. None of them cared about the news per se; they used their papers like artillery, to pound their enemies and advance their own goals. Thomson was one of the three. Robert Ewing, owner of the *States* and newspapers in Monroe and Shreveport, was another. Unlike Thomson, Ewing had no interest in joining clubs; his interests lay elsewhere. Both a Democratic national committeeman and a ward leader, he had been described by one mayor as "the most insatiable patronage grabber" in New Orleans.

The third man was Esmond Phelps, a member of the Boston and Louisiana Clubs who was rumored to have been Comus. A past president of the Louisiana bar and southern amateur tennis champion, Phelps had red hair, a good-natured disposition that hid his competitiveness, and a belly just beginning to go to fat. In the city's legal community only Blanc Monroe had more stature. Phelps had led the effort in 1924 to defeat Thomson's wife, Genevieve, when she ran for Congress; Phelps had convinced even society women who were active in politics to oppose her. But his first love was the *Times-Picayune*, whose board he controlled. His father, Ashton Phelps, had edited the paper (his great-grandson would be its publisher in the 1990s), and, though nominally Esmond's authority was limited to his board seat, he spent hours at a time at the paper several days a week.

Yet Phelps, Ewing, and Thomson cooperated on one thing: suppressing news unfavorable to the city. In 1924, when a Greek sailor with bubonic plague was cared for in a New Orleans hospital, all the papers helped the New Orleans Association of Commerce control the flow of news both within and outside the city. In 1925 the papers helped the Association of Commerce circulate seventy-two different articles boosting New Orleans, including one claiming that it was one of the healthiest cities in America. In 1926 the newspapers and the Association of Commerce again agreed "to refrain from publishing anything in connection with" a controversial port policy.

On April 8, as the local Red Cross began building boats, Thomson called a meeting of the Safe River Committee, including Phelps and Ewing, "to avoid the dissemination of incorrect or alarming information." The next day every paper ran a reassuring page-1 story. The headlines in Thomson's own paper read, "River Warning Not Alarming; Levees Can Care for Stage Expected to Exceed 1922 Level." The idea was to calm the city.

The city was not calm. No headline, or lack of one, could hide the Mississippi River. "River rats" had built shacks on stilts on the batture, outside the protection of the levees. The rising water was isolating these shacks, and wakes from barges and ships threatened to swamp them. In 1922 an anonymous telegram published in the papers had warned, "The next boat that comes down at . . . high speed will need two pilots, as we intend to kill the first one." This year there were no such warnings. There were simply rifle shots. The boats slowed. Then, on April 13, a sudden rise swept hundreds of shacks away. No word appeared in any paper, yet news, and fear, spread—particularly among the elite, since many river rats worked in the fine homes of St. Charles Avenue.

An exodus began, especially to the Gulf Coast and the high bluffs of Natchez. Business died. Those in power clamped down even tighter control on the news. But the river still rose.

Isaac Cline headed the U.S. Weather Bureau office at New Orleans. A former physician and an art collector who lived in the French Quarter, in 1900 he had run the Weather Bureau office in Galveston, then the largest city in Texas, when a hurricane had swept the sea over it. Estimates of the number of dead ranged from 3,000 to 12,000. Waves had pounded Cline's own home to pieces; he, his wife, and their children were on the second floor when it collapsed. His wife had drowned, but he had kicked his way to the surface gasping for air, and pulled his two young daughters onto his roof. They were washed onto the mainland and survived. Transferred to New Orleans, in 1903 he had issued warnings of a then-record 21-foot river stage. Superiors in Washington had ordered him to withdraw his warning. He had refused, insisting that his warning would save lives. The river reached 20.7 feet even with crevasses upstream and he did save lives. Even so, only intervention from Louisiana's congressional delegation prevented his being fired. In 1915 his insistent warnings of another hurricane had saved hundreds more lives, and he had become a local hero.

Now, in early April, Cline began issuing "Flood Bulletins."

The papers did not publish them.

Furious, he called reporters into his office on April 14, even before the terrible Good Friday storm, and demanded to know why. They said they were writing the stories but their editors weren't printing them. Cline called a man involved in the censorship and charged: "You're jeopardizing lives of men, women, and children. You may control the press but we have the mails, the telegraph, the telephone, the radio and you cannot suppress the distribution of flood warnings. We are going to see to it that the people behind the levees are warned that they are threatened with great danger."

Cline was not worried about New Orleans itself. He agreed with Kemper that a great flood—and this already looked like a great flood—would break levees hundreds of miles upriver and relieve the city. But people in vulnerable areas read and relied on New Orleans papers; the lack of warning there would create a false sense of security. His angry protest was conveyed to Thomson, who relented somewhat, printing that afternoon, "Heavy Rains Raise River; Weather Bureau Advises of Rising Stages . . . The bureau urged 'all persons interested to take necessary precautions against still higher stages during the next two weeks.' "

The story did not satisfy Cline. Late that afternoon he met with business leaders to demand honesty in future stories. They assured him of it. They were lying. Nor did they tell him that Thomson had already called an emergency meeting about the river. Butler had been out of the city and had sent Canal Bank Vice President Dan Curran, a close friend of LeRoy Percy, as his representative. Hecht and Pool had attended. In that meeting, for the first time, Thomson had talked seriously about dynamiting the levee. If the situation worsened, he said, he would travel to Washington and see the president himself.

No one had protested against the enormity of the act Thomson was suggesting. It was illegal, and it would destroy the livelihoods of thousands of people. Nor had anyone questioned the authority, right, or ability of those in the meeting to perform this illegal act. Nor, although they had been discussing the most public business, business that involved federal, state, city, and parish governments, had anyone protested the fact that no public official had been present.

After the meeting, Thomson had informed levee board president Guy Deano, who in turn privately advised Klorer, the city councilman and river engineer, "The Emergency Committee had conferences . . . and plans have been worked out by them."

That evening it began to rain again. The Good Friday storm had begun.

IN NEW ORLEANS rainwater must be pumped *up,* over the levees, into either the river or Lake Pontchartrain, both of which are often higher than much of the city. In 1913 an engineer named Albert Baldwin Wood designed and built pumps capable of moving 47,000 cubic feet of water a second, roughly half the low-water flow of the Mississippi itself, through subterranean canals buried under the "neutral ground," the city's term for the tree-lined islands that transform so many New Orleans streets into boulevards. These remarkable pumps were copied around the world, and still operate today.

But on April 15, Good Friday, lightning temporarily knocked out some of the pumps, and the rains that delivered 14.96 inches of water in eighteen hours put 4 feet of water in part of the city. It was the fifth storm since January more severe than any storm in the preceding ten years. Even after the pumps finally cleared the water, there was chaos. Many streets were paved with wooden blocks; the blocks had floated away, leaving an impassable checkerboard quagmire. Every basement downtown, including the vaults of every bank, still held several feet of water.

It was only a hint of a real flood, without the roar of a great crevasse, without the power of the river undermining buildings and roaring through streets like some nightmarish monster. The city shook with fear.

While the torrents were still falling, Marcel Garsaud, a former Army colonel and levee engineer who was now manager of the Dock Board, called Hecht, the board president, and said they needed to discuss the river situation immediately. Hecht also asked Butler, Pool, who that year headed the New Orleans Clearing House Association, several other bank presidents, and General Allison Owen, president of the Association of Commerce to come to an emergency meeting.

Thomson was not invited. Possibly Hecht kept him out because he was not a member of the inner sanctum. Possibly Garsaud objected because of Garsaud's bitter feelings toward Kemper, whom Thomson might have brought. Garsaud was prickly, bristled at any offense, and although the two engineers agreed on policy, Kemper had recently rebuked him for his mistaken calculations on the industrial canal, and for playing "politics" and creating discord, writing, "I have been in this game, Colonel, much longer than you have. For a long time I fought a lone fight. . . . You have set us back several years."

Those who did belong to the inner sanctum gathered in Hecht's office at the Hibernia Bank. Outside, the rain lashed the windows; the wind shook them. Hecht, a cigar aficionado, lit one. So did several others. The smoke filled the room. The windows were opaque with condensation, isolating them from the world outside.

Garsaud announced that he had just talked to Cline. The rain could continue for hours. "If the levees up river hold, the Mississippi could reach a stage of 24.5 feet here," Garsaud said. "In my opinion a stage above 24 feet could well cause a crevasse." Then Garsaud suggested that they could eliminate any doubt about the safety of New Orleans by dynamiting the levee elsewhere, if the men present deemed it wise.

Everyone present knew that Thomson had already begun planning for this eventuality, but it was not his decision. It was theirs. They were bankers, mostly. Bankers had a history of taking charge in city crises. During the 1905 yellow fever epidemic, the U.S. Surgeon General refused to help the city without a guarantee of $250,000. The mayor had lacked the authority to make any such commitment. Charles Janvier, then president of the Canal Bank, a member of the Board of Liquidation, and chairman of the state Democratic Party's Central Committee, had made two telephone calls, then gave the guarantee, and federal resources had poured into the city to fight the outbreak.

Now all of the bankers present had received wires from correspondent banks in New York and elsewhere, inquiring about the city's safety. Implicit in the inquiry was the question of investment risk, a life-and-death question to them.

Butler had replaced Janvier at both the bank and the Board of Liquidation. Nothing could be done if he opposed it. Butler was the key.

IN MANY WAYS James Pierce Butler was the coldest of the men present. He stood six feet five inches tall, with broad gangly shoulders, a balding head, and a deep voice. His size intimidated. He grew up on Ormond, the family plantation in Natchez, Mississippi. Five ancestors had been officers in the Revolutionary War, two of them generals. His mother often attended balls in New Orleans and took him to the opera there; sometimes they stayed in the city for months. Her brother-in-law was Dr. William Mercer, one of the city's most popular and wealthy citizens. (Before the Civil War, Mercer had routinely paid off the debts of his friend Henry Clay; during the war he used his well-known Union sympathies to shield his Confederate friends; after the war, in 1872 he helped found the krewe of Rex, when he hosted Grand Duke Alexis of Russia on gold dinner service.)

Butler's upbringing was also earthy. In spring he planted and learned what turned soil smelled like. In summer he walked down rows of shoulder-high cotton through a sea of waving white bolls. In winter he butchered hogs, felt warm blood on his hands, hung the flesh in the smokehouse. He matured early. When he was only thirteen, his father fell ill. His older brother Pierce was away at Tulane. Jim handled the plantation. When Pierce graduated from Tulane and went on to the Sorbonne, Jim said, "You all make a mighty fuss over Brother, and I will do better."

Jim also went to Tulane, then Tulane Law School. But instead of pursuing the law, he went into banking. He did well. While he was rising at the Canal Bank, he also rose socially and inherited Mercer's gleaming white marble mansion on Canal Street. The mansion was thick with rich woods, elegant molding and wainscoting, extravagant sconces, chandeliers, and ceiling medallions. Jim sold it to the Boston Club, which has occupied it ever since. After becoming president of the bank, the largest in the South, he also became president of the Boston Club.

Yet Butler's social position came entirely from his presidency of the bank and his family background, and not from charm or friendships. He had no intimates and no confidants, male or female, not even his brother, who had become the popular dean of Tulane's Newcomb College. Indeed, before Jim became Boston Club president, Pierce had resigned from the club, calling it "really quite off my beat." Because their wives had genuine contempt for one another, Butler almost never even saw his brother. Nor did Jim confide in his wife, whom he had married when she was in college; he was already successful and considerably older. She liked the security. Her father was an alcoholic who had drunk his way through a fortune, forcing her mother to take in boarders; Butler's wife became a demanding woman, willful, greedy, and grasping.

As a result, Butler lived a lonely existence. His daughter married impetuously to escape the house. Even his Boston Club presidency was unpleasant. By tradition, club presidents served two consecutive one-year terms. Butler grew tired of a feud between members associated with the Whitney and Canal Banks and, alone in club history, served only one. Herman Kohlmayer, then a rising New Orleans banker and later chairman of the Chicago Commodities Exchange and member of the board of the New York Stock Exchange, recalls: "He was an unattractive man, unattractive mentally. I would take a drink with the other fellows, young as I was, but it was impossible with Butler. He had no fun in him."

Butler filled his time working long hours; when he was home, he ruminated, sitting alone in the solarium of his St. Charles Avenue home, saying little. One thing he did have was a rootedness, a sense of place. Returning from New York on the Crescent Limited once, he sat with a prominent New Orleans architect and told him: "I really want to build a beautiful building before I die. I want it to be the bank's building."

The building was under construction in 1927; it would be his legacy. (Seventy years later the *New Orleans Times-Picayune* called it "elegant" and "distinguished for its fine construction.") Another legacy would be his decision on dynamiting the levees.

BUTLER TURNED to the men in the room and said they needed information on several issues, some legal, some technical. Addressing Garsaud, he said, "You say 'if the levees above us hold.' There is little chance of that, is there?"

"They will probably not hold," Garsaud conceded. "But the pressure will be intense here in any event. It is possible that water could flow out through any levee breaks and return to the river."

Hecht raised another point. Even if no river water entered New Orleans, the flood could destroy the city financially. People were building boats, tying them to their porches, stocking groceries. To liquidate inventories, wholesale suppliers were cutting prices in half and begging customers around the country to buy. Daily, hundreds of thousands of dollars were being withdrawn from banks. If the fear grew great enough, if a run developed on a bank, it would hurt, and perhaps even destroy, weaker banks. Short-term credit was disappearing, period. Long term, if the nation's businessmen lost confidence in the safety of New Orleans, serious damage could result. Rival ports were hungry. The Illinois Central recently had—for the first time—shipped a load of molasses from Gulfport, Mississippi. U.S. Steel was planning to ship exports out of Mobile, Alabama.

Pool's bank was the most vulnerable in the city; he had aggressively loaned money to sugar planters. A crevasse on the river's west bank could destroy them, and his bank. Dynamiting the levee on the east bank might also relieve them. Pool argued: "The people of New Orleans are in such a panic that all who can do so are leaving the city. Thousands are leaving daily. Only dynamite will restore confidence."

Butler knew the power of the river. As a boy, he had watched his father cut a canal from St. Catherine's Creek on their property to the Mississippi. It had been a mistake. The creek quickly grew into a powerful river itself and scoured out acres of their plantation. The creek had awed him, and the Mississippi had seemed like God. He knew what floods were.

Now they were discussing purposefully loosing the Mississippi River on their neighbors. It was a horrible thing, a thing that ran against everything he had been raised to believe. How real was the threat to New Orleans? The threat to its business was real enough, but how real was the threat of the river? Or did it matter?

"I believe," Butler said coolly, not explicitly deciding but allowing momentum to gather more force, "the appropriate step at this point is to involve the authorities."

GARSAUD WENT from his meeting with Butler and Hecht to see Mayor Arthur O'Keefe. O'Keefe had become mayor a year earlier after the death in midterm of Martin Behrman, who had dominated the city for the preceding twenty-four years. O'Keefe, by contrast, was a weak figure, a huge fat man who had triumphed in patronage wars over other ward leaders and would not even seek reelection. The city's elite held him in contempt. Speaking at the dedication of Le Petit Theater du Vieux Carré, whose creation by society women signaled the beginning of the restoration of the French Quarter, O'Keefe declared, "This is a wonderful thing for New Orleans, the kind of thing we should be proud of, like our new garbage incinerator." He was also, as Behrman had been before him, particularly susceptible to bankers' influence. Though both were products of a city machine called simply "the Ring," Behrman had been a founding member of the Association of Commerce and vice president of the American Bank, the most political of all the banks. As soon as O'Keefe became mayor, the same bank immediately named him to a vice presidency.

O'Keefe understood the stakes in the flood. Thomson had already spoken to him. Now Garsaud repeated his warning that, if the levees above the city held, the river would exceed a 24-foot stage. O'Keefe called in Klorer, whom the levee board had just given emergency authority over all city levees. Klorer spoke of the panic already flooding the city. Hundreds of families were fleeing to the Gulf Coast. A large Pythian convention was in town. Many conventioneers had arrived in the morning, looked up at the hulls of ships above the tops of the houses, then taken the next train out.

O'Keefe agreed to do whatever the bankers recommended.

Meanwhile, the New Orleans papers continued trying to keep the city calm, reporting only that "more than five inches" of rain had fallen that Good Friday. Triple that amount had. The papers also quoted George Schoenberger, chief engineer for the state of Louisiana, saying, "I am resting easy tonight."

Far above the city, levees along the Mississippi's tributaries were washing out one after another, like dominoes. On Saturday, April 16, the first mainline levee on the Mississippi yielded, at Dorena, Missouri.

Ironically, that helped to confirm Kemper in his opinion that upriver levees could not hold, and that therefore the city of New Orleans was in no danger. But no one sought Kemper's opinion. Garsaud was a bitter rival and had Hecht's ear. Thomson already knew his opinion and did not find it useful. And even if Kemper was right about the river, that did not answer the bankers' concerns about investor confidence.

On Sunday, April 17, there was another exodus from the city, but this one included some who were not fleeing. Garsaud and O'Keefe got on a train for St. Louis. They would meet with the Mississippi River Commission early Monday morning. Thomson took it upon himself to board a train for Washington, to see the president. O'Keefe had asked Butler to go to Washington but, hearing that Thomson had gone, "Mr. and Mrs. James P. Butler motored to their country home outside Natchez for the weekend," as one paper reported. It would be Butler's last peace for months.

CHAPTER NINETEEN

DYNAMITING THE LEVEE downriver from New Orleans would turn 10,000 people into refugees; depending on the volume of water that was loosed, it could also destroy all of St. Bernard Parish and all of Plaquemines Parish that lay on the east bank of the river. (Both the city of New Orleans and Plaquemines Parish straddle both sides of the river.) Although only a line on a map—no bayou, no canal, no natural boundary of any kind—separated St. Bernard Parish and New Orleans, they had nothing in common. But the river was now making them as intimate as predator and prey.

In St. Bernard, the town of Arabi bordered on New Orleans. None of its handful of streets were paved, but their surfaces of crushed shell hardened like concrete. Drainage was in open ditches along the streets; eels made a home of these ditches and wrapped around the legs of any children who slipped in. For drinking water people still used cisterns, which had been outlawed across the line in New Orleans because they bred mosquitoes.

But Arabi thrived. The largest sugar refinery in the world operated there and employed 1,500 people. Several hundred more jobs came from the stockyards, acres of cattle and pigs, and the largest abattoirs in the South. The smell of blood and rotting meat mixed with the delicious sweetness of the cane. In summer, in the heavy heat of Louisiana, the smells hung in the air like grit stuck to sweat, and drew swarms of rats and clouds of insects.

Arabi also had gambling casinos: the River View, the 118 Club, the 102 Club, the Candlelight Club (a converted grammar school), and, the finest and largest, the Jai Alai Club, with turrets flying pennants like a moorish castle, 3,000 seats, and a magnificent dance floor. The Jai Alai gave away a car a week in a drawing: Henry

James and Tommy Dorsey played there. All the clubs were illegal, all operated openly (indeed, they advertised in the newspapers), and all were clustered within a few blocks of New Orleans. Slot machines, also illegal, were in nearly every bar and grocery store in the parish.

Below Arabi the parish became rural, then marsh. Of St. Bernard's 617 square miles, 544 were swamp or marsh. On the good land Italians grew vegetables and oranges, from which came a wine popular during Prohibition; bootleggers added carbonation and sold it as champagne. The swamp was thick with cypress, oak, hanging moss, and alligators and water moccasins; bayous were covered with velvety green scum. The marsh was a trembling prairie of grass. It appeared solid, but only an experienced man feeling his way with a long pole could walk on it; a wrong step sank a man hip-deep in muck. Plaquemines Parish, below St. Bernard, was similar—a narrow strip of solid land near the ribbon of river, then a marsh that merged gradually with sea, where Eads had built his jetties.

Barren as it seemed, the marsh teemed with fishermen, trappers, and bootleggers, most of them "Islenos." They, their language, and their name came from the Canary Islands in the 1700s, when Spain controlled Louisiana. The largest Isleno town was called Delacroix Island; not actually an island, it was also called "The End of the World." The road stopped there. It had a school but no electricity, no post office, no telephone. Yet in the twenties, the Islenos made good money. Small fortunes came legally, large ones illegally. Louisiana produced more fur for coats than the rest of the United States combined, or Canada and Russia. And St. Bernard produced far more than any other parish in Louisiana. Muskrats, or simply "rats," brought as much as $3 for a top-quality pelt, and the best trappers could bring in 150 pelts a day. The governor made $7,500 a year; the best trappers easily made that much in the season from November to March.

The parish also ran a thriving import business. It imported alcohol. Surrounded by the sea, with an intricate system of waterways that no outsider could navigate, the trappers took their boats out to freighters anchored offshore and loaded as many as 1,000 cases of whiskey onto their fishing boats. Canals and bayous ran all through the parish; along every one of them were homes storing whiskey. Al Capone and lesser gangsters visited St. Bernard, where they were amused by Sheriff L. A. Meraux and his deputies, who charged a toll on all whiskey traversing the parish, and by Manuel Molero, one of the largest bootleggers in the South. Meraux and Molero ran the parish. Both were extraordinary men, and they hated each other.

Meraux could be a charming sophisticate, speak perfect Parisian French, and discuss premier vintages. He could abruptly turn foulmouthed, violent, terrifying. Six feet four inches and at least 300 pounds, he had a big, broad head—dark eyes, a broad forehead, thinning light brown hair, a wide mouth, and chubby cheeks that gave him a baby-faced appearance. He had a kindly demeanor but anger, the kind before which men trembled, could explode from him without warning. "Meraux had a studied, careful ruthlessness," notes William Hyland, a parish historian. "He could be rude, crude, despicable, and disgusting, and the next moment display the polish of a Grandee of Spain." He was also a physician who began his career determined to do good.

After graduating from Tulane Medical School, he studied in London, Paris, and Berlin, then settled at Johns Hopkins University to do research; Johns Hopkins was possibly the finest institution for medical research in the world at the time. When the 1905 yellow fever epidemic struck New Orleans, he returned to help and worked at Charity Hospital. But he then fell victim to yellow fever and almost died, and he never returned to research. He started a practice, and observed. What he saw did not please him. He later said, "I used to study people and mankind disappointed me. I found out what people would stoop to."

He became a ruthless real estate entrepreneur, and the largest taxpayer and landowner in the parish. His appetites were enormous. For breakfast he ate a dozen eggs, piles of biscuits, slabs of bacon. His lunches were light, but at dinner he would eat several whole chickens, then an entire strawberry shortcake, or an entire cream cheese mold. His appetite for money and power was equally enormous. His home, just inside the St. Bernard parish line, was a mansion built in 1808 and once owned by sugar planter Alexander de Lesseps, cousin of the builder of the Suez Canal. It had a colonnaded porch, windows of cut glass, and was called Château des Fleurs—Castle of Flowers—because of the extensive gardens on all four sides of the house. It had a small racetrack in the rear, a walkway to the levee in the front, a gazebo on the levee from which to view the river.

Hungry for power too, he used his medical practice to take it, traveling to the farthest reaches of the parish at all hours and often treating people for free. And wherever he went, he gave lollipops to children. "Every one of those lollipops is a vote," he snorted once. People called him "Doc." He ran for sheriff.

Meanwhile, deputies of his opponents were setting up roadblocks and hijacking liquor shipments, then selling it themselves. Bootleggers, including Doc's younger brother Claude, a former Tulane football star and lawyer, issued public warnings that they would tolerate no more hijackings.

On April 20, 1923, a caravan of three large trucks loaded with Claude Meraux's liquor started toward New Orleans. At a narrow bridge, three deputies ordered them to stop. Two of the deputies were shot. One of the trucks drove over their bodies, killing them.

Claude was indicted as an accessory and fled to Paris. Then Doc was elected sheriff. Claude returned from France, ran for district judge for St. Bernard and Plaquemines Parishes in the next election, and won. The Meraux family now controlled St. Bernard, especially with Doc's ally Leander Perez, who controlled Plaquemines, as district attorney for both parishes. Their opponents writhed in their net, fought back, and tried to impeach both Claude and Perez over charges including "oppression." They survived, and consolidated their power. (A decade later, a second impeachment effort would oust Claude, but Perez' control would last into the 1960s and CBS' 60 Minutes would investigate his sons.)

But Doc was the leader. He was a study in corruption; having started out good, he was truly corrupt. One night he invited a Prohibition agent to join him for his nightly coffee and beignets in New Orleans at the Morning Call. Meraux said, "I heard you take money from people. I heard Manny Molero has you fixed."

"I've got a few friends down there," the agent replied.

Meraux promised him $10,000 a month for advance warning of roadblocks. Prohibition agents had a starting salary of $1,186 a year. But the agent was honest. Meraux, three of his deputies, a New Orleans police captain, and thirty others were later arrested and charged in bootlegging. His deputies pleaded guilty, but charges against him were dropped.

He used his jail as his personal dungeon, made alliances with the most conservative elements of New Orleans society—Blanc Monroe put him on the board of the Whitney Bank, the most conservative in the city—and prospered. He had almost everything.

His one rival in the parish was Manuel Molero, a squat, nearly illiterate Isleno from Delacroix Island, barely fluent in English. But Molero was intelligent, with an eye for arcana; he later devised a complex maneuver to cut oil taxes that was copied by the Chase Manhattan Bank, which learned of it through the Canal Bank. A man who was among New Orleans' most prominent bankers says, "He had absolutely no education, had a terrible Spanish accent you could barely understand. [He and his partner] were the biggest bootleggers around, really thugs, running shiploads of booze. But he was very smart, and very proper in business dealings." Recalls a New Orleans attorney: "Molero was very principled, with a pound-wise as opposed to penny-foolish approach. He could sense long-term advantages. I picture him smoking a cigar, thinking things out, and coming to a conclusion. He stuck with his plan. Determined. He would persevere."

As a young man, Molero bought vegetables in St. Bernard and sold them at a huge profit at the French Market in New Orleans. He bought a truck, then a second one, then a fleet that serviced dozens of New Orleans restaurants and grocers. When Prohibition came, it was only natural that he distribute whiskey—and he sent it even to Chicago.

In the fall of 1926, Perez and Meraux tried to take control of the trappng business from the Islenos. The trappers asked Molero for his help. The result was "the Trappers' War." Perez and Meraux sent a gunboat mounted with machine guns down to Delacroix. The trappers sank the gunboat, killed one deputy, and shot others. The governor refused Meraux's request for help, and in fact became friendly with Molero. The trappers won the war. Meraux never filed any charges against them.

A few weeks later the rising river transformed them all, Meraux, Molero, Perez, and the trappers and fishermen and bootleggers, into allies.

On Monday, April 18, Garsaud and O'Keefe walked into an open hearing of the Mississippi River Commission. Immediately, it went into executive session. While O'Keefe remained silent, Gersaud explained their plan to dynamite the levee and create an emergency spillway near Poydras, the site of the 1922 break. Would the commission approve?

Colonel Charles Potter, commission president, went off the record, discussed the issues with his colleagues, hinted that they would approve if the emergency worsened, then back on the record formally replied that the commission could not even consider the request until three conditions were met. First, the War Department must approve. Second, the State of Louisiana would have to make the request. Third, the city would have to absolve the commission of any liability for damages and arrange to compensate victims of the crevasse fully for any and all losses.

Garsaud and O'Keefe, satisfied, boarded an overnight train to New Orleans. While they slept, a skiff carrying several men approached too close to the levee near Poydras. Guards opened fire. One man was killed, two others wounded. The *New York Times* seemed to shrug: "Residents had been warned not to approach the levees after dark." No New Orleans paper mentioned the killing in St. Bernard. Violence there was common anyway.

The next morning, April 19, the establishment of New Orleans gathered together in City Hall, a magnificent structure bedecked with columns designed by the city's most famous architect, James Gallier. In the splendor of the city council chamber grimly sat the presidents of the Cotton Exchange, the Board of Trade, the Stock Exchange, the Dock Board, the Association of Commerce, the levee board, all the banks, the men who ran the newspapers, and a few individual business leaders. Only one councilman, Klorer, was present, along with the mayor and two congressmen. No representatives of St. Bernard and Plaquemines Parishes, which would be flooded by the proposed crevasse, were invited.

The meeting marked the beginning of an extraordinary week. It began with O'Keefe naming Butler chairman of an ad hoc Citizens Flood Relief Committee, comprised of all the private citizens present. This committee had no legal authority of any kind, but it, and Butler, would take charge of everything involving the flood and New Orleans from then on, including the effort to determine the policy of the United States government.

There was no discussion of the decision to dynamite the levee. It was simply assumed they would pursue that end. Before the week was out, both of Louisiana's senators and several of its congressmen would do Butler's bidding. Butler would even be authorized to sign one congressman's name to any telegram, without checking with him first. O'Keefe also said that he, Pool, and H. Generes Dufour, the attorney for the Board of Liquidation and Hecht's closest friend, would see Governor Oramel H. Simpson, whose reelection campaign was just getting under way.

On April 21, the crevasse at Mounds Landing made clear that the Mississippi River was sweeping everything before it, threatening to reclaim all of its natural floodplain.

The city reacted with panic. The *Tribune* declared on page 1: "Rumors! A rumor was circulated throughout the city that the newspapers of the city were not revealing the entire truth regarding the river and levee conditions; that news was being withheld from the public, that news was being censored. There is no truth in them, of course. The Morning Tribune and The Item are giving readers all the information they possess." The *Times-Picayune* agreed: "There is no reason for alarm in New Orleans. Hundreds of false reports . . . circulated in New Orleans. Needless to say none of these was true. The

Times-Picayune is . . . giving its readers as complete and accurate information as possible."

But the newspapers were ignored. Every day hundreds of people were climbing the levee to see the river. It was angry, wide, high, and fast, swirling in whirlpools, the current sweeping logs, lumber, the bodies of mules and horses past. In some stretches it had risen higher than the levee and was contained by planks backed by thick walls of sandbags. The crest was at least two weeks away.

General Allison Owen, president of the Association of Commerce and a member of the Citizens Committee, publicly declared: "New Orleans is not affected in the slightest degree by the present high level of water in the Mississippi . . . New Orleans feels absolutely safe from any threat of flood from the river." Privately, he worried, "We have never seen such a panic, such an amount of hysteria."

THERE WAS ANOTHER response to the Mounds Landing crevasse as well. Even before it, the Red Cross had established refugee camps, set up a headquarters in Memphis, and transferred all its disaster personnel into the flooded regions. Yet the numbers of refugees—70,000 before Mounds Landing—the geographic reach of the flood, and the disruption of transportation created logistic problems far beyond its capacity to cope. Six governors had beseeched President Calvin Coolidge for help, but he had done nothing.

Now Coolidge had to act. At a cabinet meeting the morning after the crevasse, he named Commerce Secretary Herbert Hoover chairman of a special committee of five cabinet secretaries to coordinate all rescue and relief efforts. Coolidge also gave Hoover authority to issue orders to the Army and Navy.

That was the situation when Thomson arrived in Washington. Despite the crisis, or because of it, he liked being there. It was home to him, more of a home than New Orleans. Here there was no Boston Club, no Louisiana Club, no Mardi Gras krewe. Here was a briar patch in which he could operate, in which many of his New Orleans peers would be lost.

Immediately after the morning cabinet meeting, Thomson presented the case for dynamiting the levee to Secretary of War Dwight Davis and Chief of Army Engineers General Edgar Jadwin. Jadwin resisted. He said levees upriver from the city would surely break, and predicted that the flood stage at New Orleans would not go above 22 or 23 feet "unless there were no further breaks." The city's levees could certainly hold such a stage.

Thomson persisted, citing the panic in the city and quoting Jadwin's predecessor about blowing a hole in a levee. The city had counted on that commitment. Was the War Department now going back on its word? And what was the cost of blowing the levee? It would flood only marsh.

Finally Davis said if he received a formal request to dynamite the levee from the governor of Louisiana, and the federal government was absolved of any responsibility, he would look "sympathetically" upon it. Later that afternoon Thomson met with Coolidge personally and received a more ambiguous response. But it was good enough. He called Butler. Then Thomson headed back to New Orleans.

Early the next morning, Saturday, April 23, Hoover, Jadwin, and Red Cross acting chairman James Fieser departed for Memphis.

While newspapers and radio stations across the United States headlined Hoover's appointment and the plight of Greenville, page 1 of Thomson's *Tribune* recounted a censored version of his meetings with Coolidge, Davis, and Jadwin, not mentioning anything about dynamiting the levee. In St. Bernard people read between the lines. They increased to 500 the number of levee guards, enough to put an armed man every 300 yards twenty-four hours a day. They trusted no one.

TWENTY THOUSAND men were working on the levees between Baton Rouge and New Orleans. Earlier, the *Times-Picayune* had reported the arrival of 640,000 sandbags in the city, supposedly enough to guarantee perfect protection. In an effort to reassure, it now reported the arrival of 6 million sandbags. The news did not reassure.

Business in New Orleans simply disappeared. The streets emptied. One national chain closed its eighteen stores in the city; its employees fled. Parents of out-of-town students at Tulane and Loyola ordered their children back home. Hotels emptied and closed off floors. Hospitals handled only life-threatening emergencies; otherwise they too were empty. The only activity was on the levee. Earlier, hundreds of people had come to the levee each day to see the river for themselves. Now thousands came.

In the Delta the waters were wreaking havoc. The Associated Press reported: "Maj. Allen said that a conservative estimate of the total drownings in the delta region was at least 200 with the possibility that the actual number would be considerably greater. . . . Property damage is estimated at $500,000,000."

There was still a public show of confidence. Parham Werlein, a prominent figure on the Safe River Committee, insisted his sister-in-law remove a boat tied to her backyard porch, saying, "Do you know what people would think if *you* had a boat?"

ON SATURDAY, APRIL 23, an oceangoing molasses tanker rammed the levee on the west bank of the river at the Junior Plantation, forty-three miles below the city. The river began to pour through the break. In New Orleans, people only suspected sabotage. In St. Bernard and Plaquemines people were convinced of it. Levee guards tensed. A reporter and photographer traveling in a small boat down the river to examine the crevasse were fired upon repeatedly. They kept their heads literally down, below the gunwales, choosing to risk a collision with floating wreckage over being shot.

Thomson returned to New Orleans Sunday morning and went straight to Butler's home on St. Charles Avenue to brief him on what had happened in Washington. Butler nodded approval, then called Dufour, whose family owned the tanker that had rammed the levee, for a report on Governor Simpson's position.

Dufour lived a few blocks up St. Charles and came over with disheartening news. Simpson had come to the city on Friday and talked with Klorer, Garsaud, and state engineers. The engineers had presented their reasons for dynamiting the levee. Simpson had asked piercing questions, complained that their predictions of danger to New Orleans were valid only if upriver levees held, and demanded to know what they thought the chances of that were. Their answers had been evasive. Simpson had proved evasive himself, returning to Baton Rouge without seeing the delegation of Dufour, Pool, and Mayor O'Keefe.

On Saturday, Dufour had finally gotten the commander of the National Guard to convince Simpson to see them. The three New Orleans men had ridden the train to Baton Rouge and entered the governor's mansion late Saturday night, just after a delegation of men from St. Bernard and Plaquemines left. Manuel Molero, who had won the trust of the governor, had complained of rumors of the plans to cut their levee. He had pleaded with Simpson not to allow it, not to sacrifice them. Simpson had listened carefully. An election was only a few months away. Flooding country people to save the city did not play well politically in rural Louisiana. Besides, there was something so foul about the idea of the government, which should be trying to protect people, destroying people's livelihoods. The idea left a bad taste in Simpson's mouth. O'Keefe, Pool, and Dufour could not convince him to agree to their plan.

Sunday morning their case weakened further when the *New Orleans States* quoted Isaac Cline, who stated that his prediction of flood height at New Orleans depended upon all levees above the city holding. He declared, "The possibility of danger to the city, with the proper precautions which are being taken, is very remote." Simpson knew Cline's history, knew that Cline would never underestimate the danger. Simpson considered Cline's statement a near guarantee that natural crevasses would relieve the city.

Later in the day Simpson received reports that the Arkansas River levee near Pine Bluff, Arkansas, had washed out. The Arkansas was now rolling south like an invading army, and would soon inundate hundreds of thousands of acres of northern Louisiana. Then came reports that the Glasscock levee above Baton Rouge was already caving into the river, with the crest more than a week away. Both crevasses, while terrible news for Louisiana, would help relieve New Orleans; the failures of those levees also strongly suggested more crevasses would follow.

Butler, Thomson, and Dufour reviewed the situation. There was one politician in New Orleans whom Simpson trusted—Paul Maloney, a former city councilman who had lost the last mayoralty race. Butler considered him a mediocrity. But he needed him now. He called Maloney and told him what was required. Maloney immediately left for Baton Rouge, but soon reported that he could do nothing with Simpson, that Simpson clung to Cline's assessment that danger was "remote," and refused to approve dynamiting the levee.

Cline had become key. Pool knew Cline well; they shared the same tastes in art. Butler asked Pool to call him. Cline later remembered: "Pool pleaded with me to go to Governor Simpson. I told Mr. Pool that I did not consider New Orleans in danger from overflow."

Pool persisted, arguing that the panic in the city and threatened confidence in its safety was every bit as deadly as the river itself. Cline refused to help and hung up.

Pool called back. Didn't Cline worry about "the mass psychology of fear" in the city? Of course he did. But he couldn't lie. He couldn't compromise the integrity of his office. Pool argued that he had the future of the city in his hands. He could save it. And what if he was wrong? The risk to life would be tremendous. Was he so certain of his predictions as that? Cline told Pool to let him think about it and hung up again.

"I knew the levees could not carry the flood waters as far as New Orleans," Cline later explained. "However, the levees were under another branch of Government service and I could not say what the flood would do to the levees. I could only say 'If the levees hold the volume of water now in sight.' "

He called Pool back and said, "You may go to Governor Simpson and tell him that I say there is another rise in the river on the way here and that if the levee is going to be opened to relieve the situation it should be opened at once."

MALONEY CARRIED THIS MESSAGE to Simpson. Simpson had been relying on Cline but could no longer. And, only a few hours earlier, he had received a confidential memo circulated by hand because, the memo stated, it was "too confidential and alarming to telephone or telegraph." It reported that the Mississippi River Commission expected the water from Mounds Landing to "flow back into the river at Vicksburg. It will swing against the Louisiana levees opposite Vicksburg, and a break is anticipated somewhere in Louisiana between Vicksburg and Natchez. . . . [This] probably would send part of the water down the Atchafalaya Outlet and thereby relieve the situation at New Orleans." But if this expected break did not occur, the commission was "genuinely alarmed about the fate of New Orleans."

Maloney asked Simpson how he could take *any* risk with the city of New Orleans. Nearly half a million people there were at the river's mercy.

It was Sunday night. The day had seemed endless. Although Simpson had yet to agree, Butler had just sent Thomson and Garsaud to Vicksburg to meet the members of the Mississippi River Commission there and ask formal permission to dynamite the levee.

Meanwhile, Butler, Hecht, and Dufour were waiting for news in the solarium of Butler's home. It was modest compared to Hecht's home on Audubon Place, and smaller than Dufour's a few blocks away. Hecht and Dufour, both sharp and inquisitive men, traded quips. They were often together, each the other's closest friend. Butler sat, humorless, not participating.

Finally, near midnight, Maloney called from the governor's mansion to say Simpson would agree to the dynamiting of the levee, under certain conditions. He would require in writing: first, a definitive statement signed by engineers that the dynamiting of the levee was absolutely necessary, and there could be no equivocating language about "if the levees hold"; second, legal opinions that he had the authority to order the levee dynamited; third, written promises from the city of New Orleans to compensate victims for all losses.

Butler immediately agreed to all conditions. Simpson, who did not get on the phone, said he would be in the city late the next day, Monday. Butler got busy. With Hecht and Dufour he called upon other men, men of the city's establishment. The city, they believed, depended upon them.

CHAPTER TWENTY

THE MOMENT OF DECISION, the moment before which contemplation had been possible, had come earlier, when Butler had allowed the process to go forward. Since then Butler and those with him had been in continuous motion, and, in motion, Butler had never reconsidered. Now he and the others began pushing to the inevitable conclusion, using all their powers. They had the power of panic. They had the power of money. They had the power of caste. They had the power of the times, when it was believed that men with money not only knew better than others but acted better.

Rumors spread about the plan for dynamiting. It barely kept pace with the fear. On Monday, April 25, the Red Cross asked every nurse to register. A sand boil erupted at the Oak Street levee uptown. At Dumaine Street in the French Quarter, the river began seeping through the levee. The same day, the first break on a Red River levee occurred, further suggesting that New Orleans would be relieved by breaks upriver. In St. Bernard more guards were added.

In New Orleans, for three hours Monday morning Dufour sat in his office with Esmond Phelps, J. Blanc Monroe and his partner Monte Lemann, and two other prominent attorneys; together they drafted a legal opinion to compel the governor to dynamite the levee. They also wrote a separate opinion for Percy Saint, attorney general of Louisiana, to give to Simpson.

Klorer was busy preparing a formal statement of engineers to give Simpson, to be signed by himself, Garsaud, Colonel William Wooten, an Army engineer, and George Schoenberger, chief of the three-man board of state engineers. One of the three state engineers protested that dynamiting the levee would be a "hysterical" and "simply ridiculous" act, and complained that New Orleans was in no danger and that the state engineers were caving in to pressure. He was kept from Simpson, and no newspaper ever quoted him.

In Vicksburg, Thomson and Garsaud met with the Mississippi River Commission onboard the commission's boat, said they represented "all the interests" of the city, and formally requested approval to cut the levee. Colonel Potter asked them to go into the back cabin. Then in private he somberly told his fellow commission members he would "prefer to wait" to see whether the expected crevasses relieved the city, but to refuse permission now that the request had been made would truly panic the city. They had to approve "for the psychological effect."

Potter then called Thomson and Garsaud back and handed them a wire to send to Simpson, with a copy to Butler: "In order to avoid the loss of life and property incidental to . . . an accidental break along the levee line, the Commission believes that it is advisable to create a break in the levee at a predetermined point or points in the State of Louisiana selected by the Governor of the State, or by his authorized agents."

Garsaud returned to New Orleans. Thomson remained in Vicksburg to see Hoover and Jadwin, who were coming downriver and would arrive the next day.

AT SEVEN O'CLOCK that evening Governor Simpson, Butler, Hecht, Dufour, Maloney, and Garsaud met in Butler's office at the Canal Bank. No representative of the city government was present. Butler laid before Simpson the documents—the legal and engineering opinions that the action was necessary, the wire from the river commission, a pledge to reimburse victims—he had requested.

Then they walked out of Butler's office into the bank's boardroom. There Mayor O'Keefe and fifty of the wealthiest men in the city waited, crowding the long mahogany table and crammed in chairs lining the wall. It was fitting that they met there rather than in City Hall. Simpson called the meeting to order, but there was no pretense about who was in charge. It was Butler.

Simpson was grimly formal, surrounded by men who controlled New Orleans and who were demonstrating that they controlled the rest of the state as well. He began to read aloud each document in its entirety. It took him almost an hour to read them, his voice punctuated by an occasional cough, the silence of his audience broken by the sound of a chair shifting or a match being struck or a man leaning backward. It was as if it mattered to say all the words, as if it would make these men understand. But they already understood.

Butler had invited two men to this meeting to represent St. Bernard and Plaquemines. He had not invited Molero, or Meraux, or Perez. Instead, the two men were John Dymond, Jr., and Simon Leopold, men of wealth and position. Their lands lay in the two parishes, but they were not truly of them. Indeed, Dymond belonged to the Boston Club. When Simpson finished, Dymond spoke up. If the levee needed to be cut, he argued, it should be cut above New Orleans. There the cut would relieve the most pressure, and there men were expending immense energies to save the levees. To destroy those levees required no dynamite; if they simply ceased trying to save them, the river would take care of the rest. The water would flow harmlessly into Lake Pontchartrain. Wasn't that morally better than sacrificing St. Bernard and Plaquemines, especially if the sacrifice turned out to be unnecessary?

But all the weight of the room, all the money and power in the room, pressed against Dymond. And he was one of them, only protesting for form. He well knew that the land upriver was far more developed, and a flood there would cause far more expensive damage. The city was not prepared to promise reimbursement for such an amount. The decision had already been made. Dymond asked at least for a written guarantee that damages would be paid.

"We can certainly do that," Butler said. "Write it, and we will all sign it."

Dymond and Leopold left the room. The fifty men remaining in the boardroom waited uncomfortably. Some sat at the table, silent. Others stood in groups of three or four, assuring each other that they were doing the right thing.

Twenty minutes later Dymond and Leopold returned with a resolution, and read it aloud. It stipulated three things. First, signatories "pledge ourselves to the people of the parishes of Plaquemines and St. Bernard to use our good offices in seeing that they are reimbursed by proper governmental agencies, the losses which they may sustain as a result of this emergency work." Second, it proposed a five-member commission to decide all reparations issues. The governor would appoint two members; the New Orleans City Council would appoint two; and the Lake Borgne Levee Board would appoint one. Third, it created a fund of $150,000 to care for the refugees.

Butler agreed quickly. The victims would get only one of five votes on the board to determine damages; the city would get two. The fund of $150,000 guaranteed less than $20 to each refugee for the destruction of his or her home, property, and livelihood. After the river went through, there would be nothing left.

The governor signed first, followed by the mayor and the president of the Orleans Levee Board; then Butler, president of the Canal Bank; Hecht, president of the Hibernia Bank; then the presidents of the other banks. Fifty-seven men signed their names to the pledge. Only six—the governor, the mayor, two councilmen, and two levee board members—were public officials. None of the officials belonged to the Boston Club. They did not have the power.

Of the fifty-one other signatories, thirty-five were members of the Boston Club. Of the sixteen who were not, most—like Edgar Stern, president of the New Orleans Cotton Exchange and son-in-law of Julius Rosenwald, who built Sears into one of the world's largest businesses—were Jews, who could not belong. The five attorneys who signed the legal opinion given to the governor and who lived in New Orleans were even more select. Three of the five reigned over Carnival as Comus; the fourth reigned as Rex; the fifth, Monte Lemann, was Jewish and could not participate in Carnival.

Butler handed Simpson a previously prepared telegram addressed to the Honorable Dwight F. Davis, Secretary of War, with copies to Colonel Charles L. Potter, President of the Mississippi River Commission, and General Edgar Jadwin, Chief of Engineers, United States Army. It read: "I have before me copy of a resolution adopted by the Mississippi River Commission at a meeting of the Commission held at Vicksburg, Mississippi, today, recommending that a break be created in the levee at some predetermined point selected by me. . . . I concur in the views and recommendations of the Commission . . . [and] hereby request and solicit the cooperation and assistance of the Mississippi River Commission, the Chief of Engineers, and the Secretary of War in the accomplishment of this imperative. . . . Your immediate approval and cooperation are requested. Time is a vital element."

Late that evening, April 25, Simpson sent the wire.

TUESDAY MORNING, April 26, the morning after 51 respectable men of New Orleans had pressured the governor to agree to dynamite the St. Bernard levee, another meeting was held at Braithwaite, a small gritty village in the lee of the levee near the St. Bernard–Plaquemines line. The village had a pulp mill, a post office, a seafood canning plant, a general store, and a baseball field and stands. Almost 600 men packed the stands. Most were trappers. A few months earlier, they were prepared to kill each other. Now they had a common enemy.

One man rose and demanded: "Where do they get the authority to drown us out, to deprive us of our homes and our living? We had enough of it in 1922. We won't stand for it. We should die fighting for our rights." Another yelled, "Let's sleep on our shotguns."

Then Meraux stood. He wore knee-high laced boots, olive-drab riding breeches, a khaki shirt, and a Colt six-shooter. Standing there a physical giant, hands on his hips, elbows out, looking impregnable and impassable, he waited for silence. When it came, he spoke calmly. He told them that he sympathized with them and respected their willingness to fight, but warned, "The levees will be broken even if they have to use force of arms to do it." He read a statement from the commander of the Louisiana National Guard: " 'If it is necessary to cut the levee at Poydras, the cut will be made by a corps of engineers backed by the whole state militia, or even United States soldiers, and we will brook no interference whatsoever from the citizens of these parishes.' " Manuel Molero, representing the Lake Borgne Levee Board, had tried to convince the governor and the Mississippi River Commission to block the dynamiting. He had failed. Fighting would stop nothing, only add dead men to the loss of property. *But they could damn well make sure New Orleans paid.*

Meraux did not say that Blanc Monroe, with whom he had had many business dealings, would be handling the claims for New Orleans.

He did say that he knew those people, and all their talk of the moral obligation of New Orleans wasn't worth a pile of pigshit. This guarantee of $150,000 *was* pigshit. Now what they all needed to do was name a committee "to see that we get proper compensation for our property."

Then Perez spoke. "New Orleans is not giving us a square deal," he said. "They have been plotting this action for the past few weeks without giving us due consideration and getting in touch with the proper officials here." The preceding night, the New Orleans bankers had met and picked two men *they* wanted to speak for St. Bernard and Plaquemines, Dymond and Leopold. "They didn't want our committee there! They didn't even want the railroad interests there! . . . This agreement has been signed by members of the Association of Commerce and by New Orleans business and bank representatives. . . . Our levees will be broken by the militia against our will. We have the right to full compensation!"

The mass meeting named a committee to go to New Orleans. Perez was on it, and Meraux had his real estate partner and three of his political puppets named. Molero could not understand English well enough to contend directly with New Orleans bankers and lawyers and was not on it, but his bootlegging partner was.

The men at Braithwaite also sent two wires. One went to the secretary of war: "The citizens and taxpayers of St. Bernard and Plaquemines parishes, in mass meeting assembled, hereby protest to the United States War Department against the granting of any permit for the cutting of the levee below New Orleans and that the necessary relief to the problem of the city of New Orleans be secured by allowing the weak points in the levee above the city of New Orleans, where great and expensive efforts are being made to prevent these breaks, to be washed out with the natural consequences following at these points."

The second wire went to Butler—not to the mayor or the governor—"vigorously protest[ing] against the action taken towards cutting the levee . . . without informing [us] of such steps and against utterly insufficient provision for compensation in full for personal and property damages."

BUTLER READ THE WIRE with concern and informed O'Keefe, who dispatched 350 men—thugs used by ward leaders, not police—armed with rifles and riot guns to guard the New Orleans levee. The possibility of preemptive sabotage was real.

Butler also had a more formal concern. The governor so far had only asked the federal government's approval. He had issued no order to blow the levee. If St. Bernard and Plaquemines complained loudly enough, he might refuse. The committee named at the mass meeting had to be placated.

That afternoon, April 26, Perez and the others from St. Bernard and Plaquemines sat down with Simpson in the boardroom of the Marine Bank. Pool, the bank's president; Butler; Hecht; Dufour; and three others also attended. As they talked, pieces of the Glasscock levee above Baton Rouge were caving into the Mississippi River. If it gave way, the Mississippi's waters would pour west and south over the land, reaching the Gulf through the Atchafalaya basin. This would relieve New Orleans.

The St. Bernard representatives knew nothing of the Glasscock situation. They demanded a legally binding pledge of reparations and scoffed at the $150,000 fund. It insulted every citizen of the two parishes and mocked the credibility of the promise of full compensation. Butler suggested the delegation from New Orleans withdraw to consider the request.

Butler and the other bankers gathered in Pool's office. Together they epitomized the establishment of the city, and of both the Old and New South. The Old South supposedly meant honor. The New

South meant money. Butler straddled the two worlds, the world of earth and honor and myth, and the world of money and reality. Hecht belonged only to the latter.

They spent an hour developing a new proposal, one far more honorable. When they returned to the boardroom, Butler spoke. He could offer no legal guarantee beyond that of the preceding night. There was no procedural vehicle to do so given the emergency. But, he emphasized sternly and formally, "The relief to be afforded is a moral obligation undertaken by each and every person at the meeting held on Monday night, as evidenced by their signed obligation to that effect."

The pledge had been signed by the governor, the mayor, the presidents of the New Orleans Board of Trade, the New Orleans Stock Exchange, the New Orleans Cotton Exchange, the Association of Commerce, and each of the city's banks. They had made this pledge not only to the citizens of the lower parishes, but to the United States government. He had given his word, personally, as well.

But he agreed that the $150,000 was grossly inadequate. New Orleans banks would provide instead a fund of $2 million, to be loaned by New Orleans banks to those in need prior to settlement of any claims. The loans would be repaid by deducting them from the reparation settlements. The city would pay the interest.

Perez and the others knew Butler, knew his reputation, knew his standing. He had never been accused, as Hecht had, of sharp practices. Perhaps they would not have accepted the word of anyone else present, but they accepted his.

They had one other demand. They refused to accept as an arbiter of reparations the commission agreed to the preceding night. This commission was to have only one member from the two lower parishes, and two from New Orleans. They would accept only a nine-member commission; the governor would appoint two members, the city would appoint three, and four would come from the lower parishes. Butler instantly agreed.

At 3:30 P.M., Tuesday, April 26, the representatives of St. Bernard and Plaquemines reluctantly accepted the arrangements. Perez said: "What else can we do? There seems to be nothing else to do but get the people out of the affected area to refugee camps . . . [and] submit peacefully to the sacrifice."

But the deed was not yet done.

IN WASHINGTON, Memphis, and elsewhere much of the story had leaked out. By now the flood filled the front pages of virtually every newspaper in America, from the *Morning Oregonian* in Portland, Oregon, to the *Press Herald* of Portland, Maine, from the *Deseret News* in Salt Lake City to the *Richmond* (Virginia) *Times-Dispatch,* from the *Los Angeles Times* to the *Boston Globe.*

Radio stations outside New Orleans were broadcasting bits and pieces of the truth. Inside the city rumors circulated through the business community, then spread beyond into the city at large. *The levee had been dynamited already. The levee had burst. The New Orleans levees were caving in. The trappers had shot Butler.* The entire city trembled with uncertainty and fear. But the New Orleans newspapers and radio stations stayed silent, giving out no information.

BUTLER, SIMPSON, HECHT, and the other New Orleans men reassembled in the boardroom of the Canal Bank. Shortly after 4 P.M., a wire from the secretary of war reached Simpson there, stating that the approval of General Jadwin, chief of engineers was needed. Butler immediately wired Thomson at the Carroll Hotel in Vicksburg: "Everything is set here to act on receipt of General Jadwin's approval. Tension is terrific. City badly upset for lack of news while incomplete reports coming in by radio. Governor Simpson urges General Jadwin communicate his approval earliest possible minute. Address Governor care of myself, Canal Bank Directors' Room."

Two and a half hours after sending Thomson the wire, Butler, Hecht, the governor, the mayor, and a dozen other men still waited in the boardroom for news. They were all exhausted. At six-thirty Butler suggested they break for dinner and return in an hour.

In Vicksburg, Thomson was not simply waiting. He knew Jadwin and Hoover were aboard the Mississippi River Commission steamer *Control,* so he chartered a speedboat, and, accompanied by Colonel Potter, head of the river commission, Louisiana Senator Joe Ransdell, Representative James O'Connor of New Orleans, and Louisiana Representative Riley Wilson, ranking member of the House Flood Control Committee, he headed upriver to meet them. Ten miles above Vicksburg, they found them. Thomson and the others climbed aboard.

Hoover, taller and better-looking than he appeared in photographs, with a sharp tongue and a penetrating mind, was in charge. He welcomed the party to a set of deck chairs laid out along the stern. But as soon as Thomson began to explain his mission, Hoover grimaced, muttered a curse, and rose. It was too dirty for him. "I have nothing to do with this," he said, walking away. "That's General Jadwin's responsibility."

Thomson made his presentation. Jadwin said he would "not object." That was all Thomson needed. The instant the steamer docked, he sent word all was settled. Then a press report quoted Coolidge denying he had authority to cut the levee. Thomson, Hoover, and Jadwin knew of it. The news was kept from Simpson. No one made any effort to contact Coolidge for clarification; they feared the answer.

At seven-thirty, when the men in the Canal boardroom returned from dinner, they were greeted with Thomson's wire. Still, Simpson refused to issue an order. The room hissed with contained hostility. It was clear Simpson did not want to do this thing. Butler called Vicksburg, tracked Thomson down at his hotel, and told him that the governor demanded an explicit statement directly from Jadwin. They needed it immediately. The city had never been so tense.

An hour and a half later Thomson called back. Jadwin was standing beside him, he said, and was sending a wire addressed to the governor at his official residence in Baton Rouge. But Jadwin refused to get on the phone, explaining, "I wish to confine my responsibility strictly to the terms as written."

Thomson read to Butler and Simpson, "The Mississippi River Commission and Chief of Engineers interpose no objection to a creation of a temporary break in the Mississippi River levee near the site of the old Poydras crevasse . . . for this emergency only." The two Louisiana congressmen got on the phone and confirmed the accuracy of Thomson's reading. Jadwin, though standing beside them, still refused to speak.

Butler, Hecht, O'Keefe, and the others in the room looked coldly at Simpson. He hesitated, but he no longer had any justification to refuse to issue the order—other than his own judgment. How much of this, he perhaps wondered, was over interest rates on city bonds, and how much over real concern for the city. But he would interpose no objection himself. He signed the order that had already been prepared.

It was 9:45 P.M., Tuesday. The levee would be dynamited at noon Friday.

NEAR MIDNIGHT Meraux met with the National Guard commander at Jackson Barracks, located on the Orleans–St. Bernard parish line. Worried that sabotage was still possible and that in that event New Orleans would pay nothing, Meraux pleaded with the commander to send out more levee guards. Leon Sarpy, then a young soldier and later rumored to be Comus, recalls with contempt, "He was on bended knee."

Molero was in Delacroix Island, urging peace. The power against them was too great. This was not like the Trappers War. They could stop nothing. They could only die, and kill.

HUNDREDS OF MILES upriver levees were bursting and 200,000 people were homeless. The rivers were still swelling.

In New Orleans at noon the next day, Klorer, Garsaud, and the state engineers met to pick the precise spot to place the dynamite. A gauntlet of national reporters gathered outside the room. The chief state engineer promised to make the site public, but when they emerged, Garsaud snapped at reporters, "We will not reveal our plans until they are carried out in view of the possibility of trouble in carrying them out should they become known."

The New Orleans Clearing House Association approved the $2 million fund Butler had promised, and sent O'Keefe a resolution it wanted the city council to adopt guaranteeing the banks against any loss. The council adopted it without discussion or change.

New Orleans was finally calming. Perhaps the city would have been safe without dynamiting the levee. But its reputation would not have been. The city's business leaders began a tremendous public relations effort emphasizing the safety of New Orleans.

The Dock Board, headed by Hecht, announced that "the high water should not materially interfere with the commerce of the port." Thomson's *Tribune* declared: "Trade Shows Flood Scare Has Passed . . . Business in the city after a few days decline resumed normalcy. Local stocks rebounded from 2 to 4 pts." Butler sent a wire to his correspondent banks: "Contrary to disquieting rumors . . . New Orleans is absolutely free of Mississippi River flood water. . . . Some of our people have been unduly alarmed but decision of Mississippi River Commission to cut levee twelve miles below New Orleans has removed all danger to city and business and all other activities are moving along in normal manner. New Orleans never has been flooded by Mississippi River and in our judgment never will be. . . . J. P. Butler."

He sent a copy of his wire to every other New Orleans bank and dozens of the city's businessmen, saying: "I would suggest you send a similar telegram to your principal business connections. . . . This is important to help correct the unfavorable publicity that has already gone out."

THAT NIGHT more than twenty men from St. Bernard visited the city, broke into smaller groups, and made several stops. One was at the home of Pool. They rang the doorbell. A servant answered, then came to the dining room quaking, saying seven men were at the door with shotguns. Pool told his family, "Don't any of you move." He left the room and talked to the men. They had come to threaten him. They were visiting all the bankers who had promised to deal honestly with the people whose homes would be destroyed. The men standing in Pool's foyer with guns said they would make sure those promises were kept. Their voices were angry, Pool's calm. But he returned to dinner shaken.

ON THURSDAY, April 28, Hoover rode down the river with Garsaud to examine the site chosen for dynamiting the next day. Their launch was flying the U.S. flag and that of the Corps of Engineers. On the levee a man squatted down and opened fire with a rifle. Hoover and Garsaud ducked low. The man fled.

A few miles downriver Hoover and Garsaud stood on the roof of the pilothouse reviewing maps, then Garsaud, waving maps in both hands and pointing, signaled to newspaper correspondents aboard an accompanying boat, "That's where it will take place."

The site was named Caernarvon, thirteen miles below Canal Street, three-quarters of a mile below the Poydras crevasse of 1922.

FRIDAY, APRIL 29, was like a holiday in the city of New Orleans. In St. Bernard and Plaquemines people were angry and frightened, but resigned. The preceding two days refugees had trudged out of the lower parishes as if leaving a war zone. The National Guard and every major retail store in the city sent trucks and vans to evacuate the 10,000 residents. Trucks were piled high with everything movable. Most of the refugees moved in with relatives in New Orleans, or Gulfport, or the part of St. Bernard—including Meraux's home— that would not go underwater. For those with nowhere else, the city designated the huge warehouse of the International Trade Exchange, known as the Intrex, as a refugee center. Whites had the fifth floor, blacks the sixth. Almost immediately, the city began treating the people as charity cases, patronizing them.

Airplanes flew in circles over the area to be flooded searching for stragglers and taking photographs. The photos were Blanc Monroe's idea. Butler had insisted he represent the city regarding reparations. Butler had chosen well. No one took advantage of Monroe. After the flood, few buildings in the region would remain standing. The aerial photographs would document what had stood there before, and prevent claimants from exaggerating their losses.

The two parishes became increasingly desolate and empty. Delacroix Island was empty, its homes deserted, the shelves of the grocery stores empty. In Violet, where deputies had ambushed Claude Meraux's whiskey shipment and died for their efforts, the buildings stood solemn and empty. At Braithwaite, where the baseball bleachers had held the mass meeting three days before, the only sounds were those of the birds.

NEW ORLEANS meanwhile was enjoying itself. The fine families, as if on a picnic, traveled down to see the great explosion that would send dirt hundreds of feet high and create a sudden Niagara Falls. Cars jammed the road down to St. Bernard, and yachts crowded the river.

But not just anyone could witness the explosion. It required an official permit. The men who had decided to dynamite the levee controlled those permits. Residents of St. Bernard could not witness the destruction of the levee, and their parish. As New Orleans writer Lyle Saxon noted: "Only the privileged with their official permits could pass the National Guard. . . . They came in automobiles, boats, and aeroplanes, eager for the big show."

The national and New Orleans media were there, of course. Every newsreel producer in the country had cameras present. Reporters, several hundred in all, from Memphis, from Houston and Dallas, from Washington, from New York, from Baton Rouge and St. Louis, were there as well. Practically every daily newspaper in the country would run the story on the front page, from Alaska to Florida. But no representative of the *St. Bernard Voice* was allowed a pass.

BUTLER DID NOT GO to the site of the explosion himself. He was too busy. At 2 P.M. in the Canal Bank boardroom he met with twenty-five men who would care for the refugees. Butler of course chaired the meeting. The St. Bernard refugees would need housing, food, and jobs for several months. The water would not be off their land until July at the earliest. Then the land would be empty of everything except caking, fetid mud.

Simultaneously, in Thomson's office the Emergency Clearing House Publicity Committee met. It planned the distribution of copies of Butler's statement about the city's safety to 2,100 banks and businesses around the country. It also scheduled regular broadcasts of Army engineers stating that the city was now entirely safe. One member reported that the Pathé newsreel company had pledged to "be very careful in handling all New Orleans pictures"; the International News Reel Company had promised to "cooperate to the fullest extent." The committee was squeezing even national news organizations into boxes. New Orleans was doing well indeed.

AT NOON, the time scheduled for the explosion, Army, National Guard, and police motorcyclists dashed about while planes circled overhead. Chaos reigned. The crowds were pushed back, then pushed farther back. They waited, then waited more. Finally, word came that the entire area was clear, that the planes had spotted no one in the lower parishes. The hundreds who had come for the show tensed. At two-seventeen the first explosion occurred.

The earth of the levee heaved, then settled. A ditch 10 feet deep and 6 feet wide opened, through which waters began to move slowly.

Two more explosions followed with little effect. Workers used picks and shovels to increase the water flow. Divers went below the river surface to lay more charges. Finally, a reasonable flow developed, but it was no monster crevasse. The dense earth of the levee mockingly recalled Humphreys, who had called the "hard blue clay" of the river bottom impervious to erosion. Much of that clay was in these levees. The crowds went away disappointed. Dynamiting would continue over the next ten days. In all, 39 tons of dynamite would be used, ultimately creating a flow of 250,000 cubic feet of water per second.

While waiting for the first explosion, Meraux had stood on the levee in his laced boots and riding breeches with his revolver in his holster, talking quietly to a group of reporters. "We're letting 'em do it because we can't stop 'em," he said. "You can't fight the Government. I have a hell of a time trying to get my people to see that. A lot of them don't see it yet. They wanted to tell the state of Louisiana to come ahead and cut the levee—but it would be cut over their dead bodies first. We managed to talk them out of that for their own good. . . . And we haven't got a line in writing of any guarantee that we're going to get anything back."

He had only the public expressions from southern gentlemen of their moral obligation. As the explosion sounded, Meraux flinched, then turned around and said, "Gentlemen, you have seen today the public execution of this parish."

THE DAY AFTER the initial dynamiting, the Glasscock levee on the west bank of the Mississippi gave way, easing pressure on New Orleans levees. Simultaneously, the Weather Bureau warned that "the greatest flood of record" was in prospect the following week for the

Ouachita and Black Rivers. Cline, as usual, did not say all he believed, that levees along these rivers would not hold, and their waters would never reach the Mississippi River. They would instead cover the land and roll, like the water from the Glasscock gap, through the Atchafalaya basin to the Gulf. As Kemper and Cline had predicted, the destruction of St. Bernard and Plaquemines was unnecessary. One day's wait would have shown it to be so.

Part Five

THE GREAT
HUMANITARIAN

CHAPTER TWENTY-ONE

Calvin Coolidge was not a fool. In his autobiography he observed that the political mind "is a strange mixture of vanity and timidity, of an obsequious attitude at one time and a delusion of grandeur at another time, of the most selfish preferment combined with the most sacrificing patriotism. The political mind is the product of men in public life who have been twice spoiled. They have been spoiled with praise and they have been spoiled with abuse. With them nothing is natural, everything is artificial."

Coolidge did not have such a mind, and national politics did not come naturally to him. Not only was he an accidental president; he had been an accidental vice president. The 1920 Republican Convention bosses had decided upon Senator Irvine Lenroot of Wisconsin for the post, but delegates, furious at the original "smoke-filled room" that had forced Harding upon them as the presidential nominee, rebelled. When Lenroot was presented, one delegate shouted, "Not on your life!" Oregon was then recognized, with the instruction to nominate Massachusetts Senator Henry Cabot Lodge for vice president. Oregon too balked. In the turmoil of 1919, Coolidge, then governor of Massachusetts, had gained prominence when he had responded to the Boston police strike by declaring, "There is no right to strike against the public safety by anybody, anywhere, anytime." Oregon announced its support not for Lodge but for "another son of Massachusetts—Calvin Coolidge!" He was swept to the nomination.

"Silent Cal," they called him, after Harding's death in 1923 made him president. He was withdrawn. Photographs of him with others seem uncentered, because the pictures were always composed around him but he could not or would not fill the central space. He became more withdrawn after his teenaged son died in agony in 1924 from an infection that developed from a blister. "The power and the glory of the presidency went with him," Coolidge said.

Even before the Mounds Landing crevasse, the governors of Oklahoma, Illinois, Missouri, Kentucky, Arkansas, and Mississippi had begged Coolidge for help and asked him to name Commerce Secretary Herbert Hoover head of a special federal rescue effort. Hoover had repeatedly solved massive logistics problems of feeding hundreds of thousands of people. But Coolidge had done nothing until he had to, until Mississippi Governor Dennis Murphree wired desperately: "Unprecedented floods have created a national emergency. . . . This territory will be water covered one to twenty feet in twenty four hours contains population 150,000. . . . Highways covered. . . . Railroad operations suspended. . . . Beyond capacity local and state agencies to relieve and control."

Finally, at 10:30 A.M. on April 22, Coolidge had called a cabinet meeting and named Hoover chairman of a special committee of five cabinet secretaries, including Treasury Secretary Andrew Mellon and Secretary of War Dwight Davis, to handle the flood emergency.

Hoover would spend sixty of the next seventy-one days in the flooded territory. For nearly all that time he would dominate the nation's front pages, newsreels, and radio waves. The flood would both test his theories about society and advance his own ambitions. For if Hoover did not have the political mind Coolidge described, he had ambition even greater than that of most politicians. That ambition had been sidetracked. The Mississippi River was offering Hoover his main chance, and he intended to seize it.

HERBERT HOOVER was a brilliant fool. He was brilliant in the way his mind could seize and grapple with a problem, brilliant in his ability to accomplish a task, and brilliant in the originality, comprehensiveness, and depth of the political philosophy he developed. He was a fool because he deceived himself. Although considering himself as objective and analytical as science itself, in reality he rejected evidence and truths that did not conform to his biases, and he fooled himself about what those biases were. He was, as former President and then-Chief Justice William Howard Taft described him, "a dreamer . . . [with] grandiose ideas."

Yet by the time Hoover arrived in Washington, the press was calling him both "the Great Humanitarian" and "the Great Engineer." It was a time when those two occupations were considered in some ways synonymous.

Born in 1874 in West Branch, Iowa, amid rolling hills thirty miles from the Mississippi River, Hoover grew up influenced by two traditions: the silence and community of Quakers and the rationalism and purpose of engineering. He was also raised in loneliness. An orphan, separated from his siblings and shifted from one relative to another, his childhood was spent on edge, and it must have seemed that any misstep would cause him to be sent away. He grew up awkward and shy, obsessed both with how others saw him and wedded to his private thoughts. The one constant was the Quaker meeting; even there his chief memory was loneliness and "the intense repression" forced upon "a ten year old boy who might not even count his toes."

At eleven he was sent to an uncle in Oregon. From Iowa he took not much more than the two woven sayings given him by his mother, which he nailed to the wall of his new room. "Leave me not, neither forsake me, Oh God of my salvation," said one; "I will never leave thee nor forsake thee," said the other.

Only at Stanford University did he finally find a home. Though he failed the entrance exam twice and won only conditional admission, once there he thrived emotionally and academically. He met his wife, Lou Henry, there; he was studying mining and she was the only woman studying geology. Stanford became, said his classmate and longtime intimate Will Irwin, "a kind of complex with him." He would later call the school's presidency his "lifetime ambition."

He also had other ambitions. If unable to make small talk socially, when fixed on a task he was neither shy nor timid, but confident and focused. As a young mining engineer on the violent and corrupt frontiers of turn-of-the-century Australia, China, and Siberia, he thrived as never before. "God deliver me from a fool," he once said. "I would rather do business with a rogue any day if he has brains." He helped to find and develop fabulously profitable mines, and during the Boxer Rebellion both he and his wife saved other lives while risking their own. When he was twenty-seven, Leland Stanford's brother called him "the highest paid man of his age in the world." When he was thirty-seven, a London mining periodical called him "a wizard of finance." At forty he owned a share of mines and oil fields in Alaska, California, Romania, Siberia, Nigeria, Burma, Tierra del Fuego, including Russo-Asiatic Consolidated, the Inter-Argentine Syndicate, the Inter-Siberian Syndicate, and Northern Nigeria Tin Mines.

But money no longer mattered so much to him. Years before, he told Stanford president David Jordan he had "run through his profession." And he was lonely still. In 1912 he confided to a young friend: "The American is always an alien abroad. His own heart is in his own country, and yet there is less and less a niche for him when he returns. . . . [In America] the esteem one hopes to build among one's associates would not be wasted. . . . I have got to the stage now where I am playing the game for the game's sake, as the counters don't interest me anymore. I am disgusted with myself." He told Will Irwin he was "as rich as any man has much right to be." He wanted to "get in the big game somewhere. Just making money isn't enough."

HOOVER'S INTEREST in "the big game" came partly from his Quaker upbringing, partly from his engineering background, and partly from raw ambition. Both engineering and the Quakers taught self-examination, a very personal truth, and responsibility to society, and engineering then represented more than simply science. It encompassed a revolutionary way of looking at the world, a kind of rationally ordered justice. Hoover preached this new gospel and served as president of three different engineering societies.

Hoover was so convinced of the moral purity of engineers that he told a friend who was writing a novel in which the villain was an engineer, "But you are trying to make a villain of him which won't do." In a mining textbook he observed, "Engineering is the profession of creation and of construction, of stimulation of human effort and accomplishment." He said engineering's "exactness makes for truth and conscience."

Indeed, Hoover matured during a period when his profession's growth was geometric and its sense of purpose messianic. From 1880 to 1920, the number of engineers in the United States zoomed from 7,000 to 136,000; in 1930 it reached 226,000. In 1913 the *Atlantic Monthly*—ironically, just as the certainty of engineering was yielding to the uncertainty of Einstein and Freud—proclaimed "machinery is our new art form," and praised "the engineers whose poetry is too deep to look poetic" and who "have swung their souls free . . . like gods."

The explosive growth of engineering changed America. Most obviously, it changed manufacturing. Eads had played some small role in that change, with his demands for precision and consistency so unheard-of that he imposed science on steelmaking, formerly an art, as Carnegie himself conceded in 1910. As enormous enterprises employing thousands of people became the rule, owners also began to think in terms of "scientific management." Frederick Taylor invented the term. A genius of efficiency, he designed a tennis racket for himself and won a national championship with it, then designed a new golf driver and putter, which was outlawed for tournament play. He designed more efficient factories and distribution systems, and he tried to design society, saying, "The same principles can be applied with equal force to all social activities: to the management of our homes, the management of our farms, the management of the business of our tradesmen, large and small, of our churches, our philanthropic institutions, our universities, and our governmental departments." He proposed "[h]armony, not discord. Cooperation, not competition."

"Taylorism" spread rapidly. The Harvard Business School opened in 1908 to teach scientific management skills; one of its founders was Frank Taussig, a nationally known economist and son of Eads' partner; as a boy he had called Eads "Uncle."

This revolution of the rational clearly influenced Hoover. Engineers claimed scientific management meant not only improved profit margins but salvation for humanity. It was a faith, a religion. The president of one engineering society declared, "[M]etaphysics has practically ceased to be considered, and empirical science is universally acknowledged as the source of all human progress . . . , the herald that brings joy to the multitudes . . . , their redeemer from despairing drudgery and burdensome labor." Said another, "The golden rule will be put into practice by the slide rule of the engineer."

Waste itself was evil, a great burden, and engineers were determined to stamp it out for the betterment of humanity. Eads had called increasing efficiency "a principle so full of benefit to humanity [as to] constitute a theme worthy of the highest effort of the philanthropist." In 1910 one engineering journal proclaimed, "The Millennium will have been reached when humanity shall have learned to eliminate all useless waste."

To eliminate waste, of course, technocrats had to have more power. As Taylor said, "The shop, and indeed the whole works, should be managed not by the manager, superintendent, or foreman, but by the planning department."

As a corollary of this new philosophy of management, engineer-philosophers also rejected the ruthless—and wasteful—competition of Social Darwinism in favor of a rational allocation of resources and goods. Hoover himself denounced brutal competition and waste: "By some false analogy to 'the survival of the fittest' many have conceived the whole business world to be a sort of economic 'dog eat dog.' . . . Industry and commerce are not based upon taking advantage of other persons. Their foundations lie in the division of labor and the exchange of products. . . . [A] great area of indirect economic wrong and unethical practises spring up under the pressure of competition and habit." The result was "economic waste through destructive competition, strikes, booms and slumps, unemployment, through failure of our different industries to synchronize and a hundred other causes which directly lower our productivity and employment."

Some engineers, in the wake of the slaughter of World War I, even redefined democracy. Henry Gantt, a prominent Taylor disciple, bluntly repudiated "the average politician's conception of democracy. His is the debating-society theory of government . . . [policies determined] not according to the laws of physics but by majority vote. . . . Real democracy consists of the organization of human affairs in harmony with natural laws." Thorstein Veblen, a Stanford faculty member whom Hoover knew, talked of engineers forming a "directorate" and leading a revolution for "a more competent management of the country's industrial system. . . . As a matter of course, the powers and duties of the incoming directorate will be of a technological nature. . . . The old order has most significantly fallen short . . . on the avoidance of waste and duplication of work; and on an equitable and sufficient supply of goods and services to consumers."

Who better to spread such rational analysis through the culture than Hoover? He was, said Morris Cooke, a prominent engineer-philosopher, "the engineering profession personified."

HOOVER HAD FIRST gotten into the big game in a large way by feeding occupied Belgium during the war. (Helping him were a select handful of young men of America's elite, including several Rhodes scholars and William Alexander Percy.) To succeed, he had manipulated two warring Great Powers, Britain and Germany, which both initially opposed his effort. He had done so largely by using the press, and he subsequently told the *Saturday Evening Post* "the world lives by phrases."

When America entered the war, Hoover returned to Washington. Woodrow Wilson named him food administrator, giving him vast if indirect powers over everything from pricing to distribution. He performed successfully enough that Louis Brandeis called him "the biggest figure injected into Washington life by the war." After the war, he ran a European relief program that fed millions. He used power well. After Polish soldiers had executed thirty-seven Jews, he ordered the Polish government to end such incidents. Since he could halt food shipments there, the government obeyed. John Maynard Keynes called him "the only man who emerged from the ordeal [of the peace conference] with an enhanced reputation."

In the aftermath of war, in Europe and America intellectuals on both right and left were asking questions about the nature of society. Hoover, as head of the American Engineering Council, entered the debate by injecting his own ideas, which merged those of the engineering profession, the Quakers, and Edmund Burke. He called for "abandonment of the unrestricted capitalism of Adam Smith," condemned "the ruthlessness of individualism," called for "ordered liberty," bemoaned "the social and economic ills" caused by "the aggregation of great wealth," and argued, "No civilization could be built or can endure solely upon the groundwork of unrestrained and unintelligent self-interest." His answer to wasteful competition was "associational" activity in which producers in each industry cooperated to cut waste and match supply and demand. Hoover's formulation answered the assault from the left on the brutality of industrialism and capitalism while recognizing some truth to the left's charges; simultaneously, he rejected mass rule, demanded room for individual initiative, and welcomed rule by an elite meritocracy. He wrote, "[T]he real need . . . can be determined only by deliberative consideration, by education, by constructive leadership. . . . [Leaders] must be free to rise from the mass; they must be given the attraction of premiums to effort. . . . The crowd is credulous, it destroys, it consumes, it hates, and it dreams—but it never builds."

In this context he said engineering's "precise and efficient thought" could devise "a plan of individualism and associational activities that will preserve . . . individuality . . . and yet will enable us to synchronize socially and economically this gigantic machine that we have built out of applied science."

THESE PUBLIC COMMENTS and many others signified his intense interest in politics, but his intense shyness when he had no defined agenda seemed to block him from running for office. Meeting people was agony. A political writer would later call him "abnormally shy, abnormally sensitive . . . and ever apprehensive that he be made to appear ridiculous. . . . He looks down so much of the time, the casual guest obtains only a hazy impression of his appearance." Hoover himself complained of "the pneumatic drill of constant personal contact."

So he initially chose to become a power behind the scenes and bought newspapers in Washington, D.C., and Sacramento, the national and state capitals. And he spoke of "those strong men [who] with practically no organization, but with definite purpose, exert a greater influence on the situation from the outside than from in." He clearly intended to be one such strong man.

Soon, however, his head was turned. Democrats expressed interest in recruiting him as a presidential candidate, and Franklin Delano Roosevelt said, "He is certainly a wonder and I wish we could make him President of the United States." But he declared himself a Republican. While claiming to have no interest in public office, he did everything possible to procure it. He asked a friend how to get a cabinet post and was advised to run for president. In 1920 he did.

It was a strange campaign of and for the elite. He did not want to be seen as seeking the nomination, so his campaign was geared toward trying to generate a draft. To this end his backers mailed 21,210 letters soliciting support from every person listed in *Who's Who*, every member of the American Institute of Mining and Metallurgical Engineers, and every Stanford alumnus. At the Republican convention, he published a daily Hoover newspaper with contributions from such major writers as Ida Tarbell, Ray Stannard Baker, Robert Benchley, Heywoud Broun, and Dorothy Parker. Louis Brandeis announced: "I am 100 percent for him. [His] high public spirit, extraordinary intelligence, knowledge, sympathy, youth, and a rare perception of what is really worthwhile for the country, would, with his organizing ability and power of inspiring loyalty, do wonderful things in the Presidency."

But he generated no support among professional politicians, and his campaign disintegrated. Harding offered him a cabinet post. Hoover chose secretary of commerce. Old Guard GOP senators balked and told Harding they would confirm him only if Andrew Mellon was named secretary of the treasury. Harding acceded and offered Hoover what he had asked for. Hoover then pretended, if only to himself, he was answering duty's call, wiring Harding, "I should prefer infinitely not to undertake the burden of public office [but] I have no right to refuse your wish and I will accept the Secretaryship of Commerce."

As commerce secretary he called for rational planning for everything from the economy to the home. Edward Eyre Hunt, another Taylor disciple, was thrilled; he noted, "Hoover sees in the Department of Commerce a great opportunity to make the work of the engineers effective on a national scale."

HARDING TOOK OFFICE during a brief but severe recession, and one of Hoover's first acts was to organize a conference on unemployment and the business cycle. The findings would yield fertile seeds that germinated later. When the economy recovered, Hoover took credit and said it proved that prosperity could be "organized"; it was simply a matter of "intelligent cooperative group effort [and] national industrial planning."

Hoover then had the Federated American Engineering Societies, of which he was past president, survey waste in American industry. The survey's methodology was farcical; reviewers discarded questionnaires that did not conform to their wishes. In not a single industry did the survey blame management for less than 50 percent of the waste; in one industry it allocated 81 percent of waste to management. Only more planning and technocrats, of course, could eliminate this problem.

Accused of standardizing all of America, he did not dispute the charge; he had his department set standards for hundreds of products, measurements, and tools, seeking standardization to increase efficiency and spur productivity leaps, simultaneously spurring mass marketing. Applying science to the home, he sponsored (and controlled) the Better Homes of America Association, a voluntary group of 30,000 women in 1,800 chapters, each with a public relations division disseminating Commerce Department advice. This group advocated everything from rationalizing domestic labor and using specialists in such things as child nurturing and juvenile delinquency to building low-cost homes, and helped get uniform building codes and zoning regulations adopted in thirty-seven states.

Hoover also spurred the growth of aviation. He controlled radio licensing and helped it grow; in 1920, Westinghouse established the first radio station, KDKA in Pittsburgh, but there would soon be hundreds. He helped make second mortgages a new financing vehicle by convincing Julius Rosenwald, who built Sears, to issue them at 6 percent interest. Banks, which had been demanding 15 percent, quickly followed. He annexed the Bureau of Mines and the Patent Office from other departments. He told the U.S. Chamber of Commerce, "We are passing from a period of extreme individualistic action into a period of associational activities." Then he tried to force the Justice Department to reinterpret anti-trust laws to accommodate his views.

Finally, Hoover built a tremendous public relations apparatus. Advertising was a new industry, expected to have vast power to mold opinion and engineer thoughts, and J. Walter Thompson was theorizing about it. Bruce Barton, a Hoover political supporter, wrote about Jesus as a salesman and called his parables "the most powerful advertisements of all time. . . . [Jesus] picked up twelve men from the bottom ranks of business and forged them into an organization that conquered the world." At the least, national advertising was knitting the country together in a web. Brand names born or made national by advertising then included Ivory Soap, Kellogg's Corn Flakes, Crisco, Old Dutch Cleanser, Campbell's soup, Milky Way, Popsicles, Heinz pickles, and Scotch tape. New lines of copy were creating moods; typical was, "Often a bridesmaid but never a bride? For halitosis, use Listerine."

Hoover believed public relations could change behavior. He used the media bluntly. In five hundred working days as food administrator he had issued 1,840 press releases. He also used the media with sophistication. Leaks and a public relations campaign were his tools to bully the steel industry into accepting the eight-hour day. (It was inefficient and wasteful to work longer, he believed.) Meanwhile, he generated a national magazine story about his accomplishments in his first two years as commerce secretary, seeing to it that all Republican senators received it, and making sure it was "not marked as coming from this office." In 1922 his book *American Individualism* appeared; in it he articulated his beliefs, which owed much to Edmund Burke. The *New York Times* judged his book "among the few great formulations of American political theory."

Yet for all this—or because of it—by 1927 his political fortunes were fading. The public had tired of his constant doings. Professional politicians and GOP insiders despised him.

If Coolidge did not seek reelection—something by no means clear in the spring of 1927, although the two-term tradition suggested he would not—the leading contenders for the 1928 Republican nomination were Frank Lowden, the former Illinois governor who had been a favorite in 1920, Vice President Charles Dawes, Senate Republican leader Charles Curtis, and Senator William Borah.

Before the flood, the *Survey*, a national magazine considered quite progressive, reviewed the chances of these and other contenders, including dark horses. It did not mention Hoover. Even after the flood began, *Literary Digest* ran a story and cartoon about candidates chasing the GOP nomination. It did not mention Hoover.

Then, on Good Friday, 1927, the same day that torrential rains were deluging the Mississippi valley, Coolidge insulted Hoover when speaking to a group of White House reporters. The front page of the *New York Times* read, "Capital Mystified over Hoover's Status with the President." Privately, Coolidge, who called Hoover "Wonder Boy," said, "That man has offered me unsolicited advice for six years, all of it bad."

But Hoover's ambition still churned. The flood was pouring through the belly of America, and it would be on every front page in the nation for weeks. Hoover could not have been unaware of his possibilities as he took charge. Since entering public life, he had mixed good works and ambition. Now he would mix them again.

Agnes Meyer, wife of Hoover's confidant Eugene Meyer, a financier and later owner of the *Washington Post* and head of the Federal Reserve and the World Bank, wrote in her diary that Hoover was "consumed with ambition. . . . The man's will-to-power is almost a mania. The idea of goodwill, of high achievement, is strong in him, but he is not interested in the good that must be accomplished through others or even with the help of others. Only what is done by Hoover is of any meaning to him. He is a big man but cannot bear rivalry of any sort."

He had immense confidence, as much as Eads. After a conversation with him in 1927, the novelist Sherwood Anderson said, "I felt, looking at him, that he had never known failure."

CHAPTER TWENTY-TWO

THE APRIL 22 CABINET MEETING in which Coolidge named Hoover head of the flood effort adjourned at lunch. Two hours later Hoover sat down in his office with the other cabinet secretaries involved, American Red Cross vice chairman James Fieser, and senior staff. Hoover had rivalries with nearly everyone present. Davis, the secretary of war, was a potential presidential candidate and also resented Coolidge having given Hoover authority to issue orders directly to the Army. Secretary of Treasury Andrew Mellon was far larger than Hoover in the world outside Washington and scoffed at his ideas. And Hoover had repeatedly tried to usurp the power of several secretaries of agriculture. Hoover ignored these rivalries now; this meeting had purpose. Even while everyone was taking their seats, he demanded a report on the situation.

DeWitt Smith of the Red Cross gave it. Exactly one week earlier, as reports had come in of the extraordinary rains, senior Red Cross officials had gathered late at night to plan for a disaster. Quickly they had concluded that they could handle the crisis in Illinois, Missouri, Kentucky, and Tennessee. But the most likely scenario in Arkansas, Mississippi, and Louisiana would be beyond their capabilities. There would be 200,000 refugees at a minimum. If other levees broke, as expected, the number of refugees could rise above 500,000.

Hoover turned to Davis, who reported gloomily, "The Army Engineers believe nothing can be done to stop further breaks in the levees, and flood conditions will grow worse hourly."

They had defined the problem. Hoover quickly shifted the discussion to organization. The Red Cross had set up a headquarters in Memphis. Smith asked that each government department appoint a senior liaison person with direct access to the secretary. Done. Hoover went further, soon wiring to Henry Baker, the Red Cross relief director in Memphis, authority "to use such government equipment as necessary and charter any private property needed."

Finally came money. The Army, Davis said, had already spent $1 million with no way to recoup it. The Red Cross had a highly developed fund-raising apparatus. Davis suggested that the president set a specific target and ask for donations from the nation. Five million dollars was agreed upon as the initial goal, although all present knew it would be insufficient and a second call would have to be issued.

Meanwhile, a special train, including a railroad car for reporters, was being put together by the Illinois Central. As soon as it was ready, Hoover, Fieser, and Jadwin left for Memphis on it. They would arrive at 7 A.M. Jadwin would stay in the flooded region only briefly, but Hoover and Fieser would spend weeks there together, sleeping more than half their nights on a boat or train.

FROM THE FIRST, Hoover's plans went beyond simply rescuing and maintaining hundreds of thousands of people. Enormous as that task would be, he intended to rebuild the region after it was devastated. Any more personal ambitions would be taken care of by the stories written and broadcast by the railroad car full of reporters. Hoover and Fieser both understood how useful the reporters would prove to all of their respective purposes. They jointly alerted all Red Cross personnel: "In the course of the next few weeks many representatives of magazines, newspapers, and feature syndicate companies will be in the flood area. . . . [G]ive these writers every possible cooperation."

Fieser separately wired Washington headquarters: "Essential push all publicity angles next week or ten days for sake of financial drive"; "Secretary Hoover is magnetic center of publicity. Wire us currently anything useful for release by Secretary in interviews enroute"; "Keep us informed all fact matter with publicity value"; "Get pictures of Coast Guard and other boats flying Red Cross flags. Send them immediately to Douglas Griesemer, Director of Publicity, Red Cross, Wash., D.C. Also suggest similar photography by news photographers."

Hoover's staff, particularly George Akerson, fed the stories and photographs to reporters accompanying Hoover. Simultaneously, Commerce Department staff in Washington assembled clips from hundreds of newspapers and wired them to Akerson. Together, Akerson and the Washington staff would create a potent publicity machine.

Hoover himself concentrated on business. From the moment he got off the train in Memphis, he sought only people who could give him information. At first, there was chaos. For days Henry Baker had been fielding frantic calls for aid. He had worked sixty straight hours in an empty office building put at his disposal. Carpenters, electricians, and telephone and telegraph technicians had banged hammers around him. The day of the Mounds Landing break Army liaison officers had arrived from each of four Army corps located in the South and Midwest. Supplies were arriving as well. Baker was being drowned in detail. Finally, a Memphis banker cleaned up the lines of communication by arranging for men in forty towns to wire daily reports on conditions in their regions.

They still had the immense problem of distributing supplies and services throughout the flooded region. Baker recommended to Hoover and Fieser that they centralize policy but decentralize execution. If they put each county Red Cross chapter in charge of relief in its area, they would save money on administration, speed reaction time, and strengthen the Red Cross by building up local chapters. Chapters already existed in most counties. Generally, they were chaired by prominent men, such men as, in Greenville, LeRoy Percy's son William Alexander Percy. And in case of scandal Baker pointed out decentralizing would put responsibility "squarely on the local community and not the national organization. . . . Therefore, criticism may be localized very definitely."

Hoover and Fieser immediately concurred, and Hoover streamlined things more. Red tape disappeared. Representatives from every federal agency, from the Army to the Public Health Service, and several governors soon sat near Baker's desk. When Baker needed something, he called to the appropriate man, who took care of it. Thirty yards away a Red Cross purchasing agent conducted a nearly continuous reverse auction; he stood on a platform and shouted out supplies and quantities needed, and dozens of suppliers shouted back bids. Four days after the Memphis headquarters opened, it had already outgrown its space; on April 24 the Red Cross moved into an enormous Ford Motor Company automobile assembly plant.

Hoover stayed away from the headquarters, instead receiving a train of visitors in his suite at the Peabody Hotel where he dealt with the larger picture. Connolly, the Army engineer in charge of the Memphis district, had pinned a map to the wall. The Memphis mayor had assigned Hoover two homicide detectives to find and bring to him whomever he wanted to see. To ease coordination with the Red Cross, Hoover also told the governors of Arkansas, Mississippi, and

Louisiana to create state flood relief commissions headed by a single "dictator" with authority over all state resources. Each governor did. In Louisiana, Hoover told the governor to name John Parker, who had served under Hoover during the war as a regional food administrator. Parker was named. The Arkansas dictator was Harvey Couch, who headed the Arkansas Power & Light Company. Mississippi's flood czar was L. O. Crosby, a lumberman with few ties to the Delta. But he had made a fortune and, like Hoover, wanted a place at a bigger table; he was bankrolling Murphree's reelection campaign, asked him for the job, and got it. Crosby would soon become one of Hoover's most obsequious supporters.

Next, with a few phone calls, Hoover convinced railroads— the Illinois Central, the Missouri Pacific, the Texas Pacific, the Southern, the Frisco—to provide free transportation for refugees and cut rates on freight during the emergency. They also fed Baker's operation information about the contents of each boxcar, so one or more cars could be cut out of any train and sent where needed.

Order finally began to emerge. Meanwhile, Hoover began assembling a rescue fleet. In the Delta the rescue operation had long since begun.

THE FORCE of the Mounds Landing break, if not the break itself, had stunned the entire Delta. The water pouring through it rooted out, undermined, and collapsed buildings, trees, railroad embankments, rose over them, washed them out. Water poured over even Egypt Ridge, named because no flood had ever risen above it.

Literally tens of thousands of people, wet and exhausted, were clinging to trees or sitting on rooftops. All waited for boats. They waited in danger and misery. It was unseasonably cold, penetratingly cold. Some died of exposure.

The storms continued. Gales turned the entire flooded region into an angry sea, churning with filthy brown foam. As far as one could see were rolling whitecaps, a sight foreign and terrifying to planters and sharecroppers alike. Waves pounded against buildings, currents ate at their foundations, the combined force sweeping them away. From the river for sixty miles east and ninety miles south spread the sea.

There were few boats. In the entire city of Greenville there were only thirty-five bateaux—double-ended, flat-bottomed boats— a few skiffs, and a handful of motors. Only six people in Greenville had an outboard motor, and elsewhere in the Delta they were even rarer. But what boats and motors existed quickly arrived, volunteered and driven by their owners; the rest were commandeered. The first rescue boat left the city soon after the break, and independent of any organization. The fastest boats with the best motors came from Arkansas, up the White River. They belonged to bootleggers who swooped down the Mississippi, lifted their boats over the levee, and spread out into the ocean the Delta had become. From Memphis came Dr. Louis Leroy, who owned, and raced, perhaps the single fastest speedboat on the river. From the Gulf Coast towns of Gulfport, Pass Christian, Biloxi, and Bay St. Louis, professional fishermen came, 120 of their boats freighted north by rail and unloaded on the edge of the flood in Vicksburg, Greenwood, Yazoo City, and a few making it to Greenville on the last train, arriving just as water roared through the streets. The "river rats" came too, men who lived on houseboats and survived by fishing and trapping and building rafts of logs, floating them downriver to the giant Greenville sawmills. They too lifted their boats over the levee and headed over what had been fields.

It was a time for individual initiative and heroism. Will B. Moore, a black man working for a Greenville lumberyard, said, "I made myself and a bunch of men, I got a committee, we just built boats, went out and caught locals." Hunter Kimbrough grew up in a planter family, made films with Sergei Eisenstein in Mexico, and was a bond salesman at the Whitney Bank in New Orleans when the flood came. He asked for leave to help. The Clearing House Association gave him $3,000 and wished him luck, and he bought two motors, took a train to Vicksburg, and got on a stern-wheel steamboat for Greenville. There he found a large steel-hulled government boat and lifted it over the levee. For the next ten days he stayed in the Percy home at night, rode through the fields by day. Herman Caillouet, a Cajun, lived in Greenville, worked for the Corps of Engineers, and had a river pilot's license. He was not one of the social elite; his wife made dresses for debutantes. But upon hearing news of the break, he put a Model T Ford engine on his own 22-foot boat and set out onto the new sea towing another 22-footer. On his first trip back to Greenville, he unloaded refugees on the levee as the water was entering the town. "I go into Jim's Café and say gimme hotcakes," he recalled. "He says, 'Water's running in here now.' 'Well I can't help that. I ain't had dinner.' He says, 'I'm fixing to leave.' 'Put 'em on,' I said, 'I'll cook 'em.' When I finished eating, the water was up to my knees, but I cooked some more." Then he went back out. Two days after the crevasse, Caillouet's wife delivered his son. He left her to go out on the water again.

He did not always succeed. A black man with two kegs of whiskey in his house would not leave though waves were crashing against it. When Caillouet returned the next day, there was no house anymore, only water. Another time he spotted a family of seven stranded in a floating house, moving with the current. He headed for them. Suddenly, the house hit something or a wave hit it and it splintered. He was only a hundred yards or so away, but . . . "I searched the boards and things . . . and never saw a soul come up, not a soul. When the house started breaking up and falling, you see, and the waves throwing that lumber over, it just covered 'em to where they couldn't come out from under. . . . Seven of them. . . . I went round and round, did not see a hand." But in three days and nights, working almost nonstop, Caillouet rescued 150 people.

Virginia Pullen remembered her father coming home from rescue work: "He found one family with two small children; they handed him the baby out of the tree. A lady and two small children and two teenage boys. He never did know if they all were the same family. She handed him the baby, and just as she handed him the baby, it breathed its last. That really upset the rescue workers—the idea that they didn't get there the day before, why didn't they push farther."

Mrs. Hebe Crittenden was one of those rescued, just as currents were undermining her house. She and a dozen of her sharecroppers could feel it shake. She recalled, "We could hear water sloshing up under the house. The coloreds started singing spirituals."

Ernest Clarke was less lucky. He and his family had had no warning until the cattle began to low. As he started to get his boat ready, the water was upon them, the rolling, deepening surf smashing his boat to bits. He fled back to his house. The water tipped the whole house over, crushing it, throwing him, his mother, his wife, and his four daughters into the water. He fought free and climbed a tree. Three days later he was rescued. At the Greenville hospital he learned his entire family had drowned. The bodies of three of his children were found later tangled in barbed wire; the fourth body was never found.

Many rescuers carried guns. One used it more than once to keep people from jumping into his boat and capsizing it. Another shot a cow that was trying to clamber aboard. Dogs were abandoned, left frightened and barking on rooftops in the vast expanse of water.

But some men were less than helpful. One planter put his black sharecroppers in his cotton gin and nailed it shut. They broke out. Just below Mounds Landing on the levee two armed white men stood with 200 blacks who sharecropped for them. A steamer stopped and lowered the gangplank, but the whites refused to allow any blacks to get aboard for fear they would not return. The captain argued with them. Finally, a physician on the steamer climbed down the gangplank. The men blocked him. He snapped: "I come here by the authority of the American Red Cross and the God of all creation. If either of you has guts enough to pull the gun you carry please start now or get out of my way and I don't believe either of you has the guts." The doctor pushed past them and the 200 black men, women, and children boarded the steamer.

Soon rescue became systematized. Large mother ships, usually paddle-wheel steamers pushing open barges that held 1,500 people, operated in the rivers and streams, not worrying about where the channel lay. Motorboats, skiffs with outboards, and even rowboats were attached to each mother ship; they penetrated inland and searched for survivors, or picked up those stranded on levees or Indian mounds. The work was always dangerous. Even where the water seemed still, a submerged fence post, or stump, or a dozen other obstacles could capsize or rip a hole in a boat.

From Greenville itself, and Greenwood and Vicksburg also, each morning at daybreak rescuers headed their boats out into the country, generally carrying a mechanic for the motor and a mailman who knew rural routes. They followed power lines down roads. Telephones still worked. People phoned in that they were trapped, or someone else was trapped. Planes flew over and acted as spotters. When a boat filled, the rescuer turned around and carried his load back to the Greenville levee or, if he was close to Greenwood, fifty miles and four hours by boat across the sea from Greenville, he took people there.

Greenwood marked the end of the flat Delta, the beginning of the hills. It was dry.

WILL PERCY WROTE: "For thirty-six hours the Delta was in turmoil, in movement, in terror. Then the waters covered everything, the turmoil ceased, and a great quiet settled down. . . . Over everything was silence, deadlier because of the strange cold sound of the currents gnawing at foundations, hissing against walls, creaming and clawing over obstacles."

The terror lasted more than thirty-six hours. Eight days after the break a desperate wire said, "The Mississippi Delta is under water from two to eighteen feet and lots of people are drowning. 250 people in vicinity of Midnight, Miss., and Louise are begging for aid and if not moved by morning will be drowned."

Then the silence did come. Out on the water there was unimaginable silence. As far as the eye could see was an expanse of brackish chocolate water. There was not the bark of a dog, the lowing of a cow, the neighing of a horse. Even the trees turned dingy, their trunks and leaves caked with dried mud. The silence was complete and suffocating.

The water seemed stagnant, but it moved. The current showed itself and became fierce when it ran over railroad embankments or suddenly collapsed a building. At cross streets in downtown Greenville currents drowned people, until submerged cars were towed to the intersections to act as breakwaters.

A few days after the crevasse it turned hot, the steaming hot of the Delta. Outside Greenville, Henry Mascagni recalled hundreds of bodies of animals floating "just swelled up. I saw three people, colored, floating, swelled up." A week after the flood, he went out on a boat. "The first thing we saw was a 350-lb hog—they had put a lot of hogs on the levee. We had no motorboat, all rowed by hand. The fellows said, 'Well there's one we can kill and bring back and feed the people.' When we got close we see it was eating on a dead black woman, and he had done eaten quite a bit of her. She was bloated up. . . . The hog had drug her right to the edge of the water, trying to get her up on the bank where he could eat her with no trouble. I never will forget it. All we did, and could do, was kill the hog. What was left of the colored woman we just pulled her down to the canal ditch and just turned her loose and it floated on off. . . . We brought the hog back, killed it, cleaned it, the people were so hungry they were eating it before it was cooked. . . . I don't know what this disease was you got from uncooked pork but I think two people died."

One report quoted a responsible Corps of Engineers employee who had personally seen "fully two hundred bodies of dead persons in the flooded area between Vicksburg and Greenville."

Meanwhile, the river continued to pour through Mounds Landing. Five weeks after the crevasse, Caillouet took two engineers to survey it in a river commission steamer 50 feet long. Some waves still stood 12 feet high. Choosing discretion over valor, the engineers told Caillouet to drop them off on the levee before he shot the crevasse. He did, then picked them up inside the break. The crevasse was three-quarters of a mile wide. (Today a 65-acre lake remains a permanent legacy.) With a lead line 100 feet long, they took soundings and found no bottom.

HOOVER HAD LITTLE IMPACT on the initial rescue effort, but as the flood rolled south and spread across the land, he listened, set policy, delegated, and organized. As each day passed, his hand was felt more and more, and the Red Cross and Army officials under him took firm control. By April 26, Colonel George Spalding, who commanded the official rescue fleet, was instructing scattered Army engineers to reject boats offered for use unless they had been carefully inspected. He also dictated such details as the amount of coal with which "[e]very relief boat should be equipped." Soon thereafter, as the waters were swelling on every river, stream, and bayou in Louisiana, Spalding controlled a fleet of 826 vessels, including Navy and Coast Guard ships, along with 27 Navy seaplanes used for spotting stranded refugees and inspecting levees. Army engineers were filing daily reports with the Red Cross about weak levees, and, given this warning, the rescue fleet then concentrated nearby.

On April 30, the day after Hoover had watched the dynamiting of the levee at Caernarvon, he was back in Memphis. There he spoke by radio to the nation in a fund-raising appeal for the Red Cross. It was his first national address, one of the first by anyone. "I am speaking to you from the temporary headquarters which we have established for the national fight against the most dangerous flood our country has ever known," he began. "It is difficult to picture in words the might of the Mississippi in flood. . . . A week ago when it broke the levee [at Mounds Landing], only a quarter of the river went through the hole. Yet in a week it poured water up to twenty feet deep over . . . an area up to 150 miles long and 50 miles wide. . . . Behind this crest lies the ruin of 200,000 people. Thousands still cling to their homes where the upper floors are yet dry. But thousands more have need to be removed in boats and established in great camps on the higher ground. Other thousands are camped upon broken levees. This is the pitiable plight of a lost battle."

Now, he warned, the struggle was continuing along battle lines to the south. "Everything humanly possible is being done by men of magnificent courage and skill. It is a great battle against the oncoming rush, and in every home behind the battle line there is apprehension and anxiety. Every night's reading of the water gauges is telegraphed to the remotest parts of those states—a sort of communiqué of the progress of the impending, threatening invasion of an enemy. It is a great battle which the engineers are directing. They have already held important levees against the water enemy. What the result of the fight may be no one knows. But the fortitude, industry, courage and resolution of the people of the south in this struggle cannot fail to bring pride to every American tonight. . . . Another week will be a great epic. I believe they will be victorious."

But almost as he spoke, a man in an airplane above Vicksburg watched as the waters that had inundated the Delta rejoined the main river and reported, "The swiftly moving current . . . [was] clearly visible as it pounded its way back into the Mississippi, from which most of it escaped two weeks ago when the levee north of Greenville gave way."

It pressed against the levee on the opposite bank. It was relentless, its weight and force immense. Two days after Hoover's broadcast, the levee at Cabin Teele, Louisiana, yielded. Now water roared over land to the west. Soon the *Memphis Commercial-Appeal* announced, "Today it is possible to go from Vicksburg to Monroe, Louisiana, by boat." Monroe was 75 miles distant. The Cabin Teele crevasse extended the width of the inland sea to 125 miles.

A *New York Times* reporter described his flight over the region: "For mile after mile all the land in view was the tops of the levees, to which thousands had fled for safety. In places the tops of giant cypress and oak trees still swayed in the breeze, the only green spots in the picture. The lake extends far into Arkansas and probably 100 miles . . . from the banks of the Mississippi into Louisiana."

These waters were draining south through the flat land into rivers already at record height, into the Tensas, the Boeuf, the Ouachita, the Red, the Atchafalaya, rivers whose waters were climbing higher and higher, pushing against walls of rising sandbags.

CHAPTER TWENTY-THREE

T HE RIVER was conquering everything.

"First the Cairo to Memphis sector was lost," reported the *New York Times*. "Next the river triumphed as it surged south through the Memphis to Vicksburg sector. Its victory has been complete and overwhelming in the sector that stretches from Vicksburg to the mouth of the Red River. Now comes the struggle to hold the levees of the Red and the Mississippi, westward in the Red for a distance of seventy-five miles. . . . Tonight 250 rescue boats are being concentrated at the mouth of the Red." "[Failure would] increase the refugee army now depending on the Red Cross for food, clothing and shelter to nearly 400,000 in six states."

In advance of the flood, Louisiana State University students were trained to operate the outboard motors for boats. Engineers set up ten wireless radio stations, and twenty-four seaplanes and twelve airplanes were used to spot stranded refugees. A hailstorm knocked out four planes in one day, the hailstones going through the propellers like bullets. No topographical maps existed, and every railroad operating in the state cooperated with Isaac Cline, who also collected details about forestation and other obstructions and devised a formula to predict the movement of the flood over land, then issued bulletins daily, and sometimes twice daily. These bulletins went straight to Hoover and were also issued publicly; they were astoundingly accurate.

Based on Cline's predictions and Army engineers' warnings about levee weak points, Hoover and Fieser set up what they called "concentration camps" in advance of anticipated crevasses, sending telegrams to mayors or chairmen of local Red Cross committees, warning them of the oncoming flood. Typically, Hoover wired L. G.

Porter of New Iberia, Louisiana, a town in Cajun country sixty miles west of the Mississippi River, "We wish that the Red Cross chapter at New Iberia would take in hand at once the construction of a camp at some point between New Iberia and Burke as your surveyors may determine laid out for 10,000 people." Included were precise instructions on building tent platforms, latrines, pipelines, drilling wells, and connecting power lines. "The National Red Cross will bear the expense, but we are depending upon your citizens to undertake the work and do its supervision on a voluntary basis."

While Hoover saw to the building of refugee camps, thousands of men struggled to save the levees. The Bayou des Glaises levee was key. If it went, others would fall like dominoes and the "Sugar Bowl" region of Louisiana would likely go under water. Much of this land, protected by ridges that had contained all previous overflows, had never been flooded.

Here men mounted one of the most intense and longest struggles against the river. It also seemed the most hopeless. The levee had not been designed to hold such a volume of water. The flood, hemmed in by hills to the west and, ironically, the Mississippi levees to the east, had formed another inland sea that reached a depth of twenty-four feet and rose five feet above the levee. Sandbags could not keep back such a height for long. On May 9 waves began to break over the top of the levee. Thousands of men piled more sandbags higher. Miraculously, they continued to hold.

Then the rains fell again. In two days the spring's final major storm dumped eleven more inches of rain on the area. On May 12 miles of the Bayou des Glaises levee simply crumbled. Hundreds of millions of tons of water began pushing through the crevasse. The waters were immense, hurtling south to the sea through the Evangeline country.

Hoover had earlier told the 105,000 people in the area to evacuate. Few had. But Hoover and the Red Cross had prepared. Thousands of trucks rolled into the area just ahead of the first wave of water. Four trains carrying boats, motors, and now-experienced rescuers headed in from different directions, and the rescue fleet entered just behind the first wave of water. All 105,000 people, along with most of their cattle, horses, and mules, were evacuated with crisp efficiency and few deaths.

Cline announced that the flood crest had itself escaped the channel of the Mississippi and was now traveling over land. It was twenty-five miles wide and "of tremendous proportions, exceeding in height the previous highest water in that basin, which was in 1882."

The Mississippi flood could never have reached New Orleans. But it was covering areas where no white man had ever seen it, heading toward Melville, Louisiana, a town on the west bank of the Atchafalaya River. Before the Bayou des Glaises water arrived there, on May 17 at 5:30 A.M. in Melville, the Atchafalaya itself broke through the levee. Guards ran through the town firing guns, shouting, "Crevasse! Crevasse!" One man clanged the church bell over and over and over. Melville's 1,000 residents fled to the levee.

Almost in the center of the town, water from the two crevasses collided. They met violently, with, as one resident said, "the sound of a thousand freight trains." The collision ripped apart a steel railroad bridge and drowned its tender, and left, according to a later Red Cross report, "immense deposits of sediment throughout the town and surrounding countryside [creating] tremendous sand dunes, practically burying the community . . . washing away houses, shifting others from foundations." The *New York Times* reported "a veritable wall of water . . . running in places thirty or more feet high, . . . sweeping everything in its path."

Later that day in Plaucheville, Louisiana, a family of nine drowned when their house collapsed, undermined by the current. Their bodies were found floating in 16 feet of water.

On May 20, Hoover, concerned about another crevasse at McCrea, Louisiana, on the east bank of the Atchafalaya, ordered the evacuation of 35,000 more people. This time they left immediately.

Engineers insisted they had a chance to win this fight, to save the east-bank Atchafalaya levee. For weeks they had been strengthening it, and the crevasse on the opposite bank had relieved some pressure. In addition, the Mississippi River was falling. It was falling only by inches a day, but from St. Paul to New Orleans, it was falling. The great crest had passed.

Now 2,500 men worked at McCrea in shifts. They used every technique, shielding the levee with lumber, backing it up with sandbags, revetting it with rocks. Repeatedly, some small part of the levee crumbled into the river, but each time hundreds of men rushed to the spot with timber, rocks, and sandbags. "They are soldiers, every one, heroes, too," Hoover said of them.

But at three-thirty in the morning of May 24, muddy water suddenly appeared behind the levee. A few moments later a stretch of levee 700 feet long crashed into the river. The river had just ripped open the last crevasse of the 1927 flood.

The current near the crevasse roared past at 30 miles an hour. An Associated Press report said: "A wall of water 40 feet high and almost 20 miles wide tonight was . . . cutting a path of desolation across the length of Louisiana. . . . Immediately behind the advancing waters scores of residents of the lower Atchafalaya were being rescued by tiny boats which ploughed precariously through the raging current to remove them from housetops. . . . Further back, along the Bayou des Glaises sector, only the swishing of the water could be heard."

The image of a 20-mile-wide 40-foot-high wall of water was hyperbole, but the Atchafalaya had breached levees on both its banks and was spreading still another sea across central Louisiana. The flood rose to 42 feet above sea level, while the land through which it flowed had an elevation of less than 10 feet. Another 150,000 more people became refugees. Hoover informed Coolidge, "All population that could be flooded is already covered."

IN JUNE came the final blow. Another flood crest began moving from Cairo south. June rises, usually coming from the Missouri, were common. As early as May 13, Hoover had wired the War Department: "Imperative that refugees be not discouraged by fear of crop destruction by . . . possibility of June rise. . . . Desirable Mississippi River Commission stretch to utmost their authority." The War Department had assured him it would protect the area from a new rise. In fact, it did nothing. It could do nothing. It, and all the people along the river, were spent.

Many areas that were flooded in March and April, especially in Missouri and Arkansas, had begun emerging from the water. People had planted cotton. Now the river poured through the breaches already made and drowned much of that cotton.

Only in one place would man even attempt to hold back the June rise. This final battle would take place in Greenville, Mississippi.

NO OFFICIAL FIGURES summarize the deaths and flooding along tributaries from Oklahoma to West Virginia, but along the lower Mississippi alone the flood put as much as 30 feet of water over lands where 931,159 people—the nation's total population was only 120 million —had lived. Twenty-seven thousand square miles were inundated, roughly equal to Massachusetts, Connecticut, New Hampshire, and Vermont combined. As late as July 1, 1.5 million acres remained underwater. Not until mid-August, more than four months after the first break in a mainline Mississippi River levee, did all the water leave the land.

An estimated 330,000 people were rescued from rooftops, trees, isolated patches of high ground, and levees. The Red Cross ran 154 "concentration camps," tent cities, in seven states—Kentucky,

Tennessee, Missouri, Illinois, Mississippi, Arkansas, and Louisiana. A total of 325,554 people, the majority of them African-American, lived in these camps for as long as four months. An additional 311,922 people outside the camps were fed and clothed by the Red Cross. Most of these were white. Of the remaining 300,000 people, most fled; a few cared for themselves, surviving on their own food and on their own property.

Deaths occurred from Kansas, where thirty-two towns and cities were inundated, to West Virginia. Officially, the Red Cross reported 246 people drowned; the U.S. Weather Bureau reported 313. (The Red Cross confidentially warned Hoover its figures on deaths were "not necessarily reliable.") Official sources attributed an additional 250 deaths indirectly to the flood. But the death toll almost certainly ran far higher. It was impossible to know how many bodies were buried beneath tons of mud, or washed out into the Gulf. The head of the National Safety Council estimated deaths in the Yazoo-Mississippi Delta alone at 1,000.

The Red Cross estimated direct economic losses at $246,000,000. The U.S. Weather Bureau put direct losses at $355,147,000. Unofficial but authoritative estimates exceeded $500,000,000; with indirect losses, the number approached $1,000,000,000, large enough in 1927 to affect the national economy.

The river itself left a legacy. The Mississippi carried only 1,500,000 cubic feet of water per second past New Orleans to the sea, while the artificial crevasse in St. Bernard carried 250,000 cfs. An additional 950,000 cfs moved down the Atchafalaya to the Gulf; had the Mississippi River Commission closed the Atchafalaya, as it had wanted to do, the increased Mississippi flow might have destroyed New Orleans.

The enormous Atchafalaya current helped create a new problem. Before the Civil War, one could cross the head of the Atchafalaya at low water on a plank 15 feet long. The river had long since enlarged, and the 1927 flood further scoured the channel, widening and deepening it, making the Atchafalaya hungry for still more water. It began threatening to claim the entire flow of the Mississippi, luring the Mississippi away from Baton Rouge and New Orleans.

And the flood made Hoover a national hero.

COOLIDGE had done nothing. After he initially refused to visit the flooded area, the governor of Mississippi wired him again: "I urgently request and insist that you make personal visit at this time. . . . I appeal to you to come and make this inspection." The *Manufacturer's Record* declared "that a visit by you to that region would be worthy of the highest statesmanship and enable you to accomplish results of untold indeed of inestimable value." A Philadelphia Republican asked "that you go forthwith to some city near the flooded district. . . . If you did this a thrill would go through the country."

Coolidge declined.

"Big Bill" Thompson, Republican mayor of Chicago, wired; Arthur O'Keefe, Democratic mayor of New Orleans, wired. The president of the Mississippi State Board of Development pleaded: "Earnestly urge that you personally visit flood sections of Mississippi. . . . Mississippi Valley needs your help now and only by personal inspection can you grasp the situation."

Coolidge declined.

Eight senators and four governors jointly and formally pleaded with him anew to come South, arguing that the public would be more responsive to the Red Cross if he did. From Greenville the governor of Mississippi begged a third time: "More than ever . . . I want again to appeal to you to come in person. Your coming would center eyes of nation and the consequent publicity would result in securing millions of dollars additional aid for sufferers."

Coolidge declined.

NBC asked him to broadcast a nationwide appeal through a historic radio hookup. (Hoover would make this and a later broadcast instead.) The Duluth Cosmopolitan Club asked him for a dozen signed photographs to auction off at a benefit for flood victims. Will Rogers asked him to "send me a telegram that I can read at our benefit for flood sufferers tomorrow night."

All these requests Coolidge declined.

For months the flood dominated the nation's newspapers. For months, every single day the *New York Times* ran at least one story on the flood. For nearly a month, every day it ran a flood story on page 1. It was page 1 in Seattle, page 1 in San Diego, page 1 in Boston, page 1 in Miami. In the interior of the country, in the Mississippi valley itself, the story was bigger. Newspaper editors later overwhelmingly named the flood the greatest story of 1927, even though on May 22, Charles Lindbergh had, temporarily, driven the flood off the front pages of their newspapers.

But if Coolidge did nothing, Hoover did everything. For months hardly a day passed without his name appearing in a heroic and effective posture, saving the lives of Americans. He was the focus of newsreels, of magazine feature stories, of Sunday supplements. The flood influenced the treatment of him on other questions as well. Almost like the president, everything he did was news. Not counting flood-related stories, references to him in the *New York Times* tripled during the three-month period after the flood, compared to the three months before the flood.

He and his staff tracked the stories around the country carefully. Twice and sometimes three times a week Hoover saw summaries of them. The report for Saturday, May 14, read: "Since the last report on this subject, written 5/10, a further vast amount of publicity and editorial comment has been forthcoming. The number of editorials received which express approbation and appreciation of Mr. Hoover has reached 153. . . . This number represents only the editorials received here and doubtless there have been hundreds of others. . . . Hartford Courant contains the following passage: 'The country admires Mr. Hoover and justly. The politicians do not appear to relish pushing him forward. Many people would be interested to see what he would do if made president, yet they are not apt to have the opportunity.' "

The May 17 summary noted: "The Magazine section of the New York Times [has] an article entitled, 'Again Hoover Does an Emergency Job' . . . ; The Boise Idaho Statesman editorial called 'Hoover to the rescue' says, 'America is sold on the organizing and directing genius of Hoover. . . . No wonder this man, who is no skilled politician, no spell-binder, no campaigner, no leader of a political clique, is persistently and continually advanced as the logical man for the swivel chair behind the big desk in the . . . White House!' The Louisville KY Herald . . . says, 'That there's no man in the country today who can do the job as well, may, some are hinting, boost that gentleman's chances for a presidential nomination.' "

The summary of May 23 noted a *Nashville Banner* editorial: " 'There is no honor in the gift of the people of which [Hoover] is not worthy'; the Oakland *Tribune* tells of renewed talk from Washington concerning Mr. Hoover, due to his being once more in the public eye . . . '[H]e is the ablest and most efficient American in public life. . . . In personal fitness for the presidency there is no other American, even remotely, in Mr. Hoover's class.' "

There was virtually no criticism of his role, although many papers attacked Coolidge. Yet the truth was not enough for Hoover. He had to embellish it. He had to be perfect, even if it required lying. In his second national radio address, just after the final crevasse in Louisiana, he said that three hundred had died before he took charge, then bragged: "I can state at once a positive fact which will give satisfaction to every American. We have not had, so far as we know, the loss of half a dozen lives since we undertook central control and coordination of all agencies of relief in this great catastrophe." Later he claimed even fewer deaths, saying, "Only three lives have been lost since the national organization initiated its action on April 20th."

He deserved credit for saving lives. Without the magnificent organization he created and led, certainly dozens, probably hundreds —and possibly thousands—more would have died.

But his claim was a lie. The lowest count of the dead after April 20 exceeded 150, including at least 83 after he personally took control in Memphis; probably many more had died. Fieser, fearing Hoover's claim would damage the credibility of the Red Cross, even warned him of his error. Hoover persisted in repeating it.

He believed he was as scientific and objective as engineering itself. He believed he made decisions based only upon facts and truth. He was lying, and most of all to himself. This flaw meant that every decision he made was built on sand. It would haunt him, but not yet.

In the meantime, the media chose not to confront him. He was a hero. Although papers across the nation had reported deaths on page 1 that clearly exceeded his claim, the staff-produced press summaries, which reported the rare negative comment, noted not a single complaint about his facts. Instead, it quoted an editorial appearing in the *New York Telegram*, the *Youngstown* (Ohio) *Telegram*, and most other Scripps-Howard papers: "Unstinted praise can be offered the Secretary of Commerce for the work he already has performed in bringing order out of chaos. . . . Only 6 lives were lost after Hoover took hold . . . 300 lives had been lost before Hoover reached the scene. There is a fine tribute in these figures."

Hoover had earlier said "the world lives by phrases," and called public relations "an exact science." The publicity and his image-making machine was doing its work. If on the eve of the flood Hoover had not even won mention as a presidential contender, now Hoover was precisely correct when he told his old friend from Stanford, Will Irwin, that, assuming Coolidge did not seek the Republican presidential nomination, "I shall be the nominee, probably. It is nearly inevitable."

He would be the nominee, that was, unless some deus ex machina destroyed his chances. A scandal, for example, could make all the publicity he had received blow up in his face. The press was creating his candidacy; it could destroy it. And one potentially explosive scandal was threatening in Greenville, Mississippi. At its center lay LeRoy Percy and his son Will.

Part Six

THE SON

CHAPTER TWENTY-FOUR

Wᴵᴸᴸᴵᴬᴹ Aᴸᴇxᴀɴᴅᴇʀ Pᴇʀᴄʏ would ultimately become a large figure in his own right. Cultured, charming, a hero in the Great War, a poet and writer, his autobiography *Lanterns on the Levee* remains in print half a century after publication. He would travel about the world, sponsor young artists and writers, make the Percy home in Greenville a salon visited by people of international renown, and encourage northern scholarship about the Delta. Dissatisfied with the quality of the local newspaper, he would recruit Hodding and Betty Werlein Carter to Greenville to start one that would win a national reputation. His influence would be felt even more directly by his adopted son and blood cousin Walker Percy, who would become a National Book Award–winning novelist, and by Walker's close friend, Civil War historian and novelist Shelby Foote. Historian Bertram Wyatt-Brown calls Will "the best of the Percys," "the subject of myths. . . . How effortless it was to idolize Will Percy." Betty Carter says simply, "Will Percy was a great man."

But if a large figure, Will Percy always felt dwarfed by his father. Short and slight, frail even and without his father's thick chest, he was also blond, blue-eyed, and strikingly handsome, even beautiful. Forty-two years old in 1927, his features retained a boyish appeal. Even several years later Walker Percy described him as "quick as a youth . . . the abiding impression was of a youthfulness." He had his father's charm and added his own. He could talk about poetry and music, recalls Foote, "in a way that made you not only know the reality of it, but also appreciate the beauty . . . in a way that made you wish the conversation would hurry up and get over with so you could go home and read Keats." He could also in an instant turn acerbic, wintry. Foote adds, "He could get as mad as anyone I've

293

ever known in my life. . . . His anger was a fearsome thing to be around."

The anger came from a deeper torment. For Will Percy could not escape the weight of his name, nor of his father, nor of the fact that he filled a place in the world that was not his and that he did not want. He had "beautiful and terrible eyes, eyes to be careful around," Walker Percy said. "Yet now, when I try to remember them, I cannot see them otherwise than as shadowed by sadness." David Cohn, a writer and national Democratic Party figure in the 1950s, called him "the loneliest man I have ever known. . . . [Loneliness] sometimes hovered as an aura about his head as he presided at his own table bright with laughter."

To protect himself, all his life the son danced mannered and intricate steps around the father. He took those steps to insulate the life he clung to, a romanticized past—perhaps symbolically, he would never learn to drive a car—from the grit of reality. But the Mississippi River would send reality flooding through his world and mark the end of the life he romanticized. It would also mark failure, his own failure, and by his standards the failure of his father and their society as well. The lifelong dance of father and son is itself that story.

EVEN AS A YOUNG BOY, Will seemed to simultaneously embrace his heritage and seek something else. From the time of his birth, two months too soon after the marriage of LeRoy and Camille Bourges, his parents reciprocated his ambivalence. Will himself would note that his arrival "overjoyed no one," including "Father and Mother." Both parents always stood apart from him, distant. Will responded with reticence, a self-containment, a resistance. As a boy, he did not play baseball or take to horses or do mischief with the children of the black servants. He disliked fishing and found hunting "even more lacerating to [my] spirit." Instead, he loved flowers and books. Nor, as he grew older, did he take to the plantation, or to gambling, or to drinking, or to any of the social vices so much a part of his father's society.

Yet the father still dominated the son's life. He dominated it not with orders or rules or discipline, but with what Will saw as his perfection. "I had not loved Father deeply, though I had admired him boundlessly," he wrote. "It was hard having such a dazzling father; no wonder I longed to be a hermit." Many years later Will worshiped small pieces of his father that appeared in others; since his father hunted and fished, for example, Will, despite his aversion to both pursuits, called fishermen and hunters "the most gentle and understanding people in the world, and I suspect anyone who isn't one or the other." Will blamed every failing, including the distance between him and his father, on himself, saying, "I must have been a hard child to get close to."

Still, Will was a Percy, and therefore a warrior. If he shared none of his father's interests, he staked out his own ground and was determined to be worthy of him. He poured his passion into perfection. Nothing less would suffice. As a teenager, he frowned on sin, resented his father's "unchurchliness," and told his Catholic mother he wanted to become a priest. (She was appalled.) Despite the fine schools in Greenville, he was privately tutored and refused to continue reading *Othello* because it was "immoral." His religiosity, he said, "was anguish and ecstasy, but mostly anguish, to me. . . . I was determined to be honest if it killed me. . . . I wanted to be completely and utterly a saint; heaven and hell didn't matter, but perfection did."

His intensity reflected a kind of masochism, a self-flagellation, a ripping at one's own flesh. It was also passionate and ferocious. With his life largely internal, he began writing poetry, which like his religiosity seemed ill suited to the son of the father. When Will was fifteen, his parents sent him away to a military school at Sewanee to become a man, but also gave him permission to enter the nearby University of the South at Sewanee instead if he qualified; he did, and began college.

By then, Will had a brother named LeRoy, six years younger and fashioned in their father's image. Outgoing, animated, everything that Will was not, young LeRoy rode his pony bareback, explored the black sections of town, and was what Will called him: "all boy, all sturdy, obstreperous charm." His parents doted on him; clearly he would be the one who would carry on the Percy tradition, thus releasing Will from it. Will himself called him "the swell brother who should be representing and perpetuating the name." But his father gave LeRoy a rifle. When he was eleven years old, another boy accidentally shot him with it, and he died. Crowds overflowed the house and yard for the funeral, while blacks lined the street outside the house paying tribute.

The death did not bring father and remaining son closer. They grieved separately. At the time, Will wrote a poem that included the line, "I am your son, and you have slain my brother." Such a critical thought about his father was rare. It only complicated their relationship further, for he still idolized his father.

His parents did not idolize him. He graduated from Sewanee

at nineteen, then spent a year in Europe. In letters home he complained that he had not heard from them, complained of "this one-sided correspondence," wrote, "Mother Dear— it was certainly good to get your letter tonight after what seemed an interminable wait," and, later, "Mother Dear, Things are progressing very pleasantly except for the fact I haven't received a line from you or father."

He needed his parents then. Europe had awakened in him something he found hypnotizing and frightening. In the Louvre, he "was always happening upon a hermaphrodite, in some discreet alcove, and I would examine the sleazy mock-modest little monster with horror and fascination." And he became "sick for a home I had never seen and lonely for a hand I had never touched."

Fleeing from that loneliness, he returned home and submitted to his heritage. His father, grandfather, and two uncles were prominent attorneys. Will went to Harvard Law, even though his father had not pushed him to do so, and found no pleasure in it. For the new, other, greater distance between father and son was showing itself most obviously in his poetry.

IF WILL'S POEMS have not endured, in his time he developed a sizable reputation. He became the editor of the Yale Series of Younger Poets, and his work was praised and solicited by such people as Allen Tate and John Crowe Ransom, leaders of the "Fugitives," southern poets who rejected industrial society in favor of a more honorable agrarian one. As an editor, he advised one poet: "[L]et your writing reflect only the wisdom of pain or of delight which life has most deeply revealed to you. Nothing else is worth your time or the time of any reader." He told a friend that poetry's "first requirement is sincerity and the single aim should be to write as though there were no audience other than the writer's own heart."

Many of his poems spoke of his father. With the one exception quoted above, in them his father was always heroic. In a poem titled "L.P.," he was asked: " 'How many trees in your forest?' / 'One:' . . . / When storms run . . . the tree bows like Jacob wrestling with God.' " In another he wrote: "There is no certain thing I can lay hold on / And say, 'This, this is good! This will I worship!' / Except my father." In his autobiography Will defined himself, shortly before his death, as only a reflection, a son. It is subtitled *Recollections of a Planter's Son*; in it he stated simply, "Father was the only great person I ever knew."

His poems also spoke of other things, and the single poem he cited as his truest was "Sappho in Levkas." It is a long poem, seventeen pages long. It sings of passion. It also speaks of confusion, vacillation, anger, torment, and his father. In it, the narrator, ostensibly Sappho, becomes obsessed with a youth and, riveted by the boy's beauty, spies on him, dreams of him, and finally loves him. For loving him, the narrator trembles equally with love and self-hatred.

> To think nobility like mine could be
> Flawed—shattered utterly—and by . . .
> A slim, brown shepherd boy with windy eyes
> And spring upon his mouth! . . .
> Before Thine eyes to strip my passion till
> Naked its evil gleams . . .
> Drinking the poison of his loveliness . . .
> To see his bending body in the dance . . .
> That lithe and burning youth . . .
> Father, it seemed not evil then—so sweet
> He was; and I, who, most of all the world,
> Loved purity and loathed lust,
> Became the mark of my own scorning . . .
> Defeat or victory alike—is utter ruin . . .
> Oh, always beauty was to me,
> Thyself half seen, my Father . . .
> And this same beauty now betrayeth me . . .
> O home! O Lesbos!
> O gods, and grant this boon!
> Bear me back home to Lesbos and the boy!
> Steep me but one short hour in his love! . . .
> I would forswear song—beauty—Zeus, my father . . .
> I would long to be
> Freed from that loneliness men call esteem.

Sappho, he made clear, truly represented his heart, and other poems expressed similar desires. In one, he wrote longingly of "some young god, / With blown, bright hair and fillet golden, came / And stretching forth the blossoming rod of beauty / Upon me wrought a pagan spell." Such desires had to torture him.

Had it not been for his father, Will might have abandoned Greenville and his name, and freed himself from the loneliness of men's esteem. But worshiping his father, he could not do so. And having finished law school, he needed to begin his adult life. His father still would not embrace him. Though LeRoy advised one young man that Greenville was "the best place in the Delta for a young lawyer to start practicing," he confided to his brother, "I am considerably bothered about Will, whether to advise him to settle here or in Memphis. On his own account I am strongly inclined to Memphis."

But in 1910 Will did return to Greenville, and his father's law firm became Percy & Percy. Will was twenty-five years old. Meanwhile, LeRoy was bestowing his favor on his nephew, Will's first cousin, LeRoy Pratt Percy, a Birmingham attorney whose own father had killed himself with a shotgun. It was this nephew with whom LeRoy now hunted and gambled and joked. It was this nephew whom LeRoy now expected to carry on the family tradition. (The nephew, like his own father, would later kill himself.)

The closeness between father and nephew, Will's cousin, must have reminded the son of his own failings. Will lived at home with his parents, and there was constant tension, violent arguments. He was not weak and could explode with ferocity and truculence. His tongue could keep even his father at bay. "But it wasn't fun," Will said. "I had attacks of nausea, but not of tears." At least some of the tension centered on his lack of interest in women. In an unpublished manuscript Will confessed: "My father and mother looked at me strangely. . . . My father said, 'It is in the spring that the seed is eager, is it not?' But my mother would cover his lips with her hands. 'Do not speak,' she would say, 'We do not know what we may be saying.' " In Greenville other people began to wonder why he did not marry, not quite saying something else.

He often returned to Europe. The Sicilian village Taormina became a favorite spot. There a German photographer had taken famous photographs of nude shepherd boys portrayed as satyrs and ancient Greeks, and English homosexuals who worshiped young male nudes had largely adopted the town. Will moved in their circle but could not embrace that life fully. Yet in Greenville there seemed nothing for him. He wrote his cousin and confidant Janet Dana Longcope: "I'm about convinced that my usefulness down here is ended, and certainly all chance for happiness is. From now on it would be a 'petering' out process, which of all things I most despise."

When the Great War began, he was in Taormina climbing Mt. Etna. The war, he told his cousin, was "the center of the world. To miss this war is to miss the opportunity of this century or to refuse the opportunity."

In 1916, BEFORE the United States entered the war, Will went to Belgium to help run Hoover's food distribution program, along with other young Americans. At thirty-one he was one of the oldest there.

Suddenly, for the first time, Will was eclipsing his father, who had never been to war. Their relationship changed. The day Will left for Europe, LeRoy wrote John Sharp Williams, who was still in the Senate, advising him on strategy for a flood control bill and confessed, "That boy of mine has gone to Belgium today and I am lonesome."

When America declared war, Will came home and joined the Army. In France he continued to write poems and sent them home. LeRoy was proud enough to show some to Williams, who in turn showed them to the president. Wilson commended them. LeRoy also sent some of Will's letters to the *Memphis Commercial-Appeal,* which published them.

More interesting were the letters LeRoy kept to himself. "Dear Father," Will wrote in the summer of 1918. "There were patches of blue corn-flowers which always remind me of mother's eyes. I lost all interest in field of fire . . . and sniffed the air and watched the very blue distant hills and before the morning was over nearly lost my job for sheer incompetence. Being competent is certainly a difficult matter, and, when the world strikes you as particularly lovely, impossible. . . . When I go up front and see the handful of youngsters that stand immediately between us and the enemy—so full of spirit and so completely 'on their own,' I return with an awful sense of their warm flesh. . . . My work, I suppose, will always be among the chess-players at the top, but my game will never be a good one for I'll never be able to think of the pieces as pawns. And as yet, I haven't seen any of the real horror."

His father, both of them knew, could see soldiers as pawns. And Will would soon see the real horror; in combat he would remain cool, determined, and controlled.

Barely a month later, he wrote: "Dear Father, . . . To be shelled when you are in the open is one of the most terrible of human experiences. You hear this rushing, tearing sound as the thing comes toward you and then the huge explosion as it strikes, and, infinitely worse, you see its hideous work as men stagger, fall, struggle or lie quiet and unrecognizable. A company broke and I saw a colonel trying to rally and direct them. So I joined him and took over the company. . . . It was a vivid, wild experience and I think I went through it calmly by refusing to recognize it as real. You couldn't see men smashed and killed around you, and bear it except by walking in a sort of sleep, as you might read Dante's Inferno. The exhilaration of battle—there's no such thing, except perhaps in a charge. It's simply a matter of will power. As for being without fear, I met no such person under this barrage, though men played their part as if they were without it."

It was a far cry from the ecstasy Andrew Humphreys had felt at Fredericksburg. Will took pride in his performance, writing his mother, "honor I deserved," but he took no pleasure in it. He had only done his duty. After the Armistice he wrote, "Dear Father, . . . This war will furnish the material for great literature for generations to come, but I'm afraid my mould is not heroic enough or else I've seen it from too near to be able to turn the horror into beauty."

He returned as a captain with the Croix de Guerre and gold and silver stars. Father and mother were proud and met him at the dock in New York. He had been to a place his father envied and could not reach. Their relationship had matured and mellowed. They became closer. Will returned home and resumed living in the family mansion on Percy Street. He and his father walked to work together each day, and talked. Will later said, "Of all my experiences, our daily walks . . . are those I least want to forget."

But they had only built a bridge across a chasm between them. The two did not so much see things differently; they saw different things. Ironically, Will, who had been through a war that made most intellectuals bitter cynics, remained the romantic. And as if to compensate for what he must have regarded as his own personal evil, in Greenville he continued to insist on moral perfection and condemned scandal. LeRoy, perhaps remembering the timing of his own marriage, tolerated human weakness and condemned no one. LeRoy understood passion; Will endured it.

They viewed blacks differently as well. LeRoy saw all men, including blacks, as pieces in a larger game. It was almost entirely a question of economics to him, and he could accept an individual Negro as a man, if not a social equal. But then he accepted few whites as social equals. He wrote John Sharp Williams: "The negroes are going to leave the South gradually more and more until the standard of wages is raised throughout the South more nearly to the level of what it is elsewhere. When the negroes once scatter throughout the United States, there would cease to be any sectional or local negro issue, and any issue there would be, would be an issue between the whites and blacks throughout the entire country."

Will had less tolerance for racial differences than his father. In 1921, while LeRoy lobbied former Senate colleagues against all immigration restrictions, Will wrote Williams, "I can't see why we should not adopt a definite policy for the exclusion of Orientals." His feelings about blacks were far more complex, beginning with a naive paternalism. In his autobiography he claimed that the Delta was settled as "slaveholders began to look for cheap fertile lands farther west that could feed the many black mouths dependent on them." His father would have considered absurd the idea that slave owners moved hundreds of miles for the good of their slaves.

Will did protect blacks out of a sense of noblesse oblige. He stopped wearing a hat because that meant tipping it to a white woman but not to a black, and later would have blacks—such as the poet Langston Hughes—as guests in his home, an extraordinary occurrence in the South of the time. Yet, unlike his father, he had difficulty seeing an individual black as a full man. To Will blacks were unknowable, primal. Their mystery and darkness drew him. He wondered, "[W]hat can a white man, north or south, say of them that will even approximate the truth?" He envied "their obliterating genius for living in the present" and noted, "The Negro's moral flabbiness is both his charm and his undoing."

He certainly knew of the liaisons between white men and black women, many semipermanent, and of the huge house on Blanton Street called "The Mansion," where nice clean colored girls entertained white gentlemen. He disapproved, even while suffering his own passion, even while continuing to travel around the world to pursue—and evade—his own dark places and the hunger that repelled him. He wrote a poem about Taormina, home of the dark-skinned young shepherd boys. In the Delta, blacks presented an opaque smiling face to whites, but they were everywhere, unnoticed but knowing everything about whites. Some, it was rumored, might know Will far too well. He called his black personal servant in Greenville "my only tie with Pan and the Satyrs and all earth creatures who smile sunshine and ask no questions and understand." Sometimes self-disgust filled him. In his poem "Medusa," he spoke of "turn[ing] to stone with terror of facing quietly a flawless mirror."

Yet he demanded respect, and got it. He was after all a Percy. But his father had never demanded respect; he had commanded it. So had LeRoy's father, William Alexander Percy, after whom Will had been named.

Indeed, by the time the first William Alexander was forty-two, he had led a regiment in war, reorganized the state's levee system, faced down a mob to stop a lynching, led the "Redemption" of the county, started a railroad, and served as Speaker of the state legislature. By the time LeRoy himself was forty-two, he had brought railroads to the Delta, hunted with the president, maneuvered with and against the Mississippi River Commission, run plantations totaling 30,000 acres, negotiated with the mayor of Rome for Italian immigrants, defended Negroes against white demagogues, advised such financiers as J. P. Morgan, and become the strongest figure in the Delta and one of the strongest in the South.

Will was known only for being his father's son, even while others of his generation had emerged as leaders, such men as Billy Wynn, also a captain in the war whose law office was in the same building as Percy & Percy. Five years earlier when LeRoy had confronted the Klan, Will had stood beside him, always steadfast, always courageous, yet still in the shadows. Even in the midst of that battle he had been busy filling their library with delicate and exquisite volumes, conducting a warm correspondence with bookshops in New York: "I understand that Harper's has published the first volume of Elie Faure's History of Art, translated by Walter Pach. Won't you please get this for me? Have you been able to find 'Nostrom' yet? . . . The dark blue limp leather edition is the one I like best."

He had accepted a few community tasks, such as raising money for good causes. Fellow alumnus Monte Lemann of Monroe & Lemann in New Orleans convinced him to raise money for Harvard Law School. And he became chairman of the Washington County Red Cross. He disliked asking for contributions, but it was his duty and he realized that only with difficulty did someone in the county refuse a Percy.

The Mississippi River had abruptly changed everything. Now, in the emergency, he suddenly had real responsibility. Now the mayor of Greenville, after a conversation with LeRoy, named Will head of a special flood relief committee. The appointment, coupled with his chairmanship of the county Red Cross, gave Will near absolute control over the county during the emergency, and over the care of tens of thousands of refugees. The job would require more of Will than he had ever given anything except his poetry. It would also put everything that mattered to him at risk.

It would be Will's chance to prove himself a true Percy, and to learn precisely what that meant. What he did would have an impact far beyond the Delta, on the nation at large.

CHAPTER TWENTY-FIVE

THE MOUNDS LANDING LEVEE broke at seven-thirty on the morning of April 21. While Greenville waited for the water to reach the city's rear protection levee, the city was in panic. Few fled by car, afraid of being caught by the water on the flat Delta land, but trains out of the city were packed. Grocery stores and wholesale suppliers of every imaginable good were packed. Meanwhile, late that morning, Will, representing the Red Cross, went to the Opera House, a three-story building one block from the levee, and sat down with Will Whittington, the Delta's congressman, General Curtis Green, head of the Mississippi National Guard, A. G. Paxton, the local National Guard commander, and Billy Wynn, a rising power in the county, to plan for the disaster. Even if Greenville remained dry, refugees from the rest of the county would inundate it. Will was nominally in charge, but the meeting was disorderly and chaotic. Paxton spoke first. He was short and officious, and he loved the military (a general in Korea, his men nicknamed him "Bullwhip Shorty"). He stated that he had "commandeered" the building where they were meeting, and spoke of assigning labor battalions as though he were moving armies about. The congressman uselessly promised to demand federal aid. Green arranged for more men and matériel to hold the protection levee. Wynn did the most useful thing: he took responsibility for setting up kitchens for refugees. When the meeting adjourned, Will returned home and began working on his poetry. He would write feverishly deep into that night. He knew it could be his last opportunity for weeks.

While he wrote, the water reached David Cober's house outside the city. Cober remembers: "We heard this storm coming through the woods. It wasn't a storm. It was the water." It came in as rolling surf first, five-foot-high breakers, crashing against the house; the house shook under the attack, then the water rose. "Our house was six or seven feet off the ground. The water came in fourteen or fifteen feet deep." The house had only one story; water entered and forced them to stand on tables. It kept rising. In the darkness of the night, Cober dove down into the swirling water looking for an ax, kept diving until he found it, then hacked a hole in the roof and his family climbed out onto it.

The Greenville protection levee stood eight feet high. The water paused briefly, then ripped the levee apart as smoothly as if unzipping it. The fire whistle went off. The sound was, Will said, "like zero made audible."

THEN CAME THE CHAOS. Water roared and hissed, the fire whistle blasted, church bells clanged, animals barked and neighed and bellowed in terror. In Newtown, the black neighborhood closest to the protection levee, hundreds of families began to wade through the rising water to the Mississippi levee, the highest ground in the Delta. Twenty-five hundred others fled to the courthouse, packed it tight. The water rose quickly to 3 feet, 5 feet, 8 feet, dark churning water, chocolate with brown foam. The currents poured into downtown, sweeping the streets empty. "Water was just rolling in, like you see the waves down in Gulfport," recalled Jesse Pollard. "They were high —you saw horses and cows floating. If you were standing on the levee, you could see people floating who had drowned. It was a sight you never forget."

One last train tried to escape. But outside the city the crevasse water was roaring over the railroad embankment, washing it away in its entirety, leaving the rails turned upright like a picket fence. A mile beyond the city limits the train derailed. It would remain there, a twisted Gargantua lying helpless, for months.

In the Percy home, father and son were on the phone long before dawn, collecting information, tracking the water, locating food supplies and boats, contracting for boats to be built. Now in the early daybreak, LeRoy told his son wearily, "Guess you better go while you can. I'll be along." Will headed for a meeting with the relief committee in the poker room of the Knights of Columbus hall. Then his mother, Camille, and the cook went out to gather what final groceries they could find.

LeRoy was finally alone. He had spent his life building the Delta. His two greatest adversaries had always been the river and the shortage of labor. The river was invading his home now, snaking down his street, *Percy* Street, flooding his garden, overflowing his tennis court—the only one in the city—climbing the steps of his porch. And he knew the river would send blacks flooding north, stripping the Delta of labor.

The life he had known was dying. It had been so at least since Vardaman had so bitterly defeated him. He expected it to die. But if he was fatalistic, he had never simply yielded to fate. One did all that one could. He could do nothing about the river. But he could still control men. He picked up the telephone.

He first tracked down the governor and said he wanted the state to guarantee Delta banks that any funds expended for relief would be repaid. Murphree agreed. Then Percy got on the phone to New York bankers and began soliciting money, both as contributions and loans.

Meanwhile, Will and the relief committee were trying to establish order. They needed to take charge of boats, food supply, drinking water, kitchens, lights, transportation, sanitation, police. But there were crossed lines of authority, not enough resources, not enough food, no shelter for the refugees.

Rescuers were depositing thousands of refugees from all over the Delta on the levee, to join the city's own thousands already there. Farmers moved cattle, mules, horses, and pigs to the levee as well. The Mississippi River lay on one side, the flood on the other. The levee crown was only 8 feet wide, its landside slope an additional 10 to 40 feet wide before touching water. A line of people already stretched north from downtown for more than a mile.

At midday LeRoy called his son, who dispatched a boat to take him to the relief headquarters. LeRoy's presence mattered. People too busy to come to the phone for Will or Paxton came to the phone for him. Though Will nominally gave the orders, Hunter Kimbrough, who stayed in the Percy home for the first ten days of the flood, recalls, "Senator Percy was in charge." Despite the shortage of boats, LeRoy had a 17-foot motorboat, a driver, and a mechanic assigned to him personally. That first day he, Will, Billy Wynn, and Paxton decided to declare "voluntary" martial law. They had no legal authority to do so. The mayor had no role in the decision, nor the city council, nor the county board of supervisors. But the next edition of the newspaper announced: "All citizens of Greenville, all refugees . . . and all property necessary in Relief work are subject to orders from this [National Guard] headquarters. . . . Disobedience will not be tolerated." The authority came from the signatures: Will, as chairman of the Washington County Relief Committee, T. R. Buchanan, the

Red Cross relief expert assigned to the county, and LeRoy for "the Citizens."

Martial law solved little. Virtually the entire county was underwater, as much as 20 feet of water. The current everywhere was ferocious. People took shelter in railroad boxcars, in the upper stories of cotton gins, oil mills, houses, and barns. Thousands clung to roofs or trees, or sat on the levee awaiting pickup. The rain and cold continued. By the second day after the crevasse, despite the several thousand, nearly all whites, who fled the city, refugees pushed Greenville's normal population of 15,000 to nearly 25,000. Every hour rescuers were bringing hundreds more in from around the county. Twenty-five thousand more people were scattered around the rest of the county. The city was cut off from supply. The National Guard had only 5,000 rations.

By now five miles of the narrow levee were crammed with refugees, almost all of them there black, and refugees were still pouring in. Thousands of head of livestock extended farther. The number of refugees and livestock would keep growing. Without shelter or dry clothes in the continuing rain, with temperatures dropping into the forties at night, with only the sparest of rations, the refugees stood in mud, sat in mud, slept in mud. The *Greenville Democrat-Times* reported: "Flood conditions continue to grow worse in Greenville as refugees continue to be brought in from outlying sections and are huddled in every available space. . . . Cold weather added to the suffering as food and water supply here becomes lower."

The situation was becoming life-threatening. Rumors began to spread of sickness, of a possible epidemic. An urgent call for typhoid serum went out. Dogs swarmed over the levee; without food or their owners, they were barking endlessly and rapidly turning wild, making rabies a real threat. The levee was a madhouse. General Malin Craig, commander of the Army's IV Corps in Atlanta, was unsympathetic to the refugees in general and shipped out tents and field kitchens only reluctantly, at a niggardly pace. But even he warned the War Department: "Conditions Greenville area critical."

Rescue barges already full began squeezing white women and children aboard in Greenville to take them to Vicksburg, where they could make rail connections elsewhere or remain in well-organized camps. The barges also removed some of the blacks to Vicksburg. Yet Greenville's population continued to grow as even more refugees arrived.

Then the city water supply became contaminated and useless. An Associated Press dispatch reported, "The situation here, with the water supply gone, most of the food destroyed, and . . . ten thousand . . . camping on the levee, was desperate." Will, as chairman of the relief committee, had tried to respond. He had just sent out an urgent plea for 20,000 loaves of bread. But even if bread came, the logistic problems were long-term, not short-term. The flood had cut off the city for weeks, possibly months. Without rail connections, supplying Greenville would be nearly impossible.

The most obvious solution was to evacuate the refugees. But evacuation would denude Washington County of its labor supply, particularly sharecroppers. They would have nothing to return to. Most of them had with them on the levee the little they had been able to salvage before the flood washed their homes away. All that remained were their debts to the planters. It could take years to replace the croppers. They might never be replaced.

The question of evacuation went to the essence of Will's concept of a worthy aristocracy, of noblesse oblige, even of honor. Keeping the refugees on the levee risked their lives. There was no question of what was right, and therefore no choice.

Yet a decision of such import had to have at least the appearance of broad support. Will did not consult Paxton, a cotton broker, or Wynn. He consulted only his Red Cross committee, Percy loyalists. Its vice chairman was Judge Emmet Harty, another bachelor who had gone to war with Will and was his closest friend in Greenville, and its members included Charlie Williams, who ran the Percy cotton compress, and Will Hardie, the manager of Percy's Trail Lake Plantation. "Whatever Senator Percy wanted, that's what white folks in this county did," says the son of another committee member, B. B. Payne.

Will told them the refugees had to be evacuated. They believed he spoke for his father. Still, several committee members objected. Will insisted. They faced a great human disaster. One could not risk hundreds of lives simply over an economic question. Grudgingly but unanimously, they approved Will's plan.

On April 23, the Greenville paper, whose owner served on Will's committee and was another longtime supporter, said, "The city will almost be evacuated within a few days." Will informed Governor Murphree, who declared, "It is the plan of state authorities to remove from Greenville all the refugees and all other persons who desire to leave the city."

But Will had not discussed the plan with his father.

Senator Percy had been focused on problems only he could resolve, most recently convincing banks in New York, New Orleans, and St. Louis to honor checks drawn on Delta banks. Will had simply assumed his father's support and made the decision himself. Evacuation was after all the right thing to do, and the only honorable option.

What they did would define their society.

On Monday, April 25, the government steamer *Control* left Greenville with 500 white women and children. The *Minnesota* loaded more than 1,000 refugees, mostly black, at the wharf. Two other steamers, the *Wabash* and the *Kappa,* were standing by. The *Sprague, Tollinger,* and *Cincinnati* were en route, each towing barges capable of carrying several thousand each. The city would be virtually emptied in a day.

Blacks who lived in Greenville protested to Will that they did not want to leave their homes. Will simply had troops round them up, later explaining, "[N]one of us was influenced by what the Negroes themselves wanted: they had no capacity to plan for their own welfare; planning for them was another of our burdens."

But he could not ignore angry planters who went to LeRoy and denounced any evacuation. LeRoy told them Will was in charge. They then stormed into Red Cross headquarters to demand that he rescind his order. Will responded bitingly, accusing them of thinking of their pocketbooks while he was thinking of the Negro's welfare. Furious now, the planters went back to LeRoy. He gave them no satisfaction. But when they left, LeRoy went to find his son.

LeRoy Percy had spent his life trying to help Delta blacks. He had opposed stripping them of the right to vote, had insisted upon educating them decently, had confronted the race-baiting politicians like Vardaman and Bilbo, had even confronted and defeated the Klan in Washington County. For all this he had earned praise from around the nation. Yet all this he had done not simply because it was right and good; self-interest had operated too. He had needed their strong backs.

Now he found Will bursting with fury on the levee. It resembled a war zone, all confusion and noise, choked with smoke from kitchens, people on litters, squalling children, and a few men with purpose struggling to establish order. White women and children massed around gangplanks waiting to board the steamboats; the barges would carry Negroes and terrified livestock. Several white men, claiming illness or urgent business, also demanded space on a steamer; the crowd hissed at them for being cowards and the National Guard turned them back. Gangs of black men under white foremen were unloading supplies. Several more gangs of men were banging hammers, building a scaffold above the floodwater to connect the

Red Cross headquarters, the second floor of the American Legion Building, the Opera House, the Cowan Hotel, and the levee.

Through the chaos, through the thickets of people, LeRoy and Will began to walk. Along the levee they walked as if alone, a study in generations. The elder could easily have been a character out of Henry James, immaculately dressed, formal, pacing through the muddy quagmire in a suit and hunting boots, a man of substance and influence and no illusions. Will, smaller physically, less of a man in every way by the standards of the Delta, had illusions of a once-great and noble South, of a brilliant and shimmering aristocracy, and of the perfection of the man beside him.

LeRoy raised the issue of the evacuation gently, asking Will if he had listened carefully to the complaints of the planters. Yes, Will replied sharply, he had heard from louts who cared more about money than about what was right. He would not be cowed by them. LeRoy agreed. One did not yield to pressure. Yet was it really necessary to send the blacks away? Could steamboats not supply the refugees on the levee? Had Will really considered the harm to the Delta of removing its labor force?

Their conversation was intense but private. Will would not be shaken, not even by his father. Despite the stream of decisions others needed from them, no one interrupted. They paced, their boots mud-caked, up the levee, turned, headed back. Neither yielded to the other.

Finally, LeRoy said that the decision was too important for Will to make alone. He had to consult the other members of his committee. Will replied that he had done so. There was no reason to speak to them again. Consult them again, LeRoy insisted. Do it for him.

Will finally agreed. They stood outside the Red Cross headquarters. Will went in and abruptly ordered the loading of the refugees to stop. The steamboat captains angrily protested that their boats and barges represented a tremendously valuable resource in the disaster. Far more than Greenville was involved. They could not simply wait; time was too valuable. Will would not budge for them either. The captains had to wait.

Instead, he summoned his committee members to an emergency meeting. But before it convened, LeRoy informed each member that Will had spoken only for himself in proposing evacuation. He asked them to oppose the evacuation now and, to prevent embarrassment to Will, not to reveal the fact that he had talked with them. With relief the members agreed. When Will convened the committee a few hours later, one after another the members said the Negroes should stay on the levee. Will was astounded. How could they reverse themselves? Why? He argued with them for two hours, but the committee members were as unyielding as he. Finally, Will capitulated, then went to tell furious ship captains that the blacks would remain on the levee.

The steamers did not leave quite empty. The *Wabash,* capable of carrying several thousand, departed with thirty-three white women and children.

ALTHOUGH WILL CLAIMED that only years later did he learn what his father had done, he had to have known what had happened. He knew these men. He understood they would have abandoned him only for his father. His father had betrayed honor and his own son, for money. There is a saying that if a man has to choose between the truth and his father, only a fool chooses the truth. Will chose not to be a fool. He wrote a poet friend how much he appreciated his father's support, that without it he would have had a "breakdown." He was forty-two years old and had been treated as less than a child. In his humiliation, he began to humiliate the black men and women at his mercy on the levee. There would be national repercussions.

THE NEXT MORNING Hoover and his traveling party arrived in Greenville on their first trip downriver. Hoover was cordial. He was pleased to meet LeRoy, of whom he had heard so much good. He spoke with Will of Belgium. Then he listened.

Hoover had already approved the evacuation plan. Now Will presented a new plan as if it were his own. Rather than evacuate the city, it would become a point of concentration. All supplies—food, clothing, tents, construction material—for the roughly 50,000 people stranded in the county would be shipped to Greenville, unloaded, and transshipped elsewhere. A refugee camp would be established on the levee; blacks from the camp would provide the workforce to move these goods.

Hoover approved, then headed south, to be met that evening by Jim Thomson in Vicksburg. Meanwhile, Will issued a public statement that, to ease the burden, "We are urging all white women and children to leave the city. White men may also go although there is a need for them to stay. . . . There is need for negro men to stay and establish the camp."

The same day Hoover visited, the first refugee death occurred in Greenville. A black man who had not eaten for days gorged himself on bananas and suddenly collapsed, dead. His body was put in a boat and rowed out into the middle of the river. Several thousand people, white and black, silently lined the levee. Stones were tied around the dead man's feet and arms. A minister said a few words. A boatman lifted the body over the gunnel. It splashed into the river and sank. But rumors spread that the National Guard had thrown him into the river alive as punishment for stealing the bananas.

There were other rumors. The police chief was a man named Red Taggart. He could be rough. On Saturday nights he would find blacks rolling dice, walk in, and nobody would move. He'd pick up all the money on the table and smile. But he treated people fair in the jail. He didn't beat people. Now, in the flood, he regularly towed black bodies found floating in the streets to the levee. Rumors spread that Taggart had caught the men looting and shot them, then towed the body through the streets as a warning. Looting had become a problem, and this rumor was useful to whites; instead of correcting it, they decreed an 8 P.M. curfew enforced only on blacks.

The truth was harsh enough. Although the Red Cross would ultimately operate 154 "concentration camps" in Illinois, Missouri, Kentucky, Tennessee, Arkansas, Mississippi, and Louisiana, only one camp would generate enough criticism to bring intense political pressure on Hoover—the camp on the levee in Greenville. And his approval of Percy's course would haunt him.

IN GREENVILLE, a week after the flooding, a very different routine for black and white had developed. Approximately 4,000 whites remained on second floors and in offices or hotels. A few hundred whites, like the Percys, continued to occupy their own homes. For whites daily life came to resemble a dreary holiday. Paperboys delivered the newspaper, which was down to four pages, by boat. The scaffolding became a boardwalk extending throughout the business section; peddlers set up stands on it and sold soda, peanuts, and popcorn. Frank's Café was accessible from the boardwalk and stayed open twenty-four hours. Rowboats were ordered to the middle of streets so motorboats could use the deeper water near the curb. City court opened. One mechanic used blocks of wood to elevate the frame of his truck five feet and drove down the shallower streets; others imitated him. Boys invented new games: they punctured the carcasses of floating cows and mules and ignited the escaping gas. The 125-room Cowan Hotel on Main Street, the Delta's finest, kept open its Blue Bird Café, poolroom, cigar stand in the lobby, and fine dining room. On its mezzanine, people constantly played the piano, sang, and danced. It had no trouble getting meat and supplies from

Armour, Swift, or Goyer. The general public could find, for the right price, most things—except sugar, which did run out—either from bootleggers or at the Roslyn Hotel, where a thriving black market operated.

But elsewhere in Greenville the situation was desperate. Two black children had been bitten by rabid dogs, and orders had gone out to shoot all dogs on the levee. Percy Bell, a prominent attorney involved in relief work (and not related to the Percys), had sent his family out of the city. Ten days after the crevasse he wrote them: "The town is a pitiful and horrifying sight. The yards with the trees and abundance of roses everywhere are really beautiful, and yet when one gets near and sees the water in the houses and furniture floating around on the inside, sees a dead mule clinging to the veranda, the horror of it strikes in. Hundreds of mules have been dragged to the levee and dumped in." In the black neighborhoods, where the water had come hard, many houses were only splinters. On Nelson Street "water [is] up to the top of all roofs, tops of porches and second stories are covered with darkeys and cats in one terrific welter."

Roughly 5,000 blacks crowded into warehouses, oil mills, and stores. Up to 13,000 more blacks lived on the levee in an elongated city that ultimately snaked more than eight miles, complete with electric lights, pipes for water, barges for latrines. Tents had finally arrived for shelter and the weather had turned warm, but the tents were not floored and cots had not arrived, so refugees still slept on the wet ground. There were no eating utensils or mess hall. Blacks had to eat with their fingers, standing or squatting on their haunches like animals. Beyond the line of tents, for more miles farther up the levee, were thousands of livestock. The stench was unbearable.

In the first hours of the flood, black and white had risked their lives to save each other. There had been a feeling of humanity, not race. Now the disparity between life for black and white seemed greater than in normal life. Blacks, who had believed Greenville to be a special place, felt betrayed.

Petty insults stirred more resentment. Whenever the steamer *Capitol* pulled away from the dock, its calliope routinely played "Bye Bye Blackbird." It was like a slap in the face to the blacks; even many whites were bothered. The blacks also resented Will's orders, which were printed every day on the newspaper's front page. First he required "groups of negroes outside of Greenville . . . [to] get to the levee and be rationed there." Leaders of the black community complained. So did whites. Bell told LeRoy that moving "all the negroes from the country to the levee . . . was utterly impossible. . . . There are not tents to shield them and nothing to feed them." And if they stayed where they were, "as soon as the water was down to a foot or two they could work through the water" and accomplish something. Within hours after the paper published his order, Will countermanded it, reversing himself again, this time publicly, further undermining his own authority.

There were more substantive problems. The food blacks received was vastly inferior to that given whites, and not much more than what was needed to stay alive. Canned peaches were sent in; none went to blacks for fear it would "spoil" them. Charlie Loeb, who ran a first-rate restaurant, slaughtered six to eight cattle a day at the main levee kitchen. Few blacks got the meat.

But the most serious grievance penetrated to the soul. The blacks were no longer free. The National Guard patrolled the perimeter of the levee camp with rifles and fixed bayonets. To enter or leave, one needed a pass. They were imprisoned.

This was true in every camp in the state. Mississippi was determined to keep its workers if it required force to do so. The governor declared, "It is our duty to return these people to their homes and every camp under our control will handle the situation in this manner." Green, the Guard commander, ordered, "[I]n no case will the camp commander release refugees without . . . an American Red Cross request in writing . . . or upon direct orders from this office." The Red Cross cooperated. A memo on "return of refugees" stated, "Plantation owners desiring their labor to be returned from Refugee Camps will make application to the nearest Red Cross representative," whereupon they "will issue passes to refugees." In Greenville, Will told planters to "furnish a list of their negro tenants" and to advise him "when they wanted the tenants returned to their homes."

Oscar Johnston did more than supply a list. He ran the Delta & Pine Land Company, the largest cotton plantation in the world, and counted among his intimates not only LeRoy and such bankers as Jim Butler and Rudolph Hecht in New Orleans, but also executives at the Chemical and Chase Banks in New York and stockholders in London. Like LeRoy, he had charm and joked, "I have seen nothing but water for the last three weeks, and what I have seen has been too muddy for bathing and too filthy to serve as a chaser." Also, like LeRoy, he had no humor when it came to labor. In an effort to hold tenants from his plantation, he established his own refugee camp, supplied by the Red Cross, patrolled by the National Guard, and managed by his foremen. But 450 of his tenants had been rescued from rooftops or the levee and taken to Vicksburg; he had the Illinois

Central make up a special train, without charge, to carry them 260 miles to his camp at Deeson.

In Greenville control was tighter still. While whites in the city could stay in their homes, Will ordered all Greenville blacks to the levee. He intended to use them. Salvador Signa, a white man, was one of those sent to round up Negroes. He wore a gun. " 'Don't give 'em anything to eat,' they told me. 'Get them to go to levee . . .' 'Hey white folks,' this nigger said. 'I's hungry.' 'Well,' I said, 'you don't have to be hungry long. You can just put your feet right in the boat and we'll take you right on up to the levee, up to the kitchen, and we'll give you all the food you want.' "

Once on the levee, blacks were worked. LeRoy, seeking more aid from the Red Cross, described the need to the press: "Here 440,000 acres of land in one county, totally submerged, touch no dry land except the remnant of the levee on the western border. Every ounce of food for man or beast has to be transported first by large boats and then distributed by all sorts of small boats over miles of yellow, ofttimes stormy water, to a hundred almost inaccessible spots, each holding from 25 to 3,000 people and their surviving livestock."

Unloading barges to feed and supply nearly 50,000 people, and thousands of animals—horses, mules, cattle, pigs, oxen, poultry —required constant labor. Reloading onto smaller boats for distribution required labor. To supply drinking water alone meant unloading thousands of 5-gallon containers, each weighing more than 40 pounds. Preparing the food, feeding livestock, sorting and distributing supplies, all required labor. Extending the boardwalk, cleaning buildings, repairing the water supply system, putting flooring under tents, all required labor. Will Percy had to get labor. Humiliated twice by being forced to reverse himself, sensitive to criticism, he had turned cold. He was not in the mood to ask black men for help. He had the National Guard.

Paxton, the Guard commander, wired the state adjutant general, "Imperative to increase guard force here. . . . Urge you order 200 additional guardsmen here at once." The additional troops came. Will used them against the blacks. And word of the treatment of black refugees began to leak out of Greenville, despite its isolation, into the North.

IN GREENVILLE blacks had believed they had a special relationship with whites, especially the Percys. LeRoy had allowed them pride. Now Will was emasculating them, turning them into cattle, with each new order stripping more pride away. Will declared, "No able-bodied negro is entitled to be fed at all unless he is tagged as a laborer."

The tags were given out with a job assignment and also used to keep track of those who had received typhoid shots; they were large, like laundry tags, worn on shirts. To wear one was humiliating. Without one, a man could get no food for himself or his family.

And in other refugee camps, even where work was forced, laborers earned wages. Will ordered that all Red Cross work be done for free. Food was the only compensation. The levee camp became a slave camp.

Salvador Signa delivered the mail and recalled: "Me and Horace both had great big guns strapped on, heavier than the [mail] bags. . . . We'd just knock on those tents and those darkies . . . we'd tell 'em, 'All right. We got some [mail sacks] to go.' Well, they'd always want to haul mail so they wouldn't have to unload that alfalfa hay on them barges in the hot sun. . . . If the sack was heavy, I'd let one darkey carry in the front and one in the back."

The Guard was far more brutal. The Guard had power of the most elemental kind. They had guns and controlled men in a camp. Even without the complication of race, such power intoxicates, creates arrogance. And there was race.

John Johnson, a black refugee, recalled: "They wasn't given too good a food from that Red Cross up there. . . . Some of the people got beat bad up there. Everybody had a gun—white kids and men, and of course you had the National Guard."

Mrs. Henry Ransom, a white, remembered: "The Guard would come along and say, 'There's a boat coming up. Go unload.' If they didn't hurry up, they'd kick them. They didn't mind taking their guns, pistols out, and knocking them over the head."

Percy McRaney, a black, said: "The colored people caught tough times around Greenville. . . . Whites were kicking coloreds and beating them and knocking them around like dogs. Hungry people, they wouldn't feed them sometimes."

Joe Reilly, a white man, remembers: "On the levee during the day you only saw women and kids. . . . The mood was sad, pitiful looking. There wasn't any singing. The men were all out working somewhere."

Mrs. Addie Oliver, a black, complained blacks were treated "just like dogs, I'll tell you. They were treated like dogs."

John Butler, a black, went from Greenville to Vicksburg and complained he had worked all night, been relieved, then was "caught" in the morning by soldiers who "carried us up there and whipped us with a gun strap." An official investigation conceded that numerous "negroes . . . were caught slipping out of camp and were . . . whipped, the men using a strap taken off of one of their rifles."

Two particular companies of the Guard, from Corinth and Lambert, Mississippi, neither of which were in the Delta, beat black refugees, beat them for back talk, beat them for trying to leave the camp. Men from these two companies were accused of theft—entering tents at will, interrupting card games, taking all the money—rape, and at least one murder. Will sent home the troops from the two companies, later conceding the Guard was "guilty of acts which profoundly and justly made the negroes fear them." But the departure of the two detachments did not soothe black feelings. Will's orders had set the tone. He could not or would not reset it. And he still needed workers.

Weeks after the levee broke, water was still pouring through both the Mounds Landing break and the city's protection levee. Will notified the Red Cross in Memphis and Vicksburg of continued food shortages, then wrote a friend that the situation resembled "the Argonne in its strain and confusion and distress." On May 12, without a satisfactory reply from Red Cross managers, LeRoy complained to the press, "To falter or fail . . . now would mean the sacrifice of human lives, the starvation of livestock, the devastation and abandonment of a once-proud county. The stake is human lives and an empire."

And it was his empire.

AT LAST sufficient supplies began to arrive. The Warrior barge line began making regular stops at Greenville; the line had been created by the federal government during World War I to move bulk cargo, and since then had become a competitor of railroads. Enormously powerful tugs pushed huge barges cabled together, and each barge carried 300 to 400 tons of food to unload and distribute.

Will needed labor more than ever. Finally, he tried a method other than force, meeting with twenty-five carefully chosen black ministers. Most Greenville blacks dismissed them as tools of the whites. He lectured them, called the cooperation of the Negroes "rotten," and warned that Negroes who did not work would be treated as "vagrants" in court. Rev. J. B. Stanton replied for the group, "We will stand by you and make conditions so that we can do our duty as men, for this is our home."

But Will's "appeal" further angered the black community. Soon he issued a new order: "The negroes in town outside of camp have done nothing toward unloading and transporting the very food they ask for and receive. This will not be tolerated. . . . 1. No rations will be issued to Greenville negro women and children unless there is no man in the family, which fact must be certified by a white person. 2. No negro man in Greenville nor their families will be rationed unless the men join the labor gang or are employed. 3. Negro men . . . drawing a higher wage [than $1 a day] are not entitled to be rationed."

Private employers had been hiring labor to repair buildings, salvage merchandise. In effect, Will was now setting the wages these private employers paid at $1 a day. Even the black workers would not want more if it meant their family would have to pay for food and clothing they would otherwise receive free.

In other camps, while much of the labor was forced, much was also performed by choice. In other camps, employers were paying blacks from $1.25 to $2 a day and the Red Cross still fed them. In other camps, blacks working for the Red Cross were also paid at this rate. In Greenville, Will was still paying nothing for Red Cross work, which included the handling of all supplies, and the work was performed by men working under guns.

IN EARLY MAY, Negro newspapers around the country began to publish stories about abuses of black refugees in Greenville. "Refugees Herded Like Cattle to Stop Escape from Peonage," blared the *Chicago Defender*. "Conscript Labor Gangs Keep Flood Refugees in Legal Bondage," the *Pittsburgh Courier* charged. "Deny Food to Flood Sufferers; Relief Bodies Issue Work or Starve Rule," the *Defender* hissed again, blaming "W. A. Percy . . . whose prejudice against members of our Race is as bitter as gall."

Word of conditions in Greenville was also spreading into the white Progressive community, the single constituency most supportive of Hoover's presidential ambitions and most concerned about the treatment of the Negro. Word had not yet gotten into the white press, which was churning about him.

CHAPTER TWENTY-SIX

IN THE 1920S, Negroes had a voice in national Republican politics. Their power was not enormous, but it was real. Part of that power came indirectly, through some of the party's whites, especially the Progressives and intellectuals, who clung to the tradition of Lincoln. Teddy Roosevelt's 1904 platform had called for reducing congressional representation for states that did not allow blacks to vote, and as late as January 1927, Senate Republicans threatened to investigate the disenfranchisement of southern blacks. In March 1927, the Supreme Court, mostly Republican appointees, had outlawed a whites-only primary. Hoover, who was opposed by virtually all the political professionals, needed Progressive support more than any other presidential candidate. It was the closest thing he had to a natural constituency.

Blacks also had power because of their votes. In the North black voters had made their presence felt in several cities, especially Chicago. Though only about 8 percent of the population, since 77 percent of blacks were registered compared to 68 percent of whites, they made up close to 10 percent of voters. Voting as a solid bloc, they were key, for example, to the election of three-term Mayor "Big Bill" Thompson, especially in the 1927 election. Thompson had Al Capone's support, his City Hall was derided as Uncle Tom's Cabin," and he courted Irish votes by demanding the burning of the public library's "pro-English" books, but Thomson's victory that year over an incumbent Irish mayor came from his 94 percent support among black voters. Similarly, in the 1924 presidential election, well over 90 percent of northern blacks voted Republican, with most of the remaining vote going to LaFollete's Progressives, not to Democrats, whose convention that year had refused to condemn the Ku Klux Klan.

In addition, the Republican presidential nominating process gave blacks power. The base of this power was, ironically, the South. Although no southern state had voted for a Republican presidential candidate since Reconstruction, few blacks voted in general elections,* and a "Lily White" Republican movement had already emerged, blacks still controlled the GOP in several states. This control meant little in the South itself. Even Republican presidents gave few federal patronage jobs to blacks, who could only direct patronage to friendly whites; in Mississippi, for example, black Republicans routinely consulted LeRoy Percy on federal appointments.

But southern states also comprised 30 percent of the delegates needed for the presidential nomination. A significant, if variable, percentage of these delegates were black. To a presidential candidate, support from such a solid bloc of delegates made a powerful base from which to climb to the nomination.

For Hoover black support or opposition was particularly important. Publicity over his handling of the flood had virtually created his candidacy, but it could evaporate in a moment if the seeming triumph exploded in scandal. A scandal over race in particular would make both the party's Progressives and its black politicians desert. Hoover had no geographic base to compensate, and party professionals still considered him a pariah. At stake was power. The flood could mean power.

CLAUDE BARNETT ran the Associated Negro Press, which syndicated stories to 135 African-American newspapers. A hustler, a man who was committed both to his own advancement and that of his race, Barnett had played an active role in past GOP presidential nominating campaigns. In early May, after spending time in the flooded areas, he warned Hoover of rumors of "injustice" and much "scandal."

From Greenville a black minister anonymously—he feared the National Guard—protested to Coolidge. Most likely the writer was Rev. E. M. Weddington, who had signed the letter praising LeRoy after his anti-Klan speech. The minister complained that whites got good clothing while half-naked and shoeless blacks got nothing, and that blacks were "being made to work under the gun, [whites] just

---

* Only in Memphis did blacks vote in large enough numbers—often 5,000 black votes were cast—to determine election outcomes. There the white political boss Edward Crump, whose brother had run LeRoy Percy's Senate campaign, cooperated with a black machine run by Robert Church.

bossing the colored men with big guns buckled to them. . . . All of this mean and brutish treatment of the colored people is nothing but downright slavery."

Soon warnings were pouring in to Hoover of problems. Kansas Republican Senator Arthur Capper, a director of the NAACP, wrote him to "voice the protest of the colored citizens of Topeka against alleged mistreatment of Negro refugees. . . . Colored people are being isolated in refugee camps where they are being held virtually prisoners under the supervision of national guardsmen. . . . [and] discriminated against in the matter of food." He enclosed a copy of the *Chicago Defender* that detailed abuses in Greenville by W. A. Percy, and called the report "reliable."

Jane Addams, the nationally prominent social worker who would soon win the Nobel Peace Prize, had supported Hoover for president in 1920. She relayed "charges of race discrimination which are being rumored" and urged him to appoint a "colored committee" to investigate.

A letter from a black Republican activist read: "It is said that many relief boats have hauled whites only, have gone to imperilled [*sic*] districts and taken all whites out and left the Negroes; it is also said that planters in some instances hold their labor at the point of a gun for fear they would get away and not return. In other instances, it is said that mules have been given preference on boats to Negroes."

Even professional Red Cross staff outside the flooded area were asking colleagues in Memphis and Vicksburg for the truth about Greenville, Mississippi.

Inevitably, ten days after Barnett's first warning to Hoover, white reporters began asking questions. Fieser, the Red Cross vice chairman who was traveling with Hoover, wired an underling, "Chicago Defender leading colored paper carries article concerning . . . Greenville. . . . Chicago Tribune is interesting itself in article and asks for statement. Rush wire reply."

HOOVER NEEDED NO ONE to explain the importance of the press. It was he who had said "the world lives by phrases" and had talked of "the club of public opinion." He also had little use for bigots and exploiters. He wired Henry Baker, head of the relief effort, and ordered him to contact every Red Cross representative in the field and find out if "colored people are being restrained in the camps against their will, second that they are being tagged for return to specific plantations, third that they are being charged by Red Cross for food. Any such action would be a negation of the spirit of the Red Cross and I do not believe it exists . . . see that no such activity exists . . . send me a report at once."

Baker had already told Barnett's Associated Negro Press, "The American Red Cross makes no distinction as to race, creed, politics or anything else in its relief work. . . . The way the Red Cross was treating the Negro in the disaster was much better than the treatment received by the Negro in normal conditions."

Then the answers to Hoover's questions began coming back from the field. In some areas, blacks were well treated. A black leader and NAACP activist in Pine Bluff replied: "Never before have I seen the colored line obliterated to the same extent. The dominant thought appeared to be to relieve suffering, save humanity, care for the needy regardless of color . . . after the Red Cross assumed charge." But several Red Cross chapters wired back not with an answer but with a "request [for] source of information." Others described a situation less than ideal: "Charges that colored refugees have been restrained in camps are true to extent that we have tried to keep them here until . . . conditions were satisfactory for return," or, "We are endeavoring to restrain the refugees from going anywhere at the present time, but this is being done because of a written order from Mississippi State Board of Health." Still others were blunt. Said one camp commander: "It is the desire of all concerned that labor be returned to places from which they were forced to leave . . . for the general good of the entire state."

Baker immediately forwarded the information to Washington. It was kept secret. But the NAACP began publicly demanding explanations, particularly about Mississippi, and particularly about Greenville.

Hoover's friend Will Irwin, a celebrated liberal journalist, had visited the flood area and defended Hoover in the black community. He reported, "I have managed to call off most of the dogs I know." But he could not call off the NAACP's Walter White, whom Irwin called "a fanatic. . . . I argued with him at length . . . but you can't make a dent on him. . . . White is literally the nigger in the woodpile and if anything can be done to placate or squelch him I think there will be no more trouble. . . . Perhaps if some of the big negroes would communicate with him they might tone him down." Using "big negroes" was precisely what Hoover had in mind. He would need them.

White, a friend of Sinclair Lewis, Clarence Darrow, and H. L. Mencken, had been scheduled to leave for Europe on a Guggenheim Fellowship but delayed his departure to investigate flood conditions. Blue-eyed, blond, and light-skinned, he went to Mississippi passing for white and began asking questions. On May 27 in New York he held a potentially devastating press conference. While praising the Red Cross, he condemned abuses he had witnessed in Vicksburg and complained he had been unable to visit Greenville. The *New York Times,* the *New York Herald Tribune,* and other northern papers ran articles repeating his charges, while *The Nation* ran an article by him. His revelations, if unanswered, could echo, spark a press frenzy, and ultimately poison the intellectual community against Hoover.

Just prior to White's press conference Hoover met with five black leaders in his suite at the Peabody Hotel in Memphis. Immediately afterward, at their suggestion, Hoover telegraphed Robert Russa Moton, who had succeeded Booker T. Washington as principal of Tuskegee Institute. The wire misspelled Moton's name "Moulton," an indignity Moton could ignore considering its contents. "With view to making certain as to the proper treatment of the colored folks in the concentration camps and with view to inquire into any complaints," Hoover said, "I would like you to advise me as to the appointment of a commission of representative colored citizens who can visit these camps and who can make investigation of any complaint or criticisms. I would be glad if you would appoint such a commission or designate to us the names of those you think should be appointed."

On May 28, the same day that newspapers carried stories about Walter White's charges, Hoover named a Colored Advisory Commission. It was comprised of sixteen prominent Negro men and two women, all suggested by Moton. Moton chaired it.

MOTON WAS the white man's biggest Negro. If he lacked the stature of Booker T. Washington, in the white world then no black man had that stature. And Moton had inherited Washington's mantle along with his title, and more than any other Negro he represented his race in the councils of the powerful. Although criticized by more aggressive and radical blacks, he felt that weight and responsibility. On his own authority, before reports of abuses had reached even the black press, he had dispatched an assistant to investigate conditions. Now he had Hoover's authority.

Those he selected for the Colored Advisory Commission resembled himself, blacks who knew how to attract white patronage. Three commission members worked directly for him at Tuskegee. The others included Barnett, who had graduated from Tuskegee and was about to become a trustee there, J. S. Clark, president of Southern University in Baton Rouge, and L. M. McCoy, president of Rust College in Mississippi. He did not choose a single representative of the NAACP, which was so influenced by Washington's rival W. E. B. DuBois and called for a more aggressive approach to race relations. Even one commission member noted privately that his colleagues were "some of the most conservative men of the country."

The most radical member was Sidney Redmond, and Moton's handling of his appointment indicated Moton's operating style. Redmond, a Jackson, Mississippi, attorney, had two years earlier led a group of blacks who petitioned the Mississippi legislature for voting rights. Governor Murphree and L. O. Crosby, the Mississippi flood "czar," objected to his appointment. Moton did not back down publicly; instead, he failed to inform Redmond when the commission was meeting, effectively eliminating him.

Hoover now told Will Irwin, who continued to warn him about the damage criticism over racial problems could cause: "[A]fter the first few days the guard had no function except to preserve order in camps. No restrictions exist on anyone coming or going from the camps. In order to make sure that nothing of the kind has or could occur I had colored committees set up at each camp and have [now] appointed a general investigating committee under Doctor Moton who are free to report what they like to any inquirer."

Hoover was deceiving not only Irwin but himself. Meanwhile, with Moton, Hoover began playing a game far more important than improving conditions for refugees in the camps. Moton understood national politics. In his position he had to be sensitive to politics. By the time Moton's commission was formed, five weeks after Mounds Landing, newspapers were filled with talk of Hoover's qualifications for the presidency. Moton could sense the likelihood of Hoover's achieving it. Hoover was offering Moton an opportunity to become important to him. Moton grabbed it. Now both men's ambitions were in play.

Greenville had started all this, and, like a festering infection, Greenville was still leaking poison into the whole.

CHAPTER TWENTY-SEVEN

Even by late May, the Mississippi River had not fallen below flood stage, and water had not entirely stopped flowing through most levee breaks. Yet regions flooded in March and April had struggled back toward a semblance of normalcy. Even with the river still in flood, land in Illinois, Missouri, Tennessee, Arkansas, and even the very highest ground in Washington County had begun coming out of the water. People had begun planting cotton in the muddy alluvium deposited by the river; they just walked down rows, dropped seed, and stamped it down with their feet.

Greenville too had struggled back toward normalcy. By late May nearly half the city was free of water. The Wineman lumber mill reopened, the first large employer to do so. The Kiwanis held their first meeting since the crevasse. And the American Legion post voted overwhelmingly not to cancel its plans to host the state legion convention, which had earlier been scheduled for July 28. Indeed, city leaders planned to use the occasion to announce the city's rebirth. LeRoy Percy was arranging to have Charles Dawes, vice president of the United States, attend, and the county health officer predicted, "By July 28 our town will be so clean it will look like a summer resort."

Then the Mississippi began rising again. It rose six feet at Cairo, with more water in sight.

The news that another flood crest was threatening the Delta brought out an angry weariness, and grit. A social worker visiting Greenville said: "Worry is not often absent, but cheer and contentment and smiles and laughter are as rare as dry land on the flooded plantations. There is grim determination on nearly every face."

The determination focused on sealing the several thousand feet of gaps in the protection levee to prevent the river from reentering the city. Closing the gaps would be a tremendous undertaking—an 8-mile-an-hour current was flowing through them—but success would spare the city a crushing physical blow, and an even more crushing spiritual one. The effort would require more than 1,000 men working twenty-four hours a day. The bulk of the workers would of course be black men.

Will tried to assemble the labor force needed, calling in the same Negro ministers he had earlier addressed. Several of them agreed to form a committee "for the purpose of working in cooperation with the Red Cross . . . under the direction of W. A. Percy. . . . We are here to work, that is to serve." But the ministers, whom the *Chicago Defender* called "jacklegs" and "Uncle Toms," produced no workers.

On May 31, LeRoy, Will, and the mayor called an extraordinary mass meeting at City Hall, extraordinary because both races were explicitly urged to attend. A city councilman announced that the city had exhausted its financial resources buying sandbags and other materials to close the protection levee. It had no money to pay laborers. But it intended to have them if it required bayonets. The city council then voted a resolution: "We propose to close the gaps in the protection levee before the coming rise. To do this free labor is required. We hope to do the work with volunteers which will be asked for tonight. If, however, sufficient volunteers do not appear available then conscription means must be used."

Only blacks would be conscripted. Those in attendance stiffened in protest. John McMiller, a black man who ran a burial association, rose. "The guns are the problem," he said. "All the white folks carry guns. If you put the guns away, we'll have a thousand colored men on the levee in the morning."

Other blacks murmured agreement. Levye Chapple, also black, stood. He ran a printing business and a newspaper (existing on white sufferance, it bore no resemblance to the *Defender*), and had worked on racial issues with LeRoy Percy. "We are citizens of Greenville, and we have leaders among our own people," he said. "We feel that the system of conscription is bad and if you will let us work out a plan I think we will get better results."

LeRoy and other city leaders agreed to let the Negroes organize themselves. It was another blow to Will's leadership. Chapple, McMiller, and others called for the black community to meet at a church immediately. Several hundred people responded. McMiller spoke first. He said that they might not like the way things had gone, things had happened that shouldn't have happened. But the

Mississippi River didn't care whether it drowned white or black. It was their neighborhoods that the water would rise highest in, their homes that water would cover. Folks had been repairing and cleaning out their homes. All that work would be washed away. They weren't saving white folks if they volunteered. They would be saving themselves. A dozen people agreed. Others reminded everyone that whites would see to it that black men worked. The question was whether they would do so on their own terms or be forced to work like slaves by men with guns.

Ignoring the organization already formed by the ministers Will had named, this meeting created the "General Colored Committee" to handle all calls for labor and deal with Will Percy and the Red Cross. No one on this committee was a tool of whites, although some were familiar to whites. Rev. C. B. Young chaired it, and its secretary was Chapple. McMiller served on it. So did Dr. Q. Leon Toler, the son of a fiercely independent black landowner who had stirred up sharecroppers. (LeRoy had once instructed his foreman, "I don't mind your being rough with Toler if you find him on the place.") Others included another doctor, a dentist, two undertakers, and a car salesman named J. R. Wiley who once went up to the Delta & Pine Land Plantation on the annual settlement day and sold nineteen cars in a few hours.

There were also men whites did not know. Emanuel Smith ran crap games and brothels and wore striped pants, nob-toed shoes with brass tips, and white shoestrings; he made sure that on Sundays the decent folks going to church on Nelson Street, past the juke joints and drug dens and whorehouses, were not harassed. A shoe repairman named J. H. Bivins took nothing from whites. A carpenter named J. D. Fowler sometimes worked for whites, but he hated them, hated them enough and talked about it enough that he was always alone—other blacks feared being seen with him.

For this committee Chapple printed handbills to be distributed throughout the city. "500 Colored Men Wanted!" they read. "This number of men must be had at once to avoid compulsory action. . . . Make your selection—Volunteer at 6 o'clock Sunday morning or be forced to go 6 o'clock Sunday evening."

Sunday morning nearly 1,000 black men appeared on the levee, along with several dozen whites overseeing the work. One white man whom blacks already distrusted wore a pistol. McMiller told W. E. Elam, the engineer in charge, "I kept my promise. You didn't keep yours." Elam walked over to the man with the gun, pulled it out of its holster, and threw it into the water.

The blacks went to work. Every day they went to work, hundreds at a time, twenty-four hours a day, day after day. For eight days they sweated in the fetid heat, driving piling by hand, filling sandbags, building tramways to carry the sandbags to the gaps, working off two barges.

On the eighth day the levee was sealed and topped. They finished just as the water began rising. It reached four sacks high on the protection levee—two feet higher than the levee itself. But the levee held. In the long struggle of man against the river that year, the closing of the Greenville protection levee marked man's only victory.

On June 7 the city celebrated at the Saenger Theater. Both black and white were invited. Red Cross stocks were combed for meat, flour, canned peaches, and even rare and valuable sugar, and hotel kitchens and restaurants prepared food. There was music and comedy on stage, laughter off it. It was the closest the city had come to pleasant relaxation since the flood fight began in March. Whites heaped praise on the black community. Will spoke. But he had become irrelevant. His speech went unreported in the paper even though the paper was run by one of his committee members. A resolution passed by the city council was read, thanking "our colored citizens for their very valuable services, so willingly rendered the citizens of Greenville, in their work on the Protection Levee. Their citizenship has been commendable." Hazlewood Farish, a prominent attorney, told the blacks: "You have the undying thanks of the people of Greenville. . . . Here in the Delta, and especially in Washington County, there has always been perfect harmony between the races and there will never be anything else. The Mississippi Delta is the best home the negro could find. Here the white people will protect your interests and care for your homes. We want you always to have the same feeling of cooperation as has existed for the last few days."

After the celebration, Chapple, McMiller, and the other members of the General Colored Committee called a meeting of "all colored citizens" at the courthouse. "The meeting is not to discuss the dark past," they declared. "We are only looking forward."

BUT THE CITY had exhausted itself and the strains did not ease. Life was actually becoming harsher. L. O. Crosby, the state's flood dictator, suggested to Hoover, "Believe food and feed rations for refugees and animals should be cut in half while water is up and no work to do." The recommendation stunned Hoover, brought back to him that Mississippi was a different world. He vetoed cutting food for people but approved cutting feed to animals. Nonetheless, worried about having enough Red Cross money to survive the winter, rations were trimmed back. All refugee camps in Mississippi spent an average of 21 cents a day per capita on food; in Washington County camps spent 15 cents. Whites kept the good Red Cross food for themselves. Giving any to blacks, said one man, would "simply teach them a lot of expensive habits and there was no sense in giving them anything which they had not had before."

And there was work to do, work that had become harder. Weeks after the protection levee was closed, the county was, Will wrote a friend, "still a wreck and a desolation . . . four feet deep under water, railroad connections cut off and 41,000 people fed by the Red Cross." As the water fell both in the river and in the city, it became too shallow to ship supplies by boat; mules and wagons had to haul everything for miles through knee-deep water and waist-deep mud. Black men tugged and pulled and waded and sweated through the muck.

Tempers grew short among both white and black. The victory at the protection levee proved anticlimactic. "We were tired out," Will confessed. "[People] grabbed. Everyone wanted what was coming to him and a little more. The deterioration of the populace affected even our . . . committeemen [who] sulked or fought among themselves or resigned; everybody criticized everybody else. . . . Here and there we discovered simple undiluted dishonesty. It was a wretched period."

As people returned to their homes and businesses, the strain only intensified. The cleanup seemed endless and hopeless. Mud was caked everywhere, four to eight inches of the alluvial deposits that had created the Delta. It gave off a thick, fetid smell, a smell like dung mixed with swamp gas. Rattlesnakes, water moccasins, frogs, insects, and spiders infested the buildings. The rot of death was everywhere. Dead fish and crawfish—tens of millions of crawfish—paved every gutter and street and decayed and stank. Percy Bell advised his family to stay away: "Every store in town, when opened to be cleaned, smells horribly, and the entrance to the Weinberg Building is like walking into a sewer. . . . Newspapers are very misleading in their reports of openings. . . . No fresh meat at all, and no telling when we will get any."

Loading supplies was "nigger work." Cleaning was "nigger work." After the closure of the protection levee, the General Colored Committee had continued to supply workers to the Red Cross, but after police again started conscripting blacks for work gangs, the committee refused to help anymore.

On Hoover's second visit to Greenville he had traveled with

Crosby, LeRoy, Will, and a few others in two boats to Leland. The boat Crosby was in caught fire; its occupants had jumped into ten feet of water. Everyone in the remaining boat, including LeRoy and Hoover, had performed in a workmanlike manner pulling them aboard, but one man later died from his injuries. The incident had forged an even tighter bond between the Percys and Hoover, and Hoover would do whatever he could for them, including this. To calm racial tensions LeRoy arranged for Hoover, on his third visit, to address the black community.

The meeting was on Nelson Street at St. Matthew's, the cultural center of the Negro community, where Langston Hughes, Leontyne Price, and other nationally prominent blacks performed or spoke when they came to town. For Hoover it was jammed with humanity. A Red Cross worker reported, "The meeting was most auspiciously opened by one of the darky brethren, who in offering prayer did nothing but rejoice for the blessing of those engaged in 'rehabilitating' his people. . . . Sitting to the left were 25 singers who moved the audience to tears [with] music that knew no notes, harmony that defied description and sincerity of spirit that dissolves any doubt." Then Hoover spoke, so softly as to be almost inaudible. The contrast with the rich, deep black voices was tangible. Yet Hoover had the power.

Afterward, Hoover went to a Rotary luncheon and a mass meeting for whites. "Outside of the great war, there has been no such calamity as this flood," he said. No one present would disagree. But again he could barely be heard, and his commendation of their heroism and leadership inspired no one.

Immediately after his visit, the same black Greenville minister who had earlier written Coolidge anonymously now wrote Hoover anonymously. He charged that only pet blacks had been allowed access to him, and recited a list of specific charges against the white community in Greenville. Hoover sent the letter to Moton. And there were still deeper currents, evil currents.

As THE FLOOD RECEDED, a surge of violence erupted against blacks. In Little Rock a black man allegedly attacked two girls. He was tied to an automobile and dragged through downtown streets crowded at rush hour, trailed by a dozen cars blowing their horns like celebrants of a football victory. Then he was thrown onto a pyre and incinerated; photographs showed police officers watching.

The mayor of Lake Providence, Louisiana, forty miles below Greenville, ordered a Negro insurance agent to work on the levee. He refused. The mayor, a newcomer to the Delta region, shot and killed him.

In Louisville, Mississippi, two blacks were accused of killing a white farmer. The sheriff arrested them. A mob "took" them from the sheriff and burned them at the stake.

In Paris, Tennessee, a "crazed negro" killed a sheriff who pushed open the door of his cabin to arrest him. A mob formed quickly and, when the black man stepped onto his porch, killed him.

In Jackson the governor had to use troops to prevent another lynching, and even then only a quick trial of an accused murderer—from arrest to sentence took five days—calmed the crowds.

In Yazoo City a black man accused of attacking a white girl disappeared. A few day's later his bullet-riddled body was found hanging from a tree limb.

The Percys had always prevented such happenings in Greenville. In the history of Washington County there had been only two lynchings, none in decades, and one of the two victims had been a white who had murdered a black. The Percys personified what the *Louisiana Weekly*, a black paper, called "a striking example of the protection which the Southern man of high standing and authority demands for the law abiding and self respecting Negro." But times were changing.

On June 14, Moton's Colored Advisory Commission wrote a draft of its preliminary report. Claude Barnett judged Greenville "the seat of what trouble there was." The report confirmed that black refugees "could not secure supplies without an order from a white person," that they found "oppression," that black "men were beaten by the soldiers and made to work under guns. That more than one wanton murder was committed by these soldiers. . . . [T]hat women and girls were outraged"—raped—"by these soldiers."

IN THE GREAT WAR, William Alexander Percy had remained cool, had performed admirably under fire. But the war had tested only his own ability to perform. The flood tested his ability to induce others to perform. He had failed in this. True, his task was difficult. Of all the counties in the entire flooded region, from Illinois to the Gulf of Mexico, Washington County was the single one that suffered the most devastating losses. Twenty-two hundred of its buildings had been completely washed away; thousands more had been damaged or destroyed. The Red Cross officially recorded 120 drownings; total deaths, including unrecorded drownings and deaths from exposure, probably were at least double that figure, possibly much higher. Officially, 11,255 mules, horses, cattle, and hogs had been lost. In total, Washington County received more than double the aid given any other county in Mississippi, triple that given any in Louisiana, quadruple that given any in Arkansas, and almost double the aid given all of Missouri, Illinois, Tennessee, and Kentucky combined.

Still, even considering the challenge, Will's leadership had fallen short. By mid-June every other Red Cross chapter in Arkansas and Mississippi, more than forty in all, had been granted increased authority and independence "as they demonstrate ability and their character is proved," as judged by Red Cross professionals. Only the Washington County chapter, headed by Will Percy, did not demonstrate sufficient ability. In July every flooded county in Arkansas, Louisiana, and Mississippi, except for one, got a public health program financed by the Rockefeller Foundation. Only Washington County, despite its desperation, was left out, omitted because Will had failed to control internal political bickering.

LeRoy Percy could not help his son. He was in Chicago serving on the executive committee of the largest river control convention ever. He was guiding Lewis Pierson, president of both the Irving Trust Company in New York and the U.S. Chamber of Commerce, other financiers, and some of the nation's leading manufacturers on a Chamber tour of the entire flooded area. He was in Arkansas meeting with a handful of peers to plan strategy on how to get the federal government to take charge of the levee system. He was trying to rebuild the Delta's finances by convincing New York, Chicago, St. Louis, and New Orleans creditors either to write off planters' debts by 25 percent "or else take over the land . . . and pay off the back taxes owed on much of it, so that the rehabilitation process could start afresh."

Meanwhile, Will's orders had encouraged abuses of blacks, and now Will could not stop those abuses. Nor could he stop the fraud, stop the stockpiling of free Red Cross supplies by distributors who would later sell them, stop the charging of black refugees for what should have been free. The national Red Cross launched a secret investigation into profiteering and theft in the county. Will learned of it and, furious, clinging ferociously to his pride, threatened to resign, writing: "I bitterly resent this. . . . If you want me to go on with the work, I will do so under one condition: that I receive a statement that there will be no secret investigation in Washington County, that all investigators will report to me. . . . If I am in charge of this county, I am in charge of all the employees in this county."

The Red Cross withdrew the investigators. But Will had lost

control. He fled into poetry. Earlier he had told the head of the Yale University Press that he had no time for his duties as editor of the Yale Series of Younger Poets and suggested someone else do the job. Since then Greenville had finally begun emptying of water, but it remained devastated and isolated while the strains of cleanup had only added to those of supply. Yet now Will asked for and received thirty-five manuscript collections of poetry.

On July 7, trying to ease black hostility, the mayor stepped forward for the first time since the crevasse; he named a Colored Aid Committee to organize a benefit performance at the Saenger Theater, "giving the entire [proceeds of the] show to the colored people for their relief work." The leaders of the General Colored Committee would run it.

The benefit would never be held. That same day two policemen, James Mosely and Pat Simmons, were assigned to collect a work crew while a truck waited to carry the crew to the levee. The policemen separated. Mosely had joined the force shortly before the flood; he knew little of Greenville's traditions, but knew intimately the treatment of Negroes in the preceding few weeks. At the corner of Delesseps and, ironically, Percy Streets, Mosely called out to a black man named James Gooden sitting on his porch. Gooden was well respected in the black community, a man known personally to the Percys. He had worked all night. Mosely ordered him into the truck. Gooden shook his head no.

Nigger, you're going to work.

No, Suh. No, Suh, I just been workin'.

Nigger, don't give no backtalk.

No, Suh, I'm not backtalkin' you.

Gooden got up from the porch, went inside his house, and closed the door. Mosely followed him into his home and pulled his gun. Gooden froze.

Nigger! Get your black ass in that truck.

White man. Don't pull no gun on me!

According to Mosely, Gooden grabbed for the gun. Mosely shot him. But Gooden told a different version to blacks who carried him to the hospital. In an effort to save his life, two white doctors amputated his arm. James Gooden died anyway.

THE NEWS swept through the black community. Seething, blacks stopped work. The unloading of barges ceased. The loading of supplies headed inland ceased. Cleaning the muck out of white businesses ceased. The white community grew nervous. There were then more than 10,000 blacks in Greenville, fewer than 4,000 whites. Will heard from "my Negro informant" that there was a possibility of violent reprisal. Rhodes Wasson recalled, "We prepared for a race riot here. . . . We thought the blacks were going to uprise. Everyone was buying guns."

To calm the Negro community, Mosely was arrested, supposedly to be held for trial. No one believed that would ever happen. The county prosecutor was still Ray Toombs, the Exalted Cyclops of the local Klan. (Mosely never was indicted.)

The city became an armed camp. Blacks and whites who lived in the city had firearms. On the levee blacks had shovels and hoes and knives within reach. In both races fear grew. It was a deep fear, not of something external that penetrated inward; this fear began at a person's core and suffused the whole, a defining fear that made people aware of who they were. But Will relished the atmosphere of fear. He had failed at everything else that defined a Percy, but he had never showed cowardice. He later wrote: "I told my informant I would call a meeting of the Negroes for that night and speak to them in one of their churches. He vehemently opposed this course, saying the Negroes were all armed and all of them blamed me for the killing. Nevertheless I called the meeting."

Chapple, McMiller, and other members of the General Colored Committee agreed to hear Percy at Mt. Horeb, a beautiful stone church with a history of intense emotions; Chapple's father had once gotten into an argument there and had been knocked through the window into the street. E. M. Weddington, college-educated, large and powerful, the probable author of the anonymous letters to Coolidge and Hoover, was pastor.

When Will arrived, the church was almost empty. Silently, one at a time, blacks began to enter. The silence was ominous. Finally, with the church full, Weddington arose and, as Will reported, "said starkly, 'I will read from the Scripture.' Without comment, he read the chapter from Genesis on the flood. It was as impressive as ice-water. Then he said, 'Join me in a hymn.' It was a hymn I had never heard . . . a pounding barbaric chant of menace. I could feel their excitement and hate mount to frenzy. . . . The preacher turned to me."

Usually, any white visitor, much less a Percy, received a fulsome introduction when addressing a colored audience. Weddington said simply, "I give you Mr. Percy, chairman of the Red Cross." Unapplauded, he mounted the pulpit and stood there representing all the power of his class and race. Before him rippled a sea of black faces, black necks, black arms.

Suddenly, it was as if everything Will could not admit to himself transformed itself into anger. He had not come to explain. Percys did not explain. If he had fallen short of the standards of the Percys, that only made him colder, sterner, angrier. "When put upon," he once observed, "I discovered that a truculent tongue did more to save than a battalion of virtues."

He spoke slowly and bitterly: "A good Negro has been killed by a white policeman. Every white man in town regrets this from his heart and is ashamed. The policeman is in jail and will be tried. I look into your faces and see anger and hatred. . . . For four months I have struggled and worried and done without sleep in order to help you Negroes. Every white man in town has done the same thing. . . . We white people could have left you to shift for yourselves. Instead we stayed with you and worked for you, day and night. During all this time you Negroes did nothing, nothing for yourselves or for us. . . . Because of your sinful, shameful laziness, because you refused to work in your own behalf unless you were paid, one of your race has been killed. You sit before me sour and full of hatred as if you had the right to blame anybody or judge anybody. . . . You think I am the murderer. I will tell you who he is. . . . I am not the murderer. That foolish young policeman is not the murderer. The murderer is you! Your hands are dripping with blood. Look into each other's face and see the shame and the fear God set on them. Down on your knees, murderers, and beg your God not to punish you as you deserve."

The bond between the Percys and the blacks was broken. The Delta, the land that had once promised so much to blacks, had become, entirely and finally, the land where the blues began.

The black audience did get down on its knees. But what they prayed for Will did not know.

AMONG THE 154 refugee camps, there were many abuses. In violation of Red Cross rules, county relief committees routinely gave planters goods; they distributed them to tenants and too often charged for them. Routinely, black refugees were not fed as well as whites. Routinely, especially in Mississippi, sharecroppers were not free to leave. There were instances of brutality. But only in Greenville were so many extreme charges made; only in Greenville did the abuses appear to be so systematic.

"My dear Percy," Hoover wrote Will two days before Gooden was killed. "You have, I think, had the largest single burden in the flood territory. We are all proud of the way which you have carried through, and I take special satisfaction in it because of its flattery to my original judgment of long ago."

The reality was different. Will Percy had failed. Red Cross professionals judged neighboring Delta counties as having "a strong relief committee which functioned in a very business-like manner," or as having done "decidedly good work," or at the least as being "decidedly satisfactory." For Will they made excuses: "No one can ever tell the story of those first days. Whatever may have been the mistakes made, much can be excused because of the horror and the panic. . . . Into the work Mr. Percy brought a rich experience in human understanding. Not always practical in his planning and somewhat at the mercy of cross-currents of local opinion, nonetheless he was deep rooted in his desire to render genuine service."

He could face the fact that he would never be his father. He could even face the fact that he had failed his father, but he could not accept that his father had failed him, not because his father had patronized him or even betrayed him, but because his father had done what Will could not admire. He could not face his father's ruthlessness, and the abnegation of everything in which Will had believed. Unless one embraces the truth, one can only be comic or tragic; one cannot be heroic. His father had often been heroic. In the war Will had been heroic. Neither his father nor he were heroic now.

Earlier Will had derided as "rabbits" those men who had fled the city. But he could not tolerate criticism; he could not tolerate public failure; he could not tolerate being treated as irrelevant; he could not tolerate the truth.

Earlier Will had withdrawn into poetry, calling for those manuscripts to review. But now, his editing responsibility unfinished, on August 31 he returned the manuscripts to New Haven, explaining he was "passing the buck" because "frankly, nervously and mentally I am so fatigued and so harassed."

Effective that same day, he resigned as head of the relief committee. Hoover returned to Greenville on September 1. Will did not see him. On September 1, Will fled Greenville. He fled at a time when Washington County most needed help, when his father was writing a friend: "Our people here have a most trying road to travel. Some will be able to make the journey and get back to some kind of prosperity, I trust, but many of them, broken and discouraged, will fail to make the journey."

By the time Hoover arrived to be briefed by LeRoy, Will was on his way to Japan. He would remain away for months, escaping Greenville, escaping the criticism, escaping the struggle, escaping.

Hoover, in his ambition, would deal with the repercussions of what the Percys had done.

Part Seven

THE CLUB

CHAPTER TWENTY-EIGHT

The GREAT RIVER was finally done with its valley. On January 1, 1927, the first of its many crests had breached flood stage at Cairo, Illinois, and began flowing south, the river rising above flood stage January 5 at Memphis, January 16 at Vicksburg, February 12 at Baton Rouge, February 13 at New Orleans. As late as June 30, Isaac Cline was still issuing daily bulletins to warn of the water.

At its angriest the Mississippi had boiled across its floodplain, crushed the works of man, and forced Nature herself to step back, forced the great Ohio to flow upstream. It had spread, said the preachers, as wide as God's arms. Then, slowly, the river fell. Like the earlier rise, the fall flowed south, toward the sea. Not until June 14 did the flood subside at Cairo, not until June 22 at Memphis, July 11 at Vicksburg, July 14 at Baton Rouge. But at New Orleans the river, unnaturally, had fallen below flood stage more than a month earlier, on June 12. It had done so because of the use of 78,000 pounds of dynamite on the levee in St. Bernard; the dynamiting had not been necessary to save New Orleans, but it had lowered the river.

While much of the lower Mississippi valley contended with the June rise, New Orleans went about its business as though the flood had never happened, aware only of summer. It was a hot summer, even for New Orleans. The elegant Saenger Theater, adorned by $25,000 chandeliers brought from one of France's great castles, put in air-conditioning for the first time and found itself jammed every performance. Elsewhere in the night heat, in the French Quarter, in the neighborhoods for the "coloreds," in the Ninth Ward shotgun houses extending down to the St. Bernard line, across the river in Algiers, men and women sat on balconies and porches to escape the heat. Along Basin Street in the remnants of Storyville, in the French

Quarter, in the steamy close clubs, the jazz music welled up and rolled through the city on its own river.

It was time to deal with the aftermath. In this too the city's elite would reveal itself. The revelation would have import.

THE MEN who ran New Orleans had succeeded. Sitting in offices, windows newly sealed against the heat and the music and cooled by the marvel of air-conditioning, they would determine what their flood did to St. Bernard and Plaquemines.

James Butler in particular would make that determination. He was not an intellectual like his brother, the Tulane professor and graduate of the Sorbonne, yet he believed that he too dealt with large questions, with the infrastructure of society, power, money, and character. Indeed, he sat at the nexus of these things. He headed the only southern bank listed as one of the world's largest. His wife was queen of the Mystic Club. He chaired the city's Citizens Flood Relief Committee. He and John Parker represented Louisiana on the Tri-State Flood Control Committee, an ad hoc group but one that also included LeRoy Percy, representing Mississippi, and Governor John Martineau, representing Arkansas. Together these few men would sit down with Hoover and plan the long-term federal response to the flood, a response that would be enormously far-reaching.

Butler also controlled what happened to the thousands of victims of the artificial crevasse. The Red Cross and Hoover had refused all responsibility for them, declaring them the city's business entirely. And the city left it to Butler. Without any legal authority, he chose an executive committee from the larger Citizens Committee to decide what the city should do. But he found even this executive committee too cumbersome. Instead, he met with an even smaller and less formal group each morning at 8 A.M. in his office, and on weekends at his home. This group included Rudolph Hecht, president of the Hibernia Bank, J. Blanc Monroe, and H. Generes Dufour. Butler, Hecht, and, later, Monroe, the attorney and banker who was representing the city in regard to reparations for the refugees, all served on the Board of Liquidation. Dufour, Hecht's one real friend, was the board's attorney.

They and their peers had always run the city sub rosa; now they ran it for all to see, assuming even ceremonial duties. When Will Rogers offered to give a benefit performance in New Orleans, it was not the mayor but Butler who accepted, expressing "my sincere appreciation of your most generous offer." Now they began to press their weight against, enfold, and suffocate those people and institutions under their control.

Butler had already created the Emergency Clearing House Publicity Committee to handle public relations for the city. The committee's first move was to bully businesses within New Orleans. Such bullying had a long history. A month before the levee was dynamited, the Association of Commerce had rebuked ninety-two firms that bought postage stamps outside the city, thereby removing the money from the local economy. As the river was rising, several companies had tried to slash their inventories. When the Otis Mahogany Company failed to get flood insurance, it told customers around the nation "we have decided to cut our prices for a few days to move out quickly a good volume of mahogany lumber, so if anything should happen our flood loss would be minimized." The publicity committee warned Otis, "This kind of letter . . . is apt to cause New Orleans considerable harm." The rebuke was written on New Orleans Clearing House Association stationery, a veiled threat that banks would hold the company accountable. The publicity committee attacked even such New Orleans boosters as Walter Parker, a board member of the Association of Commerce and executive director of the Safe River Committee, who was admonished for sending clients of the brokerage firm Fenner & Beane an estimate of the reparations New Orleans would owe. Meanwhile, local newspaper editors were advised, "[A]ny announcements or developments tending to improve the popular impression of conditions here should be given prominent headlines." The papers all promptly began running repeated headlines, "City Out of Danger."

Then the public relations machine turned outward in an extraordinary effort to convince the world that New Orleans had never been threatened by the Mississippi River. The publicity committee had already distributed Butler's affirmation of the city's safety to 2,100 banks and investment firms, scheduled repeated broadcasts of Army engineers stating that the city was in no danger, and forced Moody's Investors Service to correct a wire it had sent. As the crisis receded, the committee contacted 265 conventions held around the country in May and June, informing them that the city had never been in danger and requesting them to pass flood control resolutions. It also distributed feature stories to 300 trade journals, wired every Chamber of Commerce in the United States, sent out 40,000 reprints of statements by General Jadwin that the city was safe, contacted the Kiwanis, Rotary, the Lions, dozens of real estate boards, and urged every large company in the city to write its clients around the world, informing them of "facts." And sometimes the committee made threats. As W. K. Seago, a sugar broker, warned one man, "New

Orleans is . . . generously helping those in actual suffering in the flooded areas and we commend her example to her TRADUCERS reminding them that their day of reckoning will come and that while the mills of the Gods grind slowly they GRIND EXCEEDING SMALL."

Simultaneously, the New Orleans committee also pressured the media directly. The *St. Bernard Voice* had been complaining that the dynamiting was unnecessary, that St. Bernard and Plaquemines were being sacrificed for "the financial interests" who worried only about investor confidence. The reporters traveling with Hoover believed it. As natural crevasses far upriver proved that the dynamiting had been unnecessary, editorials from Springfield, Massachusetts, to Kalamazoo, Michigan, began to criticize the city. The *Memphis Commercial-Appeal* wrote mockingly of "New Orleans 'Babbitry.' . . . If New Orleans is ever flooded the world will not know it unless there is some outside newspaper man there. The newspapers of New Orleans have not told their own people the actual situation. It's business depression that's feared. Many leaders of the town had much rather take a chance at loss of life and destruction of property than face the possibility of the grain market slumping a couple of notches, the price of cotton falling 50 to 100 points, or New Orleans stocks going under the least of a strain."

The city's financial interests responded aggressively enough that the *Memphis Commercial-Appeal* apologized and agreed to print no more such stories. Then the city began to reach out. Butler's committee had already wrung promises of cooperation from every national newsreel company. Now it contracted with two clipping services covering hundreds of papers, each of which was "carefully reviewed for mis-statements." It got corrections printed by the *New York Times,* the *New York Sun, Literary Digest,* the *Atlanta Journal,* the *Cincinnati Enquirer,* the *Birmingham News,* United Press, and dozens of others. Alvin Howard, a director of the *Times-Picayune,* informed Butler that "the famous writer" Richard Child was in town writing for the *Saturday Evening Post.* He suggested that top businessmen and journalists contact him and try to influence the story. They did.

And the committee asked Jim Thomson to help. Through his national political connections and ownership of papers in Virginia as well as New Orleans, he was well known in the newspaper community. He convinced executives of the wire services to cooperate and wrote to *Editor and Publisher,* a trade magazine for newspaper executives, the Southern Newspaper Publishers Association, and elsewhere that "a citizens committee representing all of the business interests of New Orleans has asked me to attempt to get before the news and picture editors throughout the United States a correction of several unfortunate and damaging impressions that experts feared for the safety of the city of New Orleans itself."

There was one other effort to improve the city's image. The Association of Commerce, whose leading members all served on Butler's Citizens Committee, had a budget of $130,000 in 1927, along with a surplus of $78,000 in its treasury. It donated $500 to the Red Cross flood relief fund. It spent $605 honoring Hoover at a luncheon. In advance of that luncheon, the association demanded that the police clear beggars from downtown streets. It later reported: "Superintendent of Police Healy inaugurated and carried forward an intensive campaign against beggars during the entire month. The effort resulted in 21 arrests."

BUT IF THE CITY succeeded in convincing the nation that, despite its insistence upon dynamiting the levee downriver to relieve pressure on itself, it had never been in danger, it was creating resentment in its neighbors.

The *New Iberia Enterprise* thanked "the noble and unselfish manner in which our sister towns have responded to our appeal in distress, and rushed trucks and men and cowboys with their own mounts to plunge headlong into the thick of the great rescue work, . . . risking their lives." From New Orleans they had gotten nothing. "What a contrast to our own metropolis, boasting the greatest population of the South, conspicuous by her failure to respond! Not a single truck, which bore the name of New Orleans! How her great dailies have played up our calamity to the world in advance of the flood, while they proclaimed their own security, purchased at so dear a price."

Even the board of the Association of Commerce conceded "in the mind of a great many of the country people New Orleans was only concerned with its own safety during the recent high water period." In response, it planned a new publicity campaign "to see if we cannot overcome the feeling that exists between the city and the country. . . . Unless we [are] able to sell the city to the country the city will always be the loser when it comes to legislation."

Perhaps this effort might have yielded at least some success, but then the city, through Butler and the men with whom he met daily, began to hammer against the refugees.

CHAPTER TWENTY-NINE

J. BLANC MONROE was not a large man, but his reach embraced all New Orleans. He was the city's leading attorney, made all important decisions for the Whitney Bank—although he was only a board member—and ruled Carnival as Comus. Physically, he resembled LeRoy Percy in his prime, distinguished-looking, his hair just turning to gray, not tall but broad-shouldered and immaculately dressed, with a presence that emanated from his self-confidence and intensity. Like LeRoy Percy, he was direct, tenacious, fierce, and, when he chose to be, charming. In both there was coldness, arrogance, smallness, and pride of family. Monroe's sister Kitty was the city's social arbiter and leading hostess and married to a Harvard friend of Will Percy; Will ushered at their wedding.

In more important ways, however, they did not resemble each other at all. LeRoy had helped build a society; Monroe merely reflected one. LeRoy had ambitions of empire; Monroe had not so much ambition as expectation, expectation that the world would bend to him.

Monroe's ancestors included two presidents, James Monroe and James Polk, one on each side of his family. His father, Frank Adair Monroe, chief justice of the Louisiana Supreme Court, had represented both Jefferson Davis and James Eads, and, like his friend Edward Douglass White, chief justice of the United States Supreme Court, had served as president of the Louisiana Club. Blanc Monroe so frequently argued cases before his father, who never recused himself, that the state legislature once considered a bill requiring recusal when a lawyer argued a case before a judge who was closely related. At a hearing on the bill, a state senator asked one witness, "You're talking about Blanc Monroe, aren't you?" Came the reply: "That's right! That's the son of a bitch I'm talking about."

Not surprisingly, given his position at the pinnacle of his society, Monroe considered the world nearly perfect. Even as a young man, in an 1899 commencement speech at Tulane University, he did not question the order of things. His subject was the legacy of the Spanish-American War, a legacy controversial enough that Speaker of the House Thomas "Czar" Reed, probably the strongest Speaker in American history, resigned from Congress to protest it. Yet Monroe gave no hint of doubt, perspective, or depth of comprehension when he proclaimed: "Into the fiercely contested struggle for empire the 'draught' of the Anglo-Saxon race is forcing us. . . . [Other] powers suddenly loom up as neighbors to be jostled against and outranked in the race for trade. . . . [T]he eagle's claws establish our claims to prestige and consideration. . . . We are powerless to resist the spirit of Americanism which exacts from us not exertion merely but the grandest efforts of our broadest men. We realize that we must indeed take up the white man's burden."

Monroe's power came from his ability, his personal force, and his business and social connections. The combination of him and his law partner Monte Lemann made the firm Monroe & Lemann a formidable one. Lemann was Jewish, had a national reputation, was a close friend and Harvard classmate of Felix Frankfurter, would brief Franklin Roosevelt on Louisiana politics and Huey Long, and once declined appointment as a judge to the U.S. Court of Appeals. In terms of legal scholarship and argument, Lemann was a better lawyer than Monroe. Yet Monroe dominated the law firm, shouted at associates, once even publicly rebuked his partner for ordering a book for the law firm, a matter of a few dollars, without asking him.

Monroe was also "social," which in New Orleans means Carnival. Not only was he once Comus, but the Atlanteans, one of the most prestigious krewes, was called "a wholly-owned subsidiary of Blanc Monroe." Lemann, being Jewish, of course never received an invitation to any Carnival event.

But if Monroe used his connections and advantages, he did not rely upon them. He worked ferociously. No one could outwork him. His eyes could chill a man. He sent bills for his time to doctors who kept him waiting. He threatened to tow the cars of people who parked in front of his house. He drove people and bullied them. An attorney who knew him well said, "I've never seen a meeting he was in that he did not dominate."

Butler had picked Blanc Monroe to represent the city, to represent the money, regarding reparations. Not only did Monroe embody the city's establishment, but he had back-channel connections to St.

Bernard Parish. Monroe had already made Sheriff Doc Meraux a director of the Whitney Bank, one of the most conservative banks in the South, though, as another board member put it, Meraux "was *tres ordinaire.*" (In the 1990s the financial magazine *Barron's* noted that the Whitney was "doing business exactly the way it had a century earlier. It offered no credit cards, had no automatic teller machines, . . . made the loans it did extend on a handshake, all under a thick coat of secrecy.") The day the decision was made to dynamite the levee, Meraux was given $5,000 by the Whitney through an intermediary, and later he filed a claim for $235,000 in reparations.

Monroe could make a deal when it served his purpose or fight when that served his purpose. When he fought, he was relentless, yielding nothing. He was the perfect choice for Butler to unleash upon the city's adversaries—the victims of the dynamiting.

NEW ORLEANS had publicly promised that citizens of St. Bernard and Plaquemines would suffer no loss. The mayor, the city council, the levee board, the presidents of every bank, every major business, of the Association of Commerce, the Cotton Exchange, the Board of Trade, and leading individuals had all pledged their civic and personal honor that this would be so.

In theory, the Reparations Commission, on which St. Bernard and Plaquemines had four votes to the city's three, with two men chosen by the governor, was to guarantee fair treatment of the victims. Commission chairman was Ernest Lee Jahncke, a Tulane classmate of Monroe who owned a shipyard. He was also one of three Americans on the International Olympic Committee and a fine sailor —later an assistant secretary of the navy, he preferred the title of "Commodore," given him by the Southern Yacht Club, to "Mr. Secretary." A man of principle, he would later oppose sending a U.S. Olympic team to Nazi Germany in 1936, and at the commission's first meeting he declared: "The words of the people of this city and of the state are pledged to the complete recompense of those who have lost their homes and property to save the city of New Orleans from grave danger. It is the function of this committee to see that full justice is done in every instance, and it will do so."

But the Reparations Commission would have no power. Indeed, when it first convened, Butler called it to order, even though he did not serve on it. He then dropped into the background, but he, Monroe, Hecht, and Dufour—the few men whom Butler had chosen and with whom he met each day—determined how the city met its moral commitment. Without consulting the mayor or a single member of either the levee board or the city council, these few men decided everything.

Butler, Monroe, Hecht, and Dufour decided to use the Orleans Levee Board, whose members were appointed by the governor, as the vehicle to pay reparations. They decided that the levee board would issue bonds to pay them. They decided the millage. They decided that Blanc Monroe would represent the city and the levee board in all reparations work. Only after the decisions were made did they inform public officials of them. (Typically, Butler invited the levee board president to a private meeting, informed him that Monroe was to be hired by the levee board, and the board president then told other board members, "The business interests suggested Mr. J. Blanc Monroe be appointed as Special Counsel of the Board"; by unanimous vote, the board promptly did so.)

More important, Butler and his colleagues decided how to handle the nearly 10,000 refugees. Roughly half stayed with friends or relatives; the city housed the rest in a warehouse lined with cots. At first, the city met its obligations well enough. Butler created subcommittees to handle food, employment, transportation, even education for the children. But as expenses rose and the Red Cross refused help, a new realism informed decisions.

The first indication of this new realism came when the members of the food subcommittee asked for "guidance" in a meeting with Butler, Monroe, and Hecht in Room 326 of the Canal Bank Building, that plush conference room with leather-backed chairs, the long table, and shining objets d'art. The subcommittee chairman explained that his subcommittee did not consider the refugees "as objects of charity. They are for the most part industrious, self-supporting and self-respecting citizens who were forced to leave, on short notice, their homes and possessions that the city of New Orleans be saved. They are crowded into the city without adequate housing, ready cash, or disinterested assistance except from the committee. . . . They [cannot] be cared for by herding in concentration camps without having a heritage of bitterness toward our city which will be long remembered." But food expenses alone were running $20,000 a week, far above what they had expected. It was only the middle of May, and the flood would likely cover the two parishes deep into August, three months away. What should their policy toward relief be?

Butler, Hecht, and Monroe decided that "relief be granted only people who had been placed in necessitous circumstances." More significantly, to cut costs, they would have John Legier, a New Orleans banker on the Reparations Commission, offer a resolution "to deduct from personal damage claims the amounts extended by way of relief for parties claiming damages."

Any money given the displaced refugees, even for food or housing, would be deducted from their settlements.

The commission promptly passed this resolution; the governor's appointees, both of whom came from New Orleans, joined the city's representatives, outvoting those from St. Bernard and Plaquemines 5 to 4. By then Butler and Monroe had taken effective control of the entire reparations process.

THE REPARATIONS PROCESS began when a flood victim filed a claim. If he or she could not reach agreement with Monroe, who technically represented the Orleans Levee Board, the Reparations Commission theoretically served as an arbitrator. The commission's decision could be appealed to the courts. But in fact Monroe dominated the entire system. He did so chiefly because he had, literally, written the commission's rules. He had done so even though the commission had its own legal adviser in Percy Saint, attorney general of Louisiana, and its own staff. And in procedure—in the rules—lay power. Monroe used it.

First, the rules stated that the firm of Monroe & Lemann would decide whether to reject a claim or settle it. (Monroe and two assistants actually did nearly all the work; his partner had little involvement.) If a claimant protested Monroe's decision to the commission itself, the commission relied heavily on the factual findings of Monroe.

Second, Monroe prevented small claimants from having legal representation. After two attorneys spoke to several claimants about representing them on a contingency basis, he, Dufour, and Esmond Phelps had the state bar association threaten them with disbarment. Saint, the attorney general, then promised publicly that for claimants who wanted an attorney, "[v]olunteer legal services will be obtained." A resulting headline read, "Legal Advice for Refugees to be Gratis." But after several attorneys offered to work pro bono for the refugees, Monroe, Dufour, Phelps, and others again went to the bar association and had it decree that such work would be "unethical" and, again, cause for disbarment. The commission, with Jahncke voting with the representatives from St. Bernard and Plaquemines, then voted to hire an attorney to help claimants. Monroe, Butler, and Dufour promptly had Saint "state the legal objections to this policy." The idea of hiring an attorney for the claimants was killed.

Third, and most important, the rules stipulated that no partial payments be made. This contradicted the policy the Reparations Commission had announced at its very first meeting, when, recognizing that few refugees had savings and even fewer had an income, it had formally resolved that "a man may file his claim as his losses become provable." Jahncke himself promised, "If a man receives forty percent of the claim immediately, he will receive sixty percent more as soon as humanly possible."

Monroe's prohibition of partial payments was an extraordinarily powerful weapon. Claims were divided into "schedules," with each schedule covering a different kind of loss—crops, equipment, housing, etc. The rules stated that once a given schedule was filed, it could not be amended; no further loss on that schedule could be added. Claimants who wanted money quickly had to limit their claim to losses they could prove while water still covered their property; after the water drained away, if more damage was found, they would get no compensation. If Monroe disputed part of a claimed loss, the claimant received nothing for that schedule. Even if Monroe accepted as valid part of the claim, the claimant received nothing. Only a complete settlement of a schedule released any money.

Most refugees needed money desperately. By refusing partial payments, Monroe was starving them into submission.

A few weeks after the levee was dynamited, Butler estimated that claims would total $2 million. Hecht estimated them at $6 million. They were both wrong. Claims would exceed $30 million. The figures made Monroe and Butler even more rigid, even more suffocating.

Typical was the case of Sigmund Tarnok, owner of a large nursery, who needed operating capital to reopen his business but resisted a settlement offer. Tarnok's attorneys brought to Monroe an independent estimate of losses confirming their claim, buttressed it with statements from two leading young businessmen whom Monroe knew, and even convinced Monte Lemann to write him a note saying, "There may possibly be something in [Tarnok's] contention."

Monroe ignored his own partner's plea, and replied to Tarnok with a threat: "[I]f the case is reopened . . . I promise I will oppose with every obstacle the payment of one penny to the Tarnok Company." Tarnok accepted a settlement of 19 cents on the dollar.

It was not only Tarnok whom Monroe pushed; he pushed everyone, and he pushed hard. The crevasse had drowned or driven away millions of muskrats and minks, and wiped out at least two full seasons of trapping. Several thousand trappers had been making between $3,000 and $8,000 each per season; a handful made even more. Compensating them could cost millions of dollars. So Monroe squeezed again. With Butler's approval, he had the state conservation commission review the trappers' claims. Trappers paid a tax on each pelt; many evaded it. If the state examined their claims, the trappers would have to minimize their losses or expose themselves to prosecution for tax evasion. One of the first trappers audited had shipped 15,000 pelts, worth from $25,000 to $35,000, out of state to avoid taxes. A group of trappers went to court to block further state review. The State of Louisiana fought the lawsuit; Monroe himself argued the case for it. He won.

Monroe pushed so hard, and won so often, that his victories themselves became a problem. On June 21, nearly two months after the crevasse, the chairman of the food subcommittee raised a question "illustrated [by] an aged negress." She had settled for and received $27, but "her home is under water. The payment of the claim does not relieve your committee of the necessity of supplying her with food."

Butler, Hecht, and Monroe discussed the situation at length at a weekend meeting in Butler's home on St. Charles Avenue. They sat comfortably in the solarium where Butler so often sat in solitude surrounded by objects that reminded him of his plantation. The street was lined with great mansions; indeed, Butler's was modest compared to his neighbors, but upstairs in his wife's bedroom was the Carnival gown that earlier that year had cost $15,000. The issue was a serious one. Paying any money to a claimant after a claim had been settled might establish a dangerous precedent. Still, they could not starve these people. Believing they were being generous, they decided to feed any refugee who received a settlement of less than $100 but could not return home.

Within a few weeks their tolerance expired. A group of black refugees pleaded for an extension of food payments, explaining that the marshes from which they had earned income—they had gathered moss and sold it as mattress filling—were waist-deep in mud. But for these people, aid had ended. They were informed, "As long as we continue to feed you, you are not going to work."

Earlier, Monroe had decided another case of extraordinary relief. It had involved the Canal Bank, so Butler had recused himself from the decision. Monroe had approved a payment of $850 to reimburse Butler's bank, the largest one in the South, for the use of its yacht *Lurline*.

THE CREVASSE VICTIMS fought back. Not all claimants were powerless. Some did have lawyers and political connections. Meanwhile, the Reparations Commission itself had begun to balk at Monroe's bullying and excesses. For some of those whom New Orleans had flooded out, the issue was survival. And they had the weight of the promises the city had made behind them.

Fifty-seven of New Orleans' leading citizens had pledged full compensation to the people of Plaquemines and St. Bernard. Butler himself had called the reparations "a moral obligation undertaken by each and every" one of those fifty-seven signatories. Each one of them had affirmed that moral obligation not only to the governor and the victims, but to the Mississippi River Commission, to the secretary of war, to the secretary of commerce, and to the president of the United States. Throughout the state, the city was being accused of breaking its word. Governor Simpson, who had been so reluctant to allow the crevasse, was well aware of the outrage among the victims.

Simpson had already declared his candidacy for reelection. In a few days, Huey Long would announce his candidacy for the same post. Long was already castigating the "plutocrats," the "self-appointed" rulers of the state—the men like Butler and Monroe. Already, Long and Monroe detested each other; five years earlier Long, then utilities commissioner, had threatened to throw Monroe in jail for contempt. Politics compelled Simpson to intervene for the crevasse victims. So did his own sense of decency. But Butler and Monroe still held a trump card. They seemed unaware of the implications of playing it.

CHAPTER THIRTY

O N MONDAY EVENING, July 25, 8 P.M., one more meeting was held in the Canal Bank's Room 326. Much had already happened in that room. Now, in its restrained elegance, gathered the political power of the state and the economic power of the city; the two powers would confront each other here. The confrontation would mark the peak of the power of New Orleans and its bankers. It also marked an exercise of power that was not atypical in the America of the time, although in few places was it as blatant as in New Orleans; such uses of power were beginning to ignite a larger political storm.

Governor Simpson had requested the meeting, hoping to find a solution to the partial-payments problem. Representing New Orleans were Butler, Monroe, Hecht, Dufour, and Lonnie Pool, along with the chairmen of Butler's subcommittees, Mayor O'Keefe, three city councilmen, and the levee board. A dozen men represented St. Bernard and Plaquemines, including Manuel Molero and four others associated with his Acme Fur Company, which owned 127,000 acres of the finest trapping land in the world. Between them sat the Reparations Commission.

Simpson convened the meeting and got directly to the point: "I have requested the Executive Committee of the Citizens Flood Committee and the members of the Reparations Commission to get together to consider certain objections that the claimants have to Regulation No. 7 of the rules and regulations adopted by the Reparations Commission."

C. A. Hartman, a member of the Reparations Commission, spoke first. He ran a large plant at Braithwaite—where the trappers had met at the baseball diamond to try to block the dynamiting— and had 400 men working now, even with part of his plant still underwater. The crevasse had caused tremendous losses and he was desperate for working capital. He explained, "The claim which we tried to enter in full was to May 31 and was not subject to additions or losses for the period covered." But Monroe had refused even to accept the claim. To get anything Hartman would have to forgo compensation for losses after May 31—despite the fact that as of this day, July 25, water still covered part of his operation.

As a result of Monroe's refusal, he continued, New Orleans banks would loan him nothing. His business was starving for capital, and, he said, many others were suffering in similar circumstances. He reminded those in the room of the promises made before the crevasse. Virtually every person in the room had pledged that no harm would come to residents of St. Bernard and Plaquemines. But harm had come to them. Then he turned to Simpson: "We ask you, as Governor of the State, by whose authority the Caernarvon crevasse was created, to give whatever assistance is in your power in behalf of all individuals or corporations for similar claims."

Then Hugh Wilkinson spoke. The Wilkinsons were the dark sheep of the city's fine families. One hundred twenty-five years before, James Wilkinson and Charles Claiborne had accepted Louisiana for the United States from the French. Ever since, the Claiborne name had been second to none in the state. But James Wilkinson had been court-martialed for his involvement in Aaron Burr's treason. Though acquitted, neither he nor his descendants were ever fully accepted in the city. Now Hugh Wilkinson frequently represented the outsiders in New Orleans against the insiders. In this instance, he represented Molero, who faced devastating losses. There would be no fur season this year, and almost certainly none the next. In the meantime, the company had spent thousands of dollars building rafts covered with clumps of marsh grass in the hope of saving some muskrats. Monroe was refusing reimbursement for even these moneys. Wilkinson argued: "It is manifestly impossible to file, under oath, a complete claim which would reasonably estimate the amount of loss to the company. We simply need operating capital to meet our maturing obligations"—the company owed $124,000—"and unless this is furnished to us by some means, we are faced with ruin. If the company cannot file a partial claim we are going to be wiped out." Then he too turned to the governor and pleaded, "In behalf of all the people of that section of the State of Louisiana, we come to you for help."

The Reparations Commission itself concurred. Jahncke, the chairman, sided with the victims and their representatives. They were five votes, a majority. Yet they could effect nothing. They were supposed to have power, but they had none. Voting to change the rule meant nothing. The commission itself had no money. The cash to pay claims came from the New Orleans banks, which were loaning claimants 80 percent of their settlements. The commission could not order the banks to make these loans. The banks did what Butler's executive committee told them to do.

Simpson turned to Butler for a response. Butler had one well prepared. He had met with the other members of his executive committee at seven-thirty that morning in his office next door to this room and, looking down upon the city of New Orleans, settled upon his answer. In that meeting they had privately agreed that they had a fiduciary responsibility to the City of New Orleans. If they allowed partial payments, then claimants could drag out their claims indefinitely and settlements would become infinitely more difficult. The Reparations Commission could make any policy statement it wanted. The banks would continue to pay nothing for partial settlements.

Butler now was hardly so blunt. Instead, he spoke of his eagerness to do what was right and his concern for the difficulties of the victims. But he was unyielding. The meeting continued for hours. Tall, gangly, cadaverous, Butler finally concluded it solemnly: "I want you all to know that as far as the New Orleans Committee is concerned, that we want to pay every just claim as promptly as possible and that we do not want any suffering afflicted upon anyone, but the money with which these claims will be paid is not our money. We have got to satisfy the members of the Orleans Levee Board."

Butler was being disingenuous. Every man in the room knew it. Butler's group had repeatedly made decisions that directly involved the levee board without consulting any member of it. Only five days earlier the board had "respectfully" asked Butler to provide minutes of his meetings so the board could document the expenditure of public money it had given him to care for the refugees. He had refused. The levee board chairman had then explained to his colleagues that Butler "did not want to give out too much information for if the people in the country found out there might be trouble at the polls." The board took no offense and promptly voted Butler's committee another $50,000; in total, it would give Butler $340,000.

Now Butler stated: "Since we are administering public money, we have got to be very careful, and we have got to be guided by the opinion of Mr. Monroe, representing the city of New Orleans. . . . I can only say we will be very happy if we can find some solution of this problem, and we will do all we can to that end, but we want to say to you frankly that we cannot have a solution that is going in any way to run counter to the advice of . . . Mr. Monroe as to what procedure can be worked out."

The meeting was over. Butler and Monroe had conceded nothing.

THE FIGHT had not been over principle; it had been over money and control. Less than a week later Butler agreed to make a partial payment to a single claimant, the British-owned Louisiana Southern Railroad, which went from New Orleans sixty miles downriver to Point à la Hache. No representative of the road had bothered to attend the July 25 meeting. Its attorney was George Janvier, who had a better way of making its case. His father had been president of the Boston Club, chairman of the state Democratic Party, and Butler's mentor and predecessor as president of the Canal Bank; when the senior Janvier had left the Board of Liquidation, Butler had also filled that seat. In a file of Butler's correspondence with a hundred people, only Janvier addressed him as "Jim." It was also in the city's interest to rebuild the railroad; without it virtually no one else in the two parishes could rebuild. On August 3, Butler and Janvier met in Butler's office. Though the railroad did not file a complete schedule, New Orleans banks loaned it the money for repairs.

Then came a final deal. In early September, Simpson called the state legislature into special session to pass a constitutional amendment to authorize legally, if retroactively, the Reparations Commission and to govern judicial procedure for cases about the Caernarvon crevasse. In the weeks since the July 25 meeting, crevasse victims had focused what political power they had on getting the legislature to force New Orleans to compensate them fairly. Immediately before the legislature convened, the *St. Bernard Voice* bitterly complained: "The City of New Orleans promised and pledged itself to stand the loss and to repay each individual his actual damage. But the city is not doing this. The city's reparation committee has been cutting and slashing each claim in half and less than half, even though these claims be absolutely accurate and justified. . . . Not one claimant is satisfied with his 'settlement.' " It then pleaded, "Here is an opportunity for a New Orleans newspaper, unafraid to lose some prestige with the bankers and financiers, to ascertain the true facts and publish the real story of the manner in which the city is repaying the residents of St. Bernard Parish."

The *Voice* was a tiny paper, but this time its audience was state legislators. Hugh Wilkinson, a state senator, distributed a copy to every member of the legislature.

The next day the New Orleans papers, far from taking up the

Voice's appeal, fired back. Thomson's *Item* and *Tribune* ran identical headlines: "Orleans to Make Good on Pay Promise; Banks Loan Currency Without Collateral Other than Spoken Word . . . History records few instances of voluntary offers such as this." The *New Orleans States* bragged, "New Orleans Makes Good on Flood Pledge; Pays Claims Although Not Liable Under Law." The *Times-Picayune* proclaimed, "City Keeps Faith Assuming Burden . . . [t]hough under no legal obligations to pay for the losses of Plaquemines and St. Bernard citizens."

New Orleans legislators made sure all these papers were widely distributed as well. The *Voice,* a weekly, could not respond.

Meanwhile, Butler had asked Dufour and Esmond Phelps to draft legislative language that a New Orleans legislator introduced. It stipulated that in any lawsuits the report of the Reparations Commission "shall be prima facie evidence of the facts." In addition, any suit would be tried without a jury in Orleans Parish—the City of New Orleans—and any appeal also had to remain in Orleans Parish.

Wilkinson had his own ideas about the wording of the legislation and drafted language that said victims would be "justly, fairly and fully compensated for losses sustained." He planned to offer his language as an amendment in committee. City representatives lobbied desperately against it, arguing that the amendment would cost the city $15 million. The day before the committee was to vote, a state senator repeated that figure on the senate floor. Wilkinson sprang to his feet, shouting, "That statement is not true! It has been widely circulated by Mr. Blanc Monroe. I object to the claims of those people in St. Bernard and Plaquemines from being prejudiced."

The fight intensified. The lieutenant governor appointed a St. Bernard representative to fill a vacancy on the committee considering the amendment. Wilkinson pushed hard, demanding equity. Butler had O'Keefe "send word to New Orleans delegates to stand firm for the Act as drawn." Still, New Orleans Senator William Davey, offended over the deduction of the cost of food and housing from the victims' settlements, seemed swayed. Butler and Hecht asked Robert Ewing, the New Orleans ward leader and owner of the *New Orleans States* as well as papers in Monroe and Shreveport, to "exercise his influence with Mr. Davey" and legislatures from outside the city.

That evening Monroe, Hecht, Phelps, and Dufour sat down with Wilkinson and Davey. They insisted that they wanted to avoid a fight, and be fair. Didn't Wilkinson know he could not win? Wilkinson conceded that, though he believed he could win in committee, he did not know what would happen on the floor. If he lost there, he threatened to sue as individuals each person who had signed the agreement promising reparations. But perhaps they could work something out. Well past midnight they were still talking, and finally an agreement was struck. Wilkinson's client, Molero's Acme Fur Company, would get $1.5 million, as well as money to pay its debts. Individual trappers, however, would have to fend for themselves.

The next day Wilkinson did not even offer his language. Without any debate whatsoever, by voice vote, the committee passed the legislation written by Dufour and Phelps. The State Senate and House, also without debate and by voice vote, did likewise, then immediately adjourned.

A few days later, after it was too late for any harmful political repercussions, Monroe moved against the trappers again. Trappers actually farmed their tracts of land, bred the animals they trapped, raised them, fed them, cared for them just as a farmer cared for chickens. But Monroe and Butler had the state commissioner of conservation claim all trapping animals as the property of the state. Thus trappers could not claim any losses for them.

To an audience of no one who mattered, the *St. Bernard Voice* sneered: "The owner or lessee of marsh lands has been making $3000 to $8000 during each trapping season . . . [but] 'Muskrats are the property of the state,' says the law. And our levee-cutting neighbors in New Orleans hide themselves behind it. It was well enough to order trappers out of their homes and to destroy the muskrats on the marsh lands, for which trappers paid princely prices and, in many cases, on which there rest heavy mortgages, but when it comes to tiding them over until their lands are replenished, that is another question and side-stepping is in order for 'Brutus is an honorable man' and muskrats are the property of the state."

IN ST. BERNARD and Plaquemines Parishes, total claims, including those that Monroe refused to accept for consideration, reached $35 million. Those he did allow to be filed totaled $12,491,041. He agreed to settlements totaling $3,897,276—but then deducted nearly $1,000,000 from these settlements for feeding and housing the claimants while they were homeless, leaving roughly $2.9 million that the city paid. Of this, $1.5 million went to Molero's company. Five other large claimants, including the Louisiana Southern Railroad, received a total of $600,000. That left roughly $800,000 to divide between 2,809 claimants, who received an average of $284 each to compensate for, in many cases, having their homes and livelihoods destroyed and having their lives disrupted for months. An additional 1,024 claimants received nothing; not a single trapper was offered any compensation for trapping losses.

The two parishes were destitute. In November 1926, trappers had gathered more than a hundred pelts a day; a year and a half after the flood, in November 1928, they were lucky to collect six. In Delacroix, the trapping center, families were literally starving. A newspaperwoman who knew the area well demanded that the Association of Commerce help these people, and threatened to write "a very good feature story for several New York newspapers" if it did not.

Monroe replied to her. He made no mention of the fact that New Orleans had forced the dynamiting of the levee and caused their loss. But he did tell her that New Orleans had been generous: "The disastrous floods of 1927 did incalculable damage to many thousands of persons in the Mississippi Delta and out of these many thousands of persons none were compensated for their losses save the inhabitants of St. Bernard and Plaquemines Parishes. The compensation of the people of these parishes was a purely voluntary act on the part of the State of Louisiana and the Orleans Levee Board."

Five hundred twenty-six claimants sued over two issues. Sixty-two suits involved the question of damages discovered after a claim had been filed. Monroe had refused to accept any such claims. The special court created by Dufour and Phelps' legislation, located in New Orleans and with New Orleans judges, decreed, "We have viewed with patience and forbearance the attempts of many claimants to foist groundless claims upon the people of New Orleans, but we must confess that these . . . ravel our nerves." The court gave the plaintiffs, the victims, nothing. Appeals courts affirmed the judgment.

The remaining suits involved the question of lost income, as opposed to damaged property. It would cover the trappers. In three test cases involving Herman Burkhardt, Alfred Oliver, and Claude Foret, a trapper and two laborers, lower courts rejected the claims and found "no cause of action."

Their attorney was Leander Perez. Arguing before the state supreme court, he established his clients' losses. He read into the record newspaper quotations of Butler and others affirming their moral and legal commitment to compensate victims for all losses. He presented the pledges signed by the bankers, by the mayor and city council, by the levee board, and argued that those pledges had the force of a legal contract.

Then Monroe began. He quoted Simpson's statement when he announced plans to dynamite the levee: " 'I am impressed with the danger, and I am determined to avert it. The people in the affected area will be removed to safety and properly cared for. No lives will be sacrificed. . . . The damage to property resulting from this act will be paid for.' " Monroe insisted that it was only for *property* that compensation would be paid. Then he dismissed all the pledges made by all the leaders of New Orleans, arguing, "The constitutional amendment fixes definitely the rights and obligations of the plaintiff and defendant herein." The amendment took precedence over the proclamations of moral obligation, of pledges of honor, of signed documents. All of that, he insisted, was "irrelevant to this case."

On December 2, 1929, the supreme court rendered its decision on the two cases. The justices stated that although the city had demanded the break, "the act of creating the crevasse nevertheless remained the act of the State, through its Governor, in the exercise of its police power. . . . [A]s observed by counsel for defendant, the sole liability of the Orleans Levee District for the results of the crevasse is the liability voluntarily assumed for it by the Legislature and people of the state, when they passed and adopted the constitutional amendment cited above."

The court declared that the amendment referred only to losses caused by " 'the encroachment of said waters.' " The court then said, "In using these words, the constitutional amendment conveys the idea that just compensation is directed to be paid for damages to what is encroached on by the waters, that is, physical property."

Yet a contemporary edition of the *Oxford English Dictionary* defined "encroach" as "to intrude usurpingly on the territory, rights or accustomed sphere of action of others." Contemporary editions of both *Black's Law Dictionary* and *Bouvier's Law Dictionary* defined it in nearly identical terms. Far from limiting damages to physical property, the word "encroach" specifically expanded it beyond physical property.

The Louisiana Supreme Court, the court from which Blanc Monroe's father had retired as chief justice, the court dominated by the New Orleans bar, had chosen to misstate the definition of a simple word, and to base its finding upon that misstatement.

The court then concluded, "The judgment is affirmed."

The plaintiffs received nothing.

The levee board promptly voted a resolution of thanks to Monroe, crediting him with success "due to the painstaking and most diligent and skillful manner in which his work was prosecuted . . . and to the great benefit of the taxpayers of Orleans Parish in general, because of the great savings affected between the amounts claimed and those settled for." It also paid him a $25,000 bonus.

No bank, business, or government agency ever made a voluntary payment to the victims to fulfill the self-proclaimed moral obligation, nor was there any organized charity drive to ease the burden of the trappers.

The word of honor of the gentlemen of New Orleans, the gentlemen of the fine clubs, the gentlemen of Carnival, was "irrelevant." J. Blanc Monroe, who belonged to the finest of those clubs, who once reigned as Comus, had declared it thus himself. But a reckoning would come.

Part Eight

THE GREAT
HUMANITARIAN

CHAPTER THIRTY-ONE

WHILE TRAPPERS in St. Bernard fought with New Orleans over reparations, upriver a different fight was going on. There the river had lingered for months, not leaving all the land until September. Then it finally fell back within its banks, languid once again, like a snake that had swallowed its prey and lay now digesting it. It left behind ruin and rot.

At the site of each crevasse it had dug out "blue holes," pockets of deep water lakes where fishing was often best and that exist still, and deposited mountains of sand over thousands of acres. In the entire flooded region 50 percent of all animals—half of all the mules, horses, cattle, hogs, and chickens—had drowned. Thousands of tenant-farmer shacks had simply disappeared. Hundreds of sturdy barns, cotton gins, warehouses, and farmhouses had been swept away. Buildings by the tens of thousands had been damaged, and in towns whole blocks had become heaps of splintered lumber, like the leavings of a tornado. In some places great mounds of sand covered fields and streets. On the fields, in the forests, in streets and yards and homes and businesses and barns, the water left a reeking muck. It filled the air with stench, and in the sun it lay baking and cracking like broken pottery, dung-colored and unvarying to the horizon.

Throughout the flooded region, as people turned toward rebuilding, there was a surge of energy, activity, and determination. Looking at the desolation in Washington County on September 1, 1927, Alfred Stone declared bravely, "We shall weather the storm. We shall stay here and see it through."

But the immensity of the rebuilding task was overwhelming. LeRoy Percy said: "Sometimes you find that you have overestimated a disaster. I see nothing to indicate that in this case. The road ahead of us is a long and very rocky one." Percy Bell wrote his sister, "Whether we are going to come back or not, nobody knows." After weeks of effort, even Stone confessed, "By and large we have quit."

The situation was nearly as bleak outside of Mississippi. One Red Cross executive complained that throughout the flooded region "[n]o real concerted effort has been made . . . to obtain independence, but rather a spirit prevails of expecting substantial help in leadership and in wealth from the outside. . . . There is an inherent something in all of us that reaches out for relief and encouragement as long as distress continues. This urge is emphasized in this disaster because of the multiplicity of needs, the recurrent ills due to nature's fickleness, and the all too prevalent desire to look on the dark side. It is just possible that there is a native indolence that fosters this latter spirit, which, in many places, is true not only of the individuals but of the whole community."

In Arkansas in October, C. C. Neal, president of the black Haygood College and an aide to the Colored Advisory Commission, reported, "Yesterday I went to Arkansas City and spent the day: it presented the worst sight I ever witnessed, wreck and ruin by water everywhere in evidence. Very little in the way of crops is to be seen but plenty of work for the winter."

In Louisiana it was the same. In October, LeRoy Percy visited New Orleans and observed, "The Boston Club was about as cheerful as a morgue." Time was not healing. Even in February 1928, a Red Cross executive visited Melville, Louisiana, and reported: "The civic authorities and individuals have made no effort on their part in clearing the property [of collapsed buildings] or making an endeavor to level the lots. Even where the houses have been raised by us out of the sand and put on a firm foundation, owners have made no attempt to fill in with sand where the depression was made by the house."

HOOVER HAD an odd reaction to the desolation. In one way he found it gratifying, for it presented him with his first great domestic challenge. He intended to meet it. Back in April in Memphis when Red Cross disaster chief Henry Baker had given him his first briefing, Baker had concluded by saying, "The public is insisting on some form of rehabilitation and our standing in the disaster field requires that we do this work." But, he warned, the disaster was so great that any aid the Red Cross could possibly offer was "so meager that the word rehabilitation would not be justified."

Hoover had other ideas. Earlier he had said that prosperity could be "organized," that it was only a matter of "intelligent cooperative group effort" and "planning." There were few places in America that seemed to offer a greater potential response to rational reorganization than the alluvial plain of the Mississippi; it had the richest soil in the world, yet it was the poorest part of the nation. The flood had put this land in his power, power such as no man in modern America had ever had. He commanded every government department, including the military, and had de facto control over state governments; martial law or a near equivalent existed in much of the flooded region; the railroads, the broadcast networks, and such companies as Standard Oil, had all volunteered to obey him; and he controlled millions of dollars. His power was only temporary, but he knew how to use it. He soon developed a plan for massive rehabilitation that reflected his sense of how the world worked, and it involved the then new concept of "human engineering." He intended to apply such engineering to the nearly 1 million people in the region and change the way they lived.

He did not understate the difficulties before him. On May 23, 1927, only hours before the final crevasse of the flood at McCrea, he told a luncheon audience in New Orleans: "We have before us perhaps the most difficult and discouraging of all periods. No longer is there the excitement of catastrophe, the stimulation of heroism and fine sacrifice. Reconstruction is always the most trying period of all disasters." Yet he was more than simply optimistic, adding, "I have said the word 'reconstruction' advisedly because I believe we may give it a new significance in the relations of North and South." Later he declared that the flood would prove "a blessing in disguise."

His comment reflected his ambition and supreme confidence. *I shall be the nominee, probably,* he had said. *It is nearly inevitable.* Given the booming economy, it also seemed nearly inevitable that he become President of the United States. If his rehabilitation plan succeeded, as president he could use it as a model to apply to other of the nation's problems.

And as grand as his goal of economic reconstruction was, he had another even more ambitious plan, one that involved race, and politics, and power.

HOOVER BEGAN by imposing his plans on the refugee camps, and he involved himself in extraordinary detail. It was almost as if, as an act of will, he intended to lift the entire region out of squalor. Most refugees, whether black Delta sharecroppers or white Cajuns, lived stunningly primitive lives amid epidemics of pellagra and venereal disease. He personally ordered the Red Cross to purchase hundreds of thousands of packets of vegetable seeds—beans, beets, squash, tomatoes—to give to refugees leaving camp so they could grow vegetable gardens, something few croppers did. He also saw to it that the refugee camps swarmed with home economists and agricultural extension agents who taught captive audiences now to sew, make soap, can vegetables, raise poultry, protect cistern water from mosquitoes, use a toothbrush, bathe, treat gonorrhea.

Hoover attended to even closer detail when it came to larger changes: he wanted to end the Delta's dependence on cotton by introducing other crops. The thought was not new, but few Delta planters had paid attention to it. Cotton, however, has to be planted in the spring; just as the June rise was ending any hope of a cotton crop for 1927, Hoover was demanding from experts a "definite program of agriculture . . . stating the end of periods when different crops can be put in." Even before getting definitive replies, he ordered the Red Cross to buy enough seed for 400,000 acres of soybeans. Agricultural scientists soon told him that planting soybeans so late was "positively contrary to not only our experience, but the leading planters of the Delta." Despite the advice, he personally contacted banks to have them "undertake to loan money on a Soya bean crop."

For the key to rebuilding, he believed, was credit. Delta cotton planters and Louisiana sugar growers had, as always, mortgaged nearly everything to plant the crops now submerged. Credit had disappeared. He was determined to supply it. Again almost as if by act of will, he began to create something out of nothing. While engineers were still fighting to hold the Bayou des Glaises levee, he was drafting a plan for private nonprofit "reconstruction corporations" in each flooded state that would loan money to planters on easier terms than would banks. He wired information on his idea to Treasury Secretary Andrew Mellon and Eugene Meyer, a financier soon to become head of the Federal Farm Loan Board (and later chairman of the Federal Reserve and owner of the *Washington Post*). To Meyer, a confidant, he said: "Am more impressed than ever with need for some kind of credit backing for situation. For your confidential information"—to guarantee confidentiality Hoover sent the telegram to Meyer's home —"some outside banks are now refusing checks on flooded banks. If there is any failure of these banks the trouble will be vastly increased."

As Hoover requested, Meyer immediately arranged for federal credit agencies to prevent any such failure. Meanwhile, Hoover himself proceeded to organize a separate reconstruction corporation in Arkansas, Louisiana, and Mississippi. Money would come not from the government but from, as he once said, those "strong men who

. . . with definite purpose exert a greater influence on the situation from the outside than from in." If his plan worked, then the flooded area would in fact be pulling itself up by its own bootstraps. And if it worked, he would have a model for economic change that could be used almost anywhere.

He wanted bankers and leading businessmen in each state to buy stock—$500,000 worth of stock each in Arkansas and Mississippi, $750,000 in Louisiana—in their state's corporation. He expected national business leaders to buy an equal amount of stock in them. The reconstruction corporations would use the capital to make loans, sell these loans at a discount to the Federal Intermediate Credit Corporation, then use the money from this sale to make more loans, repeating the process until each corporation's loan portfolio amounted to quadruple its capital.

Hoover threw all his personal force into raising money. In mid-May, even before the river had finished its war dance through Louisiana, he met with Mississippi bankers in Jackson. He explained the plan and asked every bank and large business to subscribe 1 percent of its capital. Governor Murphree reminded everyone, "You are not called upon to donate, but to invest some of your money in the integrity of these people, and I know that you will do that." Will Whittington, the congressman from the Delta, said, "The best help that can be given any people is that help which enables them to help themselves." Then, with all the fervor of a revival meeting, to cheers and foot-stomping, one pledge after another was announced. But there was a hollowness to the meeting; pledges were soon broken and few new ones made. Hoover met a second time with Mississippi bankers and this time was more emphatic: "You are upon the firing line! We are discussing economic questions but in fact we are discussing the problems of men, women, and children. . . . We have in our charge the responsibility of the welfare of these thousands of people. It is the duty of leadership!" Yet he could not move them. Out of 500 banks in Mississippi, only 115 gave anything at all. Less than half the quota he had set was actually subscribed. In Arkansas the numbers were worse.

He would not be thwarted. On May 24, he called a meeting of thirty Memphis bankers and businessmen at the Peabody and told them their quota was $200,000, half for the Arkansas corporation, half for Mississippi's. Those assembled shifted uncomfortably. One man protested. Suddenly, Hoover began to curse, his words as rough as those he had used decades before to miners a thousand miles from civilization. Then he made a simple promise. About 25,000 black refugees were in camps in Memphis. It was 2 P.M. He gave them to 5 P.M. that day to deliver pledges for the money. "If not," he warned, "I'll start sending your niggers north, starting tonight."

Immediately after the meeting he told the head of the Mississippi reconstruction corporation, "Have talked with Memphis people and I am sure they will assist." He was right. By five o'clock he had his $200,000.

Forty-eight hours later Hoover was in Washington to raise more money, only now he was unwilling to risk the humiliation of public failure. Before proceeding, he asked for help from Lewis Pierson, president of New York's Irving Trust Company and the U.S. Chamber of Commerce. Pierson, intensely interested in the flooded region, had already created a committee to develop a Chamber position on how to prevent any future Mississippi River disaster. The committee had thirteen members, including steel executives, bankers, and manufacturers spread from Los Angeles to New York, but it would be dominated by four men who had been friends for decades: LeRoy Percy; John Parker; Jacob Dickinson, the former secretary of war and Illinois Central executive; and Alfred Stone. Three of those four had joined Teddy Roosevelt in that bear hunt of so long ago. Now, at Hoover's request, Pierson sent out a handful of telegrams about his plan, noting: "This telegram for yourself only until you phone Hoover . . . or phone me. We must have psychology of situation right before making any announcements."

Once the response guaranteed success, Hoover acted quickly. On May 30, Coolidge signed a letter Hoover had drafted asking "the business interests of America under the leadership of the Chamber of Commerce of the United States . . . to secure to these loan corporations subscriptions of capital." Only four days later, on June 3, Pierson brought together forty-eight of the most powerful men in America. Some were Hoover's enemies, such as Judge E. H. Gary of U.S. Steel, who resented Hoover's earlier use of the press to force him to grant steelworkers an eight-hour day. More were Hoover's friends, such as Owen Young, the president of General Electric, who shared much of Hoover's engineering-based philosophy; Julius Rosenwald of Sears, a great benefactor to blacks whose son-in-law was president of the New Orleans Cotton Exchange; and L. A. Downs, president of the Illinois Central, who was allowing Hoover to use his road's finest private car. Also present were the most senior executives of such companies as Proctor & Gamble, Kennecott Copper, Allied Chemical, General Motors, Ford, Dodge, Standard Oil of New Jersey, Marshall Field & Company, the Pennsylvania Railroad, and the leading banks of New York, Boston, Philadelphia, and Chicago.

These men were powerful indeed, and their companies represented a significant percentage of the national economy. Hoover assured them that businessmen in the flooded region were generously buying stock in the reconstruction corporations. He also reminded them that the situation was desperate, and warned, "We cannot afford nationally to have a business or financial prairie fire starting from here after the flood." Then he read a telegram from Red Cross Vice Chairman James Fieser to the head of the Arkansas Reconstruction Corporation, noting, "[L]arge planters who have been able to supply tenants and sharecroppers so far are finding credit exhausted and are unable to secure loans from the [Federal] Intermediate Credit Bank. . . . [There is] growing alarm." Finally, he told them that if men like themselves cooperated with the blessing of the government, they could achieve nearly anything. He easily raised his goal: $1.75 million.

Added to the money raised in the South, and with rediscounting by federal credit agencies, Hoover had created $13 million in credit. Even though Arkansas and Mississippi had not met their quotas, he considered this total sufficient. By comparison, the Red Cross would spend less than $17 million to rescue, house, feed, and clothe nearly 700,000 people, many of them for as long as ten months, and rebuild and furnish several thousand homes as well.

Hoover was certain these reconstruction corporations would succeed, but his vision soon collided with financial and political realities. One was the reality of capitalism itself, for his plan was flawed at its core. The other was the fact that it ran the length of a fault line in American thought about the role of government and how much responsibility it had for its citizens—and it helped move that line.

FORTY YEARS earlier President Grover Cleveland, a Democrat, had vetoed an emergency appropriation of $10,000 for drought victims in Texas, declaring that the government had no "warrant in the Constitution . . . to indulge a benevolent and charitable sentiment through the appropriation of public funds . . . [for] relief of individual suffering which is in no manner properly related to the public service." Twenty years earlier, during Teddy Roosevelt's presidency, the federal government had required New Orleans banks to give that $250,000 guarantee before the surgeon general would help fight the yellow fever epidemic.

Since then the role of the federal government had expanded enormously, yet it had still stopped short of large-scale direct aid to suffering individuals. Nor did Hoover believe in direct aid. He had seen the new Soviet state, knew of its mass murders, and flatly rejected the idea that "any economic or social system will function and last if founded upon altruism alone."

But Hoover had also said, "The most potent force in society is its ideals," and that "no civilization based upon unrestrained self-interest could endure." He had repeatedly predicted, as in a speech to the U.S. Chamber of Commerce, that the country was "in the midst of a great revolution," that extreme individualism was giving way to what he called "associational activities" and "voluntary organization" that would mitigate the harshness of society.

He believed that government should help individuals indirectly, by providing leadership without coercion. He believed that society's strong men—outside of government—had a responsibility to gather together and create good, and that they had the leverage to move a society. He believed in aggressive and structured voluntarism. He once said that government could "best serve the community by bringing about cooperation in a large sense between groups. It is the failure of groups to respond to their responsibilities to others that drives government more and more into the lives of the people."

The nation's response to the flood disaster seemed to confirm his beliefs—initially. Of the 33,849 people in the Red Cross flood effort, only 2,438 were paid. He later said: "I made ninety-one local committees to look after the Mississippi flood. You say, 'A couple of thousand people are coming. They've got to have accommodations. Huts, watermains, sewers. Streets. Dining halls. Meals. Doctors. Everything.' . . . So you go away and they simply go ahead and do it. Of all those ninety-one committees there was just one that fell down." In the nation at large, the outpouring of sympathy and contributions was overwhelming. Every movie theater chain in the country hosted benefits, and 17,000 theaters took collections at performances for weeks. The Elks, Masons, American Legion, and virtually every other fraternal group in the country raised money. The National Congress of Parents and Teachers sought donations from 18,000 chapters. A toothbrush manufacturer donated 4,500 toothbrushes. The Singer sewing-machine company offered its products at 50 percent discount with free shipping. Hollywood stars, especially Will Rogers, gave dozens of benefits. A Polish-American society raised money from several thousand schoolchildren in Poland. NBC radio and individual stations across the country gave free time to Hoover and repeatedly urged listeners to give to the Red Cross. The *New York Times* wrote, "[Radio's] possibilities have often been discussed, but never before had it been asked to tap this field and exploit its possibilities to [this] extent." Ultimately, tens of millions of Americans donated money for relief. The Red Cross and Hoover also performed magnificently during the initial stages of the flood.

But the rehabilitation effort highlighted a hole in the fabric of the society. Refugees leaving camps who were totally destitute and who owned farms or rented them outright, or who sharecropped on plantations smaller than two hundred acres, were to receive some household and farming equipment, seed for crops, and, if their home had been destroyed, their tents and camp bedding. They were also given two weeks' supply of food and seed for a vegetable garden. Then they were on their own. Sharecroppers on large plantations would not get even that much from the Red Cross; planters were supposed to provide for them. Oscar Johnston, who ran the huge Delta & Pine Land Company, was asked for a list of what a tenant family of four who had lost absolutely everything would need. He provided a detailed nine-page inventory that reveals much about how sharecroppers lived: "1 dipper 1 baking pan 4 forks 4 spoons 1 large spoon . . . 4 joints of stove pipe 1 elbow for stove pipe 1 cooking stove . . . 1 suit overalls 4 pair shoes . . . two beds and springs." Johnston estimated that replacing an entire household's clothes, furniture, and effects for a family of four would cost $77.42, but suggested that most families would get less. In fact, the total value of goods refugees took out of camp averaged only $27 in Arkansas (no figures are available for Louisiana and Mississippi). It would hardly rebuild the lives of even sharecroppers.

The government itself would do nothing to help flood victims recover. The Treasury that year collected a record surplus of $635 million, yet in a disaster that affected almost 1 percent of the nation's population, the government would not even create a loan-guarantee program. Indeed, the War Department dunned the Red Cross for months to pay for blankets refugees had kept and the cost of cleaning supplies that were returned. (Hoover finally ordered the War Department to desist, reminding it, "The supplies and services of the Government Departments were placed at my disposal . . . and are not chargeable to the Red Cross.")

Hoover's reconstruction corporations amounted to the only organized program for rehabilitation. The approach epitomized his beliefs. Many agreed that the government should do nothing. Direct aid had always been considered charity, and charity stigmatized recipients. In 1922 as governor, John Parker had refused all outside help—even national Red Cross help—in dealing with 35,000 flood refugees. Now Tennessee Governor Austin Peay rejected Red Cross rehabilitation aid in his state. "He felt that the people in the local communities should be expected to provide for themselves, rather than depend on outside assistance," reported a disgusted Red Cross official.

But the immensity of this disaster and the government's lack of response marked a dividing line, a watershed. The debate over aid crystallized over two questions: the adequacy of Hoover's program, and the separate but related issue of calling a special session of Congress, which would be expected to appropriate money for flood victims.

Congress was not scheduled to meet until January 1928. Members of both parties from every geographical region pushed Coolidge to call a special session. Coolidge refused. Democratic Senator James Reed of Missouri wired: "I feel warranted in asking whether you will not reconsider your decision now that nearly one half million people" —the number was then still increasing—"have been driven from their homes. . . . With the utmost deference I ask you to give further consideration to this grave situation." Coolidge refused. Reed Smoot, of Coolidge's own party and chairman of the Senate Finance Committee, met with him and told the press he believed Coolidge had changed his mind. Coolidge denied it. Critics pointed out that, three years out of five, the river rose enough in the fall, even though short of flood stage, to pour through existing gaps in the levees, leaving the region helpless. The Red Cross refused to spend money on levees, and Coolidge's chief budget official ruled that the Army, with its funds exhausted, could not legally spend a penny to repair them. Legally, Congress *had* to pass an appropriations bill. Coolidge illegally ordered the Mississippi River Commission to spend money.

The *New York Times* applauded Coolidge's refusal to convene Congress and deemed Hoover's program sufficient: "Fortunately, there are still some things that can be done without the wisdom of Congress and the all-fathering Federal Government." The *San Antonio Express* wrote: "Frequent demands that Congress be called into special session to deal with the problems of relief and rehabilitation have been heard. [Hoover's financing plan] conclusively shows that such a step is not necessary. Private capital can supply the needed credit and is displaying an encouraging readiness to do so." The *Fall River* (Massachusetts) *Globe,* added, "The new spirit in which the master business minds of the day associate themselves with the public welfare is illustrated in the recent action of the officials of the Chamber of Commerce of the United States . . . an excellent example of enlightened selfishness." And the *Chicago Journal of Commerce* warned: "If the federal government were to set aside funds to be used for disaster relief . . . the appropriations might climb to appalling heights. . . . If relief of sufferers were to become a government task, the self-respect of the recipients of funds would be decidedly damaged. And the moral injury would have definite effects on the material fortunes of a recipient in after life . . . [causing] a rapid sapping of his initiative and [he] may spend the rest of his life demanding more aid as his right."

Most of the country's newspapers, however, disagreed. Hoover had created $13 million in credit; that worked out to less than $20 for each victim. The *Ames* (Iowa) *Tribune & Times* argued: "The total amount is but a bagatelle. . . . It is rather difficult to understand why the president refuses to avail himself of the sole agency through which either adequate measures of relief or of financing rehabilitation credits can be accomplished—an extra session of Congress." The *Camden* (New Jersey) *Courier,* said, "[Hoover's plan] is good—yes, but it is nothing remarkable. . . . It is a makeshift move." Norfolk's *Virginian Pilot* wrote that the appeal to private capital "is a worthy one that deserves to succeed, but it is impossible to contemplate this arrangement without wondering whether the situation might be more effectively met by government action." The *Providence* (Rhode Island) *Tribune* declared, "The indifference of the Government does not coincide with the ideals which it frequently pronounces and for which it is exalted." The *Jackson Clarion-Ledger* asked: "Why make a charity out of plain duty? . . . Not a dime has the government appropriated. The truth of the matter is that it has been necessary to school President Coolidge day by day a bit more towards the realization of the immensity of the catastrophe. . . . This new demand for aid from private citizens and corporations comes at a time when Secretary Mellon is announcing a surplus of millions in the Treasury. Why then should this tremendous burden be saddled on the people when the government has ample means to bear it?" The *Sacramento Bee* called for a special session "without delay, even if it spoils President Coolidge's plans for a care-free summer vacation." The *Houston Chronicle* asked, "Why should we ask the United States Chamber of Commerce to become responsible for flood relief?" The *Paducah* (Kentucky) *News-Democrat* observed: "It is hardly possible that this private credit arrangement will be sufficient to put the refugee population of 700,000 back at work. . . . Either [President Coolidge] has the coldest heart in America or the dullest imagination, and we are about ready to believe he has both."

All over the country, newspapers were rocking the administration with criticism. Every Scripps-Howard paper ran an editorial insisting Congress be called. Every Hearst paper did the same. Franklin

Roosevelt received much press for saying, "With due deference to Mr. Hoover I cannot believe that he really means that [the Red Cross fund] is adequate to meet more than the demands for the next few weeks."

The *St. Louis Star,* the *New York Evening World,* the *Birmingham News,* and dozens of others were echoing the demand. Papers that backed both political parties demanded it. Hoover's staff warned him: "At least four-fifths of the editorials coming in advocate such a session," and again, "Editorial comment on the question of a special session continues heavily favorable to a special session. . . . There continues to be considerable criticism of the attitude of the President."

The sentiment defined a watershed, when the nation first demanded that the federal government assume a new kind of responsibility for its citizens. But the government was not yet prepared to accept such responsibility.

LEROY PERCY had been among those calling for Congress to meet, and his voice had resonated throughout the Mississippi valley. On May 19, Hoover met with him in Baton Rouge and said that Coolidge was adamant. No amount of pressure would get him to convene Congress. Hoover promised that the Red Cross would care for the Delta's immediate needs. More important, he also promised major legislation in which the federal government assumed responsibility for the Mississippi River. He then asked Percy to mute his criticism. Percy had sought such legislation for years. Hoover accompanied his promises with a veiled threat: if Percy did not restrain his attacks, Hoover could not promise that the legislation would ever become law. Coolidge might veto it, and by the time a new president entered the White House, Congress might have lost its sense of urgency. After the meeting Percy told the Associated Press, "We regard as settled that there will be no extra session of Congress called at this time and we would deem continued agitation of the question extremely hurtful."

The next day in New Orleans, Hoover asked Butler to publicly oppose a special session. Butler agreed and saw to it that the city's leaders joined in that opposition. Soon after, the *New York Times* wired thirty men in the flooded area—including Percy and nine New Orleans leaders—to "send us collect your opinion on . . . [an] extra session of Congress." All were men of prominence, men like Percy and Butler, men who dealt with Hoover. Overwhelmingly, they opposed it. The *Times* printed their opinions prominently, and the administration used them as ammunition. Meanwhile, L. O. Crosby, the flood "dictator" in Mississippi, reported to Hoover, "Since Senator Percy has seen the light . . . sentiment is growing much stronger in support of your plans." As a result, Hoover advised Coolidge, "[I] seem to have at least temporarily stopped the press campaign for an immediate session for relief purposes."

He was correct. The push for an extra session dissipated, along with the criticism of the reconstruction corporations. Then Hoover simply declared success. Rebuking Sinclair Lewis, he told a Rotary club in New Orleans: "We rescued Main Street with Main Street. . . . The cooperative spirit of Main Street is what is putting the Mississippi Valley back on its feet after the flood. The people of the valley are settling their own problems of rehabilitation without a great deal of outside help. It is upon such independence and self-government that is based the greatness of the United States."

The press moved on. Hoover did not. First he rebutted even indirect criticism of his actions. No newspaper had criticized him personally; to the contrary, many papers that had demanded a special session and attacked Coolidge had also, like those in the Scripps-Howard chain, pointedly offered him "unstinted praise." Yet Hoover let nothing pass unanswered. To every newspaper that called his plan inadequate, and to dozens of individuals who had criticized it as well, he wrote identical but personalized lengthy responses which often ran as special articles. No paper was too small for his attention. Even weeklies in such places as Bowie, Arizona; Bremen, Indiana; Blaine, Washington; Electra, Texas; and Hartwood, Nebraska, received his rebuttal. To each editor he insisted that each individual victim had been cared for, that he had personally sat in on meetings when the reconstruction corporations had decided to loan enormous amounts to large planters, sawmill owners, manufacturers, and concluded, "I have thought upon explanation you would perhaps be willing to correct any misapprehension."

To the country he was a hero, reclaiming the title he had earned in his European relief efforts, the Great Humanitarian. When he returned to Washington after one trip through the flood states, Will Rogers joked, "Bert's just resting between disasters."

BUT HOOVER'S PROCLAMATION of success did not equal success, and he had failed to address the real problem. He had only created credit. Credit involved risk. Private capital demanded either collateral enough to mitigate that risk or return enough to compensate for it. The devastated areas could not pay a high return, and planters had no collateral, since they had already mortgaged their land to plant the crop destroyed by the waters. Therefore, ironically, the reconstruction corporations had greater difficulty loaning money than they had had raising it.

In Greenville, Hoover's program came under direct attack. Billy Wynn criticized the plan publicly: "We challenge the statement in the press that it will meet the need." While Percy himself said nothing publicly, his refusal to defend the plan did not go unnoticed. Privately, W. H. Negus, president of the First National Bank of Greenville on whose board LeRoy Percy sat, described the situation clearly to the head of Mississippi's reconstruction corporation: "There is, in fact, a super-abundance of bank funds. What this section is short of is banking collateral and that is the reason and necessity for 'rehabilitation.' Unless your corporation can furnish such need, which appears unlikely, it will do very little business, if any."

Once again Hoover, refusing to be thwarted, intervened. First he convinced the St. Louis Intermediate Credit Bank to ignore its regulations and discount new crop mortgages even if a prior lien existed, so long as the lien holder agreed not to foreclose before the new crop was harvested. To further ease credit he also had the Red Cross promise to reimburse the reconstruction corporations for half of any losses. Percy, after the New Orleans bankers Hecht and Pool asked for assistance, and Alfred Stone also helped; they convinced Percy's old friend and college classmate Tom Davis, head of the New Orleans Federal Intermediate Credit Bank, to suspend payments due on flooded land.

Meanwhile, Crosby answered criticism by lying to reporters. He said the Mississippi Reconstruction Corporation had, only two weeks after being organized and while flood water still covered nearly all the Delta, loaned out $100,000. In fact, months after his assertion, it had loaned only $50,000—and half of that went to the State of Mississippi to pay the National Guard. There was simply no demand for the loans, because there was no collateral available. Privately, Crosby informed Hoover: "It has been a source of much worry to me that an appreciation . . . [of] the great service you are rendering . . . has not been made manifest in as strong degree as I should like to see it. . . . For some reason the people in the flooded area have been difficult to arouse to their opportunities." Nor was there much demand for loans in Arkansas and Louisiana.

Hoover could admit neither error nor failure. Earlier he had proceeded with massive soybean plantings despite scientific advice against it. Now he told Butler, "I have the feeling that while there is not much demand for [the credit corporation's] services . . . yet its very existence has accomplished two-thirds of what we set out to do."

In fact, his massive financing effort accomplished next to nothing. In the end, the Mississippi corporation made loans amounting to barely 5 percent of what Hoover had envisioned, and the Arkansas and Louisiana corporations did little better. The experience was pregnant with implications regarding the ability of the private sector alone to meet a crisis, but Hoover paid little attention to them. Instead, having declared success, Hoover was advancing to something far more ambitious than simple economic rehabilitation, something that would directly advance his own ambitions as well.

CHAPTER THIRTY-TWO

THE RED CROSS treaded ever so lightly when it came to race. After a 1921 race riot in Tulsa left 9,000 blacks homeless, for example, James Fieser ordered a Red Cross professional assigned to help them "to pull out as quickly as possible." The man refused, instead took a leave of absence, and continued to help the blacks without salary "at great uneasiness" to Fieser and the national organization.

In the first days of the flood, Red Cross headquarters similarly ordered Henry Baker, the on-scene disaster chief, to avoid Red Cross involvement in the issue of using the National Guard to keep black refugees in the camps. Hoover, despite his attention to other camp details, also initially avoided entanglement in race. When a Red Cross aide suggested telling planters that if they waived all 1927 tenant debts, the Red Cross would feed their tenants through the crop year, Fieser instantly rejected the proposal, replying it was "unwise to become too involved in local conditions."

But as word of abuses of blacks in the camps had spread through the North, Hoover had created the Colored Advisory Commission and named Robert Moton chairman. Fieser had not objected. Moton, Fieser felt sure, would embarrass no one and would prove useful. Yet in return Moton had something large in mind.

ROBERT RUSSA MOTON stood well over six feet tall and towered over most men, but his slumped shoulders, rumpled appearance, and pudgy physique conveyed little force. He looked like a man who belonged in a study, smoking a pipe and pondering a problem, yet he was arguably the single most powerful black man in the United States, and what he pondered was the future of his race in American society. A man whom the Percys and their class would have commended, he personified the mythos of race relations that they expounded. During the Civil War, his father, a slave, had found himself behind Union lines but rather than claiming his freedom, he had returned to slavery because, his son explained approvingly, "he had given his definite promise he would stand with [his master] Colonel Womack until the war was over."

Whether his father really had kept his word at the cost of freedom or Moton told the story simply to please southern whites, Moton did believe that the moral force of honorable behavior would ultimately compel white men to behave honorably as well. He was no Gandhi, who used moral force like an anvil breaking the hammer; he confronted no one, trusted powerful white men, made himself useful to them, and patiently awaited them. Yet in his own way he did everything possible to advance his race, and in a most difficult time he danced a most delicate dance. For this, radicals in his race called him naive and even dangerous.

Moton rose in the world through ability, hard work, and the influence of his powerful mentors. He had a sense of dignity, but also of caste. He did not have pride. Fellow students at Hampton Institute were Native Americans and he could not understand their pride. Once a visiting Army general wanted to shake hands with the son of an Indian chief whom he had killed in battle. Moton brought the student forward and introduced him "with all the deference due to the General's position. . . . The general greeted this boy of seventeen years of age very cordially, unusually so for the ranking general of the United States Army. . . . Paul looked him straight in the eye, did not salute, and refused to shake hands with him. I thought he had not observed the general's outstretched hand and in a whisper I said, 'The general wants to shake hands with you,' but in typical Indian fashion he said, 'Know it.' " Moton confessed he was "very much humiliated" by the incident.

He considered pride a luxury too expensive to indulge. Wasn't the experience of the Indians proof? Whites were wiping them out. Wasn't it better to bend to the white wind, to make progress and survive even if that meant keeping one's thoughts to one's self? So he held his thoughts back. He did so even in his book titled *What the Negro Thinks,* telling whites, "Negroes have always met the familiar declaration, 'I know the Negro' with a certain faint, knowing smile. . . . [T]here are vast reaches of Negro life and thought of which white people know nothing whatever, even after long contact with them, sometimes on the most intimate terms . . . which reflects the persistent effort of the Negro on the concealment of his thoughts and feelings. . . . The Negro has always been quite chary of disclosing all his thoughts to the white man. He seldom tells all the truth about such matters; a great deal of it may not find its way into this volume."

A protégé of Booker T. Washington, Moton was a conciliator, and not only with whites. He once tried to bring the two great rivals Washington and W. E. B. Du Bois together, and with them the race. When Washington died, Moton succeeded him as principal of Tuskegee Institute in Alabama and also took command of what was called "the Tuskegee machine," a machine built upon cooperating with, and not confronting, the white power structure. Teddy Roosevelt had helped create this machine by giving Washington nearly total control over relevant federal patronage jobs. Although Moton never attained Washington's stature or influence, he still proved useful to whites. During World War I even Woodrow Wilson, who had imposed segregation on the federal bureaucracy and endorsed the film *Birth of a Nation,* had relied on Moton when black troops in France grew angry over the difference between how the French and their own countrymen treated them. At Wilson's request Moton had gone to France and oiled the waters, and Wilson had thanked him for "the wholesome advice" he gave black soldiers "regarding their conduct during the time they will remain in France . . . [and] as to how they should conduct themselves when they return to our own shores."

Back in Alabama, Moton carefully did not offend. Unlike at some black colleges, whites visiting Tuskegee were completely segregated, even entering chapel through a private door and sitting separately. Other black leaders, including some moderates, condemned Moton for this. When whites asked Moton to broadcast a radio appeal urging blacks to remain in the South, he did so, saying: "Whatever might be said to the contrary, the white man of the South loves the Negro. Many who have gone North have not found conditions as they had expected. . . . There is less reason now for Negroes to leave the South than ever before, because the basic sentiment in the South today, official and otherwise, is determined that the fundamental desires of the black man shall be assured him."

He had confronted whites only once, over the issue of hiring Negro physicians for a new hospital for black veterans at Tuskegee. Many black leaders nationally, such as Du Bois, raised their voices loudly. Moton exerted all the influence he possessed, but only privately—albeit successfully. Few black leaders knew how hard he had worked, and few gave him any credit. To white leaders, however, he had proved his reliability and proved he would do nothing that would hurt them.

In return for all his efforts, Moton whispered in the ear of national politicians. In 1922, while LeRoy Percy was wrestling with the Klan, and tens of thousands of Klansmen were preparing to march down Washington streets, William Howard Taft chose Moton to give the chief address at the dedication of the Lincoln Memorial, symbolizing Moton's status in white eyes. And the Tuskegee machine, if somewhat eroded after Washington's death, still gave him power. Long before the flood, Hoover had informed Moton he would "be pleased to see you any time that you come to Washington." Coolidge was also willing to meet with him or his representatives.

Equally important, Moton whispered in the ears of philanthropists. He served on boards with Andrew Carnegie, William Howard Taft, and John D. Rockefeller, Jr. George Eastman, founder of Eastman Kodak, gave $5 million to Tuskegee. An even larger giver was Julius Rosenwald of Sears, whose many philanthropic acts included, at least partly as a result of Moton's influence, building more than 6,000 "Rosenwald schools" for rural southern blacks.

It was this access to money that gave Moton the most power. When the black Kittrell College desperately needed $15,000 "to save an embarrassing situation," it called upon Moton to raise it. When the all-black Delta town of Mound Bayou, Mississippi, was foundering, Moton promised its leader Eugene Booze to raise $100,000 for him. (Booze then asked Moton "the proper approach to Mr. John D. Rockefeller, Jr." for a $1 million contribution.)

Now Hoover was intimating that he had large plans to help Negroes. And if Hoover became president—what possibilities that could afford! Now Moton was playing at a level higher even than Washington had, with the highest potential stakes for the race. It was up to Moton to play the game well.

IN EARLY JUNE in Memphis the Colored Advisory Commission met for the first time. Moton divided the members into small groups and sent each into different areas of the flood zone. Their trips were strenuous. One investigator reported: "Our train took six hours to go eleven miles, the water up to the lower steps of the car; the train in utter darkness the lights having failed, the Jim Crow coach half occupied by whites, and the remainder packed with Negroes some sitting three in a seat, aisles filled with men standing and the noise of the water boiling over the track, terrifying one woman until she screamed and put down the window to shut out the sound, with the people refusing to sing because of what seemed to be a sullen resentment at their treatment. It was an experience which will long cling to me."

Despite the difficulties, the several groups quickly visited dozens of camps. In some, when they presented papers signed by senior Red Cross officials, whites muttered, called them "nigger," and made certain they talked to no refugees alone; at least once, commission members left a camp hurriedly for fear of being kept there and forced to work. In other camps, including Greenville, whites treated them with utmost courtesy.

After ten days commission members reunited, prepared a preliminary report, and on June 14 presented it to Hoover and Fieser. It confirmed charges that Negroes were systematically being held in camps against their will and forced to work. In isolated places, the National Guard had also stolen, raped, and probably committed murder. One investigator separately sent a summary to the Justice Department asking for a criminal investigation. Yet Moton released only a much-censored version to the press with the most minor recommendations, for example "that a screened structure with tables and seats be erected for the serving of food at Greenville." He also wrote an inoffensive story for release to the Associated Press and told Hoover, "You may feel free to make any changes or additions that may seem desirable to you."

Claude Barnett did syndicate a story through his Associated Negro Press to over one hundred black newspapers stating that "members of the commission were bitter in their comment on conditions in several camps, particularly at Greenville, Mississippi." But he explained apologetically to Hoover that Greenville had received so much publicity that "the truth must be admitted" or their report would have no credibility, and pointed out that his story praised the national Red Cross as "eminently fair and just in its orders." Hoover reassured him that the story was "constructive."

The first phase had gone well for everyone. Hoover and Fieser, pleased, made good use of Moton's press release to defuse criticism. For Moton the worst abuses of the Guard had been ended, and Hoover and Fieser had promised to implement the report's recommendations. Barnett also assured Moton that they had trumped their rivals: "The [Chicago] Defender demands 'a probe of flood conditions.' It is a weak and hollow cry, used to bolster their attempt to take credit."

But Moton had a larger goal in mind than maneuvering against more radical competitors in the black community. He had been willing to mute public criticism of the Red Cross, and indirectly of Hoover, to further another goal. Hoover had told Barnett that "something substantial can be accomplished." Hoover had also hinted to J. S. Clark, president of Southern University, that he would do something, and Clark told Moton, "I am of the opinion that the work of our Committee is going to be far-reaching." Moton himself had gotten a similar message from Hoover. Excited, he told a confidant, "It is my frank opinion that, as a result of the flood, the position of the Negro as an individual farm owner is going to be considerably strengthened."

The essence of Moton's hopes lay not in the implementation of any specific recommendation of the commission report but in a more general plea. "We were face to face with one of the greatest labor questions of America, the relation between the planters and these tenant farmers," Moton wrote. "We were interested in a song that these people sang in the levee camps—that the flood had washed away the old account. They felt that the flood had emancipated them from a condition of peonage. . . . We are strongly convinced that something ought to be done permanently to relieve the hopeless condition under which these people have lived all these years. They ought not to be permitted to go back to this hopeless situation . . . if there is rehabilitation."

HOOVER ENCOURAGED the commission to think he would help the Negro. He intended to, and also needed their help. So far, they had given it. The flood had brought new attention to the plight of the Negro in the South; the sudden explosion of lynchings in May and June in Arkansas, Tennessee, Mississippi, and Louisiana, compounded by the sympathy for flood refugees, was sparking new calls for federal antilynching legislation and new criticism of the Red Cross. Moton and his commission had defused some of those attacks with their first report. Still, Hoover noted, "We are having great difficulty through the North . . . in connection with the colored people."

On July 8, the day after a policeman murdered a black in Greenville, Moton, Barnett, and several other members of the commission met again with Fieser and Hoover, this time in Fieser's Washington office, to present a more complete, second report, far more damning than the earlier press release or even than the preliminary draft. Moton reviewed it with Hoover and Fieser, doing most of the talking, gently noting that perhaps too little had been done since the first report, elaborating where necessary, and answering their questions while Barnett and the others remained silent. Moton neither said nor implied that he might release this potentially explosive document to the press. On the contrary, in order to protect the Red Cross and Hoover, Moton had prepared only three copies and had even refused to give any to other commission members; two copies he kept, one he gave to Hoover. But he also asked about rehabilitation and made a veiled reference to Hoover's hints of ambitious plans.

The next day Hoover received Moton privately in his office. By then they both knew he could very well be the next president of the United States. Indeed, his chances were increasing daily. Coolidge could legally run again, but tradition limited presidents to two terms. He had had them. And rumors were rife that Coolidge's enemies were about to launch a campaign to force his retirement. Soon one GOP senator would publicly declare his opposition to a third term and a wire-service story would proclaim, "Underground Forces Working Against Calvin; Hoover Boom Is Growing . . . The widespread subterranean alienation from Mr. Coolidge which has long existed among professional Republican politicians will come to the surface in successive explosions. . . . As soon as the next Senate meets, it will consider an anti-third term resolution."

Now Moton sat alone with Hoover; it was a heady feeling, and one filled with promise for the future. It became headier when Hoover reviewed an idea that he had not wanted to discuss before the others. He said that the flooded region suffered from a "background of bankrupt economics." The plantation system and dependence on cotton had wasted the richest land in the world. Then he outlined a comprehensive, and revolutionary, plan, a plan that could remake the face of the Delta. A memorandum he wrote that day, July 9, proposed "a subdivision of the land into smaller holdings and the building up of small farm ownership." (Almost certainly neither he nor Moton realized that less than thirty years earlier, blacks had owned two-thirds of the farms in the Delta.) Those large plantations experiencing difficulties would disappear, to be replaced by, ultimately, tens of thousands of small farms. The program would nominally serve "both white and colored farmers," but in reality it was designed for blacks. A "land resettlement corporation" would be created to issue first mortgages for the purchase of twenty-acre farms, and second mortgages for purchasing animals and equipment and to provide working capital. Hoover estimated that an initial capital of $4.5 million, properly rediscounted, would allow nearly 7,000 families to buy and equip farms. Repayments and profits would be plowed into new loans, allowing rapid expansion. Theoretically, the program could increase exponentially and transform the entire region. Hoover reasoned that white plantation owners would support the plan because it would decrease the supply of available land and therefore raise all land values. "If it were possible to save from the Mississippi flood fund a sum of [several] millions of dollars," he stated, "we would be justified in applying it to this purpose as a part of the whole rehabilitation of the flood territory."

Moton left the office ecstatic. He believed that Hoover's proposal could lift a large number of blacks out of poverty, and create both a black middle class and a promised land in the Mississippi Delta. He believed also that Hoover had the power to implement this plan—and would very likely soon have far more.

On August 2, Coolidge announced he would not seek reelection.

Before the flood, prominent southern Republicans, both black and white, had stated that their convention delegates would not support Hoover for the nomination under any conditions. Now many of the same men were promising Hoover their support regardless of his opponent.

Meanwhile, Moton began to hint at the resettlement plan in speeches. In late August black businessmen gathered in St. Louis at the annual meeting of the National Negro Business League, an association closely linked to the Tuskegee machine, founded by Booker T. Washington, and presided over by Moton. Many of the attendees had scratched out a tiny pile of money from black poverty and death, running penny savings banks, or funeral homes, or burial societies that became insurance companies. Few were radicals, even by the standards of the day. Many were Republican activists. They were, like Moton, hopeful. Now Moton gave them real hope. After this meeting they scattered across the country, committed to Hoover, because of what Moton told them.

"I am not at liberty to give you details but you will hear about it soon," he said, his words stirring curiosity and interest. "But the Red Cross fund will doubtless be the instrument for doing something in behalf of the negro more significant than anything which has happened since Emancipation."

YET HOOVER had only been holding out a tantalizing carrot. He already knew that the Red Cross fund would serve no such purpose. Only Moton did not know it. Assuming that the Red Cross did support the resettlement idea, Moton had invited Fieser to the meeting of black businessmen. Fieser had already explicitly told Hoover the Red Cross could not support it, but sat there, the only white man in a sea of black, smiled at a fulsome introduction, and accepted enthusiastic applause. Then he wrote an angry letter to Hoover.

In it he cited ten specific objections to the plan, beginning with the fact that "newspaper publicity [from] people like Senator Percy [has] created a state of mind that the fund is inadequate to meet even those items we have accepted as our responsibility." The Red Cross had to husband its money because its original policy of giving refugees just two weeks' supply of food upon leaving camp had to be abandoned; it was now "certain . . . that considerable numbers of people must be fed through the winter." Finally, should they implement the resettlement plan, there was "the possibility of a gorilla [sic] warfare or financial persecution or ostracism which would drive the negro beneficiaries off the land." He flatly declared it "impossible for the Red Cross to undertake such a program."

MOTON NEVER LEARNED of Fieser's position. Hoover continued to hold out the promise of the resettlement plan. Moton continued to respond to it.

Arthur Kellogg was managing editor of the *Survey,* a leading Progressive magazine, and a Hoover supporter. Sympathetic to blacks, Kellogg knew Moton and judged him harshly but perhaps accurately when he told Hoover, "A great many people had hoped that the introduction of northern workers, money and ideas would blast the crust of inertia in the Delta. I presume there wasn't time. . . . Perhaps a committee [might have] with a more forceful man at its head than Dr. Moton who, poor soul, has to raise the money for his school both North and South and finds himself a plump, middle-aged gentleman, riding precariously on the narrow side of a 2x4."

Moton felt differently. In Hoover he believed he had found the solidity of rock, of real power. *I shall be the nominee, probably,* Hoover had said. *It is nearly inevitable.* Trusting in Hoover, through the fall of 1927, Moton advanced Hoover's presidential candidacy at every opportunity, and exerted all the influence at his command to suffocate all criticism of Hoover among blacks and insure black support for his nomination. He was intent on seeing that there would be no sudden explosion of scandal from the flood that could in any way harm Hoover's chances. And Hoover continued to use him.

CHAPTER THIRTY-THREE

WHILE HOOVER and Moton pursued their agendas, nature imposed its own upon them, through the refugees. They were beset upon by plagues.

The first plague fell upon their crops. When the refugees finally left the camps, they planted alfalfa, wheat, peas, and the largest crop, soybeans. Hoover had insisted on the soybeans even after agricultural scientists had strongly advised against it. Everything had grown well initially, and Red Cross officials had beamed with pride. But then came a drought, followed by an infestation of insects and worms punctuated by an early freeze. Only 20 to 25 percent of the limited crops planted were harvested; the soybeans were nearly all lost. God was mocking everything the Delta's people had done that year.

The second plague fell upon the people. Tens of thousands developed pellagra. The disease, caused by poor diet, begins by draining energy from its victims (it accounted for at least some of the "laziness" ascribed to blacks by white southerners). But the disease can also become ugly and dangerous. Sores erupt on the skin and form a thick black crust. Victims become morose, hallucinate, feel as if a fire burns in their heads and spines. Untreated, pellagra kills. At the end of every winter, tenant farmers all over the South, white and black, were on the verge of developing the disease, but normally in the spring their diet improved enough to stave it off. In 1927 in the Red Cross camps the refugees' diet did not improve and pellagra became rampant. Initially, Red Cross officials denied all responsibility, but as the number of the afflicted grew to 50,000 in the Delta alone, they brought in experts who distributed tons of yeast (Washington County received one-third of the total for Mississippi). The yeast helped immeasurably, but a U.S. Public Health Service report concluded, "[A]ny attempt to remove the conditions which are fundamentally responsible for the prevalence of pellagra would involve a revolution of dietary habits and of the entire economic and financial system as it exists."

For the final plague was race. There had been discrimination in the camps, and there was discrimination in their closing. In Vicksburg, for example, the Red Cross had built different camps for different races; the black camp closed seven weeks earlier than the white camp. Blacks were sent home to work even while fields were still covered by a foot of water. Later, discrimination became even more blatant. By then the earlier sense of shared disaster and common humanity had dissipated; attitudes reverted to those common in the region.

Hoover and Fieser had specifically ordered that "all aid be given directly to sufferers." Victims were supposed to get enough feed, seed, tools, clothes, basic furnishings to start again; some of the totally destitute who had lost farm animals were even to get a mule or hog or a few chickens. But Hoover's policy was honored in the breach. Throughout the flooded territory, county Red Cross chairmen, sometimes with the explicit approval of a national Red Cross staff person, gave supplies to planters for distribution. Some planters did simply distribute the goods to their tenants for free. Some charged for the goods, or subtracted the value of the supplies from old debts, or shifted a mortgage from a drowned mule to a Red Cross–supplied mule. And some simply stole the supplies for their own use. Blacks who owned farms, their tenants, and tenants on plantations with absentee owners got almost nothing. Even official Red Cross policy discriminated against tenants of absentee owners, assuming that owners living outside the Delta were not destitute and could take care of those tenants.

From late summer through early fall, Moton focused on getting supplies to struggling tenant farmers, continually sending reports to Hoover with details of abuses. Hoover continually denied that there were any systemic problems, and told him to forward each report of abuse to the Red Cross for handling on a case-by-case basis.

In November, Du Bois wrote in the NAACP's magazine *Crisis*: "We have grave suspicions that the [Moton] committee . . . will be sorely tempted to whitewash the whole situation, to pat Mr. Hoover loudly on the back, and to make no real effort to investigate the desperate and evil conditions of that section of our country. . . . The one fatal thing for them to do, and the thing for which the American negro will never forgive them, is spineless surrender to the Administration and flattery for the guilty Red Cross." The words were harsh and biting. Du Bois concluded with the promise, "Next month we shall have more to say."

Now Moton's own credibility was at stake. Barnett warned him, "The Crisis had a white woman investigator covering the flood district recently . . . [who] was conversant with one particularly bad situation. I think we ought to beat them to any publicity on both bad and good." So Moton prodded Hoover once more, asking for another investigation and wiring, "Suggest that Red Cross release news story about Commission . . . at once."

Irritatedly, Hoover told Fieser "the colored complex has again arisen." But he also recognized that Du Bois could conceivably stir up the white press and black Republicans and finally agreed to authorize a November inspection tour by the Colored Advisory Commission. On December 12 this final report was presented to Hoover, Fieser, and half a dozen Red Cross officials in Fieser's Washington office. Moton did not make the presentation; an automobile accident prevented him from attending, so Claude Barnett and Albion Holsey, Moton's deputy, discussed it instead. Moton was accustomed to meeting men with power. Barnett was not. Perhaps because of this, perhaps to show that he was not intimidated, or perhaps because he simply thought he was among friends, he spoke more candidly, even brashly, than he might otherwise have.

For three hours, beginning late in the afternoon and continuing into the evening, Barnett and Holsey reviewed the report. It stated that local officials had "frequently nullified" national Red Cross policies, that landlords were routinely stealing supplies designated for tenants, that black landowners were refused supplies, that thousands of colored victims had yet to receive clothing needed for the winter, that tenants who tried to leave plantations were being whipped. Blacks had refused to talk to commission members because "their lives would be in danger . . . [but] the facts are known and admitted by Red Cross officials in some of the communities. . . . We urgently recommend that the Red Cross on its own initiative investigate the conditions which are set forth in these reports. . . . Confidential investigators from Washington would be able to make some interesting discoveries."

Hoover and Fieser had expected praise. They were startled at first, then grew increasingly angry. They were being rebuked, unusual enough for either of them. And they were being rebuked by Negroes, indeed, by the assistants of a Negro. Still, they revealed little of their anger.

Barnett left the meeting pleased, confiding to a colleague: "I think we beat [the NAACP] to it on the flood thing. They can now rave, but we have done our duty by everybody around Mr. Hoover." A few days later Hoover promised Moton that the charges would be "vigorously investigated and remedies applied." Naively, Barnett told Moton, "I felt Secretary Hoover would rise to the occasion but this is better than my most sanguine hopes."

But Hoover was not a man who took criticism well. Though he promised action to Moton, he also conveyed extreme displeasure.

DESPITE THE PAIN from his automobile accident, Moton decided to come to Washington immediately. At stake was not only the fate of the flood victims and his personal relationship with Hoover, who seemed closer to the presidency every day, but the resettlement plan. Moton knew also that he had misjudged Hoover. The report had been written as if to one who saw things the same way. Hoover apparently did not see things the same way. It was a mistake no man in Moton's position could make often and survive.

Moton arrived in Washington in the evening, and early the next morning, while most men were still eating breakfast, went to Hoover's office. He was not kept waiting. Hoover did not manipulate people in that petty way. But now it was Hoover's turn to hold little back. Coldly, he told Moton the report had "disappointed" him. It was a powerful word, *disappoint,* a word impossible to rebut. Then Hoover critiqued it in detail, complaining especially of its failure to credit the good the Red Cross had done.

Moton replied fulsomely, praising Hoover's "consistently wise and patriotic service." He apologized for not being in attendance when the report was first tendered, explaining, "The presence of some of us who were absent might perhaps have given a little different atmosphere to the meeting, but I want to assure you there was no intention on the part of those present to indict the National Red Cross in any way." Then he made a literally unbelievable statement: "I had not seen the report as presented to you. I saw it afterwards."

Even if somehow Moton had not read the report, he had to have read the summary. It was only seven pages long and included some of the bluntest criticism, and it was in the form of a letter from him to Hoover. He had signed it—before his accident. By disowning it, he could not have humbled himself more completely and abjectly.

Hoover listened to Moton's explanations, told him to see that the report was rewritten and to write a press release, then dismissed him absently. After the meeting, Hoover called Fieser. With some smugness and a still smoldering anger, he said he "laid Dr. Moton out." And although Moton had submitted meekly, Hoover still told an aide to bring "another element of the colored world into the picture."

A few days later Moton, unaware that Hoover was looking elsewhere, sent him a letter of further apology and enclosed for his approval a press release fully endorsing the actions of the Red Cross. Hoover replied, "I have received your letter . . . and was much pleased to read the statement."

Later Barnett pleaded with Fieser, "I feel very strongly that the changes suggested [in the report] should not be made . . . because of the state of mind of the colored people of the country as it regards the flood. . . . I beg leave to respectfully protest the change and to urge the use of the original." Moton did not second this protest, and Fieser and Hoover ignored it.

Meanwhile, commission member J. S. Clark told Fieser: "Neither Dr. Moton nor I had seen the final report that was submitted. . . . The Red Cross deserves unlimited praise for the service it is rendering." Then Clark reminded Fieser also of "the program that will not only feed, cloth [sic] and shelter the people, but will enable them to be established more firmly than before." He was referring, of course, to Hoover's resettlement plan.

THERE HAD BEEN no mention of the plan in months, except when Moton had reminded Hoover of it. Moton still did not know that Fieser had rejected it as "impossible." But Moton did know that Fieser was now cool toward everyone associated with the Colored Advisory Commission. He did know that resettlement had been Hoover's own idea. He did know that Hoover, despite reminders, had done nothing to pursue it. And he finally understood what had never been said: the Red Cross would do nothing to implement it. Concerned yet still hopeful, he told Hoover he planned to approach several philanthropists and asked permission to use Hoover's name. Hoover agreed, and told him to ask William Schieffelin, a trustee of Tuskegee who owned a chemical company, to host a luncheon in New York where Hoover could present his plan to major donors to charity.

Moton did. Schieffelin invited a select gathering, including J. C. Penney, the banker Paul Warburg, and John D. Rockefeller, Jr. Schieffelin then told Hoover they were all looking forward to hearing him "outline the plan to make good lands in the South available to Negro tenants."

Hoover knew all the invitees well—indeed, immediately after

his election as president later that year, he would go deep-sea fishing at Penney's Florida estate—yet on January 12, 1928, he replied, "I feel it would be undesirable to have a luncheon for the purpose of meeting me to discuss such a plan as you mention."

Schieffelin sent Hoover's note to Moton. He was stunned. Hoover was abandoning him. But he said nothing, and instead turned to Julius Rosenwald, another Tuskegee trustee. Rosenwald, a short, heavy-set man with iron gray hair, did not give money away for dreams and required enterprises he supported to meet high standards, but he had already given millions to help build rural black schools; he would ultimately contribute to building 6,000. Rosenwald also had a long relationship with Hoover, having worked with him to, among other things, make second mortgages a viable financial instrument; Hoover had done him such favors as get him good seats for Coolidge's inauguration. More important, while Hoover was declining Schieffelin's invitation, Rosenwald was giving $5 million to resettle European refugees on farms. For this act, Hoover congratulated him on "a great experiment in human engineering, and you and I have watched together the fruition of so many enterprises born of a realization that the welfare of other human beings is the concern of all of us."

A similar amount would finance the entire project in the Delta. The prospect excited Moton with possibilities. Now Moton placed his fate in Hoover's hands, hoping Hoover would personally ask Rosenwald to finance the project by himself. Though Hoover was not above personally asking for money for projects he cared about, though a direct personal request from him would be far more difficult to reject, Hoover did not ask Rosenwald himself. And, though Rosenwald was a Tuskegee trustee, Moton was never given an opportunity to present the plan—Hoover's plan, exactly the way Hoover had written it—directly to Rosenwald. Instead, the plan was presented to Rosenwald's assistant Edwin Embree, who replied: "Mr. Rosenwald's reaction is, to say the least, not actively favorable. He has had somewhat unfortunate experiences in somewhat similar projects, notably one I believe called Baldwin Farms near Tuskegee."

THOUGH MOTON had dignity, he had never been burdened by pride. His very first day at Hampton Institute had taught him to eschew pride, when an instructor had given him his admissions examination; it had been how well he swept a classroom, not how well he learned in it. After Rosenwald's rejection, he reminded Hoover, gently, that both the resettlement plan and the Schieffelin luncheon were Hoover's own ideas, and pleaded with him to bring the plan back to life. "A word from you with half a dozen gentlemen, in my opinion, would settle the matter in an hour so far as the financial end of it is concerned," he wrote. "You will I know, forgive me for this seeming persistence in the matter, but if you could make the trip to New York as you had one time suggested it would assure success at the start."

Hoover finally agreed to attend the Schieffelin's luncheon, then postponed it. Now desperate, Moton began to thrash about, writing Hoover again that the luncheon would be with people who "could finance the scheme with ease. . . . I was not sure you wished me to push the thing further. I would be glad to have instructions as to your wishes in the matter."

In reply, Hoover sent him a copy of the old letter from Rosenwald's assistant rejecting the idea. He said nothing else, and made no mention of the luncheon. It was never held.

All his life Moton had been forced into a smiling, accepting patience. He still did not abandon hope and wrote Rockefeller, "You are the kind of American citizen that I think of whenever I take off my hat to the Stars and Stripes, and I can properly put Mrs. Rockefeller in the same category not because of any worldly possessions you possess but rather the spirit which you manifest toward every phase of human betterment."

Rockefeller thanked him for the sentiments. But without Hoover's imprimatur, there would be no money for the land resettlement. The proposal that was to be the greatest boon for the Negro race since Emancipation lay waiting, and perhaps dying. Perhaps it was already dead.

BY NOW it was March 1928. Moton likely rationalized that Hoover was so deeply enmeshed in his campaign for the presidential nomination that he could not spare the time for the resettlement question now. But if he became president of the United States . . .

Moton was determined to do all in his power to help Herbert Hoover achieve that ambition. His help could make a difference. Through the spring of 1928, despite primary victories and a commanding lead among Republican hopefuls, Hoover remained anathema to party professionals. If the Republican National Convention did not nominate him on the first ballot, it might not nominate him at all. Hoover's opponents, led by former Illinois Governor Frank Lowden, the favorite for the nomination until the flood had elevated Hoover, struggled to form an alliance to block him. On March 31, 1928, the *New York Times* spoke of a "plan to deadlock the convention and select a compromise candidate against Mr. Hoover." LeRoy Percy, who knew something of such a strategy from his victory in the Mississippi legislature over Vardaman, had been watching the maneuvering for months and observed that other candidates' "popularity grows by contact; Hoover's diminishes." He judged: "All of the regular Republicans will oppose him. I don't believe he can get the nomination. If so, of course he will be elected." He also believed, "No man in public life has more enemies than Hoover."

Hoover fought back with his usual style, pretending to be above politics (and fooling himself with the pretense), keeping his own hands clean. But his aides, particularly George Akerson, did what was required. Tough, even ruthless, they made deals, violated clear ethical standards, and looked the other way while people acting for Hoover broke the law. They used people. They used Moton.

In the black community Moton, Barnett, and the Tuskegee machine shielded Hoover, answered charges that Hoover had allowed the abuses of black refugees, did everything possible to advance him. Their impact was felt. "Would it be possible for us to have Neale [sic] in New York on March 30, for an address," Akerson asked, referring to C. C. Neal, a small cog in the Tuskegee machine who had earlier helped move black Missouri Republicans into Hoover's column. And no black man worked harder than Barnett, who had experience in both Chicago ward politics and presidential campaigns. He had become a campaign aide reporting to Akerson as early as January 1928; he traveled constantly, poured himself into the campaign, and simultaneously threw the influence of syndicated stories in his Associated Negro Press into the battle. Shortly before the convention, Akerson told Barnett: "Both Secretary Hoover and I have known of your devoted interest, and he appreciates as I do the fine continued work you are doing in his behalf. The battle is almost over. . . . Please be assured that you are counted one of the very closest friends of this organization, and we are very glad of your help."

But Moton was the key. Moton mattered. A Negro political operative recruited by Hoover told Moton he did not want to work "against the RACE for the sake of the MAN," asking "just what you think of him." A black New Jersey politician asked for information "regarding Mr. Hoover in connection with the Mississippi flood, concerning good done the Colored people." As the convention neared, Akerson's requests of Moton became constant. Oscar DePriest, who was not in Hoover's camp, dominated Chicago black wards and that year would become the first black congressman elected in this century. Akerson instructed Moton to handle him, as well as to contact "Mr.

J. C. Mitchell . . . [who] has a tremendous influence with the three colored delegates from St. Louis"; to contact Scipio Jones, a black lawyer and key to the entire Arkansas delegation, "and find out exactly how he stands on Hoover"; to issue "a statement to the Colored Press in Chicago . . . call[ing] attention to the satisfaction which the colored leaders in the South had over the handling of Mississippi relief by Mr. Hoover." At the convention itself Moton was given charge of black delegates.

Hoover won the nomination on the first ballot. The flood had swept him to it; the flood had returned him to his countrymen's consciousness, made him once again a hero, once again the Great Humanitarian. With Moton's help no scandal had erupted and black Republican delegates had fallen in line. The election would come in a few more months. Moton was willing to wait for the resettlement plan and other boons to the race, as well as to the Tuskegee machine, a little longer.

Part Nine

THE LEAVING
OF THE WATERS

CHAPTER THIRTY-FOUR

F ROM CAIRO, ILLINOIS, to the Gulf of Mexico, and from New Orleans to Washington, D.C., all across the floodplain of the Mississippi River and beyond, the 1927 flood left a watermark. It changed things. Some changes, direct and tangible ones, came immediately; others, less direct and less tangible, came more slowly.

The first change occurred even before the flood did most of its damage, when the levee below New Orleans was dynamited. The dynamite exploded not only the levee but the levees-only policy, ending forever the argument over whether levees alone could control the Mississippi River, and forcing an admission even from Army engineers that nothing could control the Mississippi. So man would have to find a way to accommodate it.

Finding that way was the final battle of the flood, and this battle was fought in Washington. All parties began in agreement that the federal government should assume responsibility for the river, but this consensus settled almost nothing, for water, like power itself, is a zero-sum game. If one has more, another has less. The levees-only policy had obscured this truth; one of its chief attractions had been its promise to protect all the land in the river's floodplain. Any new plan would have to allow the river to spread over some land, somewhere. Congress would have to decide whose lands that would be, and the decision would have to combine engineering and politics.

The scope of the legislation also had to be defined, along with who would pay for it. At the least, this legislation would seek to contain the lower Mississippi; at the least, it would be the most ambitious and expensive single piece of legislation Congress had ever passed. Many wanted to make it far more comprehensive and include the entire Mississippi River system. The governor of New Mexico wanted Congress to include in the legislation the prevention of floods on the Canadian River. A senator and two mayors from Oklahoma demanded that the bill solve flooding and shipping problems on the Arkansas, Cimarron, and Canadian. The governor of North Dakota complained about the Missouri; a congressman from Montana complained about the Milk; the governor of Kansas spoke of thirty-two towns and cities inundated in his state, some of which had been flooded seven times from September 1926 to April 1927; congressmen from Pittsburgh and Cincinnati wanted floods on the Ohio addressed.

But it was not Congress or the White House that decided these things. They were settled in a more intimate forum by the Tri-State Flood Control Committee. This committee, like so many others that exercised power, was an ad hoc group, a handful of men, from Arkansas, Louisiana, and Mississippi. Their names were familiar, and they made decisions binding upon each state's representatives, and they had influence far beyond their states. John Parker was committee vice chairman and with Jim Butler spoke for Louisiana. LeRoy Percy spoke for Mississippi and served as secretary. Arkansas Governor John Martineau spoke for his state and chaired the committee. They, and Hoover, were the ones who mattered.

On September 12, 1927, a month after Coolidge had declared that he would not seek reelection, these men gathered at the home of Colonel John Fordyce in Hot Springs, Arkansas. By the time they met, the political forces demanding legislation were already coming together. In June, several thousand people, among them nearly 150 senators, governors, and congressmen, had attended the Chicago Flood Control Conference; its sole purpose was to generate momentum and pressure for a bill. After it adjourned, a small executive committee had been formed, including Percy, to lobby for a bill. Since then Percy had traveled constantly, meeting privately with northern governors and congressmen, seeing Coolidge and General Jadwin in Washington, hosting Vice President Charles Dawes in Greenville, guiding a U.S. Chamber of Commerce delegation through the flooded region. It seemed that everywhere, as the Associated Press reported, "[i]t remained for the old Roman of the Delta, Senator Leroy [sic] Percy of Greenville, Mississippi, to sound the keynote of these problems."

Now, in Hot Springs, Percy and his colleagues on the Tri-State Committee were to decide the broad outlines of a bill they would unanimously support. Present were Hoover, Percy, Martineau, Butler, and two others who were among the wealthiest men in the South. All except Hoover were men who could manifest extraordinary grace and charm, but now they had come together to make decisions. They shared little small talk, little comment on difficult travel schedules, not even a discussion of refugees or crops. Their interest was containing the river. What they settled upon would more closely resemble what actually became law than would the initial proposals later made by Coolidge, the House, or the Senate.

IT WAS a palatial setting, the house with tall Corinthian columns and silent smiling black servants, yet it also had a rustic quality, and not far back of the house a pack of hunting dogs barked. Outside the sun blazed, but shade nestled close to the house. The shade, high ceilings, and whirring fans kept the inside cool. The town itself, its main street packed with hotels, several of them elegant, was a resort enveloped in a vast mountain forest. The springs drew the visitors, but good shooting could be found close by. It was the shooting Percy could not forget. Here twenty-five years before he had watched impotently as his young son LeRoy Percy, Jr., died in agony from an infection after a shooting accident. He had avoided Hot Springs since then, but this was not a time for sentiment.

That became clear soon enough as they discussed federal help for the victims. Percy warned that giving relief to victims would "set a precedent" and make passage harder. It could also excite jealousy in members of Congress whose states had suffered in the past without receiving federal relief. They might exorcise their jealousy by losing interest in legislation. Therefore, he concluded, "I am not willing to [support] any other measure which would detract in any way from the Government taking over control of the levees."

Martineau agreed and made another point: "I believe if Congress were to pass a measure giving relief to those damaged they would feel they had done their duty and . . . this general plan of [river legislation] . . . would have to wait months and maybe years."

No one disagreed. The question was settled. Later Hoover personally drafted a statement for the head of each state's rehabilitation committee to release, saying, "No relief to flood sufferers by action of Congress is desirable but rather all efforts should be concentrated on formulation and passage of adequate flood control measures."

The next question was, who would pay for the massive engineering works necessary? Historically, states or local entities had always had to match with cash, land, or rights-of-way the money the federal government spent. But requiring local contributions could cripple any effort to deal with the river. In 1927, before the flood, the Mississippi River Commission had had $5 million on hand for emergency levee work, but 40 percent had gone unspent because local levee boards could not make their matching contributions. Now far more levee districts were destitute and would remain so for the foreseeable future. Yet the levee system could only be as strong as its weakest link; a crevasse in one levee district could threaten hundreds of thousands of people in other levee districts.

Percy, Butler, Martineau, and the others pressed Hoover to agree to waive any local contributions. Hoover agreed with them on the goal but warned that both Congress and the White House "are going to hesitate to let go of the requirement of local contribution for fear of future demand for this sort of thing. . . . It is a question of tactics."

Butler suggested a solution: "Wouldn't it be better for us to consider those amounts expended . . . already as a contribution already made, so we can get by this point of future contributions?"

Percy nodded an emphatic yes. "I will give you one district," he said, speaking of his own Mississippi Levee Board. "In July, 1926, the Government had spent $13,500,000 in five years and the district in that time spent $22,537,000." Overall, he added, Arkansas, Louisiana, and Mississippi had spent $168 million, while the federal government had given only $61 million.

The strategy was decided. They would argue that since in the past states and local levee boards had outspent the federal government, the local contribution had already been made. Thus waiving local contributions in this instance would not set a precedent; it would simply give credit for money already spent.

They then moved on to the final issue, the scope of the bill. On this point they disagreed. Martineau wanted a broad bill to include tributaries. One reason was parochial; many of his state's problems came not from the Mississippi itself but from its tributaries, chiefly the Arkansas, White, and St. Francis Rivers. He also argued: "I believe we have a better chance politically if we take the whole of the Mississippi and all of its tributaries. . . . [The more] troubles you take care of in this bill, the more support you will have for it, provided you can get enough troubles to take care of to have the support of a majority of the Congress."

But such a project would be immense. Hoover objected, warning: "What I am trying to do is cut off the flood plain of Kansas, Illinois, Tennessee, and other places. . . . Pittsburgh is getting ready to attach themselves and Kansas is getting ready. North Dakota has got a scheme and they are all going to be right down hanging them on your hatracks. . . . I am afraid the whole country will rebel against an enormous program." Certainly, Coolidge would rebel. If they pursued too comprehensive a bill, they would get nothing. Then Hoover reassured Martineau that a narrow bill would protect his state: "All of the overflows in Arkansas would come within my definition of the flood plain of the lower Mississippi. . . . It is a well defined flood plain from an engineering standpoint."

Martineau did not yield. He argued that if they limited the bill they would be seen as selfish. That too could lead to the defeat of legislation.

Once again Butler stepped in with a solution. The War Department was developing a flood control plan that would cover only the lower Mississippi. The War Department would be the ones narrowing the bill, eliminating help elsewhere, and making enemies. Butler suggested that if everyone in the room agreed to use the War Department plan as the framework for legislation, they would have clean hands. "It seems to me," he said, "that is our answer: 'This isn't our bill, this is a bill that was investigated and is what the engineers are now ready to do. . . . ' We may have to promise support on some bill but that won't be a part of our bill. Deal with the flood plain of the lower Mississippi and take on such additional things as expediency might demand. . . . Suppose the Illinois River comes along with a meritorious claim from the standpoint of votes, it can be tacked on, if it is necessary and expedient to do it."

"I agree with Mr. Butler," Hoover said. So did Percy.

Finally, Martineau too yielded. There were no more issues to resolve, since they did not intend to involve themselves in technical engineering issues. Now they had only to spread their message. Percy noted, "The U.S. Chamber of Commerce have fixed a committee meeting in New York to formulate plans. I am on that committee."

Martineau mentioned that the executive committee of the Chicago conference had also scheduled a meeting to formulate a legislative strategy and pointed out, "Senator Percy is on that."

So were Hecht and Thomson, whom Butler would speak to. With Percy they would convince both groups to unite behind what had just been agreed to. So in this room in Arkansas these half-dozen men, none of whom served in Congress, had largely decided the fate of the most comprehensive and expensive piece of legislation Congress had ever considered.

It had taken barely half an hour.

THE PATH was not smooth, but legislation moved down it. In the fall of 1927, Butler and Percy began spending weeks at a time in Washington, both of them staying at the Mayflower Hotel on Connecticut Avenue a few blocks above the White House and the War Department. The governor of Mississippi designated Percy, not any elected representative, to speak officially for the state. Repeatedly, they saw the secretary of war and Coolidge himself, and were reassured. Also in the fall, Jim Thomson, uninvited by Butler, simply moved to Washington with his wife, Genevieve, both of them comfortable there, moving in the highest congressional circles. But Thomson was still not one of the insiders in New Orleans, and though he had spent almost six years pushing the White House, the War Department, and Congress on river issues, he was reduced, he confessed angrily, to "following what I interpret to be the lines suggested in newspaper interviews by Messrs. Hecht and Butler." Yet despite his displeasure, he too devoted his lobbying energies to supporting the plan decided upon by Hoover, Percy, Butler, and Martineau.

Everything was coordinated. As one strategy document noted, "The first three days [of congressional hearings] will be devoted to a mammoth demonstration that the business interests of the United States demand that Congress give flood control legislation rights-of-way over everything." On a daily basis Butler, Percy, or Thomson met with the Senate leadership and senators from their own states, and, in the House, with Frank Reid of Illinois, chairman of the House Flood Control Committee, or Louisiana's Riley Wilson, the committee's ranking Democrat, whom Butler and other New Orleans financial leaders now were supporting for governor.

The only obstacle was the White House and the Corps of Engineers. Representing Coolidge, Jadwin submitted a proposal developed by the Army that became known as "the Jadwin Plan." It was the least expensive proposal, and therefore Coolidge liked it, but the chief engineer of every single levee board on the lower Mississippi signed a letter attacking it, and 94 percent of the 300 witnesses who testified before the House criticized it. In his own House testimony, Jadwin dismissed all the criticism, and all competing ideas, contemptuously. One congressman asked, "You do not expect us to accept any plan simply because you present it, and to shut our minds to any other thoughts?"

"Yes," Jadwin answered bluntly. "I think you ought to do it."

The members shook their heads incredulously. Then Representative Will Whittington, from the Delta, observed that information Jadwin had given the committee stated that the Mississippi River in its natural state, without any levees, did not flood the Yazoo-Mississippi Delta. Whittington inquired, "Am I to be told that [the Delta] is not subject to overflow from any floods of the Mississippi River? . . . As a matter of history, is not that entire Yazoo basin subject to overflow from the floods of the Mississippi River?"

Jadwin said, "The [data] is the best authority I have on that, Judge, and that indicates that it is not subject to overflow in its natural state."

Whittington guffawed. "That is news to us."

But Butler's warning had been prescient. The Jadwin plan, for all its meanness, was proving useful in focusing the attention of the Congress on the lower Mississippi alone. It seemed that each of the thirty-one states whose rivers drained into the Mississippi wanted something. Even states whose waterways did not drain into the Mississippi wanted something. A California congressman said, "Coming from the Imperial valley, [far] below the uncontrolled waters of the Colorado River, I have an appreciation of the menace of floods as great as anyone in Congress . . . [but] the Boulder Dam project is not going to be used to embarrass or harass you in the advancement of your legislation." The audience applauded and stamped its feet in approval. He continued, "We expect to give to your problem of the Mississippi the same sympathetic and earnest and helpful consideration that we expect you of the Mississippi Valley to give to the problems of other parts of the country when they in turn are presented to Congress."

The Jadwin Plan kept the bill narrow, and Coolidge was threatening to veto broader legislation. Slowly, the bill advanced. Finally, on March 28, 1928, a bill Butler and Percy supported came to a vote in the Senate. In less than an hour and a half it passed unanimously, even though it called for "the greatest expenditure the government has undertaken except in the World War," the *New York Times* reported. "For a measure of such importance, concededly one of the most important before Congress in years, the speed with which the Senate acted is believed to be a record. . . . Today, however, the wheels were greased and the leaders of the two parties demanded quick action and got it."

But while the House and Senate ironed out differences, Coolidge promised to veto any bill that did not require local contribution. For the next six weeks Congress fought with Coolidge over the question. The *Times* wrote that "President Coolidge has never shown as much opposition to a measure pending in Congress than he has to this." The *Wall Street Journal* said, "The White House has been stirred as seldom or never before. . . . Now there emerges a new portrait of the Chief Executive—in quite belligerent outline and color."

The situation required a final exertion of influence. Every interest in the Mississippi valley applied pressure. Butler, Hecht, and Percy helped those outside the valley see that it was in their interest to apply pressure as well. Levee boards owed $819,642,000 in bonds, and repayment would be jeopardized if the region's economy did not recover. The Investment Bankers Association of America lobbied intensely for the president to sign the bill, and the American Bankers Association resolved: "The disastrous flood that visited the Mississippi Valley in 1927 is by far the most overwhelmingly destructive calamity experienced by our country in generations. . . . It is the profound conviction of the American Bankers Association representing 20,000 American banks that the control of the Mississippi River is a national problem, should be solved by the nation, and that, cost no matter what it may be, should be borne exclusively by the nation. The bill . . . should be enacted into law without further delay."

Coolidge finally relented. He accepted the argument Butler had advanced in Hot Springs, and announced that in consideration of the moneys already paid by states and local governments, he would waive further contributions by them. The total cost of the plan was set at $300 million, but even those citing that estimate conceded that the real cost would run to $1 billion.

On May 15, 1928, Coolidge finished his lunch and was about to leave for a vacation. His secretary reminded him that he had promised to sign the bill before leaving the city, handed it to him, and he signed it. There was no ceremony, no commemorative pens, no gathering of smiling congressmen and senators and interested parties and photographers.

Still, the event did not pass unnoticed. Declared Illinois Congressman Frank Reid, a gritty man who had resisted White House pressure for weeks and generally disliked hyperbole: "The bill changes the policy of the federal government which has existed for 150 years. It is perhaps the greatest engineering feat the world has ever known. . . . It is the greatest piece of legislation ever enacted by Congress."

The law had many flaws. Civilian engineers condemned it with virtual unanimity both for its engineering and its policy of niggardly compensation for use of private land, and Hoover privately "unburdened" himself that it exemplified "the viciousness of Army engineers." Yet the men who controlled the lower Mississippi valley embraced it anyway. They would fix what required fixing later; the law would be changed almost continuously over the next ten years. More important, the law declared that the federal government took full responsibility for the Mississippi River.

In so doing, even in the narrowest sense, the law set a precedent of direct, comprehensive, and vastly expanded federal involvement in local affairs. In the broadest sense, this precedent reflected a major shift in what Americans considered the proper role and obligations of the national government, a shift that both presaged and prepared the way for far greater changes that would soon come.

THE DAY AFTER Coolidge signed the bill into law, the board of directors of the Canal Bank met in Room 326, where so much had happened, voted for a resolution of thanks to James Pierce Butler, and heaped praise on him. He was visibly moved and replied: "I did not expect this action on the Board's part. . . . I possibly have been away more than I can reconcile, but I was in the fight and I felt that I had to see it through. I want to thank you for all that you said and to say that I will never let another matter take me away from my very pleasant duties at the Bank as much as this work has done." Later the *New Orleans Times-Picayune* would award Butler its Loving Cup, given annually to the person who did the most for the city in the year.

Meanwhile, New Orleans Mayor Arthur O'Keefe, the 300-pound ward heeler and grocer, declared that the coming Sunday should be a day of thanksgiving and prayer in the city. A special Te Deum was sung in St. Louis Cathedral in the French Quarter, and special services were held at the St. Charles Christian Church uptown, at Christ Church in the Garden District, and at dozens of other churches and synagogues. It was rumored that the minister at Trinity Church would ask the congregation to applaud and thank James Thomson, who had just returned to the city from seven months in Washington lobbying full-time for the legislation. Thomson almost never attended church but did this Sunday. The minister spoke of the bill but did not mention him. Thomson sat silently as the service closed, then left quickly with his wife, saying nothing.

A week after the bill was signed, Congressman Reid joined the swashbuckling and corrupt Chicago Mayor Big Bill Thompson on a trip to New Orleans. A crowd estimated in the thousands greeted them, sirens and steamboat whistles sounded salutes, the police and fire department's brass bands played, and the crowd—turned out by the city's political machine—cheered. Reid said that without Jim Thomson there would have been no bill.

For Reid there would be an evening banquet in his honor

attended by five hundred people, a reception at the elegant City Hall, a reception at Thomson's paper, and a cruise of Lake Pontchartrain on a yacht. There was no invitation to dine at the Boston Club.

But the power of the clubs had already waned, although perhaps no one at Reid's banquet yet realized it. Reid and Big Bill had arrived in New Orleans at seven-fifty on Monday evening, May 20, having attended the inauguration of the governor in Baton Rouge earlier in the day. The governor was not Simpson, nor Riley Wilson, the congressman who had bet his political future on the flood control bill and Butler's support. The new governor was Huey Long.

LONG REPRESENTED a new kind of flood, an inundation that the city had never faced before. Butler informed Hecht, Dufour, and Monroe that he "had had a talk with Mr. Long, who seemed to have some wrong impressions about certain features both as to the facts and the law" regarding the dynamiting of the levee and the situation in St. Bernard and Plaquemines. Nothing changed regarding those payments, but the equation of power shifted. The two parishes, which shared a congressional seat with New Orleans, supported Long in everything he did and helped him wrest control even of city affairs from the city.*

The bankers, the lawyers, the members of the Boston Club and Comus and Momus and Rex and the other Carnival krewes, suddenly found themselves confounded by Long, who treated them as they had treated St. Bernard. They despised him. In the evenings they literally sat around their drawing rooms discussing ways to murder him. He laughed and stripped them of power and forced New Orleans to its knees. Once the Board of Liquidation, led by Monroe, told him they could not approve a bond issue he wanted because, it informed him, it had discovered a technicality that would make the issue illegal. Long replied that if that was the case, then their new discovery must apply to bonds already issued, and therefore they need not be repaid. The board went into executive session, studied the question anew, and found that it had been in error.

---

* In one St. Bernard election eight Long-backed candidates, running for national, statewide, and local office, received a combined 25,216 votes to none for their opponents. Earlier Doc Meraux had predicted each of those opponents would get two votes. When Long asked him, "What happened to those two votes?" Meraux replied, "They changed their mind at the last minute." In another election Long called Meraux to ask the result; Meraux replied, "We're still voting." Long began yelling at him, "We've already won! For God's sake, stop counting!" And Plaquemines leader Leander Perez helped Long survive an impeachment attempt.

Meanwhile, Jim Thomson never stopped trying to help the city or work himself into its inside; in a successful effort to generate money, publicity, and tourists, he was largely responsible for creating the Sugar Bowl. But he was never invited to join the Boston Club or the Louisiana Club, or any of the exclusive Carnival krewes. Despite the violent objections of his editor, he had his two papers support Huey Long; in return state employees had to subscribe to his papers. Supporting Long only confirmed his outsider status. Years later a friend asked him one of those questions that usually elicit a joke, and sometimes a longing: if he had his life to live over, what would he do differently? Bitterly Thomson replied, "I'd never have come to New Orleans."

WHEN THE FLOOD CONTROL LAW passed, the New Orleans Association of Commerce planned a campaign to guide the coming boom, the boom so certain to follow. New Orleans had once been the wealthiest city in America, and association members were confident it would be again. But the city did not boom. Instead came decline, and the first to fall were the banks.

The first collapse was of the Marine Bank. Leonidas Pool, once Rex, was Marine's president; he had gotten Isaac Cline to convince the governor to dynamite the levee, and he had been one of those visited by men from St. Bernard carrying shotguns just before the dynamiting. Pool had gambled millions of dollars in loans to sugar plantations early in 1927. The flood made his "sugar paper," as he called it, worthless. In June 1928, on a Saturday night without any advance notice, the Canal and Marine Banks "merged." Pool died soon after. His daughter, who went to live in Greenville among the people her father had called "the aristocrats of the earth," said the bank failure and the flood killed him.

Butler's Canal Bank, already the South's largest, grew even larger after the merger. But its growth was like the swelling around an infection; Pool's losses were too large for even it to absorb. When the Depression hit, it reeled. In 1931 its board reelected Butler president, then less than one month later, under the command of a controlling faction representing Chase Manhattan, it ousted him. Butler returned to Natchez, to his family's plantation. He too died young. George Champion, later president of Chase Manhattan, ran the bank, but even he could not save it. It closed.

Other New Orleans banks were also weak, weaker perhaps than those in any other city of consequence in the country. After the 1933 bank "holiday" in the Depression, only a single New Orleans bank reopened as the same institution. That was the Whitney, the conservative Whitney, dominated by Blanc Monroe and on whose board sat Doc Meraux.

Rudolph Hecht survived. He became president of the American Bankers Association, a figure important enough in Washington that the Gridiron Club would build a skit around him. But his Hibernia Bank disappeared, one of those that failed to reopen after the bank holiday, although a new bank reopened with the same name and still under his control. Its collapse and Hecht's questionable dealings led to the most involved litigation in New Orleans history, and in a cross-examination still talked about half a century later among New Orleans lawyers, Hugh Wilkinson proved Hecht a perjurer. But Hecht went on, unperturbed, traveling around the world and doing international business. In 1939, after telling the groundskeeper at his retreat in Pass Christian, Mississippi, to allow some visiting bankers to view his Japanese garden, he was driving back to New Orleans when he ran over a three-year-old boy and kept going. The child died. Witnesses described the car and gave a partial license plate number, and police stopped him less than an hour later. Human blood and flesh were found on his car. But the witnesses were Negroes. He argued that witnesses described the car as black and his was blue. It was dark navy blue. "I know absolutely nothing about the accident," he said, "and it is inconceivable to me that my car could have struck the child. . . . [The police] felt it their duty to make a charge against me on the statement of this Negro, whereupon my friends in Gulfport signed a $5000 bond for me and I returned to New Orleans." A Mississippi grand jury declined to indict him.

NEW ORLEANS had never been open, not in the way cities in the West were, where "old money" was measured in months, nor even in the way cities in the East were, where immigrants could muscle their way into first political and then economic power. New Orleans had been exclusive from the first. When the United States initially gained sovereignty over the city, the existing French and Spanish elite had mocked the Americans, who in turn created their own institutions, including the Carnival krewes. Over the next century, the Americans with their money took precedence over the remnants of the European society, and also took over their pretensions. But before the flood New Orleans had at least accepted transfusions of fresh blood. After the flood the city grew ever more insular. The Boston Club and the finest Mardi Gras krewes closed even more tightly about themselves and seemed to take special pride in excluding newcomers, especially oil company executives. And the city's elite held grudges: Russell Long, Huey's son, was elected six times to the U.S. Senate and chaired the Finance Committee for many years, but was never invited to the Comus ball.

The social conservatism intertwined with the financial conservatism; the one magnified the effect of the other. In the 1970s, a local economic study concluded: "[The] social system excludes executives recently transferred to New Orleans and discourages their participation in community issues. . . . A narrow circle of wealth-holders . . . represent a closed society whose aims are to preserve their wealth rather than incur risks in an effort to expand it. . . . This development has reduced the opportunities." At the same time, Eads Poitevent, a bank president and Boston Club member, conceded: "The long-established New Orleans financial community has often been accused of being a conservative aristocracy that was tight-fisted and wanted to keep things as they have always been. To some extent, that is absolutely true." As a result, business in the city did not expand; it shrank. Local companies found it more difficult to grow. Large companies looking for headquarters, or even a regional headquarters, put their operations in Houston or Atlanta. Only one Fortune 500 company, Freeport McMoran, has its headquarters in New Orleans.

And so the city decayed. Before the flood New Orleans had vastly more economic activity than any city in the South. Decades later, while in the newest New South such cities as Charlotte and Miami—not to mention Atlanta, Dallas, and Houston—thrived and grew, New Orleans fell far behind its old competitors, and banks even in Memphis now dwarf those in New Orleans. Meanwhile, the city's social and business elite increasingly went separate ways; in the early 1990s not a single bank president belonged to the Boston Club.

New Orleans had become even more ingrown, and it was dying. Only the port, created by the great river and Eads, remained vital. The city had become a place for tourists, and picture postcards. Perhaps all this had nothing to do with the 1927 flood. Or perhaps it did.

CHAPTER THIRTY-FIVE

ONE MONTH AFTER Calvin Coolidge signed into law the bill to contain the Mississippi River, the Republican National Convention chose Herbert Hoover as its nominee for president of the United States. His nomination was another legacy of the flood.

Moton continued to have high hopes that Hoover would help the race and dispatched his deputy Albion Holsey to work full-time for Hoover's presidential campaign, informing Hoover that Tuskegee would continue to pay Holsey's salary "as a form of contribution from Tuskegee to your campaign." After the convention, Hoover met with Moton, who then told his secretary, "Hoover said that anything I said would be approved." Hoover and he had discussed the creation of a new Colored Voters Division of the Republican National Committee. Moton had emphasized how important it was "that the right type of man be selected to head the colored division," and recommended the president of the National Negro Bar Association to the job.

But once again Hoover was merely using him. Earlier, after receiving the Colored Advisory Commission's final report, Hoover had told an aide to call in "another element of the colored world." Now Hoover ignored Moton's suggestion, installing a member of this other element as head of the new division, and making both Holsey and Claude Barnett report to this rival. Nor were Moton's other suggestions often approved. Hoover had the nomination already, and Republicans believed the black vote belonged to them by default. In presidential politics it had always belonged to the Republican nominee. Lincoln had freed the slaves. Democrats had destroyed Reconstruction, enacted the Jim Crow laws, stripped the vote from blacks, opposed antilynching legislation. Only four years before, the Democratic National Convention had voted down a resolution condemning the Klan; in doing so it had reaffirmed the historic link between blacks and Republicans.

In addition, since the same southerners who supported the Klan would not vote for a Catholic, Al Smith's nomination provided an opportunity for both a historic Republican landslide and to create a competitive Republican Party in the South—a "lily white" Republican Party. After securing the nomination with black support, Hoover now moved to build such a party. It was not the first such move by Republicans, but it was the first such move taken by a presidential candidate at the beginning of a campaign.

It began with a deal made with white Mississippi Republicans at the national convention, a deal known to Hoover when he talked with Moton. The white Mississippians had sought credentials. Instead, an assistant attorney general who chaired the credentials committee seated Perry Howard, a black Republican national committeeman from Mississippi who supported Hoover and was well known nationally. But the whites did not protest. A few weeks later the same assistant attorney general who had seated Howard indicted him for selling patronage jobs. (A white Mississippi jury later acquitted him.)

The incident, combined with continued attacks from the *Chicago Defender* on Hoover's role in flood relief, aroused anger among blacks. Barnett and Holsey were traveling through states where the black vote was of consequence and took note of "uncertainty in many sections as to [Hoover's] attitude toward the Negro in the Mississippi disaster." They warned that a campaign aimed at shoring up support should begin immediately, or "there will be a heavy defection in the Negro vote."

No such campaign was mounted. Instead, as Hoover's aides pursued the new southern strategy—the precursor of a much later one—a wedge opened between blacks and the Republican Party. And if Hoover's aides were duplicitous, blacks were far more expert than whites at playing a double game, at presenting a smiling face. As Barnett saw his own and Moton's advice ignored, in July, a few days after Howard's indictment, Barnett wrote George Brennan, a member of the Democratic National Committee: "You, more than any man I have met, white or black, have a comprehensive knowledge of the advantages which the Negro would gain by splitting his vote and becoming something of a factor in the Democratic Party. . . . A remarkable latent sentiment exists for 'Al' Smith which an educational campaign can develop into real support. . . . I can't serve myself but I am sending you two of the best publicity men in the country. Percival L. Prattis and R. Irving Johnson who will present this letter. . . . They know the game."

Only a week earlier Prattis, Barnett's deputy at the Associated Negro Press, had told Barnett: "I am out-and-out for Hoover. . . . I can use my vacation and . . . Raise Hell for Hoover, believe me." Barnett now ordered Prattis, for the good of the race, to take Johnson and together offer themselves to Brennan and work for Al Smith. They did.

In the 1920 campaign Harding received an estimated 95 percent of the black vote, even higher in Harlem. In 1924, Coolidge received marginally less, but more than three-quarters of the votes he lost went not to Democrats but to Robert LaFollette, who ran as a Progressive. In 1928, by contrast, Hoover lost an estimated 15 percent of the black vote. Such black papers as the *Chicago Defender,* the *Baltimore Afro-American,* the *Boston Guardian,* the *Louisville News,* the *Norfolk Journal and Guide,* all endorsed Smith. Noted one political scientist, "Democrats made deeper inroads on the Republicanism of Negro voters than in any previous national election."

Hoover won the presidency in a historic landslide. He even carried Texas, Tennessee, Florida, North Carolina, and Virginia, the first time since Reconstruction that any southern state voted Republican.

Hoover's election did give Moton one thing that he had worked for: access to the White House, more than any black man other than a servant had ever had. He even dined in the White House once, a politically significant event, and over the next several years he would be in constant communication with President Hoover, making many recommendations regarding southern whites and northern Negroes for posts ranging from federal judge to "a competent woman to work full-time in the Department of Child Welfare." In one four-month period they would exchange twenty-one letters. But Hoover would follow few of his recommendations and do little for blacks in his administration. There would be no land resettlement scheme, nor anything like it. There would be only repeated promises. Hoover would even nominate a man to the Supreme Court so racist that a Senate controlled by his own party rose in protest. Moton declined Hoover's request that he endorse the nominee, who was then rejected by the Senate. Even Moton had finally had enough; he rebuked Hoover, the president, informing him that blacks doubted "your personal concern for the welfare and progress of one tenth of the citizens of the United States." Hoover replied with more promises, then approved severe cuts in the 10th Cavalry, a famous black combat unit, that would force black combat soldiers to become servants to white officers. Moton declared this "repugnant to all self-respecting Negroes."

Moton had little use for Franklin Delano Roosevelt, observing that if Roosevelt "has done anything for the Negro as Governor of New York, I have not heard of it." Barnett thought Roosevelt's election would be "fatal" to the race.

Even so, in 1932, Moton refused to endorse Hoover for reelection. That year Hoover still received an overwhelming majority of the black vote, but he had driven a wedge between Republicans and even the most loyal black leaders that was splitting them asunder.

GREENVILLE CHANGED TOO. There, when the 1928 river legislation became law, LeRoy Percy gave no speeches. None were needed. Parties and celebrations went on for days. Business boomed at Muffuletto's, the finest restaurant in the state. Drummers lucky enough to be in town laid their trunks open in the display rooms at the Cowan Hotel and made money. Bootleggers from the White River came down in the fast steel boats with which they had rescued thousands and made money too. And men and women paraded up and down the crown of the levee, looking down at the river, throwing empty bottles and cigarettes into the enemy they still feared, some even daring to think that man would finally vanquish it.

But the celebration had a hollowness. Greenville had changed. Earlier, two weeks before Christmas, 1927, Hoover had returned to the city, meeting with Red Cross county chairmen from the Delta in the Elysian Club, that stately and columned building with its long porch, yellow brick walls, and the hedge in front where people hid corn whiskey during dances. The club was part of the fabric of Greenville. In summer, fans had blown air over 300-pound blocks of ice for cooling, and its card room was filled with memories of planters gambling entire loans they had just taken out to cover a year's crops. The club had smelled of fear then, the fear of wives clinging terrified to the wall. A few days after Hoover's visit, the club hosted a Christmas dance. Then it closed forever.

The Delta was beaten down in a way it had never been. As late as March 1928, almost a year after the Mounds Landing crevasse, the Red Cross was still feeding 12,000 people in Washington County alone. There was no money. The Young Men's Hebrew Association followed the Elysian Club into memory. The days when the biggest touring shows, big as Buffalo Bill's Wild West Show, came to Greenville, the days of Enrico Caruso playing in the Opera House, were over.

Greenville also took on a sullenness it had not had. Everything the blacks had endured changed things; the murder of James Gooden had changed things. Levye Chapple, who had organized the General Colored Committee and who had close connections to the Percys, left for Chicago. Though he later returned, most of the thousands of others who left did not. The Reverend E. M. Weddington had signed the letter of praise and thanks to LeRoy Percy during the Klan fight and pastored to Mt. Horeb, the church where Will Percy had castigated the black leadership; he left for Chicago and did not return. One man at a time, one family at a time, in an accelerating flood, blacks left Greenville and the Delta and did not return. They worked all week, took their pay, and left. Every Saturday night crowds of blacks gathered at the Y&MV railroad station to see who was leaving and say goodbye. It was cheaper than the movies, and far more intense. It was also exciting; even those who were remaining felt all the possibilities of the world.

White planters worried about the departures. In July 1927, Alex Scott, son of LeRoy Percy's old ally Charles Scott, warned: "A great deal of labor from the flooded section after being returned to the plantations is going north. It is thus a serious menace and it is going to offer a tremendous problem to all of us." He was correct. Three months later LeRoy Percy informed L. A. Downs, the president of the Illinois Central: "The most serious thing that confronts the planter in the overflowed territory is the loss of labor, which is great and is continuing. I would hesitate to give an accurate estimate of the loss of labor in Washington County but I am quite sure that thirty per cent is too small. If eventually we get by with a loss of fifty per cent I shall consider it fortunate." Oscar Johnston's 60,000-acre plantation produced only 44 bales of cotton in 1927 (only his aggressive trades in cotton futures early in the flood avoided losses in the millions). Nearly all bridges and buildings on the property had been washed away, and ditches and drainage canals had been filled with sand. Workers did not want to face the rebuilding task. Even though he canceled all old debts, even though he had established a refugee camp near the plantation to keep his workers close by, even though the Illinois Central had moved hundreds of his tenants from the Vicksburg refugee camp 260 miles to that camp, he had no workers with whom to rebuild. "Labor was completely demoralized and the plantation was left almost completely without labor," he reported to his shareholders.

By early 1928 the exodus of blacks from Washington County,

and likely the rest of the Delta, did reach 50 percent. Ever since the end of Reconstruction, blacks had been migrating north and west, out of the South. But it had been only a slow drain, with the South losing about 200,000 blacks between 1900 and 1910. During World War I "the Great Migration" began; the South lost 522,000 blacks between 1910 and 1920, mostly between 1916 and 1919. Now from the floodplain of the Mississippi River, from Arkansas, from Louisiana, from Mississippi, blacks were heading north in even larger numbers. In the 1920s, 872,000 more blacks left the South than returned to it. (In the 1930s the exodus fell off sharply; the number of blacks leaving Arkansas, Louisiana, and Mississippi fell by nearly two-thirds, back to the levels of the early 1900s.)

The favorite destination for Delta blacks was Chicago. They brought the blues to that city, and there the black population exploded, from 44,103 in 1910 to 109,458 in 1920—and 233,903 in 1930. Certainly not all of this exodus came from the floodplain of the Mississippi River. And even within that alluvial empire, the great flood of 1927 was hardly the only reason for blacks to abandon their homes. But for tens of thousands of blacks in the Delta of the Mississippi River, the flood was the final reason.

THERE WERE other changes in Greenville. For the Percys Greenville became a dark place. In 1929, LeRoy's wife, Camille, was dying. Even so, LeRoy left her sickroom to visit his deeply depressed nephew LeRoy Pratt Percy in Birmingham. The nephew was a few years younger than his cousin Will, about the age of LeRoy's own long-dead son, and LeRoy and his nephew had hunted together, gambled together, joked together, even talked of the law together. LeRoy the elder had become closer to his nephew than to his own son. In July 1929, LeRoy Pratt Percy did what his own father had done twelve years before. He killed himself with a shotgun. The death stunned LeRoy, who felt not only the loss but his own failure to prevent it. His nephew left a widow and three boys.

Again, Will fled. While his parents grieved, he traveled to the Grand Canyon. He remained there for months. Shortly after he returned, in October 1929, his mother died. Three days later, Will and his father went to the resort of French Lick, Indiana; it was a family favorite, only this time it held no life. On their return LeRoy became ill. Will took him off the train and rushed him to Memphis Baptist Hospital. An old friend who visited him there laughed, "I never expected to find you among the Baptists," and later recalled, "I think that was the last time he ever smiled."

LeRoy improved enough to return to Greenville but remained

morose. He hardly ate, hardly spoke. President Hoover sent condolences for his wife's death and added, "I am happy to know that you are making so good a recovery." But he was not recovering. His old colleague John Sharp Williams, the warrior who had vanquished Vardaman so many years before and who had finally retired from the Senate, spoke of his own determination to remain in this world "even if only on its outskirts" and pleaded with LeRoy to keep him company.

LeRoy would not. In his home full of echoes, he and his son waited for death. On Christmas Eve, 1929, LeRoy Percy, son of the Gray Eagle, died quietly. With his passing, a time in history also passed.

All of white Greenville fell into deep mourning. But blacks told each other that on his deathbed he had said, "No matter what you do, keep your foot on the black moccasin's head. If you take it off he's going to crawl away."

AFTER HIS FATHER'S DEATH Will wrote: "One of the pleasantest places near the home town is its cemetery. I come here not infrequently because it is restful and comforting. I am with my own people."

Will had always found comfort in the past, about which he could weave a personal mythology, rather than with the present or future, which required him to engage realities. His father's death gave him both an object of devotion, and freedom. He escaped into himself less now; it had perhaps become less necessary. He had always been prolific, but since the flood he had written hardly any poems. Now he stopped altogether.

In the cemetery he built a shrine; in the midst of the Depression, at a cost of $25,000, he commissioned Malvina Hoffman to sculpt a statue of a knight standing in armor and mail weary and subdued, yet unvanquished, his hands resting upon a great broadsword. A tablet quotes a poem by Matthew Arnold: "They outtalked thee, hissed thee, tore thee . . . / Charge once more then and be dumb! / Let the victors, when they come, / When the forts of folly fall, / Find thy body by the wall!"

It was now Will's responsibility to live honorably. His cousin's widow and her three children moved from Birmingham into the Percy home, now Will's alone, and after her death—perhaps another suicide, perhaps an unpremeditated but opportunistic seizing of death, or perhaps simply an accident—Will adopted the three children, his cousins, Walker, LeRoy, and Phinizy. He was still nothing like his father. But his house was full. His father's allies continued as his allies. He had the power of money; in one Depression year, a time when a family could live well on $1,500 a year, his personal checkbook balance ranged as high as $19,829 and never fell below $3,700. And he began to come into his own largeness.

For Will was a large man, only in different ways than his father had been large. His father had once said, "Hypocrisy is the pet vice of Americans, and bunk their favorite diet." Will's life became not hypocritical but paradoxical. As his adopted son Walker, the novelist, said, "Though he loved his home country, he had to leave often to keep loving it." He traveled constantly to escape the Delta and also brought the outside world to the Delta. Unhappy with the pedestrian views of the existing newspaper—even though its owner had supported his father in the Klan fight and him during the flood—he recruited Hodding Carter and his wife, Betty Werlein Carter, to start a new newspaper that soon took over the older one, and later became a national symbol of heroic journalism. His house became a salon, choked with artifacts and objets d'art from Italy, Japan, Tahiti. An enormous Capehart record player sat in the living room; it was designed, although it rarely worked, to automatically lift records and turn them over. Dorothy Parker visited, William Faulkner visited, Stephen Vincent Benet visited, even Langston Hughes, the poet laureate of the Harlem Renaissance, visited. (Will introduced him by saying Hughes had "risen above race," but Hughes then proceeded to read, Walker Percy recalled, "the most ideologically aggressive poetry you can imagine.")

Will lent his weight to other battles too. As the thirties moved into darkness, he opposed Oscar Johnston's efforts to sell surplus cotton to the Japanese, protesting: "To furnish [Japan] with munitions of war is the rankest form of stupidity . . . [and] so completely indecent I don't understand it. . . . The most dangerous doctrine that can be taught in our country is the doctrine now being taught by Oscar Johnston, that is America will carry on as usual after the Allies are defeated and will do business with Germany."

Then there were the blacks. Everything in the Delta always came back to the blacks. Will patronized blacks in ways his father would not have considered, failed to understand them in ways his father could not have. Once several black ministers asked him for a contribution to build a Negro YMCA. Will offered to help build a beautiful facility on one condition: that Greenville Negroes combined their nearly fifty Baptist churches into one. He did not hear from them again. "Their virtues, to Mr. Will, had almost nothing to do with freedom," Shelby Foote recalled. "It had to do with dignity, and suffering injustice in a better way than most people can."

Yet in his own way, Will shielded blacks as his father would have. In 1937 the Mississippi River rose again and tested the new flood control plan. Ultimately, the river was contained, but while it was rising, whites wanted to call out the National Guard to protect the levees and keep blacks working on them. Will prevented it. He recalled the brutality of the Guard in 1927 and warned: "If the Negroes of this county knew the guards were coming, there would be a general exodus. . . . I have pledged them I would do all in my power to keep the National Guards out of the county now and during a flood as long as they behave like decent citizens."

He protected black suspects from beatings by the police, even winning damages for at least one victim. He wrote contracts for his sharecroppers on Trail Lake, his plantation, ordered that they be treated decently (his foreman largely ignored his order), and even proposed that the federal government perform audits to see that sharecroppers were not cheated. He defended that proposal to another planter, arguing that "dishonesty practiced by landlords in this section in their settlements with their tenants . . . is widespread and disruptive of interracial relations . . . making the tenant distrust or even hate the white man."

And when black men had sex with willing white women, Will protected those blacks too, seeing that they were only hustled out of Greenville and not whipped or lynched. The white men had their black whores on Blanton Street, but the entire white Delta shivered at the possibility of a white woman desiring, submitting to, a black man. For at issue was not only love and pleasure but power; in the sultriness of the Delta, sex represented everything.

Always Will had hated this part of himself, the part he had discovered in Europe and written about so long before: *To think nobility like mine could be / Flawed — shattered utterly — and by . . . / A slim, brown shepherd boy with windy eyes / And spring upon his mouth! / . . . and I, who, most of all the world, / Loved purity and loathed lust, / Became the mark of my own scorning.* He had always had desires. He had not indulged them in Greenville but his father was dead, and perhaps his father was appeased by the sculpture by his grave.

Rumors about Will spread through his town. He preferred the women and garden clubs to men and hunting, or poker, or golf. He took young men, both white and black, on trips to Europe and Tahiti, or bought them cars, paid for their flying lessons. "You know he never married," people said of him, raising their eyebrows.

Some rumors were not acceptable. The rumors said that blacks had a power over Will. That his chauffeurs, young black men, showed their power to him. One, Ford Atkins, he had called *my only tie with Pan and the Satyrs and all earth creatures who smile sunshine and ask no questions and understand.* Atkins' mother was Will's cook; she became sullen and alcoholic, and he fired her. When Ford once addressed him in a way that was too familiar, Will instantly fired him too. Soon he hired a chauffeur named Senator Canada whose nickname "Honey" came from his charm, not his skin color. Honey had jet black skin, flashing teeth, and wore a mink tie. There were rumors about Will and Honey too. Honey spread them himself, going into the poolroom on Nelson Street, parking Percy's enormous black car by the door, and shooting pool. Outside, it was said, Will lay on the floor in the backseat to avoid being seen. Then Honey said, "I got to take my who' home," laughed, dropped his pool cue, got into the car, and drove away.

THE FIRST SENTENCE of Will Percy's autobiography *Lanterns on the Levee* reads, "My country is the Mississippi Delta, the river country." The river had created the Delta, and the white man—the Percys and men like them—had brought the blacks to the Delta to clear it and tame it and transform it into an empire. Together they had done that. They had built that empire.

Will believed he was watching that empire disintegrate. Near the end of his autobiography, completed only months before his death in 1941, he wrote: "The old Southern way of life in which I had been reared existed no more and its values were ignored or derided. A tarnish has fallen over the bright world; dishonor and corruption triumph; my own strong people have become lotus-eaters; defeat is here again, the last, the most abhorrent."

He seemed to accept that defeat, if only because he accepted the absurd and, finally, himself. The final chapter of his autobiography is titled "Home," and it is about the cemetery. He wrote: "I wish a few others out there, under the cedars, could be in this plot of ours. . . . I should like to bring from that far corner where the poor sleep well one brown-eyed lad who sleeps alone there, for he had loved me." Then he wrote, "I know that the wickedness and the failures of men are nothing and their valor and pathos and effort everything."

A SOCIETY does not change in sudden jumps. Rather, it moves in multiple small steps along a broad front. Most of these steps are parallel if not quite simultaneous; some advance farther than others, and some even move in an opposite direction. The movement rather resembles that of an amoeba, with one part of the body extending itself outward, then another, even while the main body stays back, until enough of the mass has shifted to move the entire body.

The Great Mississippi River Flood of 1927 forced many small steps. Even in the narrowest and most direct sense the flood's legacy was felt in Washington, in New Orleans, in Greenville, in every community along the banks of the Mississippi River and its tributary rivers, and in the nation's black community. Even in terms of just physical issues, the 1927 flood created a legacy of new problems that engineers must deal with today. But the flood also left a far larger, if more ambiguous and less tangible, legacy.

Like the blues music born in the Delta, languid and roiling at the same time, it penetrated to the core of the nation, washed away surface, and revealed the nation's character. Then it tested that character and changed it. It marked the end of a way of seeing the world, and possibly the end of that world itself.

It shifted perceptions of the role and responsibility of the federal government—calling for a great expansion—and shattered the myth of a quasi-feudal bond between Delta blacks and the southern aristocracy, in which the former pledged fealty to the latter in return for protection. It accelerated the great migration of blacks north. And it altered both southern and national politics. The changes would not all come quickly. But they would come.

In 1927 the Mississippi River had gone coursing once again over the land it had created, reclaiming the empire the Percys had taken. Then the waters left. In their wake black Delta sharecroppers looked north to Chicago and west to Los Angeles, and out onto the freshly replenished fields. There, in the fields, the Mississippi had deposited one more layer of earth upon the land.

Appendix:

THE RIVER TODAY

Today what the Corps of Engineers calls "Project Flood" protects the lower Mississippi River valley from a flood considerably greater, the Corps says, than that of 1927. In its present form this plan has finally ended in compromise the great and bitter rivalry of James Eads, Andrew Humphreys, and Charles Ellet begun so long ago. But the plan itself has created a major new problem, and it also has serious flaws.

Over the years Project Flood has undergone many changes, but its engineering backbone remains the original 1928 law, the Jadwin Plan, which set standards for levees far higher and thicker than those of 1927, but did not rely on levees alone. Instead, it embodied the chief principle articulated by Ellet, that the river cannot be contained within levees. So in addition the Corps has built reservoirs on several Mississippi tributaries, and also allows the Mississippi itself room to spread out through a series of various flood control features.

On the main river, the plan's northernmost flood control feature is a "floodway," essentially a parallel river 5 miles wide and 65 miles long, running from Birds Point, Missouri, south to New Madrid, Missouri. The river enters it through a "fuse-plug" levee, a levee lower than those surrounding it that is designed to blow out in a great flood. (If it holds, the Corps will dynamite it.) This floodway diverts a maximum flow of 550,000 cubic feet of water per second. It has been used only once, in 1937. At New Madrid the water returns to the Mississippi.

For the next 250 miles of river, to the mouth of the Arkansas, the Jadwin Plan originally called for only stronger levees to contain the water. At the mouth of the Arkansas, where in 1927 the river carried its greatest volume, Jadwin wanted to build a second, massive floodway that would have run for 155 miles and inundated 1.3 million acres, in effect duplicating the natural flooding that had occurred before the Corps closed the Cypress Creek outlet in 1921. Not surprisingly, this plan aroused intense opposition in Arkansas and Louisiana, intense enough to force a search for another solution.

Eads had one. He had always insisted that shortening the river by making "cutoffs," cutting across the neck of horseshoe bends, would move water much faster and thus lower flood heights. For decades the Corps and most civilian engineers had rejected Eads' argument, but after the 1927 flood William Elam, an engineer for the levee board in Greenville, took up Eads' call. The Corps and the Mississippi River Commission resisted, but Hoover, then president, was convinced that the proposal deserved a test. When Jadwin retired in 1929, the secretary of war recommended ten different men as chief of engineers. Hoover refused to nominate any of them and finally hand-picked the man he wanted, General Lytle Brown. The hydraulics laboratory previously opposed by the Corps was built, and tests there and observations of a natural cutoff confirmed Eads' predictions. In the 1930s and 1940s the Mississippi River Commission made cutoffs that shortened the river by more than 150 miles, largely by eliminating a series of sharp curves called "the Greenville bends." The cutoffs worked dramatically, and lowered flood heights 15 feet, obviating the need for the floodway that Jadwin had proposed.

The next feature of Project Flood appears at a point called Old River, halfway between Natchez and Baton Rouge, where the Atchafalaya begins to flow from the Mississippi to the sea. Here, Project Flood is designed to handle its maximum flow of 3,030,000 cubic feet per second by dividing the water.

To direct this flow, the Corps built the Old River Control Structure and, 20 miles south, the Morganza floodway, immense masses of concrete and steel designed to divert approximately 600,000 cfs each into the Atchafalaya. In 1963 a massive dam sealed off the natural flow between the Mississippi and the Atchafalaya; since then the Old River structure has controlled the flow between the two rivers. The Morganza structure has been opened only once, in the 1973 flood.

In total, Project Flood sends 1,500,000 cfs—the water diverted from the Mississippi plus all the flow of the Red River—down the Atchafalaya River, and two floodways that parallel it, to the sea. The plan allows 1,500,000 cfs to continue down the Mississippi toward New Orleans. This exactly reverses the old policy called for by the levees-only theory; prior to the 1927 flood, the Corps of Engineers had planned to separate the Atchafalaya entirely from the Mississippi, and send all flood water past New Orleans.

The final flood control feature is a concrete spillway at Bonnet Carré, 30 miles above New Orleans, designed to subtract a final 250,000 cfs from the Mississippi when it is in flood; guide levees direct the outflow across 7 miles of land into Lake Pontchartrain. This spillway was first used in 1937, when it carried 318,000 cfs, the most it has ever handled; it was also opened in 1945, 1950, 1973, 1975, 1979, and 1983. According to plan, then, no more than 1,250,000 cfs will pass the city of New Orleans.

But Project Flood has several weak spots, and its solutions have created at least one new problem. First, the Corps claims its plans will handle a flood greater than that of 1927, 11 percent greater in the vicinity of the Mounds Landing crevasse. This claim is based on the Corps' official 1927 reading of 2,544,000 cfs at the mouth of the Arkansas. In fact, James Kemper and several other civilian engineers independently measured the flow there at over 3,000,000 cfs. Even Army engineers, before being ordered by Jadwin to design an inexpensive plan, unofficially put the flow at over 3,000,000 cfs. This flow exceeds the design capacity of Project Flood by more than 100,000 cfs.

In addition, the levee system falls short of its design specifications. In 1996 there were 1,608 miles of main-stem Mississippi levees; 304 miles of those levees did not meet the design height. Most of these low levees fell only 1 to 2 feet below grade, but several miles of the levee system between Greenville and Vicksburg, on both the east and west banks, fell 6 feet short.

Another problem exists with the cutoffs. The river has not accepted them as final. In the fifty years since cutoffs shortened the river by 150 miles, the river has regained roughly one-third of that length and eroded some of the benefits.

But the greatest problem by far is the Atchafalaya, which offers a much shorter route to the sea, and a steeper slope, than the main channel of the Mississippi. The 1927 flood sent vast amounts of water down it, scouring it out, deepening it, building a channel capable of accommodating—and hungry for—far more water than it had ever carried. Project Flood puts even more water down it. Kemper warned that "the inevitable consequence" of this approach would be that the Atchafalaya "will soon become the main stream [of the Mississippi], and the river past New Orleans a deteriorating outlet."

Kemper was not merely theorizing. The mouth of the Mississippi River has shifted many times. Twenty-five years after his warning, it became obvious that he was right, and in 1954 Congress passed emergency legislation to give the Corps money to prevent the Atchafalaya from claiming the entire Mississippi River. Keeping the Mississippi in its old channel has become by far the most serious engineering problem the Corps of Engineers faces. The Old River Control Structure was built to solve it, but the 1973 flood almost destroyed the structure by scouring out a hole 75 feet underwater that came close to causing its collapse. Many engineers believe that sooner or later, no matter what man does, the Mississippi will shift its channel to the Atchafalaya. And a finger of the sea will climb north past New Orleans, north to Baton Rouge.

So the story ends as it began, with man determined to assert his will over the river.

Notes

Abbreviations of Frequently Cited Sources

AAH   Andrew Atkinson Humphreys

AAHP   Andrew Atkinson Humphreys Papers, Historical Society of Pennsylvania, Philadelphia

ACP   Association of Commerce Papers, Special Collections, Earl Long Library, University of New Orleans

ALP   James B. Eads, *Addresses, Letters, and Papers of James B. Eads*

CBP   Claude Barnett Papers, Chicago Historical Society

CP   Caplan Papers, Louisiana State Museum, History Division, New Orleans

D&PLCP   Delta & Pine Land Company Papers, Special Collections, Mitchell Library, Mississippi State University, Starkville

ECHPC   Emergency Clearing House Publicity Committee, in Caplan Papers, Louisiana State Museum, History Division, New Orleans

ECP   Elmer Corthell Papers, Special Collections, John Hay Library, Brown University, Providence, Rhode Island

EP   Eads Papers, Missouri Historical Society, St. Louis

FC   Friends of the Cabildo Oral History Collection, Louisiana Room, New Orleans Public Library

GD-T   *Greenville Democrat-Times*

HFCCH   *House Flood Control Committee Hearings,* 70th Congress, 1st Session, November 1927 through January 1928

HHPL   Herbert Hoover Presidential Library, West Branch, Iowa

JBE   James Buchanan Eads

JC-L   *Jackson Clarion-Ledger*

LC   Library of Congress, Washington, D.C.

LL   William Alexander Percy, *Lanterns on the Levee: Recollections of a Planter's Son*

LP   LeRoy Percy

MC-A   *Memphis Commercial-Appeal*

MDAH   Mississippi Department of Archives and History, Jackson

M&LP   Monroe & Lemann Papers, Offices of Monroe & Lemann, New Orleans

NA   National Archives, Washington, D.C.
NOCA   New Orleans City Archives, Louisiana Room, New Orleans Public Library
NOI   *New Orleans Item*
NOS   *New Orleans States*
NOT   *New Orleans Tribune*
NOT-P   *New Orleans Times-Picayune*
NYT   *New York Times*
P&H   Andrew Atkinson Humphreys and Henry Abbot, *Report on the Physics and Hydraulics of the Mississippi River*
PFP   Percy Family Papers, Mississippi Department of Archives and History, Jackson
RCP   Red Cross Papers, Record Group 200, National Archives, Washington, D.C.
RRMP   Robert Russa Moton Papers, Special Collections, Tuskegee University Library, Tuskegee, Alabama
SBV   *St. Bernard Voice*
TUL   Special Collections, Howard-Tilton Library, Tulane University, New Orleans
WAP   William Alexander Percy

PROLOGUE

13   "The roaring Mississippi": *MC-A,* April 15, 1927.
14   "rainy": Henry Waring Ball diaries, MDAH.
14   "at 12 it commenced": Ibid.
15   from 6 to 15 inches: *GD-T,* April 16, 1927.
15   greatest rainfall ever: "Report of the Sewage and Water Board of New Orleans, July 1927"; *GD-T,* April 16, 1927; *NYT,* April 16, 1927; Ball diaries, MDAH, April 15 and 16, 1927.
15   put on their gun boots: Interview with Florence Sillers Ogden on Mississippi Public Television, "The Flood of 1927," complete transcript of interview in MDAH; interview with Frank Hall, December 16, 1992.
16   "I saw a whole tree": Interview with William Jones, March 2, 1993; interview with Moses Mason, March 1, 1993; *GD-T,* April 21, 1928.
16   3 million cubic feet of water: *Bulletin of the American Railway Engineering Association* 29, no. 297 (July 1927); report of Army engineers quoted in *NOT-P,* April 25, 1927.

CHAPTER ONE

22   "one of the most": Quoted in Todd Shallat, *Structures in the Stream,* p. 175.
22   "commanding talents": Quoted in David McCullough, *The Great Bridge,* p. 347.
22   five greatest engineers: *Universal Engineer* 55, no. 1 (1932), cited in Florence Dorsey, *Road to the Sea: The Story of James B. Eads and the Mississippi River,* p. 307n.

23   Washington Irving was impressed: Charles van Ravensway, *St. Louis: An Informal History of the City and Its People, 1764–1865*, p. 208.

24   "towering ambition": Emerson Gould, *Fifty Years on the Mississippi*, p. 485.

24   "more dangerous than": Quoted in Floyd Clay, *A Century on the Mississippi*, p. 11.

24   "The history of the world": Mentor Williams, "The Background of the Chicago River and Harbor Convention," p. 223.

25   credited as its inventor: See for example *Webster's Biographical Dictionary* (Springfield, Mass.: G. & C. Merriam & Co., 1956), p. 460.

25   "From young manhood": Louis How, *James B. Eads*, pp. 54–57.

25   "the personal magnetism": Dorsey, p. 130.

26   Eads put on the bell: Dorsey, p. 16; How, pp. 3–8.

26   "I had occasion to descend": Eads, *ALP*, p. 153.

27   need not join the gold rush: How, p. 19.

27   "It requires little": Dorsey, p. 30.

27   "To an Absent Husband": Published in *Davenport Gazette*, August 17, 1948, EP.

27   "I do hope and pray": JBE to Martha Eads, August 16, 1852, Churchill Library.

27   "dangerous and exposed places": Dorsey, pp. 32–33.

27   "whose previous pursuits": Quoted in Joseph Gies, *Bridges and Men*, p. 150.

28   "iron muscles": How, p. 55.

28   "Really he seems": Ibid., pp. 54–57.

28   "Never let even a pawn": How, p. 11.

28   "shut[ting] so emphatically": Ibid., pp. 54–57.

28   "Fortune favors the brave": Ibid., p. 57.

29   "Whatever credit is due": Gould, p. 592.

29   Eads argued for building: L. U. Reavis, *St. Louis: The Future Great City of the World*, p. 177; Dorsey, p. 49.

29   "confidential": Bates to JBE, April 16, 1861, EP.

30   "is greatly superior": Quoted in Dorsey, p. 65.

30   "Only give me": Ibid., p. 84.

30   possibly had access: John Kouwenhoven, "The Designing of the Eads Bridge," p. 547.

31   devoted an entire chapter: James McCabe, *Great Fortunes and How They Were Made*, pp. 209–220.

CHAPTER TWO

32   "ran wild": Henry Humphreys, *Andrew Atkinson Humphreys*, p. 26.

33   "a source of great": Ibid., p. 35.

33   First he blocked a rival: AAH to C. Graham, November 21, 1858, AAHP; Gary Ryan, "War Department Topographical Bureau, 1831–1863," Ph.D. diss., p. 201.

33   "serious irregularity . . .": Abert to Secretary of War, quoted in Ryan, p. 188.

33   "capitoline guards": Ryan, p. 199.

33   "I went to science": Henry Humphreys, p. 190.

34 "very pleasant": Catton, *Grant Takes Command,* p. 231.

35 "It is a work": Henry Humphreys, p. 190.

35 "To sound knowledge": Ibid., p. 57.

35 "the work of my life": AAH to Charles Lyell, May 28, 1866, AAHP.

36 In 1835: The best brief discussion of early engineering is an essay by Terry Reynolds, "The Engineer in 19th Century America," in Terry Reynolds, ed., *The Engineer in America;* see also Richard Kirby and Philip Laurson, *Early Years of Modern Civil Engineering.*

36 "not above 3": Gene Lewis, *Charles Ellet, Jr.: The Engineer as Individualist,* p. 10.

36 "The wind was high": Quoted in McCullough, *The Great Bridge,* p. 77.

36 he built a catwalk: Ibid., p. 77.

37 "At the mouth": *P&H,* p. 94.

37 physicist Werner Heisenberg: James Gleick, *Chaos,* p. 121.

38 Engineering theories and techniques: Interview with James Tuttle, Mississippi River Commission, in Vicksburg, October 14, 1993.

38 "running *upstream*": AAH to Lee, March 18, 1851, AAHP.

39 During floods: D. O. Elliott, *The Improvement of the Lower Mississippi River for Flood Control and Navigation,* vol. 1, p. 94.

39 for the last 450: Martin Reuss, Army Corps of Engineers, Humphreys Engineering Center, Springfield, Virginia, supplied these figures.

39 At least some geologists: Philip King, *The Evolution of North America,* p. 77.

39 Over thousands of years: Harold Fisk, *Geological Investigation of the Alluvial Valley of the Lower Mississippi,* p. 11.

39 this sedimentary deposit: Elliott, vol. 1, p. 17.

40 a book arguing: William Elam, *Speeding Floods to the Sea.*

41 "Concentration of force": *Report of the Louisiana Senate Standing Committee on Levees and Drainage,* March 21, 1850.

42 "The public mind here": AAH to Capt. J. J. Lee, March 18, 1851, HP.

42 "We have been to see": Ellet to his mother, March 2, 1851, quoted in Lewis, p. 139.

42 "I cannot understand": AAH to Lee, March [illegible day], 1851, AAHP; see also Todd Shallat, *Structures in the Stream,* p. 176.

43 "a most active partisan": AAH to Lee, November 12, 1851, AAHP.

43 "What is the reason": Undated note, AAHP.

43 "The clay itself": *P&H,* p. 98.

44 "The opinions of Frisi": AAH to Lee, March 18, 1851, AAHP.

44 "Facts of great interest": Ibid.

44 "Never was there": AAH to Lee, April 22, 1851, AAHP.

44 "You see how": AAH to Lee, May 2, 1851, AAHP.

44 his superiors reprimanded him: See for example AAH to Lee, April 6, 1851, AAHP.

44 "a lesion of Enervation": Certificate of Surgeon Randall, Mississippi Delta Survey records, NA, Record Group 77 (hereafter, RG).

44 Ellet began: Ibid., pp. 32–33.

45 "fail to give": Charles Ellet, *Report on the Overflows of the Delta of the Mississippi,* 32nd Cong. 1st sess., 1852, Sen. Exec. Doc. 20; see also, House Doc., vol. 24, 63rd Cong., Doc. 918, which includes Ellet's report reprinted, p. 27.

45 "a delusive hope": Ibid., p. 28.
45 "The water is supplied": Ibid., p. 28.
45 he proposed a comprehensive: Ibid., pp. 32–33.
45 "The continued illness": Ibid., p. 24.

CHAPTER THREE

47 "desirous of taking": AAH recounts this in a letter to Charles Lyell, May 28, 1866, AAHP.
47 "the work of my life": Ibid.
47 "schooled": Henry Humphreys, p. 324.
48 "an extremely neat man": Harold Round, "A. A. Humphreys," *Civil War Times Illustrated* 4 (February 1966).
48 "I do like": Catton, *Grant Takes Command,* p. 231.
48 "Gentlemen": Bruce Catton, *Glory Road* (Garden City, N.Y.: Doubleday, 1952), pp. 72, 280.
48 "The charge of my": AAH to his wife, December 14, 1862, AAHP.
49 "I felt like": Quoted in Henry Humphreys, p. 190.
49 "In ten or fifteen": Ibid., p. 179.
49 "The division has made": Ibid.
49 "General Humphreys": Round, "A. A. Humphreys."
49 "It is acknowledged": Henry Humphreys, p. 182.
49 "The space occupied": Richard Wheeler, *Witness to Gettysburg,* p. 207.
49 "The newspaper correspondents": Henry Humphreys, pp. 200–202.
49 "Why, anyone who": Ibid., p. 190.
50 "I prefer infinitely": Ibid., pp. 200–202.
50 "My mortification": Ibid., p. 202.
50 "I know that": AAH to his wife, February 26, 1865, AAHP.
50 "I have good reason": AAH to his wife, November 25, 1864, AAHP.
50 "I do not believe": Humphreys to J. de Peyster, June 1, 1883, AAHP.
50 "The reputation justly due": Henry Humphreys, p. 219.
50 "Its publication constitutes": *New Orleans Daily Crescent,* January 30, 1866.
51 *Report upon the Physics:* The complete title reads *Report upon the Physics and Hydraulics of the Mississippi River; upon the Protection of the Alluvial Region Against Overflow; and upon the Deepening of the Mouths: Based upon Surveys and Investigations Made Under the Acts of Congress Directing the Topographical and Hydrographical Survey of the Delta of the Mississippi River, with Such Investigations as Might Lead to Determine the Most Practicable Plan for Securing It from Inundation, and the Best Mode of Deepening the Channels at the Mouths of the River.*
51 "I am on the verge": Quoted in Steve Rosenberg and John M. Barry, *The Transformed Cell* (New York: Putnam, 1992), p. 7.
51 "the crowning proof": *P&H,* p. 324.
51 " 'I approve much' ": Ibid., title page.
51 "Every river phenomenon": Ibid., p. 30.
52 "The investigations": Ibid., pp. 404–407.

52   "The legitimate consequences": Ibid., pp. 30, 186, 387.

52   "would, if executed": Ibid., p. 381.

52   "The investigations of": Ibid., p. 394.

52   "The task of criticism": Ibid., p. 310.

52   "admirably executed": Ibid., pp. 120, 199, 219.

53   "Mr. Ellet's is": Ibid., p. 219.

53   even today his data: Hunter Rouse and Simon Ince, *History of Hydraulics,* pp. 177–79.

53   "groundless": *Report of the Joint Committee on Levees,* Louisiana State Legislature, 1850, Louisiana State Museum, History Division, New Orleans.

53   "It has been *demonstrated": P&H,* p. 417.

CHAPTER FOUR

55   "far more onerous": AAH to Senator Henry Wilson, January 26, 1869, AAHP.

55   "be relieved from duty": AAH to Secretary of War John Schofield, March 9, 1869, and March 13, 1869, AAHP.

55   He sought to have: See AAH to Secretary of War, November 2, 1876, AAHP.

55   Humphreys relieved: For more on this incident, see Arthur Frazier, "Daniel Farrand Henry's Cup Type 'Telegraphic' River Current Meter," pp. 541–565.

56   "It may be properly": *Missouri Republican,* June 25, 1854.

56   Chicagoans charged: Wyatt Belcher, *The Economic Rivalry Between St. Louis and Chicago, 1850–1880,* p. 23.

56   But as a result: A famous lawsuit funded by St. Louis steamboat interests sought the destruction of the bridge, which would have choked railroad and western development. Abraham Lincoln argued for the railroads and won a hung jury; the bridge stayed and others were built.

57   twenty-two Chicago firms: Belcher, p. 157.

57   His experience with: Howard Miller and Quinta Scott in *The Eads Bridge* suggest that Eads was simply lucky in his choice of steel, and in the development of chromium steel. More likely he knew the metal fairly well, chiefly from his European travels, a probable visit to the Krupp works, and artillery experience. See also John Kouwenhoven, "The Designing of the Eads Bridge," passim.

57   "impossible . . .": Dorsey, p. 96.

58   roughly one out of every: McCullough, *The Great Bridge,* p. 390.

58   "I cannot consent": Calvin Woodward, *History of the St. Louis Bridge,* pp. 15–16.

58   "unqualified disapproval": Dorsey, p. 105.

58   "It is absolutely certain": Elmer Corthell, "Remarks to the Western Society of Engineers, June 4, 1890, Missouri Historical Society.

59   "Anyone who can": Miller and Scott, pp. 78–85.

59   He charmed: Frederick Finley, letter to editor, *St. Louis Globe-Democrat,* July 9, 1950; Gies, pp. 165–166.

59   "have constant control": How, p. 15.

60 "about our confidential": Kouwenhoven, "The Designing of the Eads Bridge," p. 535.
60 "The very machinery": Dorsey, p. 130.
61 a product he helped develop: John Kouwenhoven, "James Buchanan Eads," p. 86.
61 "It is necessary": Walter Lowrey, "Navigational Problems at the Mouth of the Mississippi River, 1689–1880," Ph.D. diss., p. 203.
62 "The solution of this problem": *NYT,* May 15, 1873.
62 "We must get ready": AAH to Cyrus Comstock, March 2, 1873, Comstock Papers, LC.
62 "a bitter and unrelenting": Corthell, "Remarks."
63 "the river interests": Calvin Woodward, p. 265.
64 "as many *hours*": Ibid.
64 "If a thousand": Ibid.
64 "The Board": Ibid., p. 270.
64 a secret agreement: See memo in Eads' handwriting dated July 1, 1874, in EP.
64 received Eads warmly: For an account of this meeting, see William Taussig, "Personal Recollections of General Grant," *Missouri Historical Society Publications* 2 (1903), pp. 1–13; also Dorsey, p. 152; Calvin Woodward, pp. 262–286.
65 "badly designed": Woodward, p. 270.
65 "[One] of those": Kirby and Laurson, p. 162.
65 "soul became immersed": Carl Condit, "Sullivan's Skyscrapers as the Expression of Nineteenth Century Technology," pp. 78–93.

CHAPTER FIVE

67 "Whatever the Delta": Robert Brandfon, *The Cotton Kingdom of the New South* (Cambridge: Harvard University Press, 1967), pp. 24–29.
67 "On the second": U. S. Grant, *Personal Memoirs of U. S. Grant,* pp. 266–271.
68 "If we make": Quoted in Benjamin G. Humphreys, *Floods and Levees on the Mississippi River,* p. 39.
68 "exhaustively treated": Letter from Secretary of War, 43rd Cong., 1st sess., House *Doc. 220,* p. 109.
68 "my death blow": Lowrey, "Navigational Problems at the Mouth of the Mississippi River, 1698–1880," Ph.D. diss., p. 376.
68 "The canal is": AAH letter, January 15, 1874, quoted in Corthell, *A History of the Jetties at the Mouth of the Mississippi,* p. 34.
69 "mud lumps": Lowrey, "Navigational Problems," p. 11.
69 "masses of tough clay": *P&H,* p. 442.
69 "If a fleet": *De Bow's Review* 18 (April 1855), p. 512.
69 "only a scattering": Capt. Fuller to Col. Stephen Long, January 24, 1859, NA, RG 77.
69 "a foolish attempt": Lowrey, "Navigational Problems," p. 201.
70 "improvement of ": Dorsey, p. 91.
70 "The West is": Lowrey, "Navigational Problems," p. 289.

70 "I am well satisfied": McAlester to Payne, October 10, 1868, quoted in ibid., p. 276.

70 "It is idle": *New Orleans Picayune,* March 6, 1869.

70 "[T]he Essayons": Lowrey, "Navigational Problems," p. 313.

70 "This is a tissue": Ibid.

71 "told me yesterday": Higby to Capt. Charles Howell, quoted in ibid., p. 313.

71 "to run us down": Howell to AAH, July 20, 1871, NA, RG 77.

71 "Its construction": Lowrey, "Navigational Problems," p. 303.

72 "are not in condition": *New Orleans Daily Times,* February 14, 1874.

72 "Can it be possible": *New Orleans Picayune,* February 8, 1874.

72 "Never was an honest": *New Orleans Daily Times,* February 15, 1874; *New Orleans Picayune,* February 15, 1874.

72 "In talking over": Corthell, "Remarks."

72 Stone's reversal: Lowrey, "Navigational Problems," p. 378.

73 "Socially Mr. Eads": *New Orleans Times-Democrat,* March 18, 1887.

73 He also bought: See memorandum of understanding in Eads hand-writing dated July 1, 1874; letter from James Wilson to JBE, July 6, 1876; memo by JBE, July 22, 1876, all in EP. The late John Kouwen-hoven collected this and a vast store of additional material on Eads; thanks to John Brown of the University of Virginia for sharing it with me.

73 single most vital issue: Lowrey, "Navigational Problems," p. 391.

73 "I need not say": Barnard to Comstock, April 14, 18, 22, and July 5, 1874, Comstock Papers, LC.

73 West Point had been using: See a superb article by Martin Reuss, "Politics and Technology in the Army Corps of Engineers," *Technology and Culture* 26, no. 1 (January 1985).

74 members of the American Society: Corthell, *A History of the Jetties,* p. 239.

74 "Every attempt": *Congressional Record,* 43rd Cong., 1st sess., pp. 5367–5368.

74 "Thirty-seven years": Quoted in Corthell, *A History of the Jetties,* p. 21.

74 "the real bed": Ibid., p. 98.

74 "The annual advance": Ibid., p. 21.

74 "absurd": JBE to S. A. Hurlbut, U.S. House, May 29, 1874, attacking Humphreys' report, in Eads, *ALP,* p. 153.

75 "We have laid": Dorsey, p. 173.

75 "Disasters and": Eads, *ALP,* p. 153.

75 he now claimed: Dorsey, p. 176.

76 The board estimated: Wright to AAH, November 30, 1874, House Exec. Doc. 25, 43rd Cong., 1st sess., pp. 1–2; and Report, Board of 1874, 43rd Cong., 1st sess., January 13, 1875, Exec. Doc. 114, quoted in Lowrey, "Navigational Problems, p. 404.

76 "The accompanying discussion": R. E. McMath to AAH, May 7, 1874, NA, RG 77.

77 "If the profession": JBE, address at a banquet in his honor at St. Louis, March 23, 1875, EP.

77 "undertake the work": Ibid.

78 "The alluvial regions": See *Annual Report of the Chief of Engineers for 1875*, pp. 540–550, esp. p. 542.

79 "By such correction": Quoted in Corthell, *A History of the Jetties*, pp. 28–34.

80 Creoles: In New Orleans, a "Creole" was a descendant of French or Spanish settlers.

80 "Captain Eads has fought": Quoted in *New Orleans Picayune*, May 12, 1875.

81 "The first indication": Quoted in Mark Twain, *Life on the Mississippi* (New York: Bantam, 1990), p. 134.

81 the deepest water: Corthell, *A History of the Jetties*, pp. 70–71.

82 "[T]ransfers of cargoes": JBE to Leovy, June 11, 1875, and January 24, 1876, Henry P. Leovy Papers, Historic New Orleans Collection.

82 "Assurance of success": *New Orleans Picayune*, June 13, 1875.

82 "any 'bloated bondholder' ": Eads to Corthell, June 11, 1875, Kouwenhoven Collection.

82 Eads would pay: Lowrey, "Navigational Problems," pp. 416–417.

84 The Dutch method: Corthell, *A History of the Jetties*, pp. 75–83.

85 a new sandbar: *New Orleans Democrat*, May 3, 5, and 10, 1876; *New Orleans Picayune*, May 10, 1876.

85 Howell pressed his attack: *New Orleans Democrat*, May 3, 5, 6, and 10, 1876; *New Orleans Picayune*, May 10, 1876.

85 "had no authority": Comstock to Secretary of War George McCrary, May 2, 1877, Comstock Papers, LC.

85 "Please instruct General Comstock": JBE to Taft, May 9, 1876, quoted in Corthell, *A History of the Jetties*, p. 100.

85 "General Comstock will": Ibid.

86 oceangoing steamer *Hudson:* The account of this incident comes from Corthell, pp. 107–109.

86 "It is not too much": Ibid., p. 108.

87 One such debate: for details see Lowrey, "Navigational Problems," p. 460.

87 "Discharge the whole force": Corthell, *A History of the Jetties*, p. 156.

87 "a marked scour": Ibid., p. 137.

87 whom he paid $5,000: JBE to Beauregard, January 2, 1877, Beauregard Papers, Louisiana State University.

88 *"The results actually attained"*: AAH to Congressman E. W. Robertson, May 1, 1878, AAHP.

88 "The Laws of Gravity": *Review of Humphreys and Abbot Report,"* pamphlet, Missouri Historical Society.

88 forty-three-page rebuttal: AAH to Abbot, October 20, 1877, AAHP.

88 "a reply might": Abbot to AAH, November 21, 1878, and November 26, 1878, AAHP.

89 "The work is done": *New Orleans Daily Times*, July 11, 1879.

89 453,681 tons were shipped: Corthell, *A History of the Jetties*, pp. 235–238; J. Thomas Scharf, *History of St. Louis City and County,* vol. 2, p. 1126; see also Kouwenhoven Collection.

89　the second-largest: Arthur Morgan, *Dams and Other Disasters,* p. 129.
89　"The present successful": Quoted in Morgan, pp. 147, 172, 175.
89　"The plan did not": Lansing Beach, "The Work of the Corps of Engineers on the Lower Mississippi," in American Society of Chemical Engineers, *Transactions,* 1924.
91　the levees rose higher: HFCCH, p. 1710.
91　"is held in place": Elliott, vol. 2, p. 44.

Chapter Seven

95　"a very cave": Percy, *LL,* p. 272.
96　"It is not like most": Twain, pp. 134–135.
97　"a jungle equal": Quoted in John C. Willis, "On the New South Frontier," Ph.D. diss., 1991, p. 18.
97　One pioneer reported: James Cobb, *The Most Southern Place on Earth,* p. 15.
97　"the fetid alligator": Ibid., p. 44.
97　"almost worth a man's life": Ibid., p. 14.
97　"Nature knows not": Alfred Stone, "The Negro in the Yazoo-Mississippi Delta," *Publications of the American Economic Association* 3, no. 3 (1902), p. 236.
97　A 1906 scientific assessment: Quoted in Brandfon, *The Cotton Kingdom of the New South,* pp. 24–29. Brandfon's book is a classic, particularly strong on the role of railroads in the Delta's development.
98　assessed values: *De Bow's Review,* October 1858, pp. 438–440.
98　In 1861: Willie Halsell, "Migration into and Settlement of Leflore County, 1833–1876," *Journal of Mississippi History,* 1947, p. 238.
98　"that great Swamp": *RP&H,* p. 24.
98　"a seething lush hell": Cobb, p. 6.
98　"a wilderness and a waste": Willis, "On the New South Frontier," Ph.D. diss., pp. 13–17; Florence Sillers, ed., *History of Bolivar County,* p. 156.
99　the most profitable: Willis, "On the New South Frontier," p. 221n.
99　"more a king": *Memphis Daily Appeal,* January 6, 1881.
99　"on the threshold": Brandfon, p. 10.
99　"The foremost branch": Quoted in Brandfon, p. 14.
100　a record harvest: Brandfon, p. 20.
100　"To facilitate trade": Eads' speech at the dedication of the grand hall of the St. Louis Merchants Exchange, December 5, 1875, EP.
100　"the salvation": Brandfon, p. 76.
100　"I [am] only trying": Fish to John Parker, May 31, 1922, quoted in Matthew Schott, "John M. Parker of Louisiana," Ph.D. diss., Parker Papers at USLL, p. 60.
100　2,365,214 Delta acres: Brandfon, p. 46.
101　the state sold 706,000 acres: C. Vann Woodward, *Origins of the New South, 1877–1913,* p. 119; see also Brandfon, pp. 49–63.
101　"The coming of": Sillers, pp. 272, 277, 321.
101　the Y&MV Railroad: Robert Harrison, *Alluvial Empire,* p. 117.
102　The Y&MV soon became: Brandfon, p. 80.

102 "Black Code": For more on the Mississippi Black Code, see Cobb; and Eric Foner, *Reconstruction.*
103 One man even credited Percy: Percy, *LL,* pp. 275–276; Foner, p. 174.
103 initially whites resisted it: Foner, p. 174; Cobb, p. 70.
103 thousands of blacks came: Vernon Wharton, *The Negro in Mississippi, 1865–1890,* pp. 107–109; Cobb, p. 83.
103 More smoothly than elsewhere: Willis, "On the New South Frontier," pp. 333–335.
104 "Public sentiment": *Greenville Times,* March 24, 1877, quoted in Willis, "On the New South Frontier," p. 335.
104 Outside the Delta: Quoted in Cobb, p. 82.
104 "with unceasing vigilance": Wharton, p. 115; Cobb, p. 70.
105 When his sister-in-law: LP to Pullman Co., October 24, 1907. Also see, for example, LP to Rigo & Co., February 16, 1909; wire to I. Aiken, July 22, 1905, all in PFP.
105 "quote a lower rate": See, for example, LP to Rigo & Co., February 16, 1909; wire to I. Aiken, July 22, 1905; to Pullman Co., October 24, 1907.
105 "While, if you should": LP to his brother Walker Percy, October 11, 1927, PFP.
105 "it has a tendency": LP to Judge George Ethridge, May 4, 1929, PFP.
105 "I think the": LP to WAP, May 31, 1929, PFP.
106 except one Wall Street: LP to Walker Percy, November 18, 1907, PFP.
106 "He read *Ivanhoe*": Percy, *LL,* p. 57.
106 "No one ever": Ibid., p. 57.

CHAPTER EIGHT

107 "bull clique": Brandfon, p. 114.
108 Probably a higher proportion: *Twelfth Census of the United States,* vol. 5, *Agriculture,* pp. 96–97, quoted in Willis, "On the New South Frontier," pp. 5, 9; interview, June 9, 1994.
108 "The South must not": *Outlook,* August 3, 1907, pp. 730–732.
108 "We are without": Quoted in Robert Brandfon, "The End of Immigration to the Cotton Fields," *Mississippi Valley Historical Review* 50 (March 1964), p. 600.
108 these partners included: Brandfon, *Cotton Kingdom,* p. 93.
109 "leave no stone unturned": Ibid., p. 153. Brandfon cites a series of letters between Fish, Percy, Percy's law partner William Yerger Scott, and U.S. Immigration Commissioner Frank Sargent on the subject in the early 1900s.
109 "the Delta's three": Ibid.
109 "the Yazoo Valley": Ibid., pp. 104–111; *The Call of the Alluvial Empire,* pamphlet, TUL.
109 over fifty in Greenville: Interview with Frank Hall, March 24, 1992; see also James Loewen, *The Mississippi Chinese,* 1971.
110 "eloquence on the subject": Ernesto R. Milani, "Sunnyside and the Italian Government," *Arkansas Historical Quarterly,* Summer 1991, p. 38; Schott, "John M. Parker of Louisiana," pp. 132–133.

110 An asthmatic and weak: Schott, "John M. Parker of Louisiana," p. 22.

110 "scarcely a genius": WAP to Camille Percy, January 9, 1905, PFP.

110 Governor Andrew Longino: Lewis Baker, *The Percys of Mississippi,* p. 25.

110 Parker also disdained: *JC-L,* November 1902, passim; Parker to Jacob Dickinson, February 25, 1924, Parker Papers, USLL; Roosevelt to Philip Bathel Stewart, November 4, 1902, in Elting E. Morison, ed., *Letters of Theodore Roosevelt* (Cambridge: Harvard University Press, 1951), vol. 3, pp. 377–380.

111 "made any direct request": Parker to Scott, May 30, 1904, quoted in Schott, p. 104; LP to Fish, November 25, 1905, PFP.

111 "in every way superior": *Manufacturer's Record,* April 7, 1904, p. 250.

111 forty-seven Delta: Randolph Boehm, "Mary Grace Quackenbos and the Federal Campaign Against Peonage: The Case of Sunnyside Plantation," *Arkansas Historical Quarterly,* Summer 1991, p. 41.

111 "Every step taken": Alfred Stone, "The Negro in the Yazoo-Mississippi Delta," pp. 236–278 passim.

112 "It is always difficult": Quoted in Rowland Berthoff, "Southern Attitudes Toward Immigration, 1865–1914," p. 346.

112 three Italians were lynched: Brandfon, "End of Immigration," p. 611.

112 "a very dirty": Report by Hall W. Sanders of Mississippi Justice Department, State Department peonage files, NA, RG 59, M862, reel 687, case 9500.

112 "I think we": J. Holland to LP, November 11, 1907; LP to Holland, October 15, 1907, PFP.

112 "*Don't Go*": *Don't Go to the Mississippi,* pamphlet, PFP.

112 a barn at Sunnyside: Boehm, "Mary Grace Quackenbos," p. 42.

112 "an unfriendly attitude": LP to Umberto Pierini, March 9, 1907, PFP.

112 he told other planters: LP to Will Dockery, March 8, 1907, PFP.

113 "Mr. Percy": LP to Ambassador Des Planches, February 14, 1907, PFP.

113 "The Italian immigrant": Quoted in Milani, "Sunnyside and the Italian Government," p. 36.

114 the first female U.S. attorney: Boehm, "Mary Grace Quackenbos," p. 45.

114 "endless and tedious": LP to Scott, n.d.

114 "Mr. Percy appears": Quackenbos to Attorney General, August 14, 1907, NA, RG 60, 100937.

115 "The whole future": Mark Sullivan, *Our Times: The United States 1900–1925,* vol. 4, *The War Begins, 1909–1914,* p. 386.

115 Roosevelt then spent: Schott, "John M. Parker of Louisiana," p. 125.

115 "at Sunnyside": Quoted in Boehm, "Mary Grace Quackenbos," p. 49.

115 "we have seen": Charles Russell, "Report on Peonage," 1908, Justice Department peonage file, NA, RG 60.

115 "I have a perfect": Quackenbos to LP, October 16, 1907, NA, RG 60.

115 "O. B. Crittenden": Ibid.

116 "rough with labor": LP to J. B. Ray, December 26, 1906, PFP.

116 "I would be willing": LP to H. B. Duncan, March 27, 1907, PFP.

116 "Those negroes": LP to J. R. Taylor, May 20, 1907, PFP.
116 "If conditions were": Sullivan, *The War Begins*, p. 384.
116 "see the South": Mark Sullivan, *Our Times: The United States, 1900–1925*, vol. 3, *Pre-War America*, pp. 128, 133, 136.
117 "I am counting on you": LP to H. Hawkings and LP to Lewis Levi, July 17, 1906.
117 "The fundamental trouble": LP to J. S. McNeilly, March 9, 1906, PFP.
117 "a positive unkindness": Albert K. Kirwan, *Revolt of the Rednecks*, pp. 144, 146.
118 "[t]hat man is a lover": *Outlook*, August 3, 1907, pp. 730–732.
118 "an intense southerner": LP to John Sharp Williams, November 30, 1907.
118 "Percy, by George": LP to WAP, April 19, 1907.
119 "I hailed": Roosevelt to LP, August 11, 1907, PFP.
119 "I believe he": LP to J. S. McNeilly, November 19, 1907.
119 "social acquaintance": LP to Lawrence Lewis, March 9, 1907, PFP.
119 Percy had urged Parker: LP to Parker, November 7, 1907, PFP.
119 Roosevelt did move: Schott, "John N. Parker of Louisiana,": p. 125; *NOT-P*, January 7, 1919.
119 Now Percy called: The following account of this meeting comes chiefly from two letters: LP to J. S. McNeilly, November 19, 1907, and LP to Roosevelt, November 13, 1907, Justice Department peonage files, NA, RG 60, 100937.
120 He then made: LP to Roosevelt, November 13, 1907, Justice Department peonage files, NA, RG 60, 100937.
120 "very amusing": Boehm, "Mary Grace Quackenbos," p. 57.
120 he gave Percy the answers: LP to J. S. McNeilly, November 19, 1907, PFP; LP to Roosevelt, November 13, 1907, Justice Department peonage files, NA, RG 60, 10937.
120 Then the president: LP to J. S. McNeilly, November 20, 1907.
120 It was part: Ibid.
120 "Fish are biting": LP to Dickinson, December 23, 1907, PFP.
121 "I am very uneasy": Roosevelt to Hart, January 13, 1908, Albert Bushnell Hart Papers, Harvard University, quoted by Boehm, "Mary Grace Quackenbos," p. 56.
121 Of 8 million: Brandfon, *Cotton Kingdom*, p. 104.
121 "Italian immigration has not": LP to M. B. Trezvant, December 26, 1913, PFP.
121 "There is no labor": LP to WAP, April 19, 1907, PFP.

Chapter Nine

122 "the representatives": W. E. B. Du Bois, *Souls of Black Folk*, edition contained in *Three Negro Classics: Up From Slavery; The Souls of Black Folk; The Autobiography of an Ex-Colored Man* (New York: Avon, 1976), p. 329.
122 "of the most reckless": William Hemphill, untitled ms., June 1905, Hemphill Family Papers, Special Collections, Duke University Library.
123 "The way these levee": Ibid.

123 "Kill a mule": For more details about levee conditions, see American Federation of Labor report of levee camp investigation, December 5, 1931; also Helen Boardman report on levee camps, August 1932, both in NAACP Papers, LC; Alan Lomax, *The Land Where the Blues Began*, pp. 212–255 passim.

123 "the negro to better": Lomax, p. 256.

123 In 1900: *Twelfth Census of the United States,* vol. 5, *Agriculture,* pp. 96–97, quoted in Willis, "On the New South Frontier," pp. 5, 9; interview with Willis, June 9, 1994.

123 Greenville had black policemen: Stone, "The Negro in the Yazoo-Mississippi Delta," p. 263.

123 "more firmly fixed": Quoted in Brandfon, *Cotton Kingdom,* p. 130.

123 In 1901: Stone kept careful records to see if the better treatment led to higher retention rates of sharecroppers. It did not. See Cobb, p. 105.

123 There, whites: William Holmes, "Whitecapping in Mississippi," pp. 165–185 passim.

124 "Today a Negro": Charles Fenn, *Ho Chi Minh,* p. 26, quoted in Wyn Craig Wade, *The Fiery Cross,* p. 203.

124 "The blacks were forced": Quoted in Cobb, p. 114.

124 "[t]he good [Negroes]": Kirwan, pp. 144, 146; McMillen, p. 224.

124 "to inflame the passions": LP to John Sharp Williams, no day, 1907, PFP.

124 "My dear Percy": Vardaman to LP, May 19, 1905, PFP.

125 "I wish you would give": John Sharp Williams to LP, April 20, 1919, Williams Collections, LC.

125 asked Percy to intervene: LP to Roosevelt, March 27, 1908, LP to Mrs. R. L. McLaurin, March 27, 1908, PFP; Baker, p. 35, p. 210n.

125 Despite opposition: LP to General J. Bell, November 2, 1909, PFP.

125 Once, at Percy's request: See LP to Fish, November 25, 1905, PFP.

125 "You cannot conciliate": William Holmes, "William Alexander Percy and the Bourbon Era in Mississippi Politics," p. 76.

126 "a life and death struggle": LP to Arthur Rice, June 18, 1910, Rice Papers, Mississippi State University Archives, quoted in Hester Ware, "A Study of the Life and Works of William Alexander Percy," M.A. thesis, p. 38.

127 "timid and third-rate": Percy, LL, p. 145.

127 "Crump": Quoted in Bertram Wyatt-Brown, *House of Percy,* p. 181.

127 "black as the night": Percy, *LL,* p. 146.

127 "Swinging perilously": William Sallis, "The Life and Times of LeRoy Percy," M.A. thesis, pp. 90–96.

128 "This is a contest": Quote kindly supplied by Bertram Wyatt-Brown.

128 "the Secret Caucus": Quoted in Kirwan, p. 197.

129 "suave and dignifiedly courteous": *NYT,* April 17, 1910.

129 "They say I'm": Sallis, "LeRoy Percy," p. 133.

129 while the Percys considered themselves: For this insight I thank William Armstrong Percy, a professor at the University of Massachusetts, Boston, interviewed October 11, 1995.

129 "looked over the": Percy, LL, p. 149.

129 "We are the low-brows": Kirwan, p. 212.

129 "When Father rose": Percy, LL, pp. 150–151.

130 "striped caterpillar": Kirwan, pp. 220–221.
130 In a final mockery: Percy, *LL,* p. 152.
130 "My dear Senator": Roosevelt to LP, November 11, 1911, PFP.
130 "will necessitate our killing": Sullivan, *Pre-War America,* p. 136.
131 "ordered . . . several hundred negroes": *NYT,* April 11, 1912.
131 "If I can keep": LP to W. W. Cain, November 19, 1912, quoted in Percy, *LL,* pp. 152–153.

CHAPTER TEN

132 More than 60 percent: Willis, "On the New South Frontier," p. 226; Ogden, p. 166.
132 The homicide rate: Hortense Powdermaker, *After Freedom,* p. 169.
132 More than 75 percent: Stone, "The Negro in the Yazoo-Mississippi Delta"; *Homicidal Deaths in Mississippi,* MDAH.
132 "Shootings were": Percy Bell, "Child of the Delta," unpublished ms., chap. 2, p. 3.
132 in 1914: Interview with Leila Clark Wynn, March 17, 1993.
133 "You are going among": Interview with Mrs. Pearl Pool Amos, January 27, 1993.
133 The biggest entertainers: Interview with Frank Hall, March 29, 1992; *Washington County the Pride of the Delta,* pamphlet, probably 1910, unpaginated, in Glen Allen (Mississippi) Public Library. LP to [illegible], November 22, 1906, PFP.
133 Enough Chinese lived: Interview with Frank Hall, March 29, 1992.
133 the two largest: *Washington County the Pride of the Delta,* pamphlet.
134 there was one club: Information kindly supplied by Bertram Wyatt-Brown.
134 "blacks tried to be": Interview with John Wiley, October 22, 1993.
134 knives, razors, and pistols: *History of Blacks in Greenville, 1863–1975;* Oral history of Daisy Green, 1975, MDAH; interview with Sylvia Jackson, February 20, 1993; interview with David Cober, February 22, 1993.
134 "passion corner": Powdermaker, p. 8; interview with Frank Hall; also, *Washington County the Pride of the Delta.*
134 In 1920 the city: "The Negro Common School, Mississippi," *Crisis,* December 1926, p. 91.
134 The teachers and facilities: Interview with Shelby Foote, March 9, 1994.
135 The city spent $17: "The Negro Common School, Mississippi," p. 91.
135 Greenville public schools: Interview with Leyser Holmes, March 2, 1993.
135 "I don't believe": Oral history of Daisy Green, 1975, p. 27.
135 "Our town has grown": LP to Lawrence McMeekin, PFP.
136 In addition, before settling: Interview with Maurice Sisson, October 22, 1993.
136 in 1923: Ezra Bowen, ed., *This Fabulous Century, 1920–1930,* pp. 105, 244.

136 "The ultimate development": Herbert Spencer, *Social Statics* (New York: D. Appleton, 1864), p. 79.

136 "flapper": Ellis Hawley, *The Great War and the Search for a Modern Order*, p. 112.

136 skirts touched the knee: Sullivan, *Pre-War America*, p. 337.

136 In 1919: Ronald Davis, ed., *The Social and Political Life of the 1920s*, p. 16.

137 "Many an American": Sullivan, *The War Begins*, p. 182.

137 150,000 people: Kenneth Harrell, "The Ku Klux Klan in Louisiana, 1920–1930," Ph.D. thesis, p. 82.

137 "Government conscripted public opinion": Robert Murray, *Red Scare: A Study in National Hysteria* (Minneapolis: University of Minnesota, 1955), p. 12.

138 a nation of informers: Wade, p. 149.

138 "If this country": LP to Dickinson, May 22, 1916, PFP.

138 "at the close": LP to Bolton Smith, June 19, 1918, PFP.

139 in none of the cases: Walter White, *A Man Called White*, p. 48; Tindall, *The Emergence of the New South*, pp. 152–154; O. A. Roberts, "The Elaine Race Riots of 1919," pp. 142–150.

139 "It is only a middling": Murray, pp. 67, 74.

139 "Free speech has been": Ibid.

139 "Silence the incendiary": Ibid.

139 "To hell with": Sullivan, *The Twenties*, p. 168.

139 the United States had two Communist parties: Murray, pp. 51–53.

139 "to maintain law and order": Ibid., p. 89.

139 "He . . . jumped off": Sullivan, *The Twenties*, see pp. 156–180 passim; Ralph Chaplin, *The Centralia Conspiracy*, p. 66.

140 "Palmer, do not let": Arthur Schlesinger, Jr., *The Crisis of the Old Order 1919–1933*, p. 42.

140 Hoover had a card file: Murray, p. 193.

140 "I myself am an American": William Katz, *The Invisible Empire*, p. 27; Murray, p. 219.

140 "fancied and certainly far distant": LP to John Sharp Williams, July 11, 1919, and LP to Pat Harrison, August 4, 1919, both in PFP.

141 "all Gods dead": F. Scott Fitzgerald, *This Side of Paradise* (New York: Scribners, 1920), p. 304.

141 "Dare to be Babbitt": Ronald Davis, p. 47.

141 "Why I Never Hire": Quoted in Ethan Morden, *That Jazz*, p. 103.

141 "the most average": Bowen, p. 218.

141 nearly 25 million tickets: Katz, p. 87.

141 "The real big purpose": Wade, p. 138.

141 "It is like": Ibid., p. 124.

142 "I am a fraternalist": Wade, p. 140; Chalmers, David, *Hooded Americanism*, p. 25.

142 he signed a contract: Stanley Coben, *Rebellion Against Victorianism*, p. 140; see also Tindall, George, *The Emergence of the New South*, p. 189.

142 "It is going to": Ibid., p. 191.

142 at least 3 million Americans: Ibid., p. 194.

142 It had 300,000 members: Harrell, "The Ku Klux Klan in Louisiana, 1920–1930," p. 66.

142 It seized control: Leonard Moore, "Historical Interpretations of the 1920s Klan," p. 352.

142 "The world broke": Quoted in Ronald Davis, p. 126.

CHAPTER 11

143 One night four: *History of Blacks in Greenville, 1863–1975,* pamphlet; also Irvin Mollison, "Negro Lawyers in Mississippi."

143 "Percy would almost": Interview with Gatewood Hamm, December 15, 1992; interview with Frank Hall, March 27, 1992.

144 "the inflammable, uneducated": Percy, *LL,* p. 228.

144 he called to his office: Percy, *LL,* p. 232.

144 "A Ku Klux orator": LP to Alfred Stone, February 27, 1922, PFP.

145 "Colonel Camp": No transcript of Camp's speech exists, but several newspaper reports, including the *Vicksburg Herald* of March 2, 1922, and the *Houston Chronicle* of March 19, 1922, paraphrased it. Percy also recounted portions of it in his speech and in letters he wrote in subsequent weeks, especially to H. H. Garwood, March 10, 1922, in PFP. So did the *GD-T, LL,* pp. 232–233, and Sallis, "The Life and Times of LeRoy Percy," pp. 150–154.

145 "Percy!": Sallis, p. 154.

145 "this eminent orator": *Houston Chronicle,* March 19, 1922.

146 "Be it resolved": Ibid.

146 "If we had Mr. Percy": E. M. Weddington et al. to LP, March 4, 1992, PFP.

146 "much stronger effect": For example, see B. McGee to LP, March 2, 1922; R. E. Montgomery to LP, March 9, 1922; William McGinley to LP, June 2, 1922; R. L. Tullis to LP, August 25, 1922; LP to Mattoon, Illinois, Knights of Columbus, August 23, 1922, all in PFP.

146 he contacted three newspaper: LP to Authors' Clipping Bureau, LP to Albert Romeike & Co., LP to Henry Romeike, Inc., all on March 7, 1922, PFP.

146 "The eagerness with which": LP to Miss A. D. Jenkins, July 21, 1922.

147 the night after being humiliated: LP to A. P. Wilkey, January 20, 1923.

147 "To all Flag": *Leland Enterprise,* March 18, 1922, PFP.

147 The town epitomized: Schott, "John M. Parker of Louisiana," p. 423.

148 more lynchings had occurred: William Hair, *The Kingfish and His Realm,* pp. 66, 130.

148 On August 24, 1992: Accounts of the Bastrop Klan come from Schott, "John M. Parker of Louisiana," esp. pp. 423–443; John Rogers, *The Murders of Mer Rouge;* Baker, *The Percys of Mississippi,* pp. 99–111; and *NOT-P* passim from September 1922 to January 1923.

148 "Louisiana has issued": *NOT-P,* April 29, 1922; *NOI,* May 2, 1922.

148 "a fight to the finish": *NOT-P,* October 31, 1922; Schott, "John M. Parker of Louisiana," p. 436.

148 Justice Department investigators: Schott, "John M. Parker of Louisiana," p. 431.

149 the Louisiana Klan invited: Thomas Dabney, *One Hundred Great Years,* pp. 415–422.

149 "You have been": Parker to LP, February 20, 1923, Parker Papers,

Special Collections, Dupre Library, University of Southwestern Louisiana, Lafayette.

149   "I am intensely uneasy": LP to Dickinson, May 14, 1923; see also LP to R. Purdy, May 14, 1923, PFP.

149   "Nothing that is founded": LP to Will McCoy, May 16, 1923.

150   "decade": Nancy McLean, *Behind the Mask of Chivalry* (New York: Oxford University Press, 1994), p. 17.

150   "Senator Percy has never": *GD-T,* June 21, 1923.

150   "All agree to stay": Undated note in Percy's handwriting, PFP.

151   "The day of kings": See copy of speech at People's Theater, April 23, 1923, PFP.

152   "[A] letter from you": LP to Alfred Stone, July 6, 1923, PFP.

152   "Senator Percy has no": Alfred Stone, *As to Senator Percy,* pamphlet, PFP.

152   One night in a rainstorm: Percy, *LL,* p. 236; *GD-T,* May 14, 1923.

152   his father likely suspected: Will Percy, "The Fifth Autumn," ms. in PFP, particularly when Will reports that his mother warned his father not to speak of sexuality.

152   "If anything happens": Percy, *LL,* p. 236.

152   "my personal injury": *GD-T,* May 14, 1923.

153   "friends among the Jews": *GD-T,* August 6, 1923.

153   Voter turnout: *GD-T,* August 8, 1923.

153   "A tremendous uproar": Percy, *LL,* pp. 238–241.

153   "Adah and Charlie": Ibid.

153   "I mourn the fact": William Howard Taft to LP, August 30, 1923, PFP.

154   "You can scarcely understand": LP to William Howard Taft, September 25, 1923.

154   "Biological laws show": Katz, *The Invisible Empire,* p. 87.

154   "the Klan virus": LP to Dickinson, May 14, 1923, PFP.

154   it elected the mayors: Wade, *The Fiery Cross,* p. 196.

155   the convention erupted in tumult: LP to WAP, June 16, 1924, PFP.

155   "mak[ing] it more difficult": LP to Dickinson, June 17, 1924, PFP.

155   Pattangall himself lost: Mordden, *That Jazz,* p. 64.

155   "I really believe": Lindsey to LP, April 25, 1925, PFP.

155   David Stephenson: John Braeman, Robert Bremner, and David Brody, eds., *Change and Continuity in Twentieth Century America: The Twenties* (Columbus: Ohio State University Press, 1968), pp. 240–41.

155   was routinely consulted: Mary Booze to John Overton, November 22, 1926, PFP.

CHAPTER TWELVE

156   "In physical and mental": "Eisenhower's General Lee," *Time,* September 25, 1944, p. 21.

157   "Levees designed to limit": E. F. Dawson, *Notes on the Mississippi River,* pp. 91–92.

158   "I was not accustomed": Speech by James Kemper to Round Table Club, April 8, 1937, New Orleans, Kemper Collection, Louisiana State Museum, Historical Division, New Orleans.

158   "The alluvial stream": *Government Control with Cooperation of Riparian States and Cities,* pamphlet (New Orleans, 1912), p. 17.

158   The *New York Times:* See *NYT,* March 28 through March 31, 1913.

158   "succeeded in getting": LP to WAP, December 27, 1916, PFP.

159   "The question of absolute": Quoted in Morgan, *Dams and Other Disasters,* pp. 260–261.

159   "[T]here is no doubt": Clarke Smith, *Survey for Spillways at or Near New Orleans,* p. 14.

159   "Whether their fears": J. A. Ockerson, *Outlets for Reducing Flood Heights,* pamphlet, reply to R. S. Taylor.

159   "are all contrary": *P&H,* p. 186.

160   The 1916 Mississippi River: HFCCH, pp. 1789–1792; James Kemper, *Floods in the Valley of the Mississippi,* p. 35.

160   He insisted that: *NOT,* April 5, 1927.

160   "The art of dam": Beach to Secretary of War, August 8, 1922, quoted in Morgan, p. 189.

160   "It is so much easier": Speech by Kemper to New Orleans Round Table, April 8, 1937, Kemper Collection, Louisiana State Museum, Historical Division, New Orleans.

161   the river rose unexpectedly: *NOT-P,* April 10, 1922.

161   the gauge at the foot: *NOT-P,* April 11, 1922.

161   in Louisiana a call: *NOT-P,* April 17, 1922.

162   "Everything possible": Wires to John Sharp Williams from Clearing House Association, J. D. Smythe, J. A. Hunt, and R. P. Crump, April 20, 1922, John Sharp Williams Papers, LC.

162   "People from Belzoni": Wire from Greenwood Chamber of Commerce to John Sharp Williams, April 25, 1922, John Sharp Williams Papers, LC.

162   "At Octavia there": John Klorer, "Report of the Inspection of the Levee Line to Mayor Andrew McShane," April 21, 1922, NOCA.

163   Three thousand city workers: Ibid.

163   "We are in": J. E. Weldon to John Parker, April 30, 1922; Parker to Weldon, May 2, 1922, Parker Papers, Special Collections, Dupre Library, University of Southwestern Louisiana, Lafayette.

163   On Esplanade Street: Interview with Louis Claverie, February 10, 1993; interview with Walter Barnett, November 15, 1992.

163   The flooding of Arkansas City: Cf., for example, *NOI,* April 10, 1922; *NOT-P,* April 10 and 11, 1922.

163   "I cannot say": Cf. *NOI,* April 14, 1922, to *NOT-P,* April 15, 1922.

164   he notified all city workers: *NOT-P,* April 18, 1922.

164   "Notify the barge line": *NOT-P,* April 25, 1922.

164   "The levees are better": *NOI,* April 19, 1922.

164   the levee abruptly caved: *NOT-P,* April 29, 1922.

164   "As for the high water": *NOT-P,* April 27, 1922.

165   "the bight of": *Report of Board of [Louisiana] State Engineers, 1922 to 1924,* pp. 58–59.

165   less than an hour: *NOI,* April 29, 1922.

165   By luck the Poydras crevasse: Testimony of John Klorer, 67th Cong., December 11, 12, 13, 14, 1922, at HFCCH; report of Board of Louisiana State Engineers, 1924, p. 58.

166 it had broken records: Kemper, *Floods in the Valley,* p. 36.

166 "A situation has": Walter Sillers, Sr., to Col. C. H. West, October 20, 1925; Sillers to LP, May 31, 1927, Sillers Papers, Delta State University Library.

166 "The Mississippi River Commission": Kemper testimony, HFCCH, p. 1710.

166 "[W]e are in reality": W. L. Head to Mississippi River Commission, March 8, 1927, NA, RG 77, case 2620, entry 521.

167 twelve floods: Undated (probably 1923) engineering report of Safe River Committee, NOCA.

168 "Some one has apparently": Beach to Harold Newman, May 12, 1922, copy in Edwin Broussard Papers, Special Collections, Dupre Library, University of Southwestern Louisiana, Lafayette.

168 When the criticism did not stop: Transcript of comments by Beach at hearings in New Orleans, August 20 and 21, 1922, Corps of Engineers Papers, NA, RG 77, entry 521; see also summary of correspondence with New Orleans Association of Commerce, NA, RG 77, entry 521.

168 "If it were my property": Ibid.

168 LeRoy Percy maneuvered: Wire from LP to Parker, August 19, 1922, Parker Papers, USL.

168 Engineers called each other: Quoted in *House Flood Control Committee Hearings,* 67th Cong., December 11–14, 1922, p. 164.

168 Percy had the Greenville: See, for example, log of correspondence under title "Flood Protection Activities of the New Orleans Association of Commerce," NA, RG 77, case 2891.

CHAPTER THIRTEEN

173 "Then God, our Lord": Garcilaso de la Vega, *The Florida of the Incas,* quoted in H. C. Frankenfield, "The Floods of 1927 in the Mississippi Basin," *Monthly Weather Review,* Supplement 29 (Washington, D.C., 1927), p. 10.

175 "to prevent the destructive": *Annual Report of the Chief of Engineers for 1926,* p. 1793.

175 "There was needed": Ibid., p. 16.

175 Only six times: John Lee, "A Flood Year on the Mississippi," *Military Engineer,* July-August 1928.

175 In October 1926: Ibid.

177 "It is no unusual": Report of Charles Ellet, reprinted in *U.S. House of Representatives Documents,* vol. 24, 63rd Cong., doc. 918, pp. 32–120.

178 the flood crest poured: D. O. Elliott, *The Improvement of the Lower Mississippi River for Flood Control and Navigation,* vol. 1, p. 91.

178 The new crest: Ibid.

178 This does not mean: Ibid., p. 92.

CHAPTER FOURTEEN

180   In Fulton, Kentucky: *MC-A,* January 4, 1927.
180   "You haint' got": *JC-L,* February 2, 1927.
180   "The Local Klan": *JC-L,* February 18, 1927.
180   Several farmers were indicted: *JC-L,* February 3, 1927.
180   Delta & Pine Land Company: *MC-A,* December 9, 1926.
181   "Cornets, trombones, bass horns": *NOT-P,* March 1 and 2, 1927.
181   "From the Rockies": Ibid.
181   That crest took: Frankenfield, "The Floods of 1927," p. 28.
181   It would remain in flood: Ibid., p. 37.
182   the White and the Little Red: *NOT,* February 3, 1927; *JC-L,* February 4, 1927.
182   A week later: *NOT,* February 14, 1927; *JC-L,* February 19, 1927.
182   "Although river stages": *NOI,* February 10, 1927.
182   March opened: *MC-A,* March 1 and 3, 1927.
182   "The virtual flood": *JC-L,* March 15 and 16, 1927.
182   Between March 17: *NOI,* March 18 and 21, 1927.
182   In January: J. S. Allen to Walter Sillers, Sr., March 1, 1927, Walter Sillers, Jr., Papers, Delta State University Library, Clarksdale, Mississippi.
182   On March 23: Minutes of Board of Mississippi Levee Commissioners, March 23, 1927, Mississippi Levee Board, Greenville.
183   "If the river": Associated Press wire report, March 24, 1927.
183   "all the water in sight": Isaac Cline, *Storms, Floods, and Sunshine,* p. 124.
184   One camp operator: Lomax, *The Land Where the Blues Began,* pp. 225–229.
184   On April 1: Lee, "A Flood Year on the Mississippi"; Frankenfield, "The Floods of 1927," p. 29.
184   "higher ups": *JC-L,* February 5 and April 7, 1927; *MC-A,* February 5 and April 7, 1927.
184   "concentration camps": Walter Sillers, Sr., to W. L. Thompson, September 20, 1927, Sillers Papers, Delta State University Library; Lee, "A Flood Year on the Mississippi."
184   In New Orleans hundreds of men: Marcel Garsaud to James Thomson, March 16, 1927, NOCA.
185   Danger areas included: Klorer to Thomson, April 10, 1927, NOCA.
185   "It is apparent": James Kemper to Walter Parker, February 1, 1927, NOCA.
185   Engineers sounding the bottom: *MC-A,* March 30, 1927.
185   Already the Yazoo: *MC-A,* March 28, 30, and 31, 1927.
185   "All levees are": *JC-L,* April 5, 1927.
185   "No serious trouble": *SBV,* March 26, 1927.
185   "report on relief": John Lee to Adjutant General, April 18, 1927, NA, RG 94.
185   Mississippi Governor Dennis Murphree: Malin Craig to Adjutant General, April 6, 1927, NA, RG 200.
185   a storm March 31: *MC-A,* April 8, 1927.

186 "The outlook was gloomy": *MC-A*, April 8, 1927.
186 "Eleven Killed Many Hurt": *NYT*, April 9, 1927.
187 the Canadian River flood: *NOI*, April 10, 1927.
187 As of April 9, 1927: Frankenfield, "The Floods of 1927," p. 28.
187 "We are in condition": *MC-A*, April 12, 1927; *JC-L*, April 10, 1927.
187 "From the forecast": Guy Deano to John Klorer, April 14, 1927, NOCA.
188 a levee in Arkansas was dynamited: *GD-T*, April 14, 1927; *NYT*, April 14, 1927.
188 "Great Flood Peril": *NYT*, April 15, 1927.
188 "The roaring Mississippi": *MC-A*, April 15, 1927.
188 "Every Available House": T. H. Caraway to Dwight Davis, April 14, 1927, NA, RG 94.
189 In the ten years: "Report of the Superintendent of the Sewerage and Water Board on the April 15 Flood," p. 10, NOCA.
189 Between 10 and 12: Ball diaries, April 15 and 16, 1927, MDAH; *NYT*, April 14–16, 1927.

CHAPTER FIFTEEN

190 In 1882: HFCCH, Committee Doc. 1, p. 25.
190 The levee itself: "The Mississippi Valley Flood, 1927," *Bulletin of the American Railway Association* 29, no. 297 (July 1927), pp. 9, 29.
192 "They gave me": Interview with William Jones, March 2, 1993.
192 "An attempt to dynamite": *GD-T*, April 6 and 16, 1927.
193 "Nothing could be": LP to Sedgwick, April 27, 1922.
193 Bill Jones remembered: Interview with William Jones, March 2, 1993.
193 "They had a bunch": Statement of Duncan Cope, "The Flood of 1927," Mississippi Public Television, transcript in MDAH.
194 "There has never been": For example, see *House Flood Control Committee Hearings,* 64th Cong., March 8, 1916, p. 26.
194 "We feel confident": *MC-A,* April 17, 1927.
194 "At Forest City": Caraway to Davis, April 18, 1927, NA, RG 94.
194 "absolutely without food": Mississippi Flood Control Association to Davis, April 18, 1927, NA, RG 94.
194 "Seven more die": *NYT,* April 17, 1927.
195 "the greatest flood in history": Wire from T. R. Buchanan to James Fieser, April 16, 1927, RCP.
195 "This is the psychological": LP to Dennis Murphree, March 24, 1927, PFP.
195 Murphree had sent: Kenneth McKellar to Dwight Davis, April 15, 1927, NA, RG 94.
195 "The levee board was": Statement of Vivian Broom, "The Flood of 1927," Mississippi Public Television, transcript in MDAH.
195 "They kept sending": Statement of Florence Sillers Ogden, "The Flood of 1927," Mississippi Public Television, transcript in MDAH.
195 If a black man refused: There are at least three confirmed incidents in Mississippi, Louisiana, and Arkansas in which blacks who refused to work on levees were killed. See *Louisiana Weekly,* March 14, 1927; *GD-T,* July 6, 1927.

196   "The first of April": Interview with Wynn Davis, February 28, 1993.

196   "They gave me charge": Statement of Frank Hall, "The Flood of 1927," Mississippi Public Television, transcript in MDAH.

196   levees averaged eighteen inches: *GD-T,* April 20, 1927.

196   that same day, April 19: *MC-A,* April 19, 1927; *NYT,* April 19, 1927.

197   Thirty years earlier: *MC-A,* April 22, 1927.

197   "The apparent slope": Report of Charles Ellet, reprinted in *House Documents,* vol. 24, 63rd Cong., doc. 918, p. 45.

197   Missouri Pacific Railroad bridge: *MC-A,* April 22, 1927.

198   In 1927 the Mississippi River: Testimony of Charles Potter, *HFCCH,* p. 1874; James Kemper, *HFCCH,* p. 2869; "The Mississippi Valley Flood, 1927," *Bulletin of the American Railway Engineering Association* 29, no. 297 (July 1927).

198   one and a half feet higher: Interview with Frank Hall, March 27, 1992.

198   pumped billions of gallons: J. S. Allen to Major J. C. H. Lee, June 23, 1927; "High Water Report East Central Sector," Mississippi Levee Board, Greenville, Mississippi.

198   On April 19: *NYT,* April 20, 1927.

198   "Stormy tonight": Ball diaries, April 20, 1927, MDAH.

198   "I'd never seen": Statement of Florence Sillers Ogden, "The Flood of 1927," Mississippi Public Television, transcript in MDAH.

199   "Is it as bad": Ibid.

199   "Forces were redoubled": *JC-L,* April 21, 1927.

199   upriver from Mounds Landing: Lee, "A Flood Year on the Mississippi," p. 112; *MC-A,* April 20 and 21, 1927.

199   "You get all": Interview with M. L. Payne, March 4, 1993.

199   "felt like jelly": Interview with William Jones, March 2, 1993.

199   "It was just boiling": Interview with Moses Mason, March 1, 1993.

200   "From dark until dawn": Lee, "A Flood Year on the Mississippi," p. 112.

200   "All night long": Statement of Florence Sillers Ogden, "The Flood of 1927," Mississippi Public television, transcript in MDAH.

200   "to arouse the labor": *GD-T,* April 21, 1927.

200   "The negroes ran": E. C. Sanders, "Report of Activities at Camp Rex," contained within *Report of Flood Relief Expedition,* Mississippi National Guard, Office of the Adjutant General, MDAH.

201   The river was overflowing: *GD-T,* April 21, 1927.

201   "You could see": Interview with William Jones, March 2, 1993.

201   "We can't hold it": A. G. Paxton, *Three Wars and a Flood,* p. 24.

201   "just seemed to move": Diary of Louise Henry Cowan, William Alexander Percy Library, Greenville, Mississippi.

201   "I took him": John Hall, Jr., oral history project taped April 13, 1977, William Alexander Percy Library, Greenville, Mississippi.

201   "I was . . .": Taped interview kindly shared by Pete Daniels with author.

201   "Levee broke": Wire from John Lee to Edgar Jadwin, April 21, 1927, NA, RG 94.

CHAPTER SIXTEEN

202 "Thousands of workers": *MC-A*, April 22, 1927.
202 "Refugees coming into Jackson": *JC-L*, April 24, 1927.
202 Judge R. C. Trimble: *JC-L*, April 22, 1927.
202 "estimated that more": *JC-L*, April 24, 1927.
202 "No lives were": Paxton, "National Guard Activities in Connection with Levee Fight and Flood Relief Expedition, Greenville, Mississippi," *Report of Flood Relief Expedition,* Mississippi National Guard, Office of the Adjutant General, MDAH; see Associated Press report in *Washington Post,* April 25, 1927; *JC-L*, April 22, 1927; Fred Chaney, "A Refugee's Story," unpublished ms., MDAH; interview with Frank Hall, March 27, 1992.
202 "We had a lead": Interview with Frank Hall, March 27, 1992.
202 The water's force: Oscar Johnston to H. W. Lee, Fine Cotton Spinners and Doublers Association, May 31, 1927, D&PLCP. The Delta & Pine Land Co., the largest cotton plantation in the world, operated the land at the site of the break. Johnston was its chief executive officer.
203 "Let's put all": Interview with William Jones, March 2, 1993.
203 "It was as if": *MC-A,* April 22, 1927; see also article by Floyd Clay, *MC-A,* July 22, 1973.
203 "[T]he water was leaping": Oral history of E. M. Barry, MDAH.
204 "An airplane kept": *Vicksburg Evening Post,* September 15, 1985.
204 "the flood water approach": Louise Henry Cowan, "Essay on Greenville, 1927," WAPL.
204 "in waves five or six": Statement of D. S. Flanagan, "The Flood of 1927," Mississippi Public Television, transcript in MDAH.
204 "When that levee broke": Statement of Sam Huggins, "The Flood of 1927," Mississippi Public Television, transcript in MDAH.
204 the water moved: Interview with Newman Bolls, March 2, 1993.
205 animals by the hundreds: Chaney, "A Refugee's Story."
205 "23 white women": *JC-L*, April 26, 1927.
205 "At 9:00, we could": Chaney, "A Refugee's Story."
205 "The water just came": Interview with L. T. Wade, "The Flood of 1927," Mississippi Public Television, transcript in MDAH.
205 "The situation is": *MC-A*, April 22, 1927.
205 "For God's Sake": *NOT-P*, April 23, 1927.
206 Mounds Landing was: American National Red Cross, *The Mississippi Flood Disaster of 1927: Official Report of the Relief Operations,* p. 47.
206 Within three hours: Chaney, "A Refugee's Story."
206 Levee board engineers: *JC-L*, April 26, 1927.
207 "The water was just rolling": Interview with Frank Hall, March 27, 1992.
207 "Everybody run": Oral history of Levye Chapple, transcript in MDAH.
207 "You could see waves": Interview with Lamar Britton, March 1, 1993.
207 "The water was coming": Statement of Mrs. Henry Ransom, "The Flood of 1927," Mississippi Public Television, transcript in MDAH.

207 Up to ten feet: Connolly to Gen. Edgar Jadwin, April 23, 1927, NA, RG 77.
208 "Louisiana waits": *MC-A,* April 23, 1927.
208 The guards: *JC-L,* April 18, 1927; *NYT,* April 19, 1927.
208 "Coolidge in Conference": *NOT,* April 23, 1927.

CHAPTER SEVENTEEN

213 FRENCH DOMINATION: George Reynolds, *Machine Politics in New Orleans, 1904–1926,* p. 11.
213 faux stone fronts: S. Frederick Starr, *Southern Comfort,* p. 261.
213 Modern poker: S. Frederick Starr, *New Orleans Unmasqued,* pp. 79, 142.
213 their own symphony: Starr, *New Orleans Unmasqued,* p. 127.
213 Women lowered baskets: Oral history of Marc Antony, FC.
214 "delight": Sherwood Anderson, "Certain Things Last," reprinted in *NYT,* December 29, 1992.
214 Billy Cabildo's: Oral history of Albert Goldstein, FC.
214 lavish parties: Oral history of Leon Mann, FC.
214 Well-dressed doormen: Oral history of Virginia Barnett, FC.
214 "Yeah, music": Quotations from Louis Armstrong exhibit, New Orleans Museum of Art, January to April 1996.
215 "without a doubt": David Cohn, *Where I Was Born and Raised,* pp. 61–62.
215 "Jazz is all": Quotations from Louis Armstrong exhibit.
215 "It was only": Quoted in Al Rose, *Storyville, New Orleans* (Tuscaloosa: University of Alabama Press, 1974), p. 94.
215 a drugstore sold cocaine: Ibid.
215 "Mardi Gras runs": Interview with Mrs. Ford T. Hardy, February 11, 1993.
216 "There is perhaps": Perry Young, *The Mistick Krewe,* pp. 212–213.
216 "[Carnival] queens are": Walker Percy, "New Orleans, Mon Amour," *Harper's Magazine,* September 1968, p. 90.
216 "Yet he values": Interview with Walter Barnett, January 28, 1993.
217 "Often the men": Interview with Mrs. F. Evans Farwell, January 23, 1993.
217 Every Rex since 1888: Phyllis Raabe, "Status and Its Impact: New Orleans Carnival, the Social Upper Class, and Upper Class Power," Ph.D. diss., p. 63.
217 the disease had killed: John R. Kemp, ed., *Martin Behrman of New Orleans, Memoirs of a City Boss,* p. 270.
217 "were largely formulated": Quoted in Landry, *History of the Boston Club,* pp. 115, 211; Angelo Miceli, *The Pickwick Club of New Orleans,* p. 70.
218 "he spoke": Interview with Ruth Dreyfous, January 5, 1993.
218 "Mother used": Ibid.
218 Rex went right on by: Oral history of Charles Kahn, FC.
218 Baron de Rothschild: Robert Tallant, *Mardi Gras as It Was,* pp. 179–180.

218   "spirit of noblesse oblige": Landry, p. 7.
219   "The aggregated amount": LP to Charles Claiborne, April 9, 1917, PFP.
219   "there is a discrepancy": M. Waterman to LP, January 9, 1923, PFP.
219   New Orleans had nearly: As measured by debits to individual accounts, cited in *Association of Commerce News Bulletin,* January 23, 1923, ACP.
219   "a compulsory reduction": LP to L. M. Pool, October 12, 1926; LP to Fenner, October 14, 1926, PFP.
220   payments on bonds absorbed: *Association of Commerce News Bulletin,* January 9, 1923, ACP; Bureau of Governmental Research (a local group), 1936 report, Special Collections, Earl Long Library, University of New Orleans.
220   the city could issue: The Sewerage and Water Board had the legal authority to issue bonds, but members of the Board of Liquidation automatically sat on it also, so in practice their approval was needed even for these bonds.
221   Twenty-four of: Raabe, "Status and Its Impact," pp. 140–141.
221   "ultra-exclusive": Young, p. 208.
221   the photograph of the Mystic Club queen: *NOT-P,* February 27, 1927.

CHAPTER EIGHTEEN

222   "Flood Water Is": *SBV,* January 1, 1927.
223   "Thomson was an": Interview with Charles Dufour, December 20, 1992.
223   a dinner was given: *NOI,* February 11, 1927.
223   The weakest levees: Memo from the Mississippi River Flood Control Association to Army Liaison Office and Red Cross, April 23, 1927, RC.
223   "it offers protection": See undated report (probably late January or early February 1927) for the National Flood Commission, NOCA.
223   "was based on": See Kemper to Walter Parker, February 1, 1927; Kemper to Thomson, February 4 and March 27, 1927, NOCA; report on levees, unsigned, March 16, 1927, NOCA; Kemper speech to Round Table Club, April 8, 1937, Kemper Collection, Louisiana State Museum, Historical Division, New Orleans.
224   "Serious settlements": Report by S. Young, chief engineer of the Dock Board, to Garsaud, March 12, 1927, NOCA.
224   "decided improvement": Klorer to Thomson, April 10, 1927, NOCA. The date is misleading; the report covers an earlier inspection.
224   twenty-four-hour patrols: *SBV,* April 9, 1927.
225   the Red Cross began: Henry Baker to Robert Bondy, May 3, 1927; two undated reports by Mrs. Charles Buck, General Chairman Women's Division Emergency Flood Relief; Ben Beekman to W. P. Simpson, July 22, 1927; all in RCP.
225   "the most insatiable": Schoot, "John M. Parker of Louisiana," Ph.D. diss., p. 104; Dabney, *One Hundred Great Years,* p. 462.
226   "to refrain from publishing": Reports of the Publicity Department,

December 16, 1924; December 18, 1925; October 10, 1926; March 6, 1927; Charles Dunbar to three publishers, October 12, 1926; all in ACP.

226 "to avoid": Thomson general letter to members of the Safe River Committee, April 8, 1927.

226 "River Warning": See *NOT, NOI, NOT-P,* and *NOS,* April 9, 1927.

226 "The next boat": *NOT-P,* April 23, 1927.

226 news, and fear, spread: Interview with Dufour.

226 Estimates of the number of dead: John Weems, *A Weekend in September* (College Station: Texas A&M University Press, 1993), pp. 114–115.

226 He had refused: Cline, p. 114.

227 "You're jeopardizing lives": Ibid., pp. 197–200.

227 "Heavy Rains Raise River": *NOI,* April 14, 1927.

227 Thomson had talked: *NOT,* April 28, 1928.

227 "The Emergency Committee": Guy Deano to John Klorer, April 14, [1927?], NOCA.

228 Albert Baldwin Wood: Sebastian Junger, "The Pumps of New Orleans," *Invention and Technology* (Fall 1992), p. 47.

228 "I have been in": Kemper to Garsaud, December 24, 1925, NOCA.

229 "If the levees up river": Minutes of Orleans Levee Board, April 20, 1927.

229 the U.S. Surgeon General refused: Kemp, p. 143.

229 Dr. William Mercer: Landry, p. 105.

230 "You all make": Pierce Butler, *The Unhurried Years,* p. 128, 162.

230 "really quite off": Pierce Butler, *Laurel Hill and Later,* p. 102.

230 Butler almost never: Interview with Laura Bayon, February 10, 1993.

230 Butler's wife: Ibid.

230 Butler grew tired: Interview with Harry Kelleher, December 1, 1992; Kelleher himself was both Rex and president of the Boston Club; his daughter was Queen of Comus.

230 "He was an unattractive": Interview with Herman Kohlmayer, December 10, 1992.

231 "I really want": Ibid.

231 "elegant": *NOT-P,* January 12, 1996.

231 Butler turned to the men: The account of this meeting comes from several interviews, including those with Pearl Pool Amos, January 27, 1993; Meyer Dressner, February 2, 1993; and Charles Dufour, November 26, 1992. Another account is found in a transcript of the *Proceedings of the Mississippi River Commission for 1926–1928,* pp. 4355–4411, at the Humphreys Engineering Center, Ft. Belvoir, Virginia. See also minutes of the meetings about the flood emergency and what became Jim Butler's quasi-official role, kept by Harry Caplan, secretary to the president of the Canal Bank, in the Caplan Papers.

The Caplan Papers, hereafter CP, are careful minutes of the executive committee of the Citizens Flood Relief Committee. The papers also include minutes of the full committee and minutes of other related meetings, as well as documents, correspondence, and news clippings. Occasionally, the minutes provide actual stenographic transcripts of the most important meetings.

231 The Illinois Central: See ongoing fight between Hecht and Bernhard related in Association of Commerce minutes—for example, April 21, 1927, and July 20, 1927, ACP. Also Walter Parker to Alfred Danziger, July 27, 1927, NOCA.

231 "The people of New Orleans": Interview with Pearl Pool Amos, January 27, 1993; see also Isaac Cline, *Storms, Floods and Sunshine*, pp. 197–200.

231 As a boy: Butler, *The Unhurried Years*, p. 73.

232 "I believe": See above, note for p. 353 regarding account of this meeting.

232 "This is a wonderful": Interview with Charles Dufour, April 1, 1993.

232 As soon as O'Keefe: John Legier to Arthur O'Keefe, May 12, 1926, NOCA.

232 the levee board had just: CP.

232 A large Pythian convention: Testimony of Leondard Kieffer, *HFCCH*, p. 255.

232 "more than five inches": See *NOT* and *NOT-P*, April 16, 1927.

233 "Mr. and Mrs. James": *NOT*, April 16, 1927.

CHAPTER NINETEEN

234 In St. Bernard: Background on St. Bernard comes chiefly from interviews with William Hyland, January 4, 1993; Matthew Reuter, February 11, 1993; Lena Torres and Manny Fernandez, December 10, 1992; and Herman Kohlmayer, December 30, 1992.

235 544 were swamp or marsh: "Historical Sketch, Inventory of the Parish Archives," 1938, p. 6, NOCA.

235 Louisiana produced more fur: Saxon, p. 331; *SBV*, August 21, 1926, cited in Glenn Jeansonne, *Leander Perez*, p. 32.

235 150 pelts a day: Description of trapping and Delacroix Island come chiefly from interviews with Joseph Campo, November 23, 1992; Lily Silvera Lopez Raiborn, November 18, 1992; William Hyland, January 4, 1993; and Matthew Reuter, February 11, 1993.

236 "Meraux had a studied": Interview with William Hyland, January 4, 1993.

236 the 1905 yellow fever: *NOT-P*, October 7, 1938; *NOI*, October 7, 1938; *SBV*, October 9, 1938.

236 "I used to study": Interview with a former Meraux employee who required anonymity, February 11, 1993.

236 the largest taxpayer: *SBV*, January 29, 1924.

236 Château des Fleurs: Interview with former St. Bernard Parish employee who desires anonymity, February 11, 1993.

236 "Every one of those": Interview with Val Dauterive, February 16, 1993.

237 a caravan of three: *SBV*, April 21, 1923; testimony quoted in *SBV*, May 19, 1923.

237 "I heard you take": Memo of agent A. Needham, May 29, 1925, Justice Department records, NA, RG 60, file reference 23-32-105.

237 Meraux promised him: Justice Department records, NA, RG 60, file reference 23-32-105; Ferdinand Estopinal to Assistant Attorney Gen-

eral, June 29, 1926; Estopinal to Attorney General, August 10 and September 13, 1926, Justice Department records, NA.

237 "He had absolutely no": Interview with Kohlmayer.

238 "Molero was very": Interview with New Orleans attorney who prefers anonymity, December 29, 1992.

238 "the Trappers' War": For the best summary of the Trappers' War, see Jeansonne.

238 until three conditions were met: testimony of Col. Charles Potter, president of the Mississippi River Commission, HFCCH, p. 2069.

239 "Residents had been warned": NYT, April 19, 1927.

239 Butler would even be authorized: Irving Gumbel to Thomson, April 22, 1927, NOCA.

239 "Rumors!": See NOI, NOT, and NOT-P, April 22, 1927.

240 "New Orleans is not affected": NOT, April 21, 1927.

240 "We have never seen": Owen testimony, HFCCH, p. 161.

240 "unless there were": NOT, April 23, 1927.

241 Thomson met with Coolidge: Ibid.; CP, same date.

241 They increased to 500: NOT, April 22, 1927.

241 6 million sandbags: Quoted in Lyle Saxon, Father Mississippi, p. 317.

241 Business in New Orleans: Quoted in ibid.

241 "Maj. Allen said": AP story as run in the Washington Post, April 25 and 26, 1927.

242 "Do you know": Interview with Betty Carter, April 5, 1995.

242 A reporter and photographer: NOT-P, April 25, 1927.

242 report on Governor Simpson's: NOS, NOT, both on April 25, 1927.

242 Their answers: NOT-P, January 9, 1928, and April 27, 1927; NOT, April 22 and 27, 1927.

242 Manuel Molero: NOT, April 27, 1927; Cline, p. 199.

242 O'Keefe, Pool, and Dufour: NOT, April 27, 1927; NOT-P, April 27, 1927.

243 "The possibility of danger": NOS, April 24, 1927.

243 "Pool pleaded with me": Cline, pp. 197–200.

243 "You may go": Ibid.

244 it was "too confidential": Memo from Mississippi Flood Control Association, Office of Adjutant General, April 23, 1927, NA, RG 94.

244 Meanwhile, Butler, Hecht, and Dufour: See narrative in CP for April 24 through April 27, 1927.

CHAPTER TWENTY

245 the river began seeping: Saxon, pp. 322, 324; interview with Harry Kelleher.

245 "hysterical": Testimony of Col. Lewis, Mississippi River Commission hearing at New Orleans, July 8, 1927, NA, RG 77.

246 "for the psychological effect": Testimony of Col. Charles Potter, president of the Mississippi River Commission, HFCCH, p. 2069.

246 "In order to avoid": Copy in CP, also NOT, NOT-P, April 27, 1927.

246 Mayor O'Keefe and fifty: The Caplan Papers are the chief source for the account of this crucial meeting. See also lengthy stories in all four

New Orleans papers over a period of several days, esp. *NOT-P, NOT, NOS,* and *NOI,* all April 27, 1927, for account of the events.

247 It stipulated three things: Ibid.

248 Of the fifty-one other: See list of Boston Club members as of December 1, 1927, available in TUL; see also Landry.

248 "I have before me": See CP; also *NOT-P, NOT, NOS,* and *NOI,* all April 27, 1927.

248 "Where do they get": *SBV,* April 30, 1927.

249 "Let's sleep on our shotguns": Ibid.

249 "get proper compensation": *NOT-P, NOT, NOI, NOS,* April 27, 1927; *MC-A,* April 26, 1927; *JC-L,* April 27 and 28, 1927.

249 "They didn't want": CP; *NOT-P, NOT, NOI, NOS,* April 27, 1927; see also *MC-A,* April 26, 1927; *JC-L,* April 27 and 28, 1927.

250 "The citizens and taxpayers": Perez and Nunez to Secretary of War, April 26, 1927, Adjutant General records, NA, RG 94.

250 "vigorously protest[ing]": CP.

251 "The relief to be": CP, April 26, 1927.

251 the representatives of St. Bernard: Account of these several discussions are most detailed in CP, in effect an abbreviated transcript, with other information in the *NOT-P, NOT, NOI, NOS,* all April 27, 1927; and *SBV,* April 20, 1927.

251 "What else can we do": *MC-A,* April 28, 1927.

252 Inside the city: *NOT,* April 27, 1927.

252 a wire from the secretary of war: Davis to Simpson, Adjutant General records, NA, RG 94.

252 "Everything is set": CP.

252 "I have nothing to do": Oral history of Turner Catledge, HHPL.

253 The news was kept from Simpson: *MC-A,* April 27, 1927.

253 "The Mississippi River Commission": *NOT,* April 27, 1927.

253 "He was on": Interview with Leon Sarpy, February 18, 1993.

254 Molero was in Delacroix Island: *NOT,* April 28, 1927.

254 "We will not reveal": *MC-A,* April 28, 1927.

254 The council adopted it: Pool to O'Keefe, April 27, 1928, NOCA.

254 "Trade Shows Flood": *NOT,* April 28, 1927.

254 "Contrary to disquieting rumors": Butler to long list of banks, April 28, 1927, copy in CP.

254 "I would suggest": Ibid.

254 That night: Oral history of Mrs. Gordon Wilson, FC.

255 On the levee: AP story published widely—for example, in *Dallas Morning News,* April 29, 1927.

255 "That's where": *MC-A,* April 29, 1927.

255 The aerial photographs: Interview with Mrs. Rose Monroe, February 17, 1993.

256 "Only the privileged": Saxon, p. 322.

256 no representative: *SBV,* May 7, 1927.

256 Emergency Clearing House: Minutes of Emergency Clearing House Publicity Committee, April 29, 1927, CP.

257 39 tons: Report by Garsaud, CP.

257 "We're letting 'em": Saxon, p. 339.

257 "Gentlemen, you have seen": Ibid., p. 324.

257   "the greatest flood": Isaac Cline, "Special Flood and Warning Bulletin," May 1, 1927, Louisiana Collection, TUL.

CHAPTER TWENTY-ONE

261   "is a strange mixture": Calvin Coolidge, *The Autobiography of Calvin Coolidge*, pp. 228–229.
261   "There is no right": Donald McCoy, *Calvin Coolidge*, pp. 119–121; Mark Sullivan, *The Twenties*, pp. 65–66.
262   "The power and": Coolidge, p. 190.
262   "Unprecedented floods": Coolidge Papers, LC.
262   "a dreamer": Richard Smith, *An Uncommon Man*, p. 107.
263   "the intense repression": Craig Lloyd, *Aggressive Introvert*, p. 4.
263   "Leave me not": George Nash, *The Life of Herbert Hoover*, p. 15.
263   "a kind of complex": Quoted in Joan Hoff Wilson, *Herbert Hoover*, p. 11.
263   "lifetime ambition": Smith, p. 30.
263   "I would rather": Nash, p. 345.
263   "the highest paid man": Quoted in Carol Wilson, *Herbert Hoover*, p. 52.
263   "a wizard of finance": Nash, p. 411.
263   At forty he owned: Schlesinger, *The Crisis of the Old Order 1919–1933*, pp. 79–85 passim.
263   "run through his profession": Joan Hoff Wilson, p. 23.
264   "The American is": Hoover to George Bancroft, quoted in Nash, p. 504.
264   "as rich as": Nash, pp. 504, 513.
264   "But you are trying": Ibid., p. 482.
264   "Engineering is": Ibid.
264   "exactness makes": Smith, p. 80.
264   the number of engineers: Edwin Layton, *The Revolt of the Engineers*, p. 3.
264   "machinery is our": Robert Wohl, *A Passion for Wings* (New Haven: Yale University Press, 1994), quoted in A. Alverez, "Lonely Passion," *New York Review of Books*, February 2, 1995, p. 7.
264   Eads had played: Andrew Carnegie, *The Autobiography of Andrew Carnegie*, p. 174.
265   "The same principles": Layton, p. 143.
265   "[h]armony not discord": Quoted in David McCullough, *The Path Between the Seas*, p. 563.
265   "[M]etaphysics has practically": Ibid., p. 59.
265   "The golden rule": Ibid., p. 67.
265   "a principle so full": Eads, St. Louis dinner, March 23, 1875, *ALP*, p. 47.
265   "The Millennium": Samuel Hays, *Conservation and the Gospel of Efficiency*, p. 124.
265   "The shop": Terry Reynolds, ed., *The Engineer in America*, p. 408.
265   "By some false": Herman Bernstein, *Herbert Hoover*, pp. 40–41.
266   "the average politician's": Layton, p. 147.

266 "directorate": See, for example, Thorstein Veblen, *Engineers and the Price System* (New York: Viking, 1921), p. 141.

266 "the engineering profession personified": Joan Hoff Wilson, p. 43.

266 "the world lives": Quoted in ibid., p. 59.

266 "the biggest figure": Schlesinger, p. 85.

266 Polish soldiers had executed: Bernstein, *Herbert Hoover,* pp. 21–22.

266 "the only man": Schlesinger, p. 83.

267 "abandonment of": Joan Hoff Wilson, p. 37.

267 "the ruthlessness": Smith, p. 93.

267 "ordered liberty": Joan Hoff Wilson, p. 7.

267 "the social and economic": William Appleman Williams, "What This Country Needs," *New York Review of Books,* November 5, 1970, p. 8.

267 "No civilization could": Hoover, *American Individualism,* pp. 19, 22–23.

267 "[T]he real need": Ibid., p. 58.

267 "precise and efficient": Quoted in Layton, pp. 189–190; Hoover, *American Individualism,* pp. 22, 58.

267 "abnormally shy": Henry Pringle, "Hoover: An Enigma Easily Misunderstood," *World's Work* 56 (June 1928), pp. 131–143.

267 "the pneumatic drill": Smith, p. 53.

267 "those strong men": Lloyd, p. 82.

268 "He is certainly": Schlesinger, pp. 79–85.

268 "I am 100 percent": Schlesinger, pp. 79–85; Gary Best, "The Hoover-for-President Boom," pp. 228, 244.

268 Old Guard GOP senators: Joan Hoff Wilson, p. 80.

268 "I should prefer": See Robert Murray, "Herbert Hoover and the Harding Cabinet" in Ellis Hawley, *Herbert Hoover as Secretary of Commerce,* p. 20.

268 "Hoover sees": Lloyd, p. 92

268 "organized": Ellis Hawley, "Herbert Hoover and Economic Stabilization 1921–22," in Hawley, *Herbert Hoover as Secretary of Commerce,* p. 65.

269 Hoover then had the Federation: Layton, p. 203.

269 the Better Homes of America Association: Joan Hoff Wilson, p. 111.

269 This group advocated: Ibid.; also, Ellis Hawley, *The Great War and the Search for a Modern Order,* p. 114.

269 He helped make second mortgages: Rosenwald to Hoover, n.d., HHPL.

269 "We are passing": Joan Hoff Wilson, p. 68.

269 "the most powerful": Michael Parrish, *Anxious Decades: America in Prosperity and Depression* (New York: Norton 1992), pp. 74–80.

270 "not marked as coming": Lloyd, p. 66.

270 "among the few": *NYT,* December 17, 1922.

270 *Literary Digest* ran a story: *Literary Digest,* May 14, 1927; note that the magazine dated its issues far in advance of actual publication.

270 "Capital Mystified": *NYT,* April 16, 1927.

270 "That man has offered": Joan Hoff Wilson, p. 124.

271 "consumed with ambition": Quoted in Richard Smith, *An Uncommon Man,* p. 144.

271 "I felt": Joan Hoff Wilson, p. 121.

CHAPTER TWENTY-TWO

272 "The Army Engineers": Unsigned Red Cross memorandum, "Conference Presidents Red Cross Committee," April 22, 1927; statement by Dwight Davis following conference, April 22, 1927; both in RCP.

273 "to use such government": Henry Baker to J. D. Cremer, August 1, 1928, RCP.

273 "In the course of": Quoted in Bruce Lohof, "Hoover and the 1927 Mississippi Flood," Ph.D. diss., p. 106.

273 "Essential push": Fieser to James McClintock, May 5, 1927; Fieser to Henry Baker, May 6, 1927; Fieser to T. R. Buchanan, May 9, 1927, all in RCP.

274 Hoover himself: Oral history of Turner Catledge, HHPL.

274 wire daily reports: F. D. Beneke to Edgar Jadwin, April 30, 1927, Office of the Adjutant General central files, NA, RG 94.

274 "squarely on": See memo from Henry Baker to Fieser, May 2, 1927, Box 741, RCP.

274 Hoover streamlined things more: Henry Baker to J. D. Cremer, August 1, 1928, RCP.

274 The Memphis mayor had assigned: Oral history of Turner Catledge, HHPL.

275 he was bankrolling: William McCain, "The Life and Labor of Dennis Murphree," unpublished ms., 1950, MDAH.

275 Crosby would soon become: Wire from Simpson to Hoover, April 27, 1927, HHPL.

275 Only six people: Interview with Frank Hall, March 24 and December 18, 1992.

276 professional fisherman came: Foster Davis to Robert Bondy, May 4, 1927, RCP.

276 "I made myself": Interview recorded by historian Pete Daniel, who kindly shared tapes of interviews he conducted for his book Deep'n as It Come.

276 The Clearing House Association: Interview with Hunter Kimbrough, November 27, 1992.

276 "I go into Jim's Café": Daniel's interview tape.

277 "I searched": Ibid.

277 "He found one family": Daniel's interview with Virginia Pullen in Vicksburg, May 13, 1975.

277 "We could hear": Tape of panel discussion at Second Levee Break Celebration, Greenville, Miss., April 1990, loaned by Jack Gannon.

278 "I come here": Quoted in Daniel, p. 17; Oscar Johnston to H. W. Lee, Fine Cotton Spinners and Doublers Assoc., May 2, 1927, D&PLCP.

278 "For thirty-six hours": Percy, LL, p. 250.

278 "The Mississippi Delta": Van de Waltman to Commerce Department, April 29, 1927, RCP.

279 "just swelled up": Oral history of Henry Mascagni, August 8, 1977, MDAH.

279 "fully two hundred bodies": Fieser to A. L. Shafer, May 7, 1927, HHPL.

279   they took soundings: Interview with Frank Hall, December 23, 1992; also Daniel's 1975 interview with Caillouet.
280   "[e]very relief boat": See, for example, Spalding to District Engineer, Louisville, Kentucky, April 26, 1927, RC, RG 2, box 740.
280   "I am speaking": Radio address, May 1, 1927, HHPL.
281   "The swiftly moving current": *NYT*, May 6, 1927.
281   "Today it is possible": *MC-A*, May 5, 1927.
281   "For mile after mile": *NYT*, May 6, 1927.

CHAPTER TWENTY-THREE

282   "First in Cairo": *NYT*, May 9, 1927.
282   "[Failure would] increase": Ibid.; *NYT*, May 10, 1927.
283   "We wish that": Quoted in Bruce Lohof, "Herbert Hoover, Spokesman for Human Efficiency," p. 694.
283   The flood, hemmed in: *Report of Board of [Louisiana] State Engineers*, 1929, pp. 98–99.
283   "of tremendous proportions": Isaac Cline, "Daily Flood Bulletin," May 12, 1927, Louisiana Collection, TUL.
284   "immense deposits": Paul Dettmer, "Final Melville Report," May 15, 1928, RCP, box 737.
284   "a veritable wall": *NYT*, May 19, 1927.
284   "Their bodies were found": *NYT*, May 17, 1927.
284   "A wall of water": AP story appearing in *MC-A*, May 24, 1927.
285   "All population": Hoover to Coolidge, May 24, 1927, HHPL.
285   "Imperative that refugees": Hoover to Jadwin, May 13, 1927, RCP.
285   The War Department: See Jadwin to Hoover, May 17, 1927; Hoover to Jadwin, June 5, 1927, RCP.
285   the flood put as much: See American Red Cross, *The Mississippi Valley Flood Disaster of 1927: Official Report of Operations* (Washington, D.C., 1928), pp. 39–46.
285   "concentration camps": Ibid.
286   "not necessarily reliable": DeWitt Smith to Hoover, January 21, 1928, RCP.
286   estimated deaths: H. C. Frankenfield, "The Floods of 1927 in the Mississippi Basin," *Monthly Weather Review*, Supplement 29 (Washington, D.C., 1927), p. 35; *MC-A*, May 30, 1927.
286   economic losses: American Red Cross, *The Mississippi Valley Flood Disaster;* Frankenfield, "The Floods of 1927 in the Mississippi Basin," p. 35.
286   The river itself: *Report of Board of [Louisiana] State Engineers*, p. 101.
286   one could cross the head: B. B. Simms to General Jeff Thompson, chief Louisiana state engineer, January 12, 1874, NA, RG 77, entry 522.
286   "I urgently request": Murphree to Coolidge, April 29, 1927, Coolidge Papers, microfilm, reel 181, LC.
287   "that a visit": Richard Edmonds to Coolidge, April 30, 1927, Coolidge Papers, microfilm, reel 181, LC.
287   "that you go": Thomas Ridgeway to Coolidge, April 25, 1927, Coolidge Papers, microfilm, reel 181, LC.

287 "Big Bill" Thompson: O'Keefe to Coolidge, April 27, 1927, Coolidge Papers, microfilm, reel 181, LC.

287 "Earnestly urge": L. O. Crosby to Coolidge, April 29, 1927, Coolidge Papers, microfilm, reel 181, LC.

287 Eight senators and four: *NYT,* May 1, 1927.

287 "More than ever": Murphree to Coolidge, May 3, 1927, Coolidge Papers, microfilm, reel 181, LC.

287 "send me a telegram": Rogers to Everett Sanders, April 30, 1927, Coolidge Papers, microfilm, reel 181, LC.

287 every single day: *NYT,* April 18 through May 10, 1927.

288 references to him: *NYT* had sixty-four nonflood references to him from April through June 1927, compared to twenty-two from January through March.

288 "Since the last report": "The Mississippi Flood and Mr. Hoover's Part in Relief Work," news summaries for May 14, 1927, HHPL.

288 "The Magazine section": "The Mississippi Flood and Mr. Hoover's Part in Relief Work," news summaries for May 17, 1927, HHPL.

288 " 'There is no honor' ": "The Mississippi Flood and Mr. Hoover's Part in Relief Work," news summaries for May 23, 1927, HHPL.

288 "I can state": Quoted in *NYT,* May 29, 1927.

289 "Only three lives": Hoover to White, June 21, 1927, HHPL.

289 "Unstinted praise": Ibid., June 17, 1927.

289 "the world lives": Joan Hoff Wilson, p. 82.

289 "I shall be": Lloyd, p. 84.

CHAPTER TWENTY-FOUR

293 "the best": Interview with Bertram Wyatt-Brown, March 1993; also, Wyatt-Brown, *The House of Percy,* pp. 192–193.

293 "Will Percy was": Interview with Betty Carter, January 16, 1996.

293 "quick as a youth": Walker Percy, Introduction to *LL,* p. viii.

293 "in a way that": Oral history of Shelby Foote, MDAH.

293 "He could get": Ibid.

294 "beautiful and terrible": Walker Percy, Introduction to *LL,* p. viii.

294 "the loneliest man": Quoted in Richard King, *A Southern Renaissance,* p. 82; David Cohn, "Eighteenth Century Chevalier," pp. 562–563.

294 "overjoyed no one": Percy, *LL,* p. 26.

294 "even more lacerating": Ibid., pp. 58, 95.

294 "I had not loved": Ibid., pp. 57, 141.

294 "the most gentle": Ibid., p. 58.

295 "I must have been": Ibid., p. 141.

295 "was anguish": Ibid., p. 79.

295 Will had a brother: Hester Ware, "A Study of the Life and Works of William Alexander Percy," M.A. thesis, p. 17.

295 "all boy": Percy, *LL,* p. 126.

295 "perpetuating the name": Percy, *LL,* p. 346.

295 Crowds overflowed the house: Ware, "A Study," p. 17.

295 "I am your son": William Alexander Percy, "A Legend of Lacedcaemon," in *Selected Poems* (New Haven: Yale University Press, 1943), p. 380.

296 "this one-sided correspondence": WAP to Camille Percy, October 6, no year, PFP.
296 "Mother Dear— it": WAP to Camille Percy, August 15, no year, PFP.
296 "Mother Dear, Things": WAP to Camille Percy, July 24, 1922, PFP.
296 "was always happening": Percy, *LL*, pp. 110–111.
296 "sick for a home": Ibid., p. 112.
296 "[L]et your writing": WAP to Audrey Bunch, September 4, 1927, PFP.
296 "first requirement": WAP to DuBose Heyward, July 14, 1923, PFP.
296 " 'How many trees' ": Ibid., "L.P.," p. 235; "Enzio's Kingdom," p. 171.
296 "Father was": Percy, *LL*, p. 270.
296 "Sappho in Levkas": WAP to DuBose Heyward, July 14, 1923, PFP.
297 *To think nobility:* William Alexander Percy, "Sappho in Levkas," in *Selected Poems*, pp. 40–56.
297 "some young god": Ibid., "To Lucrezia," p. 15.
297 "the best place": LP to C. B. Adams, August 17, 1917, PFP.
297 "I am considerably": LP to his brother Walker Percy, July 8, 1908, PFP.
298 "I had attacks": Percy, *LL*, p. 126.
298 "My father and mother": William Alexander Percy, "The Fifth Autumn," PFP.
298 "Will moved in their": For a summary of Will's involvement with this community, see Wyatt-Brown, pp. 208, 218–222.
298 "I'm about convinced": WAP to Janet Dana Longcope, n.d., Special Collections, Louisiana State University Library.
298 "the center of": WAP to Janet Dana Longcope, n.d., Special Collections, Louisiana State University Library.
299 "That boy of mine": LP to John Sharp Williams, November 14, 1916, John Sharp Williams Papers, LC.
299 "There were patches": WAP to LP, August, 31, 1918, PFP.
299 "Dear Father": WAP to LP, October 4, 1918, PFP.
300 "honor I deserved": WAP to Camille Percy, November 11, 1918, PFP.
300 "The negroes": LP to John Sharp Williams, August 4, 1919, John Sharp Williams Papers, LC.
300 "I can't see": See WAP to John Sharp Williams, February 16, 1921, John Sharp Williams Papers, LC.
300 "slaveholders began": Percy, *LL*, p. 5.
301 "[W]hat can a white": Ibid., p. 22.
301 "their obliterating genius": Ibid., p. 309.
301 Some, it was rumored: Interview with David Cober, February 25, 1993.
301 "my only tie": Percy, *LL*, p. 296.
301 "turn[ing] to stone": William Alexander Percy, "Medusa," in *Selected Poems*, p. 244.
302 "I understand": WAP to Brick Row Book Shop, February 25 and March 7, 1922, PFP.
302 Fellow alumnus Monte Lemann: See Lemann to WAP, October 21, 1926; WAP to Lemann, October 26, 1926, PFP.

CHAPTER TWENTY-FIVE

303 Will returned home: Percy, *LL*, p. 247.

303 "We heard this storm": Interview with David Cober, February 25, 1993.

304 "like zero made audible": Percy, *LL*, p. 250.

304 "Water was": Interview with Jesse Pollard, March 3, 1993.

304 "Guess you better": Percy, *LL*, p. 251.

305 "Senator Percy": Interview with Hunter Kimbrough, January 5, 1993; interview with Frank Hall, December 18, 1992; see also Paxton, *Three Wars and a Flood*, p. 24.

305 "All citizens": Mississippi National Guard, *Report of Flood Relief Expedition*, MDAH; Paxton, p. 25.

306 "Flood conditions": *GD-T*, April 23, 1927.

306 Rumors began to spread: *JC-L*, April 24, 1927.

306 "Conditions Greenville": Gen. Malin Craig to A.G., April 23, 1927, NA, RG 94, Office of the Adjutant General.

306 the city water supply: Mississippi National Guard, *Report of Flood Relief Expedition*, MDAH.

306 "The situation here": *NOT*, April 25, 1927.

307 "Whatever Senator Percy": Interview with M. L. Payne, March 4, 1993.

307 "The city will": *GD-T*, April 23, 1927.

307 "It is the plan": *NOS*, April 23, 1927.

308 the government steamer *Control*: *NOT, GD-T*, and *NOT-P*, all April 25, 1927.

308 "[N]one of us": Percy, *LL*, p. 258.

308 Will responded bitingly: Ibid., p. 257.

308 he found Will: The following account comes chiefly from Percy, *LL*, p. 257; the *GD-T*, April 23 through April 29, 1927; and Oral history of Joe Rice Dockery, December 13, 1979, MDAH.

310 Finally, Will capitulated: Percy, *LL*, pp. 257–258.

310 The *Wabash*: *GD-T*, April 26, 1927.

310 "breakdown": WAP to Gerstle Mack, May 15, 1927, PFP.

310 "We are urging": *GD-T*, April 26, 1927.

310 the first refugee death: Percy Bell to "Dear Folks," April 30, 1927, kindly supplied by Charles Greenleaf Bell.

311 Rumors spread that Taggart: Interview with David Cober, February 25, 1993; Oral history of Salvador Signa, December 1, 1976, MDAH.

311 Approximately 4,000 whites: Mississippi National Guard, *Report of Relief Expedition*, MDAH.

311 Paperboys delivered: Oral history of Reed Dunn, Mississippi Oral History Program, University of Southern Mississippi.

311 peddlers set up stands: Oral history of Frank Ciolino, August 22, 1978, MDAH.

311 Rowboats were ordered: *Memphis Courier-Appeal*, April 29, 1927.

311 people constantly played: Oral history of Theodore Pountain, MDAH.

312 a thriving black market: Oral history of Salvador Signa, MDAH.

312 "The town is": Percy Bell to "Dear Folks," April 30, 1927.

312   Roughly 5,000 blacks: Mississippi National Guard, *Report of Flood Relief Expedition,* MDAH.
312   Up to 13,000: Memo of C. P. Doe to DeWitt Smith, January 6, 1928, RCP.
312   "Bye Bye Blackbird": Oral history of Ernest Waldauer, MDAH.
312   "groups of negroes": *GD-T,* April 28, 1927.
312   "all the negroes": Percy Bell to "Dear Folks," April 30, 1927.
313   The food blacks received: Interview with Frank Carlton, February 24, 1993; Oral history of Ernest Bueller, March 17, 1977, MDAH.
313   "It is our duty": *MC-A,* April 28, 1927.
313   "[I]n no case will": *JC-L,* April 30, 1927.
313   "Plantation owners": Undated memo of A. L. Shafer, titled "Return of Refugees," to national Red Cross representative in Mississippi, RCP.
313   "furnish a list": *JC-L, Memphis Courier-Appeal,* May 18, 1927.
313   "I have seen nothing": "Statement to Shareholders," April 1, 1928, D&PLCP; Johnston to Hicks & Co., May 9, 1927, D&PLCP.
313   In an effort: Johnston to H. Lee, April 26, 1927, D&PLCP.
314   a special train: Johnston to H. Lee, May 2, 1927, D&PLCP.
314   " 'Don't give 'em' ": Oral history of Salvador Signa, MDAH.
314   "Here 440,000 acres": *MC-A,* May 12, 1927.
314   Unloading barges: Oral history of Ernest Waldauer, MDAH.
314   "Imperative to increase": Paxton to Green, April 27, 1927, quoted in *JC-L,* April 28, 1927.
314   "No able-bodied negro": *GD-T,* May 9, 1927.
315   all Red Cross work: In his autobiography Will justifies his position by claiming the Red Cross prohibited payment to recipients of its bounty. This was not the case. See Percy, *LL,* pp. 258–269.
315   "Me and Horace": Oral history of Salvador Signa, MDAH.
315   "They wasn't given": Oral history of John Johnston, MDAH.
315   "The Guard would": Oral history of Mrs. Henry Ransom, MDAH.
315   "The colored people": Oral history of Percy McRaney, MDAH.
315   "On the levee": Interview with Joe Thomas Reilly, December 16, 1992.
315   "just like dogs": Oral history of Addie Oliver, MDAH.
315   "caught": Mississippi National Guard, *Report of Flood Relief Expedition,* MDAH.
316   Two particular companies: Interview with David Cober, February 25, 1993; interview with Lamar Britton, March 1, 1993; draft report of Colored Advisory Commission, June 4, 1927, HHPL; "Final Report," April 6, 1928, NA, RC, box 744.
316   "guilty of acts": WAP to Johnston, February 11, 1937, D&PLCP.
316   continued food shortages: *GD-T,* May 9, 1927.
316   "the Argonne": WAP to Gerstle Mack, May 15, 1927, PFP.
316   "To falter or fail": *MC-A,* May 12, 1927.
316   "rotten": *GD-T,* May 16, 1927.
316   "We will stand": Ibid.
316   "The negroes in town": *GD-T,* May 24, 1927; note, orders containing a misprint appeared on May 23.
317   employers were paying: See, for example, Oscar Johnston to V. E. Cartledge, June 30, 1927, D&PLCP.
317   "Refugees Herded": *Chicago Defender,* May 6, 1927.

317   "Conscript Labor": *Pittsburgh Courier,* May 14, 1927.
317   "W. A. Percy . . .": *Chicago Defender,* June 4, 1927.

CHAPTER TWENTY-SIX

318   77 percent of blacks: Henry Lee Moon, *Balance of Power: The Negro Vote* (Garden City, N.Y.: Doubleday, 1948), pp. 48–50.
318   94 percent support: Ibid.
318   the 1924 presidential election: Harold Gosnell, *Negro Politicians,* pp. 28–30; see also Harold Gosnell, *Champion Campaigner,* p. 212; and Nancy Weiss, *Farewell to the Party of Lincoln,* pp. 11, 31.
319   black Republicans: See, for example, GOP National Committee-woman Mary Booze to John Overton, GOP State Committee, and Perry Howard, January 22, 1926, PFP.
319   Only in Memphis: Moon, p. 176.
319   "injustice": Barnett to Hoover, May 4, 1927, HHPL.
319   "being made to work": Anonymous letter to Coolidge, May 9, 1927, RCP, box 743.
320   "voice the protest": Capper to Hoover, May 10, 1927, HHPL.
320   "charges of race": Jane Addams to Hoover, May 16, 1927, quoted in wire from Lawrence Richey to George Akerson, May 18, 1927, HHPL.
320   "It is said": Sidney Redmond to Coolidge, April 30, 1927, Coolidge Papers, LC.
320   Even professional Red Cross: Ruth Thomas to Earl Kilpatrick, May 20, 1927, RCP, box 743.
320   "Chicago Defender": Wire from Fieser to Henry McClintock, May 14, 1927, RCP; see also William Baxter to Henry Baker, May 19, 1927, RCP, box 743.
320   "colored people": Hoover to Baker, May 13, 1927, HHPL.
321   "The American Red Cross": Baker to William Pickens, May 13, 1927, RCP, box 743.
321   "Never before": Mrs. L. M. Moore, Treasurer of Pine Bluff branch of NAACP, to NAACP Headquarters, May 18, 1927, NAACP Papers, LC.
321   "request [for] source": see Baker to McClintock, summary of responses, May 14, 1927, RCP, box 743.
321   "Charges that colored": See, for example, responses from N. R. Bancroft, Deeson, Mississippi, and Monticello, Arkansas (unsigned), to Baker, May 13, 1927, RCP, box 743.
321   "It is the desire": Monticello, Arkansas (unsigned), to Baker; Camp Commander, Yazoo City, to Baker, both May 13, 1927, RCP, box 743.
321   the NAACP began publicly: See, for example, wires from White to Bolton Smith and to John Clark, both on May 12, 1927; NAACP Papers, LC.
321   "I have managed": Irwin's letter was quoted in a telegram from Hoover's aide Lawrence Richey to George Akerson, June 9, 1927, HHPL.
322   northern papers ran articles: *NYT* and *New York Herald Tribune,* May 28, 1927.

322 "With view to": Hoover to R. R. Moulton [Moton], May 24, 1927, HHPL; memoir written by Henry Baker, RCP, box 743; Hoover to Robert Bondy, May 21, 1927, HHPL.

323 "some of the most": Sidney Redmond to Attorney General John Sargent, July 5, 1927, U.S. Dept. of Justice records, peonage file, NA.

323 he failed to inform Redmond: Redmond to Hoover, January 5, 1928, HHPL.

323 "[A]fter the first": Hoover to Will Irwin, June 10, 1927, HHPL.

CHAPTER TWENTY-SEVEN

324 "By July 18": *GD-T,* May 25, 1927.

324 "Worry is not": Margaret Wells Wood, Social Hygiene Lecturer, to Valeria Park, M.D., "Special Report," July 10, 1927, RCP, box 740; see also "Social Hygiene and the Mississippi Flood Disaster," *Journal of Social Hygiene* 13, no. 8, pp. 455–457.

324 "for the purpose": *GD-T,* May 31, 1927.

325 "We propose": Ibid.

325 "The guns are": Interview with Maurice Sisson, October 22, 1993; interview with John Jackson, March 9, 1993.

325 Levye Chapple: Interview with Chapple's granddaughter, Katherine Bradbury Thompson, March 9, 1993.

325 "We are citizens": Draft report of Colored Advisory Committee, June 1927, RCP, box 744; interview with Maurice Sisson, October 22, 1993; interview with John Wiley, October 22, 1993.

325 Chapple, McMiller, and others: *GD-T,* June 1, 1927; interview with John Wiley, October 22, 1993; interview with Maurice Sisson, October 22, 1993; interview with John Jackson, March 9, 1993; draft report of Colored Advisory Committee, June 1927, RCP, box 744; interview with Mildred Commodore, McMiller's daughter, August 3, 1995.

326 The question was: Interview with John Wiley, October 22, 1993; interview with Maurice Sisson, October 22, 1993; interview with John Jackson, March 9, 1993; draft report of Colored Advisory Committee, June 1927, RCP, box 744.

326 "I don't mind": LP to J. B. Ray, December 28, 1906, PFP; see also Willis, "On the New South Frontier," pp. 147–149.

326 Emanuel Smith: Interview with John Wiley, October 22, 1993; interview with Maurice Sisson, October 22, 1993.

326 J. D. Fowler: Ibid.

326 "500 Colored Men Wanted": Draft report of Colored Advisory Committee, June 1927, RC, box 744.

326 "I kept my": Interview with Mildred Commodore.

327 On the eighth day: *JC-L,* June 17, 1927.

327 "our colored citizens": City Council minutes of June 7, 1927.

327 "You have": *GD-T,* June 13, 1927.

327 "all colored citizens": Ibid.

327 "Believe food": Crosby to Hoover, June 15, 1927, HHPL.

327 He vetoed cutting: Ibid.; Hoover to Crosby, June 16, 1927, HHPL.

328 spent an average of 21 cents: "Report of the Special Committee," June 22, 1927, RCP, box 735.
328 "simply teach": Memo from C. P. Doe to DeWitt Smith, January 6, 1928; Percy Bell to "Dear Folks," April 30, 1927.
328 "still a wreck": WAP to L. P. Soule, June 22 and 27, 1927, PFP.
328 "We were tired": Percy, LL, p. 26.
328 "Every store": Percy Bell to Bessie Bell, May 15, 1927, supplied by Charles Greenleaf Bell.
329 The boat: Crosby to Hoover, November 10, 1927, HHPL; also, MC-A, June 30, 1927.
329 "The meeting was": A. L. Shafer, "Narrative Report of Flood Conditions," July 2, 1927, RCP.
329 "Outside of the great": Ibid.; JC-L, June 14, 1927.
329 the same black Greenville minister: See the anonymous letter to Hoover dated July 2, 1927, HHLP. Compare it to the anonymous letter to Coolidge, May 14, 1927, RCP, box 743. In both letters the writer describes himself similarly; the typewriter, misspellings, and grammatical constructions appear identical.
329 In Little Rock a black man: MC-A, May 5, 1927.
329 The mayor of Lake Providence: Louisiana Weekly, May 14, 1927.
330 two blacks were accused: GD-T, June 13, 1927.
330 "crazed negro": JC-L, June 18, 1927.
330 In Jackson, the governor: See JC-L, June 18 to June 22, 1927.
330 In Yazoo City: JC-L, July 8, 1927.
330 "a striking example": Louisiana Weekly, April 23 1927.
330 "the seat of": Undated Barnett speech in fall 1927 in Chicago, CBP.
330 "could not secure": Draft report of Colored Advisory Commission, June 4, 1927, HHLP; "Final Report," April 6, 1928, RCP, box 744.
330 Washington County: "Statistical Summary of Losses," RCP, box 735.
331 "as they demonstrate": Baker to Fieser, June 16, 1927, RCP, box 735.
331 internal political bickering: Report of Malinde Havey, Directory of Nursing, Mississippi Valley Flood Disaster, July 13, 1927, RCP, box 735.
331 "or else take": LP to L. A. Downs, September 10, 1927, PFP.
331 The national Red Cross: George Stricklin to Red Cross Headquarters, Memphis, May 25, 1927, RCP, box 738.
331 "I bitterly resent": WAP to Crosby, July 15, 1927, NA, RG 2, box 738.
332 Will asked for and received: WAP to L. P. Soule of Yale University Press, May 19, June 22, and June 27, 1927, PFP.
332 "giving the entire": MC-A, July 8, 1927.
332 Gooden told a different version: Interview with Frank Hall; interview with Rev. R. T. Strong, February 26, 1993; GD-T, July 9, 1927; draft report of Colored Advisory Commission presented to Hoover, December 12, 1927, RCP.
332 two white doctors: Greenville City Council minutes, September 6, 1927.
333 "We prepared": Interview with Rhodes Wasson, December 16, 1992; Margaret Wells Wood, Social Hygiene Lecturer, to Valeria Parker, M.D., "Special Report," July 10, 1927, NA, RG 2, box 740; see also "Social Hygiene and the Mississippi Flood Disaster," Journal of Social Hygiene 13, no. 8, pp. 455–457.

333 "I told my informant": Percy, *LL*, p. 267.
333 Chapple's father: Interview with Sylvia Jackson, March 7, 1993.
333 "said starkly": Ibid., pp. 267–268.
334 "When put upon": Percy, *LL*, p. 126.
334 "A good Negro": Ibid., pp. 267–268.
334 "My dear Percy": Hoover to WAP, July 5, 1927, HHPL.
335 "a strong relief": Summary report by A. Shafer and R. Thrush, September 8, 1928, RCP, box 737.
335 "No one can": Ibid.
335 "passing the buck": WAP to George Day, August 31, 1927, PFP.
335 "Our people here": LP to Judge Horace Oakly, August 22, 1927, PFP.

CHAPTER TWENTY-EIGHT

340 "my sincere appreciation": Minutes of Emergency Clearing House Publicity Committee meeting, May 11, 1927, CP.
341 the Association of Commerce: Minutes of Association of Commerce board meeting, March 16, 1927, ACP.
341 "we have decided": See exchange of letters between Emergency Clearing House Publicity Committee and Otis Mahogany Co., May 13, 1927, CP.
341 Walter Parker: Minutes of Emergency Clearing House Publicity Committee meeting, May 13, 1927, CP (hereafter, ECHPC minutes).
341 "[A]ny announcements": Minutes of Association of Commerce board meeting, May 3, 1927, ACP.
341 forced Moody's Investors Service: ECHPC minutes, May 16, 1927, CP.
341 the committee contacted 265: See Association of Commerce papers, esp. *News Bulletin*, May 10, 1927.
341 "New Orleans is": Ibid.
342 editorials from Springfield: See ECHPC minutes, May 19, 1927, CP.
342 "New Orleans 'Babbitry' ": *MC-A*, May 2, 1927.
342 It got corrections printed: ECHPC minutes, May 11, 1927, CP.
343 "a citizens committee": Copy in ECHPC minutes, May 11, 1927, CP.
343 a budget of $130,000: Figures come from Finance Committee report, December 31, 1927, ACP.
343 "Superintendent of Police Healy": Civic Bureau of Association of Commerce report, August 1, 1927, ACP.
343 "the noble and unselfish": Undated editorial, probably mid-June 1927, from *New Iberia Enterprise*, ACP.
343 "in the mind of a great": Minutes of the executive committee of the Association of Commerce board meeting, October 5, 1927, ACP.

CHAPTER TWENTY-NINE

344 "You're talking": interview with Harry Kelleher, December 10, 1992.
345 "Into the fiercely contested": Graduation speech, 1899, clipping in Williams, Monroe, and Blanc Family Papers, HNOC.

345　publicly rebuked his partner: Interview with Stephen Lemann, November 7, 1992.

345　"a wholly-owned subsidiary": Interview with Stephen Lemann, April 6, 1995.

345　He worked ferociously: Interview with Harry Kelleher, December 10, 1992.

345　"I've never seen": Interview with Stephen Lemann, April 6, 1995.

346　*tres ordinaire*: Interview with Marianne Patton Atkinson, February 20, 1993.

346　"doing business exactly": Andy Zipser, "Hidden Value in the Bayou," *Barron's,* October 4, 1993.

346　Meraux was given $5,000: St. Bernard Policy Jury minutes, April 27, 1927; "Summary of Claims," M&LP. Thanks to Robert Harvey, president of Orleans Levee Board and Stephen Lemann for access to these papers.

346　"The words of": Reported in the minutes of the meeting of the executive committee of the Citizens Flood Relief Committee, n.d., CP. (Hereafter, these minutes will be referred to as "executive committee minutes.")

347　decided to use: See, for example, executive committee minutes, May 13, 1927, CP.

347　"The business interests": Orleans Levee Board minutes, May 10, 1927, Orleans Levee Board.

347　"as objects of charity": Executive committee minutes, May 11, 1927, CP.

347　"relief be granted": Ibid.

347　"to deduct from personal": Ibid.

348　the governor's appointees: Reported in executive committee minutes, May 17, 1927, CP.

348　the rules stated: Executive committee minutes, May 14, 1927, CP.

348　"[v]olunteer legal services": Clipping of unidentified newspaper, probably *NOI,* May 8, 1927, in CP.

348　"unethical": See executive committee minutes, May 11, 1927, CP.

348　"state the legal objections": Executive committee minutes, June 14, 1927, CP.

349　"a man may file": Reported in executive committee minutes, n.d., CP.

349　Only a complete settlement: Ibid., July 25, 1927.

349　Butler estimated that claims: Ibid., May 17 and 18, 1927.

349　Claims would exceed $30 million: *SBV,* August 15, 1929.

349　"There may possibly be": Lemann to Monroe, June 11, 1927.

349　"[I]f the case is": Undated memo in Orleans Organization Caernarvon Reparations files, M&LP.

350　One of the first trappers audited: Executive committee minutes, June 27 and 29, 1927, CP.

350　"illustrated [by] an aged negress": John Wegman to Executive Committee, June 21, 1927, CP.

350　they decided to feed: Wegman to Executive Committee, July 20, 1927; executive committee minutes, August 1, 1927, CP.

350　"As long as we continue": Wegman to Butler, August 13, 1927, CP.

350　Monroe had approved a payment: Orleans Levee Board minutes, May 23, 1927, Orleans Levee Board.

CHAPTER THIRTY

352 "I have requested": Simpson's statement and the subsequent account of and quotations from this meeting are all from detailed minutes of the meeting in executive committee minutes , July 25, 1927, CP.

353 "It is manifestly impossible": In addition to minutes of the meeting (July 25, 1927) in CP, see memo dictated by Monroe re his conversations with Wilkinson, June 3, 1927, M&LP.

354 The banks would continue: Executive committee minutes, June 29, 1927, CP.

354 "did not want to give": Orleans Levee Board minutes, July 20, 1927, and May 26, 1928, Orleans Levee Board.

354 it would give Butler $340,000: Orleans Levee Board minutes, May 26, 1928, Orleans Levee Board.

355 the railroad did not file: Executive committee minutes, August 3, 1927, CP.

355 "The City of New Orleans": SBV, September 3, 1927.

356 "Orleans to Make": NOI and NOT, September 4, 1927.

356 "New Orleans Makes Good": NOS, September 4, 1927.

356 "City Keeps Faith": NOT-P, September 4, 1927.

356 "shall be prima facie": Executive committee minutes, September 7 and 8, 1927, CP; see also memo dictated by Monroe re his earlier conversations with Wilkinson, June 3, 1927, M&LP.

356 "justly, fairly and fully": Executive committee minutes, September 7 and 8, 1927, CP; see also minutes of the Delacroix Corporation, formerly Acme Fur Company (thanks to Dorothy Benge, granddaughter of Manuel Molero, for opening them to me), November 11, 1927, to December 12, 1928; interview with Hugh Wilkinson, Jr., December 30, 1992; NOT, NOT-P, September 7 through September 11, 1927.

356 "That statement": NOT, NOT-P, September 8, 1927.

357 Molero's Acme Fur Company: Executive committee minutes, September 8–10, 1927, CP.

357 "The owner or lesse": SBV, September 24, 1927, and July 7, 1928.

357 Those he did allow to be filed: Figures are from "Summary of Claims Filed, Dec. 31, 1928," M&LP; also Monroe to Levee Board, June 1929; both in ML. NOT-P, December 30, 1928.

357 an average of $284 each: "Summary of Claims Filed," M&LP.

358 they were lucky to collect six: NOT, January 14, 1929, and SBV, January 14, 1929.

358 "a very good feature": Lou Wylie to Association of Commerce, January 22 and 30, 1929, ACP.

358 "The disastrous floods": Monroe to Wylie, January 25, 1929, M&LP.

358 "We have viewed": Case 175,097, Mumphrey Bros. v. Orleans Levee Board, transcript of argument and finding in M&LP.

358 "no cause of action": Test cases included Herman Burkhardt v. Board of Orleans Levee Commissioners, no. 178,420, Civil District Court, Division F; Charles Aduler v. Board of Levee Commissioners, no. 175,991, ODC; and John Williams v. Levee Board, no. 175,463, ODC. Also, Alfred Oliver v. Board of Orleans Levee Commissioners, no. 30,134, 169 La 438; Foret v. Board of Orleans Levee Commissioners,

no. 30,063, La 427; and *Fabre v. Levee Board,* no. 30,088, 170 La 210.

358 " 'I am impressed' ": See Monroe to Lou Wylie, January 25, 1929, M&LP; *Burkhardt v. Board of Orleans Levee Commissioners; Oliver v. Board of Orleans Levee Commissioners; Foret v. Board of Orleans Levee Commissioners.*

359 "irrelevant to this case": *Burkhardt v. Board of Orleans Levee Commissioners.*

359 "the act of creating": See opinion, *Foret v. Board of Orleans Levee Commissioners,* M&LP.

359 "The judgment is affirmed": Ibid.

359 "due to the painstaking": Resolution of Orleans Levee Board, January 7, 1930, M&LP.

CHAPTER THIRTY-ONE

363 50 percent of all animals: "Economic Effects of the Mississippi Flood," *Editorial Research Reports,* quoted in Arthur Frank, *The Development of the Federal Program of Flood Control on the Mississippi River,* p. 194.

363 "We shall weather": Stone to Crosby, September 1, 1927, RCP.

363 "Sometimes you find": LP to Judge D. H. Minor, May 31, 1927, PFP.

364 "Whether we are going": Percy Bell to Bessie Bell, May 12, 1927, courtesy of Charles Greenleaf Bell.

364 "[n]o real concerted effort": Memo from McCarty to Hoover and Fieser, September 1, 1927, RCP.

364 "Yesterday I went to Arkansas City": C. C. Neal to Mrs. Monroe, October 7, 1927, RRMP.

364 "The Boston Club was": LP to L. L. Myles, October 11, 1927, PFP.

364 "The civic authorities": Memo from McCarty to Robert Bondy, February 28, 1928, RCP.

364 "The public is insisting": See memo from Henry Baker to Fieser, May 2, 1927, RCP, box 741.

364 "organized": Ellis Hawley, *Herbert Hoover as Secretary of Commerce,* p. 65.

365 "We have before us": "Summary of Secretary Hoover's Statement at the First Meeting of the Louisiana Reconstruction Commission," May 23, 1927, HHPL.

365 "a blessing in disguise": *NOS,* September 7, 1927.

365 He personally ordered the Red Cross: Robert Bondy to John Cremer, May 24, 1927, RCP.

366 home economists and agricultural extension agents: Robert Bondy to John Cremer, May 24, 1927, RCP; see also several reports by T. M. Campbell, an African-American agricultural extension worker, Department of Agriculture files, NA, RG 16, entry 17.

366 "definite program of agriculture": "Inter-office Memorandum," typed with Hoover's handwritten notes, June 10, 1927, HHPL.

366 "positively contrary": R. S. Wilson to C. W. Warburton, June 25, 1927, NA, RG 16, Secretary of Agriculture records, entry 17.

366 "undertake to loan money": Hoover to Christie Benet, June 13, 1927,

HHPL; Benet to Hoover, June 14, 1927, HHPL; Hoover to DeWitt Smith, June 14, 1927, HHPL.

366 "Am more impressed than ever": Hoover to Meyer, May 8, 1927, HHPL.

366 Meyer immediately arranged: Wire from George Scott to Hoover, May 8, 1927, HHPL.

367 quadruple its capital: Hoover, "Memorandum for Credit Arrangement for Mississippi Flood Region," May 5, 1927, HHPL.

367 "You are not called upon to donate": JC-L, May 10 and 11, 1927.

367 "You are upon the firing line!": See handwritten notes by Hoover for June 13, 1927, meeting in Jackson, Mississippi, HHPL.

367 only 115: JC-L, May 19, 1927.

367 Less than half the quota: The final total raised in Mississippi was $315,000, including the $100,000 from Memphis. See Memorandum from John Cremer to H. Stuart Crawford, secretary to Coolidge, September 17, 1927, RCP.

367 In Arkansas, the numbers: Cremer to Hoover, September 17, 1927, RCP. Cremer states the total raised in Arkansas was $672,000, but this figure includes $100,000 from Memphis bankers and $500,000 from national sources. See below.

368 "If not": Oral history of Turner Catledge, HHPL. Note: Catledge incorrectly stated the amount. Hoover wired that the total was $200,000; see Hoover to Coolidge, May 24, 1927, HHPL.

368 "Have talked with Memphis": R. E. Kennington to Hoover, May 12, 1927, and undated reply handwritten by Hoover, HHPL.

368 By five o'clock: MC-A, May 27 and 30, 1927.

368 "This telegram for yourself": Pierson to Robert Ellis, May 26, 1927, HHPL.

368 "the business interests": Coolidge to Pierson, May 30, 1927, HHPL.

368 Pierson brought together: Ibid.

369 Hoover assured them: Hoover to W. H. Sullivan, May 30, 1927; Hoover to Crosby, May 30, 1927; both in HHPL.

369 "We cannot afford nationally": See Hoover to Pierson, May 28, 1927, HHPL.

369 "[L]arge planters who": Fieser to H. C. Couch, May 26, 1927, HHPL.

369 "warrant in": Quoted in Bruce Lohof, "Herbert Hoover and the 1927 Mississippi Flood Disaster," Ph.D. diss., p. 160.

370 "any economic or": Hoover, American Individualism, p. 19.

370 "The most potent force": Ibid.

370 "in the midst": quoted in Joan Hoff Wilson, Herbert Hoover, p. 68.

370 government could "best serve": Quoted in William Appleman Williams, "What This Country Needs," New York Review of Books, November 5, 1970, pp. 7–8.

370 "I made ninety-one": quoted in Lohof, "Herbert Hoover, Spokesman for Human Efficiency," p. 693.

370 "[Radio's] possibilities have": NYT, May 15, 1927.

371 They were also given: DeWitt Smith memo, September 3, 1927, RCP.

371 a detailed nine-page inventory: Johnston to Robert Bondy, May 9, 1927, D&PLCP.

371 the total value of goods: DeWitt Smith memo, September 3, 1927, RCP.

371   a record surplus: Associated Press report, June 1, 1927, appearing in *MC-A*.

371   the War Department dunned the Red Cross: See, for example, C. P. Summerall, acting secretary of war, to John Barton Payne, July 12, 1927, Adjutant General files, NA, RG 94.

371   "The supplies and services": Hoover to John Barton Payne, forwarded to Gen. E. E. Booth, June 7, 1927, NA, RG 94.

371   "He felt that": "Lower Mississippi River Flood, May–July 1927," U.S. Department of Agriculture records, NA, RG 16, entry 16; memo from E. Douglas to Henry Baker, May 20, 1927, RCP.

372   "I feel warranted": Reed to Coolidge, May 14, 1927, Coolidge Papers, LC.

372   Coolidge illegally ordered: *NOT-P*, June 23, 1927; memo from Lawrence Richey to Akerson, same date, HHPL.

372   "Fortunately, there are still": *NYT*, May 31, 1927.

372   "Frequent demands": *San Antonio Express*, June 5, 1927.

372   "The new spirit": *Fall River* (Massachusetts) *Globe*, June 1, 1927.

372   "If the federal government": Enclosed in memo from John Barton Payne of Red Cross to Everett Sanders, May 4, 1927, Coolidge Papers, LC.

373   "The total amount": *Ames* (Iowa) *Tribune & Times*, May 31, 1927.

373   "[Hoover's plan] is good": *Camden Courier*, June 6, 1927.

373   "is a worthy one": *Virginian Pilot* (Norfolk), May 31, 1927.

373   "The indifference of": *Providence Tribune*, June 5, 1927.

373   "Why make a charity": *JC-L*, May 31, 1927.

373   "without delay": *Sacramento Bee*, May 19, 1927.

373   "Why should we ask": *Houston Chronicle*, May 31, 1927.

373   "It is hardly possible": *Paducah* (Kentucky) *News-Democrat*, June 8, 1927.

374   "With due deference": Quoted in May 17 press summary, HHPL.

374   "At least four-fifths": Press summary, undated, also June 7 and June 17, 1927, HHPL.

374   "We regard as settled": AP story appearing in *JC-L*, May 19, 1927; see also two wires from Mississippi Senator Pat Harrison to Hoover, May 18, 1927, HHPL.

374   "send us collect": *NYT* to John Klorer, May 20, 1927, NOCA.

375   "Since Senator Percy has": Crosby to Hoover, May 20, 1927, HHPL.

375   "[I] seem to have": Hoover to Coolidge, July 5, 1927, HHPL.

375   "We rescued Main Street": *NOS*, September 7, 1927.

375   he wrote identical: See, for example, Hoover to Benjamin Marsh, June 15, 1927; letters to newspapers went out over a period of time; a large number were sent out on July 12, 1927, copies in HHPL.

375   "I have thought": Hoover to the editor of the *Journal-Press*, Blaine, Washington, July 12, 1927, HHPL.

375   "Bert's just resting": Quoted in Richard Norton Smith, *An Uncommon Man*, p. 17.

376   "We challenge the statement": *MC-A*, June 22, 1927.

376   "There is, in fact": W. H. Negus to R. E. Kennington, May 24, 1927, HHPL.

376   he convinced the St. Louis: Hoover to Crosby, May 31, 1927, HHPL.

376 he also had the Red Cross: Hoover to R. E. Kennington, May 24, 1927, HHPL.
376 they convinced Percy's: Stone to Hoover, September 23, 1927, HHPL.
376 He said the Mississippi: *MC-A*, June 23, 1927.
376 months after his assertion: Memo from John Cremer to H. Stuart Crawford, secretary to Coolidge, September 17, 1927, RCP.
376 "It has been a source": Crosby to Hoover, July 2, 1927, HHPL.
376 "I have the feeling": Hoover to Butler, July 5, 1927, HHPL.
377 the Mississippi corporation: Ibid. See also "Report of Mississippi Rehabilitation Corporation," 1929, RCP.

CHAPTER THIRTY-TWO

378 "to pull out": Carol Fennelly, "History of the National Red Cross," unpublished ms., p. 6, American Red Cross Archives, Wash., D.C.
378 Red Cross headquarters: Ibid., p. 33.
378 "unwise to become": DeWitt Smith to Fieser, June 17, 1927; Fieser to DeWitt Smith, June 20, 1927, RCP.
379 "he had given his": Robert Russa Moton, *Finding a Way Out,* p. 12.
379 "with all the deference": Ibid., p. 128.
379 "Negroes have always met": Robert Russa Moton, *What the Negro Thinks,* pp. 1, 9, 67.
380 "the wholesome advice": Quoted in Moton, *Finding a Way Out,* p. 265.
380 "Whatever might be said": William Hughes and Frederick Patterson, eds., *Robert Russa Moton,* p. 182.
381 "be pleased to see": George Akerson to Moton, September 21, 1926, RRMP.
381 "to save an embarrassing": C. C. Spaulding to Moton, November 26, 1928, RRMP.
381 Moton promised its leader: Moton to Booze, February 20, 1930, RRMP.
381 "the proper approach": Booze to Moton, July 2, 1929, RRMP.
381 "Our train took six": Undated draft report of first Colored Advisory Commission, RRMP.
382 One investigator separately sent: Sidney Redmond to John Sargent, July 5, 1927, Justice Department records, peonage file, NA RG 60.
382 "You may feel free": Moton to Hoover, June 14, 1927, RCP.
382 "the truth must": Barnett to Hoover, June 14, 1927, HHPL.
382 "constructive": Barnett to Albion Holsey, June 17, 1927, RRMP.
382 "The [Chicago] Defender demands": Barnett to Moton, June 18, 1927; Barnett to Albion Holsey, June 17, 1927; both in RRMP.
382 "something substantial": Ibid.
383 "I am of the opinion": Clark to Moton, June 14, 1927, RRMP.
383 "It is my frank": Moton to Lester Walton, July 13, 1927, RRMP.
383 "We were face to face": Draft report by Moton, June 13, 1927, RRMP.
384 Moton had prepared only three: Jesse Thomas to Holsey, July 9, 1927; Holsey to Thomas, July 23, 1927; both in RRMP.
384 he also asked about rehabilitation: For background on this meeting, see "Memorandum of Conference Between Officials of the Red Cross

and Members of Colored Commission," July 8, 1927, RCP. See also Hoover to Crosby, July 8 and 12, 1927, HHPL; Moton to Clark, July 2, 1927, and Holsey to Thomas, July 23, 1927, both in RRMP.

384 "Underground Forces": Consolidated Press story, July 23, 1927, as it appears in MC-A.

384 "background of bankrupt economics": Memorandum, typed, with changes in Hoover's handwriting, July 9, 1927, HHPL.

384 Hoover estimated: Ibid.; also note in the memorandum that Hoover used a figure of $1–$2 million, with each million dollars enough for 1,500 families. In a letter to Crosby on July 12 (copy in HHPL) he called for initial capital of $4.5 million.

385 "If it were possible": Memorandum, July 9, 1927, HHPL.

385 Now many of the same men: Consolidated Press story, July 23, 1927, as it appears in MC-A; see also NYT, August 4, 5, and 16, 1927.

385 "I am not at liberty": Fieser to Hoover, August 27, 1927, HHPL.

386 "newspaper publicity": Ibid.

386 Moton never learned: There is no reference to Fieser's position in any Moton correspondence either with Hoover, with any member of the Colored Advisory Commission, or with his assistants.

386 "A great many people": Arthur Kellogg to Hoover, July 13, 1927, HHPL.

CHAPTER THIRTY-THREE

387 Only 20 to 25 percent: LP to L. A. Downs, September 10, 1927; WAP to LP, February 9, 1928, both in PFP.

387 tons of yeast: July 16, 1927, report, U.S. Public Health Service, NA, RG 90, Mississippi Flood, box 3, p. 9; Wesselius to Baker and Smith, July 23, 1927; Drs. Hugh Cumming and William DeKleine to local health officials, August 12, 1927; DeKleine to DeWitt Smith, September 23, 1927; all letters in RCP, boxes 735 and 740.

388 "[A]ny attempt to remove": July 16, 1927, report, U.S. Public Health Service, NA, RG 90, Mississippi Flood, box 3, p. 34.

388 the black camp closed: Camps for blacks in Vicksburg closed July 1; the white camp stayed open until August 22. See Crisis, February 1928, p. 42.

388 county Red Cross chairmen: Moton to Robert Bondy, June 18, 1927, RCP; draft report of Colored Advisory Commission, December 1927, RRMP; for a specific example, see flood sufferer to Hoover, July 25, 1927, HHPL.

388 official Red Cross policy: See June 26, 1927, memo signed by Hoover and Fieser, which states, "Cabins to only be erected upon properties of resident ownership," RCP.

388 "We have grave suspicions": Crisis, November 1927.

389 "Next month we shall": Ibid.

389 "The Crisis had a white": Barnett to Moton, November 19, 1927, RRMP.

389 "Suggest that Red Cross": Moton to Hoover, November 16, 1927, RCP, box 734.

389 "the colored complex": See Moton to Hoover, October 1, 1927,

RRMP; Hoover, DeWitt Smith to Robert Thrush, October 13, 1927, RCP; Hoover to Smith, November 3, 1927, RCP; November 7, 1927, memo by Smith, RCP, box 734.

389 "frequently nullified": Untitled summary addressed to Hoover, signed by Moton, December 12, 1927, RRMP; another copy in RCP.

390 "I think we beat": Barnett to Thomas, January 6, 1928, CBP.

390 "vigorously investigated": Hoover to Moton, December 17, 1927, HHPL.

390 "I felt Secretary Hoover": Barnett to Moton, January 6, 1928 (incorrectly dated), CBP.

390 "The presence of": Moton to Hoover, January 4, 1928, RRMP.

391 "laid Dr. Moton out": Fieser to DeWitt Smith, December 19, 1927, RCP.

391 "another element": Hoover to Fieser, December 22, 1927, RCP.

391 "I have received": Moton to Hoover, January 9 and 12, 1928; Hoover to Moton, January 13, 1928; both in HHPL.

391 "I feel very strongly": Barnett to Fieser, March 20, 1928, CBP.

391 "Neither Dr. Moton nor I": Clark to Fieser, January 11, 1928, RCP.

391 "outline the plan": William Schieffelin to Hoover, January 9, 1928, HHPL.

392 "I feel it would": Hoover to Schieffelin, January 12, 1928, HHPL.

392 "a great experiment": Hoover to Rosenwald, February 13, 1928, HHPL.

392 "Mr. Rosenwald's reaction": Edwin Embree to Hoover, March 1, 1928, HHPL.

393 "A word from you": Moton to Hoover, January 18, 1928, RRMP.

393 "could finance the scheme": Moton to Hoover, February 27, 1928, RRMP.

393 Hoover sent him a copy: Hoover to Moton, March 11, 1928, HHPL.

393 "You are the kind": Moton to John D. Rockefeller, Jr., June 16, 1928, RRMP.

393 "plan to deadlock": *NYT*, March 31, 1928.

394 "popularity grows by contact": LP to Pat Harrison, August 30, 1928, PFP.

394 "I don't believe": LP to Will Stimmel, September 15, 1927, PFP.

394 "No man in public life": LP to "Willie," probably his nephew William Armstrong Percy, June 30, 1928, PFP.

394 people acting for Hoover: See, for example, correspondence between Fletcher Chenault, *Arkansas Gazette* reporter, and Akerson, from October 6, 1927, to May 6, 1928, in HHPL, which detail Chenault's spying for the Hoover campaign and manipulating his stories to help Hoover. After the election Chenault asked Akerson for a job. Regarding illegal payoffs, especially in the South, see Donald Lisio, *Hoover, Blacks and Lily-Whites,* passim.

394 "Would it be possible": Akerson to Harvey Couch, March 22, 1928; see also Neale to Couch, February 22, 1928, both in Akerson Papers, HHPL.

394 a campaign aide: Barnett to Akerson, January 17, 1928, CBP.

394 "Both Secretary Hoover": Akerson to Barnett, May 15, 1928, HHPL.

394 "just what you": J. M. Lee to Moton, February 11, 1928, RRMP.

394   "regarding Mr. Hoover": Bernie mentions to Moton, August 29, 1928, RRMP.
394   Akerson instructed Moton: Holsey to Akerson, June 6, 1928, HHPL.
394   "Mr. J. C. Mitchell": Akerson to Moton, May 1, 1928, HHPL.
395   "and find out exactly": Akerson to Moton, March 27, 1928, HHPL.
395   "a statement to": Akerson to Moton, September 24, 1928, HHPL.

CHAPTER THIRTY-FOUR

400   "[i]t remained for": Clipping quoted in undated report of Mississippi River Flood Control Association, PFP.
400   Present were Hoover, Percy, Martineau, Butler: All information about this meeting and quotes from it below come from a stenographic transcript of the meeting in CP.
401   "No relief to flood": This statement is dated September 30, 1927, HHPL.
402   40 percent had gone unspent: Arthur Frank, *The Development of the Federal Program of Flood Control on the Mississippi River,* p. 195.
404   The governor of Mississippi: LP to Governor Murphree, December 21, 1927, PFP.
404   Repeatedly, they saw: October 25, 1927, executive committee minutes, CP.
404   "following what I interpret": Thomson memo, October 22, 1927, included in CP.
404   "The first three days": Mississippi River Flood Control Association confidential bulletin of October 24, 1927, included in CP.
404   the chief engineer of every single: Governor-elect Huey Long to Edwin Broussard, February 22, 1928, Edwin Broussard Papers, Dupre Library, Special Collections, University of Southwestern Louisiana; Frank, p. 229.
404   In his own House testimony: *HFCCH,* January 1928, p. 3723.
405   "Coming from the Imperial": Ibid., p. 25.
405   "the greatest expenditure": *NYT,* February 22 and March 29, 1928.
405   "President Coolidge has": *NYT,* February 22, 1928.
405   "The White House has": *Wall Street Journal,* April 24, 1928.
406   Levee boards owed: Frank, p. 237.
406   "The disastrous flood": Resolution of American Bankers Association, April 18, 1928, copy in CP.
406   the real cost would run: *NYT,* February 22 and March 29, 1928.
406   "The bill changes the policy": *NOS,* May 15, 1928.
406   "the viciousness of Army engineers": L. T. Berthe to John Klorer, February 22, 1929, NOCA.
407   "I did not expect this": Minutes of the board of Canal Bank, May 16, 1928, CP.
407   an evening banquet in his honor: see *NOT-P, NOI,* and *NOT,* May 20 through May 24, 1927.
408   25,216 votes to none: See Glen Jeansonne, *Leander Perez: Boss of the Delta,* pp. 71–72; T. Harry Williams, *Huey Long,* pp. 539–540, 589–590.

408 Once the Board of Liquidation: Interview with Otis Alexander, secretary of the Board of Liquidation, January 25, 1996.
409 "I'd never have come": Interview with Betty Carter, November 25, 1993.
409 "merged": *NOT-P*, June 24, 1928.
409 the flood killed him: interview with Pearl Amos, February 12, 1993.
409 its board reelected Butler: *NOT-P*, January 22 and February 20, 1931.
410 "I know absolutely nothing": *NOI*, May 11, 1939.
410 A Mississippi grand jury declined: *NOT-P*, *NOI*, and *NOT*, May 11 and 12, 1939.
410 Russell Long, Huey's son: Interview with Russell Long, April 4, 1996.
411 "[The] social system excludes": Task Force on the Economy, "The Economy," *Framework for the Future*, vol. 2 (New Orleans: Goals to Grow, 1971), p. 207, quoted in Raabe, "Status and Its Impact," Ph.D. diss., p. 189.
411 "The long-established New Orleans": Raabe, p. 162.
411 not a single bank president: Interview with Francis Doyle, former president of First National Bank of Commerce, December 23, 1992.

CHAPTER THIRTY-FIVE

412 "as a form of contribution": Moton to Hoover, August, 7, 1928, HHPL.
412 "Hoover said that": Quoted in Lisio, p. 98.
412 "that the right type": Moton to Hoover, June 22, 1928, RRMP.
413 a deal known to Hoover: For details on Howard, see Lisio, esp. pp. 50–71.
413 "uncertainty in many sections": Barnett and Holsey, "Report of Survey of Sentiment Among Negro Voters," July 18, 1928, CBP.
413 "You, more than any": Barnett to George Brennan, July 20, 1928, CBP.
414 "I am out-and-out": Prattis to Barnett, July 18, 1928, CBP.
414 Hoover lost an estimated 15 percent: Harold Gosnell, *Negro Politicians*, pp. 28–30.
414 "Democrats made deeper inroads": Henry Moon, *Balance of Power: The Negro Vote*, p. 49.
414 "a competent woman": See memo of July 3, 1929, filed under Moton and "Farm Matters," HHPL; memo of January 15, 1930, Moton and Colored Question file, HHPL; see also January 1, 1930, to April 30, 1930, Moton file, HHPL.
414 "your personal concern": Moton to Hoover, March 9, 1931, RRMP.
415 "repugnant to all": Quoted in Lisio, p. 248.
415 if Roosevelt "has done anything": Quoted in Lisio, p. 269.
415 the Red Cross was still feeding: *GD-T*, March 1, 1928.
416 Every Saturday night: Interview with Sylvia Jackson.
416 "A great deal of labor": Alex Scott to Johnston, July 4, 1927, D&PLCP.
416 "The most serious thing": LP to L. A. Downs, September 10, 1927, PFP. Percy routinely provided such information to senior executives of

banks, brokerage houses, and the like; his assessments represented cold business judgments, not rhetoric.

416 "Labor was completely": Report to shareholders, April 1, 1928, D&PLCP.

417 "the Great Migration": E. Marvin Goodwin, *Black Migration in America from 1915–1960*, p. 10; see also C. Horace Hamilton, "The Negro Leaves the South," pp. 273–295; Carter Woodson, *A Century of Negro Migration.*

417 In the 1930s the exodus: Simon Kuznets et al., *Population Redistribution and Economic Growth, United States, 1870–1950: Demographic Analysis and Interrelations* (Philadelphia: American Philosophical Society, 1964), vol. 1, pp. 88–99; vol. 3, p. 106.

417 "I never expected": Quoted in Wyatt-Brown, p. 256.

418 "I am happy": Hoover to LP, November 12, 1929, PFP.

418 "even if only on": John Sharp Williams to LP, December 21, 1929, PFP.

418 "No matter what": Interview with Moses Mason, March 1, 1993.

418 "One of the pleasantest": Percy, *LL*, pp. 344–345.

418 at a cost of $25,000: Wyatt-Brown, p. 258.

419 his personal checkbook balance: See checkbook ledger in PFP.

419 "Hypocrisy is the pet": LP to Pat Harrison, August 24, 1928, PFP.

419 "he had to leave often": Percy, *LL*, p. ix.

419 "the most ideologically": Oral history of Walker Percy, MDAH.

419 "To furnish [Japan]": WAP to Oscar Bledsoe, June 7, 1940; WAP to Billy Wynn, June 22, 1940, D&PLCP.

419 Will offered to help: Cohn, *Where I Was Born and Raised,* pp. 270–293 passim.

419 "Their virtues": Oral history of Shelby Foote, MDAH.

420 "If the negroes": WAP to Johnston, February 22, 1937, D&PLCP.

421 he fired her: Wyatt-Brown, pp. 265–267; see also Percy, *LL*, pp. 285–297 passim.

421 "I got to take": Interview with David Cober, February 23, 1993; Cober, a black man, drove for Billy Wynn. Mrs. Millie Commodore, the daughter of John McMiller, spoke of constant rumors of Will having affairs with black drivers. Four other people in separate interviews reported rumors of an affair Will had with Ford Atkins, but they insisted upon anonymity.

421 "My country is": Percy, *LL*, p. 3.

421 "The old Southern way": Ibid., pp. 312, 343.

421 "I wish a few others": Ibid., p. 346.

421 "I know that": Ibid., p. 347.

APPENDIX

424 Hoover refused to nominate: Arthur Morgan, *Dams and Other Disasters*, p. 211.

424 The cutoffs worked: William Elam, *Speeding Floods to the Sea*, p. 83; interview with Newman Bolls, for more than twenty years engineer for the Mississippi Levee Board, February 22, 1993.

425   measured the flow there: HFCCH, p. 2869; Association of Railway Engineers, *The Flood of 1927*, pamphlet, NOCA.

425   304 miles of those levees: Interview with Stan McAlpin, Army Corps of Engineers, Vicksburg office, July 25, 1996.

425   "the inevitable consequence": HFCCH, p. 2881.

Selected Bibliography

Major Collections of Primary Sources

Chicago Historical Society
Claude Barnett Collection

Winston Churchill Memorial and Library, Westminster
College, Fulton, Missouri
　Eads Letters

Delta State University Library, Cleveland, Mississippi
　Walter Sillers Jr. Papers

Dupre Library, Special Collections,
University of Southwestern Louisiana, Lafayette
　Edwin Broussard Papers
　John Parker Papers

John Hay Library, Brown University, Providence, Rhode Island
　Elmer Corthell Papers

Historic New Orleans Collection
　Henry P. Leovy Papers
　Mississippi Flood Insurance Collection
　Williams, Monroe, and Blanc Family Papers

Historical Society of Philadelphia
　Andrew Atkinson Humphreys Papers

Herbert Hoover Presidential Library, West Branch, Iowa
　George Akerson Papers
　Hoover Papers

Howard-Tilton Library, Tulane University
Louisiana Collection:
Isaac Cline, "Official Stage Forecasts 1927"

Special Collections:
P. G. T. Beauregard Papers
Rudolph Hecht Papers
John Klorer Papers
Lyle Saxon Papers
Stern Family Papers

Library of Congress, Washington, D.C.
Cyrus B. Comstock Papers
Coolidge Papers
Warren G. Harding Papers
NAACP Papers
John Sharp Williams Papers

Earl Long Library, Special Collections, University of New Orleans
Association of Commerce Papers
Henry Dart Papers
Task Force on the Economy, "The Economy," *Framework for the Future,* vol. 2

Louisiana State Museum, Historical Division, New Orleans
Harry B. Caplan Collection
James Kemper Collection

Mississippi Department of Archives and History, Jackson
Fred Chaney, "A Refugee's Story," Unpublished Manuscript
"The Flood of 1927," Mississippi Public Television, Transcripts of Interviews
National Guard Report on Activities During Flood of 1927
Oral History Collection
Percy Papers
Henry Waring Ball Diaries

Mississippi State University Library, Starkville
Delta & Pine Land Company Papers

Missouri Historical Society, St. Louis
James B. Eads Papers

National Archives, Washington, D.C.
Agriculture Department Papers, Record Group 16, Entries 16 and 17
Commerce Department Miscellaneous Records, Record Group 40, Box 615
Red Cross Papers, Record Group 200, Boxes 733–745

State Department Archives, Record Group 59, Microfilm Roll 539, Microcopy M862

U.S. Army, Corps of Engineers, Record Group 77

U.S. Army, Office of the Adjutant General, Record Group 94, Box 2417

U.S. Public Health Service, Record Group 90, Box 3

NEW ORLEANS PUBLIC LIBRARY, LOUISIANA ROOM
Martin Behrman Papers
Walter Carey Papers
Friends of the Cabildo Oral History Collection
John Klorer Papers
New Orleans City Archives
Arthur O'Keefe Papers
Safe River Committee of 100 Papers

ORLEANS PARISH LEVEE BOARD, NEW ORLEANS
Levee Board Minutes
Orleans Organization Caernarvon Reparations Records, at Law Offices of Monroe & Lemann

WILLIAM ALEXANDER PERCY LIBRARY, GREENVILLE, MISSISSIPPI
Oral History Collection

TUSKEGEE INSTITUTE LIBRARY, TUSKEGEE, ALABAMA
Albion Holsey Collection
Robert Russa Moton Collection

UNIVERSITY OF NORTH CAROLINA LIBRARY, CHAPEL HILL
John Parker Papers

PRINCIPAL NEWSPAPERS

Chicago Defender
Greenville Democrat-Times
Jackson Clarion-Ledger
Louisiana Weekly (New Orleans)
Memphis Commercial-Appeal
Missouri Republican (St. Louis)
New Orleans Daily Times
New Orleans Item
New Orleans Picayune
New Orleans States
New Orleans Times-Picayune
New Orleans Tribune
New York Daily Tribune
New York Herald
New York Times
Pittsburgh Courier
St. Louis Globe-Democrat

Books

Abbott, Henry. *Memoir of Andrew Atkinson Humphreys, 1810–1883.* Washington, D.C.: National Academy of Sciences, Biographical Memoirs 2, 1886.

Abert, J. W. *Report of Lieutenant J. W. Abert of His Examination of New Mexico in the Years 1846–47.* Albuquerque, 1962.

Alexander, Charles. *The Ku Klux Klan in the Southwest.* Lexington: University of Kentucky Press, 1965.

Arthur, Stanley. *Old Families of Louisiana.* Baton Rouge: Louisiana State University Press, 1971.

Ayres, Quincy, and Daniels Scoates. *Land Drainage and Reclamation.* New York: McGraw-Hill, 1939.

Baker, Lewis. *The Percys of Mississippi.* Baton Rouge: Louisiana State University Press, 1983.

Barber, William. *From New Era to New Deal: Herbert Hoover, The Economists, and American Economic Policy, 1921–1933.* Cambridge, Eng.: Cambridge University Press, 1985.

Baritz, Loren, ed. *The Culture of the Twenties.* Indianapolis: Bobbs-Merrill, 1970.

Belcher, Wyatt. *The Economic Rivalry Between St. Louis and Chicago, 1850–1880.* New York: Columbia University Press, 1947.

Bell, Percy. "Child of the Delta." Unpublished ms. courtesy of Charles Bell.

Beman, Lamar. *Flood Control.* New York: H. W. Wilson Co., 1928.

Bernstein, Herman. *Herbert Hoover: The Man Who Brought America to the World.* New York: Herald-Nathan Press, 1928.

Birmingham, Stephen. *Our Crowd.* New York: Harper & Row, 1967.

Boeger, E. A., and E. A. Goldenweiser. *A Study of Tenant Systems of Farming in the Mississippi Delta.* USDA Bulletin 337, January 13, 1916.

Bowen, Ezra, ed. *This Fabulous Century, 1920–1930.* Alexandria, Va.: Time-Life Books, 1985.

Brandfon, Robert. *The Cotton Kingdom of the New South.* Cambridge, Mass.: Harvard University Press, 1967.

Bullock, Henry. *A History of Negro Education in the South.* Cambridge, Mass.: Harvard University Press, 1967.

Burner, David. *Herbert Hoover: A Public Life.* New York: Knopf, 1979.

Butler, Pierce. *Laurel Hill and Later.* New Orleans: Crager, 1954.

———. *The Unhurried Years.* Baton Rouge: Louisiana State University Press, 1948.

Carnegie, Andrew. *The Autobiography of Andrew Carnegie.* Northeastern University Press, 1986.

Carter, Hodding. *The Lower Mississippi.* New York: Rinehart, 1942.

———. *Where Main Street Meets the River.* New York: Rinehart, 1953.

Cash, W. H. *The Mind of the South.* New York: Vintage, 1969.

Catton, Bruce. *Grant Takes Command.* Boston: Little, Brown, 1968.

———. *A Stillness at Appomattox.* Garden City, N.Y.: Doubleday, 1957.

Chalmers, David. *Hooded Americanism: The History of the Ku Klux Klan.* New York: New Viewpoints, 1981.

Chapin, Elizabeth. *American Court Gossip, or Life in the National Capital.* Marshalltown, Iowa: Chapin & Hartwell Bros., 1887.

Chaplin, Ralph. *The Centralia Conspiracy.* 1920. Reprint, Seattle: Shorey Book Store, 1971.

Clay, Floyd. *A Century on the Mississippi: A History of the Memphis District.* Washington, D.C.: U.S. Army Corps of Engineers, 1986.

Cline, Isaac. *Storms, Floods, and Sunshine.* New Orleans: Pelican Publishing, 1945.

Cobb, James. *The Most Southern Place on Earth.* New York: Oxford University Press, 1992.

Coben, Stanley. *Rebellion Against Victorianism: The Impetus for Cultural Change in 1920s America.* New York: Oxford University Press, 1991.

Cohn, David. *Where I Was Born and Raised.* Boston: Houghton Mifflin, 1948.

Conaway, James. *Judge: The Life and Times of Leander Perez.* New York: Knopf, 1973.

Coolidge, Calvin. *The Autobiography of Calvin Coolidge.* New York: Cosmopolitan Book Co., 1929.

Cooper, William J., et al., eds. *A Master's Due: Essays in Honor of David Herbert Donald.* Baton Rouge: Louisiana State University Press, 1985.

Corthell, Elmer. *A History of the Jetties at the Mouth of the Mississippi.* New York: J. Wiley, 1881.

Cowdrey, Albert. *Land's End.* Washington, D.C.: U.S. Army Corps of Engineers, 1977.

Coyle, Elinor. *St. Louis: Portrait of a River City.* St. Louis: Folkstone Press, 1966.

Dabney, Thomas. *One Hundred Great Years: The Story of the Times-Picayune from Its Founding to 1940.* Baton Rouge: Louisiana State University Press, 1944.

Daniel, Pete. *Deep'n as It Come: The 1927 Mississippi River Flood.* New York: Oxford University Press, 1977.

———. *Shadow of Slavery.* Urbana: University of Illinois, 1972.

Data in the State Engineer's Office Relating to Irrigation, Water Supply, Hydrology, and Geology of the Canadian River Basin. Santa Fe, 1925.

Davis, Allison; Burleigh Gardner; and Mary Gardner. *Deep South: An Anthropological Study of Caste and Class.* Chicago: University of Chicago Press, 1959.

Davis, Ronald, ed. *The Social and Cultural Life of the 1920s.* New York: Holt, Rinehart & Winston, 1972.

Dawson, E. F. *Notes on the Mississippi River.* Calcutta: Thacker, Spink & Co., 1900.

Dickins, Dorothy. *A Nutritional Investigation of Tenants in the Yazoo-Mississippi Delta.* Mississippi Agricultural Experiment Station Bulletin 254. Mississippi A&M College, Starkville, 1928.

Dollard, John. *Caste and Class in a Southern Town.* New Haven: Yale University Press, 1937.

Dorsey, Florence. *Road to the Sea: The Story of James B. Eads and the Mississippi River.* New York: Rinehart, 1947.

Eads, James B. *Physics and Hydraulics of the Mississippi River.* Pamphlet. New Orleans, 1876.

———. *Review of Humphreys and Abbot Report.* Pamphlet. Washington, D.C., 1878.

Elam, William. *Speeding Floods to the Sea.* New York: Hobson Book Press, 1926.

Elliott, D. O. *The Improvement of the Lower Mississippi River for Flood Control and Navigation.* 3 vols. Vicksburg: Mississippi River Commission, 1932.

Embree, Edwin, and Julia Waxman. *Investment in People: The Story of the Julius Rosenwald Fund.* New York: Harper, 1949.

Emerson, Edwin. *Hoover and His Times: Looking Back Through the Years.* Garden City, N.Y.: Doubleday, 1932.

Faulkner, John. *Dollar Cotton.* New York: Harcourt Brace & Co., 1942.

Faulkner, William. *The Wild Palms.* New York: Random House, 1939.

Fenn, Charles. *Ho Chi Minh.* New York: Scribners, 1973.

Ferrell, John. *From Single to Multi-Purpose Planning: The Role of the Army Engineers in River Development Policy, 1824–1930.* Washington, D.C.: U.S. Army Corps of Engineers, 1976.

Final Report of the Colored Advisory Commission, The. Washington, D.C.: American National Red Cross, 1929.

Fisk, Harold. *Fine Grained Alluvial Deposits and Their Effects on Mississippi River Activity.* Vicksburg: Mississippi River Commission, 1947.

———. *Geological Investigation of the Alluvial Valley of the Lower Mississippi.* Vicksburg: Mississippi River Commission, 1944.

Foner, Eric. *Reconstruction.* New York: Harper & Row, 1988.

Foote, Shelby. *The Civil War: A Narrative.* Vol. 1. New York: Vintage, 1986.

Frank, Arthur. *The Development of the Federal Program of Flood Control on the Mississippi River.* New York: Columbia University Press, 1930.

Frankenfield, H. C. "The Floods of 1927 in the Mississippi Basin." *Monthly Weather Review,* Supplement 29. Washington, D.C., 1927.

Franklin, John Hope, ed. *Three Negro Classics: Up from Slavery by Booker T. Washington, Souls of Black Folk by W. E. B. Du Bois, Autobiography of an Ex-Colored Man by James Weldon Johnson.* New York: Avon, 1976.

Fuess, Claude. *Calvin Coolidge: The Man from Vermont.* Boston: Little, Brown, 1940.

Garsaud, Marcel. *Removal of Eleven Miles of Levee on the Mississippi River Below Point à la Hache.* St. Louis, 1925.

Gleick, James. *Chaos.* New York: Viking, 1989.

Glymph, Thavolia, and John Kushna, eds. *Essays on the Post-Bellum Southern Economy.* College Station: Texas A&M Press, 1985.

Goodwin, E. Marvin. *Black Migration in America from 1915–1960.* Lewiston, N.Y.: Edwin Mellen Press, 1990.

Gosnell, Harold. *Champion Campaigner.* New York: Macmillan, 1952.

———. *Negro Politicians.* Chicago: University of Chicago Press, 1935.

Gould, Emerson. *Fifty Years on the Mississippi.* St. Louis: Nixon-Jones, 1889.

Grant, U. S. *Personal Memoirs of U. S. Grant.* New York: C. L. Webster, 1885.

Green, A. Wigfall. *The Man Bilbo.* Baton Rouge: Louisiana State University Press, 1963.

Grossman, James. *Land of Hope: Chicago, Black Southerners, and the Great Migration.* Chicago: University of Chicago, 1989.

Haas, Edward. *Political Leadership in a Southern City: New Orleans in the Progressive Era, 1896–1902.* Ruston: McGinty Publications, Louisiana Tech University, 1988.

Hair, William. *The Kingfish and His Realm: The Life and Times of Huey P. Long.* Baton Rouge: Louisiana State University Press, 1991.

Harrison, Robert. *Alluvial Empire.* Little Rock: Delta Fund, in cooperation with U.S. Department of Agriculture, 1961.

———. *Levee Districts and Levee Building in Mississippi.* Stoneville, Miss., 1951. (In cooperation with the Bureau Agricultural Economics, U.S. Department of Agriculture, USDA.)

Hawley, Ellis. *The Great War and the Search for a Modern Order: A History of American People and Their Institutions, 1917–1933.* New York: St. Martin's, 1979.

———. *Herbert Hoover and the Historians.* West Branch, Iowa: Hoover Library, 1989.

———. *Herbert Hoover as Secretary of Commerce: Studies in New Era Thought and Practice.* Iowa City: University of Iowa Press, 1981.

Hays, Samuel. *Conservation and the Gospel of Efficiency: The Progressive Conservation Movement, 1890–1920.* Cambridge, Mass.: Harvard University Press, 1959.

Hewson, William. *Principles and Practices of Levee Building.* New York, 1860.

Hicks, J. D. *The Populist Revolt.* Minneapolis: University of Minnesota, 1931.

History of Blacks in Greenville, 1863–1975. Pamphlet. National Homecoming, July 1975, W. A. Percy Library, Greenville, Miss.

Hobbs, G. A. *Bilbo, Brewer, and Bribery in Mississippi Politics.* Memphis: Dixon-Paul Printing Co., 1917.

Hofstadter, Richard. *Age of Reform.* New York: Knopf, 1956.

———. *Social Darwinism in American Thought, 1860–1915.* Boston: Beacon Press, 1967.

Holmes, Williams. *The White Chief: James Kimble Vardaman.* Baton Rouge: Louisiana State University Press, 1970.

Hoover, Herbert. *American Individualism.* Garden City, N.Y.: Doubleday, 1922.

———. *Challenge to Liberty.* New York: Scribners, 1934.

———. *Memoirs of Herbert Hoover.* New York: Macmillan, 1952.

Hoover, Irwin. *Forty-two Years in the White House.* New York: Houghton Mifflin, 1934.

How, Louis. *James B. Eads.* Boston: Houghton Mifflin, 1900.

Hughes, William, and Frederick Patterson, eds. *Robert Russa Moton.* Chapel Hill: University of North Carolina Press, 1956.

Humphreys, Andrew Atkinson and Henry Abbot, *Report upon the Physics and Hydraulics of the Mississippi River.* Philadelphia: Lippincott, 1861.

Humphreys, Benjamin G. *Floods and Levees on the Mississippi River.* Washington, D.C., 1914.

Humphreys, Henry. *Andrew Atkinson Humphreys.* Philadelphia: John C. Winston Co., 1924.

———. *Andrew Atkinson Humphreys at Fredericksburg.* Philadelphia: John C. Winston Co., 1896.

Irwin, Will. *Herbert Hoover: A Reminiscent Biography.* New York: Century Co., 1928.

Jackson, Kenneth T. *The Ku Klux Klan in the City, 1915–1930.* New York: Oxford University Press, 1967.

Jahncke Service, Inc. *The First 75 Years*. Pamphlet. New Orleans, 1950.

Jeansonne, Glenn. *Leander Perez: Boss of the Delta*. Baton Rouge: Louisiana State University Press, 1977.

Katz, William. *The Invisible Empire*. Seattle: Open Hand Publishing, 1987.

Kemp, John R., ed. *Martin Behrman of New Orleans: Memoirs of a City Boss*. Baton Rouge: Louisiana State University Press, 1977.

Kemper, James. *Floods in the Valley of the Mississippi*. New Orleans: National Flood Commission, 1928.

———. *Rebellious River*. Boston: Humphries, 1949.

Key, V. O. *Southern Politics in State and Nation*. New York: Vintage, 1949.

King, Philip. *The Evolution of North America*. Princeton: Princeton University Press, 1959.

King, Richard. *A Southern Renaissance: The Cultural Awakening of the American South*. New York: Oxford University Press, 1980.

Kirby, Richard, and Philip Laurson. *Early Years of Modern Civil Engineering*. New Haven: Yale University Press, 1932.

Kirwan, Albert K. *Revolt of the Rednecks: Mississippi Politics 1877–1925*. Lexington: University of Kentucky Press, 1951.

Korn, Bertram. *Early Jews of New Orleans*. Waltham, Mass.: American Jewish Historical Society, 1969.

La Cour, Arthur. *New Orleans Masquerade: Chronicles of Carnival*. New Orleans: Pelican Publishing, 1952.

Laborde, Adras. *A National Southerner: Ransdell of Louisiana*. New York: Benziger, 1951.

Landry, Stuart. *History of the Boston Club*. New Orleans: Pelican Publishing, 1938.

Langsford, E. L., and R. H. Leavell. *Plantation Organization in Operation in the Yazoo-Mississippi Delta*. USDA Bulletin no. 682. Washington, D.C., May 1939.

Layton, Edwin. *The Revolt of the Engineers: Social Responsibility and the American Engineering Movement*. Cleveland: Case Western Reserve University Press, 1971.

Lemann, Nicholas. *The Promised Land: The Great Black Migration and How It Changed America*. New York: Knopf, 1991.

Lewis, Gene. *Charles Ellet, Jr.: The Engineer as Individualist*. Urbana: University of Illinois Press, 1968.

Liggett, Walter. *The Rise of Herbert Hoover*. New York: H. K. Fly Co., 1932.

Lisio, Donald. *Hoover, Blacks, and Lily-Whites: A Study of Southern Strategies*. Chapel Hill: University of North Carolina Press, 1985.

Lloyd, Craig. *Aggressive Introvert: A Study of Herbert Hoover and Public Relations Management, 1912–1932*. Columbus: Ohio State University Press, 1972.

Loewen, James. *The Mississippi Chinese: Between Black and White*. Cambridge, Mass.: Harvard University Press, 1971.

Lomax, Alan. *The Land Where the Blues Began*. New York: Pantheon, 1993.

Losses and Damages Resulting from the Flood of 1927. Memphis: Mississippi River Flood Control Association, 1927.

Louisiana Engineering Society. *Government Control with Cooperation of Riparian States in Construction of Levees*. Pamphlet. New Orleans, 1912.

Luthin, James. *Drainage Engineering*. New York: Wiley, 1966.

Marks, Carole. *Farewell, We're Good and Gone: The Great Black Migration.* Bloomington: Indiana University Press, 1989.

McCabe, James D. *Great Fortunes and How They Were Made.* Philadelphia, New York, and Boston, 1871.

McCoy, Donald. *Calvin Coolidge.* New York: Macmillan, 1967.

McCullough, David. *The Great Bridge.* New York: Simon & Schuster, 1972.

———. *The Path Between the Seas.* New York: Simon & Schuster, 1977.

McHenry, Estill, ed. *Addresses, Letters, and Papers of James B. Eads,* together with a biographical sketch. St. Louis: Slawson & Co., 1884. (This is a collection of primary sources of Eads' papers.)

McMillen, Neil. *Dark Journey.* Urbana: University of Illinois Press, 1990.

McPhee, John. *Control of Nature.* New York: Farrar, Straus & Giroux, 1989.

Miceli, Angelo. *The Pickwick Club of New Orleans.* New Orleans: Pickwick Press, 1964.

Miller, Howard, and Quinta Scott. *The Eads Bridge.* Columbia: University of Missouri Press, 1979.

Mills, Gary B. *Of Men and Rivers: The Story of the Vicksburg District.* Vicksburg, Miss.: U.S. Army Corps of Engineers, 1976.

Mississippi Valley Flood Disaster of 1927: Official Report of Relief Operations, The. Washington, D.C.: American National Red Cross, 1927.

Mitchell, Broadus. *The Rise of Cotton Mills in the South.* Baltimore: Johns Hopkins University Press, 1921.

Moffit, M. E. *Twenty Years of Progress in Public Education in Mississippi.* Pamphlet. Jackson, 1931.

Moon, Henry Lee. *Balance of Power: The Negro Vote.* Westport, Conn.: Greenwood Press, 1977.

Moore, D. D. *Louisianans and Their State.* New Orleans: Louisiana Historical and Biographical Association, n.d. (c. 1919).

Moore, Leonard. *Citizen Klansmen: The Ku Klux Klan in Indiana, 1921–1928.* Chapel Hill: University of North Carolina Press, 1991.

Moore, Norman. *Improvement of the Lower Mississippi River and Its Tributaries 1931–1972.* Vicksburg: Mississippi River Commission, 1972.

Mordden, Ethan. *That Jazz.* New York: Putnam, 1978.

Morgan, Arthur. *Dams and Other Disasters: A Century of the Army Corps of Engineers in Civil Works.* Boston: Little, Brown, 1971.

Morgan, Chester. *Redneck Liberal: Theodore Bilbo and the New Deal.* Baton Rouge: Louisiana State University Press, 1970.

Morrill, Park. *Floods of the Mississippi River.* Washington, D.C.: U.S. Weather Bureau, 1897.

Moton, Robert Russa. *Finding a Way Out.* Garden City, N.Y.: Doubleday, 1921.

———. *What the Negro Thinks.* Garden City, N.Y.: Doubleday, 1929.

Myrdal, Gunnar. *An American Dilemma.* New York: Harper, 1944.

Nash, George. *The Life of Herbert Hoover.* Vols. 1 and 2. New York: Norton, 1983.

Nash, Lee. *Understanding Herbert Hoover: Ten Perspectives.* Stanford, Calif.: Hoover Institution Press, 1987.

Nash, Roderick. *The Nervous Generation: American Thought 1917–1930.* Chicago: Rand McNally, 1970.

Noble, David F. *America by Design.* New York: Knopf, 1977.

Ockerson, J. A. *Outlets for Reducing Flood Heights.* Pamphlet. Mississippi River Commission, 1915.

Osborn, George. *John Sharp Williams.* Baton Rouge: Louisiana State University Press, 1943.

Paxton, A. G. *Three Wars and a Flood.* Pamphlet. Greenville, Miss., n.d.

Percy, William Alexander. *Enzio's Kingdom and Other Poems.* New Haven: Yale University Press, 1924.

——. *Lanterns on the Levee.* New York: Knopf, 1941.

——. *Sappho in Levkas and Other Poems.* New Haven: Yale University Press, 1915.

——. *Selected Poems.* New Haven: Yale University Press, 1930.

Powdermaker, Hortense. *After Freedom: A Cultural Study in the Deep South.* New York: Viking, 1939.

Price, Daniel. *Changing Characteristics — Negro Population.* Washington, D.C.: Department of Commerce, 1965.

Price, Willard. *The Amazing Mississippi.* New York: John Day Co., 1963.

Prothro, James. *Dollar Decade: Business Ideas in the 1920s.* Baton Rouge: Louisiana State University Press, 1954.

Pursell, Carroll, ed. *Technology in America: A History of Individuals and Ideas.* Cambridge, Mass.: MIT Press, 1981.

Reavis, L. U. *St. Louis: The Future Great City of the World.* St. Louis: Nixon-Jones Publishing Co., 1876.

Redfern, Ron. *The Making of a Continent.* New York: Times Books, 1983.

Reynolds, George. *Machine Politics in New Orleans: 1897–1926.* New York: AMS Press, 1968.

Reynolds, Terry, ed. *The Engineer in America.* Chicago: University of Chicago Press, 1991.

Roberts, B. S. *On a Plan for Reclaiming the Waste Lands of the Mississippi River.* Washington, D.C., 1870.

Rogers, John. *The Murders of Mer Rouge.* St. Louis: Security Publishing, 1923.

Rouse, Hunter, and Simon Ince. *History of Hydraulics.* New York: Dover, 1957.

Rowland, Dunbar. *History of Mississippi: The Heart of the South.* Chicago: S. J. Clarke Publishing, 1925.

Sandburg, Carl. *The Chicago Race Riots, July, 1919.* New York: Harcourt, Brace & World, 1919.

Saxon, Lyle. *Father Mississippi.* New York: Century Co., 1927.

Scharf, J. Thomas, *History of St. Louis City and County.* St. Louis, 1883.

Schlesinger, Arthur, Jr. *The Crisis of the Old Order 1919–1933.* Boston: Little, Brown, 1957.

Schriftgiesser, Karl. *This Was Normalcy.* Boston: Little, Brown, 1948.

Schubert, Frank. *Vanguard of Expansion: Army Engineers in the Trans-Mississippi West, 1819–1879.* Washington, D.C.: U.S. Army Corps of Engineers, 1980.

Shallat, Todd. *Structures in the Stream.* Austin: University of Texas, 1994.

Sillers, Florence. *History of Bolivar County.* Jackson, Miss.: Behrman Bros., 1946.

Sindler, Allan. *Huey Long's Louisiana: State Politics 1920–1952.* Baltimore: John Hopkins University Press, 1966.

Sitterson, J. Carlyle. *Sugar Country: The Cane Industry in the South, 1873–1950.* Lexington: University of Kentucky Press, 1953.

Smith, Clarke. *Survey for Spillways At or Near New Orleans.* Pamphlet. Mississippi River Commission, 1914.

Smith, Richard. *An Uncommon Man.* New York: Simon & Schuster, 1984.

Souchon, Edmond. *Reminiscences of Captain James B. Eads of Jetties Fame.* Pamphlet. New Orleans, 1915.

Southern Alluvial Land Association. *The Call of the Alluvial Empire.* Pamphlet. Jackson: Mississippi Department of Archives and History, 1919.

Stackpole, Edward. *The Fredericksburg Campaign.* Harrisburg, Pa.: Military Service Publishers, 1957.

Starr, S. Frederick. *New Orleans Unmasqued.* New Orleans: Dedeaux, 1985.

———. *Southern Comfort.* Cambridge, Mass.: MIT Press, 1989.

Stearn, Colin, et al. *Geological Evolution of North America.* New York: Ronald Press, 1979.

Steinman, David, and Sharon Watson. *Bridges and Their Builders.* New York: Dover, 1957.

Stone, Alfred. *Studies in American Race Relations.* New York: Doubleday, 1908.

Sullivan, Mark. *Our Times: The United States 1900–1925.* 6 vols. New York: Scribners, 1932–35.

Tallant, Robert. *Mardi Gras as It Was.* Gretna, La.: Pelican Publishing, 1989.

———. *Romantic New Orleans.* New York: Dutton, 1950.

Tatum, Elbert. *The Changed Political Thought of the Negro, 1915–1940.* 1951. Reprint, Westport, Conn.: Greenwood Press, 1974.

Tindall, George. *The Emergence of the New South, 1913–1945.* Baton Rouge: Louisiana State University Press, 1967.

Tolson, Jay. *Pilgrim in the Ruins.* New York: Simon & Schuster, 1992.

Townsend, Col. C. McD. *Flood Control of the Mississippi River.* Pamphlet. St. Louis, 1913.

———. *The Flow of Sediment in the Mississippi River and Its Influence on the Slope and Discharge.* Pamphlet. St. Louis, 1914.

Turwitz, Leo, and Turwitz, Evelyn. *Jews in Early Mississippi.* Jackson: University Press of Mississippi, 1983.

Tuttle, William. *Race Riot: Chicago in the Red Summer of 1919.* New York: Atheneum, 1970.

Twain, Mark. *Life on the Mississippi.* New York: Harper, 1903.

Underwood, Felix. *Health Progress Among Mississippi Negroes.* Pamphlet. Jackson, Miss., 1939.

U.S. Department of Commerce, Bureau of the Census. *Historical Statistics of the United States, Colonial Times to 1970.* Pt. 1.

U.S. House Committee on Flood Control. *House Flood Control Committee Hearings.* 6 vols. 70th Cong., 1st sess.

van Ravensway, Charles. *St. Louis: An Informal History of the City and Its People, 1764–1865.* St. Louis: Missouri Historical Society, 1991.

Vance, Rupert. *Human Geography of the South.* Chapel Hill: University of North Carolina Press, 1935.

Wade, Wyn Craig. *The Fiery Cross.* New York: Simon & Schuster, 1987.

Ware, Caroline. *Greenwich Village, 1920–1930.* Boston: Houghton Mifflin, 1935.

Waskow, Arthur. *From Race Riot to Sit-In: 1919 and the 1960s*. Garden City, N.Y.: Doubleday, 1967.

Weiss, Nancy. *Farewell to the Party of Lincoln: Black Politics in the Age of FDR*. Princeton: Princeton University Press, 1983.

Wharton, Vernon. *The Negro in Mississippi, 1865–1890*. Chapel Hill: University of North Carolina Press, 1947.

Wheeler, Richard. *Witness to Gettysburg*. New York: Harper & Row, 1987.

Whipple, A. W. *Explorations and Surveys, 1853–54*. Extract from the Preliminary Report for a Railway Route Near the 35th Parallel from the Mississippi River to the Pacific Ocean. Vol. 3. Washington, D.C.: U.S. Army Corps of Engineers.

White, Walter. *A Man Called White: The Autobiogrpahy of Walter White*. London: Victor Gollancz, 1948.

———. *Rope and Faggot*. Reprint, New York: Arno Press, 1968.

White, William Allen. *A Puritan in Babylon: The Story of Calvin Coolidge*. New York: Macmillan, 1938.

Williams, T. Harry. *Huey Long*. New York: Knopf, 1969.

Wilson, Carol. *Herbert Hoover: A Challenge for Today*. New York: Evans Publishing, 1968.

Wilson, Joan Hoff. *Herbert Hoover: Forgotten Progressive*. Boston: Little, Brown, 1974.

Wilson, Tippy Pool. *In the Bend of the River*. New Orleans: Pelican, Gretna, La., 1984.

Wolfe, Harold. *Herbert Hoover: Public Servant and Leader of the Loyal Opposition*. New York: Exposition Press, 1956.

Woodman, Harold. *King Cotton and His Retainers: Financing and Marketing the Cotton Crop of the South, 1800–1925*. Lexington: University of Kentucky Press, 1968.

Woodson, Carter. *A Century of Negro Migration*. New York: Russell & Russell, 1969.

Woodward, C. Vann. *Origins of the New South, 1877–1913*. Baton Rouge: Louisiana State University Press, 1951.

———. *The Strange Career of Jim Crow*. New York: Oxford University Press, 1965.

———. *Tom Watson, Agrarian Rebel*. New York: Macmillan, 1938.

Woodward, Calvin M. *History of the St. Louis Bridge*. St. Louis: G. I. Jones & Co., 1881.

Wright, Gavin. *Old South, New South: Revolutions in the Southern Economy Since the Civil War*. New York: Basic Books, 1986.

Wright, Richard. *Eight Men*. Cleveland: World Publishing, 1961.

———. *12 Million Black Voices*. New York: Thunder's Mouth Press, 1988.

———. *Uncle Tom's Children*. New York: Harper, 1938.

Wyatt-Brown, Bertram. *The House of Percy*. New York: Oxford University Press, 1994.

Yeo, Herbert. *Canadian River Investigation*. Pamphlet. Santa Fe, 1928.

Young, Perry. *The Mistick Krewe*. New Orleans: Carnival Press, 1931.

ARTICLES

Adams, Holmes. "Writers of Greenville." *Journal of Mississippi History* 32 (August 1970).

Berthoff, Rowland. "Southern Attittudes Toward Immigration, 1865–1914." *Journal of Southern History* 17 (August 1951).

Best, Gary. "The Hoover-for-President Boom." *MidAmerica* 53 (October 1971).

Brandfon, Robert. "The End of Immigration to the Cotton Fields." *Mississippi Valley Historical Review* 50 (March 1964).

Cohn, David. "Eighteenth Century Chevalier." *Virginia Quarterly Review* 31 (Fall 1955).

———. "How the South Feels." *Atlantic Monthly* 177 (January 1944).

———. "I Kept My Name." *Atlantic Monthly* 181 (April 1948).

———. "The River I Knew." *Virginia Quarterly Review* 35 (Spring 1959).

Condit, Carl. "Sullivan's Skyscrapers as the Expression of Nineteenth Century Technology." *Technology and Culture* 1 (April 1959).

Creel, George. "The Carnival of Corruption in Mississippi." *Cosmopolitan Magazine*, 1911.

De Peyster, John Watts. "A. A. Humphreys." *Magazine of American History* 16 (October 1886).

Drumm, S. M. "Robert E. Lee and the Improvement of the Mississippi River." *Missouri Historical Society Collections*, 1929.

Frazier, Arthur. "Daniel Farrand Henry's Cup Type 'Telegraphic' River Current Meter." *Technology and Culture* 5 (Fall 1964).

Ginzl, David. "Lily Whites versus Black and Tans: Mississippi Republicans During the Hoover Administration." *Journal of Mississippi History* 42 (August 1980).

Godfrey, Stuart. "Notes from a Mississippi Flood Diary." *Military Engineer,* November–December 1927.

Hamilton, C. Horace. "The Negro Leaves the South." *Demography* 1 (1964).

Harrison, Robert. "Formative Years of the Yazoo-Mississippi Delta Levee District." *Journal of Mississippi History* 13 (March 1952).

Hartley, C. W. S. "Sir Charles Hartley and the Mouth of the Mississippi." *Louisiana History* 24, no. 3 (Summer 1983).

Hofstadter, Richard. "Herbert Hoover and the Crisis of American Individualism." In *The American Political Tradition.* New York: Knopf, 1949.

Holmes, William. "Vardaman." *Journal of Mississippi History,* 1969.

———. "Whitecapping in Mississippi." *Journal of Southern History* 35 (May 1969).

———. "William Alexander Percy and the Bourbon Era in Mississippi Politics." *Mississippi Quarterly* 26 (Winter 1972–1973).

Kazin, Michael. "The Grass-Roots Right: New Histories of U.S. Conservatism in the Twentieth Century." *American Historical Review* 97 (February 1992).

Kelley, Arthell. "Levee Building and the Settlement of the Yazoo Basin." *Southern Quarterly* 1 (July 1963).

Kirby, Jack Temple. "The Southern Exodus, 1910–1960: A Primer for Historians." *Journal of Southern History* 49 (November 1983).

Kouwenhoven, John. "The Designing of the Eads Bridge." *Technology and Culture* 23 (October 1982).

———. "The Eads Bridge: The Celebration." *Missouri Historical Society Bulletin,* April 1974.

———. "Downtown St. Louis as James Eads Knew It." *Missouri Historical Society Bulletin,* April 1977.

———. "James Buchanan Eads: The Engineer as Entrepreneur." In Carroll Pursell, eds., *Technology in America: A History of Individuals and Ideas.*

Lee, John. "A Flood Year on the Mississippi." *Military Engineer,* July-August 1928.

Lohof, Bruce. "Herbert Hoover, Spokesman for Human Efficiency: The Mississippi Flood of 1927." *American Quarterly* 22 (Fall 1970).

———. "Herbert Hoover's Mississippi Valley Land Reform Memorandum." *Arkansas Historical Quarterly* 24 (Summer 1970).

May, Henry F. "Shifting Perspectives on the 1920s." *Mississippi Valley Historical Review* 63 (December 1956).

McMillen, Neil. "Perry Howard, Boss of Black-and-Tan Republicanism in Mississippi, 1924–1960." *Journal of Southern History* 48 (May 1981).

"Memoir of James B. Eads." *Transactions of the American Society of Civil Engineers* 17 (March 1887).

Mills, Gary. "New Life for the River of Death: Development of the Yazoo River Basin, 1873–1977." *Journal of Mississippi History* 41 (November 1979).

Mollison, Irvin. "Negro Lawyers in Mississippi." *Journal of Negro History* 15 (January 1930).

Moore, Leonard. "Historical Interpretations of the 1920s Klan." *Journal of Social History* 24 (Winter 1990).

Mowry, George. "The South and the Progressive Lily White Party of 1912." *Journal of Southern History* 6 (1940).

Murfree, W. L. "The Levees of the Mississippi." *Scribner's Magazine,* July 1881.

"Negro Common School in Miss., The." *Crisis* 32 (December 1926).

"Negro Migration from Mississippi." In *Negro Migration 1916–1917 Reports.* Washington, D.C.: U.S. Department of Labor, 1919.

Olson, James. "The End of Voluntarism." *Annals of Iowa* 41 (Fall 1972).

Osborn, George. "John Sharp Williams Becomes a United States Senator." *Journal of Southern History* 6 (May 1940).

Percy, LeRoy. "A Southern View of Negro Education." *Outlook* 86 (August 3, 1907).

Rable, George. "The South and the Politics of Anti-Lynching Legislation, 1920–1940." *Journal of Southern History* (May 1985).

Rainwater, P. L. "The Autobiography of Benjamin G. Humphreys, 1808–1882." *Mississippi Valley Historical Review,* 1934.

Reuss, Martin. "Politics and Technology in the Army Corps of Engineers." *Technology and Culture* 26 (January 1985).

Roberts, O. A., Jr. "The Elaine Race Riots of 1919." *Arkansas Historical Quarterly* 19 (Summer 1960).

Round, Harold. "A. A. Humphreys." *Civil War Times Illustrated* 4 (February 1966).

Satchfield, Lamar. "Those Famous Bobo Bear Hunts." *Delta Scene Magazine* 1, no. 2 (Spring 1974).

Schofield, Kent. "The Public Image of Herbert Hoover in the 1928 Campaign." *MidAmerica* 51 (October 1969).

Schuyler, George. "Freedom of the Press in Mississippi." *Crisis,* October 1936.

Shallat, Todd. "Andrew Atkinson Humphreys." *APWA Reporter* 49, no. 1 (January 1982).

Shideler, James H. "Herbert Hoover and the Federal Farm Board Project, 1921–25." *Mississippi Valley Historical Review* 41 (March 1956).

Sillers, Walter. "Flood Control in Bolivar County, 1883–1924." *Journal of Mississippi History,* 1947.

"Sketch of James B. Eads." *Popular Science Monthly* 28 (October 1884), pp. 544–552.

Smith, John David. "Alfred Holt Stone: Mississippi Planter and Archivist/Historian of Slavery." *Journal of Mississippi History* 45 (November 1983).

Snyder, Howard. "Negro Migration and the Cotton Crop." *North American Review* 219 (January 1924).

———. "Plantation Pictures." *Atlantic Monthly,* February 1921.

Stone, Alfred. "The Negro Farmer in the Mississippi Delta." *Southern Workman,* October 1903.

———. "The Negro in the Yazoo-Mississippi Delta." *Publications of the American Economic Association,* 3rd series, vol. 3. New York, 1902.

———. "A Plantation Experiment." *Quarterly Journal of Economics* 19 (February 1905).

Thoburn, James. "The Naming of the Canadian River." *Chronicles of Oklahoma* 6 (December 1928).

Thomson, T. P. "The Story of the Canal Bank, 1831–1915." Baton Rouge: Louisiana Historical Society Publications, vol. 7, 1924.

Williams, Mentor. "The Background of the Chicago River and Harbor Convention." *MidAmerica,* October 1948.

Zipser, Andy. "Hidden Value in the Bayou." *Barron's,* October 4, 1993.

DISSERTATIONS AND THESES

Balsamo, Larry. "Theodore Bilbo and Mississippi Politics, 1874–1932." Ph.D. diss., University of Missouri, 1967.

Dileanis, Leonard. "Herbert Hoover's Use of Public Relations in the U.S. Food Administration, 1917–1919." M.A. thesis, University of Wisconsin, 1969.

Garcia, George. "Herbert Hoover's Southern Strategy and the Black Reaction." M.A. thesis, University of Iowa, 1972.

Harrell, Kenneth. "The Ku Klux Klan in Louisiana, 1920–1930." Ph.D. thesis, Louisiana State University, 1966.

Hathorn, Guy. "The Political Career of C. Bascom Slemp." Ph.D. diss., Duke University, 1950.

Jones, Mina. "The Jewish Community in New Orleans: A Study of Social Organization." B.A. thesis, Tulane University, 1925.

Lohof, Bruce. "Herbert Hoover and the 1927 Mississippi Flood Disaster." Ph.D. diss., Syracuse University, 1968.

Lowrey, Walter. "Navigational Problems at the Mouth of the Mississippi River, 1698–1880." Ph.D. diss., Vanderbilt University, 1956.

Raabe, Phyllis. "Status and Its Impact: New Orleans Carnival, the Social Upper Class, and Upper Class Power." Ph.D. diss., Pennsylvania State University, 1972.

Ryan, Gary. "War Department Topographical Bureau, 1831–1863." Ph.D. diss., American University, 1968.

Sallis, William. "The Life and Times of LeRoy Percy." M.A. thesis, Mississippi State University, 1957.

Schott, Matthew. "John M. Parker of Louisiana." Ph.D. diss., Vanderbilt University, 1969.

Sherman, Audry. "A History of the New Orleans Cotton Exchange." M.A. thesis, Tulane University, 1934.

Ware, Hester. "A Study of the Life and Works of William Alexander Percy." M.A. thesis, Mississippi State University, 1950.

White, John. "The Port of New Orleans Since 1850." M.A. thesis, Tulane University, 1924.

Williams, Robert. "Martin Behrman." M.A. thesis, Tulane University, 1952.

Willis, John C. "On the New South Frontier: Life on the Yazoo-Mississippi Delta 1865–1920." Ph.D. diss., University of Virginia, 1991.

Wrighton, Fred. "Negro Migration and Income in Mississippi." Ph.D. diss., Mississippi State University, 1972.

Acknowledgments and Methodology

THIS BOOK began twenty years ago, in 1977. At the time I was living in New Orleans and writing a column for *The Vieux Carre Courier,* a weekly owned by Phil Carter, who was also involved in his family's paper in Greenville, Mississippi. That April, Phil ran a special issue on the fiftieth anniversary of the 1927 flood. I grew up in Rhode Island and had never heard of it before, but it added to a fascination I already had with the Mississippi River. I remember reading about the flood, then walking a few hundred yards from the paper on Decatur Street to the levee and watching the river roll past. Ever since I have wanted to write something about the flood. Five years ago I finally decided to do so and began working full-time on it.

I would like to explain my methodology, particularly where I quote conversations that occurred nearly three-quarters of a century ago. I was remarkably lucky to discover detailed minutes and even exact transcripts of many of these conversations. In this regard, an extraordinarily rich source was the Harry B. Caplan Papers at the Louisiana State Museum in New Orleans. I have also used quotes based on either contemporaneous notes, memoranda, and letters written by participants, and, in the case of some public meetings, newspaper accounts. In addition, I interviewed approximately 125 people. My thanks go to all of them. Most of these people supplied background information about the characters important to this book or about a place and time, but a few of those interviewed also recalled comments made by the people in the book in particularly memorable situations. I did use these quotes.

I would like to give special thanks to the late Herman Kohlmayer and Frank Hall. They both exerted considerable effort to help me, and both combined intelligence with intimate knowledge of events and personalities. Their assistance made this book better than it would otherwise have been.

Next I would like to thank Phil Carter, who has been extremely helpful and gracious in the course of my working on this book. Neither he nor anyone else is responsible for anything in the book. If there are any mistakes, they are mine. If there is offense given, I have given it. This is not simply a pro forma disclaimer. To the contrary, when Phil realized that I was headed down one particular path he objected. But that was the way my research, and I believe the truth, took me. Nonetheless, I wish to thank him and everyone else who helped me.

In Washington, my good friend Bob Dawson (an old Tulane football connection) introduced me to the right people to get me started. Martin Reuss, a historian with the Army Corps of Engineers, was exceptionally helpful—both personally and through his writings. Pete Daniel at the Smithsonian Institution, author of *Deep'n as It Come*, which is also about the 1927 flood, generously shared with me information, photographs, and taped interviews he conducted. In Vicksburg, Michael Robinson, now with the Mississippi River Commission, showed me around and taught me much. Bertram Wyatt-Brown of the University of Florida shared with me his research for his book *House of Percy*. John K. Brown of the University of Virginia spent much time going through papers assembled by the late John Kouwenhoven about James Buchanan Eads for me. I look forward to his biography of Eads. At the University of Southwestern Louisiana, I. Bruce Turner was exceptionally helpful. In St. Louis at the Missouri Historical Society, I much appreciate the efforts of Ms. Wendi Perry, who went through many papers for me. At the Hoover Library in West Branch, Iowa, Pat Wildenberg deserves special mention for guiding me through the collection and responding to telephone queries later.

In New Orleans, Betty Werlein Carter helped me to understand that city as well as Greenville, Mississippi. Dorothy Benge took me under her wing and led me through St. Bernard Parish. Exceptionally helpful also were city archivist Wayne Everad at the New Orleans Public Library; also there I thank Irene Wainwright and Andrea Ducros. At Tulane University's Howard-Tilton Library, Joan Caldwell has become a friend. At the Orleans Levee Board, Gary Benoit put out special effort. At the Earl Long Library of the University of New Orleans, Clive Hardy and Marie Window did likewise. Laura Bayon shared family lore and photographs. Robert Brown at the district office of the Army Corps of Engineers and Captain Edward Morehouse, commander of the U.S. Dredge *Wheeler*, escorted me on a trip down to the mouth of the Mississippi and the remains of Port Eads. The late Stephen Lemann, whom I remember with great fondness, offered me cooperaton and guidance. At the Louisiana State Museum, director James Sefcik was extremely kind.

In Greenville, many thanks to Clint Bagley and Bern and Frankie Keating, and also special thanks to the Washington County Library system for use of its excellent oral history collection. Most important, Sylvia Jackson took me by the hand and introduced me to people who would not have spoken openly without her endorsement of me. Newman Bolls and his son Patrick Bolls gave generously of their time and knowledge. In Jackson, Mississippi, at the Mississippi Department of Archives and History, I appreciate the support of Hank Holmes and the entire research staff, along with the permissions they gave for use of material in their collections.

My agent Raphael Sagalyn did an outstanding job in finding the best editor for this book, and I also appreciate his willingness to accommodate some of my more unusual requests.

At Simon & Schuster, I am sincerely grateful to my editor, Alice Mayhew. She did more than what even a good editor does. From my first contact with her, I was more than just impressed with her grasp of what I was trying to do in this book. In fact, she sometimes saw it more clearly than I did, and kept me on track. Elizabeth Stein, whose title now may be only associate editor but who clearly will be someone of consequence in publishing, lent her considerable talents to my cause. Her suggestions were universally well thought out.

And I want to thank my wife, Margaret Anne Hudgins. Every day she went through archival material with me, and her tenacity in tracking down details exceeded my own. (I hope she forgives me for not including anything about the Santa Fund.) Her insight into character and general sense of the workings of the world added dimensions that would have escaped me otherwise. Anne, thank you. (So.) Finally, I want to acknowledge the cousins—Rose Fulford Hudgins and Jane Fulford Warren—whose love and support was always there for me.

—JOHN M. BARRY
New Orleans
January, 1997

Index

Butler, James Pierce, Jr. *(cont.)*
    public relations efforts of,
        340–43, 374
    on reparations policies, 250–
        251, 256, 340, 343, 345–
        358, 408
    social position of, 221, 229–
        230, 313
Butler, John, 315
Butler, Pierce, 230

Cabin Teele, crevasse at, 281
Caillouet, Herman, 276–77,
    279
caisson disease (bends), 59
Camp, Joseph, 144, 145–46,
    147
Campbell, Cora, 201
Canada, Senator (Honey), 421
Canal Bank, 221, 223, 229,
    230, 237, 248, 347, 350,
    355, 407, 409
Cannon, Joseph (Uncle Joe),
    108, 111, 119, 125
Capone, Al, 235, 318
Capper, Arthur, 320
Caraway, T. H., 188, 194
Carnegie, Andrew, 25, 58, 59,
    60, 264, 381
Carnegie Foundation for
    International Peace, 106,
    155
Carson, Kit, 23
Carter, Betty Werlein, 293, 419
Carter, Granville, 179
Carter, Hodding, 293, 419
Case, Calvin, 25
Catchings, Thomas, 114
Cather, Willa, 142
cfs (cubic feet per second)
    (second-feet), 176–77

Champion, George, 409
Chaney, Fred, 205
chaos theory, 37
Chaplin, Charlie, 180
Chapple, Levye, 207, 325, 326,
    327, 333, 416
Chicago, Ill.:
    black voters in, 318
    commercial development of,
        56–57
    southern black migration to,
        417
Child, Richard, 342
Chinese immigrants, 109–10
Christian fundamentalism,
    136, 140
Church, Robert, 319n
Citizens Flood Relief
    Committee, 239, 240,
    343, 352
Civil War:
    Delta destruction from, 98
    military shrinkage after, 55
    naval engineering in, 29–
        30
Claiborne, Charles, 353
Clark, J. S., 322, 383, 391
Clarke, Edward, 142
Clarke, Ernest, 277
Clay, Cassius, 103
Clearing House Association,
    276
Cleveland, Grover, 138, 369
Cline, Isaac, 163, 226–27, 229,
    242–44, 258, 282, 283,
    339, 409
Coastal Survey, U.S., 33–34
Cobb, Stephen, 73
Cober, David, 303–4
Cohn, David, 135, 294
Coleman, Lizzie, 135
Collier, Holt, 110

Faulkner, William, 95, 213, 419
Fenner, Charles, 219
Fieser, James, 241, 272, 273, 274, 282, 289, 369, 378, 382, 383, 385–86, 388–391
Fillmore, Millard, 37
Fink, Mike, 23
First Amendment, 138
Fish, Hamilton, 108
Fish, Stuyvesant, 100, 102, 108–9, 110, 113, 120
Fitzgerald, F. Scott, 141
Flad, Henry, 57, 60
Flanagan, Mrs. D. S., 204
flood dynamics:
    crest height and, 176
    current velocity variations in, 177–78
    measurement units for, 176–177
    of multiple crests, 178
floodways, 423–24
Foote, Andrew, 30
Foote, Shelby, 111, 135, 293–294, 419
Fordyce, John, 400
Foret, Claude, 358
Forshey, Caleb, 43, 53, 72, 75
Fowler, J. D., 326
Frankfurter, Felix, 345
Franklin, Benjamin, 51
French Quarter (Vieux Carré), 213–14, 232
Freud, Sigmund, 136
fuse-plug levees, 423

Gager, E. V., 86–87
Gallier, James, 239
Gantt, Henry, 266

Garsaud, Marcel, 228, 229, 231, 232, 233, 238, 242, 244, 245, 246, 254, 255
Gary, E. H., 368
General Colored Committee, 326, 327, 328, 332, 333, 416
Geological Survey, U.S., 62, 88
Gibson, Charlie, 203
Gifford, Walter, 179–80
Gleick, James, 37
Goddard, Robert, 136
Gooden, James, 332, 334, 416
Gould, Emerson, 28–29
Grady, Henry, 99–100
Grant, Ulysses S., 30, 50, 64–65, 67, 87, 98
Greeley, Horace, 64
Green, Curtis, 195, 205, 303, 313
Greenville, Miss.:
    blacks in government jobs of, 123
    as cotton port, 107, 133
    decline of, 415–16
    flooding of, 207–8, 275–79, 285, 303–7, 311–12, 324, 325
    levees of, 107, 130, 192–94, 303, 324–27
    race relations in, 134–35, 143–47, 179, 308–17, 319–20, 321, 325–29, 330, 332–34, 382, 416, 418, 419–20
    relief efforts in, 303, 304, 305–17, 319–23, 376, 382, 415
    social classes in, 132–34
Griesemer, Douglas, 273
Griffith, D. W., 141

Humphreys, Andrew
   Alexander:
   background of, 32–34
   canal proposal urged by, 64,
      68, 73, 75
   in Civil War, 47–50, 68
   Eads Bridge opposed by, 56,
      62–65
   on effectiveness of levees, 78,
      79, 90, 91, 157
   engineering career of, 21–22,
      33–36, 46, 55, 88
   European deltaic rivers
      studied by, 46
   jetty construction and, 84,
      85
   leadership style of, 48–49,
      55–56, 70
   political strategies of, 62, 68,
      75, 76, 88
   professional rivalries of, 47,
      55–56, 62–66, 67, 72,
      73–77, 79, 80, 82, 87–90,
      96, 157, 159, 423
   report on Mississippi
      produced by, 21–22, 35,
      36–37, 42–44, 45–47,
      50–54, 68, 78, 88, 98, 257
Hunt, Edward Eyre, 268
Hyland, William, 236

Illinois Central, 100, 101, 102,
   106, 108–9, 110, 176,
   205, 206–7, 231, 273, 368
Illinois River, 175, 181, 403
immigrants, 109–15, 119–21,
   137, 140, 218
Irving, Washington, 23
Irwin, Will, 263, 264, 289,
   321, 323
Islenos, 235, 238

Italian immigrants, 109–10,
   111–15, 119–21, 218

Jackson, Miss., development
   of, 126
Jadwin, Edgar, 175, 201, 246,
   273, 341, 400, 404–5,
   423–24, 425
   levee dynamiting and, 240,
      241, 248, 252–53
Jahncke, Ernest Lee, 346, 348,
   349, 353
Janvier, Charles, 229, 355
jazz music, 137, 214–15
Jews, social discrimination
   against, 133, 218–19,
   221, 248, 345
Johnson, John, 315
Johnson, R. Irving, 414
Johnston, Oscar, 313, 371,
   416, 419
Jones, Bill, 192, 193, 199
Jones, Scipio, 395
Jordan, David, 263

Kansas, 1927 floods in, 175,
   186–87, 400
Kellogg, Arthur, 386
Kelvin, William Thomson,
   Lord, 22
Kemper, James, 158, 160, 166,
   167, 185, 198, 222–24,
   227, 228, 233, 258, 425–
   426
Keynes, John Maynard, 266
Keystone Bridge Company, 58,
   60
Kimbrough, Hunter, 276,
   305
Kirby, Richard, 65

sandbars at mouth of, 34–35, 61–62, 67, 69–77
sediment load of, 39, 40, 41, 67, 81
shifts in route near mouth of, 425–26
sinuosity of, 38, 40, 163, 165, 197
slope of, 37
states' responsibility for, 34
three main deltaic channels of, 76, 80–81
turbulent effects combined in, 37–39, 91, 177, 197
valley of, 21, 35, 91–92
velocity of, 15–16, 38–39, 176–78, 197–98
Mississippi River, flood control for:
agricultural production and, 67–68
federal long-range legislation on, 374, 399–407, 409
Gulf canal vs. jetty proposals on, 61–62, 68–77
jetty/cutoff combination advocated for, 78–79
levees-only policy for, 45, 90–92, 156–59, 399, 425
levees vs. outlets proposed for, 39–45, 52–54, 425
modern facilities for, 423–25
racial attitudes and, 131
South Pass jetties built for, 76, 79–87
for Southwest Pass, 76, 84
Mississippi River, 1927 flood of, 173–209
cleanup efforts after, 324, 328
current velocity of, 15–16, 197–98

deaths from, 202, 203, 204, 205, 277, 278, 279, 284, 285, 286, 288–89
Delta flooding in, 185, 195–208, 275–81, 286
duration of, 181, 285, 324
dynamiting of levee during, 238–58, 286, 339, 408, 409
economic losses from, 286
emergency preparations during, 182–86, 192–96, 198–201, 206–8, 282–83, 324–27, 402
federal responses to, 179, 194–95, 240, 268–75, 279–80, 286–89, 366–77
in Greenville, 13–17, 207–8, 275–79, 285, 303–7, 311–12, 324, 325
levee conditions and, 181–182, 183, 184–85, 186, 189, 198–201, 223–24, 232, 282, 283
Mounds Landing crevasse in, 196–206, 239, 240, 244, 275, 279, 280, 303, 425
1926 rainfall and, 173–76
progress of, 179, 181–89, 194–208, 233, 257–58, 275, 280–85, 324, 339
reconstruction programs after, 363–77
refugees from, 184, 185–86, 187, 188, 194, 205–6, 240, 255, 256, 272–78, 282–83, 285–86
relief programs for, 305–17, 319–23, 327–32, 334–35
reparations policy and, 246, 247, 248–52, 255, 257, 340, 346–60

New Orleans, La., 213–33
architecture of, 213, 239
artificial outlets proposed
near, 41, 167–68, 188,
208–9
commercial interests of, 80,
219–21, 223, 225–26,
231, 237–38, 409–10,
411
economic decline of, 409–11
evacuation problems
encountered in, 162
flooding in, 34, 74–75, 223–
224, 228, 245
jazz culture of, 214–15
jetty construction below, 74–
75, 79–80, 89
levee conditions in, 162–63,
164–65
Mardi Gras in, 181, 215–17,
221, 248, 345, 410–11
natural levee as foundation
for, 40
news controlled in, 187–88,
225–27, 232–33, 239–40,
252, 256–57, 342–43, 356
1922 flood threat for, 162–
165, 167
1927 flood and, 187–88,
222–58, 339
population groups within,
213–15
power establishment in, 17,
208, 217, 220–21, 222–
223, 229, 232, 239, 244–
248, 340, 355, 374, 407,
408
precipitation levels for, 15,
181, 182, 189, 228, 232–
233
public relations efforts for,
340–43

railroads in, 100, 355
refugee center in, 255
in reparations process, 340,
345–60, 408
shipping traffic volume
through, 89
social elite of, 79, 181, 214,
215, 216–21, 237, 248,
360, 408–9, 410–11
yellow fever epidemic in,
217, 229, 236, 369
New Orleans Cotton
Exchange, 79, 110, 368
New South, 147, 250–51

Ockerson, J. A., 159
O'Connor, James, 252
Ogden, Florence Sillers, 195,
200
Ohio River, 36, 175, 181, 339,
400
O'Keefe, Arthur, 254, 287,
407
levee dynamiting and, 239,
242–43, 246, 253
political career of, 232
reparations policy and, 352,
356
on river policy, 232, 233,
238, 250
Oliver, Addie, 315
Oliver, Alfred, 358
outlets (spillways) (waste
weirs), 40–42, 52–54, 90,
91, 159, 167–68, 425
Owen, Allison, 228, 240

Palmer, A. Mitchell, 138, 140
Panama Canal, 114, 122
Parker, Dorothy, 268, 419

Parker, John M.:
  background of, 110, 219
  as governor, 109, 148, 371
  on hunts with T. Roosevelt,
    110–11, 115
  on long-range river policy,
    340, 368, 400
  1922 flood and, 148, 163,
    164
  plantation holdings of, 109,
    219
  on racial issues, 112, 148,
    149
  relief effort run by, 275
  social position of, 217
  southern banking and, 119
Parker, Walter, 341
Pass à l'Outre, 80
Pasteur, Louis, 22, 51
Pattangall, William, 155
Paxton, A. J., 199, 201, 303,
    305, 314
Payne, B. B., 199, 307
Peay, Austin, 371–72
pellagra, 365, 387–88
Penney, J. C., 391, 392
Percy, Camille Bourges, 113,
    114, 144, 294, 304, 417
Percy, Charles, 95, 98
Percy, LeRoy, 104–35
  in banking sphere, 14, 106,
    119, 123, 155, 161, 183,
    206, 302, 305, 307, 376
  death of, 417–18
  family relationships of, 16,
    105, 106, 110, 113, 294–
    300, 308–9, 310, 401,
    417
  flood control efforts and,
    130–31, 156, 158, 161–
    162, 166, 168, 206, 301,
    340, 368

  on Hoover's nomination, 394
  Ku Klux Klan fought by, 16,
    143–56, 160, 308, 319,
    416
  labor shortage and, 108,
    109–23, 140, 149, 305,
    313, 416
  law practice of, 104–5, 106,
    135, 143
  levee board appointments
    and, 125, 166, 168
  on long-range river policy
    legislation, 340, 400–406
  1927 flood and, 14, 15, 16–
    17, 183, 192, 195, 206–7,
    208, 304–6, 329, 331,
    363–64
  patrician background of, 16,
    129, 130, 146–47
  physical appearance of, 13,
    105, 106, 151, 309, 344
  plantation holdings of, 105,
    109, 111, 112, 113, 115,
    117, 133, 219–20, 301,
    307
  political and social milieu of,
    17, 108, 109, 110–11,
    113, 114, 115, 119–20,
    124–25, 128, 133, 134,
    153, 155, 161, 188, 195,
    198, 214, 219, 221, 227,
    301–2, 313, 319, 324,
    329, 394
  power wielded by, 17, 106,
    114, 119, 125, 130, 131,
    143–44, 150, 208, 301,
    302, 307
  as public speaker, 117–18,
    128, 129–30, 145–46,
    149, 151–52, 161, 415
  racial views of, 108, 111–12,
    116–19, 123, 124, 129,